*

AMERICAN WRITERS SERIES
*
HARRY HAYDEN CLARK
General Editor

*

★ AMERICAN WRITERS SERIES ★

Volumes of representative selections, prepared by American scholars under the general editorship of Harry Hayden Clark, University of Wisconsin. Volumes now ready are starred.

AMERICAN TRANSCENDENTALISTS, *Raymond Adams, University of North Carolina*

*WILLIAM CULLEN BRYANT, *Tremaine McDowell, University of Minnesota*

*JAMES FENIMORE COOPER, *Rober E. Spiller, Swarthmore College*

*JONATHAN EDWARDS, *Clarence H. Faust, University of Chicago, and Thomas H. Johnson, Lawrenceville School*

*RALPH WALDO EMERSON, *Frederic I. Carpenter, Harvard University*

*BENJAMIN FRANKLIN, *Frank Luther Mott, University of Iowa, and Chester E. Jorgenson, Wayne University*

*ALEXANDER HAMILTON AND THOMAS JEFFERSON, *Frederick C. Prescott, Cornell University*

*BRET HARTE, *Joseph B. Harrison, University of Washington*

*NATHANIEL HAWTHORNE, *Austin Warren, Boston University*

*OLIVER WENDELL HOLMES, *S. I. Hayakawa, University of Wisconsin, and Howard Mumford Jones, Harvard University*

*WASHINGTON IRVING, *Henry A. Pochmann, Mississippi State College*

*HENRY JAMES, *Lyon Richardson, Western Reserve University*

*HENRY WADSWORTH LONGFELLOW, *Odell Shepard, Trinity College*

JAMES RUSSELL LOWELL, *Norman Foerster, University of Iowa, and Harry H. Clark, University of Wisconsin*

*HERMAN MELVILLE, *Willard Thorp, Princeton University*

*JOHN LOTHROP MOTLEY, *Chester P. Higby and B. T. Schantz, University of Wisconsin*

THOMAS PAINE, *Harry H. Clark, University of Wisconsin*

*FRANCIS PARKMAN, *Wilbur L. Schramm, University of Iowa*

*EDGAR ALLAN POE, *Margaret Alterton, University of Iowa, and Hardin Craig, Stanford University*

*WILLIAM HICKLING PRESCOTT, *William Charvat, New York University, and Michael Kraus, College of the City of New York*

*SOUTHERN POETS, *Edd Winfield Parks, University of Georgia*

SOUTHERN PROSE, *Gregory Paine, University of North Carolina*

*HENRY DAVID THOREAU, *Bartholow Crawford, University of Iowa*

*MARK TWAIN, *Fred Lewis Pattee, Rollins College*

*WALT WHITMAN, *Floyd Stowall, University of Texas*

JOHN GREENLEAF WHITTIER, *Harry H. Clark, University of Wisconsin, and Bertha M. Stearns, Wellesley College*

Pen drawing by Kerr Eby, after
a mezzotint by John Sartain

WILLIAM HICKLING PRESCOTT

ÆT. *c.* 60

William Hickling Prescott

REPRESENTATIVE SELECTIONS, WITH
INTRODUCTION, BIBLIOGRAPHY, AND NOTES

BY

WILLIAM CHARVAT

Assistant Professor of English
New York University

AND

MICHAEL KRAUS

Assistant Professor of History
College of the City of New York

AWS

AMERICAN BOOK COMPANY
New York · Cincinnati · Chicago
Boston · Atlanta

E. P. I

Charvat and Kraus's Prescott

Made in U. S. A.

PREFACE

As in the case of the Motley volume in this series, the general editor thought it appropriate to use the services of two editors in the preparation of this anthology of Prescott—one from the field of American literature, the other from the field of history. In the writing of the Introduction, the editors divided responsibility. Mr. Charvat wrote the sections on Backgrounds, the Art of History, Style, Literary Criticism, and Reputation; Mr. Kraus did those on Historical Attitudes, Scholarship, and Political Ideas.

The editors have departed from the general plan of the series in presenting the selections, not under the headings of the volumes from which they were taken, but under topical headings. They have done this from a conviction that it would be unwise to attempt to demonstrate in an anthology Prescott's power of depicting a historical era. Even if they had managed to arrange coherent abridgements of the historian's four long major works, they would not have felt that these were a satisfactory substitute for the reading of one of the originals. They believe that it is impossible for a student to get a just idea of the majestic sweep of Prescott's narrative without reading at least one of his works from beginning to end. On the other hand, they felt that it would be useful to illustrate, by means of the topical plan, the wide variety of Prescott's materials and his versatility. For the student who wishes to see at a glance the proportional representation of Prescott's works under this plan they have provided in an appendix a second table of contents (see p. 464) in which the selections are listed in the order of their appearance in the original works. He will note therein that considerable space is given to Prescott's miscellaneous writings, collected and uncollected. The reasons for this are two. First, the editors wished to emphasize Prescott's importance as a literary critic, a fact which has been recognized by some literary historians but never adequately demonstrated in an anthology. Second, inasmuch as this text is intended for students of Prescott, they wished to make easily available such materials as illustrate the historian's theories and scholarship, and his opinions on matters related to history.

Prescott's voluminous footnotes have been omitted from this text because they would have displaced about a quarter of his narrative. However, on pages 134–149 the student will find a passage as originally documented by Prescott, illustrating his methods of citation, his presentation of proof, and his commentary.

For convenience, page references to *The Conquest of Mexico* and *The Conquest of Peru* are made to the easily accessible reprint of both those works in one volume of the Modern Library "Giants." Since there is no such recent reprint of Prescott's other works, references to them are made to the original editions.

The editors are grateful to Professor H. H. Clark, general editor of the American Writers Series, for much valuable advice and criticism.

W. C.
M. K.

CONTENTS

WILLIAM HICKLING PRESCOTT

I. BACKGROUNDS

1. Early Cultural Environment

The career of William Hickling Prescott (1796–1859) coincided with the height of the Romantic Movement, and his first work appeared in 1837, the year of *The American Scholar* and *Twice-Told Tales*. But mere dates are often misleading, for in 1837 Prescott was forty-one years old. He belongs not with the major romantics, but with the precursors of romanticism, who, born in the last decades of the eighteenth century, came to maturity before or about 1815.[1] During his adolescence, therefore, he was subject to the influence of certain cultural phenomena which help to explain the difference in the climates of opinion in which the two groups developed.

In the first decade of the nineteenth century our literary atmosphere was predominantly British and neoclassical.[2] We had not yet created a native literature, and the new English romantics were not yet generally accepted. Byron and Scott were read in the first decade, but the most revolutionary of the romantics—Wordsworth and Coleridge in the first decade, and Shelley and Keats in the second—were for the most part ignored. In their most impressionable years Prescott's group read Cowper, Pope, Milton, Addison, Thomson, and the histories of the eighteenth-century rationalists. At college they

---

[1] This group includes Irving, Cooper, Bryant, Kennedy, and Prescott's close friend, George Ticknor.

[2] On the culture of the period 1790–1810, see I. W. Riley, *American Philosophy: The Early Schools* (New York, 1907); H. M. Ellis, *Joseph Dennie and His Circle* (Austin, Texas, 1915); H. M. Flewelling, *Literary Criticism in American Periodicals, 1783–1820* (unpub. dissertation, University of Michigan, 1931).

were taught Scottish realistic philosophy and Scottish aesthetics. The classical element in Prescott's education was particularly strong because of his boyhood studies in the private school of the English-born Dr. J. S. J. Gardiner, who had been the student of Dr. Samuel Parr, one of the most pedantic of eighteenth-century classicists.

Prescott's group were exposed, in their youth, to the world-wide reaction against the French Revolution. The great movement of French liberalism in political, social, and religious thought, springing from Rousseau, the Encyclopedists, the Physiocrats, and their English disciples, and sponsored in America by Jefferson, Paine, and Freneau, received a serious setback when it became apparent that such thought was a potential threat to government, property, and organized religion. In consequence of the reaction, the skepticism of the school of Hume, the idealism of Berkeley, and the materialism of the Priestley group were banished from the colleges, "safe and sane" Scottish philosophy was imported,[3] and a wave of religious enthusiasm and revivalism swept the country. Although, in the 1820's, Unitarianism made a respectable compromise with Deism and sponsored a new type of humanitarianism, a tendency to link atheism and liberal social thought persisted, and except for Bryant the older generation never lost their slightly apprehensive attitude toward social revolution or their distaste for both idealistic and skeptical philosophies.[4]

[3] I. W. Riley, *op. cit.*, pp. 475–476. The influence of this philosophy on teaching at Harvard during Prescott's time is discussed by Benjamin Rand in "Philosophical Instruction in Harvard University, 1639–1900," *Harvard Graduates' Magazine*, XXXVII, 29–46 (December, 1928). See also William Charvat, *The Origins of American Critical Thought, 1810–1835* (Philadelphia, 1936).

[4] Charvat, *op. cit.*, chap. ii. Ticknor reflected the reaction when he wrote that in his boyhood he read an American edition of Paul Henri Mallet's *Considerations on the French Revolution*, which gave "a direction to my opinions on that subject which I think has not been materially altered since" (*Life, Letters, and Journals*, II, 274). For Prescott's opinion of the French Revolution, see p. cix, below.

Most of Prescott's group grew up in an atmosphere of Federalist culture. Because, under shifting economic and social pressures, Federalism changed its position on specific issues such as national unity, the tariff, and even constitutionalism, it is not easily defined; but in general Federalists stood for government by the educated and the well-to-do, limitations on the democratic process, and protection of economic interests by a Constitution and a Supreme Court not easily subjected to popular pressure. When the Federalist party was formed after the Revolution it had a particularly strong growth in New England because these attitudes were in accord with the traditions of seventeenth-century theocracy. With Harvard and Yale as its bulwarks, Federalism permeated upper-class thought by allying itself with religion and literature. Intellectual Boston was ruled from 1787 to 1815 by such Federalist spokesmen as Fisher Ames and H. G. Otis, whose politics were echoed by poets who fused their religious and political attitudes with their poetic art.[5] As a boy Prescott lived in Salem, long the center of Federalist politics. In the Salem of 1801, said Judge Joseph Story, "the great preponderance of the wealth, rank, and talent" was Federalistic, and Prescott's father was "the ablest and most accomplished of the federal leaders."[6] After the passage of the Embargo Act (1808) the elder Prescott became a member of an exclusive group of Essex County *emigrés* living in Boston, whose "opinions, or rather prejudices, were the standard of 'right thinking' in Eastern Massachusetts,"[7] and who punished devi-

---

[5] V. L. Parrington, *The Connecticut Wits* (1926), and *Main Currents in American Thought* (1927), I, 357–382; Henry Adams, *History of the United States during the Administration of Thomas Jefferson*, I, 75–107.

[6] *Life and Letters of Joseph Story*, ed. W. W. Story (Boston, 1851), I, 96, 197. Judge William Prescott was born in 1762, received degrees from Harvard in 1783 and 1815, and became a Harvard overseer. He began law practice at Salem in 1789, and succeeded H. G. Otis on the Bench of Common Pleas, 1818. He died in 1844.

[7] S. E. Morison, *Maritime History of Massachusetts* (Boston, 1921), p. 167.

ators from Federalist orthodoxy by social ostracism.[8] It was
this group which convened the Hartford Convention of 1814,[9]
to which Prescott's and Longfellow's fathers were delegates,
and which young George Ticknor attended. When it is observed that Prescott's revered schoolmaster, Gardiner, was a
virulent Federalist partisan, and that Harvard in his day was
manned by Federalists, it is clear that he was thoroughly exposed to the thinking of the party. By the time he reached his
majority the party was almost defunct, but its spirit was perpetuated in the Whig party of Daniel Webster,[10] among whose
most loyal supporters and friends were Ticknor and the Prescotts.

These three phenomena—neoclassicism, conservative reaction, and Federalism—grew weaker with time, and had little
influence on the generation which followed Prescott's. The
historian was affected by two other forces, however, which grew
stronger in the nineteenth century and which influenced both the
older and younger romantics—Industrialism and Unitarianism.

When the elder Prescott practiced law in the port of Salem
(1789–1808), shipping was the most profitable business in New
England and a potent force in national politics. But the Embargo and the War of 1812 permanently injured the shipping
business of the small ports,[11] and a number of merchants and

---

[8] S. E. Morison, *Maritime History of Massachusetts* (Boston, 1921)
p. 129.

[9] This was strictly a movement of the "ruling aristocracy of New
England," twenty-two of the twenty-six delegates being college
graduates and lawyers, and nine of them jurists. Morison, *The Life
and Letters of Harrison Gray Otis*, II, 137. On Judge Prescott's attitude toward the Convention, see George Ticknor, *Life of William
Hickling Prescott* (Boston, 1864), p. 456. This work will be referred
to hereafter as Ticknor.

[10] After the party ceased to exist as a state organization in 1825,
the mass of the Federalists joined the National Republican, later the
Whig party. All of the surviving Federalist leaders of 1814 were
Whigs in 1840. See Morison, *Harrison Gray Otis*, II, 248.

[11] Salem's fleet numbered 182 in 1807, 57 in 1815. Morison, *Maritime History of Massachusetts*, p. 217.

lawyers, among them the Prescotts, moved to Boston,[12] which was expected to absorb much of the future development of New England commerce. The removal brought Judge Prescott into contact with the powerful new force of manufactures. Partly as a result of the War of 1812, which tended to force New England capital into new channels, the lagging factories of Massachusetts were reorganized in the years following 1813.[13] For the first time they came under the direct management of experienced merchants like Francis Lowell who sought to protect their own investments. Through the banking houses which centered in Boston, the old merchant class and the new industrialists were merged, and the shipping and textile groups were united to form a new aristocracy of wealth.[14] Within twenty years Judge Prescott and his son added lucrative railroad and manufacturing investments to their holdings in shipping and insurance,[15] and when the historian married Susan Amory and his children married into the Peabody and Lawrence families, he had connections with three of the most important financial and industrial dynasties in the country.

It is easy to assume a connection between these circumstances and Prescott's tendency—deplored by Theodore Parker—to ignore the common people in his histories.[16] Yet it must be recognized that inasmuch as the worst effects of the Massachusetts factory system did not become apparent until about 1850,

[12] A. B. Darling, *Political Changes in Massachusetts, 1824–1848* (New Haven, 1925), chap. i.

[13] C. F. Ware, *The Early New England Cotton Manufacture* (Boston, 1931), p. 61.

[14] Darling, *op. cit.*, chap. i.

[15] Vera Shlakman ("Economic History of a Factory Town," *Smith College Studies in History*, Vol. XX, 1935, appendix) lists a W. Prescott as an incorporator of the Boston Insurance Co. in 1831; a W. H. Prescott as officer or stockholder of the Taunton Manufacturing Co.; and a Prescott Manufacturing Co. in Lowell. See also Ware, *op. cit.*, pp. 302, 321. For an idea of the high profits yielded by such investments, see *ibid.*, p. 152.

[16] See pp. cxvi–cxvii, below.

after the influx of a foreign proletariat, there is no reason why Prescott's stake in industrialism should have disturbed his social conscience during his productive years. On the other hand, it is natural that he did not join with Thoreau and Parker in their protest against the cultural effects of industrialism, and that he belonged to the party most closely affiliated with business interests. These interests created for the Whigs political problems on which Prescott was forced, as we shall see, to take a stand.

In this period, Unitarianism had such a powerful growth in Eastern Massachusetts among the upper classes that it may be considered one of the peculiar elements in the culture of Prescott's group. By 1805 it had gained control of the Harvard Divinity School, and by 1815 a contemporary observer could say that most of the Boston clergy and well-to-do laymen were Unitarians.[17] Although, doctrinally, right-wing Unitarianism adhered to such basic dogma as the Christian miracles, it encouraged a rationalistic solution of ethical and religious problems and considerable tolerance towards other forms of worship. Culturally, it repudiated the real or fancied antipathy between Protestantism and art by supporting some of the most important critical magazines of the time, in all of which Prescott's group had a hand.[18]

Prescott came under the influence of the great Unitarian leader, William Ellery Channing, in early childhood when his mother brought him to repentant tears by reading to him Channing's sermon on "The Duties of Children."[19] But his affilia-

[17] C. H. Faust, "The Background of Unitarian Opposition to Transcendentalism," *Modern Philology*, XXXV, 297–324 (February, 1938). For a history of the sect, see G. W. Cooke, *Unitarianism in America* (Boston, 1902).

[18] The *Monthly Anthology*, the *General Repository and Review*, the *North American Review*, and the *Christian Examiner*. See F. L. Mott, *A History of American Magazines, 1741–1850*, for a detailed account of these periodicals.

[19] Ticknor, p. 5. Channing admired the historian as "a quiet student . . . the more to be honoured because he has carried on his

tion with the sect was no mere inheritance, for as Channing said in 1831, Unitarians "think each for himself." In 1819 Prescott deliberately accepted "Christian revelation." In 1829 the death of his daughter led him to review the grounds of his decision.[20] It is striking proof of the rationalistic spirit of the sect that at this time he conducted his re-examination with the aid of his father, "an old and learned lawyer," who, "on all matters of evidence, had a tendency to skepticism rather than credulity"; and that in the process he weighed Hume, Gibbon, and Jenyns against Watson, Brown, Butler, and Paley. Finding no authority in the New Testament for the "doctrines commonly accounted orthodox," he rejected them; but he decided that the Gospels were authentic, and that even if they were not, they embodied the best system of morals for happiness now and hereafter. Though he resolved after this never to trouble himself again about these fundamentals, in 1837 he went over the problem once more and reaffirmed his old conclusions.[21] At

great work amidst outward prosperity, which has relieved him from all necessity of labour and opened to him all the indulgences of life" (*Correspondence of W. E. Channing and Lucy Aikin* [Edinburgh, 1874], p. 328). The fact that Prescott was a member of the First Congregational Church of Boston (Ticknor, p. 445) need cause no confusion, inasmuch as in its early stages in New England, Unitarianism was merely a liberal form of Congregationalism. Prescott said specifically that he was a Unitarian (Ticknor, p. 313).

[20] Ticknor, pp. 90–91.

[21] *Ibid.*, p. 164. These final investigations may have risen out of his studies of Cardinal Ximenes' Polyglot Bible. (See *Ferdinand and Isabella*, III, 321–326.) They may also have had some connection with the contemporary controversy over Biblical criticism, for there are references in the footnotes of this section to the Biblical studies of James Marsh, student of German "higher criticism" and philosophy, and of Andrews Norton, conservative Unitarian leader, whose *Evidences of the Genuineness of the Gospels* (1837) Prescott called a "noble specimen of scholarship." But that Prescott was little interested in the controversy is evident in his statement, at about this time, that "the study of polemics or biblical critics will tend neither to settle principles nor clear up doubts, but rather confuse the former and multiply the latter."

that time he stated the credo from which he never thereafter departed:

To do well and act justly, to fear and to love God, and to love our neighbors as ourselves—in these is the essence of religion. For what we can believe, we are not responsible. . . . For what we do we shall indeed be accountable. The doctrines of the Saviour unfold the whole code of morals by which our conduct should be regulated.

These attitudes may be restated as (a) belief in a benevolent Deity, (b) emphasis upon conduct rather than creed, (c) acceptance of New Testament ethics, and (d) belief in immortality.[22] The serene tone of Prescott's works must be attributed in part to the fact that by 1837, the year of the publication of his first book, he had determined upon the fundamentals of his religion and ethics.

These principles were too broad to affect seriously his judgment of religious factors in history, yet there has been considerable critical confusion on the matter. J. Q. Adams said that Prescott the historian seemed to be without religion,[23] and a modern critic that he was one of the three American historians who celebrated the triumph of the Protestant faith over Catholicism.[24] Some contemporary critics called him anti-Catholic; others, including Archbishop Hughes of New York, commended him for his treatment of the Church. Prescott himself, amused by these contradictions, commented that they entitled him to "pass for a very liberal Christian."[25]

---

[22] His attitude in this matter is stated more fully in Ticknor, p. 375. In this connection, note his interest in spiritualism when it was in vogue (*ibid.*, pp. 91–92, note).

[23] Ticknor, p. 232.

[24] Allan Nevins, in *American Writers on American Literature*, edited by John Macy (New York, 1931), p. 226.

[25] Roger Wolcott, ed., *The Correspondence of William Hickling Prescott, 1833–1847* (Boston, 1925), p. 583. This work will be referred to hereafter as *Correspondence*.

These difficulties are solved if we recognize that he preferred Christianity to paganism, Protestantism to Catholicism, and Unitarianism to all other Christian sects. In his histories, his Unitarianism is perceptible chiefly in his disapproval of fanaticism, and in occasional comments on ancient conceptions of the afterlife.[26] In the larger matter of Protestant psychology his bias is more obvious, for he made no special effort to conceal it. Indeed, when his Mexican translators so altered his religious sentiments that he was made "to talk like a good son of the Pope," he protested that he had a right to have his "Protestant heresies at least preserved in a Note at the bottom of the page in the original English."[27] The depth of his Protestantism is indicated by his belief, as will be shown, that the Reformation was one of the great steps in the progress of civilization. But that he was not a "Protestant historian" is even more evident in the fact that his works concern not the triumphs of Protestantism but those of Catholic Christianity over the heathen.

On the whole, Protestantism was a far more dynamic force in his life than in his works. Temperate always in his judgment of others, he was a merciless critic of himself. If one recalls his statement that a "new standard of moral excellence was formed" by the Christian doctrine which "inculcated that the end of being was best answered by a life of active usefulness, and not by one of abstract contemplation, or selfish indulgence, or passive fortitude,"[28] there can be no question that his career was radically affected by his religious training. The fortitude implicit in his victory over physical handicaps is obvious enough,

---

[26] Note especially his statement that "the absence of all physical torture [in the Aztec conception of the afterlife] forms a striking contrast to the schemes of suffering so ingeniously devised by the fancies of the most enlightened nations" (*Mexico*, p. 40, and note. See also *Peru*, p. 777).

[27] *Correspondence*, p. 533.

[28] *Miscellanies*, p. 93.

but his moral triumph over himself is, in a sense, even more significant. Like Franklin he kept careful watch over his character. In Ticknor's words,[29]

He made a record of everything that was amiss, and examined and considered and studied that record constantly and conscientiously. It was written on separate slips of paper,—done always with his own hand,—seen only by his own eye. These slips he preserved in a large envelope, and kept them in the most reserved and private manner. From time to time . . . he took them out and looked them over, one by one. If any habitual fault were, as he thought, eradicated, he destroyed the record of it; if a new one had appeared, he entered it on its separate slip, and placed it with the rest for future warning and reproof. This habit, known only to the innermost circle of those who lived around his heart, was persevered in to the last. After his death the envelope was found, marked, as it was known that it would be, "To be burnt." And it *was* burnt. No record, therefore, remains on earth of this remarkable self-discipline. But it remains in the memory of his beautiful and pure life.

In all his connections, then, Prescott belonged to the aristocracy of New England. A Harvard graduate, a Federalist, a Unitarian, an offshoot of the wealthy professional and commercial class, he was conscious of his inherited social prestige, and he moved easily in a society as exclusive as that of Philadelphia or London, in which "few names had risen to prominence since the Revolution."[30] From 1640 his ancestors had been prominent farmers, soldiers, and judges, and many had been educated at Harvard.[31] Like Holmes, Prescott took open pride in his family's place in society. He loved to contemplate the fact that his and his wife's ancestors fought on opposite sides in the Revolution, and that three generations of William Prescotts had occupied the same room at Harvard. "I have a right to

---

[29] Ticknor, pp. 152–153.
[30] Morison, *Maritime History of Massachusetts*, p. 128.
[31] See Ticknor, Appendix A, "The Prescott Family."

take an honest pride, or at least satisfaction, in my descent," he wrote Griswold in 1845,[32] and he studied his genealogy and ordered his coat of arms engraved on the family plate.[33]

It was characteristic of New England aristocracy in those days, however, that it considered social usefulness as important as wealth and breeding, and that in Prescott's youth there was no really leisured class.[34] When Holmes defined the man of family as a descendant of "a member of his Majesty's Council for the Province, a Governor or so, one or two Doctors of Divinity, [and] a member of Congress, not later than the time of top-boots with tassels,"[35] and stipulated the instinct for scholarship as a prerequisite for Brahminism,[36] he implied that wealth and social prestige carried with them an obligation of social leadership or cultural distinction. In a world in which presidents like Jefferson and the Adamses were scholars, it is not surprising that the socially élite were often professional men of such distinction as Holmes in medicine, Longfellow in teaching, and Channing in the ministry.

Prescott had reason to be aware of this tradition, for at least five of his forebears had held public positions, but for him the problem of a career was difficult. "God knows how poorly I am qualified to be a merchant," he wrote about 1818. The law,

[32] Rollo Ogden, *William Hickling Prescott*, American Men of Letters Series (Boston, 1904), p. 2.

[33] *Correspondence*, p. 619.

[34] Prescott observed in 1839 that "a person in our country who takes little interest in politicians or in making money—our staples, you know—will be thrown pretty much on his own resources, and if he is not fond of books he may as well go hang himself, for as to a class of idle gentlemen, there is no such thing here" (*Correspondence*, pp. 71–72). Similarly, Hawthorne observed that his countrymen anticipated "nothing but evil of a young man who neither studies physic, law, nor gospel, nor opens a store, nor takes to farming, but manifests an incomprehensible disposition to be satisfied with what his father left him" (G. E. Woodberry, *Life of Hawthorne* [1902], p. 43).

[35] *The Autocrat of the Breakfast Table* (Riverside edition), p. 20.

[36] *Elsie Venner* (Riverside edition), pp. 4–6.

of course, was his natural inheritance, and for a time after leaving college he studied in his father's office. But changing social conditions were making the law a less attractive profession than it had been for men of his class. Politics was becoming a vulgar scramble which was distasteful to the genteel, and gentlemen who entered the law could not assume that it was a straight road to the bench or to the foreign legations.[37] Because of the pressure of a growing middle class, which politicians like Jackson and Van Buren knew how to control, the aristocracy could no longer depend on its prestige alone for political preferment.

Even the law, however, was eliminated from Prescott's field of choice by the results of an accident. In his junior year at Harvard, a crust of bread thrown by a roistering student destroyed the sight of his left eye.[38] Treatment by specialists here and abroad did not help, and a vacation at his uncle's home at St. Michael's in the Azores proved that rest would not cure him. When oculists warned him that much reading would render him totally blind, he gave up reading for the law, and began to go out into Boston society, in which he was notably popular. In the year 1819, at the age of twenty-three, Prescott was a man-about-town,—handsome, gay, popular—but with no plans, and with adequate means and excuse for a life of idleness.

2. *Prescott's Problem and the Solution*

That Prescott became an eminent historian instead of a parasite was due not only to patrician traditions, but to his character and to the opportunities which were developing in the intellectual world of the 1820's.

[37] For data on this phenomenon, see A. B. Darling, *op. cit.*, and D. R. Fox, *The Decline of Aristocracy in the Politics of New York* (New York, 1919).

[38] For a description of his case by one of his doctors, see James Jackson, *Another Letter to a Young Physician* (Boston, 1861), pp. 130–156. See also Ticknor, pp. 19–22, 28–32; and *Correspondence*, pp. 298–299, 301–302.

Prescott's character was not simple. In college days, Ticknor hints, he was something of a gay blade,[39] but the Puritan impulse was strong, and, as we have seen, he made elaborate rules for the regulation of his conduct. He was not naturally industrious. He "learned his lessons well in boyhood, because he respected Dr. Gardiner, and was sure to be punished if he neglected them. At college he considered a moderate amount of scholarship necessary to the character of a gentleman, and came up to his own not very high standard with a good deal of alacrity. And he had always desired to gratify his father, whose authority he felt to be gentle as well as just. . . ."[40] When he left college, however, these compulsions were no longer effective. Yet the social code required that he work, and his deep-rooted Protestantism impelled him, in spite of all obstacles and temptations, to turn his life to some account. "It is of little moment," he wrote in 1822, "whether I succeed in this or that thing, but it is of great moment that I am habitually industrious."[41] Accordingly, in spite of the doctors' warnings that his right eye was weakening, he set about a career which called for much writing and the assimilation of an enormous number of books and manuscripts. Once he had decided to become a scholar, he budgeted the time during which he was permitted to use his good eye, hired secretaries[42] to read to him, and bought an instrument called a noctograph,[43] for guiding his hand while writing. Even with these facilities his work was

[39] Ticknor, p. 17.

[40] *Ibid.*, p. 142.

[41] *Ibid.*, p. 141.

[42] Prescott's secretaries had, of course, an important role in his work. They are listed and discussed by Ticknor (pp. 80–82), who got some of them from his own language classes at Harvard. The most important was John Foster Kirk, a competent historian himself, who accompanied Prescott to Europe in 1850, edited Prescott's work, and became editor of *Lippincott's*. See the article on Kirk in *Dictionary of American Biography*.

[43] See Ticknor for a description (pp. 123–125) and a picture (p. 121) of the instrument.

not easy, for readers were slower than his own eye, and the noctograph gave no opportunity for a clear correction of errors. In addition to his eye trouble, he was subject to headaches and rheumatism which hampered him severely. Thus, although he was not sightless, and objected to that description, he may be placed with the great company of blind and near-blind historians—Parkman,[44] Thierry, Szaynocha, and the Marquis Capponi.

In the struggle for self-mastery, he reverted to his methods of college days, when he had forced on himself a program of study. Now he established a system of "pecuniary mulcts and penalties, by which he punished himself with a moderate fine which he paid to charity";[45] or he made bets with his friends and secretaries that he would accomplish certain tasks in a specified time. Proof that during most of his life he had to call in the aid of some outside stimulus to rouse himself to the proper exertion of his faculties is abundant in his memoranda. Yet so well did he succeed in his efforts to acquire the habit of work that by 1850 he was incapable of enjoying leisure, and he wrote from Europe, whither he had gone for a much-needed rest, that it was "hard work to make a *life* of pleasure." [46] His enormous achievement, then, is doubly remarkable in view of his natural proclivity to idleness.

A second factor in the solution of his problem was the situation in American letters in the first two decades of the nineteenth century. In effect it was a period of transition in author-public relationships comparable to the Age of Johnson in English letters, when the aristocratic patron was displaced by the magazine editor and the bookseller.[47] Though there was little

[44] See the account of Parkman's similar ailments by W. L. Schramm, ed., *Parkman* (American Writers Series), pp. xxiv–xxxi.

[45] Ticknor, p. 143.

[46] *Ibid.*, p. 305.

[47] See A. S. Collins, *The Profession of Letters, A Study of the Relation of Author to Patron, Publisher, and Public, 1780–1832* (New York,

or no patronage in America, and no professional author class, there were many professional men who were amateurs in literature and who formed literary clubs to further their common interest. These clubs were important not only because they created a literary atmosphere in the urban centers, but because they published and supported magazines and miscellanies as vehicles for their work.[48]

At loose ends in the year 1818, Prescott gathered about him a group of his Harvard contemporaries to form a society called "The Club," which met to read and criticize papers of their own composition. As "the only member who had neither profession nor ostensible pursuit," Prescott was nicknamed "the gentleman."[49] In their magazine, *The Club Room*,[50] which went through only four issues before it expired in 1820, appeared Prescott's first literary attempts, two of them sentimental story-essays in the *Sketch-Book* manner, the third an editorial in which he took pains to deny that the magazine was an imitation of Irving's *Salmagundi*, although his denial reproduced the facetious tone of that periodical. These productions have no intrinsic value, but the experience gave him direct contact with the problems of essay technique and led to his writing the first important analysis of the historical development of the

---

1929). Note Prescott's recognition of this "unhappy interim between patronage and democracy," in his "English Literature of the Nineteenth Century," *North American Review*, XXXV, 170 (July, 1832); and his belief that public patronage is the only kind that can be "received without some sense of degradation" (*Miscellanies*, p. 135).

[48] Such were the Friendly Club (Brown's *Monthly Magazine*), the Anthology Club (*Monthly Anthology*), the Literary Club (Dennie's *Farmer's Museum*), and the Tuesday Club (*Portfolio*). See F. L. Mott, *op. cit.*, and F. L. Pattee, *The Development of the American Short Story*, pp. 28–29.

[49] Ticknor, p. 57. For a list of the members, see *ibid.*, p. 55.

[50] *The Club Room*, February, March, April, July, 1820. Prescott edited the magazine, and contributed the leading article and "Calais" in March, and "The Vale of Alleriot" in April. For discussion, see Ticknor, pp. 56–57, and F. L. Pattee, *op. cit.*, pp. 34–36.

essay.[51] It also taught him that he had no bent for the lighter forms of literature.

When, in 1821, Prescott determined upon a life of letters, and began to write critical articles on English literature, the vehicle for these was another "gentlemen's" magazine, the *North American Review*,[52] with which he was to be associated for the rest of his life. Established in 1815 by members of the Harvard-Federalist-Unitarian group that had sponsored the *Monthly Anthology*, the *Review* was the organ of Prescott's own social set, and during his career he was a friend or acquaintance of most of its editors and contributors. More important, however, is the fact that early in its life the *Review* came under the influence of a new literary phenomenon which may be considered a third factor in Prescott's literary development. Up to 1820 the *Review* was nationalistic, if not "provincial and parochial";[53] but with the assumption of the editorship in that year by the brilliant young Edward Everett its internationalism became so pronounced as to earn for it the epithet of "the North Unamerican." As one of the group—all of them friends of Prescott—who went to Germany for graduate study in the second decade,[54] Everett brought to the *Review* an enthusiasm for European literature and history, and for German scholarly methods which was symptomatic of a profound change in American scholarship and education. Under German inspiration this movement was to result in the creation of an effective modern language curriculum in the universities, the expansion and reform of libraries, new research methods, and scientific methods in historical research. A vehicle of this movement, the *Review* printed "hundreds and eventually thousands of

[51] Discussed below, pp. xcvii–xcviii.

[52] See Mott, *op. cit.*, pp. 219–261, for full discussion.

[53] *Ibid.*, pp. 222–224, 228–229.

[54] The European experiences of the group have been recorded in detail by O. W. Long in *Literary Pioneers* (Cambridge, 1935). The group included Ticknor, Cogswell, Bancroft, Everett, and Motley.

pages"[55] of material on European literature, society, and politics, in which the German influence was sufficiently obvious to occasion complaints from some of the older contributors that "the North American is becoming too partial to the Germans at the expense of our worthy brethren, the English."[56]

Prescott's contributions to the *Review* began (1821) under Everett's editorship, but his most direct contact with the new influence came through George Ticknor, who was in many ways the leader of the Göttingen group. Ticknor and Prescott first met in 1808 in Dr. Gardiner's school, where they shared a common interest in old literature. Thereafter their paths were separate but nearly parallel. Ticknor, having already graduated from Dartmouth (1807), took to the law, but with a characteristic instinct for new trends, he sensed that Germany was developing a fresh approach to scholarship. The American publication of Madame de Staël's *De l'Allemagne* in 1813 inspired a general interest in the new Germany to which Ticknor responded.[57] He got letters of introduction from John Adams to Thomas Jefferson, who, in turn, gave both him and Everett letters to friends in Europe.[58] Thus the internationalism of the eighteenth century provided the links for the new movement.[59]

---

[55] Mott, *op. cit.*, p. 228.

[56] J. S. Bassett, ed., "Correspondence of George Bancroft and Jared Sparks, 1823–1832," *Smith College Studies in History*, II, 73 (January, 1917).

[57] H. G. Doyle, "George Ticknor," *Modern Language Journal*, XXII, 5 (October, 1937). Note also Emma Jaeck, *Madame de Staël and the Spread of German Literature* (New York, 1915).

[58] O. W. Long, *Thomas Jefferson and George Ticknor: A Chapter in American Scholarship* (Williamstown, Mass., 1933).

[59] There had been, of course, earlier German-American relationships. See Michael Kraus, *A History of American History* (New York, 1937), pp. 191–192, and Jaeck, *op. cit.* Irving's early visit (1804–1806) to Europe had been culturally unproductive (Pochmann, *Irving*, p. xviii), but note his interest in European belles lettres in 1813–1815 (*ibid.*, p. xxx) and his friend Brevoort's service in supplying European liaisons (*ibid.*, p. xxxi, note).

Four years of travel, and of study under such teachers as Heyne and Wolf, taught Ticknor (as he wrote Jefferson) that the study of antiquity might be a "liberal science" rather than a "mechanical art";[60] that American libraries were inadequate; and that the study of modern languages was a major desideratum in American colleges.   Upon his return in 1819 he assumed at Harvard the Smith Professorship of French and Spanish Language and Literature and built up the department which was to train such men as Lowell, Norton, and Child.   With Jefferson and others he led the effort to modernize the whole college curriculum in the middle 1820's;[61] he was the central figure in the founding of the Boston Public Library in the 1850's; and, following his own convictions about scholarship, he devoted a good part of the rest of his life to the writing of a *History of Spanish Literature* (1849) which, it was said, not six men in Europe were capable of reviewing.[62]

It was no accident that within a year after Ticknor's return, Prescott decided on a career of scholarship and that he chose Spanish history as his special subject in 1826.   Ticknor took no credit for the course of studies which Prescott laid out for himself in October, 1821, but it is significant that by 1823 Prescott was studying French and Italian literature, reading European criticisms and histories of literature with which Ticknor's group must have become familiar when they were abroad,[63] and carrying on an elaborate scholarly correspondence with his mentor on the subject of Italian literature.   It is likely also that Ticknor communicated to Prescott something of his own enthusiasm for German, for the latter determined in 1822 to learn the lan-

[60] Doyle, *op. cit.*, p. 11.

[61] On this subject see Doyle, *op. cit.*; Louis Snow, *The College Curriculum in the United States* (New York, 1907); G. P. Schmidt, "Intellectual Cross-Currents in American Colleges, 1825–1855," *American Historical Review*, XLII, 46–67 (October, 1936); W. T. Foster, *The Administration of the College Curriculum* (New York, 1911).

[62] See *Life, Letters, and Journals of George Ticknor*, II, 254.

[63] Ticknor, pp. 58–62.

guage, which he "deemed more important to the general scholarship at which he aimed than any other modern language." [64]
Eye trouble forced him to give up this plan in 1824, but thereafter he kept in touch with German criticism and scholarship through translations.[65]

Ticknor's part in Prescott's final choice of Spanish history was considerable. He had studied at Göttingen at a time when it was a center of Spanish studies, and had been tutored by the eminent Spanish scholar Condé at Madrid. On his return to America he had worked up a course of lectures on Spanish literature for his students at Harvard. As Ticknor tells it, "Thinking simply to amuse and occupy my friend at a time when he seemed much to need it, I proposed to read him these lectures in the autumn of 1824 . . . and in November he determined, as a substitute for the German, to undertake the Spanish, which had not previously constituted any part of his plan of study." [66]
Ticknor helped him prepare a study list, and gave him the run of his Spanish library.

The year 1825 was a period of indecision for Prescott. He contemplated writing a history of Italian literature, American history, Roman history, and biography, debating their advantages in his private memoranda. It was characteristic of the man that in spite of his dislike for digging into "latent, barren antiquities," in spite of his ignorance of legal and institutional philosophy, he "subscribed," on January 19, 1826, to the subject of the reign of Ferdinand and Isabella.[67]

---

[64] *Ibid.*, p. 68.

[65] In Prescott's histories there are few references to titles in the German language. On translations available in his time, see B. Q. Morgan, *A Critical Bibliography of German Literature in English Translation, 1481–1927* (Stanford, 1938), especially under the headings of Ranke, Raumer, Schiller, Niebuhr, Müller, and Heeren. F. W. Lembke kept him informed of important German works in his field (*Correspondence*, p. 51–52).

[66] Ticknor, pp. 70–71.

[67] *Ibid.*, p. 76.

"Dedicated" would have been a better word. For the rest of his life his devotion to Spanish history was such that his biography must be written largely in terms of his literary career. A few trips to Washington, New York City, and Albany, a triumphal visit to England in 1850,[68] occasional evenings with the "Club" (which, however, always ended for Prescott at ten o'clock),[69] entertainment of distinguished visitors, such as the Calderóns, the Charles Lyells, Lord Carlisle, Dickens, and Thackeray at one of his three homes[70]—these are the high points of his nonworking hours. No hobby, like Parkman's rose-growing, none of Bancroft's and Motley's adventures in politics and statesmanship. Even his daily horseback ride was "business," for he composed history in his head as he galloped.[71]

3. Contemporary Interest in Spanish Subjects

The choice was a good one. For the rest of his career Prescott worked painstakingly on a theme as grand as Gibbon's— the rise and decline of a great empire. This was not Prescott's plan when he began his first work, but before he died he had depicted Spain's rise to world power under Ferdinand and Isabella (1474–1517), its conquest of Mexico (1519–1521) and of Peru (1524–1550), and the beginning of its decline under Philip II (1556–1574). Only a history of the reign of Charles V was lacking to make Prescott's works a saga of the most brilliant century in Spain's history, and this, at least, he contributed

---

[68] For a detailed account of the trip, see Ticknor, pp. 299–341.

[69] H. T. Peck, *William Hickling Prescott*, English Men of Letters Series (New York, 1905), p. 92.

[70] Ticknor devotes chap. xxvi to Prescott's homes. These were at Tremont Street, Bedford Street, and Beacon Street, successively, in Boston; the ancestral country home at Pepperell; and the cottages at the shore—first at Nahant, then at Lynn.

[71] *Ibid.*, pp. 127 and 149.

to by writing a new conclusion to Robertson's history of Charles (1769).[72]

The literary exploitation of Spanish history by Irving, Prescott, and Motley had its special background. The antiquarianism of Hurd and Warton had, of course, directed attention to the riches of the popular and formal literature of medieval Spain, and Gothic fiction and drama had drawn heavily upon Latin backgrounds. Of particular significance is the use made of Spanish history by the rationalists and the primitivists. For believers in the concept of the Noble Savage,[73] the stories of Spain's conquests in the New World were arsenals of evidence that Catholic civilization spoiled whatever it touched. In the 1780's and 1790's this concept merged with French revolutionary ideology[74] to produce a great vogue of Spanish history as a literary subject.[75] Early anti-Spanish accounts of the destruction of the Inca and Aztec societies, such as those of the Inca, Garcilasso de la Vega (1540–1616), and of Bishop Bartolomé de las Casas (1474–1566),[76] were the sources[77] of dramas on the

---

[72] Prescott was often urged to write an entirely new history of his period, but declined. (See Ticknor, pp. 372, 406.) His addition to Robertson's *The History of the Reign of Charles V* (III, 325–510) appeared in the Boston edition of 1857. Inasmuch as almost all of the material in his continuation appeared in his own *Philip II*, Book I, chaps. i and x, references hereafter will be to the latter.

[73] See H. N. Fairchild, *The Noble Savage* (New York, 1928).

[74] Note the popularity in America of such primitivistic and anti-Christian propaganda as Constantin Volney's *Les Ruines, ou Méditation sur les Révolutions des Indes* (1791) and Guillaume Raynal's *Histoire des Indes* (1772). See H. M. Jones, *America and French Culture* (1927), p. 404, and Bernard Faÿ, *The Revolutionary Spirit in France and America* (1927), pp. 8–11.

[75] See Fairchild, *op. cit.*, and Benjamin Bissell, *The American Indian in English Literature of the Eighteenth Century* (Yale Studies in English, Vol. LXVIII).

[76] For convenient accounts of the work of these historians, see Prescott's *Peru*, pp. 879–882, and *Mexico*, pp. 203–209.

[77] Through Jean François Marmontel's *Les Incas* (1777), an important source of drama on this subject (Bissell, *op. cit.*, p. 148).

Incas by Kotzebue,[78] which, in turn, were translated and adapted
by English[79] and American[80] playwrights. An even more common source for primitivistic literature was *The History of America* (1777) by Prescott's great predecessor in the field, William
Robertson (1721–1793),[81] whose work was used by Joel Barlow
in the *Columbiad* (1807),[82] by W. G. Simms in *The Vision of
Cortes* (1829),[83] and by R. M. Bird in his Spanish plays and
novels.[84]

In the nineteenth century several factors contributed toward
a new phase of interest in Spain. Napoleon's raids on the
Peninsula naturally aroused British sympathy, which was expressed in verse by Wordsworth, Byron, Landor, and others.
The literary phase received fresh impetus from German scholarship in the field of early Spanish literature.[85] Southey's work

[78] *The Virgin of the Sun* (1791), *The Spaniards in Peru* (1795).

[79] Bissell, *op. cit.*, pp. 154–155.

[80] William Dunlap's adaptations held the American stage for forty
years. See A. H. Quinn, *A History of American Drama from the
Beginning to the Civil War*, pp. 97–99.

[81] Bissell, *op. cit.*, p. 165.

[82] T. A. Zunder, *Early Days of Joel Barlow* (New Haven, 1934),
pp. 87, 220. Note also that C. B. Brown contemplated epics on
Mexico and Peru (Quinn, *American Fiction*, p. 26).

[83] See the preface. Simms says that the poem is part of a longer
work which he had destroyed; and that he wonders why a field so
full of genuine romance has not been drawn upon oftener by poets.
Note also Simms' novels on Spanish themes—*Pelayo* (1838); *The
Damsel of Darien* (1839), the material for which was drawn from
Irving's *Companions of Columbus; Count Julian* (1845); and *Vascon-
celas* (1854).

[84] *Oralloossa* (1832), a blank verse tragedy on the sufferings of the
Peruvians; *Calavar, or the Knight of the Conquest* (1834), and its
sequel, *The Infidel, or the Fall of Mexico* (1835). Bird was learned in
the language and history of Spain. See Quinn, *History of American
Drama from the Beginning to the Civil War*, p. 238; and C. B. Williams,
introduction to Bird's *Nick of the Woods* (New York, 1939).

[85] Particularly Friedrich Bouterwek's *Geschichte der neuern Poesie
und Beredsamkeit* (Göttingen, 1801–1819) which included a history
of Spanish literature often published separately in translation. For
Prescott's recognition that this was a pioneer work, see *Miscellanies*,

in the first decade was to have a direct influence on Prescott,[86] who read his translation of the *Amadis* as a boy and who, in his *Conquest of Mexico*, quoted frequently from *Madoc* (1805), a poem on the legendary origins of the Aztecs.

Spanish materials had, therefore, been extensively explored by literary men before Prescott began his first work in 1826, and the literary appeal of the subject had been firmly established. From the point of view of historical scholarship, however, the American historians were motivated chiefly by the publication of new source materials which followed upon the opening of the Spanish archives in 1780. In this field the work of Muñoz, Don Vargas Ponçe, Navarrete, Llorente, and Condé made the rewriting of Spanish history not only possible but necessary.[87] Prescott and Irving seem to have marked out provinces for themselves almost simultaneously. A month after Prescott decided on his subject (January, 1826), Irving arrived in Madrid to find the scholarly world excited over Navarrete's first volume of his *Coleccion de los viages* . . . At Edward Everett's suggestion, and with the aid of Obadiah Rich, Irving began a translation of the work which he soon turned into a supposedly original *Life and Voyages of Columbus* (1828).[88] A year later he brought out his *Conquest of Granada*, which, Prescott said, "superseded all further necessity for poetry, and unfortunately for me, for history." [89] Thus Prescott

p. 643. Note also K. F. Eichhorn's *Geschichte der Kultur und Litteratur der neuern Europa* (Göttingen, 1796–1811).

[86] On Southey's Spanish studies, see Oliver Elton, *A Survey of English Literature, 1780–1880*, II, 1–12. Note Prescott's comment that the necessity of an English version of Condé's great *History of the Domination of the Arabs in Spain*, published in the 1820's, would be superseded by Southey's use of the material in the *Cabinet Cyclopaedia* (*Ferdinand and Isabella*, I, 315).

[87] Treated more fully in section iii, below.

[88] S. T. Williams, *Washington Irving*, I, 303. On Irving's understatement of his debt to Navarrete, see *ibid.*, II, 299–301, and *Ferdinand and Isabella*, II, 134, 509.

[89] *Ferdinand and Isabella*, II, 109.

found that two of the most brilliant portions of his story had been robbed of their novelty while he was making his "tortoise-like progress."[90] A more serious situation was averted later when Irving, upon learning that Prescott was at work on the *Conquest of Mexico*, gave up his own plans in that field.[91] Prescott's opportunity to be generous in similar circumstances came in 1847, when Motley, hearing of Prescott's intention of writing a history of the reign of Philip II, asked him if he had any objection to his writing on the war of the Netherlands—"the cream of my subject," as Prescott put it. Prescott not only agreed, but offered Motley his source books, for he inclined to take the broad, if practical, view that a simultaneous working of the soil would augment the crop.[92]

How, in spite of his semi-blindness, Prescott met such competition in his own field is an interesting story. His wealth, of course, made it possible for him to buy not only the new works, most of them expensive, but the best editions of old ones. The acquisition of manuscript materials, however, was another problem. Realizing at the very start that he would not be able to use his own eyes in the foreign archives, but increasingly anxious to base his work on original sources, Prescott made use of social connections without which access to European libraries and manuscript collections would have been impossible. Thanks to the circumstance that in those days many American consuls and

---

[90] *Ferdinand and Isabella*, I, xi–xii.

[91] Prescott acknowledged the sacrifice handsomely in his preface to *Mexico*, but Irving wrote, "I doubt whether Mr. Prescott was aware [that I] gave him up my bread" (G. S. Hellman, *Washington Irving, Esquire* [1925], p. 236). S. T. Williams (*op. cit.*, II, 105) wonders at the lack of negotiations or of offers of compromise of any sort from Prescott, but Prescott's correspondence (Ticknor, pp. 166–173) shows that he wrote Irving as soon as he knew of the latter's plans, though he probably suspected them earlier. See also *Correspondence*, p. 48.

[92] *Correspondence*, p. 663. See Motley's account of the incident in Ticknor, pp. 278–280.

ambassadors were not only men of family but men of culture,[93] Prescott had entrée to the places and people most valuable to him.

His most useful friend was George Ticknor, who had powerful connections in literary and political circles throughout Europe. Through Ticknor came Prescott's contacts with the Italian historian, the Marquis Capponi;[94] with the English historian, Henry Hallam;[95] with the distinguished Spanish scholar, Pascual de Gayangos. Ticknor's importance in his friend's career is best illustrated, perhaps, by his handling of review copies of *Ferdinand and Isabella*. From Paris he wrote in 1838, "One I sent instantly to Julius . . .; one to Von Raumer . . . with a request to review it; one to Guizot . . .; one to Count Circourt, who will write a review of it . . .; one to Fauriel, the very best scholar in Spanish literature and Spanish history alive . . . whom I have also asked to notice it . . . another, for a man named Doudan, who will review it in 'Revue Française.'" In England he went to the headquarters of Spanish scholarship, Lord Holland's house, in order to get the work reviewed in the *Edinburgh*. "It was fully agreed that Allen should write it, if Napier could persuade him to do so,—which I do not anticipate; that otherwise a review by a young Spaniard, by name Gayangos, which I know Allen will propose, shall be accepted; and, if both of these fail, that then the subject shall be given to Dunlop, the author of the *History of Fiction*." In the course of the negotiations, Lord Holland, Sydney Smith, Jeffrey, and Allen all wrote to Napier in Ticknor's behalf.[96]

Such friends, such opportunities cannot be lightly dismissed

[93] On this subject, see R. E. Spiller, *The American in England* (New York, 1926), especially chap. iv. For details on Prescott's scholarly friends and agents, see section iii, below.

[94] Ticknor's *Life, Letters, and Journals*, II, 56; and see *Correspondence*, p. 59.

[95] *Correspondence*, p. 35.

[96] Ticknor's *Life, Letters, and Journals*, II, 142-143, 161, 162.

in an estimate of Prescott's work and career. If, in the long run, he has had greater success with the general reader than either Motley or Irving (as historian), the fact must be attributed in part to the circumstances of his life and environment. Protected from financial pressure, he could afford to incubate his studies longer than Irving; well-adjusted to his time and community, and concerned with the reform of himself rather than of the world, he had none of Motley's political partisanship or philosophic bias; heir to New England's heritage of scholarship and its political prestige, he found the doors of the world's libraries and muniment rooms open to his helpers, and influential friends ready to serve as eyes and agents. But it is no small compliment to say that he deserved all of his good fortune.

II. ATTITUDES TOWARD HISTORY

When Prescott was at work on his *Ferdinand and Isabella*, a distinguished visitor to America, Alexis de Tocqueville, was writing his observations on the characteristics of historians in democratic ages. He noted that historians catering to an aristocratic society were wont to attribute occurrences to the will of certain individuals, and even events of the utmost importance apparently flowed from "very slight accidents"; the least significant causes were analyzed with deep wisdom but the greatest were often left unnoted. Characteristics the reverse of these were observed in historians living in democratic ages. In their eyes the individual has scarcely any influence over man's progress and even to petty incidents "great general causes" were assigned. But it is exceedingly difficult to trace out these causes, often complex and hidden, in relation to specific events. Intellectual weariness begets vague generalizations and the historians soon prefer to talk about "the characteristics of race, the physical conformation of the country, or the genius of civilization—which abridges his own labors, and satisfies his reader far better at less cost." [97]

Prescott was an aristocrat writing in a democratic age and his works reveal the distinctive features attributed by de Tocqueville to historians belonging in each period. Prescott, however, would never have said as did his contemporary, George Bancroft, that he liked "to watch the shouts of the multitude but had rather not scream with them." [98] And yet, of course, he was not immune to the pervasive intellectual influences that colored the thinking of his generation.

No one factor was more significant than the writings of Sir Walter Scott, who hovered like a protecting deity over his English and American idolaters. For them he was beyond all others "the true Romantic historian," [99] and Prescott was only one of many who acclaimed Scott for giving "new charms to history by embellishing it with the graces of romance." [100] While Prescott may conveniently fit into the category of romantic historians (where he has always been placed), analysis of his reading and critical preferences reveals him to be kin to the remote and near past as well as to the immediate present. He belongs, too, in the tradition of American historiography— a tradition with well-established principles followed by leading practitioners of the art before Prescott lived. In his writing and in his more private remarks, one can study the forces which affected his development—rationalism, romanticism, democracy, Christianity, and the idea of progress.

The conventional classical training experienced by Prescott gave him an appreciative understanding of the ancient Greek and Latin historians. He was particularly impressed with their

[97] Alexis de Tocqueville, *Democracy in America* (trans. Henry Reeve, 2 vols. in one, n.d.), II, 90–93.

[98] Quoted in Kraus, *op. cit.*, p. 235.

[99] T. P. Peardon, *The Transition in English Historical Writing, 1760–1830* (New York, 1933), pp. 214–216.

[100] *Miscellanies*, p. 279.

ability "to stir the imaginations of their readers." Herodotus and Livy "bestowed infinite pains on the costume, the style of their history, and . . . made everything subordinate to the main purpose of conveying an elegant and interesting *narrative.*" [101] Prescott delighted in their poetry which infused every manifestation of their creative life, including historical composition. But while he was enthusiastic over the liveliness of their imagination, he claimed for his own generation a greater rationalism, a more matured historical judgment. Also, in contrast to pagan preference for "abstract contemplation or selfish indulgence," Christian doctrine (by which Prescott really meant Puritanism) "inculcated that the end of being was best answered by a life of active usefulness." [102]

In tracing the genealogy of the historians of his own time, Prescott said that the line of descent began with Voltaire, for he was the first to arrange into a regular system "the present laws of historic composition." [103] Voltaire was defended against charges of inaccuracy, although scolded for his "pernicious philosophy." Departing from the conventional chronological ordering of events (an arrangement which monastic chroniclers had bequeathed to eighteenth-century historians), Voltaire's "work was distributed on the principle of a *Catalogue raisonné,* into sections arranged according to their subjects, and copious dissertations were introduced into the body of the narrative." Chapters on letters, religion, manners, etc., were to be found in his *Essai sur les Mœurs . . .*, and in his *Age of Louis the Fourteenth* separate sections contain materials on court life and governmental policies.[104] Prescott spoke enthusiastically of Jacques N. A. Thierry's plan of historical composition. The spirit of an age he agreed could best be

[101] *Miscellanies,* p. 89.

[102] *Ibid.*, p. 93.

[103] *Ibid.*, p. 96.

[104] *Ibid.*, p. 99. Cf. Prescott's similar arrangement in his *Ferdinand and Isabella.*

captured by a study of the minstrelsy and legends of a period, "even more than in set historical records."[105]   Prescott's opinion of Sismondi was also very high; "there is no one of the historians of our generation for whom I have felt greater admiration than for him," he once wrote to a friend.[106]

The most influential historian in Prescott's intellectual growth was the Abbé de Mably, whose *De l'étude de l'histoire* he had read a number of times.   Mably was favored because of his "wide views," the "directness and good faith of his politics," in short his brand of moral didacticism.   Prescott went on to say that he liked especially Mably's realization that history should have dramatic interest as well as utility, by letting events tend to some obvious point or moral, very much as writers of romances or dramas would do.   Prescott expressly indicated that he intended to apply that principle in his own historical writing.[107]

Prescott admired greatly the narrative powers and the gift for brilliant generalization possessed by the French, but he seemed to prefer the English historians.   He admitted their lapses from impartiality but he claimed for them on the whole a superior integrity.   No one more clearly revealed the principles of modern history than did Gibbon.   His erudition was enormous and his glowing style kindled "a corresponding warmth in the bosom of his reader."[108]

Prescott might be thrilled intellectually from reading Voltaire and respond almost physically to the exhilaration of Gibbon, but his spirit, the abode of his moral being, remained unmoved, if not resentful.   And this is what marks him off from thoroughgoing rationalists.   Prescott, like earlier American

[105] *Correspondence*, p. 140.

[106] *Ibid.*, p. 405.

[107] Ticknor, pp. 94-95.

[108] *Miscellanies*, pp. 103, 105.   See Prescott's preference for English historians because they did not interpolate imaginary speeches in their narratives, as did Italian historians (*Mexico*, p. 618).

historians, Thomas Hutchinson, Jeremy Belknap, and Ebene-
zer Hazard, found no room for the miraculous in his narratives.
Belknap, the historian of New Hampshire, once wrote to his
friend Hazard that they ought to be together to laugh at Cotton
Mather's *Wonders of the Invisible World*.[109] They agreed with
Montesquieu in attributing major influence to the factor of environment—geography (mainly climate), government, and
religion. Man was the author of his own evil, the result of his
institutional shortcomings. But education, and especially the
study of history, would transform the world of evil into a
world of good. The idea of progress, subscribed to with whole-
hearted enthusiasm by eighteenth-century rationalists, led inevitably to the irrational acceptance of the perfectibility of
man.[110] Above all, wrote Benjamin Rush, "let our youth be
instructed in the history of the ancient republics, and the progress of liberty and tyranny in the different states of Europe."
A more careful investigation of the laws underlying national
development was proposed by Nathaniel Chipman. Historians formerly had been too largely interested in battles and sieges
and political intrigues. A more fundamental understanding of
civilization was to be gained by studying the "history of man
in society," for it would liberate man from "fanaticism and
superstition." History also would reveal the folly and vice of
war.[111]

Almost half a century separated Prescott from these American forerunners who were so close to the spirit of Voltaire.
The French Revolution had intervened and the reaction had
set in. Benevolent minds were easily led astray said Prescott,
by focusing "too exclusively" on contemporary evils and "in-

[109] "Belknap Papers," *Collections of the Massachusetts Historical
Society*, 5th ser., III, 198, Oct. 22, 1789.
[110] E. Fueter, *Geschichte der neueren Historiographie*, pp. 434–483;
J. B. Bury, *The Idea of Progress* (1932), chap. vii.
[111] A. O. Hansen, *Liberalism and American Education in the Eighteenth Century* (New York, 1926), pp. 56–57, 99, 153.

dulging in indefinite dreams of perfectibility."[112] Conservatives with property interests drew back from the abyss of infidelity which led to social chaos, and the once enthroned Voltaire was banished by the pious and the frightened. Religious revivals in America from the close of the eighteenth century on revitalized religious feeling among the masses. In more decorous manner the group to which Prescott belonged also refashioned its city of God.

It should be remembered that Voltairian rationalism never sank such deep roots in America nor in England as it did in France and elsewhere on the continent. And Prescott's taproot was in Anglo-American soil. Even in the heyday of Voltaire's triumph, Jonathan Mayhew, one of Boston's most intelligent clergymen, characterized his work with the same reserve later expressed by Prescott. Mayhew was writing of the *Philosophical Dictionary* and the *Philosophy of History* and thought them very fine literary performances: "I have read them with delight, as containing much useful learning, many fine observations on antiquity, & written throughout in a most spirited entertaining & masterly way: so that I would not be long without them for twice their value"—but Mayhew disagreed vigorously with their religious ideas.[113] Prescott's generation had recaptured something of that earlier religious feeling (albeit on a more rarefied plane) and the want of faith in the extreme rationalist historians was repellent. They were too self-conscious to attack the earlier group on the ground of being anti-religious (for that would be a confession of their own piety and orthodoxy) so they criticized them for moral defects. Skepticism in Gibbon and in Voltaire prevented their works from being suffused "with a generous moral sentiment";[114] Voltaire leaves

[112] See "Memoir of C. B. Brown," in *Miscellanies*, p. 10; also pp. 41–42.

[113] Bancroft, *Transcripts*, Jan. 7, 1766 (New York Public Library).

[114] *Miscellanies*, p. 104.

the impression of a "baleful withering skepticism"; neither he nor his readers ever experience "the glow of patriotism, or moral and religious enthusiasm."[115] The egotism of Gibbon marred his style so that the author often overshadowed his material. Thoroughgoing rationalists believed that the age soon to come would be the logical culmination of history's unfolding—for in it all institutions would have passed a searching examination at the bar of reason and emerged newly purified. Prescott could never employ reason so ruthlessly—much had to be taken on faith. In so far as the more determined rationalists believed history should teach us something, should "take us somewhere," [116] Prescott was in agreement with them; he differed in the direction.

Prescott feared the withering effects of the skepticism of Voltaire, but they had this faith in common—that man was destined to indefinite progress. And this faith would scarcely brook any criticism, particularly in the new world. With Americans it was a belief adhered to with religious intensity, and doubters were heretics and scorned as such. This was the one creed that transcended sectarian differences and its celebrants were peasants fleeing from Europe, real estate speculators flocking westward, workers in the cities, ministers, and historians. The American scene itself, it was argued, with its more fertile soil for the growth of libertarian and equalitarian sentiments would inspire new interpretations in history. William Ellery Channing thought the history of the human race was to be rewritten. "Men imbued with the prejudices which thrive under aristocracies and state religions, cannot understand it," he said. "Past ages, with their great events and great men, are to undergo, we think, a new trial and to yield new results. It is plain that history is already viewed under new aspects, and we believe that the true principles for studying

[115] *Miscellanies*, p. 98.
[116] J. B. Black, *The Art of History* (London, 1926), p. 21.

and writing it are to be unfolded here."[117] George Bancroft, Prescott's friend and fellow historian, thought that our historical literature should have running through it "a vein of public feeling, of democratic independence, of popular liberty."[118] In his writing he associated directly the United States with the idea of progress; "the trust of our race," he declares, "has ever been in the coming of better times."[119]

Prescott was more reserved in his expression of similar thoughts, but they may be found scattered through his writings. They are not a fundamental theme in his work, sometimes being convenient pegs from which dangle comparisons of the relative merits of primitive and modern civilizations and Catholic and Protestant societies. Non-Christian peoples while admittedly contributors to civilization were, on the whole, wisely removed to make room for followers of Christianity. Arabs in Spain had made real contributions to civilization but they were doomed to decay having exhausted their creative powers. Therefore they were succeeded by a people "whose religion and more liberal form of government . . . qualified them for advancing still higher the interests of humanity."[120] Aztecs and Incas, too, followed the Arabs of Spain into eclipse. Belief in human sacrifice was a prime cause of the undoing of the Aztecs and there was no need to lament their collapse. In describing individual Aztec chieftains Prescott often does them justice by noting their dignity and courage, but when writing of the mass of the people he has less detachment. "The Empire of the Aztecs," he concludes, "did not fall before its time."[121] Their fate gives striking proof "that a government, which does not rest on the sympathies of its subjects, cannot long abide;

[117] Quoted in Kraus, *op. cit.*, pp. 181–182.
[118] Letter to Jared Sparks, in H. B. Adams, *The Life and Writings of Jared Sparks* (1893), II, 192, note 1.
[119] Bancroft, *History of the United States* (1852), III, 398.
[120] *Ferdinand and Isabella*, II, 105–106.
[121] *Mexico*, p. 613.

that human institutions, when not connected with human prosperity and progress, must fall,—if not before the increasing light of civilization, by the hand of violence; by violence from within, if not from without."[122]   Incas, although progressive in many respects, had built a society in which individual initiative had been strait-jacketed, thus leaving the people defenseless in the face of the adventurous, aggressive Spaniards.   With all its limitations of fanatical prejudices, Catholicism was a brand of morality superior to that of brutish paganism, said Prescott, and therefore was a force for progress.   Mohammedanism too, "with its doctrines of blind fatality," its despotism and "sensual religion," was inimical to cultural advance; Christianity quickened and elevated the soul "by the consciousness of its glorious destiny." [123]   On at least one occasion, however, Prescott paused to note the moral dangers to the whites so ruthlessly using their superior strength in conflict with natives everywhere in the world.   The European feels that he has a natural right to the obedience of natives; "wherever the civilized man and the savage have come in contact, in the East or in the West, the story has been too often written in blood." [124]

But while Prescott was partial to Christianity in general, as against non-Christian believers, he had his preferences within Christianity.   They were, despite a strong attempt at maintaining impartiality, for Protestant Christianity.   The Inquisition in Spain had bound the minds of the curious and covered with ashes the sparks of intellectual revolt.[125]   No great pro-

---

[122] *Mexico*, p. 615.

[123] *Miscellanies*, p. 295; *Ferdinand and Isabella*, p. 286.   A distinguished French reviewer of *Ferdinand and Isabella* thought that the war against Granada was "not to be justified by the code of a Christian civilization" (Ticknor, pp. 112–113).

[124] *Peru*, pp. 1037–1038.

[125] Cf. *Philip II*, I, 445–448, one of the clearest expressions by Prescott of the effects of the Inquisition in Spain.

gressive achievements could be expected from such a society with all its abuses of feudalism, "already far exhausted and hastening to decay." The next tremendous step in the advance of mankind came with the Reformation which "gave an electric shock to the intellect, long benumbed under the influence of a tyrannical priesthood. It taught men to distrust authority, . . . to search for themselves and to take no guide but the reason which God had given them." Freedom of action followed hard upon freedom of inquiry. Struggles in behalf of civil liberty in the eighteenth and nineteenth centuries succeeded earlier battles over religious issues.[126] Prescott defended the Reformation against the strictures of Chateaubriand. Admittedly Catholicism furnished a favorable atmosphere for the finest achievements in the fine arts, but its main appeal was to the senses. But with the growth of Protestantism, "reason took the place of sentiment—the useful of the merely ornamental";[127] "the cold abstractions of Protestantism" prevented it from making much of an impression on primitive peoples; a higher degree "of refinement and mental culture" was needed to comprehend the faith of Protestants.[128] American Protestantism had reached the greatest heights. True, in the first flush of their enthusiasm, Puritans had been intolerant of other beliefs and they deserved censure, though not too harsh, for it. But here in this new land was "no feudal tyrant to grind the poor man to the dust on which he toiled, no Inquisition to pierce into the thought, and to make thought a crime."[129]

Prescott found superior virtues in the process of expansion as practiced by Anglo-Saxon peoples in America. Unlike the natives of southern Europe they were not motivated by avarice, "nor the more specious pretext of proselytism; but independence,—independence, religious and political." They were con-

---

[126] *Miscellanies*, pp. 298–299.
[128] *Mexico*, p. 159.
[127] *Ibid.*, p. 268.
[129] *Miscellanies*, p. 299.

tent with a "life of frugality and toil," following the slow but
sure path of social progress; "No golden visions threw a deceitful halo around their path, and beckoned them onwards through
seas of blood to the subversion of an unoffending dynasty."
The communities established by the Portuguese and Spaniards,
"shooting up into the sudden splendors of a tropical vegetation, exhibited, even in their prime, the sure symptoms of
decay." But while Prescott gives the palm to Anglo-Saxons
for their type of settlement, he makes partial amends by concluding that seemingly, by providential dispensation, the discovery of the western hemisphere was made by "the two races
best fitted to conquer and colonize" it.[130]

Prescott, we have noted, was heir to the Enlightenment of
the eighteenth century and to its beliefs in natural laws. One
of those (not always clearly formulated) was the tendency to
civil and political liberty. Prescott's friend Bancroft believed
firmly in this idea and in an address before the New York Historical Society he phrased it in these words: "As a consequence
of the tendency of the race towards unity and universality, the
organization of society must more and more conform to the
principle of freedom."[131] Writers of Prescott's generation
sometimes dimly anticipated theories of the later school represented by Edward A. Freeman and Herbert B. Adams, ad-
vocates of the "germ theory" of politics which traced libertarian
ideas back to early dwellers in German forests—a sort of fanciful gene in the racial protoplasm which transmitted its characteristics down through the years. The first settlers, said
Prescott, "brought with them the living principle of freedom,
which would survive when their generation had passed
away."[132] Concentration of power in earlier civilizations, Inca,

[130] *Peru*, p. 830.
[131] Bancroft, *The Necessity, the Reality and the Promise of the
Progress of the Human Race* (New York, 1854).
[132] *Miscellanies*, p. 300.

Moorish, and Spanish, made progress impossible. What could Mohammedans know, asked Prescott, "of the finer moral relations ... developed only under free and beneficent institutions?" [133] Despotism was a stony soil for such tender plants as civil and religious liberties, but in the long run persecution was impotent even when used in behalf of good as against evil.[134] "The seeds of liberty, though dormant, lay deep in the heart of the nation waiting only the good time to germinate." That time had arrived, thought Prescott, and the ultimate flowering of liberal principles was assured.[135]

Prescott's writings, we have seen, registered the winds of doctrine that blew across his generation—romanticism, rationalism, the idea of progress, and the virtues of Christian as against non-Christian civilizations. Despite his apparent preoccupation with the inculcation of a proper morality through history, this was, it seems, a secondary consideration in his art. The primary objective was to tell a picturesque story or narrate a tale with mounting crescendos and magnificent climaxes. The scientific method was to be followed in accumulating materials, but the writing of the historical narrative belonged in the field of belles lettres.[136] Thus it is clear why Scott of all the romantics should have been among the most favored. His Tory benevolence was something that Prescott understood,[137] and as a literary artist no one ever surpassed him in the painting of battle scenes; "he had a natural relish for gunpowder; and his mettle roused, like that of the war-horse, at the sound of the trumpet." [138] Prescott understood the glamorous appeal of scenes of war and of courtly splendor. The attractiveness of

[133] *Ferdinand and Isabella*, I, 304.
[134] *Ibid.*, II, 456.
[135] *Ibid.*, III, 447.
[136] *Mexico*, p. 616.
[137] *Miscellanies*, p. 225.
[138] *Ibid.*, p. 284. Cf. Prescott's own "relish for gunpowder," in his pages of battle scenes.

Scott was reenforced by the achievement of M. de Barante, author of the *Histoire des ducs de Bourgogne*. Barante was critical of modern writers who inadequately exploited the older chroniclers; "they tell the reader how he should feel, instead of making him do so." By the proper choice of selections from the older historians Barante projected his modern reader into the life of the past,[139] and Prescott thought it wise to emulate him. The American historian may not have expressed the thought as directly as did Macaulay who wished to supplant the latest novel on milady's table with his history, but his object was very similar. Half in jest, he noted, too, his popularity among children. The *Conquest of Mexico*, he remarked to a correspondent, "is a child's story as much as any of Monk Lewis's tales of wonder." [140] History, then, should instruct us to achieve a higher degree of morality and as a branch of literature it should also entertain.

III. PRESCOTT'S SCHOLARSHIP

New Englanders, George Bancroft once pointed out, "have always been a documentary people."[141] Their collections of materials for the historian have been plentiful and their historical-mindedness has often been a subject of comment. A tradition running back for a hundred years before the appearance of *Ferdinand and Isabella*, had emphasized, too, the need of diligence in ferreting out sources and of scrupulous care in naming references. Thomas Prince, in his *Chronological History of New England* (1736) stated his credo: "I would not take the least iota upon trust: if possible, I examined the original authors I could meet with. . . . I cite my vouchers to every passage."

---

[139] *Miscellanies*, p. 107. Cf. Woodrow Wilson's opinion that historians should know no more of the period they are describing than the generation which then lived.

[140] *Correspondence*, p. 447.

[141] *North American Review* (April, 1838), p. 476.

Men and women of literary tastes turned easily to writing history and if it happened to be that of another country it might almost be laid to accident rather than to design. Even then there was an infusion of so much of the native spirit that, though the historian's canvas might be foreign, his frame was New England's.

In the first days of January, 1826, Prescott committed himself to a study of the age of Ferdinand, for this was the period that contained "the germs of the modern system of European politics"; Henry VII and Louis XI were instrumental in overturning the old system. In every respect, thought Prescott, it was "an interesting and momentous period of history; the materials authentic, ample." After weighing with some care the difficulties to be met with, Prescott wrote in his diary, January 19, 1826, that he subscribed to the history of the reign of Ferdinand and Isabella;[142] it was a decision he was never to regret despite the years of labor it entailed.

Once having made his decision Prescott planned a systematic survey of European history in the fifteenth and sixteenth centuries, with particular attention to the years during which Ferdinand ruled. With critical ears he listened to the reading of all the original sources he could lay his hands on, and in his wide-flung net he caught all the authorities who had published anything of importance on the reign of Ferdinand and Isabella. He placed particular dependence on the biography of Isabella by Don Diego Clemencin.[143] Temporarily turned aside from his immediate purpose by the preparation of an article on Washington Irving's *Conquest of Granada*, Prescott returned to his studies and in the fall of 1829 began the composition of his work.

From the fullness of his knowledge and the enthusiasm for his theme words seemed to cascade until they overran the limits

---

[142] Ticknor, pp. 75–76.
[143] *Ibid.*, p. 96.

he had set for himself. But what appeared to be a carefree out-
pouring of language was actually the thoughtful estimate of
events and personalities Prescott reluctantly gave to the world.
In a light mood he wrote to George Bancroft that he was nearing the end of his work; "I have little more to do than bury
and write the epitaphs of the Great Captain, Ximenes, and
Ferdinand. Columbus and Isabella are already sent to their account. So my present occupation seems to be that of a sexton,
and I begin to weary of it."[144] Ten years of intense application
had gone by when, at Christmas, 1837, the three volumes of
A History of the Reign of Ferdinand and Isabella were published.
Its success was instantaneous, partly because of the immense
personal popularity of the author but also because the solidity
of its achievement was readily recognized.

Prescott hesitated for only a brief while before plunging into
the further ramifications of his Spanish theme. His plans for
research matched in grandeur the accomplishments of his heroes.
They embraced narratives of the conquests of Mexico and Peru
and an elaborate investigation of the age of Philip the Second.
Prescott's friend Pascual de Gayangos had noted often that a
study of Philip would break new ground, for there was scarcely
anything of value in the field.[145]

With his characteristic fervor Prescott set to work gathering
needed materials for his *Mexico*. In some respects he thought
that this subject was superior to the story of Columbus for the
"perilous adventures and crosses with which the enterprise is
attended, the desperate chances and reverses and unexpected
vicissitudes, all serve to keep the interest alive."[146] But before
he could write the pages that narrated the exciting details of the
conquest, Prescott felt it necessary to lay a foundation with the
early traditions and history of Mexico. This introduction in-

---

[144] Ticknor, pp. 97–98, June 17, 1835.
[145] *Ibid.*, p. 191, and *Correspondence*, p. 167.
[146] *Ibid.*, p. 187.

volved him in the most difficult part of his subject, for the evidence was conflicting, and after two years of hard labor he was ready to call quits with the pre-Spanish history of Mexico.

A few weeks after publication of *The Conquest of Mexico* (1843), Prescott started on the *Peru*. "I shall work the mine, however, at my leisure," he promised himself.[147] His mine of materials was more complete than that on Mexico, and despite the more leisurely gait he had promised himself his composition proceeded at a rapid rate. The two volumes were published in 1847.

Prescott allowed himself a brief period of loafing before beginning on *Philip II*. Standard works by Robertson, Watson (whose history of Philip II was held in contempt by Prescott), and the greatly esteemed Ranke were read to him. He was justly proud of his own possessions of books and manuscripts relating to this subject, "a truly precious collection of rarities," he claimed. He toyed for a moment with the idea of writing up a single brilliant episode in Philip's reign but he rather preferred a *kulturgeschichte* of the entire period. And yet the choice he finally made did not substantially differ from his original impulse for he intended to stress "the most important and interesting features of the reign, and bring these, and these only, into as clear a light as possible." He would avoid "wearisome research" into constitutional, financial and ecclesiastical details, treating them sparingly, and using them merely as background "to the great transactions of the reign."[148] Instead of concentrating on one incident the historian decided to bring together a series of specifically selected episodes. Thus with his mind made up he began the composition of *Philip II* in the last days of July, 1849.

He counted his treasures in great events and great men; "the

[147] *Ibid.*, p. 231.

[148] *Ibid.*, p. 293. Prescott, like other historians, subscribed more in theory than in practice to the notion of relating events and personalities to their historical backgrounds.

war with the Turks, and the glowing battle of Lepanto; the bloody revolt of the Moriscos; the conquest of Portugal, . . . the gallant days of the Armada." He had a good gallery of portraits—"Don John of Austria, frank and chivalrous; the great Duke of Alva, a name of terror; William of Orange, the Washington of Holland; Farnese, the greatest captain of his times; Don Sebastian, the theme for romance rather than history"; and of course the dominant personality of Philip himself. There is more than a touch of the eighteenth-century Gothic atmosphere of horror that he threw around Philip, "the master-spirit, who, in the dark recesses of the Escorial, himself unseen even by his own subjects, watches over the lines of communication which run out in every direction to the farthest quarters of the globe."[149]

While he worked on the *Philip*, he brought out a continuation of Robertson's *Charles the Fifth*, which had not sufficiently dealt with the life of the emperor following his abdication. Prescott depreciated this work, done at the suggestion of his publishers, but excused it on the ground that people who liked a complete series needed it "to fill up the gap betwixt 'Ferdinand' and 'Philip.'"

Prescott, in the main, leaps from peak to peak in the achievements of individuals. He had many heroes and heroines but few villains.[150] Like his younger contemporary, Francis Parkman, he wished to project before his readers "a certain ideal of manhood, a little medieval, but nevertheless good."[151] The Spaniard, wrote Prescott, was always a Crusader. "He was in

[149] Ticknor, pp. 293–294.

[150] A contemporary observed as one of Prescott's charms "that his worst characters are so fully developed that we perceive their humanity as well as their rascality. They never appear as bundles of evil qualities, but as men" (E. P. Whipple, *Essays and Reviews*, II, 180).

[151] Kraus, *op. cit.*, p. 273. Cf. Prescott's remark, "I am afraid that I can't make a *preux chevalier* out of Pizarro" (*Correspondence*, p. 513).

the sixteenth century, what Coeur de Lion and his brave knights were in the twelfth," but the latter fought for the Cross and glory, whereas the Spaniard fought for the Cross and gold.[152] But not all Spaniards were seen in this light. Philip had much less appeal for Prescott than had Isabella. The events in Philip's reign were great enough, but to the historian "there was not much true greatness of soul in those who conducted them. I am sorry for this, as one likes a noble character for his canvas."[153] With all his good nature Prescott couldn't wash Philip "even into the darkest French gray. He is black and all black."[154]

In the *Mexico*, which probably had the greatest appeal for Prescott, he dealt with material so overladen with an air of romanticism, that it was difficult to treat it as sober history. There was great temptation in writing about it to escape the "severe rules prescribed by historical criticism," but he successfully avoided it and vigorously sought to distinguish fact from fiction.[155] Prescott tells the story as if he himself scarcely believed, despite its authentication by the many sources at his command. In fact so carried away is he by the seeming fantasy of it all that he includes anecdotes that he himself only half believes.[156] "This half civilization breed," he wrote, "makes a sort of mystification like twilight in which things appear as big again as they are, and all distorted from the truth."[157]

Historians of a later day too easily assumed that the romantic school was seduced from the truth by the glamour of their materials. It is true that Prescott's approach on occasion put a premium upon types of sources not quite so highly prized by later scholars; "I have always found a good, gossiping chronicle or memoir the best and most fruitful material for the historian," he once stated to a friend.[158] While it is obvious that

---

[152] *Peru*, p. 988.   [153] *Correspondence*, pp. 565–566.
[154] Ticknor, p. 414.   [155] *Mexico*, preface, p. 4.
[156] *Ibid.*, p. 426.   [157] *Correspondence*, p. 115.   [158] Ticknor, p. 190.

at many points corrections can be made of their work and new angles made to cast a different light on their subjects, yet in the main the version left us by the best of these historians may well be fairly truthful. In Prescott's case we have the word of one of the best of modern scholars in the field, R. B. Merriman, that the *Conquest of Mexico* is "still the best book on the subject with which it deals," although new material of great value is to be found in Manuel Orozco y Berra's *Historia Antigua y de la Conquista de México.* For the specialist Orozco y Berra's work has greater usefulness than Prescott's on the Aztec period as it is far more detailed in its archaeologic and ethnographic studies.[159] Another distinguished historian of Latin America, Diego Barros Arana, informs us that although he consulted original sources and documents, some of which were unknown to Prescott, he followed consistently the latter's interpretation of the Mexican conquest.[160] A third historian in a detailed work on Mexico likewise indicated his high regard for Prescott upon whom he leaned heavily for the story of the conquest.[161]

Merriman's verdict is equally favorable to the *Conquest of Peru*—it "remains the standard authority"[162] and recent works add little to it. A half century after the appearance of the *Conquest of Peru*, an English historian of wide reputation, Clements R. Markham, said that his generation depended almost entirely upon Prescott for information on the Incas.[163]

It was to be expected that Spaniards would read with close

[159] Orozco y Berra's work is in four vols. (Mexico City, 1880).

[160] Diego Barros Arana, *Compendio de Historia de América* (Santiago, 1865), Pt. 2, p. 223, and p. 310, note 8.

[161] Lúcas Alamán, *Disertaciones sobre la historia de la República Mejicana desde la época de la conquista* (Habana, 1873), I, 37, note 1.

[162] R. B. Merriman, *The Rise of the Spanish Empire in the Old World and in the New* (New York, 1918), III, 539, 616.

[163] Justin Winsor, *Narrative and Critical History of America*, I, 269. For a discussion of Markham's scholarship, see article by B. W. Diffie in *Hispanic American Historical Review*, XVI; also article by B. W. Diffie and Harry Bernstein in *ibid.*, XVII.

critical attention the volumes of Prescott and it is particularly significant that Spanish reviewers in general appreciated the American's impartiality and his mastery of materials. In a gay mood Prescott once wrote to Gayangos that he had spent so much time in Spanish history that he felt as if he were a Spaniard.[164] In a symposium dealing with Prescott's works held in *La Ilustración* (July 30, 1893) a noted historian and statesman, Antonio del Castillo, said that for half a century "no historian had equalled Prescott in popularity in Spain"; his first books "fell on us like a spring shower." It is a fact worth noting that Prescott, besides entertaining Spaniards, stimulated them to new researches in the history of their own country.[165] With becoming pride the American wrote that with the exception of Irving he had done as much as any alien to portray Spain in the most favorable light for the admiration of students of history.[166]

Merriman's opinion of the *Ferdinand and Isabella* was also very favorable. In composing his own work Professor Merriman used the vast mass of Prescott materials in the Harvard University Library: "I have thus had the opportunity to follow, step by step, the process of the composition of his masterpiece and can testify to the profound learning, deep insight, and above all to the unfailing honesty with which his work was done. Such errors as he made were due to lack of material. . . ."[167] Although a distinguished scholar, Altamira, has rewritten much of the history of Spain in the fifteenth and sixteenth centuries in the modern spirit, a leading Spanish bibliography speaks of the *Ferdinand and Isabella* and the *Philip II* as still the best works on their respective periods.[168]

[164] C. L. Penney, *Prescott, Unpublished Letters to Gayangos in the Library of the Hispanic Society of America* (1927), p. 64 (October 9, 1846).

[165] J. De Lancey Ferguson, *American Literature in Spain* (1916), pp. 148–157.   [166] *Correspondence*, p. 468.   [167] Merriman, *op. cit.*, I, xii.

[168] See Rafael Altamira y Crevea, *Historia de España y de la civilización española* (6 vols. in 5, last two by Don Pio Zabala y Lera

The general background for the interest of Irving and Prescott in Spanish history is fairly apparent. The theme of the Noble Savage was interwoven with Spanish history in dramas by Kotzebue which were translated and adapted by English and American playwrights.[169] William Robertson, Prescott's distinguished predecessor in the field of Hispanic history, set a high standard with *The History of America* (1777), and Americans in considerable numbers became familiar with it in reprintings or in extracts found in periodicals. Colonial libraries included Spanish volumes on their shelves, and standard Spanish histories were translated and published on this side of the ocean. Some few Americans, like Dr. William Bentley, dealt authoritatively with Hispanica, but Americans were on more familiar ground in the area of economic relations.[170] The Peninsular campaigns in the Napoleonic wars focused attention on Spain, and Robert Southey's writings on Spanish history were well known and admired by Prescott.[171] German scholarship in these years also turned its attention with marked success to Spanish themes.[172]

The more immediate influence stemmed from the revisions that Spaniards themselves were making of their own history. They, too, were stimulated in the post-Napoleonic era to rewrite the narrative of their past in nationalistic terms. The incompleted work of Juan Baptiste Muñoz (*History of the New World*, 1793) was carried on by Martín Fernández de Navarrete, who brought out the first volume of his documents of Spanish voy-

[Barcelona, 1929], 4th ed.); *Bibliografía de la Historia de España* (Gerona, 1921), pp. 225, 247–248.

[169] Bissell, *op. cit.*, pp. 148, 154–155.

[170] For cultural relations see the paper by Harry Bernstein, "Las Primeras Relaciones Intelectuales entre New England y el Mundo Hispánico," in *La Revista Hispánica Moderna*, Tomo V, núm. 1.

[171] See *Ferdinand and Isabella*, I, 315 note.

[172] Friedrich Weber, *Beiträge zur Charakteristik der älteren Geschichtschreiber über Spanisch-Amerika* (Leipzig, 1911).

ages in 1825. Irving made use of this material immediately in his *Life and Voyages of Columbus* (1828) and it is no coincidence that Prescott should have finally determined in 1826 to devote himself to Spanish history. Important works by other historians testified to the renewal of interest in this great theme. Juan Antonio Llorente brought out the records of the Inquisition in 1814; in 1820 José Antonio Condé began publication of a standard work on the Spanish Arabs. Shortly after, the Mexican Carlos Maria Bustamente brought out his new editions of old Spanish histories. Publications of documents and bibliographical contributions swelled the volume of historical materials.[173] In 1837 Henri Ternaux-Compans began his translations of original documents relating to the discovery of America. A few years earlier a new phase of Mexican archaeology began (1830) with the publication of Lord Kingsborough's *The Antiquities of Mexico*. It is clear then that Prescott was not in "terra incognita."

Prescott's scholarship must be measured in the light of materials readily available, the more inaccessible documents, and finally by sources unknown in his day. The materials in print that were readily accessible were fairly numerous and becoming more so at the time Prescott made his decision to write on the history of Spain and her empire. Von Humboldt's investigations were of inestimable value to students and are still of fundamental importance. Clavigero's work on Mexico and especially Navarrete's volumes on the age of discovery lightened the task of many scholars. American officials in the diplomatic service abroad sent Prescott vast quantities of materials, and his agents opened doors that had been immovable to most earlier students. A transplanted American, Obadiah Rich (who had

---

[173] José T. Medina, *Biblioteca Hispano-Americana, 1493–1810* (Santiago de Chile), VI, cvii; and Justin Winsor, *op. cit.*, I, iv. In the preface to *Peru*, Prescott mentions a number of scholars whose researches aided him.

earlier aided Washington Irving in Spain), gave great bibliographical assistance to Prescott. Arthur Middleton, a class-
mate, who was in the legation at Madrid, was very helpful
to him. The German scholar, Friedrich Wilhelm Lembke,
searched the archives of Spain for him, but the most valuable
assistance was rendered to Prescott by Pascual de Gayangos,
one of the most learned Spanish historians of the nineteenth
century. Prescott recorded his sources for the *Mexico* as including, in addition to printed works, a huge mass of materials
from the archives of the Royal Academy of History in Madrid
totaling some "five thousand folio pages of manuscript, and
making the most authentic basis for a history of the Conquest,
and one to which previous historians native or foreign have
not had access."[174] For his *Philip the Second*, Prescott had in
his library over 370 printed volumes on the period and about
twenty-five folio volumes of manuscript materials—in Ticknor's opinion one of the richest collections made on any subject of historical research.[175]

Prescott followed well-established American practice in
searching out original sources, and all his volumes are soundly
based on the best materials available to an indefatigable scholar.
Criticism which grew in volume after his generation had passed,
noted that Prescott's range of materials was too narrowly conceived—he belonged as Edward Eggleston observed derisively
to the "drum and trumpet" school of history. Prescott believed with Ranke that the historian "must take just what
Father Time has given him, just what he finds in the records
of the age, setting down neither more nor less."[176] But the
historian cannot take *everything* that has been left to him—there

---

[174] *Correspondence*, pp. 345–346, and preface to *Mexico*. The *Correspondence* has many letters from Rich, Gayangos, and others who
aided Prescott.

[175] Ticknor, pp. 287–288.

[176] *Miscellanies*, p. 286.

is the necessity of choosing from among the records of the past. And in the judgment of Theodore Parker and others Prescott chose wrongly. A Virginia contemporary complained that histories of kings and statesmen were plentiful but the "people rarely appear upon the stage," and he believed that the time had arrived for a history of the mass of the people.[177] Parker noted the class bias of Prescott and criticized excessive space given to military affairs. If a historian must write on this subject, he urged that more attention be given to the technique of raising and provisioning armies. Prescott, said Parker, paid no heed to changes in the life of the people and while omitting important developments such as the growth of towns, found room for many frivolous details. In Parker's judgment the work was "not written in the philosophy of this age."[178] In justification of Prescott it should be remembered that he did include in his *Ferdinand and Isabella* chapters (xix, xx) on science and literature (with Ticknor's assistance), and in his other volumes similar chapters appeared.[179] However, they were unrelated generally to the rest of the narrative for they were not fundamentally germane to Prescott's purpose—storytelling. Even in his final work, the *Philip II*, which was intended to be a comprehensive social and political history, it is still mainly the history of the chevalier, the swashbuckler, and the statesman.

Philip is a mixture of the old history and the new—old in the sense of emphasizing romantic incidents and glorifying chivalric ideals; new in stressing the things appealing to Ranke—political development, growth of the state, diplomatic maneuvers.

---

[177] *Virginia Historical Register* (1848), I, 69; II, 210. Prescott himself gently criticized Irving's *Conquest of Granada* for not choosing a wider range of materials (*Miscellanies*, pp. 108–109).

[178] Theodore Parker, "Prescott as an Historian," in *The American Scholar*.

[179] See the course of study mapped out by Prescott for his *Ferdinand and Isabella*. It included geography, civil and ecclesiastical history, and statistical information of an economic nature (Ticknor, p. 79).

But the reader senses that Prescott's dramatic and narrative powers are declining in the *Philip*. He had little zest for this work and his materials seemed to engulf him. While he intended to have a main thread in the work (Philip's influence on most of the developments in his reign), the reader does not grasp this significance. Events seem too great for Philip (and almost for Prescott, too) to handle. The historian could deal with the conflicts of arms but not so easily with the conflicts of ideas.[180]

Prescott was thought to be particularly vulnerable in his materials on the Aztecs and Incas. Modern archaeological research has indeed modified the picture that he has left us of their civilization.[181] Most recent judgments, however, make the point that, given the limitations of the materials at his command, Prescott's version of these pre-Spanish civilizations is fairly accurate. Herbert J. Spinden and Baron Erland Nordenskiöld, two of the best modern authorities in the field, believe in the remarkably high quality of Central and South American Indian culture.[182] But scholars have exhumed civilizations older than those known to Prescott, and they maintain that the Aztec civilization, though very advanced, was copied from peoples who had preceded them. The Aztecs bear the same relation to the Mayans which in earlier centuries the Romans had borne to the Greeks. Another point emphasized in recent studies is that the peak of Aztec power had passed when Cortés came.[183] Philip A. Means, probably the best-known student of Andean civilization, is especially enthusiastic over Prescott's pages on the Incas.[184]

[180] For Prescott's dependence on Ranke see Ticknor, pp. 289–290.

[181] See section viii of this introduction for a detailed historical discussion of opinion on Prescott's archaeology.

[182] See papers by Spinden and Nordenskiöld in *The American Aborigines*, ed. by Diamond Jenness (Toronto, 1933).

[183] H. J. Spinden, *Ancient Civilizations of Mexico and Central America* (1922).

[184] *New England Quarterly*, October, 1931; Prescott understood the indebtedness of the Aztecs to earlier civilizations (see *Mexico*, p. 612).

While it is true that Prescott leaned very heavily on Spanish sources his skepticism dictated caution. Where authoritative chroniclers spoke of great chieftains "who could muster a hundred thousand vassals each on their estates," Prescott wrote: "Without relying on such wild statements, it is clear, from the testimony of the Conquerors, that the country was occupied by numerous powerful chieftains. . . ."[185] He spoke, too, of the "imperfection of the sources," whence his outline of the civil and military polity of the Aztecs was drawn.[186] Weighing his materials on the Incas, Prescott suggested that possibly Sarmiento may have formed too high an estimate of their attainments: "It is not improbable, that, astonished by the vestiges it afforded of an original civilization, he became enamored of his subject, and thus exhibited it in colors somewhat too glowing to the eye of the European."[187] As for the charge that he pursued the method of analogy in depicting early American society, Prescott expressly stated that "analogies lead sometimes to very erroneous conclusions." "It is chimerical," he writes, "to look for much in common—beyond a few accidental forms and ceremonies—with [the] aristocratic institutions of the Middle Ages."[188] Despite this caution on the use of analogy, Prescott's language, however, conveys the impression that he is thinking in European terms, for he speaks of nobles, palaces, privy councils, etc.

Like most historians Prescott professed his belief in impartiality. The historian must love truth "under all circumstances" and be ready "to declare it at all hazards."[189] Prescott was rarely at a loss to characterize the sources on which he based his own narrative. Torquemada the Franciscan, who left a chronicle of Aztec civilization, was adjudged a bigot in describing pagan culture, although due recognition is granted his "mani-

---

[185] *Mexico*, p. 21.   [186] *Ibid.*, p. 32.
[187] *Peru*, p. 822.   [188] *Mexico*, p. 22.
[189] *Miscellanies*, p. 88.

fest integrity" in gathering the facts.[190] The Abbé Clavigero, a
Jesuit, conducted his discussion temperately and "with good
faith" despite an excess of nationalist feeling.[191] The native
chronicler, Ixtlilxochitl, although too credulous and a national
partisan, has the "appearance of good faith and simplicity."[192]
Las Casas, always pleading the cause of the persecuted native,
wrote his works dominated by that one idea.[193]

Prescott is always at pains to remind the reader that he is
judging men and their institutions in the light of their own
contemporary standards. To answer the anticipated criticism
made by his American and English readers whose moral standard differed greatly from that of the sixteenth century, and who
would expect the historian to condemn ruthlessness, Prescott
said that he did not hesitate "to expose in their strongest colors
the excesses of the Conquerors." On the other hand he gave
them "the benefit of such mitigating reflections as might be
suggested by the circumstances and the period in which they
lived." He aimed to present a picture "in its proper light, and
to put the spectator in a proper point of view for seeing it to
the best advantage," "to surround him with the spirit of the
times" and make him "a contemporary of the sixteenth century."[194] Prescott drew a sharp distinction between the actor
and the act; the former was to be judged by the changing
standards of the age, while the act was to be judged by "the
immutable principles of right and wrong." In the last analysis
Prescott falls back, rather lamely, upon the position that "the
real question is whether a man was sincere."[195]

[190] *Mexico*, p. 34.   [191] *Ibid.*, p. 35.
[192] *Ibid.*, p. 116.   [193] *Ibid.*, pp. 207–208.
[194] Preface to *Mexico*, p. 6.
[195] Ticknor, p. 214; it is lame because nearly every fanatic may be
justified on the ground of sincerity. See Lembke's support of Prescott's point of view in historical judgments (*Correspondence*, pp. 88–
89); also Whipple (*op. cit.*, II, 155), commending Prescott for his
"hatred of wrong, modified by charity for the wrongdoer."

The massacre of Cholula by Cortés is told in horrified language, but Prescott adds that to judge the action fairly we must transport ourselves to the age when it happened. Explaining sixteenth-century ethics he notes that pagans, like all religious infidels, were sinful in Christian eyes, and their lands proper regions for expropriation by the Holy See or its representatives. Besides the Conquerors were no worse than the English and French during their struggle in the Iberian peninsula in the Napoleonic wars.[196] The advance in moral standards, at least in theory, should of itself "teach us charity" and make us "more distrustful of applying the standard of the present to measure the actions of the past."[197] But Prescott was not always consistent in applying this standard of measurement. He judges Christians by their own contemporary standards, but not Mohammedans and aborigines by *their* codes; the latter two are measured by Christian standards.

Prescott was, for his day, particularly free of nationalistic prejudices. European observers commented warmly on this virtue and noted how far short their own historians fell in this regard.[198] Although he was criticized for his anti-Catholicism, students generally praised his freedom from religious and political bias.[199] On occasion he nodded, as when he doubted that historians could write satisfactorily on alien countries (forgetting his own masterly contribution to Spanish history), but rarely was he guilty of any major chauvinism.[200] He believed that that nation was poor indeed which had no distinguished men of letters to tell its story, but he did not press the point. Boundaries were no barriers to the community of learned men. He truly belonged to one of the oldest bands of international fellowship—the fraternity of scholars.

[196] *Mexico*, p. 277. [197] *Ibid.*, pp. 350–351.
[198] *Correspondence*, pp. 72–73. [199] *Ibid.*, pp. 107, 583.
[200] *Miscellanies*, p. 310.

IV. PRESCOTT AND THE ART OF HISTORY

1. General Characteristics

Without neglecting the philosophical values or the scientific requirements of history, Prescott was primarily a craftsman. His study of the great historians had taught him that though historical philosophies were mutable, artistic narrative had a perennial appeal. Characteristically, he developed his theory of the art on the basis of the achievements of the great artists of the past. Herodotus and Livy had emphasized the narrative values of history, and Tacitus and Thucydides had deepened its biographical content and dramatized it.[201] It was Voltaire, however, who effected a "revolution in the structure . . . of history by substituting the topical for the chronological arrangement." Thereby he had adapted the art of history to its proper philosophical function, for his method "enabled the reader to arrive more expeditiously at the results, for which alone history is valuable," and provided the means for the writer to convey "his own impressions."[202] Voltaire's contemporary, Gabriel de Mably, had even more influence on Prescott through his theory, set forth in *De l'étude de l'histoire* (1778) that the essential lessons of history should be made palatable for the reader by the use of graphic descriptions, imaginary speeches by the chief personages, and a central, controlling moral.[203] Prescott rejected the idea of speeches, but he liked

[201] *Miscellanies*, pp. 89–90.

[202] *Ibid.*, p. 99. On the topical arrangement see also comments in *Ferdinand and Isabella*, I, vii–viii; *Mexico*, pp. 308, 310; *Philip II*, I, xii–xiv; II, 343. If, at such a late date, Prescott's emphasis on an old and elementary principle of historical composition seems peculiar, it should be noted that his contemporaries, Bancroft and Hildreth, used the chronological method. See *Marcus W. Jernegan Essays in American Historiography* (Chicago, 1937), pp. 15, 30.

[203] See E. A. Whitfield, *Gabriel Bonnot de Mably* (London, 1930), pp. 67–68.

the "notion of the necessity of giving an interest as well as utility to history, by letting events tend to some obvious point or moral; in short, by paying such attention to the development of events tending to this leading result, as one would in the construction of a romance or a drama."[204]

The next great change in the art of history came to Prescott indirectly. This was the romantic principle of subjectivism which derived from the speculations of Rousseau and was first embodied in Friedrich Schiller's *Geschichte des Abfalls der Vereinigten Niederlande von der Spanischen Regierung* (1788).[205] Rejecting the objectivity of the rationalists, Schiller believed that the apprehending of historical material was an emotional as well as an intellectual process. When historical data were examined sympathetically, individual men and women emerged, and history was revealed to be a quarry for the novel and the drama. Schiller demonstrated that by careful selection of the facts history could be turned into art without perversion of the facts. Like Prescott, he chose his themes from the periods which offered the most color and the most heroes.

All of this accords with Prescott's practice, but though he drew upon Schiller's work in his own *Philip II*, the new approach came to him through the French narrative artists who adopted it before he began the study of history. The French historians, indeed, had gone further than Schiller in developing specific techniques for the graphic and imaginative reconstruction of the past, and it was from them chiefly that Prescott drew his theory. Sismondi taught him primarily the use of a central theme as a means of organizing and unifying masses of incongruous materials. In his *Republiques Italiennes* (1807) he "succeeded in unravelling the intricate web of Italian politics . . . by keeping constantly in view the principle [of the rise and de-

---

[204] Ticknor, p. 95.

[205] See Fueter, *op. cit.*, p. 499; and G. P. Gooch, *Germany and the French Revolution* (London, 1920).

cline of liberty]."[206] The same technique, Prescott found, had been used by Antonio de Solís (1610–1686), whose *Conquista de Méjico* (1684) was one of Prescott's chief sources. This work was centered in "one great theme [the Conquest of Mexico] . . . which shed its light . . . over his whole work. . . . Instead of the numerous episodes, leading like so many blind galleries, to nothing, he took the student along a great road, conducting straight toward the mark. . . . The work, thus conducted, affords the interest of a grand spectacle,—of some well-ordered drama, in which scene succeeds to scene, act to act . . . until the whole is consummated by the grand and decisive *dénouement* . . ., the fall of Mexico."[207] Similarly, Bancroft had brought unity out of the affairs of thirteen separate colonies by tracing the development of independence.[208] Prescott was careful to distinguish, however, between this artistic unity, which merely dictates the choice and disposition of parts, and the philosophic unity, sought by the rationalists, which selects or suppresses evidence in order to bear out a preconceived hypothesis.[209]

The next most important influence was Barante, who, in his *Histoire des ducs de Bourgogne* (1824), set forth his theory of the use of original sources. A disciple of Scott, Barante sought to "restore to history the interest that the historical novel has

[206] *Ferdinand and Isabella*, II, 328.

[207] *Mexico*, p. 617.

[208] *Miscellanies*, pp. 306, 338.

[209] See his discussion of Las Casas, in *Mexico*, p. 208. Though Prescott was familiar with A. W. Schlegel's literary criticism (see section v, on criticism) he did not acknowledge that in history writing he was influenced by Schlegel's principle of unity of effect. There is no evidence that he was a reader of *Blackwood's*, through which Schlegel's influence came to England and to Poe (see Margaret Alterton's *The Origins of Poe's Critical Theory* [Iowa City, 1925]). But note his statement that "*unity of interest* [is] the only unity held of much importance by modern critics" (preface to *Mexico*, p. 6).

borrowed from it" by quoting and summarizing freely the ancient chronicles which were the basis of his narrative.[210]   Prescott gladly acknowledged his indebtedness,[211] and illustrated the principle ably, especially in his works on Mexico and Peru, by his use of the records of the Conquistadors and their contemporaries.   He perceived, like Barante, that the rationalistic love of generalization had robbed history of its potential vivacity and graphic freshness,[212] and he joined his romantic contemporaries in their attempt to re-create sympathetically the spirit of the past by making abundant use of the records of eyewitnesses.   For this he was to be attacked later by the archaeologists.

Thus, three elements of Prescott's theory of the art of history may be traced to the work of precursors and contemporaries: (1) dramatic form and purpose, (2) unity through a central theme, and (3) the use of graphic details drawn from primary sources.   A fourth element, the use of biography, he derived from traditional and contemporary practice in general, and from the necessities of his theory as a whole.   Prescott had always been interested in this phase of history; indeed in 1825 he contemplated it as a field of scholarship because of "the deeper interest which always attaches to minute differences of character, and a continuous, closely connected narrative."[213]   Even after he had published his first work he was inclined to think that the history of persons was more appealing than that of nations, because "Instead of a mere abstraction, at once we see a being like ourselves. . . .   We place ourselves in his position, and see the passing current of events with the same eyes."[214]   Naturally, then, the biographical element in his work was large, and

[210] G. P. Gooch, *History and Historians in the Nineteenth Century*, pp. 174–175.
[211] *Peru*, p. 728.
[212] *Miscellanies*, pp. 107–108.
[213] Ticknor, p. 75.
[214] *Miscellanies*, p. 176.

it is to be noted that the titles of all of his histories are names of
individuals. His individuals, however, have no such role as
those of Carlyle's "heroes," who are "intuitively aware of the
Divine Idea beneath appearances; and have an intimation of the
universal processes going on behind the curtains of prosaic existence."[215] When Prescott said of Cortés that he was "not
merely the soul, but the body" of the conquest,[216] he meant
only that he was a superb leader and that he embodied the best
characteristics of Spanish chivalry. His sole attempt to analyze
philosophically the secret of leadership in history was inspired
by the least admirable part of Cardinal Ximines' career. "Moral
energy," he wrote, "when stimulated by some intense passion
or ambition" constitutes the chief requisite of leadership, and
"when associated with exalted genius . . . conveys an image of
power, which approaches, nearer than anything else on earth,
to that of a divine intelligence. It is, indeed, such agents that
Providence selects for the accomplishment of those great revolutions, by which the world is shaken to its foundations. . . ."
But such an individual can be either the "scourge or the benefactor of his species," and Ximines' marvelous inflexibility of
purpose became an instrument of persecution.[217] This is as
close as Prescott ever came to finding a harmonizing principle
in one of his personages. Motley, disciple of Carlyle, might
have been thinking of Prescott when he said, "If a writer cannot get at the unity [of a character], let him give us the multi-
plicity from which we may extract it."[218] Content to leave
subtle interpretations to others, Prescott desired only to describe his people accurately and vividly. And he did not believe in hiding their defects. "A frank exhibition of the minor

[215] L. M. Young, *Thomas Carlyle and the Art of History* (Philadelphia, 1939), p. 81.

[216] *Mexico*, p. 681.

[217] *Ferdinand and Isabella*, II, 402.

[218] Quoted by Higby and Schantz, eds., *Motley* (American Writers
Series), pp. xxix–xxx.

blemishes" of a character, he said, tends to secure the reader's confidence in the "general fidelity of the portraiture." [219]

2. *The Reign of Ferdinand and Isabella*

The external form of Prescott's first history is topical, the various sections illustrating by turn military, political, religious, cultural, and biographical history. Prescott's problem was the discernment of a central theme. Lacking a theory of historical forces, he refused to invent one to explain the rise of imperial Spain; but two concepts afforded a certain philosophical unity—nationalism and progress. The first is illustrated chiefly in Part I (1406–1492)—the period of the unification of the kingdoms of Spain under one monarchy, the development of a national culture, and the reform of internal administration. Prescott's inherited Federalism is reflected, perhaps, in his description of the "glorious *union*, which brought together the petty and hitherto discordant tribes of the Peninsula under the same rule; and, by creating common interests and an harmonious principle of action, was silently preparing them for constituting one great nation,—one and indivisible, as intended by nature." [220] The idea of progress is illustrated in Part II (1493–1517) by the discoveries and conquests of united Spain. "Whatever be the amount of physical good or evil immediately resulting to Spain from her new discoveries . . . the ancient limits of human thought were overleaped; the veil which had covered the secrets of the deep for so many centuries was removed; another hemisphere was thrown open; and a boundless expansion promised to science. . . ." [221] Even the conquest of Granada and the victories over Italy represented the triumph of a superior state

---

[219] *Miscellanies*, p. 179. See also *Mexico*, p. 619. On this point, compare George Bancroft, who ordered the engravers of a portrait of Franklin to remove a wart (M. A. DeWolfe Howe, ed., *Life and Letters of George Bancroft*, I, 236).

[220] *Ferdinand and Isabella*, III, 107; see also II, 103.

[221] *Ibid.*, II, 503.

over more backward and degenerate nations.[222] An introductory section on Castile and Aragon before Ferdinand and Isabella, and a concluding chapter on the achievements of these sovereigns round out the theme of the emergence of a brilliant and powerful monarchy from a "barbarous age." [223]

Prescott did not, however, try to relate all of his materials to these basic concepts. There is a constant interplay between environmental and race factors, traditions, international stresses, military technology, and personalities which indicates his essential pluralism.[224] The Inquisition and the persecution of Jews and Arabs are revealed as impediments to progress and the seed of Spain's later degeneration. The biographical portraits are numerous and follow a regular pattern. Appearing usually at the end of a character's career, these always consist of a rather formal catalogue of his traits,[225] a comparison of his ethics with the accepted code of the age, a review of his accomplishments, and perhaps a contrast with a similar figure in another era or country. Thus Ferdinand is described as representative of the age,[226] and Isabella as superior to it and to Queen Elizabeth, with whom she is compared at some length.[227] Gonsalvo de Cordova is the representative military genius,[228] and Cardinal Ximines is described as the great statesman and churchman of the sixteenth century, the superior of Cardinal Richelieu, with whom he is contrasted.[229]

[222] *Ferdinand and Isabella*, II, 105–106; III, 110–111.
[223] *Ibid.*, III, 496.
[224] For example, Gonsalvo de Cordova's victory at Naples is attributed to military, racial, and personal factors (*ibid.*, III, 160–163).
[225] This reflects, perhaps, the influence of phrenology, which was popular in Prescott's time. Note his statement that Scott's "cranium . . ., to judge from his busts, must have exhibited a strong development of the organ of veneration" (*Miscellanies*, p. 223).
[226] *Ferdinand and Isabella*, III, 389–403.
[227] *Ibid.*, III, 183–205.
[228] *Ibid.*, III, 377–382.
[229] *Ibid.*, III, 418–428.

3. The Conquest of Mexico

Because *Ferdinand and Isabella* is the multifarious history of
a nation, it lacks the continuously dramatic quality of Prescott's
second work, the *Conquest of Mexico*.[230] He approached the
new subject with enthusiasm, for it was, he said, "an epic in
prose . . . the most poetic subject ever offered to the pen of
the historian," and "superior to the Iliad in true epic proportion." [231] "The natural development of the story . . . is precisely what would be prescribed by the severest rules of art.
The conquest of the country is the great end always in view of
the reader. From the first landing of the Spaniards on the soil,
their subsequent adventures, their battles and negotiations, their
ruinous retreat, their rally and final siege, all tend to this grand
result, till the long series of events is closed by the downfall of
the capital . . . all moves steadily forward to this consummation.
It is a magnificent epic, in which the unity of interest is complete." [232]

Perfect as the subject was, however, Prescott's sense of scholarly integrity created several problems of form. A full understanding of the conquest was impossible without a description
of the Aztec civilization, a labor which cost him as much
time as the rest of the history. Moreover, because Cortés
was the "soul" of the conquest, and because there was much
new material on his life, Prescott felt obliged to complete the
story of his life after the conquest. These necessities resulted
in a threefold division, embodying "philosophic," historical,
and biographical themes, which, in Prescott's opinion, was
slightly incongruous.[233] The postscript on Cortés' later life
was particularly troublesome, for Irving's *Columbus*, wherein

[230] Prescott studied, as models for the work, Voltaire's *Charles XII*,
Livy's *Hannibal*, and Irving's *Columbus* (Ticknor, pp. 186–187).
[231] Ogden, pp. 137, 154.
[232] Preface to *Peru*, p. 727.
[233] Preface to *Mexico*, pp. 5–6.

the discovery of America comes early in the work, was a warning of the danger of an anticlimactic effect.[234] "The mind, previously occupied with one great idea, that of the subversion of the capital, . . . may find it difficult, after the excitement caused by witnessing a great national catastrophe, to take an interest in the adventures of a private individual. . . . To prolong the narrative is to expose the historian to the error so much censured by the French critics in some of their most celebrated dramas, where the author by a premature *dénouement* has impaired the interest of his piece." He hoped, however, that these incongruities had less weight in practice than in theory, inasmuch as he had preserved the romantic principle of *"unity of interest*—the only unity held of much importance by modern critics."[235]

These hopes were justified, for the work is a masterpiece of unified construction. It is divided into seven books, the first six containing about one hundred pages each, the last (the later life of Cortés) considerably shortened in order to minimize the impression of anticlimax. Book I (View of the Aztec Civilization), far from impairing unity, aids it, for it serves a triple purpose: (a) its descriptions of the politics, religion, economics, and culture of the Aztecs supply a vivid and concrete background for the Conquest, and permit exclusive attention to the Conquest itself in later chapters; (b) it inspires pity and wonder that a civilization, in some respects so advanced, should have been destroyed by a few hundred Spaniards; (c) the exposure of the despotism and cannibalism of the Aztecs provides an excuse for their destruction by the hero of the work. By relegating to an appendix a discussion of the origins of Mexican civilization (which, in Prescott's time, was a matter of guesswork) he preserved the factual integrity of the whole section.

[234] Ticknor, p. 187.
[235] Preface to *Mexico*, pp. 5–6.

Each of the succeeding sections has its own tone and structural unity. Book II (Discovery of Mexico) begins with a suitably compressed review of the colonial policy of Charles V, and closes with Cortés' burning of his fleet—a symbol of the individualism of the adventurers who implemented that policy. The mood of Book III (March to Mexico) is comparatively quiet. There is much scenic description, and the climactic reception of the Spaniards by the Emperor is outwardly cordial. The tempo quickens in Book IV (Residence in Mexico) from the descriptions of Aztec magnificence at the beginning, to the rising of the Mexicans at the end. In Book V (Expulsion from Mexico) the action reaches a preliminary climax at Chapter III (the account of the terrible "Noche Triste"), and then drops, as if in preparation for the rise to the grand climax in Book VI (Siege and Surrender of Mexico) which terminates in philosophical reflections on the conquest. As Prescott hoped, he had aroused such interest in his hero that the final chapter on Cortés is not an anticlimax. Indeed it is the concentration of interest in one dominating personality that makes this work dramatically superior to *Ferdinand and Isabella*. The contradictions of Cortés' character made him interesting, his knight-errantry made him representative, and his superb leadership, his courage, and his constancy of purpose made him successful. Except for the unfortunate Emperors, Montezuma and Guatemozin, the other characters are of interest only in their relations to him as companions, rivals, and traitors.

Artistically, the *Conquest of Mexico* is the best of all of Prescott's works. Having established in *Ferdinand and Isabella* his attitude toward Spanish civilization, he was able in this work to concentrate on the story. He poured into it not only his erudition but a wealth of illustrative material from literature and travel books. He quoted from Spanish and Italian poetry; drew parallels from the classics; persuaded his friend Madame Calderón de la Barca, then resident in Mexico, to send him information on Mexican flora;[236] combed Humboldt for lively sociological materials; and quoted long passages from Southey's *Madoc* whenever he felt that his own prose failed to do justice to the poetic possibilities of his subject. His footnotes are rich in allusion, comparison, and comment; and his bibliographical notes contain valuable discussions of the art and science of history. In general, he spared no pains to make the work not only authoritative but vivid and lively, and to bring it into relation with the culture of the average reader.

4. The Conquest of Peru

The form of this work was a more difficult problem. "The action," he said in the preface, "so far as it is founded on the subversion of the Incas, terminates long before the close of the narrative. The remaining portion is taken up with the fierce feuds of the Conquerors, which would seem, from their very nature, to be incapable of being gathered round a central point of interest. The conquest of the natives is but the first step, to be followed by the conquest of the ... rebel Spaniards, themselves,—till the supremacy of the Crown is permanently established. ... By fixing the eye on this remoter point, the successive steps will be found leading to one great result, and ... unity of interest [is] preserved." As Prescott admitted in his memoranda, this solution was logical rather than effective. It was difficult to give the story a place in the philosophical pattern of his works, for the conquest of a cultured and humane race by a gang of "banditti"[237] was poor evidence of progress.

[236]*Correspondence*, pp. 150, 167, 248, 251. Madame Calderón's *Life in Mexico* (London, 1843), which was written at Prescott's suggestion, was considered so accurate that American officers in the Mexican War used it as a guidebook. Prescott wrote a very short preface for it, and reviewed it in *Miscellanies*, pp. 340–360. The correspondence between the two is lively and informative.

[237]Ogden, p. 154.

The struggle lacked dignity. The vanquished, unlike the Aztecs, were feeble, and the attackers were "the scum of [Spanish] chivalry."[238] "I must look at some popular stories of highwaymen," he wrote in comic despair.[239]

The external form of the work resembles that of the *Conquest of Mexico*, except that it lacks a supplementary chapter on the origins of Peruvian civilization. It is divided into five books, covering culture, discovery, conquest, civil wars, and settlement. These, individually, have the unity of content but not the clean-cut dramatic drive of the corresponding books in the *Conquest of Mexico*. They are episodes, in which villains triumph over innocents and are, in turn, subdued by stronger forces; and the reader is held not by interest in the fortunes of a hero, but by the simple appeal of adventure in an exotic environment.

5. *The Reign of Philip II*

Prescott's last work was a severe test of his powers of organization and synthesis, and, if it is fair to judge an unfinished book, it cannot be said that he was entirely successful. This was due in part to the state of his eyes and health. For a time in 1848 he was inclined to concur in his doctor's advice to work no more; but idleness was intolerable, and the subject, which he had been contemplating since 1835,[240] was seductive. After considering a plan to treat only one of the episodes of Philip's reign, he decided to write memoirs of Philip, in which he would skim the cream of incident and character. The whole of Book I was written on this plan, but meanwhile Ticknor's urgency and a refreshing trip to Europe gave him the courage to attempt a regular history from Book II on.[241]

[238] *Peru*, p. 1232.
[239] Ticknor, p. 259; see also *Correspondence*, p. 513.
[240] *Correspondence*, p. 5.
[241] Ticknor, pp. 283, 293–295.

Even when the work was in the memoir stage, however, he sought a unifying theme. In the general scheme of his works, the reign of Philip was to represent the first step in the decline of Spain, just as that of Ferdinand was the last in its rise.[242] But in the unfinished form of *Philip II*, this decline does not emerge as a dynamic factor. Moreover, Prescott was far more interested in the colorful events and personalities of the reign than he was in such a negative concept. The problem was how to weave these rich materials into a pattern. The subject, he said, embraces such a "variety of independent, not to say incongruous, topics that it is no easy matter to preserve anything like unity of interest in the story." Thus, the revolt of the Netherlands, which in itself had the qualities of "unity, moral interest, completeness, and momentous and beneficent results," runs along through the whole of Philip's reign, "continually distracting the attention of the historian, creating an embarrassment something like that which arises from what is termed a double plot in the drama." Nevertheless, he felt that a "dominant principle . . . controlled all the movements of the complicated machinery . . . and impressed on them a unity of action." This principle is to be found in the "policy of Philip, the great aim of which was to uphold the supremacy of the Church, and, as a consequence, that of the crown. . . . It was this policy, almost as sure and steady in its operation as the laws of Nature herself, that may be said to have directed the march of events through the whole of his long reign; and it is only by keeping this constantly in view that the student will be enabled to obtain a clue to guide him through the intricate passages in the history of Philip, and the best means of solving what would otherwise remain enigmatical in his conduct."[243]

It is one thing, however, to tell readers to keep a unifying

[242] Ticknor, p. 190; *Correspondence*, p. 119.

[243] *Philip II*, I, xii–xiii; see also Prescott's discussion of the problem in Ticknor, pp. 283, 293.

principle in view; it is quite another to use that principle organically. *Philip II* must be read not as an analysis of a period and a reign but as a collection of brilliant episodes. Even the several units of the work lack singleness of purpose. This does not matter in Book I (the latter days of Charles V, the early days of Philip, the English alliance, and the wars with the Pope and with France), because, as Ticknor observed, the memoir technique serves as a "graceful vestibule" to the body of the work, and because within the section there is an easy transition toward the regular historical method.[244] Books II and III, dealing with Philip's troubles in the Netherlands, also have at least unity of subject matter. But Book IV is a mélange including a view of the Ottoman Empire, the siege of Malta, the story of Don Carlos, and the death of Isabella, and each of these subjects is exploited for its own narrative values. The same is true of Book V,—the rebellion of the Moors and the wars with the Turks. These attractive subjects took such disproportionate space in the general scheme that the subjects of Book IV crowded those of Book V out of the second volume, so that he needed five or six volumes when he intended only three.[245] Of Book VI, on the domestic affairs of Spain, only two chapters were written.

More than anywhere else, the decline of Prescott's energy and enthusiasm in his later years is evident in his bibliographical comments, which are short and unadventurous, and in his footnotes, which are perfunctory and lacking in generous allusiveness. *Philip II* has charm, but it must be sought in the style, not in the structure and spirit of the whole.

The artistic effectiveness of Prescott's work must be attributed in part to orderliness and precision of method, and skillful articulation of parts. Each book, each section, each chapter is

[244]Ticknor, p. 347.   [245]*Ibid.*, p. 403.

so carefully planned that the reader is never for a moment lost in the mazes of the past. It has been well said of *Ferdinand and Isabella* that it "had been planned like a battle and built as stoutly as a Salem clipper, destined to sail through many enchanted minds for generations to come."[246] This may be said, even more appropriately, of the *Conquest of Mexico*, and to some extent of the *Conquest of Peru* and *Philip II.* The classical love of form and proportion has never borne better fruit in our literature.

V. PRESCOTT'S STYLE

If Prescott's style has attracted less attention in modern criticism than it did in his own day,[247] it is because in literary history we are apt to emphasize change rather than convention. Prescott seems to have written conventionally in a period of stylistic revolt; yet it can be shown not only that his style was in harmony with his material—which is the best criterion—but that in an arduous struggle to achieve a suitable style he grappled with the problems which disturbed the whole romantic generation. If his achievement was not revolutionary, it was because he himself was not. "Innovation," he wrote, "is not reform in writing any more than in politics."[248]

One reason for his concern with the problem of style was, of course, his awareness that he was a *literary* historian. He was convinced that "*no* work in any of the departments of the belles-lettres can dispense with excellence of style. . . . If this be wanting, a work . . . can hardly be popular, for it cannot give

[246] Van Wyck Brooks, *The Flowering of New England* (New York, 1936), p. 135.

[247] Hallam wrote Prescott, "Your style appears to me to be nearly perfect" (Ticknor, p. 226). See also the review of the *Conquest of Mexico* by G. T. Curtis, *Christian Examiner*, XXXVI, 197–226 (March, 1844).

[248] Ticknor, p. 224.

pleasure or create interest,—things essential in every kind of composition which has not science *exclusively* for its end."[249]

His struggle with the problem went through three phases. The first began in 1821 when he decided to be a scholar. At this time he made a systematic survey of the whole history of English prose, studying, "as if he had been a school-boy," Blair's *Rhetoric*, Murray's *Grammar*, Johnson's Preface to his *Dictionary*, and the chief writers from Ascham to Jeffrey, taking notes and making judgments all the way.[250] Though he resolved at this time to imitate no one and to create a style suited to himself, this thorough grounding in the tradition of English prose before the Romantic period had a lasting effect upon him. As codified by Hugh Blair in his *Lectures on Rhetoric and Belles Lettres* (1783)[251] the academic rules emphasized simplicity, clarity, propriety, and precision; decreed the proper use of balance, antithesis, and metaphor; and discouraged "common" or "low" diction. Prescott's prose is in accord with these rules, for the characteristic pattern of his rhetoric is the single clause or sentence, followed by paired clauses in balance or antithesis or by a series of parallelisms. Yet he strove to avoid the worst faults of this kind of style, and even as he studied Blair he criticized his own articles in *The Club Room* because they contained "Too many adjectives; too many couplets of substantives, as well as adjectives, and perhaps of verbs; too set; sentences too much in the same mould . . . sentences balanced by *ands, buts,* and semicolons; too many precise, emphatic pronouns, as *these, those, which,* &c., instead of the particles *the, a,* &c." [252]

---

[249] *Ibid.*, p. 224. See the discussions of style in *Motley* (pp. **xx–xxi**) and *Parkman* (p. lvi) in American Writers Series.

[250] Ticknor, pp. 59–60. The results of these studies are embodied in Prescott's article, "Essay Writing" (1822), discussed in section vi, below.

[251] See Charvat, *op. cit.*, pp. 44–47, 111–112, for the contents, background, and importance of this popular rhetoric.

[252] Ticknor, p. 219.

The second phase of his development began when Richard Ford, in a review of *Ferdinand and Isabella* in 1839,[253] complained that his style was too formal. The rebuke was deserved, for as late as 1837 Prescott was capable of writing, "It is high time to terminate our lucubrations."[254] After a careful rereading of his book, Prescott concluded that "the reader may take my style for better or worse, as it now is formed." He decided, however, that the second volume "affords examples of words not so simple as might be," and that unless something is to be "gained in the way of strength or of coloring it is best to use the most simple, *unnoticeable* words to express ordinary things; ex.gr. 'to send' is better than 'to transmit'; 'crown descended' better than 'devolved'; 'guns fired' than 'guns discharged'; 'to name' or 'call' than 'to nominate'; 'to read' than 'peruse'; 'the term,' or 'name,' than 'appellation,' and so forth."[255] Thus did Prescott take part in the contemporary reaction against Latinity in English diction.[256]

In the third phase, represented in memoranda of 1844,[257] Prescott seems to have repudiated, in theory, at least, the standardizing tendencies of the eighteenth-century rhetorics. "How many varieties of beauty and excellence there are in this world! As many in the mental as the material creation, and it is a pedantic spirit, which, under the despotic name of taste, would reduce them all to one dull uniform level. . . . The form of expression is so nicely associated with the idea expressed, that it is impossible to say how much of [the writer's] success is owing to the one or to the other. . . . The best rule is to dispense with all rules except grammar, and to consult the natural

[253] *Quarterly Review*, LXIV, 1–58 (June, 1839).

[254] *Miscellanies*, p. 243.

[255] Ticknor, p. 222.

[256] On this subject, see Charvat, *op. cit.*, pp. 115–117. Note a similar tendency in Irving, described in *Irving* (p. lxxiv) in American Writers Series.

[257] Printed in Ticknor, pp. 223–224.

bent of one's genius." In this attack on rules Prescott was not rebelling against traditional prose, but expressing a romantic principle—that the function of language is self-expression as much as communication. When he rejected Johnson's dictum that "whoever would write in a good style, &c., &c., must devote his days and nights to the study of Addison" (sic), he meant only that "one man's style will no more fit another, than one man's coat, or hat, or shoes will fit another." Thus, by 1844, Prescott had reached the conviction that the great stylists were great because they followed the "natural suggestions of their genius"; and that "a man's style, to be worth anything, should be the natural expression of his mental character," even at the "hazard of violating the conventional tone of the most chaste and careful writers. It is this alone which can give full force to his thoughts."[258]

In stylistic practice, Prescott modified rather than rejected the traditional principles of English prose, and an analysis of representative paragraphs reveals how skillfully he made the stately eighteenth-century rhythms and syntax serve his central purpose—which was to write "philosophic" but readable history. His method varied with his material. Here is a typical military passage, describing the panic which fell upon the Spaniards when they realized they were trapped during the bloody "Noche Triste":[259]

---

[258] This critical principle corresponds to Prescott's doctrine of historical judgment of men and events. Thus in a defense of Solís' style against those who thought it "tumid, artificial, and verbose," he warned the foreign critic to "beware how he meddles with style, that impalpable essence which surrounds thought as with an atmosphere, giving it its life and peculiar tone of color, differing in different nations, like the atmospheres which envelope the different planets of our system" (*Mexico*, p. 617). Thus also he ridiculed Lord Brougham's criticism of W. E. Channing's style on the ground that the latter's "fine gossamer" was as appropriate to him as Brougham's style was to the critic (Ticknor, pp. 223-224).

[259] *Mexico*, pp. 445-446.

The tidings soon spread from man to man, and no sooner was their dreadful import comprehended, than a cry of despair arose, which for a moment drowned all the noise of conflict. All means of retreat were cut off. Scarcely hope was left. The only hope was in such desperate exertions as each could make for himself. Order and subordination were at an end. Intense danger produced intense selfishness. Each thought only of his own life. Pressing forward, he trampled down the weak and the wounded, heedless whether it were friend or foe. The leading files, urged on by the rear, were crowded on the brink of the gulf. Sandoval, Ordaz, and the other cavaliers dashed into the water. Some succeeded in swimming their horses across. Others failed, and some, who reached the opposite bank, being overturned in the ascent, rolled headlong with their steeds into the lake. The infantry followed pellmell, heaped promiscuously on one another, frequently pierced by the shafts, or struck down by the war-clubs of the Aztecs; while many an unfortunate victim was dragged half-stunned on board their canoes, to be reserved for a protracted, but more dreadful death.

The scientific historian might well object to such subjective interpolations as "a cry of despair," and "drowned all the noise of conflict"; to such philosophizing as "intense danger produced intense selfishness"; and to the numerous adjectives which Prescott could have drawn only from his imagination. But such coloring was the prerogative of the romantic historian, and the modern reader can have little objection to a passage which is supported by eight authorities (several of whom were eyewitnesses), all of them tested for their reliability in the bibliographical essays.[260] In form, the paragraph is closely knit,

[260] J. B. Black (in *Art of History*, pp. 126–128) thinks Robertson's style superior to Prescott's and Irving's because of his greater objectivity, and cites as examples the latter's use of the same source material that Robertson used for the description of Cortés' first view of the vale of Mexico (in Prescott's *Mexico*, p. 286, last paragraph). He fails to note, however, that Prescott's sensuous detail is based not only on the primary sources, but on the observations of modern travelers who had surveyed the scene.

every sentence contributing to the theme of terror and chaos. The more generalized material of the first half reaches a climax in the statement, "Each thought only of his own life," which is illustrated by the concrete descriptions of the second half. Discarding, for a moment, the leisurely rhythm of balanced clauses, Prescott reproduces in short, almost staccato, sentences of parallel structure the rapid movement of the action described. Ornament is restricted to alliteration.

He used this dramatic, pictorial technique frequently in passages dealing with social history. Thus his paragraph in *Philip II* on the Turkish janizaries[261] is a skillfully compressed history of an institution, made vivid by pictorial elements:

The most important of these various classes was that of the janizaries, whose discipline was far from terminating with the school. Indeed, their whole life may be said to have been passed in war, or in preparation for it. Forbidden to marry, they had no families to engage their affections, which, as with the monks and friars in Christian countries, were concentrated on their own order, whose prosperity was inseparably connected with that of the state. Proud of the privileges which distinguished them from the rest of the army, they seemed desirous to prove their title to them by their thorough discipline and by their promptness to execute the most dangerous and difficult services. Their post was always the post of danger. It was their proud vaunt that they had never fled before an enemy. Clad in their flowing robes, so little suited to the warrior, armed with the arquebuse and the scimitar,—in their hands more than a match for the pike or sword of the European,—with the heron's plume waving above their heads, their dense array might ever be seen bearing down in the thickest of the fight; and more than once, when the fate of the empire trembled in the balance, it was this invincible corps that turned the scale and by their intrepid conduct decided the fortune of the day. Gathering fresh reputation with age, so long as their discipline remained unimpaired they were a match for the best soldiers of Europe. But in time this admirable organization experienced a change. One Sultan allowed them to marry; another, to bring their sons into the corps; a third opened the ranks to Turks as well as Christians; until, forfeiting their peculiar character, the janizaries became confounded with the militia of the empire. These changes occurred in the time of Philip the Second; but their consequences were not fully unfolded till the following century.

Here the Rationalist's interest in causation is combined with the Romantic's love of the picturesque: the opening analysis of the strength of the corps, which supplies the groundwork for the account of the decline of the corps at the end of the paragraph, is followed by a physical description which turns an abstraction into a picture. As the subject matter is varied, so is the sentence structure. One complex and one simple sentence lead to two long parallel structures, the rhythm of which is terminated by a short simple sentence. A slightly longer one is followed by a very long complex one. The same pyramidal structure is then repeated, and the paragraph closes with a compound structure which closes off the rhythm of the whole.

In passages of a more purely philosophical or generalizing cast, the method changes again:

Never was there a persecution which did its work more thoroughly. The blood of the martyr is commonly said to be the seed of the church. But the storm of persecution fell as heavily on the Spanish Protestants as it did on the Albigenses in the thirteenth century, blighting every living thing, so that no germ remained for future harvests. Spain might now boast that the stain of heresy no longer defiled the hem of her garment. But at what a price was this purchased! Not merely by the sacrifice of the lives and fortunes of a few thousands of the existing generation, but by the disastrous consequences entailed forever on the country. Folded under the dark wing of the Inquisition, Spain was shut out from the light which in the sixteenth century broke over the rest of Europe, stimulating the nations to greater enterprise in every department of knowledge. The genius of the people was rebuked, and their spirit quenched, under the malignant influence of an eye that never slumbered, of an unseen arm ever raised to strike. How could there be freedom of thought, where there was no freedom of utterance? Or freedom of utterance, where it was as dangerous to say too little as too much? Freedom cannot go along with fear. Every way the mind of the Spaniard was in fetters.[262]

Here Prescott's love of intellectual freedom leads him into exclamation and interrogation; and moral, like martial, excitement finds its expression in short sentences. But the most striking characteristic of the passage is the quantity of metaphor—six figures in one short passage. If such excess may be traced to the influence of the rhetorics, which emphasized this type of ornament, it may be justified to some extent by the abstractness of the material. A lover of the concrete, Prescott turned naturally to metaphor when his subject led him into speculation.

On the score of diction it is clear that Prescott's merit lay in precision rather than in originality or idiomatic quality. Any page of his work contains such clichés as "bloody deed," "calm the passions of the multitude," "consigned to their kindred dust," and his favorite words were "gloomy," "chimerical," "superstition." There is little in the diction of his histories to indicate that he was an American writer, and when, occasionally, he was accused of Americanisms he defended them on the ground of respectable though remote English ancestry.[263] For his lack of nativism in language there were several reasons. One was his respect for traditional and contemporary English culture. His correspondence with English aristocrats was vo-

---

[262] *Philip II*, I, 445–446.
[263] See *Correspondence*, pp. 123–124; 659–660. Note Lowell's use of the same argument in his introduction to the *Biglow Papers*, Second Series (1866).

luminous and deferential,[264] and he was inclined to admit the superiority of British civilization in general.[265] Another was his reliance on the British literary market. "After all," he wrote, "my market and my reputation rest principally with England."[266] He contemplated publishing his first work in England only,[267] and he determined to do nothing about American publication which would interfere with securing English copyright.[268]

The effect of these attitudes on his language is clear. He wished to "write his language not only as is current in his own land, but so that it shall pass current among the best judges in his Father-land";[269] but he also felt that the Father-land had the right to establish the norm. "We cannot have two standards of purity, and until our culture becomes superior to that of England, we must defer to the metropolis of the Anglo-Saxon race," he wrote in his memoir of John Pickering;[270] and he conceded to a critic of his diction that "We cannot guard too carefully against . . . innovations, liable to spring up in a coun-

---

[264] Note, for example, his letters to the Earl of Carlisle (Ticknor, pp. 350–352, and *Correspondence, passim*). Note also his anxiety to maintain friendly relations with England during the antislavery controversy (*Correspondence*, pp. 538, 582, 586).

[265] See especially Ticknor, p. 255; and *Correspondence*, pp. 71–72. Though he received several honorary degrees in America, it was not until Oxford honored him that he felt like a "*real* doctor" (Ticknor, p. 314).   [266] Ogden, p. 103.

[267] "Sparks advises me to print it here. I may perhaps do so." (*Correspondence*, p. 5).

[268] *Correspondence*, p. 6.

[269] *Ibid.*, p. 659.

[270] *Memoir of the Hon. John Pickering* (1848), p. 12. The purpose of Pickering's *A Vocabulary or Collection of Words Peculiar to the United States* (Boston, 1816) was to preserve "the English language in its purity throughout the United States" by calling attention to departures from the standard, and by distinguishing these from American survivals of obsolete English forms. Note Pickering's defense of formal style in his review of *Ferdinand and Isabella*, *New York Review*, II, 308–341 (April, 1838), especially p. 339.

try where an active, inventive population, less concerned with books than business, is very likely to corrupt the pure waters of 'English undefiled' in their homely every-day vocations."[271] Whatever his theories in the matter, however, he had a natural inclination toward raciness of idiom. In his letters he used such Americanisms as "whopper-jawed," "cotton to," "quiddle," "die game," "take it easy," and "bungling," and his private memoranda yield such passages as this: "Finished Abridg. Hist. of F. & I. Io Triumphe! . . . About one tenth of the vol. written *de novo*—the rest docked, scissored, sweated, headed, and tailed. I shied, like a skittish horse at a leap, and find 'tis a mud puddle only."[272]

In general, Prescott's style represents a modification of traditional English prose rather than any radical departure from it. His syntax and diction, and his use of alliteration and metaphor seem a little old-fashioned, even for his time, but they give his prose dignity and an air of deliberate art. The absence of any startling qualities in his style had certain advantages which rebels like Carlyle could not claim for theirs. Having no private or revolutionary principles to urge, he had no need to create a new idiom or to come between his readers and his materials. Confronted with no peculiarities of expression or surprises of rhythm, syntax, or structure, the reader is never distracted from the story itself and can enjoy the sweep and general outline of the histories as a whole.

In conclusion, the effect of his blindness on his style should be noted. Unable to make alterations or erasures on his noctograph, Prescott was compelled, as Ticknor says,[273] to "prepare everything, down to the smallest details, in his memory, and to correct and fashion it all while it was still held there in silent

[271]*Correspondence*, p. 124. See also *ibid.*, p. 660.
[272]Ogden, p. 140. Note Ogden's claim that Ticknor, in printing parts of Prescott's memoranda, bowdlerized his language.
[273]Ticknor, pp. 229–230.

suspense." One need not agree with Ticknor that this was "among the principal causes of the grace, ease, and attractiveness of his style," but it is likely that the circumstance explains in part his use of the balanced sentence structure and the rhythmic period. These devices, like rhyme and meter in poetry, are mnemonic aids, and with their help he was able to carry "what was equal to sixty pages of printed matter in his memory for many days, correcting and finishing its style as he walked or rode or drove for his daily exercise." Certainly his blindness helps to account for the exquisite articulation of his paragraphs in which each sentence has its special function in relation to the whole unit.

VI. PRESCOTT AS LITERARY CRITIC

Prescott was a successful and representative critic in his time. All but one of his twenty-one full length essays appeared in the *North American Review*, and his *Biographical and Critical Miscellanies* (1845), in which fourteen of these were reprinted, had a sale of 13,000 copies in England and America by 1860.[274] The value of his criticism for the modern reader may be better estimated if it is understood from the start that it was, for the most part, either a by-product of his studies during his apprentice years, or a reluctant discharge of obligation to his author-

[274] Ticknor, p. 247. See Bibliography, section ii, for a complete listing of collected and uncollected reviews. Prescott also wrote a "considerable number" of short articles for newspapers in his early career, but he did not wish these remembered (Ticknor, p. 256). Ogden (p. 66) seems to have seen Prescott's list of these in manuscript. Allibone's (*Critical Dictionary of English Literature*, II, 1673) attribution of "Tales from the German" (*North American Review*, XLVI, 156–161 [January, 1838]) to Prescott is indefensible, inasmuch as the reviewer claims a good knowledge of the German language. Prescott said in his journal, September, 1853 (Ogden, pp. 65–66) that he had written a review of Hillard's *Six Months in Italy* for the *National Intelligencer*, but I have been unable to locate a file of this periodical.

friends. We need not look to it for significant evaluations of American culture in his time, for he was primarily interested only in such European literature as might be useful as background for his historical writings; nor need we expect to find in it intuitive or appreciative criticism, for Prescott thought of himself as a scholar whose function it was to inform.[275] His aesthetic criteria, which he assumed rather than argued, were appropriate to his time, class, and region, and he made no attempt to explore their limits. It is pointless, therefore, to compare him with contemporaries like Bryant, Channing, W. H. Gardiner, R. H. Dana, Willard Phillips, and the *Christian Examiner* group, whose interests were aesthetic and philosophical.[276]

The relation of his criticism to his apprenticeship is clear. When, in 1821, he decided upon a life of scholarship, he recorded in his journal:

I will write a review no oftener than once in three numbers of the "No. American Review"—no *oftener*, and *print* only what I think will add to my reputation. . . . In the interim I will follow a course of reading and make the subjects of my reviews, as far as I can, fall in with this course. . . . Pursue this course till I am thirty. . . . Mem. I will never engage to write for a number.[277]

One need only compare Ticknor's description of his studies[278] with a chronological list of his reviews to see how closely he followed his plan.

[275] Note his comment in his essay on Cervantes: "Don Quixote is too familiar to the reader to require any analysis; but we will enlarge on a few circumstances attending its composition but little known to the English scholar, which may enable him to form a better judgment for himself" (*Miscellanies*, p. 148).

[276] On these and other critics of the period, see Charvat, *op. cit.*, chap. viii.

[277] Ogden, pp. 63–64.

[278] Ticknor, chaps. v and vi.

When his apprenticeship ended in 1837, he lost interest in criticism—in fact, grew contemptuous of it. Of the six long essays he wrote between 1837 and 1850, three (on Cervantes, Scott, and Chateaubriand) were stopgaps between historical writings, and three (on Bancroft, Calderón, and Ticknor) were reviews of books by friends. These latter seem to have made him embarrassingly conscious of the cliquishness of American periodical criticism, for when he reviewed his friend Bancroft's *History* he wrote Sparks, "What a humbug the business of reviewing is! When will the honest public see through a millstone?"[279] Later he wrote in his journal, "It is impossible for one who has done that sort of work himself to have any respect for it. How can one critic look another in the face without laughing?"[280]

The judgment was too severe. If his reviews today lack the intrinsic value of Lowell's work in the same field, they are indispensable not only for an understanding of Prescott's mind, but of the intellectual history of America. In Prescott's criticism two major foreign influences came together, modified by American needs and by each other. The first of these was Scottish criticism,[281] which had dominated American periodicals since the founding of the *Edinburgh Review* in 1802. Deriving from Scottish "common sense" philosophy and aesthetics, this criticism was based on (1) a conception of criticism as a judicial process by which literature is subjected to prevailing moral, social, and aesthetic criteria; (2) an assumed "standard of taste," drawn, supposedly, from the accumulated aesthetic experience of mankind; (3) acceptance of a system of "associations" by which aesthetic reactions to external phenomena were standardized. The value of this criticism lay in its social quality; its danger in its rigidity. It was a healthy antidote to the excesses

[279] *Correspondence*, p. 179.

[280] Ticknor, p. 255. For similar comments see *Correspondence*, pp. 534, 547, and Ogden, pp. 65–67.

[281] On this subject, see Charvat, *op. cit.*, chap. iii.

of the Romantic poets, but it delayed the general appreciation they deserved.

Its influence on Prescott is most definite in his early work. In 1821 he accepted Jeffrey and Gifford as the leading critics of the period,[282] and even after he had come to think less of the group he continued to give them credit for having brought philosophy and liberal speculation into English criticism.[283] His 1821 essay on Byron[284] best represents their influence, for in it he applies the associational concept to the Byron-Pope controversy; rejects the Cockney and Lake schools of verse and the "false principles in poetry which have been gaining ground in England in the last ten years"; and attacks Byron's immorality. Throughout his criticism he enforced the contemporary ban on revolutionary and skeptical attitudes in literature, and on mysticism and unintelligibility.

After 1830, however, there is evidence in his work of increasing alienation from the assumptions of Scottish criticism. Though he never wholly lost the habit of thinking of poetry in associational terms, he seems to have begun to doubt that the concept operated as universally as the rhetoricians had believed. Thus he conceded in 1834[285] that Wordsworth and Coleridge had not been popular because "they seem to rely on deeper sensibilities than most men possess," and that he himself had acquired a much greater respect for Wordsworth.[286] In an attack on Johnsonian criticism in 1838 he made the significant statement that in such cold-blooded analysis "all the effect that relies on *impression* goes for nothing."[287] The spirit

[282] Ticknor, p. 60.

[283] "English Literature of the Nineteenth Century," *North American Review*, XXXV, 181–182 (July, 1832), and *Miscellanies*, p. 194.

[284] "Byron's Letters on Pope," *North American Review*, XIII, 450–473 (October, 1821).

[285] *Miscellanies*, p. 56.

[286] "English Literature of the Nineteenth Century," *North American Review*, XXXV, 170–175 (July, 1832). [287] *Miscellanies*, p. 247.

of this dictum is in harmony with his changing attitude toward style. He had also begun to question the right of critics to judge for the general public. In 1832 he felt that the British periodicals had lost their authority by indulging in sensationalism, brutal personalities, and party squabbles.[288] In 1837 he denied that the judgments of any "private circle, however well-qualified by taste and talent," had any effect on the opinions of the great public.[289] In 1839 he repudiated, in effect, all contemporary periodical criticism as a "secret tribunal, . . . whose business is rather to convict than to examine."[290]

More important, his scholarly studies had made him aware that the British had failed to keep up with developments in the comparative criticism of European literature. In this movement—a growth of the last fifty years, he said in 1825—aesthetic criteria had been widened to embrace "the character, the wants of different nations and ages . . .; from the local beauties peculiar to each, the philosophic inquirer has deduced certain general principles of beauty applicable to all; petty national prejudices have been extinguished; and a difference of taste, which for that reason alone was before condemned as a deformity, is now admired as a beautiful variety in the order of nature." For this improvement he gave contemporary British criticism little credit.[291] He acknowledged the profound importance of Hurd's and Warton's distinction between the Gothic and the classical—a principle which "set all things right—"[292] and he had read Ritson, Ellis, Percy, and the *Northern Antiquities;*[293]

[288] "English Literature of the Nineteenth Century," *op. cit.,* pp. 181–185; *Miscellanies,* p. 194.

[289] *Miscellanies,* p. 132.

[290] *Ibid.,* p. 260.

[291] *Ibid.,* pp. 633–635.

[292] *Ibid.,* p. 451, and note; see also *ibid.,* p. 634, note.

[293] Ticknor, p. 61. He also gave Warton, Johnson, and Campbell credit for "an accurate inventory" of British "poetical wealth," and Drake and Dunlop for "limited researches" in English prose (*Miscellanies,* p. 635).

but except for Hallam's *Introduction to the Literature of Europe* (1837–1838) England had made no contribution to the study of continental literature.[294] The English, he thought, were potentially the best critics in the world,[295] but the wit, sarcasm, and national vanity which characterized their contemporary periodicals were hardly conducive to a "just, impartial estimate of foreign literature."[296]

It was the Germans, he felt, who deserved credit for modern historical criticism of literature, and theirs is the second of the great influences on Prescott. "They have . . . done wonders in this department," he wrote in 1832,[297] "and have extended their critical wand over the remotest regions, dispelling the mists of old prejudice, and throwing the light of learning on what before was dark and inexplicable. . . . No nation has done so much to lay the foundations of that reconciling spirit of criticism, which, instead of condemning a difference of taste in different nations as a departure from it, seeks to explain such discrepancies by the peculiar circumstances of the nation."

The German influence seems to have come to Prescott chiefly through Friedrich Bouterwek (1766–1828) and August Wilhelm Schlegel (1767–1845). He believed that the former's *Geschichte der neuern Poesie und Beredsamkeit* (1801–1819), part of a great history of modern European letters projected "by a literary association in Göttingen," entitled him to "great credit as the earliest pioneer in this untrodden field of letters."[298] Schlegel's *Lectures on Dramatic Art and Literature* had become available in an American edition in 1818, which Prescott had read with relish in 1823.[299] There are more references in his reviews to Schlegel than to any other critic.[300] What he admired in the

---

[294] *Miscellanies*, pp. 258, 635.   [295] *Ibid.*, pp. 635, 637–638.
[296] *Ibid.*, pp. 259–260.   [297] *Ibid.*, p. 254.
[298] *Ibid.*, p. 643.   [299] Ticknor, p. 61.
[300] E.g., *Miscellanies*, pp. 255–257; 403; 541; 621, note; 631; 635, note; 702; 713.

German's work is indicated by his statement that he "has made himself so intimately acquainted with the peculiar circumstances of [Shakespeare's] age and country, that he has been enabled to speculate on his productions as those of a contemporary."[301] Prescott's similar effort to relate literature to the environment in which it was produced—to study it as a product of national character, political institutions, religion, and traditions—is evident throughout his essays.

Yet he never felt intellectually at ease with the Germans. He questioned their moral soundness, and above all he disliked their "taste for theories and system building," their tendency to "carry their fantastic imagination beyond the legitimate province of the muse into the sober fields of criticism," their "cold-blooded enthusiasm . . . which spurs them on over the plainest barriers of common sense until even the right becomes wrong." Schlegel, for example, "calls on us to admire, in contradiction to the most ordinary principles of taste and common sense," Shakespeare's "notorious blunders in geography and chronology" and his "villainous puns and quibbles."[302]

Prescott, then, applied British moralism and common sense to German methods of genetic criticism. Just as, in his histories, he judged individuals by a double standard of the "lights of their age," and of a "universal" moral law which was really an assumption of his own ethical and intellectual environment, so in his criticism he tried to do justice to the aesthetic standards of other times and countries without violating certain presumably universal "principles of taste and common sense" which were actually aesthetic and ethical standards acquired from his

[301] E.g., *Miscellanies*, pp. 255–256.

[302] *Ibid.*, pp. 254–255. Prescott's attitudes toward German criticism should be compared with George Bancroft's (in *Literary and Historical Miscellanies* [Boston, 1855], especially p. 179), for though the latter was enthusiastic about German poets and novelists, he was suspicious of the critics. For other opinions, see S. H. Goodnight, *German Literature in American Magazines Prior to 1846* (Madison, 1907).

own background. When he said, for example, that the German critics "are too often sadly wanting in . . . taste," he meant that their over-subtlety carried them past "the plainest barriers of common sense."[303] When he condemned Calderón's moral tone, and added that a "disregard of the obvious laws of morality is a violation of the principles of taste,"[304] he was voicing Anglo-Saxon didacticism.

How British attitudes and German methods came together in his work is easily apparent. "French and English Tragedy" (1823)[305] is a discussion of dramatic literature in terms of national character; but that his appreciation of the form was conditioned by his Puritanism is evident when he says elsewhere that the decline of the drama is a "consequence of the advance of civilization" because "with the progress of education and refinement, men become less open to, or, at least, less dependent on the pleasures of sense, and seek their enjoyment in more elevated and purer sources."[306] The implication of this remark is confirmed by his admiration of Molière (somewhat at the expense of Shakespeare).[307] His three essays on Italian literature —"Italian Narrative Poetry" (1824),[308] "Da Ponte's Observations" (1825),[309] and "Poetry and Romance of the Italians" (1831)[310]—are factual and scholarly histories of a national literature in terms of racial character and institutions, but he does not neglect to comment adversely on the amorality and the exclusively diverting purpose of Italian poetry.[311] "Scottish

[303]*Ibid.*, p. 255.   [304]*Ibid.*, p. 713.

[305]*North American Review*, XVI, 124–156 (January, 1823).

[306]*Miscellanies*, p. 136–137.

[307]*Ibid.*, pp. 361–409.

[308]*Ibid.*, pp. 410–485.

[309]*Ibid.*, pp. 596–638. This is Prescott's rejoinder to Lorenzo Da Ponte's reply to the first Italian article. See Ticknor, pp. 248–249.

[310]*Ibid.*, pp. 486–567. Written 1827–1828, but delayed in publication because Prescott sent it first to an English periodical which failed to print it.

[311]E.g., *ibid.*, pp. 478, 482.

Song" (1826)[312] is an admirable evaluation of a popular literature in terms of racial, geographical, and political influences,
with references to Spanish, Icelandic, German, and classical
analogues, but it ends with the contented reflection that this
barbarous "mythology," which was "venerated by man in the
infancy of society," has "become the sport of infants in an age
of civilization, furnishing a pleasing example of the progress of
the human intellect, and a plausible coloring for the dream of
perfectibility." "Chateaubriand's English Literature" (1839)[313]
contains excellent comparative estimates of English, German,
and French criticism, and of pagan, Catholic, and Protestant
arts, but the objective attitude wears thin in his long refutation
of Chateaubriand's statement that the Reformation "restricted
genius in poetry, eloquence, and the arts [and] checked heroism
in war."

"Cervantes" (1837)[314] and "Ticknor's Spanish Literature"
(1850)[315] represent the German influence at its best. In them
the combination of biographical, textual, and racial-historical
analysis demonstrates that in criticism as in historical writing
his method was eclectic. To effect an understanding of Cervantes' work, Prescott described (1) his personality, social position, and career; (2) culture and society in the reign of Philip II,
the phenomenon of chivalry, and the relation between Spanish
fiction and the national character; and (3) the evolution of a reliable text of *Don Quixote*. He followed much the same plan
in his review of Ticknor, but in addition to being an excellent
short history of the subject, this essay is significant for his final
statement of his ideals in scholarship. Accepting Bouterwek
as the modern pioneer in the field of Spanish literary history,

---

[312] *Miscellanies*, pp. 568–595.
[313] *Ibid.*, pp. 245–293.
[314] *Ibid.*, pp. 123–175.
[315] *Ibid.*, pp. 639–729. Prescott revised Ticknor's work for him
before publication (Ticknor, p. 284).

Prescott judged that Ticknor's connections in Spain had given him the advantage over the Germans in source materials. In calling his friend's great work "a complete record of Spanish civilization, both social and intellectual," he implied that Ticknor had made successful use of German methods of cultural integration; but in stating that Ticknor's style was "clear, classical, and correct, with a sustained moral dignity" and "free from any tendency to mysticism—from vagueness of expression, a pretty sure indication of vague conceptions in the mind of the author," he also implied that Ticknor had avoided the worst faults of German criticism. Thus this "standard work on Spanish literature" was, to Prescott, the ideal union of German methods and British morality and common sense.

Of the uncollected *North American Review* essays, two are especially interesting for their comments on style and romanticism. "Essay Writing" (1822)[316] appears to be the first American history and critique of the essay form.[317] Conscious of the fact that the *Sketch-Book* "forms an epoch in the history of this kind of literature," Prescott was moved to review two products of the Irving influence—Dana's *Idle Man* and his own group's *The Club Room*—in the light of the development of English prose. Though he believed that English style reached its peak in the work of Johnson, Burke, Gibbon, and Robertson, Prescott thought of prose expression as a cyclical phenomenon in which decay alternates with excellence. The "mystical" and "unintelligible" prose of Coleridge, and of Lockhart in his early work, represented a decline which was

---

[316] *North American Review*, XIV, 319-350 (April, 1822).

[317] F. L. Pattee (*Development of the American Short Story*, pp. 19-20) says that Prescott was "the first critic clearly to recognize that a new literary form had arisen," and calls his essay a "remarkable analysis." Prescott got his materials on the eighteenth-century essay from Nathan Drake's monumental *Essays* (5 vols., London, 1810). For earlier American criticism of the essay, see H. M. Ellis, *Joseph Dennie and His Circle*.

reflected in Dana's essays. That Prescott in 1822 was still under the influence of the conservative reaction against romantic impressionism is apparent in his judgment that Dana's sentence, "A tree lays itself out upon the air" was "affected, quaint, and feeble"; and in finding this sentence as perplexing as Locke's blind man's comparison of the idea of scarlet with the sound of a trumpet, he revealed his stubborn adherence to the conventional system of associations. But there is perspicacity in his perception that the originality of the *Sketch-Book* lay in its combination of sentiment, humor, and "exquisite but artificial language," and in its lack of moral purpose; and modern critics agree with his statement that Irving's style is "the very worst model in the world for the imitation of writers . . . who, wanting genuine sensibility, will only expose the beggarly condition of their thoughts the more by arraying them in this gorgeous apparel."

That Prescott's perspective on the Romantic Movement improved is obvious in his "English Literature of the Nineteenth Century" (1832).[318] In a threefold discussion of poetry, fiction, and general prose, he identified Scott and Wordsworth as the key figures of the movement. Rejecting the latter's rustic theory, Prescott yet found significance in his attempt to "reconcile man with himself and his destiny by furnishing him with a key to his present condition." As a humanist Prescott deplored Byron's total want of principle and attacked the imitators of Byron, who live in luxury but are determined to be miserable and to "indite Spenserian stanzas on the vanities and nothingness of life . . . a sort of whining much easier to write than to read." There was nothing new in his belief that American poetry can only be a new variety of English poetry, but in view of the fact that he antedated Emerson and Whitman, there is vision in his judgment that our greatest poetic materials must be nature and democratic man: "If all this be not sufficient to warm the poet's vision, the fault must lie with him." Prescott's essentially social and moral attitude toward literature is again reflected in his opinions of Scott's fiction. He believed that the novel of character was a significant feature of the age, and that Scott not only was "possessed of power sufficient to affect the moral destinies of his age," but also of "the inclination to give that power a uniformly beneficent direction." Prescott's concluding thought on the relation between literature and society is that democracy corrupts literature temporarily in that the increased demands of the literate tempt authors into rapid and careless writing, but that though "literature loses something in this way, the cause of society may be thought to gain more."

Prescott's preference for the novel is made clear in other essays, and his opinion of the form was dominated by his love of Scott, whom he called "Shakespeare in prose."[319] "Sir Walter Scott" (1838),[320] the most unreservedly sympathetic of his essays, is almost entirely biographical in content, and similar to his historical character analyses in method. In "Novel Writing" (1827),[321] only nominally a review of two contemporary novels, he attributes England's superiority in character portrayal to its free institutions, which permit the existence of many classes and varieties of people. Here and elsewhere he states his central conviction about the novel, that delineation of character is its chief province, an attitude which is in logical accordance with his emphasis on individuals in his histories.

Prescott had little interest in or knowledge of American fiction, for except for some incidental and unenlightening com-

---

[319] *Miscellanies*, p. 199.

[320] *Ibid.*, pp. 176–244. For other comments on Scott, see *ibid.*, pp. 279–286.

[321] *North American Review*, XXV, 183–203 (July, 1827).

ments on Cooper and Irving,[322] his only essay on the subject is his "Charles Brockden Brown, the American Novelist" (1834).[323] Primarily a biographical work based on William Dunlap's *Life of Brown* (1815), its chief interest for the modern reader lies in his reflections on social and philosophical radicalism during the period of French Revolutionary influence,[324] and on style.[325] There is some merit, however, in his opinion that the modern writer on the supernatural must dispense with Gothic machinery and rational explanations and rely on the creation of a convincing atmosphere.[326]

In summation, Prescott's criticism represents, (1) the decline of exclusive British influence, and the beginning of the scholarly historical criticism that stemmed from Germany; (2) the application of basic moral and social criteria, less narrow than those which characterized the more conservative criticism of his time, but appropriate nevertheless to his time and environment; (3) the development of a critical principle of historical judgment which is in harmony with the spirit of his histories. Valuable in their time for their factual content, these essays are today striking evidence of the cosmopolitanism of romantic culture. Considered in relation to the whole history of American criticism, they come at the beginning of the genteel tradition which was to flower in the humanistic essays of Lowell in the 'sixties and 'seventies, and to be reborn in the

[322] In "English Literature of the Nineteenth Century," *op. cit.*, pp. 170–191.

[323] *Miscellanies*, pp. 1–56. First published in Jared Sparks, ed., *Library of American Biography* (Boston, 1834), I, 117–180. That the essay as a whole is not inspiring is to be expected in view of Prescott's statement that "he could not have finished one of [Brown's novels] except as a job" (Ogden, p. 70).

[324] *Ibid.*, pp. 10, 14.

[325] *Ibid.*, pp. 54–56.

[326] *Ibid.*, pp. 22–26. On this subject, see also pp. 578–581. There is no evidence that Prescott was aware of Poe's and Hawthorne's achievements in the supernatural. Note Prescott's own clumsy attempt in ghost fiction, "Calais," in *The Club Room* (March, 1820).

work of the New Humanists in the twentieth century.[327]   Opposed to the egotism of the romantic rebels, seeking standards which had been disappearing since the beginning of the Industrial Revolution, concerned lest art be divorced from morality and a healthy social spirit, this school, from Prescott to Irving Babbitt, has sought, as Norman Foerster has put it, to "disengage the permanent from the transitory elements in tradition."[328]   Then as now such criticism is an antidote to the provincialism which seems inevitably to accompany national achievement.

VII. POLITICAL IDEAS

Prescott's life spanned the period of triumphant Federalism, its decline, and the rise of Jacksonian democracy.   In these years religious changes of a like magnitude upset the ordered society of Federalist Congregationalism that had believed so long in the security of its own orthodoxy.   Prescott was not so inflexible as Timothy Dwight or Fisher Ames who tenaciously held on to the past, but his spirit was uneasy in the presence of an exuberant democracy.   The wellborn and the intellectually elite were the natural leaders of society, he believed, and all others were rather presumptuous in aspiring to leadership.   It was disconcerting to see people taking the Declaration of Independence literally, and this new generation of Americans, aided by programs of public-supported education was encouraged to articulate more clearly its demands and aspirations.

New leaders, new ideas, new people (for in Prescott's later life New England experienced its second colonization, this time largely from Ireland)—all these combined to produce a terrific

---

[327] On this subject see Norman Foerster, *American Criticism* (1928), especially pp. 223–262; and G. E. De Mille, *Literary Criticism in America* (1931).

[328] Foerster, *op. cit.*, p. 235.

impact on the citadel of New England traditionalism. There were some within the citadel who affected to disdain the *hoi polloi* without; there were others who timidly ventured forth to meet this new world in the making. Prescott was of this latter group, for he believed in the necessity of change, but his tempo was confessedly slow—his social lag was a full generation. He said as much in a letter to a friend: "A Conservative of our day is as much of a Liberal in his politics as a Democrat of the time of Jefferson, while a Democrat of the present day— Lord help us!"[329]

As a historian committed to a belief in the idea of progress, which of course means change, he reluctantly adjusted himself to the transformation in American life. In the letter quoted above, Prescott said that "the tendency to a more and more democratic complexion has been checked by peculiar circumstances from time to time, but has gone on pretty steadily nevertheless." Jackson, headstrong, "very ignorant, but with an accurate knowledge of characteristics of his countrymen, and a mind of invincible resolution" hurried along the process. He stretched the "prerogatives of the executive beyond any of his predecessors" but "he was a democrat at heart." But Prescott criticized his vulgarization of "the high posts of Government by a continual appeal and reference to the mob in his actions and discourse" and he feared that Jackson had "spread a contempt for constitutional forms and usages, which is most hazardous to liberty in its truest sense."[330] Prescott commented with bitterness on Jackson's retirement: "The evil he has done will not pass away with him."[331]

Prescott was a firm believer in constitutional government but one senses that his approach was that of an obstructionist, using all the parliamentary devices available to slow up the process of

[329] *Correspondence*, p. 500, Sept. 15, 1844.
[330] *Ibid.*, p. 501.
[331] *Ibid.*, p. 15.

social change. He was, in his correspondence at least, distinctly a snob, believing that the lower classes should keep their place.[332] He believed that if "suffrage could be limited to those who have property at stake, and the press could be conducted by honest men, this would be a perfect government." And then, as if to shake himself out of this pessimism, he added, "as it is, it is only the best—the least bad—in the world."[333] He had strong distaste for money-grubbing, a failing which he attributed to his own country; "the science of spending," he thought, was to be found in Europe.[334]

The apologetic note that appears in Prescott's correspondence reflecting his political environment in America sometimes seems stronger when he writes to Europeans living under monarchical regimes, almost out of deference to a superior ordering of existence. He was "born a republican," he once remarked. "But I am not a fierce one," he hurried to add, "and in my own country indeed am ranked among what in England would correspond with the conservatives."[335] This estimate of himself was confirmed by his closest friend, Ticknor, who was a little more specific. During Prescott's whole life, "as his father always did," he belonged to the conservative school of Hamiltonian Federalism.[336] That party names changed did not affect the accuracy of this judgment, for many of the Whigs of the 1830's and 1840's were Federalists writ large. Security for wealth was definitely a fundamental consideration with Prescott.[337] His view was dictated by sectional as well as economic considerations, and as a New Englander he strongly resented the influence exerted by the South and the West in national affairs.[338]

Possibly because of his aversion to politics as carried on in

[332] *Ibid.*, p. 121.
[334] *Ibid.*, pp. 71, 188, 597.
[336] Ticknor, p. 359.
[333] *Ibid.*, p. 513, Nov. 3, 1844.
[335] *Ibid.*, p. 333, Jan. 30, 1843.
[337] *Correspondence*, p. 144, also p. 12.
[338] *Ibid.*, p. 597.

the democratic era Prescott left no comprehensive statement of his views on the issues that troubled his generation. But in his correspondence and conversation and sometimes, unobtrusively, in his writings, he indicated his position on contemporary problems. The democratization of American life forced from him a grudging acceptance of changing mores, and he was not pleased when the Whigs had to adopt the technique of their opponents to win votes. "Every man is a patriot, and guns and hurrahs are splitting the air in all directions," he wrote anent the election in 1840. "But it is a glorious victory," he said to Jared Sparks, "though I agree with you a log cabin and hard cider are indifferent qualifications for the presidency. But these are words to gull the many, who love to be gulled."[339]

Opposed as he was to *enthusiasm* (whether it appeared in politics or religion) Prescott deplored the procedure, the manner of getting things done, even while he approved of the objectives. He liked the fight that John Quincy Adams was waging in Congress against slavery. Sarcastically he spoke of "the chivalrous South, which rages and roars like a mad bull." But even while "planting himself on the right ground," Adams half makes it wrong "by the manner he defends it." The North welcomed his leadership, fighting an "arrogant South," although he was "a very qualified blessing." "But it is a pity," said Prescott, "to bring the great local divisions of the land into conflict more than is necessary."[340] He belonged to the considerable group of prosperous Northerners who preferred in general, to soft-pedal controversial issues in the 1840's. "One thing is certain," he wrote to George Sumner, "we never were so prosperous, in a material sense, as now, if we don't spoil our prosperity by a muddling legislature. . . ."[341] He did not go as far as Abbott Lawrence in appeasing the South, at

[339] *Correspondence*, p. 178.
[340] *Ibid.*, pp. 419–420, to Edward Everett, Dec. 23, 1843.
[341] *Ibid.*, pp. 549–550, Aug. 14, 1845.

this time, but temperamentally they seem not to have been far apart.[342] Emerson did not believe that New England agreed to accept Southern slavery because of the tiresome constitutional argument of "misleading Whig parties and good-boy states-men," but tolerated it rather because of material considerations. It was cotton thread, said Emerson, which "holds the union to-gether: unites John C. Calhoun and Abbott Lawrence. Patri-otism is for holidays and summer evenings with music and rockets, but cotton thread is the *union*."[343]

The major parties seemed to be breaking up and new Whigs, like Sumner, Palfrey, and Charles Francis Adams gradually as-serted themselves with more spirit in the late 1840's, refusing to let the Boston merchants speak for the whole party.[344] Pres-cott seems to have drifted over to this newer group, but what-ever vigorous opinions he had were mainly on the slavery issue. He was like so many in their unwillingness to face fundamental questions in the late 1840's, finding the only safe topics of con-versation to be railroads and California gold. These, said Emerson, engrossed alike "farmers, merchants, boys, women, saints, philosophers, and fools."[345]

Although Prescott would have preferred to let sleeping dogs lie, he did communicate to his friends his judgments on the cur-rent scene. He was strongly opposed to the acquisition of Texas, less from dislike of imperialism[346] than from fear of an increase of the slave owners' influence in national politics. In a letter supporting the Rev. W. E. Channing's stand against the annexation of Texas, Prescott said such enlargement of

---

[342] Prescott appears to have approved of Lawrence in general (*Correspondence*, p. 199). Prescott was introduced to Calhoun by Lawrence with the wish that whatever their political differences, they might be personal friends (Darling, *op. cit.*, p. 336). See also Prescott's *Memoir of the Honorable Abbott Lawrence* (1856).

[343] Quoted in Darling, *op. cit.*, p. 336.

[344] *Correspondence*, p. 292; Darling, *op. cit.*, pp. 337–339.

[345] Darling, *op. cit.*, p. 359.   [346] *Correspondence*, p. 577.

our domain "for the criminal purpose of extending and indefinitely perpetuating slavery" would dishonor and degrade the nation. It would also disturb the balance of the states to the advantage of the South, and slave owners, said Prescott, "cannot be expected to prove a temperate majority." Collisions between the two sections were likely, and eventually, separation, unless the free states, in a debased mood, submitted. And rather than accept such degradation for the North, Prescott made (what was for him) a very unusual statement: "I am disposed to think a peaceable separation would be preferable to a continuance of the Union, under the preponderating power the annexation would give the slave States over the free provided the latter could be brought to unite in another government."[347]

As time went on he did not abate his antagonism to the extension of slave territory but he gradually accommodated himself to the thought that by negotiation the claims of "beggarly Mexico" would be bought off and then with Texas voluntarily joining the Union, there would be no excuse for European interference in the affair.[348] He did not believe that the administration of Polk, much as he disliked it, would go to war with Mexico nor risk one with England and France over Texas. When the Texans finally decided to throw themselves into the arms of Brother Jonathan, he accepted the situation with poor grace, wishing rather that Texas "had thrown herself to the devil, where indeed it is probable most of her population at

[347] "Letters to Dr. Channing on Slavery and the Annexation of Texas, 1837," Fulmer Mood and Granville Hicks, eds., *New England Quarterly*, V, 600–601 (July, 1932).
[348] *Correspondence*, pp. 519–520, Nov. 30, 1844. A friendlier reference to Mexico is found in a letter to a fellow historian Lúcas Alamán, wishing his country were as tranquil as the United States: "Mexico has the elements of a great nation, but these seem to be in too disorderly a condition to allow the country any fair prospect of developing its natural resources. Yet I trust the time may come . . ." (*Correspondence*, p. 584).

some time or other will go."[349] Because this territorial acquisition was made "in contempt of constitutional law, and in disregard of the great principles of international justice" it was "the most serious shock yet given to the stability of our glorious institutions."[350]

On the related issue of territorial expansion in Oregon, Prescott was more complacent. It is true that this too, was somewhat disturbing, leading him to soliloquize on the tendency of all states to self-aggrandizement, but he found it easier to stomach the addition of more free territory to the Union. "What is the reason that nations are so greedy of territorial acquisition?" he asked one correspondent. "Our nation above all, that has got ten times as much now as it can cover? I suppose it is on the same principle that a land proprietor likes to add a piece more to round off his corners. There will always be corners."[351] He was quite certain that England and the United States would find an amicable solution to the problem, but in his correspondence there is an undertone suggesting just the slightest irritation with John Bull. Writing to George Sumner on the Oregon question he said that "we must hope for the best. Hope belongs to republics, and the 'guess and fear' of the poet should be reserved for the crazy time-eaten policies of the Old World."[352]

The growing tensions of the 1850's made it much harder for Prescott and his fellow Whigs to wait patiently for the gradual solution of the slavery question, which in an earlier year seemed so obvious. When he was writing about slavery in his *Conquest of Mexico*, he inserted a reference to the nineteenth century, observing how risky it would be to deal strongly with slavery in the United States lest the whole political fabric be endangered.

[349] *Ibid.*, p. 547, note 5; also p. 577.

[350] *Miscellanies*, pp. 304–305, note.

[351] *Correspondence*, p. 520; also p. 538; see Prescott's criticism of European imperialism in *Peru*, pp. 1037–1038.

[352] *Ibid.*, pp. 549–550; also pp. 545–546, 597.

Admitting the evils of the institution, Prescott said he might "nevertheless hesitate to adopt a remedy, until he [was] satisfied that the remedy itself [was] not worse than the disease. That such a remedy will come with time, who can doubt, that has confidence in the ultimate prevalence of the right, and the progressive civilization of his species?"[353] Like many another Whig Prescott swallowed the Compromise of 1850 out of a desire to preserve the Union, but again, like many another Northern Whig, he gagged at the Fugitive Slave Law. He joined in the efforts to nullify the act by aiding runaway slaves. His dislike of the Kansas-Nebraska Act, which "seemed so much like double dealing," capitulating to the South, made it easier to look with complacency upon the sabotage of the Fugitive Slave Law.[354] He was sufficiently shaken out of his traditional political groove to join thousands of other Whigs in a shift to the Republican candidate, Fremont, in the election of 1856. A truer index to his sentiments, however, was the preference for a distant era: "I belong to the sixteenth century," he said, "and am quite out of place when I sleep elsewhere."[355]

In fact contemporary politics, generally, was distasteful to him (he once called it a "dirty trade"), and his lifelong friend, Ticknor, tells us that he took little interest in the political questions of his time.[356] He gently chided his friend and political opponent, George Bancroft, for mixing in politics, affecting astonishment at his simultaneous wooing of "the fair Muse of history and the ugly strumpet of faction with the same breath." "Why do you coquet with such a troublesome termagant as politics . . .?" he asked. "I can't say I comprehend the fascination of such a mistress; for which, I suppose, you will commiser-

[353] *Mexico*, p. 678.

[354] Ogden, pp. 202–203.

[355] Peck, pp. 89–90. Cf. Prescott's remarks in 1844: "I take refuge from these political squabbles among the Andes, where I am trying to dig out a few grains of Peruvian gold" (*Correspondence*, p. 520).

[356] *Correspondence*, p. 54; Ticknor, p. 358.

ate me."[357] There is more than a touch of cynicism in his observations on the passing political scene. On one occasion he remarked that the phrase "the good sense of the people" had more of humbug in it "than he once thought."[358] He wrote to a friend that a great gathering of Whigs was to be held on Bunker Hill "where Mr. Webster, etc., etc., are to fill them with —patriotism, not bread and cheese, which they are to return and pick up among the good people of Boston. . . . Whiggery is a good thing in the abstract, but in the concrete we may have too much of a good thing." He comforted himself with the assurance that "this is the machinery by which revolutions are effected" in the United States and he was thankful "that muskets make no part of it, as among our South American brethren."[359] Nevertheless he was fearful of huge crowds subjected to excited oratory, even when Whig, "for a mob after all is an inflammable mass, and when inflamed is not easily controlled." Discussing the process of presidential selection, Prescott thought that one term, extending for six years (with the president ineligible for re-election) would be an improvement in American political life.[360]

Apparently Prescott disapproved of contemporary social changes achieved through violence. He coldly condemned the French Revolution and its historian Carlyle. "After a very candid desire to relish him," said Prescott, "I must say I do not at all. I think he has proceeded on a wrong principle altogether. The French Revolution is a most lamentable comedy (as Nick Bottom says) of itself, and requires nothing but the simplest statement of facts to freeze one's blood."[361] But Prescott's blood did not freeze, it was rather warmed, contemplating the revolutions achieved by the Protestant Reformation and the Americans in 1776. To Prescott, obviously, these latter were

[357] Ticknor, p. 361; *Correspondence*, p. 162.
[358] *Correspondence*, p. 3.   [359] *Ibid.*, p. 153, Sept. 1, 1840.
[360] *Ibid.*, p. 502.   [361] Ticknor, p. 362.

progressive movements, and besides had happened sufficiently long ago to have been glossed with a patina of comfortable respectability. The French Revolution (an alien uprising, Celtic in origin, no Anglo-Saxons would conduct a revolution on this pattern)[362] was too devastating in its results and perhaps, too recent, to view with serenity.

It is clear that Prescott could not be classed with the pacifists, then growing in number in the western world. He may not have been as enamored of war as was his fellow historian, Parkman, who wrote once that the military instincts are "always strongest in the strongest and richest nature,"[363] but he did proclaim that war was sometimes justifiable. Surely in his histories he often made war appear very romantic. To one correspondent who had maintained that all wars were dishonorable Prescott answered a vigorous, "No! by all those who fell at Marathon; by those who fought at Morgarten and Bannockburn; by those who fought and bled at Bunker's Hill; in the war of the Low Countries against Philip the Second,—in all those wars which have had—which are *yet* to have—freedom for their object,—I can't acquiesce in your sweeping denunciation, my good friend."[364]

But one of the lessons that history, and particularly the history that Prescott studied and wrote, teaches us is that the evils of war are so great that nations should be willing to submit to extreme sacrifices "save that of honor, before authorizing an appeal to arms." The desire to avoid the calamities of war by resorting to "peaceful congresses and impartial mediation, is on the whole, the strongest evidence, stronger than that afforded by the progress of science and art, of our boasted advance in civilization."[365] He saw as one of the best guarantees of prog-

[362] J. B. McMaster's distinction; see Kraus, p. 383.
[363] Quoted in Kraus, p. 289.
[364] Ticknor, p. 377.
[365] *Mexico*, p. 278; *Ferdinand and Isabella*, III, 342.

ress and peace in the world, collaboration between England and the United States, "the only two great nations where constitutional liberty exists."[366]

There were, of course, obstacles in the path of Anglo-American friendship. Texas and Oregon were two, fortunately removed—the tariff and repudiation of debts to England were others. Prescott saw with misgivings the strain on Anglo-American relations created by the defaulting states and anxiously looked to them to make the *amende honorable*.[367] Prescott, as a fairly orthodox Whig, believed in the value of a protective tariff for American industry. But he was not particularly vigorous in his espousal of it and he found it possible to write rather lightly when England and America lowered their tariff barriers. A note, faintly wry, crept into his remark to a correspondent in England that she would be "monstrously annoying in forcing" her free trade system on the rest of the world. "Master Bull," said Prescott, "is a canny chiel, and when he has climbed up to the top of the building has no objection to kicking away the scaffolding by which he has got up, and by which his younger brethren are trying to get up."[368] He was happy that the war clouds gathering because of the Oregon dispute had blown over and he had no doubt that "Mr. Bull and Jonathan will shake hands and be better friends than before, our cotton jackets, woollens, etc., at the north being thrown in as a kind of peace offering. Peace or war, the Yankees—the *genuine* Yankees—have always to pay for it."[369]

Prescott, like so many others in his circle, especially George Ticknor and Edward Everett, was a strong Anglophile. Despite his deprecation of imperialistic tendencies, particularly if slavery was the beneficiary, his sentiments generally favored an

[366] Ticknor, p. 353.

[367] *Correspondence*, p. 421.

[368] *Ibid.*, pp. 585–586, to T. J. Phillips, March 30, 1846. Cf. also p. 519, to Lord Morpeth.

[369] *Ibid.*, pp. 581–582, to Mrs. Charles Lyell, March 22, 1846.

Anglo-Saxon hegemony in the world. They were not so marked as those of some contemporaries (surely not so crude as those of Edward Freeman) but obviously they did give comfort to English correspondents with like beliefs. He mourned over the conquest of Mexico but expressed pride in the achievements of American troops. And when it looked as though Mexico itself might be added to American territory he asked what we should do with Mexicans. "It will be a heavy drag on our republican car, and the Creole blood will not mix well with the Anglo-Saxon." "The Mexicans are such poor creatures," thought Mrs. Charles Lyell, that she was sure "it is for their good that they should be conquered, and have Yankee schools. If only, Southern slavery could be shut out. We should like to send you four millions of Irish to fill up your newly acquired territories." [370] One of the chief claims of "the Anglo-Saxon race in both hemispheres" to the gratitude of man, said Prescott, was its ability to apply science to the useful arts. [371]

Prescott's conservatism naturally made him hostile to the revolutionary movements of 1848. He distrusted the ability of the illiterate millions "to exercise the full extent of political power that can be claimed by a democracy of long standing," and of universal suffrage in France and Italy he was frankly contemptuous. But added to this conservative mistrust in the working of democracy was the belief that this form of government would be further handicapped if tried by Latin or Slavic peoples. "Liberty and equality seem to be too great stimulants for some constitutions. They suit the Anglo-Saxon better than any." [372] Ideas such as these were to gain greater currency in the later years of the century and historians in Europe and America were to be among their leading protagonists.

---

[370] *Correspondence*, p. 634, April 30, 1847; p. 642; p. 637, May 17, 1847.

[371] *Mexico*, p. 78.

[372] Penney, pp. 77, 82.

Prescott had that warm attachment to his native land which is so often strengthened by travel abroad. He had a tender regard for England, but its carefully cultivated, tame beauty, he told his wife, made him homesick for a "ragged fence, or an old stump . . . to show that man's hand had not been combing Nature's head so vigorously. I felt I was not in my own dear, wild America."[373] Prescott's faith in America rarely faltered although it wobbled when Democratic administrations were in power. The million, he said, sinned "more from ignorance than design. The design is in the knaves who dupe them."[374] Despite the "bad hands" guiding our government under Polk, "we go ahead like a great lusty brat that will work his way into the full size of a man, from the strength of his constitution, whatever quacks and old women may do to break it."[375] America is so young and vigorous that it easily throws off ailments "that would prostrate an old and debilitated state."[376] The New World is the true soil for republican institutions and our own example may prepare the European mind to eventually acquire them. Prescott fervently hoped we would be "true to ourselves for the future." This is our *mission*, he proclaimed, "the most momentous ever intrusted to a nation."[377]

VIII. PRESCOTT'S REPUTATION

Prescott's success in authorship was one of the wonders of the Golden Day. His first work was greeted by a chorus of applause, not only from American periodicals—which was to be expected—but from European critics and historians, one of whom, an authority on Spanish history, conceded that it was "the first historical work which British-America has yet produced," and that it need not fear comparison with anything

[373] Ticknor, p. 300. [374] *Correspondence*, p. 513.
[375] *Ibid.*, p. 629. [376] *Ibid.*, p. 48.
[377] *Miscellanies*, pp. 297, 303.

written in Europe since 1800.[378] In this the Royal Academy of
History at Madrid concurred by electing him to membership.[379]
The *Conquest of Mexico* earned him the place in the French
Institute left vacant by the death of Navarrete,[380] membership
in the Royal Society of Berlin, congratulations from such no-
tables as Humboldt and Hallam, and over one hundred and
thirty favorable American newspaper reviews in the space of a
month.[381] By 1850 his fame was such that his vacation in England turned out to be, according to Ticknor, "the most brilliant
visit ever made to England by an American citizen not clothed
with the *prestige* of official station."[382] By 1857 he had received
four honorary degrees, and had been elected to twenty-seven
historical and philosophical societies.[383] All told, over 91,000
copies of his works had been sold by 1860.[384]

Under the circumstances, it is more useful to modify Ticknor's statement that criticism of Prescott was all of "one tone
and temper" than to document it. There was dissent from three
sources: (1) from Catholic critics; (2) from the Transcendentalists; (3) after his death, from the new school of "realistic"
archaeologists.

That Prescott, on the whole, gave little offense to Catholics
is evident from the popularity of translations of his works in
Latin countries.[385] But although Protestants like J. Q. Adams
and Guizot[386] believed that he was unbiased in his treatment of

---

[378]Richard Ford, in the *Quarterly Review*, LXIV, 58 (June, 1839).
For the reception of *Ferdinand and Isabella*, see Ticknor, pp. 110–113;
and the excerpts from criticisms in Allibone, *op. cit.*, p. 1665.

[379]See interesting details on this in *Correspondence*, pp. 63, 84, 85.
[380]See Ticknor, pp. 239–240; and *Correspondence*, pp. 543–544.
[381]Ticknor, p. 205.
[382]*Ibid.*, p. 339. For a full account of this trip, see *ibid.*, pp. 299–341.
[383]See *ibid.*, Appendix D, for a list of these honors.
[384]Compiled from figures in Ticknor, pp. 247, 405, 407; and Peck,
p. 95.
[385]Ferguson, *American Literature in Spain*, pp. 148–157.
[386]See his article on Prescott, *Edinburgh Review*, CV, 42 (January,
1857).

the Church, it was natural enough for some Catholic critics to wish for more sympathetic treatment of Spanish religious and imperialist history. Prescott's Mexican translator, Lúcas Alamán, thought he savored "something of the old Puritan acid in [his] anti-Catholic strictures"; a Madrid translator condemned his hostility to the Inquisition; a Baltimore Catholic journal called him a Deist;[387] and M. J. Spalding accused him of hating the "religion of the Conquerors."[388] On the other hand, Archbishop Hughes commended his treatment of Catholicism;[389] the Catholic *Dublin Review* found him unbiased;[390] and even Spalding admitted that Prescott tried to be just. Clearly, he was innocent of Motley's violent Protestant partisanship.

The Transcendentalists were, almost without exception, either hostile or indifferent. Emerson, frankly contemptuous, reflected bitterly when the historian died that the public "thinks Prescott the very Muse of History," while it ignores Carlyle's biography of Frederick—"a book that is a Judgment Day . . . for its moral verdict on men and nations and manners of modern times."[391] Margaret Fuller, admitting the richness and freshness of Prescott's materials, regretted that they should have been first presented to the public by one who "possesses nothing of the higher powers of the historian."[392] Orville Dewey thought Prescott wanting in "moral nerve" because he does not "make us shudder at the names of Cortés and Pizarro."[393]

But the only detailed and sustained attack from this group was by Theodore Parker, whose two essays, "The Character of

---

[387] All three opinions were reported by Prescott (*Correspondence*, p. 583).

[388] *United States Catholic Magazine*, III, 487 (August, 1844). See also J. B. Culemans, "A Revaluation of Early Peruvian History," *Catholic Historical Review*, II, 157–167 (July, 1916).

[389] Ticknor, p. 232.

[390] *Correspondence*, p. 583.

[391] *Journals*, IX, 195 (May, 1859).

[392] *Art, Literature, and the Drama* (Boston, 1874), p. 303.

[393] *Autobiography and Letters* (Boston, 1883), p. 190.

Mr. Prescott as an Historian" and "Prescott's Conquest of Mexico,"[394] constitute the one really searching criticism to which Prescott's work was subjected in his lifetime. Having devoted to these essays seven months' work, which included a reading of all the available sources which Prescott had used,[395] Parker was qualified to state, at least from the Transcendentalist's point of view, the shortcomings of the historian's work.

He began by listing the qualifications of the modern historian. A historian is to a nation what a biographer is to a man. He must describe the origin of the nation's people, its ideas, philosophy, literature, laws, religion, industry, sources and use of revenues, social classes, influence on the rest of the world, and the daily life of the masses. Only thus can "history become Philosophy teaching by experience." Asserting that history is essentially subjective, Parker found that the work of strong historians reflects their own character; that of weak ones (like Prescott), the prejudices of their environment. The criterion of modern history is the "spirit of humanity." This spirit is possessed by Niebuhr, Schlosser, Sismondi, Michelet, Bancroft,[396] Grote, and Macaulay, but not by Prescott or (curiously enough) by Carlyle, who, "Himself a giant, . . . writes History in the interest only of giants." From the point of view of content, he found *Ferdinand and Isabella* inadequate on law, revenue, military organization, the life of the common people, and intellectual (but not literary) history. He found the *Conquest of Mexico* much less vulnerable on the score of content. In the

---

[394] *Massachusetts Quarterly Review*, II, 215–248, 437–470 (March, September, 1849). The two articles cover *Ferdinand and Isabella* and *Mexico*, successively. An intended third on *Peru* was never written.

[395] O. B. Frothingham, *Theodore Parker* (Boston, 1874), p. 397.

[396] But cf. Parker's statement that "Bancroft has elevated no man" (Frothingham, *op. cit.*, p. 441). Emerson thought him "thin" (*Heart of Emerson's Journals*, ed. Bliss Perry, p. 208). Bancroft is sometimes considered a Transcendental historian. See R. B. Nye, "The Religion of George Bancroft," *Journal of Religion*, XIX, 229–230 (July, 1939).

matter of interpretation, Parker deprecated Prescott's high rating of Isabella and Cortés, his failure to abuse the "atrocious" Ferdinand sufficiently, his lack of emphasis on the conflict of Spanish and Indian cultures, his defense of Spanish imperialism, his belief in the religious sincerity of the Conquerors, and his lack of sympathy for the natives. He found Prescott's portraits lacking in distinctness, and his language commonplace and full of clichés. In general, Prescott is a "well-bred gentleman of letters," who "lacks philosophy to a degree exceeding belief." He writes with the "average sense of mankind, with their average of conscience—and his judgment, the average judgment of a trading town, is readily accepted by the average of men." He "writes as one with little sympathy for mankind," and "seems to think that Spain belonged to Ferdinand and Isabella."

On the credit side, Parker placed Prescott's "niceness of literary culture," his accuracy and scholarship, his "just and hearty horror" of Aztec sacrificial rites, and his lack of bigotry.

Modern criticism of the romantic historians tends to accept these accusations of too exclusive attention to political and military history, too little concern for social and economic data, and avoidance of the dry and commonplace. These were failings, or at least traits, of the age. But the historian, like any other artist, has the right to choose his own subjects, and Prescott's main interest lay in exciting events and eras. *Ferdinand and Isabella* is, after all, the story of a monarchy, not a sociological history of Spain, and *Mexico* and *Peru* are accounts of two great adventures. Moreover, the fact that these histories were conceived as works of literature, written with due regard for form and proportion, and in relation to a controlling central theme, precluded extended ventures into related fields. Yet whenever it was appropriate, Prescott supplied background materials. Thus, in *Ferdinand and Isabella* he devoted more than two full chapters to the literature and learning which flourished under the sovereigns, and in *Mexico* and *Peru* he provided vivid and detailed introductory accounts of Indian civilization.

It is difficult to refute Parker's criticism, for he and the historian represented irreconcilable points of view. Parker's passions—for the people, for freedom, for "Natural Right and Justice"— his frank partisanship, his lack of a sense of humor (which made him impatient of such "frivolous" matters as the brilliance of a royal pageant), these were fundamentally incompatible with Prescott's dislike of reformism, his detachment, and his literary purpose. There is room in the world for both Parkers and Prescotts, and the critic and the historian, each in his fashion, made valuable contributions to American culture.

The most damaging attack on Prescott came from the field of archaeology after his death. In studying Aztec and Inca cultures for the introductory sections of his *Mexico* and *Peru*, Prescott made use of the best materials that were available at the time, including the records of the Spaniards who invaded America, and the newest studies in the anthropology, archaeology, and ethnology of Indian races. Within a decade after his death, the evolutionary method was applied to these disciplines, with the result that for a time archaeological conclusions in the field of ancient Indian culture were based upon observation of existing Indian tribes, and all sixteenth-century Spanish accounts of Indian culture were discredited. The new approach did not go unchallenged at the time, and it has been shaken—indeed, almost demolished—by modern science and scholarship. Yet Prescott's reputation has never recovered from the attack on the so-called "romantic" archaeology, and modern commentators still repeat the old judgment that he and his whole generation were ignorant of archaeological science.[397] The controversy, therefore, deserves review.

[397] For example, Ruth Putnam, in *CHAL*, II, 129; G. P. Gooch, *History and Historians in the Nineteenth Century*, p. 414; G. M. Dutcher and others, *Guide to Historical Literature*, p. 1066.

In the first place, Prescott's contemporaries were not un-critical of the Spanish sources. In 1840, Lewis Cass, in a review attacking contemporary French archaeology in America,[398] stated that the Conquistadors had described a state of society "far more advanced" than could be proved by an examination of Aztec and Inca remains. This skeptical note appeared again in 1845, when Albert Gallatin indicated, in his important summary of Central American archaeology,[399] numerous incon-sistencies in the records of the Conquerors and minor errors in Prescott's use of these sources. Inasmuch as Gallatin was later cited against the Romantics by the evolutionists, it should be pointed out that he and Prescott respected each other's work.

This critical attitude toward sources was put on a controversial plane in 1859 by Robert A. Wilson in *A New History of the Conquest of Mexico*, a sensational denunciation of the Spaniards and all their accounts of the Aztecs, and of Prescott's acceptance of their testimony. Wilson's chauvinistic and anti-Catholic spirit, and his revival of Las Casas' ancient denunciations of Spanish abuses, did not merit the respect of scholars, and no one troubled to refute the devastating criticism of his work by J. F. Kirk, Prescott's secretary and editor-to-be.[400] But one

---

[398] *North American Review*, LI, 396–433 (October, 1840).

[399] "Notes on the Semi-Civilized Nations of Mexico, Yucatan, and Central America," *Transactions of the American Ethnological Society*, I, 1–352 (1845). Gallatin founded the American Ethnological Society in 1842. On this aspect of his career, see J. A. Stevens, *Albert Gallatin* (1900), pp. 387 ff. For Prescott's relations with Gallatin, see *Correspondence*, pp. 542, 655; and *Mexico*, pp. 702, 712.

[400] *Atlantic Monthly*, III, 518–525, 633–645 (April, May, 1859). Kirk not only exposed the weakness of Wilson's methods and conclusions, but pointed out that his chief authorities—Rousseau, St. Hilaire, and Gallatin—had a high opinion of Prescott, and that Wilson had asked Prescott for the use of his library. Ticknor commended Kirk's articles in *Proceedings of the Massachusetts Historical Society*, IV, 277–282 (April, 1859) and in *Papers Discussing the Comparative Merits of Prescott's and Wilson's Histories* (Boston, 1861). The latter contains three letters from Prescott to Wilson, one of which Wilson

element of his theory attracted attention. Wilson rejected the traditional picture of Aztec civilization on the theory that all American Indian tribes had a common culture, and that the present low state of North American tribes proved that the Spaniards had exaggerated the progressiveness of the Aztecs.

In the next phase of the controversy, the study of existing tribes was linked with the evolutionary hypothesis by a group —led by Lewis Henry Morgan[401]—who came to be known as the "Discouragists." On the theory that "the history of the human race is one in source, one in experience, and one in progress," [402] Morgan rejected all evidence of high civilization among the Aztecs, calling "the whole series of Spanish and American histories . . . delusive and fictitious so far as Indian society and government are concerned." [403] The Aztecs "were thoroughly and essentially Indian," and their culture "simply exhibited a more advanced development of those primary ideas of civilization and social life which were common to the whole Indian family." [404]

Morgan did not attack Prescott (for whom he had high regard[405]) until the publication of H. H. Bancroft's *Native Races of the Pacific* (1875), which he called "a crime against ethnological science," [406] convinced him that the romantic myth of Aztec

---

had reprinted as a testimonial in his book. In 1859 Prescott's *Peru* was attacked by Lambert A. Wilmer in his *Life . . . of Fernand De Soto* (Philadelphia, 1859), pp. 2–4. Like Wilson, Wilmer was a Las Casas partisan.

[401] For an analysis of his work, see B. J. Stern, *Lewis Henry Morgan* (Chicago, 1931). For his place in American thought, see R. H. Gabriel, *The Course of American Democratic Thought*, pp. 163–168; in anthropology, see V. F. Calverton, ed., *The Making of Man* (Modern Library, 1931), pp. 4–30. Note that Parkman approved Morgan's work (Stern, *op. cit.*, p. 110).

[402] L. H. Morgan, *Ancient Society* (1878), p. vi.

[403] Stern, *op. cit.*, p. 116.

[404] *Ibid.*, p. 109.

[405] *Ibid.*, p. 116.

[406] *Ibid.*, p. 116.

magnificence must be exploded. This he attempted to do in his sensational "Montezuma's Dinner" (1876).[407] Proclaiming Bernal Diaz' description of Montezuma's sumptuous dining customs a monstrous exaggeration,[408] Morgan substituted a picture of squalid savages huddled around a common pot. Montezuma was not an hereditary emperor, but an elective war-chief; his "empire" was a confederation of Indian tribes; his "palace" was a communal house. In general (his argument ran) the Spaniards had interpreted Indian culture in terms of their own, and Bancroft and Prescott had perpetuated their distortions.

Morgan's disciple, A. F. A. Bandelier,[409] continued the attack more moderately, but on substantially the same theory. In his archaeological reports Bandelier tried to establish the theory that ancient Mexico was a military democracy originally based on communal living. Reviewing historical interpretations of the Aztecs in his *Romantic School of American Archaeology* (1885), he concluded, "A school of historical literature which pretends to write history without the aid of judicious criticism creates illusion, propagates fiction, and may deservedly be called the romantic school in American aboriginal history." In a later article[410] he attacked the traditions of Peruvian archaeology,

---

[407] *North American Review*, CXXII, 265–308 (April, 1876). See H. H. Bancroft's bitter attack on the "men of Morgan" in *The Early American Chroniclers* (San Francisco, 1883). "It seems to me ridiculous for the superficial readers of a few books to criticize the result of such thorough researches as Prescott's. . . . I for one can testify to his general thoroughness and accuracy" (p. 25).

[408] For Prescott's use of this material, see selection below, pp. 150–158.

[409] See T. T. Waterman, "Bandelier's Contribution to the Study of Ancient Mexican Social Organization," *University of California Publications in American Archaeology and Ethnology*, XII, 249–282 (February, 1917); Stern, *op. cit.*, *passim*; Peck, pp. 153–165.

[410] "The Truth About Inca Civilization," *Harper's Monthly Magazine*, CX, 632–640 (March, 1905). For fuller details on the attack on Inca traditions, see Peck (pp. 163–165), who reflects the influence of the Discouragists.

stating that the companions of Pizarro had described Peruvian social organization in feudal terms; that Peru was not an empire but a group of tribes; that the Inca was not a divine, hereditary ruler, but a war-chief chosen by a council; that the nobles were not nobles; and that Inca religion was not monotheistic, but polytheistic and fetichistic.

The influence of the Discouragists—particularly Morgan— was so great that for decades their devaluation of Prescott's work was generally accepted.[411]   Charles Eliot Norton, president of the American Archaeological Society, wrote Carlyle in 1880 that the "wild fancies . . . current ever since the days of the Spanish Conquerors" had been confirmed by the "amiable Prescott . . . in his pleasant romantic narrative."[412]   Henry Adams was Morgan's enthusiastic supporter.[413]   John Fiske, carrying the torch of evolution into history, wove the new realism into his *Discovery of America* (1891),[414] in which he referred to Prescott only in rather scornful footnotes.

It would be pointless to deny that Prescott's picture of Indian civilizations has been modified by later scholarship; that he was an amateur in archaeology; and that he had never examined archaeological remains himself.[415]   But a revaluation of his work must take into account the following facts:

(1) Morgan's hypotheses have been outmoded.[416]   It is now clear that whereas Prescott worked objectively on the basis of available evidence, Morgan fitted facts into a preconceived theory.   Even contemporary evolutionists thought him extreme.

---

[411]"Almost every radical thinker in the nineteenth century cited Morgan as final authority" (Calverton, *op. cit.*, p. 6).   "His idea of progress from savagery to barbarism to civilization entered into the fabric of the thought of the people" (Gabriel, *op. cit.*, p. 168).

[412]*Letters of Charles Eliot Norton* (Boston, 1913), II, 112.

[413]Stern, *op. cit.*, p. 116.

[414]See Volume I, Chapter I, for Fiske's review of the controversy.

[415]Neither had Morgan.

[416]Stern, *op. cit.*, pp. 127–128; Calverton, *op. cit., passim*; Gabriel, *op. cit.*, p. 165.

Bandelier wrote him in 1873[417] that evidence pointed to "an intellectual development [in Peru] superior to many states of the old world," and the English anthropologist, E. B. Tylor, believed that Morgan had "built up a structure of theory wider and heavier than his foundations will bear." [418]

(2) The Spanish sources have recovered most of their former authority. Even Bandelier believed, as he wrote Morgan,[419] that "Both branches, the ethnological (the present) and the historical (the past) [are] parallel." Fiske thought Morgan "too much inclined to dismiss the whole story" of the Conquistadors as a fairy tale, and deplored his captious criticisms of Diaz' observations.[420] Modern archaeology gives more and more credence to Spanish testimony. The distinguished scholar, Paul Radin, wrote in 1920 that because of the influence of the Morgan-Bandelier group, "who were supremely critical of anything that seemed to credit the ancient Mexicans with a high degree of culture, we in America have been uncritically skeptical of the historical authenticity of the sources relating to these people."[421] P. A. Means, our chief authority on Peruvian sources, has sifted all of the records of Inca civilization and given most of those upon which Prescott relied a high rating.[422]

(3) The Aztecs and the Incas are now credited with a much

[417] Stern, *op. cit.*, p. 114.

[418] *Ibid.*, p. 198.

[419] *Ibid.*, p. 112.

[420] *Discovery of America*, I, 126–129. E. B. Tylor believed that when the most unreliable chroniclers were eliminated, and the more valuable ones severely criticized, "it does not seem to us that the history thus extracted from these sources is much less reliable than European history of the same period" (*Anahuac* [London, 1861], p. 147).

[421] "The Sources and Authenticity of the History of the Ancient Mexicans," *University of California Publications in American Archaeology and Ethnology*, XVII, 132 (1920).

[422] "Biblioteca Andina," Part I: Chroniclers of the Sixteenth and Seventeenth Centuries who treated the Pre-Hispanic History and Culture of Andean Countries, *Transactions of the Connecticut Academy of Arts and Sciences*, XXIX, 271–525 (May, 1928).

higher civilization than the Discouragists allowed, and the sociological observations of the Spaniards have been declared generally accurate. E. B. Tylor, who traveled in Mexico, admitted that although at the start he believed the Conquerors had exaggerated, actually they had had "no eyes for the wonderful things around them. . . . What we saw of Mexico tended generally to confirm Prescott's History of the Conquest, and but seldom to make his statements improbable."[423] Among modern scholars, Means finds Prescott's account of the Peruvian political, economic, social, and religious system still "unimpeachable," and concludes that aside from his political terminology, which is easily corrected, and allowing for new information, Prescott's description of the Inca Empire "is as good and as trustworthy as any modern account."[424] Radin, accepting the findings of modern archaeologists on the clan-council organization of the earlier Aztecs, nevertheless confirms the Spaniards in asserting that by the time of the conquest, "Montezuma [had broken] with custom . . . to change the ruler from an elected chief to a king, a change . . . foreshadowed in the elaborate court and the palaces of the chiefs who preceded Montezuma."[425] Recent studies of ancient Mexican art seem to accept almost without reservation the picture of Aztec culture which Prescott records in his history.[426]

(4) Although Prescott worked only from printed sources in archaeology and ethnology, he was both thorough and critical in his use of materials from these fields. In spite of his dislike

[423] *Anahuac*, p. 147.

[424] "A Re-examination of Prescott's Account of Early Peru," *New England Quarterly*, IV, 645–662 (October, 1931).

[425] Quoted by Stern, *op. cit.*, p. 128.

[426] See, for example, L. E. Schmeckebier, *Modern Mexican Art* (1939); the *Catalogue* of the exhibition of Twenty Centuries of Mexican Art (Museum of Modern Art, New York, in collaboration with the Institute of the Anthropology and History of Mexico, Mexico City, 1940); and G. C. Vaillant, *Aztecs of Mexico* (1941). In all of these works the conquerors are cited extensively.

of what he called "philosophical" research,[427] he spared no
pains to gather and collate all available material on such special
subjects as ancient mathematics, astronomy, language, and
architecture. For example, in studying Mexican philology, he
not only absorbed the contemporary works of Gallatin and
Du Ponceau, but wrote to a Mexican specialist requesting new
light on Aztec writing;[428] and in dealing with ethnological
problems he mastered the best current works on craniology.[429]
One need only read the footnotes to the background sections
of the *Conquest of Mexico* to realize that he had a remarkable
grasp of scholarship in fields related to history. Still more important, his attitude toward these materials was critical and his
method comparative. The best specific defense against the
claims of the Discouragists is that Prescott was fully aware of
exaggerations and misinterpretations in the Spanish chronicles,
and that in using these records he was careful to balance testimony and to compare them with the results of later archaeological investigations. One wonders if the author of "Montezuma's
Dinner" read Prescott's warning to his readers that "the picture of Montezuma's domestic establishment . . . as delineated
by the Conquerors" was probably "too highly colored . . . by
the proneness to exaggerate, which was natural to those who
first witnessed a spectacle so striking to the imagination";[430] or
his judgment that in the works of Garcilasso de la Vega, long

---

[427] The introduction and appendix of *Mexico* cost him "twice as
much labor, and nearly as much time as the remainder of the history"
(Preface). The problem of ethnological origins, which he found a
"confounded hard and bothering subject" (*Correspondence*, p. 115),
was particularly distasteful because the lack of solid evidence begot
a "sort of mystification like twilight." He was inclined to think with
Humboldt that such matters are beyond the limits of history and
perhaps even of philosophy (*Mexico*, pp. 117, 692).

[428] *Correspondence*, pp. 66–68. The letter is excellent evidence of
his desire to be thorough and accurate.

[429] See *Mexico*, p. 705; and note his learned commentary on this
aspect of Bancroft's work, in *Miscellanies*, pp. 334–336.

[430] *Mexico*, p. 325.

accepted as an authority on Inca society, "the material splendors of the monarchy . . . become heightened . . . into the gorgeous illusions of a fairy tale";[431] or his explicit rejection of those "Spanish writers who are fond of tracing analogies to European institutions." [432]   Under the circumstances, it is not enough to say, with Peck, that "If one cares to know how the Old World first understood the New, he will read Prescott," [433] or even that "his story represents the most accurate information then attainable."   It appears now that the information then attainable is reliable when used critically; that, as one modern archaeologist puts it, "[Prescott's] fine imagination, coupled with a singular sense of proportion, carried him far nearer the truth than might . . . be expected . . . of one equipped with the meager critical apparatus of the time";[434] and that even though many of his details have been corrected, his general conclusions have been verified by modern investigators.   The carefulness of Prescott's scholarship is obvious; but that he had the good sense to listen to the evidence of witnesses, as his so-called "realistic" critics refused to do, is a paradoxical tribute to him and to "romantic" history.

None of the attacks on Prescott had very much effect on his general readers.   Partly because of the detachment and lack of moral earnestness which Parker deplored, Prescott succeeded so well in bringing out the romantic qualities inherent in his material that the appeal of his work has become permanently established.   One proof of this is the use that has been made of

[431] *Peru*, p. 881.   Gallatin held the same opinion; see *Correspondence*, p. 543.

[432] *Mexico*, p. 22.

[433] Quoted by Peck, p. 157.

[434] T. A. Joyce, in his introduction to Prescott's *Conquest of Mexico* (New York, 1922), I, xx.   This introduction contains a useful review of archaeological science, and detailed criticism of Prescott's contribution.   For other modern summaries of American archaeology, see Joyce's *Mexican Archaeology* (London, 1914) and *South American Archaeology* (London, 1912).

his books by writers of other forms of literature. In his own time, *Ferdinand and Isabella* was used by J. F. Cooper in his *Mercedes of Castile* (1840).[435] *The Conquest of Mexico* was the chief source of two popular novels of 1845,[436] and probably of two anonymous plays on Montezuma published in 1846 and 1847.[437] But the *Mexico* had its greatest indirect popular influence through Lew Wallace's *The Fair God* (1873), an historical novel which by 1905 had a sale of 145,750.[438] Having, as a boy, "devoured [Prescott's *Mexico*] preface, text, notes, and appendix," Wallace used it as the skeleton of his romance and filled in with material from Prescott's sources.[439] Later, when the vogue of historical fiction was in full swing, there were dozens of novels, both juvenile and adult, on Cortés, the Pizarros, chivalry in fifteenth-century Spain, and Don John of Austria;[440] and it is probable that like G. A. Henty, who heartily

[435] D. M. Goodfellow, "The Sources of *Mercedes of Castile*," *American Literature*, XII, 318–328 (November, 1940).

[436] J. T. Flanagan and R. L. Grismer, "Mexico in American Fiction Prior to 1850," *Hispania*, XXIII, 307–318 (December, 1940). The novels were J. H. Ingraham's *Montezuma, the Serf*, and Edward Maturin's *Montezuma, the Last of the Aztecs*.

[437] *Montezuma, or the Conquest of Mexico*, and *The Battle of Mexico, or the Halls of Montezuma*. Listed by A. H. Quinn in *A History of American Drama, from the Beginning to the Civil War*, pp. 442, 443. James Russell Lowell contemplated using *Mexico* as the basis of a tragedy to be submitted in one of Forrest's prize competitions (Scudder, *op. cit.*, I, 274).

[438] Lew Wallace, *Autobiography* (New York, 1906), II, 893.

[439] *Ibid.*, I, 88–89. Wallace began his novel in 1849 (I, 890).

[440] See G. A. Baker, *A Guide to Historical Fiction* (pp. 168–170, 372–376), for a list of novels on the Spanish subjects treated by Prescott. Since few of the authors troubled to acknowledge their sources, it would require tedious collation to establish their indebtedness. Prescott's popularity with children has been constant. He noted the fact in 1844 (*Correspondence*, p. 447), and it has been confirmed by the publication of at least six versions of *Mexico* and *Peru* for children. See, for example, editions of *Peru* by Henry Gilbert (1916), and of *Mexico* by Henry Gilbert (1914), H. W. Banks (1916 and 1926), Andrew Lang (1932), and the Junior Literary Guild (1934).

acknowledged his debt to Prescott in his *By Right of Conquest* (1890),[441] many of these writers found Prescott's histories convenient sources of information. In our own time, Jakob Wasserman has deemed Prescott's *Peru* worthy of literal translation into a part of one of his stories.[442]

Today Prescott's reputation stands secure. His scholarly soundness has been confirmed by modern specialists in his field, and his artistry and charm have been rediscovered by readers of popular editions of two of his works. He has, it is true, been comparatively neglected by modern literary critics, perhaps because in his whole career he touched upon the American scene in only a few essays. But a new generation of critics is realizing that a true evaluation of American culture of the past must embrace writers like Prescott who, in getting out of their age, carried American ideals and traditions with them. His work adds to the mounting evidence that the main line of American thought has been anything but narrowly nationalistic,[443] and its value can no longer be obscured by critics too exclusively preoccupied with nativism.[444]

[441] Henty says in his preface that Prescott's "admirable" work "far surpasses in interest any volume of fiction."

[442] "Das Gold von Caxamalca," in *Der Geist des Pilgers* (1923). Arpad Steiner, in "William H. Prescott and Jakob Wasserman," *Journal of English and Germanic Philology*, XXIV, 555–559 (October, 1925), says that two-thirds of the story is literal and unacknowledged translation from Prescott's *Peru*.

[443] See especially Harry H. Clark, "Nationalism in American Literature," *University of Toronto Quarterly*, II, 492–519 (July, 1933).

[444] V. L. Parrington, for instance, who seemed to think Prescott peculiar for writing Spanish history "while Jacksonianism was in full swing" (*The Romantic Revolution in America*, p. 438).

CHRONOLOGICAL TABLE

1796. Born at Salem, Massachusetts, May 4, to William Prescott and Catherine Greene Hickling Prescott. Second of seven children.

1803–08. Attended private schools in Salem.

1808. Family moved to Tremont Street, Boston.

1808–11. Attended Rev. J. S. J. Gardiner's school, with George Ticknor and William H. Gardiner, who later became his financial advisor and executor. Read at the Boston Athenaeum.

1811. Admitted to sophomore class in Harvard. Cared little for studies, but aspired to the "character of a cultivated gentleman." In his junior year the sight of his left eye was destroyed during a dining-hall frolic. Elected to Phi Beta Kappa.

1814. Graduated from Harvard. Read Latin poem at Commencement, and entertained five hundred friends under marquee on campus. Began study of law in father's office.

1815. Rheumatic inflammation of right eye stopped all studies. In September sailed for St. Michael's, Azores, to visit grandfather Thomas Hickling, U. S. Consul.

1816–17. Traveled in England (saw oculists), France, Italy. Too ill, part of the time, to make the most of his trip.

1817. Returned to America. Family moved to Bedford Street. Determined to give up law. Became popular man-about-town.

1820. May 4, married Susan Amory, daughter of powerful merchant. Lived with parents as long as they were alive. Edited *The Club Room*.

1821. Began systematic studies of literature and history.

1824. Began study of Spanish under Ticknor's inspiration. Daughter born.

1826. January 19, determined to write history of Ferdinand and Isabella. Eye troubles delayed him. Ordered books and hired first secretary, James English.

1829. Daughter died. October, began writing *Ferdinand and Isabella*.

1836. June, finished writing *Ferdinand and Isabella*.

1837. *Ferdinand and Isabella* published, Christmas. Began to gather materials on conquest of Mexico.

1838. Discovered Irving was contemplating work on Conquest; wrote him December 31.

1839. January 18, Irving ceded subject to Prescott. Began extensive correspondence with Gayangos; acquired services of Lembke.

1842. Visited New York. Met Irving.

1843. December, *Conquest of Mexico* published.

1844. February, began *Conquest of Peru*. Visit to New York. Father died December 8.

1845. *Miscellanies* published. Moved to Beacon Street.

1846. Visit to Washington and New York. Severe eye trouble. Visit to Albany.

1847. *Peru* published.

1848. Began studies for *Philip II*. Arranged to divide the field with Motley.

1850. Entertained in Washington by President Taylor, Webster, and others. Four months in Europe. Extensively entertained by English aristocracy; presented at court; made Doctor of Civil Law at Oxford; met Macaulay, Peel, Wellington. Paris. Belgium. Holland.

1852. Mother died.

1853. Purchased summer home at Lynn.

1855. Published first two volumes of *Philip II*.

1856. Published continuation of Robertson's *Charles V*. Health began to decline.

1858. Attack of apoplexy. Published third volume of *Philip II*.

1859. January 28, died in Boston, of an apoplectic stroke.

SELECTED BIBLIOGRAPHY

I. COLLECTED WORKS

Works, ed. J. F. Kirk. 16 vols. Philadelphia: 1874. (In addition to Kirk's emendations, this edition contains Prescott's important revisions of the *Conquest of Mexico* on the basis of Mexican emendations of his work. See Ticknor, p. 436 f., and *Correspondence*, p. 583.)

Works, ed. W. H. Munro. Montezuma Edition. 22 vols. Philadelphia, 1904.

There is no good bibliography of Prescott, but see those printed in *The Cambridge History of American Literature*, II, 500–501, and in Allibone, *A Critical Dictionary of English Literature and British and American Authors*, III, 1663–1675. For translations of Prescott's works, see Ticknor, Appendix E.

II. SEPARATE WORKS

(Starred items were reprinted in *Biographical and Critical Miscellanies*.)

The Club Room (February, March, April, July, 1820), Boston. Edited by Prescott. He contributed "Calais" and the leading article (March), and "The Vale of Alleriot" (April).

"Byron's Letter on Pope," *North American Review*, XIII, 445–473 (October, 1821).

"Essay Writing," *North American Review*, XIV, 319–350 (April, 1822).

"French and English Tragedy," *North American Review*, XVI, 124–156 (January, 1823).

"Mr. Sprague's Prize Poems," *North American Review*, XIX, 253–256 (July, 1824).

*"Italian Narrative Poetry," *North American Review*, XIX, 337–389 (October, 1824).

*"Da Ponte's Observations," *North American Review*, XXI, 189–217 (July, 1825).

"Leisure Hours at Sea," *North American Review*, XXII, 453–455 (April, 1826). (Short notice of poems by William Leggett.)

*"Scottish Song," *North American Review*, XXIII, 124–142 (July, 1826).

"Novel Writing," *North American Review*, XXV, 183–203 (July, 1827).

*"Molière," *North American Review*, XXVII, 372–402 (October, 1828).

*"Historical Composition," *North American Review*, XXIX, 293–314 (October, 1829). (Reprinted in *Miscellanies* as "Irving's Conquest of Granada.")

*"Asylum for the Blind," *North American Review*, XXXI, 66–85 (July, 1830).

*"Poetry and Romance of the Italians," *North American Review*, XXXIII, 29–81 (July, 1831).

"English Literature of the Nineteenth Century," *North American Review*, XXXV, 165–195 (July, 1832).

*"Charles Brockden Brown," in Jared Sparks, ed., *Library of American Biography*, I, 117–180 (Boston: 1834). (Reprinted in *Miscellanies* as "Memoir of Charles Brockden Brown, the American Novelist.")

*"Spanish Literature in America," *North American Review*, XLV, 1–34 (July, 1837). (Reprinted in *Miscellanies* as "Cervantes.")

A History of the Reign of Ferdinand and Isabella, the Catholic. 3 vols. Boston and London: 1837. (Dated 1838. For contemporary reviews, see W. H. Gardiner in *North American Review*, XLVI, 203–291 [January, 1838]; F. W. P. Greenwood in *Christian Examiner*, XXIV, 99–111 [March, 1838]; John Pickering in *New York Review*, II, 308–341 [April, 1838]; Pascual de Gayangos in *Edinburgh Review*, LXVIII, 376–405 [January, 1839]; Richard Ford in *Quarterly Review*, LXIV, 1–58 [June, 1839]; anonymous reviewer in *Dublin Review*, XIII, 308–346 (November, 1842); P. Fredet in *United States Catholic Magazine*, II, 449–463 [August, 1843]).

*"Sir Walter Scott," *North American Review*, XLVI, 431–474 (April, 1838).

"Kenyon's Poems," *North American Review*, XLVIII, 401–415 (April, 1839).

*"Chateaubriand's English Literature," *North American Review*, XLIX, 317–348 (October, 1839).

*"Bancroft's United States," *North American Review*, LII, 75–103 (January, 1841).

"Mariotti's Italy," *North American Review*, LIV, 339–356 (April, 1842).

A History of the Conquest of Mexico, with a Preliminary View of the Ancient Mexican Civilization and the Life of Hernando Cortes. 3 vols. New York and London: 1843. (For contemporary reviews, see H. H. Milman in *Quarterly Review*, LXXIII, 187–235 [December, 1843]; G. S. Hillard in *North American Review*, LVIII, 157–210 [January, 1844]; G. T. Curtis in *Christian Examiner*, XXXVI, 197–226 [March, 1844]; *Dublin Review*, XVI, 45–65 [March, 1844]; J. G. Cogswell in *Methodist Quarterly Review*, IV 284–310 [April, 1844]; M. J. Spalding in *United States Catholic Magazine*, III, 409–426, 477–493 [July–August, 1844]; S. M. Phillips in *Edinburgh Review*, LXXXI, 434–473 [April, 1845]).

*"Madame Calderón's Life in Mexico," *North American Review*, LVI, 137–170 (January, 1843).

Madame Calderón de la Barca, *Life in Mexico*. Boston: 1843. (Preface, I, iii–iv, by Prescott).

Biographical and Critical Miscellanies. New York and London: 1845. (Revised and enlarged edition, 1850.)

A History of the Conquest of Peru, with a Preliminary View of the Civilization of the Incas. 2 vols. New York and London: 1847. (For contemporary reviews, see *Blackwood's Edinburgh Magazine*, LXII, 1–20 [July, 1847]; *Democratic Review*, XXI, 129–140 [August, 1847]; *Quarterly Review*, LXXXI, 317–351 [September, 1847]; C. W. Upham in *Christian Examiner*, XLIII, 253–269 [September, 1847]; Francis Bowen in *North American Review*, LXV, 366–400 [October, 1847]; *Dublin Review*, XXIII, 322–340 [December, 1847]; *Southern Quarterly Review*, XIII, 136–187 [January, 1848]).

Memoir of the Honorable John Pickering, LL.D. Cambridge: 1848. (Also in *Massachusetts Historical Society Collections*, ser. 3, X, 204–224 [1849]).

"Spanish Literature," *North American Review*, LXX, 1–56 (January, 1850). (Reprinted in 1850 edition of *Miscellanies* as "Ticknor's History of Spanish Literature.")

A History of the Reign of Philip the Second. 3 vols. Boston and London: 1855–1858. (For contemporary reviews see *Blackwood's Edinburgh Magazine*, LXXIX, 421–438 [April, 1856]; M. Guizot in *Edinburgh Review*, CV, 1–45 [January, 1857]; James Woodhouse in *Southern Literary Messenger*, XXII, 144–155 [February, 1856]; G. E. Ellis in *Christian Examiner*, XL, 274–295 [March, 1856]. "Battle of Lepanto" [from Book V, Chapters X and XI,] printed in advance of book publication in *Atlantic Monthly*, I, 138–148 [December, 1857]).

Memoir of the Honorable Abbott Lawrence, prepared for the National Portrait Gallery. Printed for private distribution. Philadelphia: 1856.

William Robertson, *The History of the Reign of the Emperor Charles V*. Boston: 1857. (Prescott added "The Life of Charles V after His Abdication," III, 325–510).

"A Letter Concerning the Reverend Dr. S. J. Gardiner," in William Buell Sprague, *Annals of the American Pulpit*, V, 365–367 (1859).

III. BIOGRAPHY AND LETTERS

Catalogue of the Valuable Library of the late William Hickling Prescott. Boston: 1871.

Eliot, Samuel. "William Hickling Prescott," *New England Magazine*, IX, 515–529 (December, 1893). (Some hitherto unpublished anecdotes, chiefly about Prescott's personality.)

Emerson, E. W. *Early Years of the Saturday Club.* Boston: 1918. (Pages 180–187 contain a few interesting reminiscences by friends.)

Hillard, G. S. *Little Journeys to the Homes of American Authors.* New York: 1896. (Prescott, pp. 131–143.)

Jackson, James. *Another Letter to a Young Physician.* Boston: 1861. (Pages 130–156 contain a description of Prescott's eye trouble by one of his physicians.)

Massachusetts Historical Society Proceedings, IV (1858–1860), pp. 167–196. (Speeches and eulogies by members of the society.)

Merriman, R. B. Article in *Dictionary of American Biography*, XV, 196–200 (1935). (This is the best short biographical sketch of Prescott.)

Mood, Fulmer, and Hicks, Granville. "Letters to Dr. Channing on Slavery and the Annexation of Texas, 1837," *New England Quarterly*, V, 587–601 (July, 1932). (Contains a long and important letter, hitherto unpublished, by Prescott.)

Ogden, Rollo. *William Hickling Prescott.* American Men of Letters Series. Boston: 1904. (A short biography, emphasizing Prescott's personality in order to correct Ticknor's stiff portrait. Valuable for use of manuscript materials unknown to or ignored by Ticknor, and for analysis of Prescott's political attitudes.)

Peck, Harry Thurston. *William Hickling Prescott*. English Men of Letters Series. New York: 1905. (No new source materials are used here, but the work is valuable for criticism and analysis of Prescott's style and content.)

Penney, Clara Louisa, ed. *Prescott, Unpublished Letters to Gayangos in the Library of the Hispanic Society of America.* New York: 1927. (Well edited, with competent notes. Supplementing Wolcott, especially for 1847–1859, it offers enlightening material on Prescott's scholarship.)

Richardson, C. B., ed. *Prescott Memorial.* New York: 1859. (Speeches delivered at several meetings in honor of Prescott.)

Ticknor, George. *Life of William Hickling Prescott.* Boston: 1864. (Reprinted in the Montezuma edition of Prescott's works. Remains the standard life of Prescott, by the friend and colleague who knew him and his work best. Ticknor did not, however, make the fullest use of the Prescott manuscripts, as works by Ogden, Wolcott, and Penney indicate. Valuable appendices on genealogy, translations, literary honors, etc.)

Wolcott, Roger, ed. *The Correspondence of William Hickling Prescott, 1833–1847.* Boston and New York: 1925. (Large, well-edited selection from the original drafts of Prescott's letters in the manuscript collection deposited with the Massachusetts Historical Society by the Prescott family. Indispensable details on Prescott's work and opinions.)

Obituaries may be found in the *Proceedings of the Massachusetts Historical Society*, IV, 167–196, 236–237, 266–271, 277–283 (1858–1860), speeches, letters, etc. by friends and members of the society; in *Proceedings of the New York Historical Society on the Announcement of the Death of Prescott* (in its *Discourses, 1852–1859*); in *Prescott Memorial* (pamphlet, 1870), speeches from several commemorative meetings, and recollections by J. F. Kirk; and in American Academy of Arts and Sciences, *Proceedings*, IV, 149–163 (1860).

IV. CRITICISM

Allibone, S. A. *A Critical Dictionary of English Literature and British and American Authors.* Philadelphia: 1858–1871. (II, 1663–1675, contains numerous excerpts from contemporary reviews of Prescott.)

Bandelier, A. F. A. *The Romantic School of American Archaeology,* a paper read before the New York Historical Society. New York: 1885. (Historically important attack on Prescott's school.)

Bassett, John Spencer. *The Middle Group of American Historians.* New York: 1917. (Prescott, pp. 211–223, 312–313. Emphasis on Prescott's success. A superficial discussion.)

Brooks, Van Wyck. *The Flowering of New England, 1815–1865.* New York: 1936. (Excellent treatment of Prescott's relation to his intellectual environment. See especially pp. 135–146, 327–331, 499–502.)

Circourt, Count Adolphe de. "William Hickling Prescott," *Bibliothèque Universelle et Revue Suisse,* IV, 597–620 (April, 1859). (By Prescott's "most important correspondent in France." See *Correspondence,* p. xvii.)

Clark, H. H. "Literary Criticism in the *North American Review, 1815–1835,*" *Transactions of the Wisconsin Academy of Sciences, Arts, and Letters,* XXX, 299–350 (1940). (A careful summary of all the literary criticism published in this periodical during the years when Prescott was writing his best essays for it.)

Da Ponte, Lorenzo. "Alcune osservazioni sull' articulo quarto publicatio nel North American Review, il mese d'ottobre dell' anno 1824." In *Economia della vita humana, tradotta dal Inglese da L. Giudelli.* New York: 1824. (Attack on Prescott's "Italian Narrative Poetry," to which Prescott replied in "Da Ponte's Observations.")

De Mille, George E. *Literary Criticism in America*. New York: 1931. (Chapter I contains a general discussion of the *North American Review* critics.)

Ferguson, J. De Lancey. *American Literature in Spain*. New York: 1916. (Prescott, pp. 148–157. "Criticism of Prescott was scanty." Data about Spanish translations.)

Fueter, E. *Histoire de l'historiographie Moderne*. Paris: 1914. (Prescott, pp. 648–651.)

Gooch, G. P. *History and Historians in the Nineteenth Century*. London: 1913. (Prescott, pp. 412–416. Good short estimate. "If [his] reserve renders his writings less vital, it saves them from the reaction which accompanies the discredit of once popular catchwords.")

Jameson, J. F. *History of Historical Writing in America*. Boston: 1891. (Prescott, pp. 113–118. Superficial.)

Joyce, T. A. Introduction to Prescott's *Conquest of Mexico*. New York: 1922. (Pp. xix–xxxiii. Excellent criticism of Prescott's archaeology.)

Means, P. A. "A Re-examination of Prescott's Account of Early Peru," *New England Quarterly*, IV, 645–662 (October, 1931). (Important and favorable revaluation by a specialist in the literature of Peru.)

Merriman, R. B. *The Rise of the Spanish Empire in the Old World and in the New*. 4 vols. New York: 1918. (See III, 564, and IV, 73, for short comparative criticisms of Prescott's works by the modern authority on Prescott's field.

—— in Allison, W. H., et al. *A Guide to Historical Literature*. New York: 1931. (P. 647, estimate of *Ferdinand and Isabella* in relation to earlier and later treatments of the subject.)

Moulton, C. W., ed. *The Library of Literary Criticism of English and American Authors*. Buffalo: 1904. (IV, 181–191 contains many excerpts from contemporary comment and criticism.)

Nevins, Allan. In John Macy, ed., *American Writers on American Literature*. New York: 1931. (Prescott, pp. 226–233. Places him as leader of American historians, but puts too much emphasis on his Protestantism.)

Parker, Theodore. "The Character of Mr. Prescott as an Historian" and "Prescott's Conquest of Mexico," *Massachusetts Quarterly Review*, II, 215–248, 437–470 (March, September, 1849). Reprinted in Parker's *Works*, ed. F. P. Cobbe (London, 1863–1870), X, 81–153, and in *The American Scholar*, ed. G. W. Cooke (Boston, 1907), 81–153. (The most significant "dissenting opinion" in Prescott's time.)

Putnam, Ruth. "Prescott and Motley," in *Cambridge History of American Literature*, II, 123–147. New York: 1918. (Pages 123–131 constitute a good brief discussion of Prescott's career and writings.)

Steiner, Arpad. "William Hickling Prescott and Jakob Wasserman," *Journal of English and German Philology*, XXIV, 555–559 (October, 1925). (Identifies unacknowledged borrowings by Wasserman from Prescott's *Peru*.)

Ticknor, George. "Papers Discussing the Comparative Merits of Prescott's and Wilson's Histories . . . also Three Letters of Prescott, commanding Wilson's Research." *Massachusetts Historical Society Proceedings*, IV (1858–1860), pp. 277–283.

Whipple, E. P. *Essays and Reviews*. 2 vols. New York: 1848. ("Prescott's Histories," based upon *Ferdinand and Isabella, Mexico*, and *Peru*, in II, 152–186, and "Prescott's Conquest of Peru," in II, 187–208, are expansions of articles that first appeared in reverse order in *Methodist Quarterly Review*, VIII, 5–28, 268–282 [January, April, 1848]).

Winsor, Justin. *Narrative and Critical History of America*, II. Boston: 1886. (See index for scattered material on Prescott's sources, manuscripts, etc.)

V. INTELLECTUAL, LITERARY, AND
SOCIAL BACKGROUNDS

Allison, W. H., et al. *A Guide to Historical Literature.* New York: 1931. (Estimates of other histories of Prescott's subjects provide means of establishing his rank in scholarship.)

American Writers Series (Harry Hayden Clark, general editor). New York: 1934 et seq. (The critical introductions and annotated bibliographies of these anthologies of major American writers make this series the best general literary reference for Prescott's period. See particularly *Parkman*, ed. by Wilbur L. Schramm; and *Motley*, ed. by C. P. Higby and B. T. Schantz.)

Becker, Carl L. *The Heavenly City of the Eighteenth-Century Philosophers.* New Haven: 1932. (Good analysis of rationalist thought.)

Black, J. B. *The Art of History.* New York: 1926. (Analysis of the art of the rationalist historians, who influenced Prescott.)

Braden, Charles S. *Religious Aspects of the Conquest of Mexico.* Durham, N.C.: 1930. (Modern scholarly discussion of a subject that interested Prescott.)

Charvat, William. *The Origins of American Critical Thought, 1810–1835.* Philadelphia: 1936. (Analysis of periodical criticism in Prescott's period. Emphasis on Scottish sources.)

Cooke, G. W. *Unitarianism in America.* Boston: 1902. (Useful for religious background of Prescott's group.)

Darling, Arthur B. *Political Changes in Massachusetts, 1824–1848.* New Haven: 1925. (Detailed information on Prescott's political milieu.)

Fairchild, H. H. *The Noble Savage.* New York: 1928. (Study of the Indian in English literature.)

Foerster, Norman. *American Criticism.* Boston and New York: 1928. (A humanist's analysis of the humanist critical tradition, to which Prescott belongs.)

Gabriel, R. H. *The Course of American Democratic Thought.* New York: 1940. (Stimulating study in American intellectual history.)

Kraus, Michael. *The History of American History.* New York: 1937. (Materials on the growth of historical writing in America. See also works by Bassett and Gooch cited above in section IV of bibliography.)

Long, O. W. *Literary Pioneers.* Cambridge: 1935. (Indispensable for study of German and Spanish influences on Prescott's contemporaries, and, indirectly, on Prescott. See especially the sections on Ticknor, Bancroft, Cogswell, and Motley.)

Merriman, R. B. *The Rise of the Spanish Empire in the Old World and in the New.* 4 vols. New York: 1918. (Because this authority made use of Prescott's books and manuscripts, his work offers an instructive contrast between modern and "romantic" methods. For contrast between Prescott and "rationalist" history, see William Robertson's *History of America* [1777], available in numerous editions.)

Morison, S. E. *Harrison Gray Otis.* 2 vols. Boston: 1913.

—— *A Maritime History of Massachusetts.* Boston: 1921. (Excellent material on Prescott's social background.)

Mott, F. L. *A History of American Magazines, 1741–1850.* New York: 1930.

——*A History of American Magazines, 1850–1865.* Cambridge: 1938. (Valuable for background of Prescott's periodical work, and for his literary milieu.)

Parrington, V. L. *The Romantic Revolution in America, 1800–1860.* New York: 1927. (Pioneer study in American intellectual history from the viewpoint of a political liberal.)

Peardon, T. P. _The Transition in English Historical Writing, 1760–1830._ New York: 1933. (Valuable material on the work of some of Prescott's friends and colleagues in history writing, especially Hallam, Milman, and Tytler.)

Stern, B. J. _Lewis Henry Morgan._ Chicago: 1931. (Good background on the development of American archaeology and anthropology.)

Ticknor, George. _Life, Letters, and Journals of George Ticknor._ 2 vols. Boston, 1876; new ed., with introduction by Ferris Greenslet (1909). (Because Ticknor's and Prescott's careers were so closely related, this work offers invaluable materials on Prescott's connections, friendships, and social contacts.)

Vaillant, George C. _Aztecs of Mexico._ New York: 1941. (Well-written, authoritative study of Aztec society. The illustrations, reproduced from Aztec and Spanish art, are an excellent accompaniment to Prescott's narrative. Bibliography, pp. 299–325. See pages 288, 295, 296 for tributes to Prescott.)

Whitney, Lois. _Primitivism and the Idea of Progress in English Popular Literature of the Eighteenth Century._ Baltimore: 1934. (Good backgrounds for Prescott's intellectual attitudes.)

Young, L. M. _Thomas Carlyle and the Art of History._ Philadelphia: 1939. (Offers interesting contrast between methods of Prescott and his contemporary.)

For current articles, the student should consult Grace G. Griffin's annual bibliography, _Writings on American History_; the annual bibliography of the _New England Quarterly_; and bibliographies in _American Literature_ and _Publications of the Modern Language Association._

★

Selections from
WILLIAM HICKLING PRESCOTT

★

I. THEORY AND PRACTICE OF HISTORY

[THE DEVELOPMENT OF HISTORICAL WRITING]
From *Miscellanies*, pp. 88–108

[From "Historical Composition" (1829), ostensibly a review of Irving's *The Conquest of Granada*, but actually a critique of historiography. Prescott had a keen understanding of the progress of historiography from ancient times to his own day. In this selection he gives the reader his own "genealogy," tracing the indebtedness of the historians of his generation to writers of the distant and more immediate past.]

Almost as many qualifications may be demanded for a perfect historian, indeed the Abbé Mably has enumerated as many, as Cicero stipulates for a perfect orator. He must be strictly impartial; a lover of truth under all circumstances, and ready to declare it at all hazards: he must be deeply conversant with whatever may bring into relief the character of the people he is depicting, not merely with their laws, constitution, general resources, and all the other more visible parts of the machinery of government, but with the nicer moral and social relations, the informing spirit which gives life to the whole, but escapes the eye of a vulgar observer. If he has to do with other ages and nations, he must transport himself into them, expatriating himself, as it were, from his own, in order to get the very form and pressure of the times he is delineating. He must be conscientious in his attention to geography, chronology, &c., an inaccuracy in which has been fatal to more than one good philosophical history; and, mixed up with all these drier details, he must display the various powers of a novelist or dramatist, throwing his characters into suitable lights and shades, disposing his scenes so as to awaken and maintain an unflagging interest, and diffusing over the whole that finished style, without which his work will only become a magazine of materials for the more elegant edifices of subsequent writers. He must be—in short,

3

there is no end to what a perfect historian must be and do. It is hardly necessary to add that such a monster never did and never will exist.

But, although we cannot attain to perfect excellence in this or any other science in this world, considerable approaches have been made to it, and different individuals have arisen at different periods, possessed, in an eminent degree, of some of the principal qualities which go to make up the aggregate of the character we have been describing. The peculiar character of these qualities will generally be determined in the writer by that of the age in which he lives. Thus, the earlier historians of Greece and Rome sought less to instruct than to amuse. They filled their pictures with dazzling and seductive images. In their researches into antiquity, they were not startled by the marvelous, like the more prudish critics of our day, but welcomed it as likely to stir the imaginations of their readers. They seldom interrupted the story by impertinent reflection. They bestowed infinite pains on the costume, the style of their history, and, in fine, made everything subordinate to the main purpose of conveying an elegant and interesting *narrative*. Such was Herodotus, such Livy, and such, too, the earlier chroniclers of modern Europe, whose pages glow with the picturesque and brilliant pageants of an age of chivalry. These last, as well as Herodotus, may be said to have written in the infancy of their nations, when the imagination is more willingly addressed than the understanding. Livy, who wrote in a riper age, lived, nevertheless, in a court and a period where tranquillity and opulence disposed the minds of men to elegant recreation rather than to severe discipline and exertion.

As, however, the nation advanced in years, or became oppressed with calamity, history also assumed a graver complexion. Fancy gave way to reflection. The mind, no longer invited to rove abroad in quest of elegant and alluring pictures, was driven back upon itself, speculated more deeply, and sought for support under the external evils of life in moral and philosophical truth. Description was abandoned for the study of character; men took the place of events; and the romance was converted into the drama. Thus it was with Tacitus, who lived under those imperial monsters who turned Rome into a charnel-house, and his compact narratives are filled with moral and political axioms sufficiently numerous to make a volume; and, indeed, Brotier has made one of them in his edition of the historian. The same philosophical spirit animates the page of Thucydides, himself one of the principal actors in the long, disastrous struggle that terminated in the ruin of his nation.

But, notwithstanding the deeper and more comprehensive thought of these later writers, there was still a wide difference between the complexion given to history under their hands and that which it has assumed in our time. We would not be understood as determining, but simply as discriminating their relative merits. The Greeks and Romans lived when the world, at least when the mind was in its comparative infancy—when fancy and feeling were most easily, and loved most to be excited. They possessed a finer sense of beauty than the moderns. They were infinitely more solicitous about the external dress, the finish, and all that makes up the poetry of a composition. Poetry, indeed, mingled in their daily pursuits as well as pleasures; it determined their gravest deliberations. The command of their armies was given, not to the best general, but ofttimes to the most eloquent orator. Poetry entered into their religion, and created those beautiful monuments of architecture and sculpture which the breath of time has not tarnished. It entered into their philosophy; and no one confessed its influence more deeply than he who would have banished it from his republic. It informed the souls of their orators, and prompted those magnificent rhapsodies which fall lifeless enough from the stammering tongue of the schoolboy, but which once awaked to ecstasy the living populace of Athens. It entered deeply even into their latest history. It was first exhibited in the national chronicles of Homer. It lost little of its coloring, though it conformed to the general laws of prosaic composition, under Herodotus. And it shed a pleasing grace over the sober pages of Thucydides and Xenophon. The muse, indeed, was stripped of her wings. She no longer made her airy excursions into the fairy regions of romance; but, as she moved along the earth, the sweetest wildflowers seemed to spring up unbidden at her feet. We would not be understood as implying that Grecian history was ambitious of florid or meretricious ornament. Nothing could be more simple than its general plan and execution; far too simple, we fear, for imitation in our day. Thus Thucydides, for example, distributes his events most inartificially, according to the regular revolutions of the seasons; and the rear of every section is brought up with the same eternal repetition of ἔτος τῷ πολέμῳ ἐτέλευτα τῷδε, ὃν Θουκυδίδης ξυνέγραψε. But in the fictitious speeches with which he has illumined his narrative, he has left the choicest specimens of Attic eloquence; and he elaborated his general diction into so high a finish, that Demosthenes, as is well known, in the hope of catching some of his rhetorical graces, thought him worthy of being thrice transcribed with his own hand.

Far different has been the general conception, as well as execution, of history by the moderns. In this, however, it was accommodated to the exigencies of their situation, and, as with the ancients, still reflected the spirit of the age. If the Greeks lived in the infancy of civilization, the contemporaries of our day may be said to have reached its prime. The same revolution has taken place as in the growth of an individual. The vivacity of the imagination has been blunted, but reason is matured. The credulity of youth has given way to habits of cautious inquiry, and sometimes to a phlegmatic skepticism. The productions, indeed, which first appeared in the doubtful twilight of morning exhibited the love of the marvelous, the light and fanciful spirit of a green and tender age. But a new order of things commenced as the stores of classical learning were unrolled to the eye of the scholar. The mind seemed at once to enter upon the rich inheritance which the sages of antiquity had been ages in accumulating, and to start, as it were, from the very point where they had terminated their career. Thus raised by learning and experience, it was enabled to take a wider view of its proper destiny—to understand that truth is the greatest good, and to discern the surest method of arriving at it. The

Christian doctrine, too, inculcated that the end of being was best answered by a life of active usefulness, and not by one of abstract contemplation, or selfish indulgence, or passive fortitude, as variously taught by the various sects of antiquity. Hence a new standard of moral excellence was formed. Pursuits were estimated by their practical results, and the useful was preferred to the ornamental. Poetry, confined to her own sphere, was no longer permitted to mingle in the councils of philosophy. Intellectual and physical science, instead of floating on vague speculation, as with the ancients, was established on careful induction and experiment. The orator, instead of adorning himself with the pomp and garniture of verse, sought only to acquire greater dexterity in the management of the true weapons of debate. The passions were less frequently assailed, the reason more. A wider field was open to the historian. He was no longer to concoct his narrative, if the scene lay in a remote period, from the superficial rumors of oral tradition. Libraries were to be ransacked; medals and monuments to be studied; obsolete manuscripts to be deciphered. Every assertion was to be fortified by an authority; and the opinions of others, instead of being admitted on easy faith, were to be carefully collated, and the balance of probability struck between them. With these qualifications of antiquarian and critic, the modern historian was to combine that of the philosopher, deducing from his mass of facts general theorems, and giving to them their most extended application.

By all this process, poetry lost much, but philosophy gained more. The elegant arts sensibly declined, but the most important and recondite secrets of nature were laid open. All those sciences which have for their object the happiness and improvement of the species, the science of government, of political economy, of education—natural and experimental science— were carried far beyond the boundaries which they could possibly have reached under the ancient systems.

The peculiar forms of historic writing, as it exists with the moderns, were not fully developed until the last century. It may be well to notice the intermediate shape which it assumed before it reached this period in Spain and Italy, but especially this latter country, in the sixteenth century. The Italian historians of that age seemed to have combined the generalizing and reflecting spirit characteristic of the moderns, with the simple and graceful forms of composition which have descended to us from the ancients. Machiavelli, in particular, may remind us of some recent statue which exhibits all the lineaments and proportions of a contemporary, but to which the sculptor has given a sort of antique dignity by enveloping it in the folds of the Roman toga. No one of the Spanish historians is to be named with him. Mariana, who enjoys among them the greatest celebrity, has, it is true, given to his style, both in the Latin and Castilian, the elegant transparency of an ancient classic, but the mass of detail is not quickened by a single spark of philosophy or original reflection. Mariana was a monk, one of a community who have formed the most copious, but, in many respects, the most incompetent chroniclers in the world, cut off, as they are, from all sympathy with any portion of the species save their own order, and predisposed by education to admit as truth the grossest forgeries of fanaticism. What can their narratives be worth, distorted thus by prejudice and credulity? The Aragonese writers, and Zurita in particular, though far inferior as to the literary execution of their works, exhibit a pregnant thought and a manly independence of expression far superior to the Jesuit Mariana.

The Italian historians of the sixteenth century, moreover, had the good fortune not only to have been eyewitnesses, but to have played prominent parts in the events which they commemorated. And this gives a vitality to their touches which is in vain to be expected from those of a closet politician. This rare union of public and private excellence is delicately intimated in the inscription on Guicciardini's monument, "*Cujus negotium, an otium, gloriosius incertum.*"

The personage by whom the present laws of historic composition may be said to have been first arranged into a regular system was Voltaire. This extraordinary genius, whose works have been productive of so much mingled good and evil, discovers in them many traces of a humane and beneficent disposition. Nowhere is his invective more keenly directed than against acts of cruelty and oppression—above all, of religious oppression. He lived in an age of crying abuses both in Church and government. Unfortunately, he employed a weapon against them whose influence is not to be controlled by the most expert hand. The envenomed shaft of irony not only wounds the member at which it is aimed, but diffuses its poison to the healthiest and remotest regions of the body.

The free and volatile temper of Voltaire forms a singular contrast with his resolute pertinacity of purpose. Bard, philosopher, historian, this literary Proteus animated every shape with the same mischievous spirit of philosophy. It never deserted him, even in the most sportive sallies of his fancy. It seasons his romances equally with his gravest pieces in the encyclopedia; his familiar letters and most licentious doggerel no less than his histories. The leading object of this philosophy may be defined by the single cant phrase, "the abolition of prejudices." But in Voltaire prejudices were too often confounded with principles.

In his histories, he seems ever intent on exhibiting, in the most glaring colors, the manifold inconsistencies of the human race; in showing the contradiction between profession and practice; in contrasting the magnificence of the apparatus with the impotence of the results. The enormous abuses of Christianity are brought into juxtaposition with the most meritorious features in other religions, and thus all are reduced to nearly the same level. The credulity of one half of mankind is set in opposition to the cunning of the other. The most momentous events are traced to the most insignificant causes, and the ripest schemes of wisdom are shown to have been baffled by the intervention of the most trivial accidents. Thus the conduct of the world seems to be regulated by chance; the springs of human action are resolved into selfishness; and religion, of whatever denomination, is only a different form of superstition. It is true that his satire is directed not so much against any particular system as the vices of that system; but the result left upon the mind is not a whit less pernicious. His philosophical romance of "Candide" affords a good exemplification of his manner. The thesis of perfect optimism in this world, at which he levels this *jeu d'esprit*, is manifestly indefensible. But then he supports his position with such an array of gross and hyperbolical atrocities, without the intervention of a single palliative circumstance, and, withal, in such a tone of keen derision, that, if any serious impression be left on the mind, it can be no other than that of a baleful, withering skepticism. The historian rarely so far forgets his philosophy as to kindle into high and generous emotion the glow of patriotism, or moral and religious enthusiasm. And hence, too, his style, though always graceful, and often seasoned with the sallies of a piquant wit, never rises into eloquence or sublimity.

Voltaire has been frequently reproached for want of historical accuracy. But if we make due allowance for the sweeping tenor of his reflections, and for the infinite variety of his topics, we shall be slow in giving credit to this charge.[1] He was, indeed, oftentimes misled by his inveterate Pyrrhonism; a defect, when carried to the excess in which he indulged it, almost equally fatal to the historian with credulity or superstition. His researches frequently led him into dark, untraveled regions; but the aliment which he imported thence served only too often to minister to his pernicious philosophy. He resembled the allegorical agents of Milton, paving a way across the gulf of Chaos for the spirits of mischief to enter more easily upon the earth.

Voltaire effected a no less sensible revolution in the structure than in the spirit of history. Thus, instead of following the natural consecutive order of events, the work was distributed, on the principle of a *Catalogue raisonné*, into sections arranged according to their subjects, and copious dissertations were introduced into the body of the narrative. Thus, in his *Essai sur les Mœurs*, &c., one chapter is devoted to letters, another to

---

[1] Indeed, Hallam and Warton—the one as diligent a laborer in the field of civil history as the other has been in literary—both bear testimony to his general veracity. [Prescott's note.]

religion, a third to manners, and so on. And in the same way, in his "Age of Louis the Fourteenth," he has thrown his various illustrations of the policy of government, and of the social habits of the court, into a detached portion at the close of the book.

This would seem to be deviating from the natural course of things as they occur in the world, where the multifarious pursuits of pleasure and business, the lights and shadows, as it were, of life are daily intermingled in the motley panorama of human existence. But, however artificial this division, it enabled the reader to arrive more expeditiously at the results, for which alone history is valuable, while, at the same time, it put it in the power of the writer to convey with more certainty and facility his own impressions.

This system was subsequently so much refined upon, that Montesquieu, in his "Grandeur et Décadence des Romains," laid no farther stress on historical facts than as they furnished him with illustrations of his particular theorems. Indeed, so little did his work rest upon the veracity of such facts, that, although the industry of Niebuhr, or, rather, of Beaufort, has knocked away almost all the foundations of early Rome, Montesquieu's treatise remains as essentially unimpaired in credit as before. Thus the materials which anciently formed the body of history now served only as ingredients from which its spirit was to be extracted. But this was not always the spirit of truth. And the arbitrary selection as well as disposition of incidents which this new method allowed, and the coloring which they were to receive from the author, made it easy to pervert them to the construction of the wildest hypotheses.

The progress of philosophical history is particularly observable in Great Britain, where it seems to have been admirably suited to the grave, reflecting temper of the people. In the graces of *narrative* they have ever been unequal to their French neighbors. Their ancient chronicles are inferior in spirit and execution to those either of France or Spain; and their more elaborate histories, down to the middle of the eighteenth century, could not in any way compete with the illustrious models of Italy. But soon after this period several writers appeared, exhibiting a combination of qualities, erudition, critical penetration, powers of generalization, and a political sagacity unrivaled in any other age or country.

The influence of the new forms of historical composition, however, was here, as elsewhere, made too frequently subservient to party and sectarian prejudices. Tory histories and Whig histories, Protestant and Catholic histories, successively appeared, and seemed to neutralize each other. The most venerable traditions were exploded as nursery tales. The statues decreed by antiquity were cast down, and the characters of miscreants whom the general suffrage of mankind had damned to infamy—of a Dionysius, a Borgia, or a Richard the Third— were now retraced by what Jovius distinguishes as "the golden pen" of the historian, until the reader, bewildered in the maze of uncertainty, is almost ready to join in the exclamation of Lord Orford to his son, "Oh, quote me not history, for that I know to be false!" It is remarkable, indeed, that the last-mentioned monarch, Richard the Third, whose name has become a byword of atrocity, the burden of the ballad and the moral of the drama, should have been the subject of elaborate vindication by two eminent writers of the most opposite characters, the pragmatical Horace Walpole, and the circumspect and conscientious Sharon Turner. The apology of the latter exhibits a technical precision, a severe scrutiny into the authenticity of records, and a nice balancing of contradictory testimony, that give it all the air of a legal investigation. Thus history seems to be conducted on the principles of a judicial process, in which the writer, assuming the functions of an advocate, studiously suppresses whatever may make against his own side, supports himself by the strongest array of evidence which he can muster, discredits, as far as possible, that of the opposite party, and, by dexterous interpretation and ingenious inference, makes out the most plausible argument for his client that the case will admit.

But these, after all, are only the abuses of philosophical history, and the unseasonable length of remark into which we have been unwarily led in respect to them may give us the appearance of laying on them greater emphasis than they actually deserve. There are few writers in any country whose judgment has not been sometimes warped by personal prejudices. But it is to the credit of the principal British historians that, however they may have been occasionally under the influence of such human infirmity, they have conducted their researches, in the main, with equal integrity and impartiality. And while they have enriched their writings with the stores of a various erudition, they have digested from these details results of the most enlarged and practical application. History in their hands, although it may have lost much of the simplicity and graphic vivacity which it maintained with the ancients, has gained much more in the amount of useful knowledge and the lessons of sound philosophy which it inculcates.

There is no writer who exhibits more distinctly the full development of the principles of modern history, with all its virtues and defects, than Gibbon. His learning was fully equal to his vast subject. This, commencing with expiring civilization in ancient Rome, continues on until the period of its final and perfect resurrection in Italy in the fifteenth century, and thus may be said to furnish the lights which are to guide us through the long interval of darkness which divides the Old from the Modern world. The range of his subject was fully equal to its duration. Goths, Huns, Tartars, and all the rude tribes of the North, are brought upon the stage, together with the more cultivated natives of the South, the Greeks, Italians, and the intellectual Arab; and, as the scene shifts from one country to another, we behold its population depicted with that peculiarity of physiognomy and studied propriety of costume which belong to dramatic exhibition; for Gibbon was a more vivacious draughtsman than most writers of his school. He was, moreover, deeply versed in geography, chronology, antiquities, verbal criticism—in short, in all the sciences in any way subsidiary to his art. The extent of his subject permitted him to indulge in those elaborate disquisitions so congenial to the spirit of modern history on the most momentous and interesting topics, while his early studies enabled him to embellish the drier details of his narrative with the charms of a liberal and elegant scholarship.

What, then, was wanting to this accomplished writer? Good faith. His defects were precisely of the class of which we have before been speaking, and his most elaborate efforts exhibit too often the perversion of learning and ingenuity to the vindication of preconceived hypotheses. He cannot, indeed, be convicted of ignorance or literal inaccuracy, as he has triumphantly proved in his discomfiture of the unfortunate Davis. But his disingenuous mode of conducting the argument leads precisely to the same unfair result. Thus, in his celebrated chapters on the "Progress of Christianity," which he tells us were "reduced by three successive revisals from a bulky volume to their present size," he has often slurred over in the text such particulars as might reflect most credit on the character of the religion, or shuffled them into a note at the bottom of the page, while all that admits of a doubtful complexion in its early propagation is ostentatiously blazoned, and set in contrast to the most amiable features of paganism. At the same time, by a style of innuendo that conveys "more than meets the ear," he has contrived, with Iago-like duplicity, to breathe a taint of suspicion on the purity which he dares not openly assail. It would be easy to furnish examples of all this were this the place for them; but the charges have no novelty, and have been abundantly substantiated by others.

It is a consequence of this skepticism in Gibbon, as with Voltaire, that his writings are nowhere warmed with a generous moral sentiment. The most sublime of all spectacles, that of the martyr who suffers for conscience' sake, and this equally whether his creed be founded in truth or error, is contemplated by the historian with the smile, or, rather, sneer of philosophic indifference. This is not only bad taste, as he is addressing a Christian audience, but he thus voluntarily relinquishes one of the most powerful engines for the movement of human passion, which is never so easily excited as by deeds of suffering, self-devoted heroism.

But, although Gibbon was wholly defective in moral enthusiasm, his style is vivified by a certain exhilarating glow that kindles a corresponding warmth in the bosom of his reader. This may, perhaps, be traced to his egotism, or, to speak more liberally, to an ardent attachment to his professional pursuits, and to his inextinguishable love of letters. This enthusiasm appears in almost every page of his great work, and enabled him to triumph over all its difficulties. It is particularly conspicuous whenever he touches upon Rome, the *alma mater* of science, whose adopted son he may be said to have been from his earliest boyhood. Whenever he contemplates her fallen fortunes, he mourns over her with the fond solicitude that might become an ancient Roman; and when he depicts her pristine glories, dimly seen through the mist of so many centuries, he does it with such vivid accuracy of conception, that the reader, like the traveler who wanders through the excavations of Pompeii, seems to be gazing on the original forms and brilliant colors of antiquity.

To Gibbon's egotism—in its most literal sense, to his personal vanity—may be traced some of the peculiar defects for which his style is conspicuous. The "historian of the Decline and Fall" too rarely forgets his own importance in that of his subject. The consequence which he attaches to his personal labors is shown in a bloated dignity of expression, and an ostentation of ornament that contrast whimsically enough with the trifling topics and commonplace thoughts on which, in the course of his long work, they are occasionally employed. He nowhere moves along with the easy freedom of nature, but seems to leap, as it were, from triad to triad by a succession of strained, convulsive efforts. He affected, as he tells us, the light, festive raillery of Voltaire; but his cumbrous imitation of the mercurial Frenchman may remind one, to make use of a homely simile, of the ass in Æsop's fable, who frisked upon his master in imitation of the sportive gambols of the spaniel. The first two octavo volumes of Gibbon's history were written in a comparatively modest and unaffected manner, for he was then uncertain of the public favor; and, indeed, his style was exceedingly commended by the most competent critics of that day, as Hume, Joseph Warton, and others, as is abundantly shown in their correspondence; but when he had tasted the sweets of popular applause, and had been crowned as the historian of the day, his increased consequence becomes at once visible in the assumed stateliness and magnificence of his bearing. But even after this period, whenever the subject is suited to his style, and when his phlegmatic temper is warmed by those generous emotions, of which, as we have said, it was sometimes susceptible, he exhibits his ideas in the most splendid and imposing forms of which the English language is capable.

The most eminent illustrations of the system of historical writing, which we have been discussing, that have appeared in England in the present century, are the works of Mr. Hallam, in which the author, discarding most of the circumstances that go to make up mere narrative, endeavors to fix the attention of the reader on the more important features of constitutional polity, employing his wide range of materials in strict subordination to this purpose.

But while history has thus been conducted on nearly the same principles in England for the last century, a new path has been struck out in France, or, rather, an attempt has lately been made there to retrace the old one. M. de Barante, no less estimable as a literary critic than as a historian, in the preliminary remarks to his "Histoire des Ducs de Bourgogne," considers the draughts of modern compilers as altogether wanting in the vivacity and freshness of their originals. They tell the reader how he should feel, instead of making him do so. They give him their own results, instead of enabling him, by a fair delineation of incidents, to form his own. And while the early chroniclers, in spite of their unformed and obsolete idiom, are still read with delight, the narratives of the former are too often dry, languid, and uninteresting. He proposes, therefore, by a close adherence to his originals, to extract, as it were, the spirit of their works, without any affectation, however, of their antiquated phraseology, and to exhibit as vivid and veracious a portraiture as possible of the times he is delineating, unbroken by any discussions or reflections of his own. The result has been a work in eleven octavo volumes, which, notwithstanding its bulk, has already passed into four editions.

[SIR WALTER SCOTT AS HISTORIAN]
From *Miscellanies*, pp. 279–287

[From "Chateaubriand's English Literature" (1839), which is, for the most part, a refutation of the French critic's judgments of English writers. This selection reveals Prescott's conception of the relation between history writing and historical romance. It is interesting to observe the points which Prescott stresses in this appreciative notice—Scott's picturesqueness, his love of battles, his romanticism.]

• We may pass over a good deal of skimble-skamble stuff about men and things, which our author may have cut out of his commonplace book, to come to his remarks on Sir Walter Scott, whom he does not rate so highly as most critics.

"The illustrious painter of Scotland," he says, "seems to me to have created a false class; he has, in my opinion, confounded history and romance. The novelist has set about writing historical romances, and the historian romantic histories."—Vol. ii., p. 306.

We should have said, on the contrary, that he had improved the character of both; that he had given new value to romance by building it on history, and new charms to history by embellishing it with the graces of romance.

To be more explicit. The principal historical work of Scott is the "Life of Napoleon." It has, unquestionably, many of the faults incident to a dashing style of composition, which precluded the possibility of compression and arrangement in the best form of which the subject was capable. This, in the end, may be fatal to the perpetuity of the work, for posterity will be much less patient than our own age. He will have a much heavier load to carry, inasmuch as he is to bear up under all of his own time, and ours too. It is very certain, then, some must go by the board; and nine sturdy volumes, which is the amount of Sir Walter's English edition, will be somewhat alarming. Had he confined himself to half the quantity, there would have been no ground for distrust. Every day, nay, hour, we see, ay, and feel, the ill effects of this rapid style of composition, so usual with the best writers of our day. The immediate profits which such writers are pretty sure to get, notwithstanding the example of M. Chateaubriand, operate like the dressing improvidently laid on a naturally good soil, forcing out noxious weeds in such luxuriance as to check, if not absolutely to kill, the more healthful vegetation. Quantities of trivial detail find their way into the page, mixed up with graver matters. Instead of that skillful preparation by which all the avenues verge at last to one point, so as to leave a distinct impression—an impression of unity—on the reader, he is hurried along zigzag, in a thousand directions, or round and round, but never, in the cant of the times, "going ahead" an inch. He leaves off pretty much where he set out, except that his memory may be tolerably well stuffed with facts, which, from want of some principle of cohesion, will soon drop out of it. He will find himself like a traveler who has been riding through a fine country, it may be, by moonlight, getting glimpses of everything, but no complete, well-illuminated view of the whole (*"quale per incertam lunam,"* &c.); or, rather, like the same traveler, whizzing along in a locomotive so rapidly as to get even a glimpse fairly of nothing, instead of making his tour in such a manner as would enable him to pause at what was worth his attention, to pass by night over the barren and uninteresting, and occasionally to rise to such elevations as would afford the best points of view for commanding the various prospect.

The romance writer labors under no such embarrassments. He may, undoubtedly, precipitate his work, so that it may lack proportion, and the nice arrangement required by the rules which, fifty years ago, would have condemned it as a work of art. But the criticism of the present day is not so squeamish, or, to say truth, pedantic. It is enough for the writer of fiction if he give pleasure; and this, everybody knows, is not effected by the strict observance of artificial rules. It is of little consequence how the plot is entangled, or whether it be untied or cut, in order to extricate the *dramatis personæ*. At least, it is of little consequence compared with the true delineation of character. The story is serviceable only as it affords a means for the display of this; and if the novelist but keep up the interest of his story and the truth of his characters, we easily forgive any dislocations which his light vehicle may encounter from too heedless motion. Indeed, rapidity of motion may in some sort favor him, keeping up the glow of his invention, and striking out, as he dashes along, sparks of wit and fancy, that give a brilliant illumination to his track. But in history there must be another kind of process—a process at once slow and laborious. Old parchments are to be ransacked, charters and musty records to be deciphered, and stupid, worm-eaten chroniclers, who had much more of passion, frequently, to blind, than good sense to guide them, must be sifted and compared. In short, a sort of Medea-like process is to be gone through, and many an old bone is to be boiled over in the caldron before it can come out again clothed in the elements of beauty. The dreams of the novelist—the poet of prose—on the other hand, are beyond the reach of art, and the magician calls up the most brilliant forms of fancy by a single stroke of his wand.

Scott, in his History, was relieved, in some degree, from this necessity of studious research, by borrowing his theme from contemporary events. It was his duty, indeed, to examine evidence carefully, and sift out contradictions and errors. This demanded shrewdness and caution, but not much previous preparation and study. It demanded, above all, candor; for it was his business, not to make out a case for a client, but to weigh both sides, like an impartial judge, before summing up the evidence, and delivering his conscientious opinion. We believe there is no good ground for charging Scott with having swerved from this part of his duty. Those who expected to see him deify his hero, and raise altars to his memory, were disappointed; and so were those, also, who demanded that the tail and cloven hoof should be made to peep out beneath the imperial robe. But this proves his impartiality. It would be unfair, however, to require the degree of impartiality which is to be expected from one removed to a distance from the theater of strife, from those national interests and feelings which are so often the disturbing causes of historic fairness. An American, no doubt, would have been, in this respect, in a more favorable point of view for contemplating the European drama. The ocean, stretched between us and the Old World, has the effect of time, and extinguishes, or, at least, cools the hot and angry feelings, which find their way into every man's bosom within the atmosphere of the contest. Scott was a Briton, with all the peculiarities of one—at least of a North Briton; and the future historian, who gathers materials from his labors, will throw these national predilections into the scale in determining the probable accuracy of his statements. These are not greater than might occur to any man, and allowance will always be made for them, on the ground of a general presumption; so that a greater degree of impartiality, by leading to false conclusions in this respect, would scarcely have served the cause of truth better with posterity. An individual who felt his reputation compromised may have joined issue on this or that charge of inaccuracy, but no such charge has come from any of the leading journals in the country, which would not have been slow to expose it, and which would not, considering the great popularity, and, consequently, influence of the work, have omitted, as they did, to notice it at all, had it afforded any obvious ground of exception on this score. Where, then, is the romance which our author accuses Sir Walter of blending with history?

Scott was, in truth, master of the picturesque. He understood, better than any historian since the time of Livy, how to dispose his lights and shades so as to produce the most striking result. This property of romance he had a right to borrow. This talent is particularly observable in the animated parts of his story—in his battles, for example. No man ever painted those terrible scenes with greater effect. He had a natural relish for gunpowder; and his mettle roused, like that of the war-horse, at the sound of the trumpet. His acquaintance with military science enabled him to employ a technical phraseology, just technical enough to give a knowing air to his descriptions, without embarrassing the reader by a pedantic display of unintelligible jargon. This is a talent rare in a civilian. Nothing can be finer than many of his battle-pieces in his "Life of Bonaparte," unless, indeed, we except one or two in his "History of Scotland:" as the fight of Bannockburn, for example, in which Burns's "Scots, wha hae" seems to breathe in every line.

It is when treading on Scottish ground that he seems to feel all his strength. "I seem always to step more firmly," he said to some one, "when on my own native heather." His mind was steeped in Scottish lore, and his bosom warmed with a sympathetic glow for the age of chivalry. Accordingly, his delineations of this period, whether in history or romance, are unrivaled; as superior in effect to those of most compilers, as the richly-stained glass of the feudal ages is superior in beauty and brilliancy of tints to a modern imitation. If this be borrowing something from romance, it is, we repeat, no more than what is lawful for the historian, and explains the meaning of our assertion that he has improved history by the embellishments of fiction.

Yet, after all, how wide the difference between the province of history and of romance, under Scott's own hands, may be shown by comparing his account of Mary's reign in his "History of Scotland," with the same period in the novel of "The Abbot." The historian must keep the beaten track of events. The novelist launches into the illimitable regions of fiction, provided only that his historic portraits be true to their originals. By due attention to this, fiction is made to minister to history, and may, in point of fact, contain as much real truth—truth of character, though not of situation. "The difference between the historian and me," says Fielding, "is, that with him everything is false but the names and dates, while with me nothing is false but these." There is, at least, as much truth in this as in most witticisms.

It is the great glory of Scott, that, by nice attention to costume and character in his novels, he has raised them to historic importance, without impairing their interest as works of art. Who now would imagine that he could form a satisfactory notion of the golden days of Queen Bess, that had not read "Kenilworth"? or of Richard Cœur-de-Lion and his brave paladins, that had not read "Ivanhoe"? Why, then, it has been said, not at once incorporate into regular history all these traits which give such historical value to the novel? Because, in this way, the strict truth which history requires would be violated. This cannot be. The fact is, History and Romance are too near akin ever to be lawfully united. By mingling them together, a confusion is produced, like the mingling of day and night, mystifying and distorting every feature of the landscape. It is enough for the novelist if he be true to the spirit; the historian must be true, also, to the letter. He cannot coin pertinent remarks and anecdotes to illustrate the characters of his drama. He cannot even provide them with suitable costumes. He must take just what Father Time has given him, just what he finds in the records of the age, setting down neither more nor less. Now the dull chroniclers of the old time rarely thought of putting down the smart sayings of the great people they biographize, still less of entering into minute circumstances of personal interest. These were too familiar to contemporaries to require it, and, therefore, they waste their breath on more solemn matters of state, all important in their generation, but not worth a rush in the present. What would the historian not give, could he borrow those fine touches of nature with which the novelist illustrates the characters of his actors—natural touches, indeed, but, in truth, just as artificial as any other part— all coined in the imagination of the writer. There is the same difference between his occupation and that of the novelist that there is between the historical and the portrait painter. The former necessarily takes some great subject, with great personages, all strutting about in gorgeous state attire, and air of solemn tragedy, while his brother artist insinuates himself into the family groups, and picks out natural, familiar scenes and faces, laughing or weeping, but in the charming undress of nature. What wonder that novel-reading should be so much more amusing than history?

[PREFACES]

[In his various prefaces, as well as in his letters, Prescott informs us about the materials on which his histories are based, and he sometimes included a summary statement of his narrative construction. The following preface from his *Philip II* is an excellent example of this procedure. Note the warmth of his acknowledgments to Gayangos and to his American friends located in strategic places who added to his collections. Note also his emphasis on a "dominant principle" to give his work a "unity of action," and his reminder that his history was more than a political narrative. The prefaces to the *Conquest of Mexico* and the *Ferdinand and Isabella* reveal the wide range of assistance granted to Prescott.]

I. From *A History of the Reign of Philip the Second*

The reign of Philip the Second has occupied the pen of the historian more frequently—if we except that of Charles the Fifth—than any other portion of the Spanish annals. It has become familiar to the English reader through the pages of Watson, who has deservedly found favor with the public for the perspicuity of his style,—a virtue, however, not uncommon in his day,—for the sobriety of his judgments, and for the skill he has shown in arranging his complicated story, so as to maintain the reader's interest unbroken to the end. But the public, in Watson's day, were not very fastidious in regard to the sources of the information on which a narrative was founded. Nor was it easy to obtain access to those unpublished documents which constitute the best sources of information. Neither can it be denied that Watson himself was not so solicitous as he should have been to profit by opportunities which a little pains might have put within his reach,—presenting, in this respect, a contrast to his more celebrated predecessor, Robertson; that he contented himself too easily with such cheap and commonplace materials as lay directly in his path; and that, consequently, the foundations of his history are much too slight for the super-structure. For these reasons, the reign of Philip the Second must still be regarded as open ground for English and American writers.

And at no time could the history of this reign have been undertaken with the same advantages as at present, when the more enlightened policy of the European governments has opened their national archives to the inspection of the scholar; when he is allowed access, in particular, to the Archives of Simancas, which have held the secrets of the Spanish monarchy hermetically sealed for ages.

The history of Philip the Second is the history of Europe during the latter half of the sixteenth century. It covers the period when the doctrines of the Reformation were agitating the minds of men in so fearful a manner as to shake the very foundations of the Romish hierarchy in the fierce contest which divided Christendom. Philip, both from his personal charac-ter and from his position as sovereign of the most potent mon-archy in Europe, was placed at the head of the party which strove to uphold the fortunes of the ancient Church; and thus his policy led him perpetually to interfere in the internal affairs of the other European states,—making it necessary to look for the materials for his history quite as much without the Peninsula as within it. In this respect the reign of Ferdinand and Isabella presents a strong contrast to that of Philip the Second; and it was the consideration of this, when I had completed my history of the former, and proposed at some future day to enter upon that of the latter, that led me to set about a collection of authen-tic materials from the public archives in the great European capitals. It was a work of difficulty; and, although I had made some progress in it, I did not feel assured of success until I had the good fortune to obtain the co-operation of my friend Don Pascual de Gayangos, Professor of Arabic in the University of Madrid. This eminent scholar was admirably qualified for the task which he so kindly undertook; since, with a remarkable facility—such as long practice only can give—in deciphering the mysterious handwriting of the sixteenth century, he combined such a thorough acquaintance with the history of his country as enabled him to detect, amidst the ocean of manuscripts which he inspected, such portions as were essential to my purpose.

With unwearied assiduity he devoted himself to the examination of many of the principal collections, both in England and on the Continent. Among these may be mentioned the British Museum and the State-Paper Office, in London; the Library of the Dukes of Burgundy, in Brussels; that of the University of Leyden; the Royal Library, at the Hague; the Royal Library of Paris, and the Archives of the Kingdom, in the Hôtel Soubise; the Library of the Academy of History, the National Library at Madrid, and, more important than either, the ancient Archives of Simancas, within whose hallowed precincts Señor Gayangos was one of the first scholars permitted to enter.

Besides these public repositories, there are several private collections to the owners of which I am largely indebted for the liberal manner in which they have opened them for my benefit. I may mention in particular the late Lady Holland, who kindly permitted copies to be made by Señor Gayangos from the manuscripts preserved in Holland House; Sir Thomas Phillips, Bart., who freely extended the same courtesy in respect to the present work which he had shown to me on a former occasion; and Patrick Fraser Tytler, Esq., the late excellent historian of Scotland, who generously placed at my disposal sundry documents copied by him in the public offices with his own hand for the illustration of the reign of Mary Tudor.

In Spain the collection made by Señor Gayangos was enriched by materials drawn from the family archives of the Marquis of Santa Cruz, whose illustrious ancestor first had charge of the Spanish armada; from the archives of Medina Sidonia, containing papers of the duke who succeeded to the command of that ill-starred expedition; and from the archives of the house of Alva,—a name associated with the most memorable acts of the government of Philip.

The manuscripts thus drawn from various quarters were

fortified by such printed works as, having made their appearance in the time of Philip the Second, could throw any light on his government. Where such works were not to be purchased, Señor Gayangos caused copies to be made of them, or of those portions which were important to my purpose. The result of his kind, untiring labors has been to put me in possession of such a collection of authentic materials for the illustration of the reign of Philip as no one before had probably attempted to make. Nor until now had the time come for making the attempt with success.

There still remained, however, some places to be examined where I might expect to find documents that would be of use to me. Indeed, it is in the nature of such a collection, covering so wide an extent of ground, that it can never be complete. The historian may be satisfied if he has such authentic materials at his command as, while they solve much that has hitherto been enigmatical in the accounts of the time, will enable him to present in their true light the character of Philip and the policy of his government. I must acknowledge my obligations to more than one person who has given me important aid in prosecuting my further researches.

One of the first of them is my friend Mr. Edward Everett, who in his long and brilliant career as a statesman has lost nothing of that love of letters which formed his first claim to distinction. The year before his appointment to the English mission he passed on the Continent, where, with the kindness that belongs to his nature, he spent much time in examining for me the great libraries, first in Paris, and afterwards more effectually in Florence. From the *Archivio Mediceo*, in which he was permitted by the grand duke to conduct his researches, he obtained copies of sundry valuable documents, and among them the letters of the Tuscan ministers, which have helped to guide me in some of the most intricate parts of my narrative. A still larger amount of materials he derived from the private library of Count Guicciardini, the descendant of the illustrious historian of that name. I am happy to express my lively sense of the courtesy shown by this nobleman; also my gratitude for kind offices rendered me by Prince Corsini; and no less by the Marquis Gino Capponi, whose name will be always held in honor for the enlightened patronage which he has extended to learning while suffering, himself, under the severest privation that can befall the scholar.

There was still an important deficiency in my collection,— that of the *Relazioni Venete*, as the reports are called which were made by ambassadors of Venice on their return from their foreign missions. The value of these reports, for the information they give of the countries visited by the envoys, is well known to historians. The deficiency was amply supplied by the unwearied kindness of my friend Mr. Fay, who now so ably fills the post of minister from the United States to Switzerland. When connected with the American legation at Berlin, he in the most obliging manner assisted me in making arrangements for obtaining the documents I desired, which, with other papers of importance, were copied for me from the manuscripts in the Royal Library of Berlin and the Ducal Library of Gotha. I have also, in connection with this, to express my obligations to the distinguished librarian of the former institution, Mr. Pertz, for the good will which he showed in promoting my views.

Through Mr. Fay I also obtained the authority of Prince Metternich to inspect the Archives of the Empire in Vienna, which I inferred, from the intimate relations subsisting between the courts of Madrid and Vienna in that day, must contain much valuable matter relevant to my subject. The result did not correspond to my expectations. I am happy, however, to have the opportunity of publicly offering my acknowledgments to that eminent scholar Dr. Ferdinand Wolf for the obliging manner in which he conducted the investigation for me, as well in the archives above mentioned as, with better results, in the Imperial Library, with which he is officially connected.

In concluding the list of those to whose good offices I have been indebted, I must not omit the names of M. de Salvandy, minister of public instruction in France at the time I was engaged in making my collection; Mr. Rush, then the minister of the United States at the French court; Mr. Rives, of Virginia, his successor in that office; and last, not least, my friend Count de Circourt, a scholar whose noble contributions to the periodical literature of his country, on the greatest variety of topics, have given him a prominent place among the writers of our time.

I am happy, also, to tender my acknowledgments for the favors I have received from Mr. Van de Weyer, minister from Belgium to the court of St. James; from Mr. B. Homer Dixon, consul for the Netherlands at Boston; and from my friend and kinsman Mr. Thomas Hickling, consul for the United States at St. Michael's, who kindly furnished me with sundry manuscripts exhibiting the condition of the Azores at the period when those islands passed, with Portugal, under the sceptre of Philip the Second.

Having thus acquainted the reader with the sources whence I have derived my materials, I must now say a few words in regard to the conduct of my narrative. An obvious difficulty in the path of the historian of this period arises from the nature of the subject, embracing, as it does, such a variety of independent, not to say incongruous, topics, that it is no easy matter to preserve anything like unity of interest in the story. Thus the Revolution of the Netherlands, although, strictly speaking, only an episode to the main body of the narrative, from its importance well deserves to be treated in a separate and independent narrative by itself.[1] Running along through the whole extent of Philip's reign, it is continually distracting the attention of the historian, creating an embarrassment something like that which arises from what is termed a double plot in the drama. The best way of obviating this is to keep in view the dominant

[1] It is gratifying to learn that before long such a history may be expected,—if indeed it should not appear before the publication of this work,—from the pen of our accomplished countryman Mr. J. Lothrop Motley, who during the last few years, for the better prosecution of his labors, has established his residence in the neighborhood of the scenes of his narrative. No one acquainted with the fine powers of mind possessed by this scholar, and the earnestness with which he has devoted himself to his task, can doubt that he will do full justice to his important but difficult subject. [Prescott's note.]

principle which controlled all the movements of the complicated machinery, so to speak, and impressed on them a unity of action. This principle is to be found in the policy of Philip, the great aim of which was to uphold the supremacy of the Church, and, as a consequence, that of the crown. "Peace and public order," he writes on one occasion, "are to be maintained in my dominions only by maintaining the authority of the Holy See." It was this policy, almost as sure and steady in its operation as the laws of Nature herself, that may be said to have directed the march of events through the whole of his long reign; and it is only by keeping this constantly in view that the student will be enabled to obtain a clue to guide him through the intricate passages in the history of Philip, and the best means of solving what would otherwise remain enigmatical in his conduct.

In the composition of the work I have for the most part conformed to the plan which I had before adopted. Far from confining myself to a record of political events, I have endeavored to present a picture of the intellectual culture and the manners of the people. I have not even refused such aid as could be obtained from the display of pageants and court ceremonies, which, although exhibiting little more than the costume of the time, may serve to bring the outward form of a picturesque age more vividly before the eye of the reader. In the arrangement of the narrative I have not confined myself altogether to the chronological order of events, but have thrown them into masses, according to the subjects to which they relate, so as to produce as far as possible a distinct impression on the reader. And in this way I have postponed more than one matter of importance to a later portion of the work, which a strict regard to time would assign more properly to an earlier division of the subject. Finally, I have been careful to fortify the text with citations from the original authorities on which it depends, especially where these are rare and difficult of access.

In the part relating to the Netherlands I have pursued a course somewhat different from what I have done in other parts of the work. The scholars of that country, in a truly patriotic spirit, have devoted themselves of late years to exploring their own archives, as well as those of Simancas, for the purpose of illustrating their national annals. The results they have given to the world in a series of publications, which are still in progress. The historian has reason to be deeply grateful to those pioneers, whose labors have put him in possession of materials which afford the most substantial basis for his narrative. For what basis can compare with that afforded by the written correspondence of the parties themselves? It is on this sure ground that I have mainly relied in this part of my story; and I have adopted the practice of incorporating extracts from the letters in the body of the text, which, if it may sometimes give an air of prolixity to the narrative, will have the advantage of bringing the reader into a sort of personal acquaintance with the actors, as he listens to the words spoken by themselves.

In the earlier part of this Preface I have made the acknowledgments due for assistance I have received in the collection of my materials; and I must not now conclude without recording my obligations, of another kind, to two of my personal friends,— Mr. Charles Folsom, the learned librarian of the Boston Athenæum, who has repeated the good offices he had before rendered me in revising my manuscript for the press; and Mr. John Foster Kirk, whose familiarity with the history and languages of Modern Europe has greatly aided me in the prosecution of my researches, while his sagacious criticism has done me no less service in the preparation of this volume.

Notwithstanding the advantages I have enjoyed for the composition of this work, and especially those derived from the possession of new and original materials, I am fully sensible that I am far from having done justice to a subject so vast in its extent and so complicated in its relations. It is not necessary to urge in my defense any physical embarrassments under which I labor; since that will hardly be an excuse for not doing well what it was not necessary to do at all. But I may be permitted to say that what I have done has been the result of careful preparation; that I have endeavored to write in a spirit of candor and good faith; and that, whatever may be the deficiencies of my work, it can hardly fail—considering the advantages I have enjoyed over my predecessors—to present the reader with such new and authentic statements of facts as may afford him a better point of view than that which he has hitherto possessed for surveying the history of Philip the Second.

BOSTON, *July*, 1855.

II. From *History of the Conquest of Mexico*

[This is a statement of materials, especially manuscript, used by Prescott in the composition of *Mexico*. He was far richer in these resources than any earlier historian of the conquest.]

As the Conquest of Mexico has occupied the pens of Solís and of Robertson, two of the ablest historians of their respective nations, it might seem that little could remain at the present day to be gleaned by the historical inquirer. But Robertson's narrative is necessarily brief, forming only part of a more extended work; and neither the British, nor the Castilian author, was provided with the important materials for relating this event, which have been since assembled by the industry of Spanish scholars. The scholar who led the way in these researches was Don Juan Baptista Muñoz, the celebrated historiographer of the Indies, who, by a royal edict, was allowed free access to the national archives, and to all libraries, public, private, and monastic, in the kingdom and its colonies. The result of his long labors was a vast body of materials, of which unhappily he did not live to reap the benefit himself. His manuscripts were deposited, after his death, in the archives of the Royal Academy of History at Madrid; and that collection was subsequently augmented by the manuscripts of Don Vargas Ponçe, President of the Academy, obtained, like those of Muñoz, from different quarters, but especially from the archives of the Indies at Seville.

On my application to the Academy, in 1838, for permission to copy that part of this inestimable collection relating to Mexico and Peru, it was freely acceded to, and an eminent German scholar, one of their own number, was appointed to superintend the collation and transcription of the manuscripts and this, it may be added, before I had any claim on the courtesy of that respectable body, as one of its associates. This conduct shows advance of a liberal spirit in the Peninsula since the time of Dr. Robertson, who complains that he was denied admission to the most important public repositories. The favor with which my own application was regarded, however, must chiefly be attributed to the kind offices of the venerable President of the Academy, Don Martin Fernandez de Navarrete; a scholar whose personal character has secured to him the same high consideration at home, which his literary labors have obtained abroad. To this eminent person I am under still further obligations, for the free use which he has allowed me to make of his own manuscripts,—the fruits of a life of accumulation, and the basis of those valuable publications, with which he has at different times illustrated the Spanish colonial history.

From these three magnificent collections, the result of half a century's careful researches, I have obtained a mass of unpublished documents, relating to the Conquest and Settlement of Mexico and of Peru, comprising altogether about eight thousand folio pages. They consist of instructions of the Court, military and private journals, correspondence of the great actors in the scenes, legal instruments, contemporary chronicles, and the like, drawn from all the principal places in the extensive colonial empire of Spain, as well as from the public archives in the Peninsula.

I have still further fortified the collection, by gleaning such materials from Mexico itself as had been overlooked by my illustrious predecessors in these researches. For these I am indebted to the courtesy of Count Cortina, and, yet more, to that of Don Lucas Alaman, Minister of Foreign Affairs in Mexico; but, above all, to my excellent friend, Don Angel Calderon de la Barca, late Minister Plenipotentiary to that country from the Court of Madrid,—a gentleman whose high and estimable qualities, even more than his station, secured him the public confidence, and gained him free access to every place of interest and importance in Mexico.

I have also to acknowledge the very kind offices rendered to me by the Count Camaldoli at Naples; by the Duke of Serradifalco in Sicily, a nobleman, whose science gives additional luster to his rank; and by the Duke of Monteleone, the present representative of Cortés, who has courteously opened the archives of his family to my inspection. To these names must also be added that of Sir Thomas Phillips, Bart., whose precious collection of manuscripts probably surpasses in extent that of any private gentleman in Great Britain, if not in Europe; that of Mons. Ternaux-Compans, the proprietor of the valuable literary collection of Don Antonio Uguina, including the papers of Muñoz, the fruits of which he is giving to the world in his excellent translations; and, lastly, that of my friend and countryman, Arthur Middleton, Esq., late Chargé d'Affaires from the United States at the Court of Madrid, for the efficient aid he has afforded me in prosecuting my inquiries in that capital.

In addition to this stock of original documents obtained through these various sources, I have diligently provided myself with such printed works as have reference to the subject, including the magnificent publications, which have appeared both in France and England, on the Antiquities of Mexico, which, from their cost and colossal dimensions, would seem better suited to a public than to a private library.

III. From *History of the Reign of Ferdinand and Isabella*

English writers have done more for the illustration of Spanish history, than for that of any other except their own. To say nothing of the recent general compendium, executed for the "Cabinet Cyclopædia," a work of singular acuteness and information, we have particular narratives of the several reigns, in an unbroken series, from the emperor Charles the Fifth (the First of Spain) to Charles the Third, at the close of the last century, by authors whose names are a sufficient guaranty for the excellence of their productions. It is singular, that, with this attention to the modern history of the Peninsula, there should be no particular account of the period, which may be considered as the proper basis of it,—the reign of Ferdinand and Isabella.

In this reign, the several States, into which the country had been broken up for ages, were brought under a common rule; the kingdom of Naples was conquered; America discovered and colonized; the ancient empire of the Spanish Arabs subverted; the dread tribunal of the Modern Inquisition established; the Jews, who contributed so sensibly to the wealth and civilization of the country, were banished; and, in fine, such changes were introduced into the interior administration of the monarchy, as have left a permanent impression on the character and condition of the nation.

The actors in these events, were every way suited to their importance. Besides the reigning sovereigns, Ferdinand and Isabella, the latter certainly one of the most interesting personages in history, we have, in political affairs, that consummate statesman, Cardinal Ximenes, in military, the "Great Captain," Gonsalvo de Cordova, and in maritime, the most successful navigator of any age, Christopher Columbus; whose entire biographies fall within the limits of this period. Even such portions of it as have been incidentally touched by English writers, as the Italian wars, for example, have been drawn so exclusively from French and Italian sources, that they may be said to be untrodden ground for the historian of Spain.[1]

It must be admitted, however, that an account of this reign could not have been undertaken at any preceding period, with anything like the advantages at present afforded; owing to the

[1] The only histories of this reign by continental writers, with which I am acquainted, are the "Histoire des Rois Catholiques Ferdinand et Isabelle, par l'Abbé Mignot, Paris, 1766," and the "Geschichte der Regierung Ferdinand des Katholischen, von Rupert Becker, Prag und Leipzig, 1790." Their authors have employed the most accessible materials only in the compilation; and, indeed, they lay claim to no great research, which would seem to be precluded by the extent of their works, in neither instance exceeding two volumes duodecimo. They have the merit of exhibiting, in a simple, perspicuous form, those events, which, lying on the surface, may be found more or less expanded in most general histories. [Prescott's note.]

light which recent researches of Spanish scholars, in the greater
freedom of inquiry now enjoyed, have shed on some of its
most interesting and least familiar features. The most important of the works to which I allude are, the History of the Inquisition, from official documents, by its secretary, Llorente;
the analysis of the political institutions of the kingdom, by such
writers as Marina, Sempere, and Capmany; the literal version,
now made for the first time, of the Spanish-Arab chronicles, by
Conde; the collection of original and unpublished documents,
illustrating the history of Columbus and the early Castilian
navigators, by Navarrete; and, lastly, the copious illustrations
of Isabella's reign, by Clemencin, the late lamented secretary
of the Royal Academy of History, forming the sixth volume of
its valuable Memoirs.

It was the knowledge of these facilities for doing justice to
this subject, as well as its intrinsic merits, which led me, ten
years since, to select it; and surely no subject could be found
more suitable for the pen of an American, than a history of that
reign, under the auspices of which the existence of his own
favored quarter of the globe was first revealed. As I was conscious that the value of the history must depend mainly on that
of its materials, I have spared neither pains nor expense, from
the first, in collecting the most authentic. In accomplishing
this, I must acknowledge the services of my friends, Mr. Alexander H. Everett, then Minister Plenipotentiary from the United
States to the Court of Madrid, Mr. Arthur Middleton, secretary
of the American legation, and, above all, Mr. O. Rich, now
American consul for the Balearic Islands, a gentleman, whose
extensive bibliographical knowledge, and unwearied researches,
during a long residence in the Peninsula, have been liberally
employed for the benefit both of his own country and of England. With such assistance, I flatter myself that I have been
enabled to secure whatever can materially conduce to the illustration of the period in question, whether in the form of
chronicle, memoir, private correspondence, legal codes, or
official documents. Among these are various contemporary
manuscripts, covering the whole ground of the narrative, none

of which have been printed, and some of them but little known to Spanish scholars. In obtaining copies of these from the public libraries, I must add, that I have found facilities under the present liberal government, which were denied me under the preceding. In addition to these sources of information, I have availed myself, in the part of the work occupied with literary criticism and history, of the library of my friend, Mr. George Ticknor, who during a visit to Spain, some years since, collected whatever was rare and valuable in the literature of the Peninsula. I must further acknowledge my obligations to the library of Harvard University, in Cambridge, from whose rich repository of books relating to our own country I have derived material aid. And, lastly, I must not omit to notice the favors of another kind for which I am indebted to my friend, Mr. William H. Gardiner, whose judicious counsels have been of essential benefit to me in the revision of my labors.

In the plan of the work, I have not limited myself to a strict chronological narrative of passing events, but have occasionally paused, at the expense, perhaps, of some interest in the story, to seek such collateral information, as might bring these events into a clearer view. I have devoted a liberal portion of the work to the literary progress of the nation, conceiving this quite as essential a part of its history as civil and military details. I have occasionally introduced, at the close of the chapters, a critical notice of the authorities used, that the reader may form some estimate of their comparative value and credibility. Finally, I have endeavored to present him with such an account of the state of affairs, both before the accession, and at the demise of the Catholic sovereigns, as might afford him the best points of view for surveying the entire results of their reign.

How far I have succeeded in the execution of this plan, must be left to the reader's candid judgment. Many errors he may be able to detect. Sure I am, there can be no one more sensible of my deficiencies, than myself; although it was not till after practical experience, that I could fully estimate the difficulty of obtaining anything like a faithful portraiture of a distant age, amidst the shifting hues and perplexing crosslights of historic testimony. From one class of errors my subject necessarily exempts me; those founded on national or party feeling. I may have been more open to another fault; that of too strong a bias in favor of my principal actors; for characters, noble and interesting in themselves, naturally beget a sort of partiality akin to friendship, in the historian's mind, accustomed to the daily contemplation of them. Whatever defects may be charged on the work, I can at least assure myself, that it is an honest record of a reign important in itself, new to the reader in an English dress, and resting on a solid basis of authentic materials, such as probably could not be met with out of Spain, nor in it without much difficulty.

I hope I shall be acquitted of egotism, although I add a few words respecting the peculiar embarrassments I have encountered, in composing these volumes. Soon after my arrangements were made, early in 1826, for obtaining the necessary materials from Madrid, I was deprived of the use of my eyes for all purposes of reading and writing, and had no prospect of again recovering it. This was a serious obstacle to the prosecution of a work, requiring the perusal of a large mass of authorities, in various languages, the contents of which were to be carefully collated, and transferred to my own pages, verified by minute reference.[1] Thus shut out from one sense, I was driven to rely exclusively on another, and to make the ear do the work of the eye. With the assistance of a reader, uninitiated, it may be added, in any modern language but his own, I worked my way through several venerable Castilian quartos, until I was satisfied of the practicability of the undertaking. I next procured the services of one more competent to aid me in pursuing my historical inquiries. The process was

[1] "To compile a history from various authors, when they can only be consulted by other eyes, is not easy, nor possible, but with more skilful and attentive help than can be commonly obtained." (Johnson's *Life of Milton.*) This remark of the great critic, which first engaged my attention in the midst of my embarrassments, although discouraging at first, in the end stimulated the desire to overcome them. [Prescott's note.]

slow and irksome enough, doubtless, to both parties, at least till my ear was accommodated to foreign sounds, and an antiquated, oftentimes barbarous phraseology, when my progress became more sensible, and I was cheered with the prospect of success. It certainly would have been a far more serious misfortune, to be led thus blindfold through the pleasant paths of literature; but my track stretched, for the most part, across dreary wastes, where no beauty lurked, to arrest the traveler's eye and charm his senses. After persevering in this course for some years, my eyes, by the blessing of Providence, recovered sufficient strength to allow me to use them, with tolerable freedom, in the prosecution of my labors, and in the revision of all previously written. I hope I shall not be misunderstood, as stating these circumstances to deprecate the severity of criticism, since I am inclined to think the greater circumspection I have been compelled to use has left me, on the whole, less exposed to inaccuracies, than I should have been in the ordinary mode of composition. But, as I reflect on the many sober hours I have passed in wading through black-letter tomes, and through manuscripts whose doubtful orthography and defiance of all punctuation were so many stumbling-blocks to my amanuensis, it calls up a scene of whimsical distresses, not usually encountered, on which the good-natured reader may, perhaps, allow I have some right, now that I have got the better of them, to dwell with satisfaction.

I will only remark, in conclusion of this too prolix discussion about myself, that while making my tortoise-like progress, I saw what I had fondly looked upon as my own ground, (having indeed lain unmolested by any other invader for so many ages,) suddenly entered, and in part occupied, by one of my countrymen. I allude to Mr. Irving's "History of Columbus," and "Chronicle of Granada," the subjects of which, although covering but a small part of my whole plan, form certainly two of its most brilliant portions. Now, alas! if not devoid of interest, they are, at least, stripped of the charm of novelty. For what eye has not been attracted to the spot, on which the light of that writer's genius has fallen?

[BATTLE OF THE KNIGHTS]

From *Ferdinand and Isabella*, Vol. III, pt. ii, chap. xi

[Part of a long section on the Franco-Spanish wars in Italy. Throughout his volumes Prescott reveals a healthy skepticism, and though he includes episodes whose authenticity he doubts even while almost wishing they were true, he generally observes the accepted historical canons. More often it is in his notes that he indicates disagreement with earlier historians.]

The war now began to assume many of the romantic features of that of Granada. The knights on both sides, not content with the usual military rencontres, defied one another to jousts and tourneys, eager to establish their prowess in the noble exercises of chivalry. One of the most remarkable of these meetings took place between eleven Spanish and as many French knights, in consequence of some disparaging remarks of the latter on the cavalry of their enemies, which they affirmed inferior to their own. The Venetians gave the parties a fair field of combat in the neutral territory under their own walls of Trani. A gallant array of well-armed knights of both nations guarded the lists, and maintained the order of the fight. On the appointed day, the champions appeared in the field, armed at all points, with horses richly caparisoned, and barbed or covered with steel panoply like their masters. The roofs and battlements of Trani were covered with spectators, while the lists were thronged with the French and Spanish chivalry, each staking in some degree the national honor on the issue of the contest. Among the Castilians were Diego de Paredes and Diego de Vera, while the good knight Bayard was most conspicuous on the other side.

As the trumpets sounded the appointed signal, the hostile parties rushed to the encounter. Three Spaniards were borne from their saddles by the rudeness of the shock, and four of their antagonists' horses slain. The fight, which began at ten in the morning was not to be protracted beyond sunset. Long before that hour, all the French save two, one of them the chevalier Bayard, had been dismounted, and their horses, at which the

Spaniards had aimed more than at the riders, disabled or slain.
The Spaniards, seven of whom were still on horseback, pressed
hard on their adversaries, leaving little doubt of the fortune of
the day. The latter, however, intrenching themselves behind
the carcasses of their dead horses, made good their defense
against the Spaniards, who in vain tried to spur their terrified
steeds over the barrier. In this way the fight was protracted till
sunset; and, as both parties continued to keep possession of the
field, the palm of victory was adjudged to neither, while both
were pronounced to have demeaned themselves like good and
valiant knights.[1]

The tourney being ended, the combatants met in the center
of the lists, and embraced each other in the true companionship
of chivalry, "making good cheer together," says an old chronicler, before they separated. The Great Captain was not satisfied with the issue of the fight. "We have, at least," said one
of his champions, "disproved the taunt of the Frenchmen, and
shown ourselves as good horsemen as they." "I sent you for
better," coldly retorted Gonsalvo.

[OBSEQUIES OF CHARLES V]

From *Philip the Second*, Bk. I, chap. ix

[In the following account, Prescott sets straight the record
of the obsequies of Charles the Fifth by pointing out the shortcomings of previous historians.]

The declining state of the emperor's health may have inspired
him with a presentiment of his approaching end, to which, we
have seen, he gave utterance some time before this, in his con-

---

[1] This celebrated tourney, its causes, and all the details of the action,
are told in as many different ways as there are narrators; and this,
notwithstanding it was fought in the presence of a crowd of witnesses, who had nothing to do but look on, and note what passed before their eyes. The only facts in which all agree, are, that there was
such a tournament, and that neither party gained the advantage.
So much for history! [Part of Prescott's note.]

versation with Gaztelu. It may have been the sober reflections which such a feeling would naturally suggest that led him, at the close of the month of August, to conceive the extraordinary idea of preparing for the final scene by rehearsing his own funeral. He consulted his confessor on the subject, and was encouraged by the accommodating father to consider it as a meritorious act. The chapel was accordingly hung in black, and the blaze of hundreds of wax-lights was not sufficient to dispel the darkness. The monks in their conventual dresses, and all the emperor's household, clad in deep mourning, gathered round a huge *catafalque*, shrouded also in black, which had been raised in the center of the chapel. The service for the burial of the dead was then performed; and, amidst the dismal wail of the monks, the prayers ascended for the departed spirit, that it might be received into the mansions of the blessed. The sorrowful attendants were melted to tears, as the image of their master's death was presented to their minds, or they were touched, it may be, with compassion for this pitiable display of his weakness. Charles, muffled in a dark mantle, and bearing a lighted candle in his hand, mingled with his household, the spectator of his own obsequies; and the doleful ceremony was concluded by his placing the taper in the hands of the priest, in sign of his surrendering up his soul to the Almighty.

Such is the account of this melancholy farce given us by the Jeronymite chroniclers of the cloister-life of Charles the Fifth, and which has since been repeated—losing nothing in the repetition—by every succeeding historian, to the present time. Nor does there seem to have been any distrust of its correctness till the historical skepticism of our own day had subjected the narrative to a more critical scrutiny. It was then discovered that no mention of the affair was to be discerned in the letters of any one of the emperor's household residing at Yuste, although there are letters extant written by Charles's physician, his major-domo, and his secretary, both on the thirty-first day of August, the day of the funeral, and on the first of September. With so extraordinary an event fresh in their minds, their silence is inexplicable.

One fact is certain, that, if the funeral did take place, it could not have been on the date assigned to it; for on the thirty-first the emperor was laboring under an attack of fever, of which his physician has given full particulars, and from which he was destined never to recover. That the writers, therefore, should have been silent in respect to a ceremony which must have had so bad an effect on the nerves of the patient, is altogether incredible.

Yet the story of the obsequies comes from one of the Jeronymite brethren then living at Yuste, who speaks of the emotions which he felt, in common with the rest of the convent, at seeing a man thus bury himself alive, as it were, and perform his funeral rites before his death. It is repeated by another of the fraternity, the prior of the Escorial, who had ample means of conversing with eyewitnesses. And, finally, it is confirmed by more than one writer near enough to the period to be able to assure himself of the truth. Indeed, the parties from whom the account is originally derived were so situated that if the story be without foundation it is impossible to explain its existence by misapprehension on their part. It must be wholly charged on a willful misstatement of facts. It is true, the monkish chronicler is not always quite so scrupulous in this particular as would be desirable,—especially where the honor of his order is implicated. But what interest could the Jeronymite fathers have had in so foolish a fabrication as this? The supposition is at variance with the respectable character of the parties, and with the air of simplicity and good faith that belongs to their narratives.

We may well be staggered, it is true, by the fact that no allusion to the obsequies appears in any of the letters from Yuste; while the date assigned for them, moreover, is positively disproved. Yet we may consider that the misstatement of a date is a very different thing from the invention of a story, and that chronological accuracy, as I have more than once had occasion to remark, was not the virtue of the monkish or indeed of any other historian of the sixteenth century. It would not be a miracle if the obsequies should have taken place some days before the period assigned to them. It so happens that we have no letters from Yuste between the eighteenth and the twenty-seventh of August. At least, I have none myself, and have seen none cited by others. If any should hereafter come to light, written during that interval, they may be found possibly to contain some allusion to the funeral. Should no letters have been written during the period, the silence of the parties who wrote at the end of August and the beginning of September may be explained by the fact that too long a time had elapsed since the performance of the emperor's obsequies for them to suppose it could have any connection with his illness, which formed the subject of their correspondence. Difficulties will present themselves, whichever view we take of the matter. But the reader may think it quite as reasonable to explain those difficulties by the supposition of involuntary error as by that of sheer invention.

Nor is the former supposition rendered less probable by the character of Charles the Fifth. There was a taint of insanity in the royal blood of Castile, which was most fully displayed in the emperor's mother, Joanna. Some traces of it, however faint, may be discerned in his own conduct before he took refuge in the cloisters of Yuste. And though we may not agree with Paul the Fourth in regarding this step as sufficient evidence of his madness, we may yet find something in his conduct, on more than one occasion, while there, which is near akin to it. Such, for example, was the morbid relish which he discovered for performing the obsequies not merely of his kindred, but of any one whose position seemed to him to furnish an apology for it. Not a member of the *toison* died, but he was prepared to commemorate the event with solemn funeral rites. These, in short, seemed to be the festivities of Charles's cloister-life. These lugubrious ceremonies had a fascination for him that may remind one of the tenacity with which his mother, Joanna, clung to the dead body of her husband, taking it with her wherever she went. It was after celebrating the obsequies of his parents and his wife, which occupied several successive days, that he conceived, as we are told, the idea of rehearsing his own funeral,—a piece of extravagance which becomes the more credible when we reflect on the state of morbid excitement to which his mind may have been brought by dwelling so long on the dreary apparatus of death.

[HUMAN SACRIFICES UNDER THE AZTECS]

From *The Conquest of Mexico*, Bk. I, chap. iii, note 28

[Prescott was generally judicious in weighing sources. This footnote illustrates his critical approach to them.]

Bishop Zumarraga, in a letter written a few years after the Conquest, states that 20,000 victims were yearly slaughtered in the capital. Torquemada turns this into 20,000 *infants*. (Monarch. Ind., lib. 7, cap. 21.) Herrera, following Acosta, says 20,000 victims on a specified day of the year, throughout the kingdom. (Hist. General, dec. 2, lib. 2, cap. 16.) Clavigero, more cautious, infers that this number may have been sacrificed annually throughout Anahuac. (Ubi supra.) Las Casas, however, in his reply to Sepulveda's assertion, that no one who had visited the New World put the number of yearly sacrifices at less than 20,000, declares that "this is the estimate of brigands, who wish to find an apology for their own atrocities, and that the real number was not above 50!" (Œuvres, ed. Llorente, (Paris, 1822,) tom. I. pp. 365, 386.) Probably the good Bishop's arithmetic, here, as in most other instances, came more from his heart than his head. With such loose and contradictory *data*, it is clear that any specific number is mere conjecture, undeserving the name of calculation.

[IMPEDIMENTS TO HISTORICAL ACCURACY]

From *Ferdinand and Isabella*, Vol. III, pt. ii, chap. xiii

[In the middle of his narrative of the Italian wars, Prescott paused to discuss the difficulty of getting truth out of the incomplete and prejudiced records of the past.]

Those, who have not themselves had occasion to pursue historical inquiries, will scarcely imagine on what loose grounds the greater part of the narrative is to be built. With the exception of a few leading outlines, there is such a mass of inconsistency and contradiction in the details, even of contemporaries, that it seems almost as hopeless to seize the true aspect of any particular age as it would be to transfer to the canvas a faithful likeness of an individual from a description simply of his prominent features.

Much of the difficulty might seem to be removed, now that we are on the luminous and beaten track of Italian history; but, in fact, the vision is rather dazzled than assisted by the numerous crosslights thrown over the path, and the infinitely various points of view from which every object is contemplated. Besides the local and party prejudices which we had to encounter in the contemporary Spanish historians, we have now a host of national prejudices, not less unfavorable to truth; while the remoteness of the scene of action necessarily begets a thousand additional inaccuracies in the gossiping and credulous chroniclers of France and Spain.

The mode in which public negotiations were conducted at this period, interposes still further embarrassments in our search after truth. They were regarded as the personal concerns of the sovereign, in which the nation at large had no right to interfere. They were settled, like the rest of his private affairs, under his own eye, without the participation of any other branch of the government. They were shrouded, therefore, under an impenetrable secrecy, which permitted such results only to emerge into light as suited the monarch. Even these results cannot be relied on as furnishing the true key to the intentions of the parties. The science of the cabinet, as then practiced, authorized such a system of artifice and shameless duplicity, as greatly impaired the credit of those official documents which we are accustomed to regard as the surest foundations of history.

The only records which we can receive with full confidence are the private correspondence of contemporaries, which, from its very nature, is exempt from most of the restraints and affectations incident more or less to every work destined for the public eye. Such communications, indeed, come like the voice of departed years; and when, as in Martyr's case, they proceed from one whose acuteness is combined with singular opportunities for observation, they are of inestimable value. Instead of exposing to us only the results, they lay open the interior workings of the machinery, and we enter into all the shifting doubts, passions, and purposes, which agitate the minds of the actors. Unfortunately, the chain of correspondence here, as in similar cases, when not originally designed for historical uses, necessarily suffers from occasional breaks and interruptions. The scattered gleams which are thrown over the most prominent points, however, shed so strong a light, as materially to aid us in groping our way through the darker and more perplexed passages of the story.

The obscurity, which hangs over the period, has not been dispelled by those modern writers, who, like Varillas, in his well-known work, *Politique de Ferdinand le Catholique*, affect to treat the subject philosophically, paying less attention to facts than to their causes and consequences. These ingenious persons, seldom willing to take things as they find them, seem to think that truth is only to be reached by delving deep below the surface. In this search after more profound causes of action, they reject whatever is natural and obvious. They are inexhaustible in conjectures and finespun conclusions, inferring quite as much from what is not said or done, as from what is. In short, they put the reader as completely in possession of their hero's thoughts on all occasions, as any professed romance-writer would venture to do. All this may be very agreeable, and to persons of easy faith, very satisfactory; but it is not history, and may well remind us of the astonishment somewhere expressed by Cardinal de Retz at the assurance of those, who, at a distance from the scene of action, pretended to lay open all the secret springs of policy, of which he himself, though a principal party, was ignorant.

No prince, on the whole, has suffered more from these unwarrantable liberties, than Ferdinand the Catholic. His reputation for shrewd policy, suggests a ready key to whatever is mysterious and otherwise inexplicable in his government; while it puts writers like Gaillard and Varillas constantly on the scent after the most secret and subtile sources of action, as if there were always something more to be detected, than readily meets the eye. Instead of judging him by the general rules of human conduct, every thing is referred to deep laid stratagem; no allowance is made for the ordinary disturbing forces, the passions and casualties of life; every action proceeds with the same wary calculation that regulates the moves upon a chessboard; and thus a character of consummate artifice is built up, not only unsupported by historical evidence, but in manifest contradiction to the principles of our nature. The part of our subject embraced in the present chapter, has long been debatable ground between the French and Spanish historians, and the obscurity which hangs over it has furnished an ample range for speculation to the class of writers above alluded to, which they have not failed to improve.

[ON FOOTNOTES]

From *Miscellanies*, pp. 325–328

[From "Bancroft's United States" (1841), a review of Volume III of Bancroft's *History of the United States*. Prescott observed closely the conventions relating to footnote citation and he was very much annoyed when scholars departed from recognized practice in documentation.]

This leads us to enlarge on what we consider a defect in our author's present plan. His notes are discarded altogether, and his references transferred from the bottom of the page to the side margin. This is very objectionable, not merely on account of the disagreeable effect produced on the eye, but from the more serious inconvenience of want of room for very frequent and accurate reference. Titles are necessarily much abridged, sometimes at the expense of perspicuity. The first reference in this volume is "Hallam, iv., 374"; the second is "Archdale."

Now Hallam has written several works, published in various forms and editions. As to the second authority, we have no means of identifying the passage at all. This, however, is not the habit of Mr. Bancroft where the fact is of any great moment, and his references throughout are abundant. But the practice of references in the side margin, though warranted by high authority, is unfavorable, from want of room, for very frequent or very minute specification.

The omission of notes we consider a still greater evil. It is true, they lead to great abuses, are often the vehicle of matter which should have been incorporated in the text, more frequently of irrelevant matter which should not have been admitted anywhere, and thus exhaust the reader's patience, while they spoil the effect of the work by drawing the attention from the continuous flow of the narrative, checking the heat that is raised by it in the reader's mind, and not unfrequently jarring on his feelings by some misplaced witticism, or smart attempt at one. For these and the like reasons, many competent critics have pronounced against the use of notes, considering that a writer who could not bring all he had to say into the compass of his text was a bungler. Gibbon, who practiced the contrary, intimates a regret in one of his letters that he had been over-ruled so far as to allow his notes to be printed at the bottom of the page instead of being removed to the end of the volume. But from all this we dissent, especially in reference to a work of research like the present History. We are often desirous here to have the assertion of the author, or the sentiment quoted by him, if important, verified by the original extract, especially when this is in a foreign language. We want to see the grounds of his conclusions, the scaffolding by which he has raised his structure; to estimate the true value of his authorities; to know something of their characters, positions in society, and the probable influences to which they were exposed. Where there is contradiction, we want to see it stated; the *pros* and the *cons*, and the grounds for rejecting this and admitting that. We want to have a reason for our faith, otherwise we are merely led blindfold. Our guide may be an excellent guide; he may have traveled over the path till it has become a beaten track to him; but we like to use our own eyesight too, to observe somewhat for ourselves, and to know, if possible, why he has taken this particular road in preference to that which his predecessors have traveled.

The objections made to notes are founded rather on the abuse than the proper use of them. Gibbon only wished to remove his own to the end of his volume; though in this we think he erred, from the difficulty and frequent disappointment which the reader must have experienced in consulting them—a disappointment of little moment when unattended by difficulty. But Gibbon knew too well the worth of this part of his labors to him to wish to discard them altogether. He knew his reputation stood on them as intimately as on his narrative. Indeed, they supply a body of criticism, and well-selected, well-digested learning, which of itself would make the reputation of any scholar. Many accomplished writers, however, and Mr. Bancroft among the number, have come to a different conclusion; and he has formed his, probably, with deliberation, having made the experiment in both forms.

It is true, the fullness of the extracts from original sources with which his text is inlaid, giving such life and presence to it, and the frequency of his references, supersede much of the necessity of notes. We should have been very glad of one, however, of the kind we are speaking of, at the close of his expedition of La Salle.

[GACHARD AND GROEN]
From *Philip the Second*, Bk. III, chap. vi

[In his very full footnotes and in brief bibliographical essays at the close of a number of chapters or books, Prescott discusses at length the work of the historians who have been his main authorities. In these discussions Prescott, while acknowledging his indebtedness, also reveals his differences with these authorities in a calm weighing of their virtues and their deficiencies. The four selections that follow are good illustrations of Prescott's method of evaluating his historical sources.]

In the part of this History which relates to the Netherlands, I have been greatly indebted to two eminent scholars of that country. The first of these, M. Gachard, who has the care of the royal archives of Belgium, was commissioned by his government, in 1844, to visit the Peninsula for the purpose of collecting materials for the illustration of the national history. The most important theatre of his labors was Simancas, which, till the time of his visit, had been carefully closed to natives as well as foreigners. M. Gachard profited by the more liberal arrangements which, under certain restrictions, opened its historical treasures to the student. The result of his labors he is now giving to the world by the publication of his "Correspondance de Philippe II.," of which two volumes have already been printed. The work is published in a beautiful form, worthy of the auspices under which it has appeared. It consists chiefly of the correspondence carried on by the Spanish government and the authorities of the Netherlands in the reign of Philip the Second,—the revolutionary age, and of course the most eventful period of their history. The official despatches, written in French, are, it is true, no longer to be found in Simancas, whence they were removed to Brussels on the accession of Albert and Isabella to the sovereignty of the Low Countries. But a large mass of correspondence which passed between the court of Castile and the Netherlands is still preserved in the Spanish archives. As it is, for the most part, of a confidential nature, containing strictures on men and things intended only for the eyes of the parties to it, it is of infinite value to the historian. Not only has it never before been published, but, with the exception of a portion which passed under the review of the Italian Strada, it has never been submitted to the inspection of the scholar. With the aid of this rich collection, the historian is enabled to enter into many details, hitherto unknown, of a personal nature, relating to the actors in the great drama of the revolution, as well as to disclose some of the secret springs of their policy.

M. Gachard has performed his editorial duties with conscientiousness and ability. In a subsequent volume he proposes to give the entire text of the more important letters; but in the two already published he has confined himself to an analysis of their contents, more or less extended, according to circumstances. He has added explanatory notes, and prefixed to the whole a copious dissertation, presenting a view of the politics of the Castilian court, and of the characters of the king and the great officers of state. As the writer's information is derived from sources the most authentic as well as the least accessible to scholars, his preliminary essay deserves to be carefully studied by the historian of the Netherlands.

M. Gachard has further claims to the gratitude of every lover of letters by various contributions in other forms which he has made to the illustration of the national history. Among these his "Correspondance de Guillaume le Taciturne," of which three volumes in octavo have already appeared, has been freely used by me. It consists of a collection of William's correspondence, industriously gathered from various quarters. The letters differ from one another as widely in value as might naturally be expected in so large and miscellaneous a collection.

The other scholar by whose editorial labors I have profited in this part of my work is M. Groen van Prinsterer. His voluminous publication, "Archives de la Maison d'Orange-Nassau," the first series of which embraces the times of William the Silent, is derived from the private collection of the king of Holland. The contents are various, but consist chiefly of letters from persons who took a prominent part in the conduct of affairs. Their correspondence embraces a miscellaneous range of topics, and with those of public interest combines others strictly personal in their details, thus bringing into strong relief the characters of the most eminent actors on the great political theatre. A living interest attaches to this correspondence, which we shall look for in vain in the colder pages of the historian. History gives us the acts, but letters like these, in which the actors speak for themselves, give us the thoughts, of the individual.

M. Groen has done his part of the work well, adhering to the original text with scrupulous fidelity, and presenting us the letters in the various languages in which they were written. The interstices, so to speak, between the different parts of the correspondence, are skillfully filled up by the editor, so as to connect the incongruous materials into a well-compacted fabric. In conducting what, as far as he is concerned, may be termed the original part of his work, the editor has shown much discretion, gathering information from collateral contemporary sources; and, by the sidelights he has thus thrown over the path, he has greatly facilitated the progress of the student and enabled him to take a survey of the whole historical ground. The editor is at no pains to conceal his own opinions; and we have no difficulty in determining the religious sect to which he belongs. But it is not the less true that he is ready to render justice to the opinions of others, and that he is entitled to the praise of having executed his task with impartiality.

One may notice a peculiarity in the criticisms of both Groen and Gachard, the more remarkable considering the nations to which they belong; that is, the solicitude they manifest to place the most favorable construction on the conduct of Philip, and to vindicate his memory from the wholesale charges so often brought against him, of a systematic attempt to overturn the liberties of the Netherlands. The reader, even should he not always feel the cogency of their arguments, will not refuse his admiration to the candor of the critics.

There is a third publication, recently issued from the press in Brussels, which contains, in the compass of a single volume, materials of much importance for the history of the Netherlands. This is the "Correspondance de Marguerite d'Autriche," by the late Baron Reiffenberg. It is a part of the French correspondence which, as I have mentioned above, was transferred, in the latter part of Philip the Second's reign, from Simancas to Brussels, but which, instead of remaining there, was removed, after the country had passed under the Austrian scepter, to the imperial library of Vienna, where it exists, in all probability, at the present day. Some fragments of this correspondence escaped the fate which attended the bulk of it; and it is gleanings from these which Reiffenberg has given to the world.

That country is fortunate which can command the services of such men as these for the illustration of its national annals,—men who with singular enthusiasm for their task combine the higher qualifications of scholarship, and a talent for critical analysis. By their persevering labors the rich ore has been drawn from the mines where it had lain in darkness for ages. It now waits only for the hand of the artist to convert it into coin and give it a popular currency.

[COUNT ADOLPHE DE CIRCOURT]

From *Philip the Second*, Bk. V, chap. viii

[From a bibliographical essay in a chapter devoted to the rebellion of the Moriscoes. Prescott's correspondence shows that he thought highly of Circourt as an authority and that he deeply appreciated that historian's encouragement. See *Correspondence*, especially p. 176.]

The most comprehensive and by far the most able history of the Moors of Spain with which I am acquainted is that of the Count Adolphe de Circourt,—"*Histoire des Arabes en Espagne.*" Beginning with the beginning, the author opens his narrative with the conquest of the Peninsula by the Moslems. He paints in glowing colors the magnificent empire of the Spanish caliphs. He dwells with sufficient minuteness on those interminable feuds which, growing out of a diversity of races and tribes, baffled every attempt at a permanent consolidation under one government. Then comes the famous war of Granada, with the conquest of the country by the "Catholic Kings"; and the work closes with the sad tale of the subsequent fortunes of the conquered races until their final expulsion from the Peninsula. Thus the rapidly shifting scenes of this most picturesque drama,

sketched by a master's hand, are brought in regular succession
before the eye of the reader.

In conducting his long story, the author, far from confining
himself to a dry record of events, diligently explores the causes
of these events. He scrutinizes with care every inch of debatable ground which lies in his path. He enriches his narrative
with copious disquisitions on the condition of the arts, and
the progress made by the Spanish Arabs in science and letters,
thus presenting a complete view of that peculiar civilization
which so curiously blended together the characteristic elements of European and Oriental culture.

If, in pursuing his speculations, M. de Circourt may be sometimes thought to refine too much, it cannot be denied that they
are distinguished by candor and by a philosophical spirit. Even
when we may differ from his conclusions, we must allow that
they are the result of careful study and display an independent
way of thinking. I may regret that in one important instance—
the policy of the government of Ferdinand and Isabella—he
should have been led to dissent from the opinions which I had
expressed in my history of those sovereigns. It is possible
that the predilection which the writer, whether historian or
novelist, naturally feels for his hero when his conduct affords
any ground for it, may have sometimes seduced me from the
strict line of impartiality in my estimate of character and motives
of action. I see, however, no reason to change the conclusions
at which I had arrived after a careful study of the subject. Yet
I cannot deny that the labors of the French historian have shed
a light upon more than one obscure passage in the administration of Ferdinand and Isabella, for which the student of Spanish
history owes him a debt of gratitude.

[LAS CASAS]

From *The Conquest of Mexico*, Bk. II, chap. viii

[Las Casas was little known to the reader of English and
Prescott felt justified in discussing at length the good Bishop's
long career and his writings.]

The state of the colonies became a common topic of discussion, not only in the council, but in the court; and the representations of Las Casas made an impression that manifested itself in the change of sentiment more clearly every day. He promoted this by the publication of some of his writings at this time, and especially of his "Brevísima Relacion," or Short Account of the Destruction of the Indies, in which he sets before the reader the manifold atrocities committed by his countrymen in different parts of the New World in the prosecution of their conquests. It is a tale of woe. Every line of the work may be said to be written in blood. However good the motives of its author, we may regret that the book was ever written. He would have been certainly right not to spare his countrymen; to exhibit their misdeeds in their true colors, and by this appalling picture —for such it would have been—to have recalled the nation, and those who governed it, to a proper sense of the iniquitous career it was pursuing on the other side of the water. But, to produce a more striking effect, he has lent a willing ear to every tale of violence and rapine, and magnified the amount to a degree which borders on the ridiculous. The wild extravagance of his numerical estimates is of itself sufficient to shake confidence in the accuracy of his statements generally. Yet the naked truth was too startling in itself to demand the aid of exaggeration. The book found great favor with foreigners; was rapidly translated into various languages, and ornamented with characteristic designs, which seemed to put into action all the recorded atrocities of the text. It excited somewhat different feelings in his own countrymen, particularly the people of the colonies, who considered themselves the subjects of a gross, however undesigned, misrepresentation; and, in his future intercourse with them, it contributed, no doubt, to diminish his influence and consequent usefulness, by the spirit of alienation, and even resentment, which it engendered.

Las Casas' honest intentions, his enlightened views and long experience, gained him deserved credit at home. This was visible in the important regulations made at this time for the better government of the colonies, and particularly in respect to the Aborigines. A code of laws, *Las Nuevas Leyes*, was passed, having for their avowed object the enfranchisement of this unfortunate race; and, in the wisdom and humanity of its provisions, it is easy to recognize the hand of the Protector of the Indians. The history of Spanish colonial legislation is the history of the impotent struggles of the government in behalf of the natives, against the avarice and cruelty of its subjects. It proves that an empire powerful at home—and Spain then was so—may be so widely extended, that its authority shall scarcely be felt in its extremities.

The government testified their sense of the signal services of Las Casas, by promoting him to the bishopric of Cuzco, one of the richest sees in the colonies. But the disinterested soul of the missionary did not covet riches or preferment. He rejected the proffered dignity without hesitation. Yet he could not refuse the bishopric of Chiapa, a country, which, from the poverty and ignorance of its inhabitants, offered a good field for his spiritual labors. In 1544, though at the advanced age of seventy, he took upon himself these new duties, and embarked, for the fifth and last time, for the shores of America. His fame had preceded him. The colonists looked on his coming with apprehension, regarding him as the real author of the new code, which struck at their ancient immunities, and which he would be likely to enforce to the letter. Everywhere he was received with coldness. In some places his person was menaced with violence. But the venerable presence of the prelate, his earnest expostulations, which flowed so obviously from conviction, and his generous self-devotion, so regardless of personal considerations, preserved him from this outrage. Yet he showed no disposition to conciliate his opponents by what he deemed an unworthy concession; and he even stretched the arm of authority so far as to refuse the sacraments to any, who still held an Indian in bondage. This high-handed measure not only outraged the planters, but incurred the disapprobation of his own brethren in the Church. Three years were spent in disagreeable altercation without coming to any decision. The Spaniards, to borrow their accustomed phraseology on these occasions, "obeying the law, but not fulfilling it," applied to the Court for further instruction; and the bishop, no longer supported by his own brethren, thwarted by the colonial magistrates, and outraged by the people, relinquished a post where his presence could be no further useful, and returned to spend the remainder of his days in tranquillity at home.

Yet, though withdrawn to his Dominican convent, he did not pass his hours in slothful seclusion. He again appeared as the champion of Indian freedom in the famous controversy with Sepulveda, one of the most acute scholars of the time, and far surpassing Las Casas in elegance and correctness of composition. But the Bishop of Chiapa was his superior in argument, at least in this discussion, where he had right and reason on his side. In his "Thirty Propositions," as they are called, in which he sums up the several points of his case, he maintains, that the circumstance of infidelity in religion cannot deprive a nation of its political rights; that the Holy See, in its grant of the New World to the Catholic sovereigns, designed only to confer the right of converting its inhabitants to Christianity, and of thus winning a peaceful authority over them; and that no authority could be valid, which rested on other foundations. This was striking at the root of the colonial empire, as assumed by Castile. But the disinterested views of Las Casas, the respect entertained for his principles, and the general conviction, it may be, of the force of his arguments, prevented the Court from taking umbrage at their import, or from pressing them to their legitimate conclusion. While the writings of his adversary were interdicted from publication, he had the satisfaction to see his own printed and circulated in every quarter.

From this period his time was distributed among his religious duties, his studies, and the composition of his works, especially his History. His constitution, naturally excellent, had been strengthened by a life of temperance and toil; and he retained his faculties unimpaired to the last. He died after a short illness, July, 1566, at the great age of ninety-two, in his monastery at Atocha, at Madrid.

The character of Las Casas may be inferred from his career.

He was one of those, to whose gifted minds are revealed those glorious moral truths, which, like the lights of heaven, are fixed and the same forever; but which, though now familiar, were hidden from all but a few penetrating intellects by the general darkness of the time in which he lived. He was a reformer, and had the virtues and errors of a reformer. He was inspired by one great and glorious idea. This was the key to all his thoughts, all that he said and wrote, to every act of his long life. It was this which urged him to lift the voice of rebuke in the presence of princes, to brave the menaces of an infuriated populace, to cross seas, to traverse mountains and deserts, to incur the alienation of friends, the hostility of enemies, to endure obloquy, insult, and persecution. It was this, too, which made him reckless of obstacles, led him to count too confidently on the coöperation of others, animated his discussion, sharpened his invective, too often steeped his pen in the gall of personal vituperation, led him into gross exaggeration and over-coloring in his statements, and a blind credulity of evil that rendered him unsafe as a counsellor, and unsuccessful in the practical concerns of life. His motives were pure and elevated. But his manner of enforcing them was not always so commendable. This may be gathered not only from the testimony of the colonists generally, who, as parties interested, may be supposed to have been prejudiced; but from that of the members of his own profession, persons high in office, and of integrity beyond suspicion, not to add that of missionaries engaged in the same good work with himself. These, in their letters and reported conversations, charged the Bishop of Chiapa with an arrogant, uncharitable temper, which deluded his judgment, and vented itself in unwarrantable crimination against such as resisted his projects, or differed from him in opinion. Las Casas, in short, was a man. But, if he had the errors of humanity, he had virtues that rarely belong to it. The best commentary on his character is the estimation which he obtained in the court of his sovereign. A liberal pension was settled on him after his last return from America, which he chiefly expended on charitable objects. No measure of importance, relating to the Indians, was taken without his advice. He lived to see the fruits of his efforts in the positive amelioration of their condition, and in the popular admission of those great truths which it had been the object of his life to unfold. And who shall say how much of the successful efforts and arguments since made in behalf of persecuted humanity may be traced to the example and the writings of this illustrious philanthropist?

His compositions were numerous, most of them of no great length. Some were printed in his time; others have since appeared, especially in the French translation of Llorente. His great work, which occupied him at intervals for more than thirty years, the *Historia General de las Indias*, still remains in manuscript. It is in three volumes, divided into as many parts, and embraces the colonial history from the discovery of the country by Columbus to the year 1520. The style of the work, like that of all his writings, is awkward, disjointed, and excessively diffuse; abounding in repetitions, irrelevant digressions, and pedantic citations. But it is sprinkled over with passages of a different kind; and, when he is roused by the desire to exhibit some gross wrong to the natives, his simple language kindles into eloquence, and he expounds those great and immutable principles of natural justice, which, in his own day, were so little understood. His defect as a historian is, that he wrote history, like everything else, under the influence of one dominant idea. He is always pleading the cause of the persecuted native. This gives a coloring to events which passed under his own eyes, and filled him with a too easy confidence in those which he gathered from the reports of others. Much of the preceding portion of our narrative which relates to affairs in Cuba must have come under his personal observation. But he seems incapable of shaking off his early deference to Velasquez, who, as we have noticed, treated him, while a poor curate in the island, with peculiar confidence. For Cortés, on the other hand, he appears to have felt a profound contempt. He witnessed the commencement of his career, when he was standing, cap in hand, as it were, at the proud governor's door, thankful even for a smile of recognition. Las Casas remembered all this, and, when he saw the Conqueror of Mexico rise into a glory and renown that threw his former patron into the shade,—and most unfairly, as Las Casas deemed, at the expense of that patron,—the good bishop could not withhold his indignation; nor speak of him otherwise than with a sneer, as a mere upstart adventurer.

It was the existence of defects like these, and the fear of the misconception likely to be produced by them, that have so long prevented the publication of his history. At his death, he left it to the convent of San Gregorio, at Valladolid, with directions that it should not be printed for forty years, nor be seen during that time by any layman or member of the fraternity. Herrera, however, was permitted to consult it, and he liberally transferred its contents to his own volumes, which appeared in 1601. The Royal Academy of History revised the first volume of Las Casas some years since, with a view to the publication of the whole work. But the indiscreet and imaginative style of the composition, according to Navarrete, and the consideration that its most important facts were already known through other channels, induced that body to abandon the design. With deference to their judgment, it seems to me a mistake. Las Casas, with every deduction, is one of the great writers of the nation; great from the important truths which he discerned when none else could see them, and from the courage with which he proclaimed them to the world. They are scattered over his History as well as his other writings. They are not, however, the passages transcribed by Herrera. In the statement of fact, too, however partial and prejudiced, no one will impeach his integrity; and, as an enlightened contemporary, his evidence is of undeniable value. It is due to the memory of Las Casas, that, if his work be given to the public at all, it should not be through the garbled extracts of one who was no fair interpreter of his opinions. Las Casas does not speak for himself in the courtly pages of Herrera. Yet the History should not be published without a suitable commentary to enlighten the student, and guard him against any undue prejudices in the writer. We may hope that the entire manuscript will one day be given to the world under the auspices of that distinguished body, which has already done so much in this way for the illustration of the national annals.

The life of Las Casas has been several times written. The two memoirs most worthy of notice are that by Llorente, late Secretary of the Inquisition, prefixed to his French translation of the Bishop's controversial writings, and that by Quintana, in the third volume of his "Españoles Célebres," where it presents a truly noble specimen of biographical composition, enriched by a literary criticism as acute as it is candid.—I have gone to the greater length in this notice, from the interesting character of the man, and the little that is known of him to the English reader. I have also transferred a passage from his work in the original to the Appendix, that the Spanish scholar may form an idea of his style of composition. He ceases to be an authority for us hereafter, as his account of the expedition of Cortés terminates with the destruction of the navy.

[SOLÍS]

From *The Conquest of Mexico*, Bk. VI, chap. viii

[Prescott pays tribute to a distinguished predecessor in the field of Mexican historiography, although he notes, too, his limitations. This is one of the best criticisms of an authoritative source to be found in the whole of Prescott's works.]

Some of the most distinguished of the national historiographers, as, for example, Herrera and Zurita, two of the greatest names in Castile and Aragon, fall under this censure. They display acuteness, strength of argument, judicious criticism, wonderful patience and industry in accumulating details for their varied and voluminous compilations; but in all the graces of composition,—in elegance of style, skillful arrangement of the story, and in selection of incidents, they are lamentably deficient. With all their high merits, intellectually considered, they are so defective on the score of art, that they can neither be popular, nor reverenced as the great classics of the nation.

Solís saw that the field was unappropriated by his predecessors, and had the address to avail himself of it. Instead of spreading himself over a vast range, where he must expend his efforts on cold and barren generalities, he fixed his attention on one great theme,—one, that, by its picturesque accompaniments, the romantic incidents of the story, the adventurous character of the actors, and their exploits, associated with many a proud and patriotic feeling in the bosom of the Spaniard,—one, in fine, that, by the brilliant contrast it afforded of European civilization to the barbaric splendors of an Indian dynasty, was remarkably suited to the kindling imagination of the poet. It was accordingly under its poetic aspect, that the eye of Solís surveyed it. He distributed the whole subject with admirable skill, keeping down the subordinate parts, bringing the most important into high relief, and, by a careful study of its proportions, giving an admirable symmetry to the whole. Instead of bewildering the attention by a variety of objects, he presented to it one great and predominant idea, which shed its light, if I may so say, over his whole work. Instead of the numerous episodes, leading, like so many blind galleries, to nothing, he took the student along a great road, conducting straight towards the mark. At every step which we take in the narrative, we feel ourselves on the advance. The story never falters or stands still. That admirable *liaison* of the parts is maintained, by which one part is held to another, and each preceding event prepares the way for that which is to follow. Even those occasional interruptions, the great stumbling-block of the historian, which cannot be avoided, in consequence of the important bearing which the events that cause them have on the story, are managed with such address, that, if the interest is suspended, it is never snapped. Such halting-places, indeed, are so contrived, as to afford a repose not unwelcome after the stirring scenes in which the reader has been long involved; as the traveler, exhausted by the fatigues of his journey, finds refreshment at places, which, in their own character, have little to recommend them.

The work, thus conducted, affords the interest of a grand spectacle,—of some well-ordered drama, in which scene succeeds to scene, act to act, each unfolding and preparing the mind for the one that is to follow, until the whole is consummated by the grand and decisive *dénouement*. With this *dénouement*, the fall of Mexico, Solís has closed his history, preferring to leave the full impression unbroken on the reader's mind, rather than to weaken it by prolonging the narrative to the Conqueror's death. In this he certainly consulted effect.

Solís used the same care in regard to style, that he showed in the arrangement of his story. It is elaborated with nicest art, and displays that varied beauty and brilliancy which remind us of those finely variegated woods, which, under a high polish, display all the rich tints that lie beneath the surface. Yet this style finds little favor with foreign critics, who are apt to condemn it as tumid, artificial, and verbose. But let the foreign critic beware how he meddles with style, that impalpable essence which surrounds thought as with an atmosphere, giving to it its life and peculiar tone of color, differing in different nations, like the atmospheres which envelop the different planets of our system, and which require to be comprehended, that we may interpret the character of the objects seen through their medium. None but a native can pronounce with any confidence upon style, affected, as it is, by so many casual and local associations, that determine its propriety and its elegance. In the judgment of eminent Spanish critics, the style of Solís claims the merits of perspicuity, copiousness, and classic elegance. Even the foreigner will not be insensible to its power of conveying a living picture to the eye. Words are the colors of the writer, and Solís uses them with the skill of a consummate artist; now displaying the dark tumult of battle, and now refreshing the mind by scenes of quiet magnificence, or of soft luxury and repose.

Solís formed himself, to some extent, on the historical models of Antiquity. He introduced set speeches into the mouths of his personages, speeches of his own composing. The practice may claim high authority among moderns as well as ancients, especially among the great Italian historians. It has its advantages, in enabling the writer to convey, in a dramatic form, the sentiments of the actors, and thus to maintain the charm of historic illusion by never introducing the person of the historian. It has also another advantage, that of exhibiting the author's own sentiments under cover of his hero's,—a more effective mode than if they were introduced as his own. But, to one trained in the school of the great English historians, the practice has something in it unsatisfactory and displeasing. There is something like deception in it. The reader is unable to determine what are the sentiments of the characters and what those of the author. History assumes the air of romance, and the bewildered student wanders about in an uncertain light, doubtful whether he is treading on fact or fiction.

It is open to another objection, when, as it frequently does, it violates the propriety of costume. Nothing is more difficult than to preserve the keeping of the piece, when the new is thus laid on the old,—the imitation of the antique on the antique itself. The declamations of Solís are much prized as specimens of eloquence. But they are too often misplaced; and the rude characters, into whose mouths they are inserted, are as little in keeping with them, as were the Roman heroes with the fashionable wig and sword, with which they strutted on the French stage in Louis the Fourteenth's time.

As to the value of the researches made by Solís in the compilation of his work it is not easy to speak, for the page is supported by none of the notes and references which enable us to track the modern author to the quarry whence he has drawn his materials. It was not the usage of the age. The people of that day, and, indeed, of preceding times, were content to take the author's word for his facts. They did not require to know why he affirmed this thing or doubted that; whether he built his story on the authority of a friend, or of a foe, of a writer of good report, or of evil report. In short, they did not demand a reason for their faith. They were content to take it on trust. This was very comfortable to the historian. It saved him a world of trouble in the process, and it prevented the detection of error, or, at least, of negligence. It prevented it with all who did not carefully go over the same ground with himself. They who have occasion to do this with Solís will probably arise from the examination with no very favorable idea of the extent of his researches; they will find, that, though his situation gave him access to the most valuable repositories in the kingdom, he rarely ascends to original documents, but contents himself with the most obvious and accessible; that he rarely discriminates between the contemporary testimony, and that of later date; in a word, that, in all that constitutes the *scientific* value of history, he falls far below his learned predecessor, Herrera,—rapid as was the composition of this last.

Another objection that may be made to Solís is his bigotry, or rather his fanaticism. This defect, so repugnant to the philosophic spirit which should preside over the labors of the historian, he possessed, it is true, in common with many of his countrymen. But in him it was carried to an uncommon height; and it was peculiarly unfortunate, since his subject, being the contest between the Christian and the Infidel, naturally drew forth the full display of this failing. Instead of regarding the benighted heathen with the usual measure of aversion in which they were held in the Peninsula, after the subjugation of Granada, he considered them as part of the grand confederacy of Satan, not merely breathing the spirit and acting under the invisible influence of the Prince of Darkness, but holding personal communication with him; he seems to have regarded them, in short, as his regular and organized militia. In this view, every act of the unfortunate enemy was a crime. Even good acts were misrepresented, or referred to evil motives; for how could goodness originate with the Spirit of Evil? No better evidence of the results of this way of thinking need be given, than that afforded by the ill-favored and unauthorized portrait which the historian has left us of Montezuma,—even in his dying hours. The war of the Conquest was, in short, in the historian's eye, a conflict between light and darkness, between the good principle and the evil principle, between the soldiers of Satan and the chivalry of the Cross. It was a Holy War, in which the sanctity of the cause covered up the sins of the Conquerors; and every one—the meanest soldier who fell in it—might aspire to the crown of martyrdom. With sympathies thus preoccupied, what room was there for that impartial criticism which is the life of history?

The historian's overweening partiality to the Conquerors is still further heightened by those feelings of patriotism,—a bastard patriotism,—which, identifying the writer's own glory with that of his countrymen, makes him blind to their errors. This partiality is especially shown in regard to Cortés, the hero of the piece. The lights and shadows of the picture are all disposed with reference to this principal character. The good is ostentatiously paraded before us, and the bad is winked out of sight. Solís does not stop here, but, by the artful gloss which makes the worse appear the better cause, he calls on us to admire his hero sometimes for his very transgressions. No one, not even Gomara himself, is such a wholesale encomiast of the great Conqueror; and, when his views are contradicted by the statements of honest Diaz, Solís is sure to find a motive for the discrepancy in some sinister purpose of the veteran. He knows more of Cortés, of his actions and his motives, than his companion in arms, or his admiring chaplain.

In this way Solís has presented a beautiful image of his hero, —but it is a hero of romance; a character without a blemish. An eminent Castilian critic has commended him for "having conducted his history with so much art, that it has become a panegyric." This may be true; but, if history be panegyric, panegyric is not history.

Yet, with all these defects,—the existence of which no candid critic will be disposed to deny,—the History of Solís has found such favor with his own countrymen, that it has been printed and reprinted, with all the refinements of editorial luxury. It has been translated into the principal languages of Europe; and such is the charm of its composition, and its exquisite finish as a work of art, that it will doubtless be as imperishable as the language in which it is written, or the memory of the events which it records.

At this place, also, we are to take leave of father Sahagun, who has accompanied us through our narrative. As his information was collected from the traditions of the natives, the contemporaries of the Conquest, it has been of considerable importance in corroborating or contradicting the statements of the Conquerors. Yet its value in this respect is much impaired by the wild and random character of many of the Aztec traditions,—so absurd, indeed, as to carry their own refutation with them. Where the passions are enlisted, what is too absurd to find credit?

The Twelfth Book—as it would appear from his Preface, the Ninth Book originally—of his *Historia de la Nueva España* is devoted to the account of the Conquest. In 1585, thirty years after the first draft, he rewrote this part of his great work, moved to it, as he tells us, "by the desire to correct the defects of the first account, in which some things had found their way that had better been omitted, and other things omitted which were well deserving of record." It might be supposed, that the obloquy, which the missionary had brought on his head by his honest recital of the Aztec traditions, would have made him more circumspect in this *rifacimento* of his former narrative. But I have not found it so; or that there has been any effort to mitigate the statements that bore hardest on his countrymen. As this manuscript copy must have been that which the author himself deemed the most correct, since it is his last revision, and as it is more copious than the printed narrative, I have been usually guided by it.

Señor de Bustamante is mistaken in supposing that the edition of this Twelfth Book, which he published in Mexico, in 1829, is from the *reformed* copy of Sahagun. The manuscript cited in these pages is undoubtedly a transcript of that copy. For in the Preface to it, as we have seen, the author himself declares it.—In the intrinsic value of the two drafts there is, after all, but little difference.

II. PHILOSOPHICAL REFLECTIONS

[EFFECTS OF RELIGIOUS FANATICISM]

From *Philip the Second*, Bk. II, chap. iii

[Prescott's concluding reflections on the persecution of Spanish Protestants. It was a characteristic of Prescott as of other contemporary historians critical of religious fanaticism to make sententious remarks by way of pronouncing benediction or malediction on the events and characters described.]

Never was there a persecution which did its work more thoroughly. The blood of the martyr is commonly said to be the seed of the church. But the storm of persecution fell as heavily on the Spanish Protestants as it did on the Albigenses in the thirteenth century, blighting every living thing, so that no germ remained for future harvests. Spain might now boast that the stain of heresy no longer defiled the hem of her garment. But at what a price was this purchased! Not merely by the sacrifice of the lives and fortunes of a few thousands of the existing generation, but by the disastrous consequences entailed forever on the country. Folded under the dark wing of the Inquisition, Spain was shut out from the light which in the sixteenth century broke over the rest of Europe, stimulating the nations to greater enterprise in every department of knowledge. The genius of the people was rebuked, and their spirit quenched, under the malignant influence of an eye that never slumbered, of an unseen arm ever raised to strike. How could there be freedom of thought, where there was no freedom of utterance? Or freedom of utterance, where it was as dangerous to say too little as too much? Freedom cannot go along with fear. Every way the mind of the Spaniard was in fetters.

His moral sense was miserably perverted. Men were judged, not by their practice, but by their professions. Creed became a substitute for conduct. Difference of faith made a wider gulf of separation than difference of race, language, or even interest.

Spain no longer formed one of the great brotherhood of Christian nations. An immeasurable barrier was raised between that kingdom and the Protestant states of Europe. The early condition of perpetual warfare with the Arabs who overran the country had led the Spaniards to mingle religion strangely with their politics. The effect continued when the cause had ceased. Their wars with the European nations became religious wars. In fighting England or the Netherlands, they were fighting the enemies of God. It was the same everywhere. In their contest with the unoffending natives of the New World they were still battling with the enemies of God. Their wars took the character of a perpetual crusade, and were conducted with all the ferocity which fanaticism could inspire.

The same dark spirit of fanaticism seems to brood over the national literature,—even that lighter literature which in other nations is made up of the festive sallies of wit or the tender expression of sentiment. The greatest geniuses of the nation, the masters of the drama and of the ode, while they astonish us by their miracles of invention, show that they have too often kindled their inspiration at the altars of the Inquisition.

Debarred as he was from freedom of speculation, the domain of science was closed against the Spaniard. Science looks to perpetual change. It turns to the past to gather warning, as well as instruction, for the future. Its province is to remove old abuses, to explode old errors, to unfold new truths. Its condition, in short, is that of progress. But in Spain, everything not only looked to the past, but rested on the past. Old abuses gathered respect from their antiquity. Reform was innovation, and innovation was a crime. Far from progress, all was stationary. The hand of the Inquisition drew the line which said, "No further!" This was the limit of human intelligence in Spain.

The effect was visible in every department of science,—not in the speculative alone, but in the physical and the practical; in the declamatory rant of its theology and ethics, in the childish and chimerical schemes of its political economists. In every walk were to be seen the symptoms of premature decrepitude, as the nation clung to the antiquated systems which the march of civilization in other countries had long since effaced. Hence those frantic experiments, so often repeated, in the financial administration of the kingdom, which made Spain the byword of the nations, and which ended in the ruin of trade, the prostration of credit, and finally the bankruptcy of the state. But we willingly turn from this sad picture of the destinies of the country to a more cheerful scene in the history of Philip.

[COMPARISON OF CIVILIZATIONS]
From *The Conquest of Peru*, Bk. II, chap. i

[An example of Prescott's familiar custom of inserting asides on the relative merits of Anglo-Saxon and Spanish culture. The balance generally favors Anglo-Saxon Protestantism.]

The character of the warrior took somewhat of the exaggerated coloring shed over his exploits. Proud and vainglorious, swelled with lofty anticipations of his destiny, and an invincible confidence in his own resources, no danger could appall and no toil could tire him. The greater the danger, indeed, the higher the charm; for his soul revelled in excitement, and the enterprise without peril wanted that spur of romance which was necessary to rouse his energies into action. Yet in the motives of action meaner influences were strangely mingled with the loftier, the temporal with the spiritual. Gold was the incentive and the recompense, and in the pursuit of it his inflexible nature rarely hesitated as to the means. His courage was sullied with cruelty, the cruelty that flowed equally—strange as it may seem—from his avarice and his religion; religion as it was understood in that age,—the religion of the Crusader. It was the convenient cloak for a multitude of sins, which covered them even from himself. The Castilian, too proud for hypocrisy, committed more cruelties in the name of religion than were ever practiced by the pagan idolater or the fanatical Moslem. The burning of the infidel was a sacrifice acceptable to Heaven, and the conversion of those who survived amply atoned for the foulest offenses.

It is a melancholy and mortifying consideration, that the most uncompromising spirit of intolerance—the spirit of the Inquisitor at home, and of the Crusader abroad—should have emanated from a religion which preached peace upon earth and good-will towards man!

What a contrast did these children of Southern Europe present to the Anglo-Saxon races who scattered themselves along the great northern division of the western hemisphere! For the principle of action with these latter was not avarice, nor the more specious pretext of proselytism; but independence—independence religious and political. To secure this, they were content to earn a bare subsistence by a life of frugality and toil. They asked nothing from the soil, but the reasonable returns of their own labor. No golden visions threw a deceitful halo around their path, and beckoned them onwards through seas of blood to the subversion of an unoffending dynasty. They were content with the slow but steady progress of their social polity. They patiently endured the privations of the wilderness, watering the tree of liberty with their tears and with the sweat of their brow, till it took deep root in the land and sent up its branches high towards the heavens; while the communities of the neighboring continent, shooting up into the sudden splendors of a tropical vegetation, exhibited, even in their prime, the sure symptoms of decay.

It would seem to have been especially ordered by Providence that the discovery of the two great divisions of the American hemisphere should fall to the two races best fitted to conquer and colonize them. Thus the northern section was consigned to the Anglo-Saxon race, whose orderly, industrious habits found an ample field for development under its colder skies and on its more rugged soil; while the southern portion, with its rich tropical products and treasures of mineral wealth, held out the most attractive bait to invite the enterprise of the Spaniard. How different might have been the result, if the bark of Columbus had taken a more northerly direction, as he at one time meditated, and landed its band of adventurers on the shores of what is now Protestant America!

[CONFLICT OF CIVILIZATIONS]
From *The Conquest of Peru*, Bk. I, chap. v

[This is a part of a general discussion of Peruvian civilization whose high achievements Prescott praises, while condemning its political and economic despotism.]

It is not easy to comprehend the genius and the full import of institutions so opposite to those of our own free republic, where every man, however humble his condition, may aspire to the highest honors of the state,—may select his own career, and carve out his fortune in his own way; where the light of knowledge, instead of being concentrated on a chosen few, is shed abroad like the light of day, and suffered to fall equally on the poor and the rich; where the collision of man with man wakens a generous emulation that calls out latent talent and tasks the energies to the utmost; where consciousness of independence gives a feeling of self-reliance unknown to the timid subjects of a despotism; where, in short, the government is made for man, —not as in Peru, where man seemed to be made only for the government. The New World is the theater in which these two political systems, so opposite in their character, have been carried into operation. The empire of the Incas has passed away and left no trace. The other great experiment is still going on,—the experiment which is to solve the problem, so long contested in the Old World, of the capacity of man for self-government. Alas for humanity, if it should fail!

The testimony of the Spanish conquerors is not uniform in respect to the favorable influence exerted by the Peruvian institutions on the character of the people. Drinking and dancing are said to have been the pleasures to which they were immoderately addicted. Like the slaves and serfs in other lands, whose position excluded them from more serious and ennobling occupations, they found a substitute in frivolous or sensual indulgence. Lazy, luxurious, and licentious, are the epithets bestowed on them by one of those who saw them at the Conquest, but whose pen was not too friendly to the Indian. Yet the spirit of independence could hardly be strong in a people who had no interest in the soil, no personal rights to defend; and the facility with which they yielded to the Spanish invader —after every allowance for their comparative inferiority— argues a deplorable destitution of that patriotic feeling which holds life as little in comparison with freedom.

But we must not judge too hardly of the unfortunate native, because he quailed before the civilization of the European. We must not be insensible to the really great results that were achieved by the government of the Incas. We must not forget, that, under their rule, the meanest of the people enjoyed a far greater degree of personal comfort, at least, a greater exemption from physical suffering, than was possessed by similar classes in other nations on the American continent,—greater, probably, than was possessed by these classes in most of the countries of feudal Europe. Under their scepter, the higher orders of the state had made advances in many of the arts that belong to a cultivated community. The foundations of a regular government were laid, which, in an age of rapine, secured to its subjects the inestimable blessings of tranquillity and safety. By the well-sustained policy of the Incas, the rude tribes of the forest were gradually drawn from their fastnesses, and gathered within the folds of civilization; and of these materials was constructed a flourishing and populous empire, such as was to be found in no other quarter of the American continent. The defects of this government were those of over-refinement in legislation,— the last defects to have been looked for, certainly, in the American aborigines.

[SUPERIORITY OF EUROPEAN TO AZTEC]
From *The Conquest of Mexico*, Bk. VI, chap. viii

[After leading up to his tremendous climax and narrating the fall of the Aztec empire Prescott reads the obsequies, regretting not too deeply its passing. While he might sorrow over cruelties perpetrated by the conquerors he never concealed his belief in the value of the victory of Christianity over paganism.]

Thus, after a siege of nearly three months' duration, unmatched in history for the constancy and courage of the besieged, seldom surpassed for the severity of its sufferings, fell the renowned capital of the Aztecs. Unmatched, it may be truly said, for constancy and courage, when we recollect that the door of capitulation on the most honorable terms was left open to them throughout the whole blockade, and that, sternly rejecting every proposal of their enemy, they, to a man, preferred to die rather than surrender. More than three centuries had elapsed, since the Aztecs, a poor and wandering tribe from the far Northwest had come on the plateau. There they built their miserable collection of huts on the spot—as tradition tells us—prescribed by the oracle. Their conquests, at first confined to their immediate neighborhood, gradually covered the Valley, then, crossing the mountains, swept over the broad extent of the tableland, descended its precipitous sides, and rolled onwards to the Mexican Gulf, and the distant confines of Central America. Their wretched capital, meanwhile, keeping pace with the enlargement of territory, had grown into a flourishing city, filled with buildings, monuments of art, and a numerous population, that gave it the first rank among the capitals of the Western World. At this crisis, came over another race from the remote East, strangers like themselves, whose coming had also been predicted by the oracle, and, appearing on the plateau, assailed them in the very zenith of their prosperity, and blotted them out from the map of nations forever! The whole story has the air of fable, rather than of history! a legend of romance,—a tale of the genii!

Yet we cannot regret the fall of an empire, which did so little to promote the happiness of its subjects, or the real interests of humanity. Notwithstanding the luster thrown over its latter days by the glorious defense of its capital, by the mild munificence of Montezuma, by the dauntless heroism of Guatemozin, the Aztecs were emphatically a fierce and brutal race, little calculated, in their best aspects, to excite our sympathy and regard. Their civilization, such as it was, was not their own, but reflected, perhaps imperfectly, from a race whom they had succeeded in the land. It was, in respect to the Aztecs, a generous graft on a vicious stock, and could have brought no fruit to perfection. They ruled over their wide domains with a sword, instead of a scepter. They did nothing to ameliorate the condition, or in any way promote the progress, of their vassals. Their vassals were serfs, used only to minister to their pleasure, held in awe by armed garrisons, ground to the dust by imposts in peace, by military conscriptions in war. They did not, like the Romans, whom they resembled in the nature of their conquests, extend the rights of citizenship to the conquered. They did not amalgamate them into one great nation, with common rights and interests. They held them as aliens,—even those, who in the Valley were gathered round the very walls of the capital. The Aztec metropolis, the heart of the monarchy, had not a sympathy, not a pulsation, in common with the rest of the body politic. It was a stranger in its own land.

The Aztecs not only did not advance the condition of their vassals, but, morally speaking, they did much to degrade it. How can a nation, where human sacrifices prevail, and especially when combined with cannibalism, further the march of civilization? How can the interests of humanity be consulted, where man is leveled to the rank of the brutes that perish? The influence of the Aztecs introduced their gloomy superstition into lands before unacquainted with it, or where, at least, it was not established in any great strength. The example of the capital was contagious. As the latter increased in opulence, the religious celebrations were conducted with still more terrible magnificence; in the same manner, as the gladiatorial shows of the Romans increased in pomp with the increasing splendor of the capital. Men became familiar with scenes of horror and the most loathsome abominations. Women and children—the whole nation became familiar with, and assisted at them. The heart was hardened, the manners were made ferocious, the feeble light of civilization, transmitted from a milder race, was growing fainter and fainter, as thousands and thousands of miserable victims, throughout the empire, were yearly fattened in its cages, sacrificed on its altars, dressed and served at its banquets! The whole land was converted into a vast human shambles! The empire of the Aztecs did not fall before its time.

Whether these unparalleled outrages furnish a sufficient plea to the Spaniards for their invasion, whether, with the Protestant, we are content to find a warrant for it in the natural rights and demands of civilization, or, with the Roman Catholic, in the good pleasure of the Pope,—on the one or other of which grounds, the conquests by most Christian nations in the East and the West have been defended,—it is unnecessary to discuss, as it has already been considered in a former Chapter. It is more material to inquire, whether, assuming the right, the conquest of Mexico was conducted with a proper regard to the claims of humanity. And here we must admit, that, with all allowance for the ferocity of the age and the laxity of its principles, there are passages which every Spaniard, who cherishes the fame of his countrymen, would be glad to see expunged from their history; passages not to be vindicated on the score of self-defense, or of necessity of any kind, and which must forever leave a dark spot on the annals of the Conquest. And yet, taken as a whole, the invasion, up to the capture of the capital, was conducted on principles less revolting to humanity, than most, perhaps than any, of the other conquests of the Castilian crown in the New World.

It may seem slight praise to say, that the followers of Cortés used no bloodhounds to hunt down their wretched victims, as in some other parts of the Continent, nor exterminated a peaceful and submissive population in mere wantonness of cruelty, as in the Islands. Yet it is something, that they were not so far infected by the spirit of the age, and that their swords were rarely stained with blood, unless it was indispensable to the success of their enterprise. Even in the last siege of the capital, the sufferings of the Aztecs, terrible as they were, do not imply any unusual cruelty in the victors; they were not greater than those inflicted on their own countrymen at home, in many a memorable instance, by the most polished nations, not merely of ancient times, but of our own. They were the inevitable consequences which follow from war, when, instead of being confined to its legitimate field, it is brought home to the hearthstone, to the peaceful community of the city,—its burghers untrained to arms, its women and children yet more defenseless. In the present instance, indeed, the sufferings of the besieged were in a great degree to be charged on themselves,—on their patriotic, but desperate, self-devotion. It was not the desire, as certainly it was not the interest, of the Spaniards, to destroy the capital, or its inhabitants. When any of these fell into their hands, they were kindly entertained, their wants supplied, and every means taken to infuse into them a spirit of conciliation; and this, too, it should be remembered, in despite of the dreadful doom to which they consigned their Christian captives. The gates of a fair capitulation were kept open, though unavailingly, to the last hour.

The right of conquest necessarily implies that of using whatever force may be necessary for overcoming resistance to the assertion of that right. For the Spaniards to have done otherwise than they did would have been to abandon the siege, and, with it, the conquest of the country. To have suffered the inhabitants, with their high-spirited monarch, to escape, would but have prolonged the miseries of war by transferring it to another and more inaccessible quarter. They literally, as far as the success of the expedition was concerned, had no choice. If our imagination is struck with the amount of suffering in this, and in similar scenes of the Conquest, it should be borne in mind, that it is a natural result of the great masses of men engaged in the conflict. The amount of suffering does not of itself show the amount of cruelty which caused it; and it is but justice to the Conquerors of Mexico to say, that the very brilliancy and importance of their exploits have given a melancholy celebrity to their misdeeds, and thrown them into somewhat bolder relief than strictly belongs to them.—It is proper that thus much should be stated, not to excuse their excesses, but that we may be enabled to make a more impartial estimate of their conduct, as compared with that of other nations under similar circumstances, and that we may not visit them with peculiar obloquy for evils which necessarily flow from the condition of war. I have not drawn a veil over these evils; for the historian should not shrink from depicting, in their true colors, the atrocities of a condition, over which success is apt to throw a false halo of glory, but which, bursting asunder the strong bonds of human fellowship, purchases its triumphs by arming the hand of man against his brother, makes a savage of the civilized, and kindles the fires of hell in the bosom of the savage.

Whatever may be thought of the Conquest in a moral view, regarded as a military achievement it must fill us with astonishment. That a handful of adventurers, indifferently armed and equipped, should have landed on the shores of a powerful empire inhabited by a fierce and warlike race, and, in defiance of the reiterated prohibitions of its sovereign, have forced their way into the interior;—that they should have done this, without knowledge of the language or of the land, without chart or compass to guide them, without any idea of the difficulties they were to encounter, totally uncertain whether the next step might bring them on a hostile nation, or on a desert, feeling their way along in the dark, as it were;—that, though nearly overwhelmed by their first encounter with the inhabitants, they should have still pressed on to the capital of the empire, and, having reached it, thrown themselves unhesitatingly into the midst of their enemies;—that, so far from being daunted by the extraordinary spectacle there exhibited of power and civilization, they should have been but the more confirmed in their original design;— that they should have seized the monarch, have executed his ministers before the eyes of his subjects, and, when driven forth with ruin from the gates, have gathered their scattered wreck together, and, after a system of operations, pursued with consummate policy and daring, have succeeded in overturning the capital, and establishing their sway over the country;—that all this should have been so effected by a mere handful of indigent adventurers, is a fact little short of the miraculous,—too startling for the probabilities demanded by fiction, and without a parallel in the pages of history.

Yet this must not be understood too literally; for it would be unjust to the Aztecs themselves, at least to their military prowess, to regard the Conquest as directly achieved by the Spaniards alone. This would indeed be to arm the latter with the charmed shield of Ruggiero, and the magic lance of Astolfo, overturning its hundreds at a touch. The Indian empire was in a manner conquered by Indians. The first terrible encounter of the Spaniards with the Tlascalans, which had nearly proved their ruin, did in fact insure their success. It secured to them a strong native support, on which to retreat in the hour of trouble, and round which they could rally the kindred races of the land for one great and overwhelming assault. The Aztec monarchy fell by the hands of its own subjects, under the direction of European sagacity and science. Had it been united, it might have bidden defiance to the invaders. As it was, the capital was dissevered from the rest of the country, and the bolt, which might have passed off comparatively harmless, had the empire been cemented by a common principle of loyalty and patriotism, now found its way into every crack and crevice of the ill-compacted fabric, and buried it in its own ruins.—Its fate may serve as a striking proof, that a government, which does not rest on the sympathies of its subjects, cannot long abide; that human institutions, when not connected with human prosperity and progress, must fall,—if not before the increasing light of civilization, by the hand of violence; by violence from within, if not from without. And who shall lament their fall?

[MOTIVES OF EUROPEAN NATIONS EXPANDING TO AMERICA]

From *The Conquest of Mexico*, Bk. VI, chap. iii

[Prescott digresses for a moment from his story of the capture of Cuernavaca to compare the objectives of the various European peoples in settling America.]

The period which we are reviewing was still the age of chivalry; that stirring and adventurous age, of which we can form little conception in the present day of sober, practical reality.

The Spaniard, with his nice point of honor, high romance, and proud, vainglorious vaunt, was the true representative of that age. The Europeans, generally, had not yet learned to accommodate themselves to a life of literary toil, or to the drudgery of trade, or the patient tillage of the soil. They left these to the hooded inmate of the cloister, the humble burgher, and the miserable serf. Arms was the only profession worthy of gentle blood,—the only career which the high-mettled cavalier could tread with honor. The New World, with its strange and mysterious perils, afforded a noble theater for the exercise of his calling; and the Spaniard entered on it with all the enthusiasm of a paladin of romance.

Other nations entered on it also, but with different motives. The French sent forth their missionaries to take up their dwelling among the heathen, who, in the good work of winning souls to Paradise, were content to wear—nay, sometimes seemed to court—the crown of martyrdom. The Dutch, too, had their mission, but it was one of worldly lucre, and they found a recompense for toil and suffering in their gainful traffic with the natives; while our own Puritan fathers, with the true Anglo-Saxon spirit, left their pleasant homes across the waters, and pitched their tents in the howling wilderness, that they might enjoy the sweets of civil and religious freedom. But the Spaniard came over to the New World in the true spirit of a knight-errant, courting adventure however perilous, wooing danger, as it would seem, for its own sake. With sword and lance, he was ever ready to do battle for the Faith; and, as he raised his old war-cry of "St. Jago," he fancied himself fighting under the banner of the military apostle, and felt his single arm a match for more than a hundred infidels!—It was the expiring age of chivalry; and Spain, romantic Spain, was the land where its light lingered longest above the horizon. ✱ ✱ ✱

There can be no doubt, that Cortés, with every other man in his army, felt he was engaged on a holy crusade, and that, independently of personal considerations, he could not serve Heaven better, than by planting the Cross on the bloodstained towers of the heathen metropolis. But it was natural that he should feel some compunction, as he gazed on the goodly scene, and thought of the coming tempest, and how soon the opening blossoms of civilization which there met his eye must wither under the rude breath of War. It was a striking spectacle, that of the great Conqueror, thus brooding in silence over the desolation he was about to bring on the land! It seems to have made a deep impression on his soldiers, little accustomed to such proofs of his sensibility; and it forms the burden of some of those *romances*, or national ballads, with which the Castilian minstrel, in the olden time, delighted to commemorate the favorite heroes of his country, and which, coming midway between oral tradition and chronicle, have been found as imperishable a record as chronicle itself.

[OBJECTIVES OF MISSIONARY AND CONQUEROR]

From *The Conquest of Peru*, Bk. V, chap. iv

[Gasca's reforms in Peru usher in a period of calm after the violence of the era of the Pizarros. The missionary begins his slow process of transforming the civilization of the Incas.]

After the dark and turbulent spirits with which we have been hitherto occupied, it is refreshing to dwell on a character like that of Gasca. In the long procession which has passed in review before us, we have seen only the mailclad cavalier, brandishing his bloody lance, and mounted on his war-horse, riding over the helpless natives, or battling with his own friends and brothers; fierce, arrogant, and cruel, urged on by the lust of gold, or the scarce more honorable love of a bastard glory. Mingled with these qualities, indeed, we have seen sparkles of the chivalrous and romantic temper which belongs to the heroic age of Spain. But, with some honorable exceptions, it was the scum of her chivalry that resorted to Peru, and took service under the banner of the Pizarros. At the close of this long array of iron warriors, we behold the poor and humble missionary coming into the land on an errand of mercy, and everywhere proclaiming the glad tidings of peace. No warlike trumpet heralds his approach, nor is his course to be tracked by the groans of the wounded and the dying. The means he employs are in perfect harmony with his end. His weapons are argument and mild persuasion. It is the reason he would conquer, not the body. He wins his way by conviction, not by violence. It is a moral victory to which he aspires, more potent, and happily more permanent, than that of the bloodstained conqueror. As he thus calmly, and imperceptibly, as it were, comes to his great results, he may remind us of the slow, insensible manner in which Nature works out her great changes in the material world, that are to endure when the ravages of the hurricane are passed away and forgotten.

With the mission of Gasca terminates the history of the Conquest of Peru. The Conquest, indeed, strictly terminates with the suppression of the Peruvian revolt, when the strength, if not the spirit, of the Inca race was crushed forever. The reader, however, might feel a natural curiosity to follow to its close the fate of the remarkable family who achieved the Conquest. Nor would the story of the invasion itself be complete without some account of the civil wars which grew out of it; which serve, moreover, as a moral commentary on preceding events, by showing that the indulgence of fierce, unbridled passions is sure to recoil, sooner or later, even in this life, on the heads of the guilty.

It is true, indeed, that the troubles of the country were renewed on the departure of Gasca. The waters had been too fearfully agitated to be stilled, at once, into a calm; but they gradually subsided, under the temperate rule of his successors, who wisely profited by his policy and example. Thus the influence of the good president remained after he was withdrawn from the scene of his labors; and Peru, hitherto so distracted, continued to enjoy as large a share of repose as any portion of the colonial empire of Spain. With the benevolent mission of Gasca, then, the historian of the Conquest may be permitted to terminate his labors,—with feelings not unlike those of the traveler, who, having long journeyed among the dreary forests and dangerous defiles of the mountains, at length emerges on some pleasant landscape smiling in tranquillity and peace.

[RAPACITY OF THE CONQUERORS OF PERU]
From *The Conquest of Peru*, Bk. IV, chap. vii

[In a short survey of the relations between the victors and the vanquished Incas, Prescott details the harsh treatment accorded the defeated.]

But the dominant passion of the Spaniard was the lust of gold. For this he shrunk from no toil himself, and was merciless in his exactions of labor from his Indian slave. Unfortunately, Peru abounded in mines which too well repaid this labor; and human life was the item of least account in the estimate of the Conquerors. Under his Incas, the Peruvian was never suffered to be idle; but the task imposed on him was always proportioned to his strength. He had his seasons of rest and refreshment, and was well protected against the inclemency of the weather. Every care was shown for his personal safety. But the Spaniards, while they taxed the strength of the native to the utmost, deprived him of the means of repairing it, when exhausted. They suffered the provident arrangements of the Incas to fall into decay. The granaries were emptied; the flocks were wasted in riotous living. They were slaughtered to gratify a mere epicurean whim, and many a llama was destroyed solely for the sake of the brains,—a dainty morsel, much coveted by the Spaniards. So reckless was the spirit of destruction after the Conquest, says Ondegardo, the wise governor of Cuzco, that in four years more of these animals perished than in four hundred, in the times of the Incas. The flocks, once so numerous over the broad tablelands, were now thinned to a scanty number, that sought shelter in the fastnesses of the Andes. The poor Indian, without food, without the warm fleece which furnished him a defense against the cold, now wandered half-starved and naked over the plateau. Even those who had aided the Spaniards in the conquest fared no better; and many an Inca noble roamed a mendicant over the lands where he once held rule, and if driven, perchance, by his necessities, to purloin something from the superfluity of his conquerors, he expiated it by a miserable death.

It is true, there were good men, missionaries, faithful to their calling, who wrought hard in the spiritual conversion of the native, and who, touched by his misfortunes, would gladly have interposed their arm to shield him from his oppressors. But too often the ecclesiastic became infected by the general spirit of licentiousness; and the religious fraternities, who led a life of easy indulgence on the lands cultivated by their Indian slaves, were apt to think less of the salvation of their souls than of profiting by the labor of their bodies.

Yet still there were not wanting good and wise men in the colonies, who, from time to time, raised the voice of remonstrance against these abuses, and who carried their complaints to the foot of the throne. To the credit of the government, it must also be confessed, that it was solicitous to obtain such information as it could, both from its own officers, and from commissioners deputed expressly for the purpose, whose voluminous communications throw a flood of light on the internal condition of the country, and furnish the best materials for the historian. But it was found much easier to get this information than to profit by it.

[CRUELTY OF PIZARRO]

From *The Conquest of Peru*, Bk. III, chap. viii

[After describing Pizarro's execution of the Inca, Prescott stops to pass judgment on the deed.]

The treatment of Atahuallpa, from first to last, forms undoubtedly one of the darkest chapters in Spanish colonial history. There may have been massacres perpetrated on a more extended scale, and executions accompanied with a greater refinement of cruelty, but the bloodstained annals of the Conquest afford no such example of coldhearted and systematic persecution, not of an enemy, but of one whose whole deportment had been that of a friend and a benefactor.

From the hour that Pizarro and his followers had entered within the sphere of Atahuallpa's influence, the hand of friendship had been extended to them by the natives. Their first act, on crossing the mountains, was to kidnap the monarch and massacre his people. The seizure of his person might be vindicated, by those who considered the end as justifying the means, on the ground that it was indispensable to secure the triumphs of the Cross. But no such apology can be urged for the massacre of the unarmed and helpless population,—as wanton as it was wicked.

The long confinement of the Inca had been used by the Conquerors to wring from him his treasures with the hard gripe of avarice. During the whole of this dismal period, he had conducted himself with singular generosity and good faith. He had opened a free passage to the Spaniards through every part of his empire; and had furnished every facility for the execution of their plans. When these were accomplished, and he remained an encumbrance on their hands, notwithstanding their engagement, expressed or implied, to release him,—and Pizarro, as we have seen, by a formal act, acquitted his captive of any further obligation on the score of the ransom,—he was arraigned before a mock tribunal, and, under pretenses equally false and frivolous, was condemned to an excruciating death. From first to last, the policy of the Spanish conquerors towards their unhappy victim is stamped with barbarity and fraud.

It is not easy to acquit Pizarro of being in a great degree responsible for this policy. His partisans have labored to show, that it was forced on him by the necessity of the case, and that in the death of the Inca, especially, he yielded reluctantly to the importunities of others. But weak as is this apology, the historian who has the means of comparing the various testimony of the period will come to a different conclusion. To him it will appear, that Pizarro had probably long felt the removal of Atahuallpa as essential to the success of his enterprise. He foresaw the odium that would be incurred by the death of his royal captive without sufficient grounds; while he labored to establish these, he still shrunk from the responsibility of the deed, and preferred to perpetrate it in obedience to the suggestions of others, rather than his own. Like many an unprincipled politician, he wished to reap the benefit of a bad act, and let others take the blame of it.

Almagro and his followers are reported by Pizarro's secretaries to have first insisted on the Inca's death. They were loudly supported by the treasurer and the royal officers, who considered it as indispensable to the interests of the Crown; and, finally, the rumors of a conspiracy raised the same cry among the soldiers, and Pizarro, with all his tenderness for his prisoner, could not refuse to bring him to trial.—The form of a trial was necessary to give an appearance of fairness to the proceedings. That it was only form is evident from the indecent haste with which it was conducted,—the examination of evidence, the sentence, and the execution, being all on the same day. The multiplication of the charges, designed to place the guilt of the accused on the strongest ground, had, from their very number, the opposite effect, proving only the determination to convict him. If Pizarro had felt the reluctance to his conviction which he pretended, why did he send De Soto, Atahuallpa's best friend, away, when the inquiry was to be instituted? Why was the sentence so summarily executed, as not to afford opportunity, by that cavalier's return, of disproving the truth of the principal charge,—the only one, in fact, with which the Spaniards had any concern? The solemn farce of mourning and deep sorrow affected by Pizarro, who by these honors to the dead would intimate the sincere regard he had entertained for the living, was too thin a veil to impose on the most credulous.

It is not intended by these reflections to exculpate the rest of the army, and especially its officers, from their share in the infamy of the transaction. But Pizarro, as commander of the army, was mainly responsible for its measures. For he was not a man to allow his own authority to be wrested from his grasp, or to yield timidly to the impulses of others. He did not even yield to his own. His whole career shows him, whether for good or for evil, to have acted with a cool and calculating policy.

A story has been often repeated, which refers the motives of Pizarro's conduct, in some degree at least, to personal resentment. The Inca had requested one of the Spanish soldiers to write the name of God on his nail. This the monarch showed to several of his guards successively, and, as they read it, and each pronounced the same word, the sagacious mind of the barbarian was delighted with what seemed to him little short of a miracle, —to which the science of his own nation afforded no analogy. On showing the writing to Pizarro, that chief remained silent; and the Inca, finding he could not read, conceived a contempt for the commander who was even less informed than his soldiers. This he did not wholly conceal, and Pizarro, aware of the cause of it, neither forgot nor forgave it. The anecdote is reported not on the highest authority. It may be true; but it is unnecessary to look for the motives of Pizarro's conduct in personal pique, when so many proofs are to be discerned of a dark and deliberate policy.

Yet the arts of the Spanish chieftain failed to reconcile his countrymen to the atrocity of his proceedings. It is singular to observe the difference between the tone assumed by the first chroniclers of the transaction, while it was yet fresh, and that of those who wrote when the lapse of a few years had shown the tendency of public opinion. The first boldly avow the deed as demanded by expediency, if not necessity; while they deal in no measured terms of reproach with the character of their unfortunate victim. The latter, on the other hand, while they extenuate the errors of the Inca, and do justice to his good faith, are unreserved in their condemnation of the Conquerors, on whose conduct, they say, Heaven set the seal of its own reprobation, by bringing them all to an untimely and miserable end. The sentence of contemporaries has been fully ratified by that of posterity; and the persecution of Atahuallpa is regarded with justice as having left a stain, never to be effaced, on the Spanish arms in the New World.

[MORALITY OF THE CONQUEST]

From *The Conquest of Mexico*, Bk. IV, chap. iii

[The seizure of Montezuma is dramatically narrated and this chapter is concluded with typical reflections aspersing the morals of Cortés and his soldiers.]

The events recorded in this chapter are certainly some of the most extraordinary on the page of history. That a small body of men, like the Spaniards, should have entered the palace of a mighty prince, have seized his person in the midst of his vassals, have borne him off a captive to their quarters,—that they should have put to an ignominious death before his face his high officers, for executing, probably, his own commands, and have crowned the whole by putting the monarch in irons like a common malefactor,—that this should have been done, not to a driveling dotard in the decay of his fortunes, but to a proud monarch in the plenitude of his power, in the very heart of his capital, surrounded by thousands and tens of thousands, who trembled at his nod, and would have poured out their blood like water in his defense,—that all this should have been done by a mere handful of adventurers, is a thing too extravagant, altogether too improbable, for the pages of romance! It is, nevertheless, literally true. Yet we shall not be prepared to acquiesce in the judgments of contemporaries who regarded these acts with admiration. We may well distrust any grounds on which it is attempted to justify the kidnaping of a friendly sovereign,—by those very persons, too, who were reaping the full benefit of his favors.

To view the matter differently, we must take the position of the Conquerors, and assume with them the original right of conquest. Regarded from this point of view, many difficulties vanish. If conquest were a duty, whatever was necessary to effect it was right also. Right and expedient become convertible terms. And it can hardly be denied, that the capture of the monarch was expedient, if the Spaniards would maintain their hold on the empire.

The execution of the Aztec governor suggests other considerations. If he were really guilty of the perfidious act imputed to him by Cortés, and if Montezuma disavowed it, the governor deserved death, and the general was justified by the law of nations in inflicting it. It is by no means so clear, however, why he should have involved so many in this sentence; most, perhaps all, of whom must have acted under his authority. The cruel manner of the death will less startle those who are familiar with the established penal codes in most civilized nations in the sixteenth century.

But, if the governor deserved death, what pretense was there for the outrage on the person of Montezuma? If the former was guilty, the latter surely was not. But, if the cacique only acted in obedience to orders, the responsibility was transferred to the sovereign who gave the orders. They could not both stand in the same category.

It is vain, however, to reason on the matter, on any abstract principles of right and wrong, or to suppose that the Conquerors troubled themselves with the refinements of casuistry. Their standard of right and wrong, in reference to the natives, was a very simple one. Despising them as an outlawed race, without God in the world, they, in common with their age, held it to be their "mission" (to borrow the cant phrase of our own day) to conquer and to convert. The measures they adopted certainly facilitated the first great work of conquest. By the execution of the caciques, they struck terror not only into the capital, but throughout the country. It proclaimed that not a hair of a Spaniard was to be touched with impunity! By rendering Montezuma contemptible in his own eyes and those of his subjects, Cortés deprived him of the support of his people, and forced him to lean on the arm of the stranger. It was a politic proceeding,—to which few men could have been equal, who had a touch of humanity in their natures.

A good criterion of the moral sense of the actors in these events is afforded by the reflections of Bernal Diaz, made some fifty years, it will be remembered, after the events themselves, when the fire of youth had become extinct, and the eye, glancing back through the vista of half a century, might be supposed to be unclouded by the passions and prejudices which throw their mist over the present. "Now that I am an old man," says the veteran, "I often entertain myself with calling to mind the heroical deeds of early days, till they are as fresh as the events of yesterday. I think of the seizure of the Indian monarch, his confinement in irons, and the execution of his officers, till all these things seem actually passing before me. And, as I ponder on our exploits, I feel that it was not of ourselves that we performed them, but that it was the providence of God which guided us. Much food is there here for meditation!" There is so, indeed, and for a meditation not unpleasing, as we reflect on the advance, in speculative morality, at least, which the nineteenth century has made over the sixteenth. But should not the consciousness of this teach us charity? Should it not make us the more distrustful of applying the standard of the present to measure the actions of the past?

[MORALITY OF WAR AND IMPERIAL CONQUEST]

From *The Conquest of Mexico*, Bk. III, chap. vii

[The massacre of the Cholulans is described in all its horror, but Prescott goes very far to find for the Conquerors some extenuating circumstances.]

This passage in their history is one of those that have left a dark stain on the memory of the Conquerors. Nor can we contemplate at this day, without a shudder, the condition of this fair and flourishing capital thus invaded in its privacy, and delivered over to the excesses of a rude and ruthless soldiery. But, to judge the action fairly, we must transport ourselves to the age when it happened. The difficulty that meets us in the outset is, to find a justification of the right of conquest, at all. But it should be remembered, that religious infidelity, at this period, and till a much later, was regarded—no matter whether founded on ignorance or education, whether hereditary or acquired, heretical or Pagan—as a sin to be punished with fire and faggot in this world, and eternal suffering in the next. This doctrine, monstrous as it is, was the creed of the Romish, in other words, of the Christian Church,—the basis of the Inquisition, and of those other species of religious persecutions, which have stained the annals, at some time or other, of nearly every nation in Christendom. Under this code, the territory of the heathen, wherever found, was regarded as a sort of religious waif, which, in default of a legal proprietor, was claimed and taken possession of by the Holy See, and as such was freely given away by the head of the Church, to any temporal potentate whom he pleased, that would assume the burden of conquest. Thus, Alexander the Sixth, generously granted a large portion of the Western hemisphere to the Spaniards, and of the Eastern to the Portuguese. These lofty pretensions of the successors of the humble fisherman of Galilee, far from being nominal, were acknowledged and appealed to as conclusive in controversies between nations.

With the right of conquest, thus conferred, came, also, the obligation, on which it may be said to have been founded, to retrieve the nations sitting in darkness from eternal perdition. This obligation was acknowledged by the best and the bravest, the gownsman in his closet, the missionary, and the warrior in the crusade. However much it may have been debased by temporal motives and mixed up with worldly considerations of ambition and avarice, it was still active in the mind of the Christian conqueror. We have seen how far paramount it was to every calculation of personal interest in the breast of Cortés. The concession of the Pope, then, founded on, and enforcing, the imperative duty of conversion, was the assumed basis— and, in the apprehension of that age, a sound one—of the right of conquest.

This right could not, indeed, be construed to authorize any unnecessary act of violence to the natives. The present expedition, up to the period of its history at which we are now arrived, had probably been stained with fewer of such acts than almost any similar enterprise of the Spanish discoveries in the New

World. Throughout the campaign, Cortés had prohibited all wanton injuries to the natives, in person or property, and had punished the perpetrators of them with exemplary severity. He had been faithful to his friends, and, with perhaps a single exception, not unmerciful to his foes. Whether from policy or principle, it should be recorded to his credit; though, like every sagacious mind, he may have felt, that principle and policy go together.

He had entered Cholula as a friend, at the invitation of the Indian emperor, who had a real, if not avowed, control over the state. He had been received as a friend, with every demonstration of good-will; when, without any offense of his own or his followers, he found they were to be the victims of an insidious plot,—that they were standing on a mine which might be sprung at any moment, and bury them all in its ruins. His safety, as he truly considered, left no alternative but to anticipate the blow of his enemies. Yet who can doubt that the punishment thus inflicted was excessive,—that the same end might have been attained by directing the blow against the guilty chiefs, instead of letting it fall on the ignorant rabble, who but obeyed the commands of their masters? But when was it ever seen, that fear, armed with power, was scrupulous in the exercise of it? or that the passions of a fierce soldiery, inflamed by conscious injuries, could be regulated in the moment of explosion?

We shall, perhaps, pronounce more impartially on the conduct of the Conquerors, if we compare it with that of our own contemporaries under somewhat similar circumstances. The atrocities at Cholula were not so bad as those inflicted on the descendants of these very Spaniards, in the late war of the Peninsula, by the most polished nations of our time; by the British at Badajoz, for example,—at Taragona, and a hundred other places, by the French. The wanton butchery, the ruin of property, and, above all, those outrages worse than death, from which the female part of the population were protected at Cholula, show a catalogue of enormities quite as black as those imputed to the Spaniards, and without the same apology for resentment, —with no apology, indeed, but that afforded by a brave and patriotic resistance. The consideration of these events, which, from their familiarity, make little impression on our senses, should render us more lenient in our judgments of the past, showing, as they do, that man in a state of excitement, savage or civilized is much the same in every age. It may teach us,—it is one of the best lessons of history,—that, since such are the *inevitable* evils of war, even among the most polished people, those who hold the destinies of nations in their hands, whether rulers or legislators, should submit to every sacrifice, save that of honor, before authorizing an appeal to arms. The extreme solicitude to avoid these calamities, by the aid of peaceful congresses and impartial mediation, is, on the whole, the strongest evidence, stronger than that afforded by the progress of science and art, of our boasted advance in civilization.

It is far from my intention to vindicate the cruel deeds of the old Conquerors. Let them lie heavy on their heads. They were an iron race, who periled life and fortune in the cause; and, as they made little account of danger and suffering for themselves, they had little sympathy to spare for their unfortunate enemies. But, to judge them fairly, we must not do it by the lights of our own age. We must carry ourselves back to theirs, and take the point of view afforded by the civilization of their time. Thus only can we arrive at impartial criticism in reviewing the generations that are past. We must extend to them the same justice which we shall have occasion to ask from Posterity, when, by the light of a higher civilization, it surveys the dark or doubtful passages in our own history, which hardly arrest the eye of the contemporary.

III. CIVIL AND RELIGIOUS POLITY

[THE COMMONS, THE REVENUES, AND RELIGIOUS POLICY]

From *Ferdinand and Isabella*, Vol. III, pt. ii, chap. xxvi

[Part of a general review of the administration of Ferdinand and Isabella. Among the fundamental beliefs of Prescott was the necessity of civil and religious freedom for the progress of mankind. He understood the role of legislatures in advancing civil progress and effecting a transition from feudalism to a strong monarchy.]

The condition of the commons under this reign was probably, on the whole, more prosperous than in any other period of the Spanish history. New avenues to wealth and honors were opened to them; and persons and property were alike protected under the fearless and impartial administration of the law. "Such was the justice dispensed to everyone under this auspicious reign," exclaims Marineo, "that nobles and cavaliers, citizens and laborers, rich and poor, masters and servants, all equally partook of it." We find no complaints of arbitrary imprisonment, and no attempts, so frequent both in earlier and later times, at illegal taxation. In this particular, indeed, Isabella manifested the greatest tenderness for her people. By her commutation of the capricious tax of the *alcavala* for a determinate one, and still more by transferring its collection from the revenue officers to the citizens themselves, she greatly relieved her subjects.

Finally, notwithstanding the perpetual call for troops for the military operations, in which the government was constantly engaged, and notwithstanding the example of neighboring countries, there was no attempt to establish that iron bulwark of despotism, a standing army; at least, none nearer than that of the voluntary levies of the hermandad, raised and paid by the people. The queen never admitted the arbitrary maxims of

Ximenes in regard to the foundation of government. Hers was essentially one of opinion, not force. Had it rested on any other than the broad basis of public opinion, it could not have withstood a day the violent shocks, to which it was early exposed, nor have achieved the important revolution that it finally did, both in the domestic and foreign concerns of the country.

The condition of the kingdom, on Isabella's accession, necessarily gave the commons unwonted consideration. In the tottering state of her affairs, she was obliged to rest on their strong arm for support. It did not fail her. Three sessions of the legislature, or rather the popular branch of it, were held during the two first years of her reign. It was in these early assemblies, that the commons bore an active part in concocting the wholesome system of laws, which restored vitality and vigor to the exhausted republic.

After this good work was achieved, the sessions of that body became more rare. There was less occasion for them, indeed, during the existence of the hermandad, which was, of itself, an ample representation of the Castilian commons, and which, by enforcing obedience to the law at home, and by liberal supplies for foreign war, superseded, in a great degree, the call for more regular meetings of cortes. The habitual economy, too, not to say frugality, which regulated the public, as well as private expenditure of the sovereigns, enabled them, after this period, with occasional exceptions, to dispense with other aid than that drawn from the regular revenues of the crown.

There is every ground for believing that the political franchises of the people, as then understood, were uniformly respected. The number of cities summoned to cortes, which had so often varied according to the caprice of princes, never fell short of that prescribed by long usage. On the contrary, an addition was made by the conquest of Granada; and, in a cortes held soon after the queen's death, we find a most narrow and impolitic remonstrance of the legislature itself, against the alleged unauthorized extension of the privilege of representation. ✳ ✳ ✳

The commons gained political consideration, no doubt, by the depression of the nobles; but their chief gain lay in the inestimable blessings of domestic tranquillity, and the security of private rights. The crown absorbed the power, in whatever form, retrieved from the privileged orders; the pensions and large domains, the numerous fortified places, the rights of seigniorial jurisdiction, the command of the military orders, and the like. Other circumstances conspired to raise the regal authority still higher, as, for example, the international relations then opened with the rest of Europe, which, whether friendly or hostile, were conducted by the monarch alone, who, unless to obtain supplies, rarely condescended to seek the intervention of the other estates; the concentration of the dismembered provinces of the Peninsula under one government; the immense acquisitions abroad, whether from discovery or conquest, regarded in that day as the property of the crown, rather than of the nation; and, finally, the consideration flowing from the personal character, and long successful rule, of the Catholic sovereigns. Such were the manifold causes, which, without the imputation of a criminal ambition, or indifference to the rights of their subjects, in Ferdinand and Isabella, all combined to swell the prerogative to an unprecedented height under their reign.

This, indeed, was the direction in which all the governments of Europe, at this period, were tending. The people, wisely preferring a single master to a multitude, sustained the crown in its efforts to recover from the aristocracy the enormous powers it so grossly abused. This was the revolution of the fifteenth and sixteenth centuries. The power thus deposited in a single hand, was found in time equally incompatible with the great ends of civil government; while it gradually accumulated to an extent, which threatened to crush the monarchy by its own weight. But the institutions derived from a Teutonic origin have been found to possess a conservative principle, unknown to the fragile despotisms of the East. The seeds of liberty, though dormant, lay deep in the heart of the nation, waiting only the good time to germinate. That time has at length arrived. Larger experience, and a wider moral culture, have taught men not only the extent of their political rights, but the best way to secure them. And it is the reassertion of these by the great body of the people, which now constitutes the revolution going forward in most of the old communities of Europe. The progress of liberal principles must be controlled, of course, by the peculiar circumstances and character of the nation; but their ultimate triumph, in every quarter, none can reasonably distrust. May it not be abused. * * *

I have elsewhere examined the policy pursued by the Catholic sovereigns in the government of their colonies. The supply of precious metals yielded by them eventually, proved far greater than had ever entered into the conception of the most sanguine of the early discoverers. Their prolific soil and genial climate, moreover, afforded an infinite variety of vegetable products, which might have furnished an unlimited commerce with the mother country. Under a judicious protection, their population and productions, steadily increasing, would have enlarged to an incalculable extent the general resources of the empire. Such, indeed, might have been the result of a wise system of legislation.

But the true principles of colonial policy were sadly misunderstood in the sixteenth century. The discovery of a world was estimated, like that of a rich mine, by the value of its returns in gold and silver. Much of Isabella's legislation, it is true, is of that comprehensive character, which shows that she looked to higher and far nobler objects. But with much that is good, there was mingled, as in most of her institutions, one germ of evil, of little moment at the time, indeed, but which, under the vicious culture of her successors, shot up to a height that overshadowed and blighted all the rest. This was the spirit of restriction and monopoly, aggravated by the subsequent laws of Ferdinand, and carried to an extent under the Austrian dynasty, that paralyzed colonial trade.

Under their most ingeniously perverse system of laws, the interests of both the parent country and the colonies were sacrificed. The latter, condemned to look for supplies to an incompetent source, were miserably dwarfed in their growth;

while the former contrived to convert the nutriment which she extorted from the colonies into a fatal poison. The streams of wealth which flowed in from the silver quarries of Zacatecas and Potosí, were jealously locked up within the limits of the Peninsula. The great problem, proposed by the Spanish legislation of the sixteenth century, was the reduction of prices in the kingdom to the same level as in other European nations. Every law that was passed, however, tended, by its restrictive character, to augment the evil. The golden tide, which, permitted a free vent, would have fertilized the region through which it poured, now buried the land under a deluge which blighted every green and living thing. Agriculture, commerce, manufactures, every branch of national industry and improvement, languished and fell to decay; and the nation, like the Phrygian monarch, who turned all that he touched to gold, cursed by the very consummation of its wishes, was poor in the midst of its treasures.

From this sad picture, let us turn to that presented by the period of our History, when, the clouds and darkness having passed away, a new morn seemed to break upon the nation. Under the firm but temperate sway of Ferdinand and Isabella, the great changes we have noticed were effected without convulsion in the state. On the contrary, the elements of the social system, which before jarred so discordantly, were brought into harmonious action. The restless spirit of the nobles was turned from civil faction to the honorable career of public service, whether in arms or letters. The people at large, assured of the security of private rights, were occupied with the different branches of productive labor. Trade, as is abundantly shown by the legislation of the period, had not yet fallen into the discredit which attached to it in later times. The precious metals, instead of flowing in so abundantly as to palsy the arm of industry, served only to stimulate it.

The foreign intercourse of the country was every day more widely extended. Her agents and consuls were to be found in all the principal ports of the Mediterranean and the Baltic. The Spanish mariner, instead of creeping along the beaten track of inland navigation, now struck boldly across the great western ocean. The new discoveries had converted the land trade with India into a sea trade; and the nations of the Peninsula, who had hitherto lain remote from the great highways of commerce, now became the factors and carriers of Europe.

The flourishing condition of the nation was seen in the wealth and population of its cities, the revenues of which, augmented in all to a surprising extent, had increased in some, forty and even fifty fold beyond what they were at the commencement of the reign; the ancient and lordly Toledo; Burgos, with its bustling, industrious traders; Valladolid, sending forth its thirty thousand warriors from its gates, where the whole population now scarcely reaches two thirds of that number; Cordova, in the south, and the magnificent Granada, naturalizing in Europe the arts and luxuries of the East; Saragossa, "the abundant," as she was called from her fruitful territory; Valencia, "the beautiful"; Barcelona, rivaling in independence and maritime enterprise the proudest of the Italian republics; Medina del Campo, whose fairs were already the great mart for the commercial exchanges of the Peninsula; and Seville, the golden gate of the Indies, whose quays began to be thronged with merchants from the most distant countries of Europe.

The resources of the inhabitants were displayed in the palaces and public edifices, fountains, aqueducts, gardens, and other works of utility and ornament. This lavish expenditure was directed by an improved taste. Architecture was studied on purer principles than before, and, with the sister arts of design, showed the influence of the new connection with Italy in the first gleams of that excellence, which shed such luster over the Spanish school at the close of the century. A still more decided impulse was given to letters. More printing presses were probably at work in Spain in the infancy of the art, than at the present day. Ancient seminaries were remodeled; new ones were created. Barcelona, Salamanca, and Alcalá, whose cloistered solitudes are now the grave, rather than the nursery of science, then swarmed with thousands of disciples, who, under the generous patronage of the government, found letters the surest path to preferment. Even the lighter branches of literature felt the revolutionary spirit of the times, and, after yielding the last fruits of the ancient system, displayed new and more beautiful varieties, under the influence of Italian culture.

With this moral development of the nation, the public revenues, the sure index, when unforced, of public prosperity, went on augmenting with astonishing rapidity. In 1474, the year of Isabella's accession, the ordinary rents of the Castilian crown amounted to 885,000 reals; in 1477, to 2,390,078; in 1482, after the resumption of the royal grants, to 12,711,591; and finally in 1504, when the acquisition of Granada and the domestic tranquillity of the kingdom had encouraged the free expansion of all its resources, to 26,283,334; or thirty times the amount received at her accession. All this, it will be remembered, was derived from the customary established taxes, without the imposition of a single new one. Indeed, the improvements in the mode of collection tended materially to lighten the burdens on the people.

The accounts of the population at this early period are, for the most part, vague and unsatisfactory. Spain, in particular, has been the subject of the most absurd, though, as it seems, not incredible estimates, sufficiently evincing the paucity of authentic data. Fortunately, however, we labor under no such embarrassment as regards Castile in Isabella's reign. By an official report to the crown on the organization of the militia, in 1492, it appears that the population of the kingdom amounted to 1,500,000 *vecinos* or householders; or, allowing four and a half to a family (a moderate estimate), to 6,750,000 souls. This census, it will be observed, was limited to the provinces immediately composing the crown of Castile, to the exclusion of Granada, Navarre, and the Aragonese dominions. It was taken, moreover, before the nation had time to recruit from the long and exhausting struggle of the Moorish war, and twenty-five years before the close of the reign, when the population, under circumstances peculiarly favorable, must have swelled to a much larger amount. Thus circumscribed, however, it was probably considerably in advance of that of England at the same period.

How have the destinies of the two countries since been reversed!

The territorial limits of the monarchy, in the meantime went on expanding beyond example;—Castile and Leon, brought under the same scepter with Aragon and its foreign dependencies, Sicily and Sardinia; with the kingdoms of Granada, Navarre, and Naples; with the Canaries, Oran, and the other settlements in Africa; and with the islands and vast continents of America. To these broad domains, the comprehensive schemes of the sovereigns would have added Portugal, and their arrangements for this, although defeated for the present, opened the way to its eventual completion under Philip the Second.

The petty states, which had before swarmed over the Peninsula, neutralizing each other's operations, and preventing any effective movement abroad, were now amalgamated into one whole. Sectional jealousies and antipathies, indeed, were too sturdily rooted to be wholly extinguished; but they gradually subsided, under the influence of a common government, and community of interests. A more enlarged sentiment was infused into the people, who, in their foreign relations, at least, assumed the attitude of one great nation. The names of Castilian and Aragonese were merged in the comprehensive one of Spaniard; and Spain, with an empire which stretched over three quarters of the globe, and which almost realized the proud boast that the sun never set within her borders, now rose, not to the first class only, but to the first place, in the scale of European powers.

The extraordinary circumstances of the country tended naturally to nourish the lofty, romantic qualities, and the somewhat exaggerated tone of sentiment, which always pervaded the national character. The age of chivalry had not faded away in Spain, as in most other lands. It was fostered, in time of peace, by the tourneys, jousts, and other warlike pageants, which graced the court of Isabella. It gleamed out, as we have seen, in the Italian campaigns under Gonsalvo de Cordova, and shone forth in all its splendors in the war of Granada. "This was a right gentle war," says Navagiero, in a passage too pertinent to be omitted, "in which, as firearms were comparatively little used, each knight had the opportunity of showing his personal prowess; and rare was it, that a day passed without some feat of arms and valorous exploit. The nobility and chivalry of the land all thronged there to gather renown. Queen Isabel, who attended with her whole court, breathed courage into every heart. There was scarce a cavalier, who was not enamored of some one or other of her ladies, the witness of his achievements, and who, as she presented him his weapons, or some token of her favor, admonished him to bear himself like a true knight, and show the strength of his passion by his valiant deeds. What knight so craven, then," exclaims the chivalrous Venetian, "that he would not have been more than a match for the stoutest adversary; or who would not sooner have lost his life a thousand times, than return dishonored to the lady of his love. In truth," he concludes, "this conquest may be said to have been achieved by love, rather than by arms."

The Spaniard was a knight-errant, in its literal sense, roving over seas on which no bark had ever ventured, among islands and continents where no civilized man had ever trodden, and which fancy peopled with all the marvels and drear enchantments of romance; courting danger in every form, combating everywhere, and everywhere victorious. The very odds presented by the defenseless natives among whom he was cast, "a thousand of whom," to quote the words of Columbus, "were not equal to three Spaniards," was in itself typical of his profession; and the brilliant destinies to which the meanest adventurer was often called, now carving out with his good sword some "El Dorado" more splendid than fancy had dreamed of, and now overturning some old barbaric dynasty, were full as extraordinary as the wildest chimeras which Ariosto ever sang, or Cervantes satirized.

His countrymen who remained at home, feeding greedily on the reports of his adventures, lived almost equally in an atmosphere of romance. A spirit of chivalrous enthusiasm penetrated the very depths of the nation, swelling the humblest individual with lofty aspirations, and a proud consciousness of the dignity of his nature. "The princely disposition of the Spaniards," says a foreigner of the time, "delighteth me much, as well as the gentle nurture and noble conversation, not merely of those of high degree, but of the citizen, peasant, and common laborer." What wonder that such sentiments should be found incompatible with sober, methodical habits of business, or that the nation indulging them should be seduced from the humble paths of domestic industry to a brilliant and bolder career of adventure. Such consequences became too apparent in the following reign.

In noticing the circumstances that conspired to form the national character, it would be unpardonable to omit the establishment of the Inquisition, which contributed so largely to counterbalance the benefits resulting from Isabella's government; an institution which has done more than any other to stay the proud march of human reason; which, by imposing uniformity of creed, has proved the fruitful parent of hypocrisy and superstition; which has soured the sweet charities of human life, and, settling like a foul mist on the goodly promise of the land, closed up the fair buds of science and civilization ere they were fully opened. Alas! that such a blight should have fallen on so gallant and generous a people! That it should have been brought on it too by one of such unblemished patriotism and purity of motive, as Isabella! How must her virtuous spirit, if it be permitted the departed good to look down on the scene of their earthly labors, mourn over the misery and moral degradation, entailed on her country by this one act! So true is it, that the measures of this great queen have had a permanent influence, whether for good or for evil, on the destinies of her country.

The immediate injury inflicted on the nation by the spirit of bigotry in the reign of Ferdinand and Isabella, although greatly exaggerated, was doubtless serious enough. Under the otherwise beneficent operation of their government, however, the healthful and expansive energies of the state were sufficient to heal up these and deeper wounds, and still carry it onward in the career of prosperity. With this impulse, indeed, the nation continued to advance higher and higher, in spite of the system of almost unmingled evil pursued in the following reigns. The glories of this later period, of the age of Charles the Fifth, as it is called, must find their true source in the measures of his illustrious predecessors. It was in their court, that Boscan, Garcilasso, Mendoza, and the other master-spirits were trained, who moulded Castilian literature into the new and more classical forms of later times. It was under Gonsalvo de Cordova, that Leyva, Pescara, and those great captains with their invincible legions were formed, who enabled Charles the Fifth to dictate laws to Europe for half a century. And it was Columbus, who not only led the way, but animated the Spanish navigator with the spirit of discovery. Scarcely was Ferdinand's reign brought to a close, before Magellan completed, what that monarch had projected, the circumnavigation of the southern continent; the victorious banners of Cortés had already penetrated into the golden realms of Montezuma; and Pizarro, a very few years later, following up the lead of Balboa, embarked on the enterprise which ended in the downfall of the splendid dynasty of the Incas.

Thus it is, that the seed sown under a good system continues to yield fruit in a bad one. The season of the most brilliant results, however, is not always that of the greatest national prosperity. The splendors of foreign conquest in the boasted reign of Charles the Fifth were dearly purchased by the decline of industry at home, and the loss of liberty. The patriot will see little to cheer him in this "golden age" of the national history, whose outward show of glory will seem to his penetrating eye only the hectic brilliancy of decay. He will turn to an earlier period, when the nation, emerging from the sloth and license of a barbarous age, seemed to renew its ancient energies, and to prepare like a giant to run its course; and glancing over the long interval since elapsed, during the first half of which the nation wasted itself on schemes of mad ambition, and in the latter has sunk into a state of paralytic torpor, he will fix his eye on the reign of Ferdinand and Isabella, as the most glorious epoch in the annals of his country.

[THE CROWN]

From *Ferdinand and Isabella*, Introduction, sec. i

[Part of an introductory review of the Castilian monarchy before the accession of Ferdinand and Isabella.]

From the preceding survey of the constitutional privileges enjoyed by the different orders of the Castilian monarchy, previous to the fifteenth century, it is evident that the royal authority must have been circumscribed within very narrow limits. The numerous states, into which the great Gothic empire was broken after the Conquest, were individually too insignificant to confer on their respective sovereigns the possession of extensive power, or even to authorize their assumption of that state, by which it is supported in the eyes of the vulgar. When some more fortunate prince, by conquest or alliance, had enlarged the circle of his dominions, and thus in some measure remedied the evil, it was sure to recur upon his death, by the subdivision of his estates among his children. This mischievous practice was even countenanced by public opinion, for the different districts of the country, in their habitual independence of each other, acquired an exclusiveness of feeling, which made it difficult for them ever cordially to coalesce; and traces of this early repugnance to each other are to be discerned in the mutual jealousies and local peculiarities, which still distinguish the different sections of the Peninsula, after their consolidation into one monarchy for more than three centuries.

The election to the crown, although no longer vested in the hands of the national assembly, as with the Visigoths, was yet subject to its approbation. The title of the heir apparent was formally recognized by a cortes convoked for the purpose; and, on the demise of his parent, the new sovereign again convened the estates to receive their oath of allegiance, which they cautiously withheld, until he had first sworn to preserve inviolate the liberties of the constitution. Nor was this a merely nominal privilege, as was evinced on more than one memorable occasion.

We have seen, in our review of the popular branch of the government, how closely its authority pressed even on the executive functions of the administration. The monarch was still further controlled, in this department, by his Royal or Privy Council, consisting of the chief nobility and great officers of state, to which, in later times, a deputation of the commons was sometimes added. This body, together with the king, had cognizance of the most important public transactions, whether of a civil, military, or diplomatic nature. It was established by positive enactment, that the prince, without its consent, had no right to alienate the royal demesne, to confer pensions beyond a very limited amount, or to nominate to vacant benefices. His legislative powers were to be exercised in concurrence with the cortes; and, in the judicial department, his authority, during the latter part of the period under review, seems to have been chiefly exercised in the selection of officers for the higher judicatures, from a list of candidates presented to him on a vacancy by their members concurrently with his privy council.

The scantiness of the king's revenue corresponded with that of his constitutional authority. By an ancient law, indeed, of similar tenor with one familiar to the Saracens, the sovereign was entitled to a fifth of the spoils of victory. This, in the course of the long wars with the Moslems, would have secured him more ample possessions than were enjoyed by any prince in Christendom. But several circumstances concurred to prevent it.

The long minorities, with which Castile was afflicted perhaps more than any country in Europe, frequently threw the government into the hands of the principal nobility, who perverted to their own emoluments the high powers intrusted to them. They usurped the possessions of the crown, and invaded some of its most valuable privileges; so that the sovereign's subsequent life was often consumed in fruitless attempts to repair the losses of his minority. He sometimes, indeed, in the impotence of other resources, resorted to such unhappy expedients as treachery and assassination. A pleasant tale is told by the Spanish historians, of the more innocent device of

Henry the Third, for the recovery of the estates extorted from the crown by the rapacious nobles during his minority.

Returning home late one evening, fatigued and half famished, from a hunting expedition, he was chagrined to find no refreshment prepared for him, and still more so, to learn from his steward, that he had neither money nor credit to purchase it. The day's sport, however, fortunately furnished the means of appeasing the royal appetite; and, while this was in progress, the steward took occasion to contrast the indigent condition of the king with that of his nobles, who habitually indulged in the most expensive entertainments, and were that very evening feasting with the archbishop of Toledo. The prince, suppressing his indignation, determined like the far-famed caliph, in the "Arabian Nights," to inspect the affair in person, and, assuming a disguise, introduced himself privately into the archbishop's palace, where he witnessed with his own eyes the prodigal magnificence of the banquet, teeming with costly wines and the most luxurious viands.

The next day he caused a rumor to be circulated through the court, that he had fallen suddenly and dangerously ill. The courtiers, at these tidings, thronged to the palace; and, when they had all assembled, the king made his appearance among them, bearing his naked sword in his hand, and, with an aspect of unusual severity, seated himself on his throne at the upper extremity of the apartment.

After an interval of silence in the astonished assembly, the monarch, addressing himself to the primate, inquired of him, "How many sovereigns he had known in Castile?" The prelate answering four, Henry put the same question to the duke of Benevente, and so on to the other courtiers in succession. None of them, however, having answered more than five, "How is this," said the prince, "that you, who are so old, should have known so few, while I, young as I am, have beheld more than twenty! Yes," continued he, raising his voice, to the astonished multitude, "you are the real sovereigns of Castile, enjoying all the rights and revenues of royalty, while I, stripped of my patrimony, have scarcely wherewithal to procure the necessaries of

life." Then giving a concerted signal, his guards entered the
apartment, followed by the public executioner bearing along
with him the implements of death. The dismayed nobles, not
relishing the turn the jest appeared likely to take, fell on their
knees before the monarch and besought his forgiveness, promising, in requital, complete restitution of the fruits of their ra-
pacity. Henry, content with having so cheaply gained his point,
allowed himself to soften at their entreaties, taking care, however, to detain their persons as security for their engagements,
until such time as the rents, royal fortresses, and whatever effects
had been filched from the crown, were restored. The story,
although repeated by the gravest Castilian writers, wears, it
must be owned, a marvelous tinge of romance. But, whether
fact, or founded on it, it may serve to show the dilapidated condition of the revenues at the beginning of the fourteenth century, and its immediate causes.

[THE FALL OF GRANADA]

From *Ferdinand and Isabella*, Vol. II, pt. i, chap. xv

[The following reflections conclude Prescott's narrative of
the War of Granada, by which Ferdinand and Isabella conquered the Moors of Spain.]

The fall of Granada excited general sensation throughout
Christendom, where it was received as counterbalancing, in a
manner, the loss of Constantinople, nearly half a century before.
At Rome, the event was commemorated by a solemn procession
of the Pope and cardinals to St. Peter's, where high mass was
celebrated, and the public rejoicing continued for several days.
The intelligence was welcomed with no less satisfaction in England, where Henry the Seventh was seated on the throne. . . .

Thus ended the war of Granada, which is often compared
by the Castilian chroniclers to that of Troy in its duration,
and which certainly fully equaled the latter in variety of picturesque and romantic incidents, and in circumstances of poetical
interest. With the surrender of its capital, terminated the

Arabian empire in the Peninsula, after an existence of seven hundred and forty-one years from the date of the original conquest. The consequences of this closing war were of the highest moment to Spain. The most obvious, was the recovery of an extensive territory, hitherto held by a people, whose difference of religion, language, and general habits, made them not only incapable of assimilating with their Christian neighbors, but almost their natural enemies; while their local position was a matter of just concern, as interposed between the great divisions of the Spanish monarchy, and opening an obvious avenue to invasion from Africa. By the new conquest, moreover, the Spaniards gained a large extent of country, possessing the highest capacities for production, in its natural fruitfulness of soil, temperature of climate, and in the state of cultivation to which it had been brought by its ancient occupants; while its shores were lined with commodious havens, that afforded every facility for commerce. The scattered fragments of the ancient Visigothic empire were now again, with the exception of the little state of Navarre, combined into one great monarchy, as originally destined by nature; and Christian Spain gradually rose by means of her new acquisitions from a subordinate situation, to the level of a first-rate European power.

The moral influence of the Moorish war, its influence on the Spanish character, was highly important. The inhabitants of the great divisions of the country, as in most countries during the feudal ages, had been brought too frequently into collision with each other to allow the existence of a pervading national feeling. This was particularly the case in Spain, where independent states insensibly grew out of the detached fragments of territory recovered at different times from the Moorish monarchy. The war of Granada subjected all the various sections of the country to one common action under the influence of common motives of the most exciting interest; while it brought them in conflict with a race, the extreme repugnance of whose institutions and character to their own, served greatly to nourish the nationality of sentiment. In this way, the spark of patriotism was kindled throughout the whole nation, and the most distant provinces of the Peninsula were knit together by a bond of union, which has remained indissoluble.

The consequences of these wars in a military aspect are also worthy of notice. Up to this period, war had been carried on by irregular levies, extremely limited in numerical amount and in period of service; under little subordination, except to their own immediate chiefs, and wholly unprovided with the apparatus required for extended operations. The Spaniards were even lower than most of the European nations in military science, as is apparent from the infinite pains of Isabella to avail herself of all foreign resources for their improvement. In the war of Granada, masses of men were brought together, far greater than had hitherto been known in modern warfare. They were kept in the field not only through long campaigns, but far into the winter; a thing altogether unprecedented. They were made to act in concert, and the numerous petty chiefs brought in complete subjection to one common head, whose personal character enforced the authority of station. Lastly, they were supplied with all the requisite munitions, through the providence of Isabella, who introduced into the service the most skillful engineers from other countries, and kept in pay bodies of mercenaries, as the Swiss for example, reputed the best disciplined troops of that day. In this admirable school, the Spanish soldier was gradually trained to patient endurance, fortitude, and thorough subordination, and those celebrated captains were formed, with that invincible infantry, which in the beginning of the sixteenth century spread the military fame of their country over all Christendom.

But, with all our sympathy for the conquerors, it is impossible, without a deep feeling of regret, to contemplate the decay and final extinction of a race, who had made such high advances in civilization as the Spanish Arabs; to see them driven from the stately palaces reared by their own hands, wandering as exiles over the lands, which still blossomed with the fruits of their industry, and wasting away under persecution, until their very name as a nation was blotted out from the map of history. It must be admitted, however, that they had long since reached their utmost limit of advancement as a people. The light shed over their history shines from distant ages; for, during the later period of their existence, they appear to have reposed in a state of torpid, luxurious indulgence, which would seem to argue, that, when causes of external excitement were withdrawn, the inherent vices of their social institutions had incapacitated them for the further production of excellence. In this impotent condition, it was wisely ordered, that their territory should be occupied by a people, whose religion and more liberal form of government, however frequently misunderstood or perverted, qualified them for advancing still higher the interests of humanity.

[THE SPANISH INQUISITION]

From *Ferdinand and Isabella*, Vol. I, pt. i, chap. vii

[Concluding reflections in a chapter on the establishment of the Inquisition in Spain. The selection is a bitter indictment of tyranny—that despotism of the spirit which nineteenth-century liberalism thought the worst of all despotisms.]

It is painful, after having dwelt so long on the important benefits resulting to Castile from the comprehensive policy of Isabella, to be compelled to turn to the darker side of the picture, and to exhibit her as accommodating herself to the illiberal spirit of the age in which she lived, so far as to sanction one of the grossest abuses that ever disgraced humanity. The present chapter will be devoted to the establishment and early progress of the Modern Inquisition; an institution, which has probably contributed more than any other cause to depress the lofty character of the ancient Spaniard, and which has thrown the gloom of fanaticism over those lovely regions which seem to be the natural abode of festivity and pleasure.

In the present liberal state of knowledge, we look with disgust at the pretensions of any human being, however exalted, to invade the sacred rights of conscience, inalienably possessed by every man. We feel that the spiritual concerns of an individual may be safely left to himself, as most interested in them, except so far as they can be affected by argument or friendly monition; that the idea of compelling belief in particular doctrines is a solecism, as absurd as wicked; and, so far from condemning to the stake, or the gibbet, men who pertinaciously adhere to their conscientious opinions in contempt of personal interests and in the face of danger, we should rather feel disposed to imitate the spirit of antiquity in raising altars and statues to their memory, as having displayed the highest efforts of human virtue. But, although these truths are now so obvious as rather to deserve the name of truisms, the world has been slow, very slow in arriving at them, after many centuries of unspeakable oppression and misery. * * *

Isabella's serious temper, as well as early education, naturally disposed her to religious influences. Notwithstanding the independence exhibited by her in all secular affairs, in her own spiritual concerns she uniformly testified the deepest humility, and deferred too implicitly to what she deemed the superior sagacity, or sanctity, of her ghostly counselors. An instance of this humility may be worth recording. When Fray Fernando de Talavera, afterwards archbishop of Granada, who had been appointed confessor to the queen, attended her for the first time in that capacity, he continued seated, after she had knelt down to make her confession, which drew from her the remark, "that it was usual for both parties to kneel." "No," replied the priest, "this is God's tribunal; I act here as his minister, and it is fitting that I should keep my seat, while your Highness kneels before me." Isabella, far from taking umbrage at the ecclesiastic's arrogant demeanor complied with all humility, and was afterwards heard to say, "This is the confessor that I wanted."

Well had it been for the land, if the queen's conscience had always been intrusted to the keeping of persons of such exemplary piety as Talavera. Unfortunately, in her early days, during the lifetime of her brother Henry, that charge was committed to a Dominican monk, Thomas de Torquemada, a native of old Castile, subsequently raised to the rank of prior of Santa Cruz in Segovia, and condemned to infamous immortality by the signal part which he performed in the tragedy of the Inquisition. This man, who concealed more pride under his monastic weeds than might have furnished forth a convent of his order, was one of that class, with whom zeal passes for religion, and who testify their zeal by a fiery persecution of those whose creed differs from their own; who compensate for their abstinence from sensual indulgence, by giving scope to those deadlier vices of the heart, pride, bigotry, and intolerance, which are no less opposed to virtue, and are far more extensively mischievous to society. This personage had earnestly labored to infuse into Isabella's young mind, to which his situation as her confessor gave him such ready access, the same spirit of fanaticism that glowed in his own. Fortunately this was greatly counteracted by her sound understanding and natural kindness of heart. Torquemada urged her, or indeed, as is stated by some, extorted a promise, that, "should she ever come to the throne, she would devote herself to the extirpation of heresy, for the glory of God, and the exaltation of the Catholic faith." The time was now arrived when this fatal promise was to be discharged.

It is due to Isabella's fame to state thus much in palliation of the unfortunate error into which she was led by her misguided zeal; an error so grave, that, like a vein in some noble piece of statuary, it gives a sinister expression to her otherwise unblemished character. It was not until the queen had endured the repeated importunities of the clergy, particularly of those reverend persons in whom she most confided, seconded by the arguments of Ferdinand, that she consented to solicit from the Pope a bull for the introduction of the Holy Office into Castile. Sixtus the Fourth, who at that time filled the pontifical chair, easily discerning the sources of wealth and influence, which this measure opened to the court of Rome, readily complied with the petition of the sovereigns, and expedited a bull bearing date November 1st, 1478, authorizing them to appoint two or three ecclesiastics, inquisitors for the detection and suppression of heresy throughout their dominions.

The queen, however, still averse to violent measures, suspended the operation of the ordinance, until a more lenient policy had been first tried. By her command, accordingly, the archbishop of Seville, cardinal Mendoza, drew up a catechism exhibiting the different points of the Catholic faith, and instructed the clergy throughout his diocese to spare no pains in illuminating the benighted Israelites, by means of friendly exhortation and a candid exposition of the true principles of Christianity. How far the spirit of these injunctions was complied with, amid the excitement then prevailing, may be reasonably doubted. There could be little doubt, however, that a report, made two years later, by a commission of ecclesiastics with Alfonso de Ojeda at its head, respecting the progress of the reformation, would be necessarily unfavorable to the Jews. In consequence of this report the papal provisions were enforced by the nomination, on the 17th of September, 1480, of two Dominican monks as inquisitors, with two other ecclesiastics, the one as assessor, and the other as procurator fiscal, with instructions to proceed at once to Seville, and enter on the duties of their office. Orders were also issued to the authorities of the city to support the inquisitors by all the aid in their power. But the new institution, which has since become the miserable boast of the Castilians, proved so distasteful to them in its origin, that they refused any co-operation with its ministers, and indeed opposed such delays and embarrassments, that, during the first years, it can scarcely be said to have obtained a footing in any other places in Andalusia, than those belonging to the crown.

On the 2d of January, 1481, the court commenced operations by the publication of an edict, followed by several others, requiring all persons to aid in apprehending and accusing all such as they might know, or suspect to be guilty of heresy, and holding out the illusory promise of absolution to such as should confess their errors within a limited period. As every mode of accusation, even anonymous, was invited, the number of victims multiplied so fast, that the tribunal found it convenient to remove its sittings from the convent of St. Paul within the city, to the spacious fortress of Triana, in the suburbs.

The presumptive proofs, by which the charge of Judaism was established against the accused are so curious, that a few of them may deserve notice. It was considered good evidence of the fact, if the prisoner wore better clothes or cleaner linen on the Jewish sabbath than on other days of the week; if he had no fire in his house the preceding evening, if he sat at table with Jews, or ate the meat of animals slaughtered by their hands, or drank a certain beverage held in much estimation by them; if he washed a corpse in warm water, or when dying turned his face to the wall; or, finally, if he gave Hebrew names to his children; a provision most whimsically cruel, since, by a law of Henry the Second, he was prohibited under severe penalties from giving them Christian names. He must have found it difficult to extricate himself from the horns of this dilemma. Such are a few of the circumstances, some of them purely accidental in their nature, others the result of early habit, which might well have continued after a sincere conversion to Christianity, and all of them trivial, on which capital accusations were to be alleged, and even satisfactorily established.

The inquisitors, adopting the wily and tortuous policy of the ancient tribunal, proceeded with a despatch, which shows that they could have paid little deference even to this affectation of legal form. On the sixth day of January, six convicts suffered at the stake. Seventeen more were executed in March, and a still greater number in the month following; and by the 4th of November in the same year, no less than two hundred and ninety-eight individuals had been sacrificed in the *autos da fe* of Seville. Besides these, the mouldering remains of many, who had been tried and convicted after their death, were torn up from their graves, with a hyena-like ferocity, which has disgraced no other court, Christian or Pagan, and condemned to the common funeral pile. This was prepared on a spacious stone scaffold, erected in the suburbs of the city, with the statues of four prophets attached to the corners, to which the unhappy sufferers were bound for the sacrifice, and which the worthy Curate of Los Palacios celebrates with much complacency as the spot, "where heretics were burnt, and ought to burn as long as any can be found."

Many of the convicts were persons estimable for learning and probity; and, among these, three clergymen are named, together with other individuals filling judicial or high municipal stations. The sword of justice was observed, in particular, to strike at the wealthy, the least pardonable offenders in times of proscription.

The plague which desolated Seville this year, sweeping off fifteen thousand inhabitants, as if in token of the wrath of Heaven at these enormities, did not palsy for a moment the arm of the Inquisition, which, adjourning to Aracena, continued as indefatigable as before. A similar persecution went forward in other parts of the province of Andalusia; so that within the same year, 1481, the number of the sufferers was computed at two thousand burnt alive, a still greater number in effigy, and seventeen thousand *reconciled*; a term which must not be understood by the reader to signify anything like a pardon or amnesty, but only the commutation of a capital sentence for inferior penalties, as fines, civil incapacity, very generally total confiscation of property, and not unfrequently imprisonment for life. * * *

The proceedings of the tribunal, as I have stated them, were plainly characterized throughout by the most flagrant injustice and inhumanity to the accused. Instead of presuming his innocence, until his guilt had been established, it acted on exactly the opposite principle. Instead of affording him the protection accorded by every other judicature, and especially demanded in his forlorn situation, it used the most insidious arts to circumvent and to crush him. He had no remedy against malice or misapprehension on the part of his accusers, or the witnesses against him, who might be his bitterest enemies; since they were never revealed to, nor confronted with the prisoner, nor subjected to a cross-examination, which can best expose error or willful collusion in the evidence. Even the poor forms of justice, recognized in this court, might be readily dispensed with; as its proceedings were impenetrably shrouded from the public eye, by the appalling oath of secrecy imposed on all, whether functionaires, witnesses, or prisoners, who entered within its precincts. The last, and not the least odious feature of the whole, was the connexion established between the condemnation of the accused and the interests of his judges; since the confiscations, which were the uniform penalties of heresy, were not permitted to flow into the royal exchequer, until they had first discharged the expenses, whether in the shape of salaries or otherwise, incident to the Holy Office.

The last scene in this dismal tragedy was the *act of faith* (auto da fe), the most imposing spectacle probably, which has been witnessed since the ancient Roman triumph, and which, as intimated by a Spanish writer, was intended, somewhat profanely, to represent the terrors of the Day of Judgment. The proudest grandees of the land, on this occasion, putting on the sable livery of familiars of the Holy Office and bearing aloft its banners, condescended to act as the escort of its ministers; while the ceremony was not unfrequently countenanced by the royal presence. It should be stated, however, that neither of these acts of condescension, or more properly, humiliation, were witnessed until a period posterior to the present reign. The effect was further heightened by the concourse of ecclesiastics in their sacerdotal robes, and the pompous ceremonial, which the church of Rome knows so well how to display on fitting occasions; and which was intended to consecrate, as it were, this bloody sacrifice by the authority of a religion, which has expressly declared that it desires mercy and not sacrifice.

The most important actors in the scene were the unfortunate convicts, who were now disgorged for the first time from the dungeons of the tribunal. They were clad in coarse woolen garments, styled *san benitos*, brought close round the neck and descending like a frock, down to the knees. These were of a yellow color, embroidered with a scarlet cross, and well garnished with figures of devils and flames of fire, which, typical of the heretic's destiny hereafter, served to make him more odious in the eyes of the superstitious multitude. The greater part of the sufferers were condemned to be *reconciled*, the manifold meanings of which soft phrase have been already explained. Those who were to be *relaxed*, as it was called, were delivered over, as impenitent heretics, to the secular arm, in order to expiate their offense by the most painful of deaths, with the consciousness, still more painful, that they were to leave behind them names branded with infamy, and families involved in irretrievable ruin.

It is remarkable, that a scheme so monstrous as that of the Inquisition, presenting the most effectual barrier, probably, that was ever opposed to the progress of knowledge, should have been revived at the close of the fifteenth century, when the light of civilization was rapidly advancing over every part of Europe. It is more remarkable, that it should have occurred in Spain, at this time under a government, which had displayed great religious independence on more than one occasion, and which had paid uniform regard to the rights of its subjects, and pursued a generous policy in reference to their intellectual culture. Where, we are tempted to ask, when we behold the persecution of an innocent, industrious people for the crime of adhesion to the faith of their ancestors, where was the charity, which led the old Castilian to reverence valor and virtue in an infidel, though an enemy? Where the chivalrous self-devotion, which led an Aragonese monarch, three centuries before, to give away his life, in defense of the persecuted sectaries of Provence? Where the independent spirit, which prompted the Castilian nobles, during the very last reign, to reject with scorn the purposed interference of the Pope himself in their concerns, that they were now reduced to bow their necks to a few frantic priests, the members of an order, which, in Spain at least, was quite as conspicuous for ignorance as intolerance? True indeed the Castilians, and the Aragonese subsequently still more, gave such evidence of their aversion to the institution, that it can hardly be believed the clergy would have succeeded in fastening it upon them, had they not availed themselves of the popular prejudices against the Jews. Providence, however, permitted that the sufferings, thus heaped on the heads of this unfortunate people, should be requited in full measure to the nation that inflicted them. The fires of the Inquisition, which were lighted exclusively for the Jews, were destined eventually to consume their oppressors. They were still more deeply avenged in the moral influence of this tribunal, which, eating like a pestilent canker into the heart of the monarchy, at the very time when it was exhibiting a most goodly promise, left it at length a bare and sapless trunk.

Notwithstanding the persecutions under Torquemada were confined almost wholly to the Jews, his activity was such as to furnish abundant precedent, in regard to forms of proceeding, for his successors; if, indeed, the word forms may be applied to the conduct of trials so summary, that the tribunal of Toledo alone, under the superintendence of two inquisitors, disposed of three thousand three hundred and twenty-seven processes in little more than a year. The number of convicts was greatly swelled by the blunders of the Dominican monks, who acted as qualificators, or interpreters of what constituted heresy, and whose ignorance led them frequently to condemn as heterodox, propositions actually derived from the fathers of the church. The prisoners for life, alone, became so numerous, that it was necessary to assign them their own houses as the places of their incarceration.

The data for an accurate calculation of the number of victims sacrificed by the Inquisition during this reign are not very satisfactory. From such as exist, however, Llorente has been led to the most frightful results. He computes, that, during the eighteen years of Torquemada's ministry, there were no less than 10,220 burnt, 6,860 condemned, and burnt in effigy as absent or dead, and 97,321 reconciled by various other penances; affording an average of more than 6,000 convicted persons annually. In this enormous sum of human misery is not included the multitude of orphans, who, from the confiscation of their paternal inheritance, were turned over to indigence and vice. Many of the reconciled were afterwards sentenced as relapsed; and the Curate of Los Palacios expresses the charitable wish, that "the whole accursed race of Jews, male and female, of twenty years of age and upwards, might be purified with fire and fagot!"

The vast apparatus of the Inquisition involved so heavy an expenditure, that a very small sum, comparatively, found its way into the exchequer, to counterbalance the great detriment resulting to the state from the sacrifice of the most active and skillful part of its population. All temporal interests, however, were held light in comparison with the purgation of the land from heresy; and such augmentations as the revenue did receive, we are assured, were conscientiously devoted to pious purposes, and the Moorish war!

The Roman see, during all this time, conducting itself with its usual duplicity, contrived to make a gainful traffic by the sale of dispensations from the penalties incurred by such as fell under the ban of the Inquisition, provided they were rich enough to pay for them, and afterwards revoking them, at the instance of the Castilian court. Meanwhile, the odium, excited by the unsparing rigor of Torquemada, raised up so many accusations against him, that he was thrice compelled to send an agent to Rome to defend his cause before the pontiff; until, at length, Alexander the Sixth, in 1494, moved by these reiterated complaints, appointed four coadjutors, out of a pretended regard to the infirmities of his age, to share with him the burdens of his office.

This personage, who is entitled to so high a rank among those who have been the authors of unmixed evil to their species, was permitted to reach a very old age, and to die quietly in his bed. Yet he lived in such constant apprehension of assassination, that he is said to have kept a reputed unicorn's horn always on his table, which was imagined to have the power of detecting and neutralizing poisons; while, for the more complete protection of his person, he was allowed an escort of fifty horse and two hundred foot in his progresses through the kingdom.

This man's zeal was of such an extravagant character, that it may almost shelter itself under the name of insanity. His history may be thought to prove, that, of all human infirmities, or rather vices, there is none productive of more extensive mischief to society than fanaticism. The opposite principle of atheism, which refuses to recognize the most important sanctions to virtue, does not necessarily imply any destitution of just moral perceptions, that is, of a power of discriminating between right and wrong, in its disciples. But fanaticism is so far subversive of the most established principles of morality, that, under the dangerous maxim, "For the advancement of the faith, all means are lawful," which Tasso has rightly, though perhaps undesignedly derived from the spirits of hell, it not only excuses, but enjoins the commission of the most revolting crimes, as a sacred duty. The more repugnant, indeed, such crimes may be to natural feeling, or public sentiment, the greater their merit, from the sacrifice which the commission of them involves. Many a bloody page of history attests the fact, that fanaticism, armed with power, is the sorest evil which can befall a nation.

[EUROPEAN POLITICS AT THE END OF THE FIFTEENTH CENTURY]

From *Ferdinand and Isabella*, Vol. II, pt. ii, chap. i

[Part of the introduction to the section of the history which deals with the foreign policy of the reign.]

The close of the fifteenth century presents, on the whole, the most striking point of view in modern history; one from which we may contemplate the consummation of an important revolution in the structure of political society, and the first application of several inventions destined to exercise the widest influence on human civilization. The feudal institutions, or rather the feudal principle, which operated even where the institutions, strictly speaking, did not exist, after having wrought its appointed uses, had gradually fallen into decay; for it had not the power of accommodating itself to the increased demands and improved condition of society. However well suited to a barbarous age, it was found that the distribution of power among the members of an independent aristocracy, was unfavorable to that degree of personal security and tranquillity indispensable to great proficiency in the higher arts of civilization. It was equally repugnant to the principle of patriotism, so essential to national independence, but which must have operated feebly among a people, whose sympathies, instead of being concentrated on the state, were claimed by a hundred masters, as was the case in every feudal community. The conviction of this reconciled the nation to the transfer of authority into other hands; not those of the people, indeed, who were too ignorant, and too long accustomed to a subordinate, dependent situation, to admit of it,—but into the hands of the sovereign. It was not until three centuries more had elapsed, that the condition of the great mass of the people was to be so far improved, as to qualify them for asserting and maintaining the political consideration which of right belongs to them.

In whatever degree public opinion and the progress of events might favor the transition of power from the aristocracy to the monarch, it is obvious that much would depend on his personal character: since the advantages of his station alone made him by no means a match for the combined forces of his great nobility. The remarkable adaptation of the characters of the principal sovereigns of Europe to this exigency, in the latter half of the fifteenth century, would seem to have something providential in it. Henry the Seventh of England, Louis the Eleventh of France, Ferdinand of Naples, John the Second of Aragon and his son Ferdinand, and John the Second of Portugal, however differing in other respects, were all distinguished by a sagacity, which enabled them to devise the most subtile and comprehensive schemes of policy, and which was prolific in expedients for the circumvention of enemies too potent to be encountered by open force.

Their operations, all directed towards the same point, were attended with similar success, resulting in the exaltation of the royal prerogative at the expense of the aristocracy, with more or less deference to the rights of the people, as the case might be; in France, for example, with almost total indifference to them, while in Spain they were regarded, under the parental administration of Isabella, which tempered the less scrupulous policy of her husband, with tenderness and respect. In every country, however, the nation at large gained greatly by the revolution, which came on insensibly, at least without any violent shock to the fabric of society, and which, by securing internal tranquillity and the ascendency of law over brute force, gave ample scope for those intellectual pursuits, that withdraw mankind from sensual indulgence, and too exclusive devotion to the animal wants of our nature.

No sooner was the internal organization of the different nations of Europe placed on a secure basis, than they found leisure to direct their views, hitherto confined within their own limits, to a bolder and more distant sphere of action. Their international communication was greatly facilitated by several useful inventions coincident with this period, or then first extensively applied. Such was the art of printing, diffusing knowledge with the speed and universality of light; the establishment of posts, which, after its adoption by Louis the Eleventh, came into frequent use in the beginning of the sixteenth century; and lastly, the compass, which, guiding the mariner unerringly through the trackless wastes of the ocean, brought the remotest regions into contact. With these increased facilities for intercommunication, the different European states might be said to be brought into as intimate relation with one another, as the different provinces of the same kingdom were before. They now for the first time regarded each other as members of one great community, in whose action they were all mutually concerned. A greater anxiety was manifested to detect the springs of every political movement of their neighbors. Missions became frequent, and accredited agents were stationed, as a sort of honorable spies, at the different courts. The science of diplomacy, on narrower grounds, indeed, than it is now practiced, began to be studied. Schemes of aggression and resistance, leading to political combinations the most complex and extended, were gradually formed. We are not to imagine, however, the existence of any well-defined ideas of a balance of power at this early period. The object of these combinations was some positive act of aggression or resistance, for purposes of conquest or defense, not for the maintenance of any abstract theory of political equilibrium. This was the result of much deeper reflection, and of prolonged experience.

The management of the foreign relations of the nation, at the close of the fifteenth century, was resigned wholly to the sovereign. The people took no further part or interest in the matter, than if it had concerned only the disposition of his private property. His measures were, therefore, often characterized by a degree of temerity and precipitation, that could not have been permitted under the salutary checks afforded by popular interposition. A strange insensibility, indeed, was shown to the rights and interests of the nation. War was regarded as a game, in which the sovereign parties engaged, not on behalf of their subjects, but exclusively on their own. Like desperate gamblers, they contended for the spoils or the honors of victory, with so much the more recklessness as their own station was too elevated to be materially prejudiced by the results. They contended with all the animosity of personal feeling; every device, however paltry, was resorted to; and no advantage was deemed unwarrantable, which could tend to secure the victory. The most profligate maxims of state policy were openly avowed by men of reputed honor and integrity. In short, the diplomacy of that day is very generally characterized by a low cunning, subterfuge, and petty trickery, which would leave an indelible stain on the transactions of private individuals.

Italy was, doubtless, the great school where this political morality was taught. That country was broken up into a number of small states, too nearly equal to allow the absolute supremacy of any one; while, at the same time, it demanded the most restless vigilance on the part of each to maintain its independence against its neighbors. Hence such a complexity of intrigues and combinations as the world had never before witnessed. A subtile, refined policy was conformable to the genius of the Italians. It was partly the result, moreover, of their higher cultivation, which naturally led them to trust the settlement of their disputes to superior intellectual dexterity, rather than to brute force, like the *barbarians* beyond the Alps. From these and other causes, maxims were gradually established, so monstrous in their nature as to give the work, which first embodied them in a regular system, the air of a satire rather than a serious performance, while the name of its author has been converted into a byword of political knavery.

At the period before us, the principal states of Italy were, the republics of Venice and Florence, the duchy of Milan, the papal see, and the kingdom of Naples. The others may be regarded merely as satellites, revolving round some one or other of these superior powers, by whom their respective movements were regulated and controlled. Venice may be considered as the most formidable of the great powers, taking into consideration her wealth, her powerful navy, her territory in the north, and princely colonial domain. There was no government in that age which attracted such general admiration, both from natives and foreigners; who seem to have looked upon it as affording the very best model of political wisdom. Yet there was no country where the citizen enjoyed less positive freedom; none whose foreign relations were conducted with more absolute selfishness, and with a more narrow, bargaining spirit, savoring rather of a company of traders than of a great and powerful state. But all this was compensated, in the eyes of her contemporaries, by the stability of her institutions, which still remained unshaken, amidst revolutions which had convulsed or overturned every other social fabric in Italy.

The government of Milan was at this time under the direction of Lodovico Sforza, or Lodovico the Moor, as he is commonly called; an epithet suggested by his complexion, but which he willingly retained, as indicating the superior craftiness on which he valued himself. He held the reins in the name of his nephew, then a minor, until a convenient season should arrive for assuming them in his own. His cool, perfidious character was stained with the worst vices of the most profligate class of Italian statesmen of that period.

The central parts of Italy were occupied by the republic of Florence, which had ever been the rallying point of the friends of freedom, too often of faction; but which had now resigned itself to the dominion of the Medici, whose cultivated tastes and munificent patronage shed a splendid illusion over their administration, which has blinded the eyes of contemporaries, and even of posterity.

The papal chair was filled by Alexander the Sixth, a pontiff whose licentiousness, avarice, and unblushing effrontery have been the theme of unmingled reproach, with Catholic as well as Protestant writers. His preferment was effected by lavish bribery, and by his consummate address, as well as energy of character. Although a native Spaniard, his election was extremely unpalatable to Ferdinand and Isabella, who deprecated the scandal it must bring upon the church, and who had little to hope for themselves, in a political view, from the elevation of one of their own subjects even, whose mercenary spirit placed him at the control of the highest bidder.

The Neapolitan scepter was swayed by Ferdinand the First, whose father, Alfonso the Fifth, the uncle of Ferdinand of Aragon, had obtained the crown by the adoption of Joanna of Naples, or rather by his own good sword. Alfonso settled his conquest on his illegitimate son Ferdinand, to the prejudice of the rights of Aragon, by whose blood and treasure he had achieved it. Ferdinand's character, the very opposite of his noble father's, was dark, wily, and ferocious. His life was spent in conflict with his great feudal nobility, many of whom supported the pretensions of the Angevin family. But his superior craft enabled him to foil every attempt of his enemies. In effecting this, indeed, he shrunk from no deed of treachery or violence, however atrocious, and in the end had the satisfaction of establishing his authority, undisputed, on the fears of his subjects. He was about seventy years of age at the period of which we are treating, 1493. The heir apparent, Alfonso, was equally sanguinary in his temper, though possessing less talent for dissimulation than his father.

Such was the character of the principal Italian courts at the close of the fifteenth century. The politics of the country were necessarily regulated by the temper and views of the leading powers. They were essentially selfish and personal. The ancient republican forms had been gradually effaced during this century, and more arbitrary ones introduced. The name of freedom, indeed, was still inscribed on their banners, but the spirit had disappeared. In almost every state, great or small, some military adventurer, or crafty statesman, had succeeded in raising his own authority on the liberties of his country; and his sole aim seemed to be to enlarge it still further, and to secure it against the conspiracies and revolutions, which the reminiscence of ancient independence naturally called forth. Such was the case with Tuscany, Milan, Naples, and the numerous subordinate states. In Rome, the pontiff proposed no higher object than the concentration of wealth and public honors in the hands of his own family. In short, the administration of every state seemed to be managed with exclusive reference to the personal interests of its chief. Venice was the only power of sufficient strength and stability to engage in more extended schemes of policy, and even these were conducted, as has been already noticed, in the narrow and calculating spirit of a trading corporation.

But, while no spark of generous patriotism seemed to warm the bosoms of the Italians; while no sense of public good, or even menace of foreign invasion, could bring them to act in concert with one another, the internal condition of the country was eminently prosperous. Italy had far outstripped the rest of Europe in the various arts of civilized life; and she everywhere afforded the evidence of faculties developed by unceasing intellectual action. The face of the country itself was like a garden; "cultivated through all its plains to the very tops of the mountains; teeming with population, with riches, and an unlimited commerce; illustrated by many munificent princes, by the splendor of many noble and beautiful cities, and by the majesty of religion; and adorned with all those rare and precious gifts, which render a name glorious among the nations." Such are the glowing strains in which the Tuscan historian celebrates the prosperity of his country, ere yet the storm of war had descended on her beautiful valleys.

[THE EMPIRE OF PHILIP]

From *Philip the Second*, Bk. I, Chap. v

[Introductory to the narrative of Philip's War with the Pope.]

Soon after Philip's arrival in Brussels took place that memorable scene of the abdication of Charles the Fifth, which occupies the introductory pages of our narrative. By this event Philip saw himself master of the most widely extended and powerful monarchy in Europe. He was king of Spain, comprehending under that name Castile, Aragon, and Granada, which, after surviving as independent states for centuries, had been first brought under one scepter in the reign of his father, Charles the Fifth. He was king of Naples and Sicily, and duke of Milan, which important possessions enabled him to control to a great extent the nicely-balanced scales of Italian politics. He was lord of Franche-Comté, and of the Low Countries, comprehending the most flourishing and populous provinces in Christendom, whose people had made the greatest progress in commerce, husbandry, and the various mechanic arts. As titular king of England, he eventually obtained an influence which, as we shall see, enabled him to direct the counsels of that country to his own purposes. In Africa he possessed the Cape de Verd Islands and the Canaries, as well as Tunis, Oran, and some other important places on the Barbary coast. He owned the Philippines and the Spice Islands in Asia. In America, besides his possessions in the West Indies, he was master of the rich empires of Mexico and Peru, and claimed a right to a boundless extent of country, that offered an inexhaustible field to the cupidity and enterprise of the Spanish adventurer. Thus the dominions of Philip stretched over every quarter of the globe. The flag of Castile was seen in the remotest latitudes,—on the Atlantic, the Pacific, and the far-off

Indian seas,—passing from port to port, and uniting by commercial intercourse the widely scattered members of her vast colonial empire.

The Spanish army consisted of the most formidable infantry in Europe; veterans who had been formed under the eye of Charles the Fifth and of his generals, who had fought on the fields of Pavia and of Muhlberg, or who, in the New World, had climbed the Andes with Almagro and Pizarro and helped these bold chiefs to overthrow the dynasty of the Incas. The navy of Spain and Flanders combined far exceeded that of any other power in the number and size of its vessels; and if its supremacy might be contested by England on the "narrow seas," it rode the undisputed mistress of the ocean. To supply the means for maintaining this costly establishment, as well as the general machinery of government, Philip had at his command the treasures of the New World; and if the incessant enterprises of his father had drained the exchequer, it was soon replenished by the silver streams that flowed in from the inexhaustible mines of Zacatecas and Potosí.

All this vast empire, with its magnificent resources, was placed at the disposal of a single man. Philip ruled over it with an authority more absolute than that possessed by any European prince since the days of the Cæsars. The Netherlands, indeed, maintained a show of independence under the shadow of their ancient institutions. But they consented to supply the necessities of the crown by a tax larger than the revenues of America. Naples and Milan were ruled by Spanish viceroys. Viceroys, with delegated powers scarcely less than those of their sovereign, presided over the American colonies, which received their laws from the parent country. In Spain itself, the authority of the nobles was gone. First assailed under Ferdinand and Isabella, it was completely broken down under Charles the Fifth. The liberties of the commons were crushed at the fatal battle of Villalar, in the beginning of that monarch's reign. Without nobles, without commons, the ancient cortes had faded into a mere legislative pageant, with hardly any other right than that of presenting petitions and of occasionally raising an ineffectual note of remonstrance against abuses. It had lost the power to redress them. Thus all authority vested in the sovereign. His will was the law of the land. From his palace at Madrid he sent forth the edicts which became the law of Spain and of her remotest colonies. It may well be believed that foreign nations watched with interest the first movements of a prince who seemed to hold in his hands the destinies of Europe, and that they regarded with no little apprehension the growth of that colossal power which had already risen to a height that cast a shadow over every other monarchy.

From his position, Philip stood at the head of the Roman Catholic princes. He was in temporal matters what the pope was in spiritual. In the existing state of Christendom, he had the same interest as the pope in putting down that spirit of religious reform which had begun to show itself, in public or in private, in every corner of Europe. He was the natural ally of the pope. He understood this well, and would have acted on it. Yet, strange to say, his very first war, after his accession, was with the pope himself. It was a war not of Philip's seeking.

IV. SOCIAL AND CULTURAL HISTORY

[AZTEC CIVILIZATION: GOVERNMENT AND NOBILITY]

From *The Conquest of Mexico*, Bk. I, chap. ii

[The first book of *The Conquest of Mexico* is a view of Aztec civilization. This study of native political life follows a description of Mexican geography. While suggesting a rather romantic view of Aztec society (a view that brought on the criticism of Lewis H. Morgan), it nevertheless reveals something of the skepticism with which Prescott handled subjects that he knew had been overlaid with a glamorous coating.]

The form of government differed in the different states of Anahuac. With the Aztecs and Tezcucans it was monarchical and nearly absolute. The two nations resembled each other so much, in their political institutions, that one of their historians has remarked, in too unqualified a manner indeed, that what is told of one may be always understood as applying to the other. I shall direct my inquiries to the Mexican polity, borrowing an illustration occasionally from that of the rival kingdom.

The government was an elective monarchy. Four of the principal nobles, who had been chosen by their own body in the preceding reign, filled the office of electors, to whom were added, with merely an honorary rank however, the two royal allies of Tezcuco and Tlacopan. The sovereign was selected from the brothers of the deceased prince, or, in default of them, from his nephews. Thus the election was always restricted to the same family. The candidate preferred must have distinguished himself in war, though, as in the case of the last Montezuma he were a member of the priesthood. This singular mode of supplying the throne had some advantages. The candidates received an education which fitted them for the royal dignity, while the age, at which they were chosen, not only secured the nation against the evils of minority, but afforded ample means for estimating their qualifications for the office. The result, at all events, was favorable; since the throne, as already noticed, was filled by a succession of able princes, well qualified to rule over a warlike and ambitious people. The scheme of election, however defective, argues a more refined and calculating policy than was to have been expected from a barbarous nation.

The new monarch was installed in his regal dignity with much parade of religious ceremony; but not until, by a victorious campaign he had obtained a sufficient number of captives to grace his triumphal entry into the capital, and to furnish victims for the dark and bloody rites which stained the Aztec superstition. Amidst this pomp of human sacrifice, he was crowned. The crown, resembling a mitre in its form, and curiously ornamented with gold, gems, and feathers, was placed on his head by the lord of Tezcuco, the most powerful of his royal allies. The title of *King*, by which the earlier Aztec princes are distinguished by Spanish writers, is supplanted by that of *Emperor* in the later reigns, intimating, perhaps, his superiority over the confederated monarchies of Tlacopan and Tezcuco.

The Aztec princes, especially towards the close of the dynasty, lived in a barbaric pomp, truly Oriental. Their spacious palaces were provided with halls for the different councils, who aided the monarch in the transaction of business. The chief of these was a sort of privy council, composed in part, probably, of the four electors chosen by the nobles after the accession, whose places, when made vacant by death, were immediately supplied as before. It was the business of this body, so far as can be gathered from the very loose accounts given of it, to advise the king, in respect to the government of the provinces, the administration of the revenues, and, indeed, on all great matters of public interest.

In the royal buildings were accommodations, also, for a numerous bodyguard of the sovereign, made up of the chief nobility. It is not easy to determine with precision, in these barbarian governments, the limits of the several orders. It is certain, there was a distinct class of nobles, with large landed possessions, who held the most important offices near the person of the prince, and engrossed the administration of the provinces and cities. Many of these could trace their descent from the founders of the Aztec monarchy. According to some writers of authority, there were thirty great *caciques*, who had their residence, at least a part of the year, in the capital, and who could muster a hundred thousand vassals each on their estates. Without relying on such wild statements, it is clear, from the testimony of the Conquerors, that the country was occupied by numerous powerful chieftains, who lived like independent princes on their domains. If it be true that the kings encouraged, or, indeed, exacted, the residence of these nobles in the capital, and required hostages in their absence, it is evident that their power must have been very formidable.

Their estates appear to have been held by various tenures, and to have been subject to different restrictions. Some of them, earned by their own good swords or received as the recompense of public services, were held without any limitation, execpt that the possessors could not dispose of them to a plebeian. Others were entailed on the eldest male issue and, in default of such, reverted to the crown. Most of them seem to have been burdened with the obligation of military service. The principal chiefs of Tezcuco, according to its chronicler, were expressly obliged to support their prince with their armed vassals, to attend his court, and aid him in the council. Some, instead of these services, were to provide for the repairs of his buildings, and to keep the royal demesnes in order, with an annual offering, by way of homage, of fruits and flowers. It was usual, if we are to believe historians, for a new king, on his accession, to confirm the investiture of estates derived from the crown.

It cannot be denied that we recognize, in all this, several features of the feudal system, which, no doubt, lose nothing of their effect, under the hands of the Spanish writers, who are fond of tracing analogies to European institutions. But such analogies lead sometimes to very erroneous conclusions. The obligation of military service, for instance, the most essential principle of a fief, seems to be naturally demanded by every government from its subjects. As to minor points of resemblance, they fall far short of that harmonious system of reciprocal service and protection, which embraced, in nice gradation, every order of a feudal monarchy. The kingdoms of Anahuac were, in their nature, despotic, attended, indeed, with many mitigating circumstances unknown to the despotisms of the East; but it is chimerical to look for much in common—beyond a few accidental forms and ceremonies—with those aristocratic institutions of the Middle Ages, which made the court of every petty baron the precise image in miniature of that of his sovereign.

[AZTEC CIVILIZATION: RELIGION]

From *The Conquest of Mexico*, Bk. I, chap. iii

[Continuing his study of Aztec culture, Prescott writes a close analysis of native religion. In this selection the author's footnotes are all reproduced in order that the reader may have an excellent example of Prescott's methods of documentation.]

In contemplating the religious system of the Aztecs, one is struck with its apparent incongruity, as if some portion of it had emanated from a comparatively refined people, open to gentle influences, while the rest breathes a spirit of unmitigated ferocity. It naturally suggests the idea of two distinct sources, and authorizes the belief that the Aztecs had inherited from their predecessors a milder faith, on which was afterwards engrafted their own mythology. The latter soon became dominant, and gave its dark coloring to the creeds of the conquered nations,—which the Mexicans, like the ancient Romans, seem willing to have incorporated into their own,—until the same funereal superstition settled over the farthest borders of Anahuac.

The Aztecs recognized the existence of a supreme Creator

and Lord of the universe. They addressed him, in their prayers, as "the God by whom we live," "omnipresent, that knoweth all thoughts, and giveth all gifts," "without whom man is as nothing," "invisible, incorporeal, one God, of *perfect perfection* and purity," "under whose wings we find repose and a sure defense." These sublime attributes infer no inadequate conception of the true God. But the idea of unity—of a being, with whom volition is action, who has no need of inferior ministers to execute his purposes—was too simple, or too vast, for their understandings; and they sought relief, as usual, in a plurality of deities, who presided over the elements, the changes of the seasons, and the various occupations of man.[1] Of these, there were thirteen principal deities, and more than two hundred inferior; to each of whom some special day, or appropriate festival, was consecrated.[2]

At the head of all stood the terrible Huitzilopotchli, the Mexican Mars; although it is doing injustice to the heroic war-god of antiquity to identify him with this sanguinary monster. This was the patron deity of the nation. His fantastic image was loaded with costly ornaments. His temples were the most stately and august of the public edifices; and his altars reeked

---

[1] Ritter has well shown, by the example of the Hindoo system, how the idea of unity suggests, of itself, that of plurality. History of Ancient Philosophy, Eng. trans., (Oxford, 1838,) book 2, ch. 1.

[2] Sahagun, Hist. de Nueva España, lib. 6, passim.—Acosta, lib. 5, ch. 9.—Boturini, Idea, p. 8, et seq.—Ixtlilxochitl, Hist. Chich., MS., cap. 1.—Camargo, Hist. de Tlascala, MS.

The Mexicans, according to Clavigero, believed in an evil Spirit, the enemy of the human race, whose barbarous name signified "Rational Owl." (Stor. del Messico, tom. II. p. 2.) The curate Bernaldez speaks of the Devil being embroidered on the dresses of Columbus's Indians, in the likeness of an owl. (Historia de los Reyes Católicos, MS., cap. 131.) This must not be confounded, however, with the evil Spirit in the mythology of the North American Indians, (see Heckewelder's Account, ap. Transactions of the American Philosophical Society, Philadelphia, vol. I. p. 205,) still less, with the evil Principle of the Oriental nations of the Old World. It was only one among many deities, for evil was found too liberally mingled in the natures of most of the Aztec gods,—in the same manner as with the Greek,—to admit of its personification by any one.

with the blood of human hecatombs in every city of the empire. Disastrous, indeed, must have been the influence of such a superstition on the character of the people.[1]

A far more interesting personage in their mythology was Quetzalcoatl, god of the air, a divinity who, during his residence on earth, instructed the natives in the use of metals, in agriculture, and in the arts of government. He was one of those benefactors of their species, doubtless, who have been deified by the gratitude of posterity. Under him, the earth teemed with fruits and flowers, without the pains of culture. An ear

---

[1] Sahagun, Hist. de Nueva España, lib. 3, cap. 1, et seq.—Acosta, lib. 5, ch. 9.—Torquemada, Monarch. Ind., lib. 6, cap. 21.—Boturini, Idea, pp. 27, 28.

Huitzilopotchli is compounded of two words, signifying "humming-bird," and "left," from his image having the feathers of this bird on its left foot; (Clavigero, Stor. del Messico, tom. II. p. 17;) an amiable etymology for so ruffian a deity.—The fantastic forms of the Mexican idols were in the highest degree symbolical. See Gama's learned exposition of the devices on the statue of the goddess found in the great square of Mexico. (Descripcion de las Dos Piedras, (México, 1832,) Parte 1, pp. 34–44.) The tradition respecting the origin of this god, or, at least, his appearance on earth, is curious. He was born of a woman. His mother, a devout person, one day, in her attendance on the temple, saw a ball of bright-colored feathers floating in the air. She took it, and deposited it in her bosom. She soon after found herself pregnant, and the dread deity was born, coming into the world, like Minerva, all armed,—with a spear in the right hand, a shield in the left, and his head surmounted by a crest of green plumes. (See Clavigero, Stor. del Messico, tom. II. p. 19 et seq.) A similar notion in respect to the incarnation of their principal deity existed among the people of India beyond the Ganges, of China, and of Thibet. "Budh," says Milman, in his learned and luminous work on the History of Christianity, "according to a tradition known in the West, was born of a virgin. So were the Fohi of China, and the Schakaof of Thibet, no doubt the same, whether a mythic or a real personage. The Jesuits in China, says Barrow, were appalled at finding in the mythology of that country the counterpart of the Virgo Deipara." (Vol. I. p. 99, note.) The existence of similar religious ideas in remote regions, inhabited by different races, is an interesting subject of study; furnishing, as it does, one of the most important links in the great chain of communication which binds together the distant families of nations.

of Indian corn was as much as a single man could carry. The cotton, as it grew, took, of its own accord, the rich dyes of human art. The air was filled with intoxicating perfumes and the sweet melody of birds. In short, these were the halcyon days, which find a place in the mythic systems of so many nations in the Old World. It was the *golden age* of Anahuac.

From some cause, not explained, Quetzalcoatl incurred the wrath of one of the principal gods and was compelled to abandon the country. On his way, he stopped at the city of Cholula, where a temple was dedicated to his worship, the massy ruins of which still form one of the most interesting relics of antiquity in Mexico. When he reached the shores of the Mexican Gulf, he took leave of his followers, promising that he and his descendants would revisit them hereafter, and then, entering his wizard skiff, made of serpents' skins, embarked on the great ocean for the fabled land of Tlapallan. He was said to have been tall in stature, with a white skin, long, dark hair, and a flowing beard. The Mexicans looked confidently to the return of the benevolent deity; and this remarkable tradition, deeply cherished in their hearts, prepared the way, as we shall see hereafter, for the future success of the Spaniards.[1]

[1] Codex Vaticanus, Pl. 15, and Codex Telleriano-Remensis, Part 2, Pl. 2, ap. Antiq. of Mexico, vols. I., VI.—Sahagun, Hist. de Nueva España, lib. 3, cap. 3, 4, 13, 14.—Torquemada, Monarch. Ind., lib. 6, cap. 24.—Ixtlilxochitl, Hist. Chich., MS., cap. 1.—Gomara, Crónica de la Nueva España, cap. 222, ap. Barcia, Historiadores Primitivos de las Indias Occidentales, (Madrid, 1749,) tom. II.

Quetzalcoatl signifies "feathered serpent." The last syllable means, likewise, a "twin"; which furnished an argument for Dr. Siguenza to identify this god with the apostle Thomas, (Didymus signifying also a twin,) who, he supposes, came over to America to preach the gospel. In this rather startling conjecture he is supported by several of his devout countrymen, who appear to have as little doubt of the fact as of the advent of St. James, for a similar purpose, in the mother country. See the various authorities and arguments set forth with becoming gravity in Dr. Mier's dissertation in Bustamante's edition of Sahagun, (lib. 3, Suplem.,) and Veytia, (tom. I. pp. 160–200.) Our ingenious countryman, McCulloh, carries the Aztec god up to a still more respectable antiquity, by identifying

We have not space for further details respecting the Mexican divinities, the attributes of many of whom were carefully defined, as they descended, in regular gradation, to the _penates_ or household gods, whose little images were to be found in the humblest dwelling.

The Aztecs felt the curiosity, common to man in almost every stage of civilization, to lift the veil which covers the mysterious past, and the more awful future. They sought relief, like the nations of the Old Continent, from the oppressive idea of eternity, by breaking it up into distinct cyles, or periods of time, each of several thousand years' duration. There were four of these cycles, and at the end of each, by the agency of the elements, the human family was swept from the earth, and the sun blotted out from the heavens, to be again rekindled.[1]

They imagined three separate states of existence in the future life. The wicked, comprehending the greater part of mankind, were to expiate their sins in a place of everlasting darkness.

---

him with the patriarch Noah. Researches, Philosophical and Antiquarian, concerning the Aboriginal History of America, (Baltimore, 1829,) p. 233.

[1] Cod. Vat., Pl. 7–10, ap. Antiq. of Mexico, vols. I., VI.—Ixtlilxochitl, Hist. Chich., MS., cap. 1.

M. de Humboldt has been at some pains to trace the analogy between the Aztec cosmogony and that of Eastern Asia. He has tried, though in vain, to find a multiple which might serve as the key to the calculations of the former. (Vues des Cordillères, pp. 202–212.) In truth, there seems to be a material discordance in the Mexican statements, both in regard to the number of revolutions and their duration. A manuscript before me, of Ixtlilxochitl, reduces them to three, before the present state of the world, and allows only 4394 years for them; (Sumaria Relacion, MS., No. 1;) Gama, on the faith of an ancient Indian MS., in Boturini's Catalogue, (VIII. 13,) reduces the duration still lower; (Descripcion de las Dos Piedras, Parte 1, p. 49, et seq.;) while the cycles of the Vatican paintings take up near 18,000 years.—It is interesting to observe how the wild _conjectures_ of an ignorant age have been confirmed by the more recent _discoveries_ in geology, making it probable that the earth has experienced a number of convulsions, possibly thousands of years distant from each other, which have swept away the races then existing, and given a new aspect to the globe.

Another class, with no other merit than that of having died of certain diseases, capriciously selected, were to enjoy a negative existence of indolent contentment. The highest place was reserved, as in most warlike nations, for the heroes who fell in battle, or in sacrifice. They passed, at once, into the presence of the Sun, whom they accompanied with songs and choral dances, in his bright progress through the heavens; and, after some years, their spirits went to animate the clouds and singing birds of beautiful plumage, and to revel amidst the rich blossoms and odors of the gardens of paradise.[1] Such was the heaven of the Aztecs; more refined in its character than that of the more polished pagan, whose elysium reflected only the martial sports, or sensual gratifications, of this life.[2] In the destiny they assigned to the wicked, we discern similar traces of refinement; since the absence of all physical torture forms a striking contrast to the schemes of suffering so ingeniously devised by the fancies of the most enlightened nations.[3] In

[1] Sahagun, Hist. de Nueva España, lib. 3, Append.—Cod. Vat., ap. Antiq. of Mexico, Pl. 1-5.—Torquemada, Monarch. Ind., lib. 13, cap. 48.

The last writer assures us, "that, as to what the Aztecs said of their going to hell, they were right; for, as they died in ignorance of the true faith, they have, without question, all gone there to suffer everlasting punishment!" Ubi supra.

[2] It conveys but a poor idea of these pleasures, that the shade of Achilles can say, "he had rather be the slave of the meanest man on earth, than sovereign among the dead." (Odyss. A. 488-490.) The Mahometans believe that the souls of martyrs pass, after death, into the bodies of birds, that haunt the sweet waters and bowers of Paradise. (Sale's Koran, (London, 1825,) vol. I. p. 106).—The Mexican heaven may remind one of Dante's, in its *material* enjoyments; which, in both, are made up of light, music, and motion. The sun, it must also be remembered, was a spiritual conception with the Aztec;

"He sees with other eyes than theirs; where they
    Behold a sun, he spies a deity."

[3] It is singular that the Tuscan bard, while exhausting his invention in devising modes of bodily torture, in his "Inferno," should have made so little use of the *moral* sources of misery. That he has not done so might be reckoned a strong proof of the rudeness of the time, did we not meet with examples of it in a later day; in which a serious and sublime writer, like Dr. Watts, does not disdain to em-

all this, so contrary to the natural suggestions of the ferocious Aztec, we see the evidences of a higher civilization, inherited from their predecessors in the land.

Our limits will allow only a brief allusion to one or two of their most interesting ceremonies. On the death of a person, his corpse was dressed in the peculiar habiliments of his tutelar deity. It was strewed with pieces of paper, which operated as charms against the dangers of the dark road he was to travel. A throng of slaves, if he were rich, was sacrificed at his obsequies. His body was burned, and the ashes, collected in a vase, were preserved in one of the apartments of his house. Here we have successively the usages of the Roman Catholic, the Mussulman, the Tartar, and the Ancient Greek and Roman; curious coincidences, which may show how cautious we should be in adopting conclusions founded on analogy.[1]

A more extraordinary coincidence may be traced with Christian rites, in the ceremony of naming their children. The lips and bosom of the infant were sprinkled with water, and "the Lord was implored to permit the holy drops to wash away the sin that was given to it before the foundation of the world; so that the child might be born anew."[2] We are reminded of Christian morals, in more than one of their prayers, in which they used regular forms. "Wilt thou blot us out, O Lord, for ever? Is this punishment intended, not for our reforma-

---

ploy the same coarse machinery for moving the conscience of the reader.

[1] Carta del Lic. Zuazo, (Nov., 1521,) MS.—Acosta, lib. 5, cap. 8.—Torquemada, Monarch. Ind., lib. 13, cap. 45.—Sahagun, Hist. de Nueva España, lib. 3, Apend.

Sometimes the body was buried entire, with valuable treasures, if the deceased was rich. The "Anonymous Conqueror," as he is called, saw gold to the value of 3000 castellanos drawn from one of these tombs. Relatione d' un gentil' huomo, ap. Ramusio, tom. III. p. 310.

[2] This interesting rite, usually solemnized with great formality, in the presence of the assembled friends and relatives, is detailed with minuteness by Sahagun, (Hist. de Nueva España, lib. 6, cap. 37,) and by Zuazo, (Carta, MS.,) both of them eyewitnesses. For a version of part of Sahagun's account, see *Appendix, Part 1. note 26.*

tion, but for our destruction?" Again, "Impart to us, out of
thy great mercy, thy gifts, which we are not worthy to receive
through our own merits." "Keep peace with all," says another
petition; "bear injuries with humility; God, who sees, will
avenge you." But the most striking parallel with Scripture is
in the remarkable declaration, that "he, who looks too curiously
on a woman, commits adultery with his eyes." These pure
and elevated maxims, it is true, are mixed up with others of
a puerile, and even brutal character, arguing that confusion of
the moral perceptions, which is natural in the twilight of civilization. One would not expect, however, to meet, in such a
state of society, with doctrines as sublime as any inculcated by
the enlightened codes of ancient philosophy.[1]

But, although the Aztec mythology gathered nothing from
the beautiful inventions of the poet, nor from the refinements
of philosophy, it was much indebted, as I have noticed, to the
priests, who endeavored to dazzle the imagination of the people
by the most formal and pompous ceremonial. The influence
of the priesthood must be greatest in an imperfect state of
civilization, where it engrosses all the scanty science of the
time in its own body. This is particularly the case, when the
science is of that spurious kind which is less occupied with
the real phenomena of nature, than with the fanciful chimeras
of human superstition. Such are the sciences of astrology and
divination, in which the Aztec priests were well initiated; and,
while they seemed to hold the keys of the future in their own

[1] ¿ Es posible que este azote y este castigo no se nos da para
nuestra correccion y enmienda, sino para total destruccion y asola-
miento?" (Sahagun, Hist. de Nueva España, lib. 6, cap. 1.) "Ye
esto por sola vuestra liberalidad y magnificencia lo habeis de hacer,
que ninguno es digno ni merecedor de recibir vuestras larguezas por
su dignidad y merecimiento, sino que por vuestra benignidad."
(Ibid., lib. 6, cap. 2.) "Sed sufridos y reportados, que Dios bien os
vé y responderá por vosotros, y él os vengarà (á) sed humildes con
todos, y con esto os hará Dios merced y tambien honra." (Ibid.,
lib. 6, cap. 17.) "Tampoco mires con curiosidad el gesto y disposicion
de la gente principal, mayormente de las mugeres, y sobre todo de las
casadas, porque dice el refran que él que curiosamente mira á la
muger adultera con la vista." (Ibid., lib. 6, cap. 22.)

hands, they impressed the ignorant people with sentiments of superstitious awe, beyond that which has probably existed in any other country,—even in ancient Egypt.

The sacerdotal order was very numerous; as may be inferred from the statement, that five thousand priests were, in some way or other, attached to the principal temple in the capital. The various ranks and functions of this multitudinous body were discriminated with great exactness. Those best instructed in music took the management of the choirs. Others arranged the festivals conformably to the calendar. Some superintended the education of youth, and others had charge of the hiero-glyphical paintings and oral traditions; while the dismal rites of sacrifice were reserved for the chief dignitaries of the order. At the head of the whole establishment were two high-priests, elected from the order, as it would seem, by the king and principal nobles, without reference to birth, but solely for their qualifications, as shown by their previous conduct in a sub-ordinate station. They were equal in dignity, and inferior only to the sovereign, who rarely acted without their advice in weighty matters of public concern.[1]

The priests were each devoted to the service of some par-ticular deity, and had quarters provided within the spacious precincts of their temple; at least, while engaged in immediate attendance there,—for they were allowed to marry, and have families of their own. In this monastic residence they lived in all the stern severity of conventual discipline. Thrice during the day, and once at night, they were called to prayers. They

[1] Sahagun, Hist. de Nueva España, lib. 2, Apend.; lib. 3, cap. 9.—Torquemada, Monarch. Ind., lib. 8, cap. 20; lib. 9, cap. 3, 56.—Gomara, Crón., cap. 215, ap. Barcia, tom. II.—Toribio, Hist. de los Indios, MS., Parte 1, cap. 4.

Clavigero says that the high-priest was necessarily a person of rank. (Stor. del Messico, tom. II. p. 37.) I find no authority for this, not even in his oracle, Torquemada, who expressly says, "There is no warrant for the assertion, however probable the fact may be." (Monarch. Ind., lib. 9, cap. 5.) It is contradicted by Sahagun, whom I have followed as the highest authority in these matters. Clavigero had no other knowledge of Sahagun's work than what was filtered through the writings of Torquemada, and later authors.

were frequent in their ablutions and vigils, and mortified the
flesh by fasting and cruel penance,—drawing blood from their
bodies by flagellation, or by piercing them with the thorns of
the aloe; in short, by practicing all those austerities to which
fanaticism (to borrow the strong language of the poet) has
resorted, in every age of the world,

"In hopes to merit heaven by making earth a hell."[1]

The great cities were divided into districts, placed under the
charge of a sort of parochial clergy, who regulated every act
of religion within their precincts. It is remarkable that they
administered the rites of confession and absolution. The secrets of the confessional were held inviolable, and penances
were imposed of much the same kind as those enjoined in the
Roman Catholic Church. There were two remarkable peculiarities in the Aztec ceremony. The first was, that, as the
repetition of an offense, once atoned for, was deemed inexpiable,
confession was made but once in a man's life, and was usually
deferred to a late period of it, when the penitent unburdened
his conscience, and settled, at once, the long arrears of iniquity.
Another peculiarity was, that priestly absolution was received
in place of the legal punishment of offenses, and authorized
an acquittal in case of arrest. Long after the Conquest, the
simple natives, when they came under the arm of the law,
sought to escape by producing the certificate of their confession.[2]

[1] Sahagun, Hist. de Nueva España, ubi supra.—Torquemada,
Monarch. Ind., lib. 9, cap. 25.—Gomara, Crón., ap. Barcia, ubi
supra.—Acosta, lib. 5, cap. 14, 17.

[2] Sahagun, Hist. de Nueva España, lib. 1, cap. 12; lib. 6, cap. 7.
The address of the confessor, on these occasions, contains some
things too remarkable to be omitted. "O merciful Lord," he says
in his prayer, "thou who knowest the secrets of all hearts, let thy
forgiveness and favor descend, like the pure waters of heaven, to
wash away the stains from the soul. Thou knowest that this poor
man *has sinned, not from his own free will*, but from the influence of
the sign under which he was born." After a copious exhortation to
the penitent, enjoining a variety of mortifications and minute ceremonies by way of penance, and particularly urging the necessity of

One of the most important duties of the priesthood was that of education, to which certain buildings were appropriated within the inclosure of the principal temple. Here the youth of both sexes, of the higher and middling orders, were placed at a very tender age. The girls were intrusted to the care of priestesses; for women were allowed to exercise sacerdotal functions, except those of sacrifice.[1] In these institutions the boys were drilled in the routine of monastic discipline; they decorated the shrines of the gods with flowers, fed the sacred fires, and took part in the religious chants and festivals. Those in the higher school—the *Calmecac*, as it was called—were initiated in their traditionary lore, the mysteries of hieroglyphics, the principles of government, and such branches of astronomical and natural science as were within the compass of the priesthood. The girls learned various feminine employments, especially to weave and embroider rich coverings for the altars of the gods. Great attention was paid to the moral discipline of both sexes. The most perfect decorum prevailed; and offenses were punished with extreme rigor, in some instances with death itself. Terror, not love, was the spring of education with the Aztecs.[2]

---

instantly procuring *a slave for sacrifice* to the Deity, the priest concludes with inculcating charity to the poor. "Clothe the naked and feed the hungry, whatever privations it may cost thee; for remember, *their flesh is like thine, and they are men like thee.*" Such is the strange medley of truly Christian benevolence and heathenish abominations which pervades the Aztec litany,—intimating sources widely different.

[1] The Egyptian gods were also served by priestesses. (See Herodotus, Euterpe, sec. 54.) Tales of scandal similar to those which the Greeks circulated respecting them, have been told of the Aztec virgins. (See Le Noir's dissertation, ap. Antiquités Mexicaines, (Paris, 1834,) tom. II. p. 7, note.) The early missionaries, credulous enough certainly, give no countenance to such reports; and father Acosta, on the contrary, exclaims, "In truth, it is very strange to see that this false opinion of religion hath so great force among these young men and maidens of Mexico, that they will serve the Divell with so great rigor and austerity, which many of us doe not in the service of the most high God; the which is a great shame and confusion." Eng. Trans., lib. 5, cap. 16.

[2] Toribio, Hist. de los Indios, MS., Parte 1, cap. 9.—Sahagun,

At a suitable age for marrying, or for entering into the world, the pupils were dismissed, with much ceremony, from the convent, and the recommendation of the principal often introduced those most competent to responsible situations in public life. Such was the crafty policy of the Mexican priests, who, by reserving to themselves the business of instruction, were enabled to mould the young and plastic mind according to their own wills, and to train it early to implicit reverence for religion and its ministers; a reverence which still maintained its hold on the iron nature of the warrior, long after every other vestige of education had been effaced by the rough trade to which he was devoted.

To each of the principal temples, lands were annexed for the maintenance of the priests. These estates were augmented by the policy or devotion of successive princes, until, under the last Montezuma, they had swollen to an enormous extent, and covered every district of the empire. The priests took the management of their property into their own hands; and they seem to have treated their tenants with the liberality and indulgence characteristic of monastic corporations. Besides the large supplies drawn from this source, the religious order was enriched with the first-fruits, and such other offerings as piety or superstition dictated. The surplus beyond what was required for the support of the national worship was distributed in alms among the poor; a duty strenuously prescribed by their moral code. Thus we find the same religion inculcating lessons of pure philanthropy, on the one hand, and of merciless extermination, as we shall soon see, on the other. The inconsistency will not appear incredible to those who are familiar with the

---

Hist. de Nueva España, lib. 2, Apend.; lib. 3, cap. 4–8.—Zurita, Rapport, pp. 123–126.—Acosta, lib. 5, cap. 15, 16.—Torquemada, Monarch. Ind., lib. 9, cap. 11–14, 30, 31.

"They were taught," says the good father last cited, "to eschew vice, and cleave to virtue,—*according to their notions of them;* namely, to abstain from wrath, to offer violence and do wrong to no man,—in short, to perform the duties plainly pointed out by natural religion."

history of the Roman Catholic Church, in the early ages of the Inquisition.[1]

The Mexican temples—*teocallis*, "houses of God," as they were called—were very numerous. There were several hundreds in each of the principal cities, many of them, doubtless, very humble edifices. They were solid masses of earth, cased with brick, or stone, and in their form somewhat resembled the pyramidal structures of ancient Egypt. The bases of many of them were more than a hundred feet square, and they towered to a still greater height. They were distributed into four or five stories, each of smaller dimensions than that below. The ascent was by a flight of steps, at an angle of the pyramid, on the outside. This led to a sort of terrace, or gallery, at the base of the second story, which passed quite round the building to another flight of stairs, commencing also at the same angle as the preceding and directly over it, and leading to a similar terrace; so that one had to make the circuit of the temple several times, before reaching the summit. In some instances the stairway led directly up the center of the western face of the building. The top was a broad area, on which were erected one or two towers, forty or fifty feet high, the sanctuaries in which stood the sacred images of the presiding deities. Before these towers stood the dreadful stone of sacrifice, and two lofty altars, on which fires were kept, as inextinguishable as those in the temple of Vesta. There were said to be six hundred of these altars, on smaller buildings within the inclosure of the great temple of Mexico, which, with those on the sacred edifices in other

---

[1] Torquemada, Monarch. Ind., lib. 8, cap. 20, 21.—Camargo, Hist. de Tlascala, MS.

It is impossible not to be struck with the great resemblance, not merely in a few empty forms, but in the whole way of life, of the Mexican and Egyptian priesthood. Compare Herodotus (Euterpe, passim) and Diodorus (lib. 1, sec. 73, 81). The English reader may consult, for the same purpose, Heeren, (Hist. Res., vol. V. chap. 2,) Wilkinson, (Manners and Customs of the Ancient Egyptians, (London, 1837,) vol. I. pp. 257–279,) the last writer especially,—who has contributed, more than all others, towards opening to us the interior of the social life of this interesting people.

parts of the city, shed a brilliant illumination over its streets, through the darkest night.[1]

From the construction of their temples, all religious services were public. The long processions of priests, winding round their massive sides, as they rose higher and higher towards the summit, and the dismal rites of sacrifice performed there, were all visible from the remotest corners of the capital, impressing on the spectator's mind a superstitious veneration for the mysteries of his religion, and for the dread ministers by whom they were interpreted.

This impression was kept in full force by their numerous festivals. Every month was consecrated to some protecting deity; and every week, nay, almost every day, was set down in their calendar for some appropriate celebration; so that it is difficult to understand how the ordinary business of life could have been compatible with the exactions of religion. Many of their ceremonies were of a light and cheerful complexion, consisting of the national songs and dances, in which both sexes joined. Processions were made of women and children crowned with garlands and bearing offerings of fruits, the ripened maize, or the sweet incense of copal and other odoriferous gums, while the altars of the deity were stained with no blood save that of animals.[2] These were the peaceful

[1] Rel. d' un gent., ap. Ramusio, tom. III. fol. 307.—Camargo, Hist. de Tlascala, MS.—Acosta, lib. 5, cap. 13.—Gomara, Crón., cap. 80, ap. Barcia, tom. II.—Toribio, Hist. de los Indios, MS., Parte 1, cap. 4.—Carta del Lic. Zuazo, MS.

This last writer, who visited Mexico immediately after the Conquest, in 1521, assures us that some of the smaller temples, or pyramids, were filled with earth impregnated with odoriferous gums and gold dust; the latter, sometimes in such quantities as probably to be worth a million of *castellanos!* (Ubi supra.) These were the temples of Mammon, indeed! But I find no confirmation of such golden reports.

[2] Cod. Tel.-Rem., Pl. 1, and Cod. Vat., passim, ap. Antiq. of Mexico, vols. I., VI.—Torquemada, Monarch. Ind., lib. 10, cap. 10, et seq.—Sahagun, Hist. de Nueva España, lib. 2, passim.

Among the offerings, quails may be particularly noticed, for the incredible quantities of them sacrificed and consumed at many of the festivals.

rites derived from their Toltec predecessors, on which the fierce Aztecs engrafted a superstition too loathsome to be exhibited in all its nakedness, and one over which I would gladly draw a veil altogether, but that it would leave the reader in ignorance of their most striking institution, and one that had the greatest influence in forming the national character.

Human sacrifices were adopted by the Aztecs early in the fourteenth century, about two hundred years before the Conquest.[1] Rare at first, they became more frequent with the wider extent of their empire; till, at length, almost every festival was closed with this cruel abomination. These religious ceremonials were generally arranged in such a manner as to afford a type of the most prominent circumstances in the character or history of the deity who was the object of them. A single example will suffice.

One of their most important festivals was that in honor of the god, Tezcatlipoca, whose rank was inferior only to that of the Supreme Being. He was called "the soul of the world," and supposed to have been its creator. He was depicted as a handsome man, endowed with perpetual youth. A year before the intended sacrifice, a captive, distinguished for his personal beauty, and without a blemish on his body, was selected to represent this deity. Certain tutors took charge of him, and instructed him how to perform his new part with becoming grace and dignity. He was arrayed in a splendid dress, regaled with incense and with a profusion of sweet-scented flowers, of which the ancient Mexicans were as fond as their descendants at the present day. When he went abroad, he was attended by a train of the royal pages, and, as he halted in the streets to play some favorite melody, the crowd prostrated themselves before him, and did him homage as the representative of their good deity. In this way he led an easy, luxurious life, till

---

[1] The traditions of their origin have somewhat of a fabulous tinge. But, whether true or false, they are equally indicative of unparalleled ferocity in the people who could be the subject of them. Clavigero, Stor. del Messico, tom. I. p. 167, et seq.; also Humboldt, (who does not appear to doubt them,) Vues des Cordillères, p. 95.

within a month of his sacrifice. Four beautiful girls, bearing the names of the principal goddesses, were then selected to share the honors of his bed; and with them he continued to live in idle dalliance, feasted at the banquets of the principal nobles, who paid him all the honors of a divinity.

At length the fatal day of sacrifice arrived. The term of his short-lived glories was at an end. He was stripped of his gaudy apparel, and bade adieu to the fair partners of his revelries. One of the royal barges transported him across the lake to a temple which rose on its margin, about a league from the city. Hither the inhabitants of the capital flocked, to witness the consummation of the ceremony. As the sad procession wound up the sides of the pyramid, the unhappy victim threw away his gay chaplets of flowers, and broke in pieces the musical instruments with which he had solaced the hours of captivity. On the summit he was received by six priests, whose long and matted locks flowed disorderly over their sable robes, covered with hieroglyphic scrolls of mystic import. They led him to the sacrificial stone, a huge block of jasper, with its upper surface somewhat convex. On this the prisoner was stretched. Five priests secured his head and his limbs; while the sixth, clad in a scarlet mantle, emblematic of his bloody office, dexterously opened the breast of the wretched victim with a sharp razor of *itztli*,—a volcanic substance, hard as flint,—and, inserting his hand in the wound, tore out the palpitating heart. The minister of death, first holding this up towards the sun, an object of worship throughout Anahuac, cast it at the feet of the deity to whom the temple was devoted, while the multitudes below prostrated themselves in humble adoration. The tragic story of this prisoner was expounded by the priests as the type of human destiny, which, brilliant in its commencement, too often closes in sorrow and disaster.[1]

[1] Sahagun, Hist. de Nueva España, lib. 2, cap. 2, 5, 24, et alibi.— Herrera, Hist. General, dec. 3, lib. 2, cap. 16.—Torquemada, Monarch. Ind., lib. 7, cap. 19; lib. 10, cap. 14.—Rel. d' un gent., ap. Ramusio, tom. III. fol. 307.—Acosta, lib. 5, cap. 9-21.—Carta del Lic. Zuazo, MS.—Relacion por el Regimiento de Vera Cruz, (Julio, 1519,) MS.

[AZTEC CIVILIZATION: MONTEZUMA'S RESIDENCES]

From *The Conquest of Mexico*, Bk. IV, chap. ii

[The long fight of the Spaniards up from the coast to Mexico City is temporarily halted with a description of the splendors of Montezuma's capital.]

Not content with the spacious residence of his father, Montezuma erected another on a yet more magnificent scale. It occupied, as before mentioned, the ground partly covered by the private dwellings on one side of the *plaza mayor* of the modern city. This building, or, as it might more correctly be styled, pile of buildings, spread over an extent of ground so vast, that, as one of the Conquerors assures us, its terraced roof might have afforded ample room for thirty knights to run their courses in a regular tourney. I have already noticed its interior decorations, its fanciful draperies, its roofs inlaid with cedar and other odoriferous woods, held together without a nail, and, probably, without a knowledge of the arch, its numerous and spacious apartments, which Cortés, with enthusiastic hyperbole, does not hesitate to declare superior to anything of the kind in Spain.

Adjoining the principal edifice were others devoted to various objects. One was an armory, filled with the weapons and military dresses worn by the Aztecs, all kept in the most perfect order, ready for instant use. The emperor was himself very expert in the management of the *maquahuitl*, or Indian sword, and took great delight in witnessing athletic exercises, and the mimic representation of war by his young nobility. Another building was used as a granary, and others as warehouses for the different articles of food and apparel contributed by the districts charged with the maintenance of the royal household.

Few readers, probably, will sympathize with the sentence of Torquemada, who concludes his tale of woe by coolly dismissing "the soul of the victim, to sleep with those of his false gods, in hell!" Lib. 10, cap. 23.

There were, also, edifices appropriated to objects of quite another kind. One of these was an immense aviary, in which birds of splendid plumage were assembled from all parts of the empire. Here was the scarlet cardinal, the golden pheasant, the endless parrot-tribe with their rainbow hues, (the royal green predominant,) and that miniature miracle of nature, the humming-bird, which delights to revel among the honeysuckle bowers of Mexico. Three hundred attendants had charge of this aviary, who made themselves acquainted with the appropriate food of its inmates, oftentimes procured at great cost, and in the moulting season were careful to collect the beautiful plumage, which, with its many-colored tints, furnished the materials for the Aztec painter.

A separate building was reserved for the fierce birds of prey; the voracious vulture-tribes and eagles of enormous size, whose home was in the snowy solitudes of the Andes. No less than five hundred turkeys, the cheapest meat in Mexico, were allowed for the daily consumption of these tyrants of the feathered race.

Adjoining this aviary was a menagerie of wild animals, gathered from the mountain forests, and even from the remote swamps of the *tierra caliente*. The resemblance of the different species to those in the Old World, with which no one of them, however, was identical, led to a perpetual confusion in the nomenclature of the Spaniards, as it has since done in that of better instructed naturalists. The collection was still further swelled by a great number of reptiles and serpents remarkable for their size and venomous qualities, among which the Spaniards beheld the fiery little animal "with the castanets in his tail," the terror of the American wilderness. The serpents were confined in long cages lined with down or feathers, or in troughs of mud and water. The beasts and birds of prey were provided with apartments large enough to allow of their moving about, and secured by a strong lattice-work, through which light and air were freely admitted. The whole was placed under the charge of numerous keepers, who acquainted themselves with the habits of their prisoners, and provided for their comfort and cleanliness. With what deep interest would the enlightened naturalist of that day—an Oviedo, or a Martyr, for example—have surveyed this magnificent collection, in which the various tribes which roamed over the Western wilderness, the unknown races of an unknown world, were brought into one view! How would they have delighted to study the peculiarities of these new species, compared with those of their own hemisphere, and thus have risen to some comprehension of the general laws by which Nature acts in all her works! The rude followers of Cortés did not trouble themselves with such refined speculations. They gazed on the spectacle with a vague curiosity not unmixed with awe; and, as they listened to the wild cries of the ferocious animals and the hissings of the serpents, they almost fancied themselves in the infernal regions.

I must not omit to notice a strange collection of human monsters, dwarfs, and other unfortunate persons, in whose organization Nature had capriciously deviated from her regular laws. Such hideous anomalies were regarded by the Aztecs as a suitable appendage of state. It is even said, they were in some cases the results of artificial means, employed by unnatural parents desirous to secure a provision for their offspring by thus qualifying them for a place in the royal museum!

Extensive gardens were spread out around these buildings, filled with fragrant shrubs and flowers, and especially with medicinal plants. No country has afforded more numerous species of these last, than New Spain; and their virtues were perfectly understood by the Aztecs, with whom medical botany may be said to have been studied as a science. Amidst this labyrinth of sweet-scented groves and shrubberies, fountains of pure water might be seen throwing up their sparkling jets, and scattering refreshing dews over the blossoms. Ten large tanks, well stocked with fish, afforded a retreat on their margins to various tribes of water-fowl, whose habits were so carefully consulted, that some of these ponds were of salt water, as that which they most loved to frequent. A tessellated pavement of marble inclosed the ample basins, which were overhung by light and fanciful pavilions, that admitted the perfumed breezes of the gardens, and offered a grateful shelter to the monarch and his mistresses in the sultry heats of summer.

But the most luxurious residence of the Aztec monarch, at that season, was the royal hill of Chapoltepec, a spot consecrated, moreover, by the ashes of his ancestors. It stood in a westerly direction from the capital, and its base was, in his day, washed by the waters of the Tezcuco. On its lofty crest of porphyritic rock, there now stands the magnificent, though desolate, castle erected by the young viceroy Galvez, at the close of the seventeenth century. The view from its windows is one of the finest in the environs of Mexico. The landscape is not disfigured here, as in many other quarters, by the white and barren patches, so offensive to the sight; but the eye wanders over an unbroken expanse of meadows and cultivated fields, waving with rich harvests of European grain. Montezuma's gardens stretched for miles around the base of the hill. Two statues of that monarch and his father, cut in *bas relief* in the porphyry, were spared till the middle of the last century; and the grounds are still shaded by gigantic cypresses, more than fifty feet in circumference, which were centuries old at the time of the Conquest. The place is now a tangled wilderness of wild shrubs, where the myrtle mingles its dark, glossy leaves with the red berries and delicate foliage of the pepper-tree. Surely, there is no spot better suited to awaken meditation on the past; none, where the traveler, as he sits under those stately cypresses gray with the moss of ages, can so fitly ponder on the sad destinies of the Indian races and the monarch who once held his courtly revels under the shadow of their branches.

The domestic establishment of Montezuma was on the same scale of barbaric splendor as everything else about him. He could boast as many wives as are found in the harem of an Eastern sultan. They were lodged in their own apartments, and provided with every accommodation, according to their ideas, for personal comfort and cleanliness. They passed their hours in the usual feminine employments of weaving and embroidery, especially in the graceful feather-work, for which such rich materials were furnished by the royal aviaries. They conducted themselves with strict decorum, under the supervision of certain aged females, who acted in the respectable capacity of duennas, in the same manner as in the religious houses attached to the *teocallis.* The palace was supplied with numerous baths, and Montezuma set the example, in his own person, of frequent ablutions. He bathed at least once, and changed his dress four times, it is said, every day. He never put on the same apparel a second time, but gave it away to his attendants. Queen Elizabeth, with a similar taste for costume, showed a less princely spirit in hoarding her discarded suits. Her wardrobe was, probably, somewhat more costly than that of the Indian emperor.

Besides his numerous female retinue, the halls and antechambers were filled with nobles in constant attendance on his person, who served also as a sort of bodyguard. It had been usual for plebeians of merit to fill certain offices in the palace. But the haughty Montezuma refused to be waited upon by any but men of noble birth. They were not unfrequently the sons of the great chiefs, and remained as hostages in the absence of their fathers; thus serving the double purpose of security and state.

His meals the emperor took alone. The well-matted floor of a large saloon was covered with hundreds of dishes. Sometimes Montezuma himself, but more frequently his steward, indicated those which he preferred, and which were kept hot by means of chafing-dishes. The royal bill of fare comprehended, besides domestic animals, game from the distant forests, and fish which, the day before, was swimming in the Gulf of Mexico! They were dressed in manifold ways, for the Aztec *artistes,* as we have already had occasion to notice, had penetrated deep into the mysteries of culinary science.

The meats were served by the attendant nobles, who then resigned the office of waiting on the monarch to maidens selected for their personal grace and beauty. A screen of richly gilt and carved wood was drawn around him, so as to conceal him from vulgar eyes during the repast. He was seated on a cushion, and the dinner was served on a low table covered with a delicate cotton cloth. The dishes were of the finest ware of Cholula. He had a service of gold, which was reserved for religious celebrations. Indeed, it would scarcely have comported with even his princely revenues to have used it on ordinary occasions, when his table equipage was not allowed to appear a second time, but was given away to his attendants. The saloon was lighted by torches made of a resinous wood, which sent forth a sweet odor and, probably, not a little smoke, as they burned. At his meal, he was attended by five or six of his ancient counselors, who stood at a respectful distance, answering his questions, and occasionally rejoiced by some of the viands with which he complimented them from his table.

This course of solid dishes was succeeded by another of sweetmeats and pastry, for which the Aztec cooks, provided with the important requisites of maize-flour, eggs, and the rich sugar of the aloe, were famous. Two girls were occupied at the further end of the apartment, during dinner, in preparing fine rolls and wafers, with which they garnished the board from time to time. The emperor took no other beverage than the *chocolatl*, a potation of chocolate, flavored with vanilla and other spices, and so prepared as to be reduced to a froth of the consistency of honey, which gradually dissolved in the mouth. This beverage, if so it could be called, was served in golden goblets, with spoons of the same metal or of tortoise-shell finely wrought. The emperor was exceedingly fond of it, to judge from the quantity,—no less than fifty jars or pitchers being prepared for his own daily consumption! Two thousand more were allowed for that of his household.

The general arrangement of the meal seems to have been not very unlike that of Europeans. But no prince in Europe could boast a dessert which could compare with that of the Aztec emperor. For it was gathered fresh from the most opposite climes; and his board displayed the products of his own temperate region, and the luscious fruits of the tropics, plucked, the day previous, from the green groves of the *tierra caliente*, and transmitted with the speed of steam, by means of couriers, to the capital. It was as if some kind fairy should crown our banquets with the spicy products that but yesterday were growing in a sunny isle of the far-off Indian seas!

After the royal appetite was appeased, water was handed to him by the female attendants in a silver basin, in the same manner as had been done before commencing his meal; for the Aztecs were as constant in their ablutions, at these times, as any nation of the East. Pipes were then brought, made of a varnished and richly gilt wood, from which he inhaled, sometimes through the nose, at others through the mouth, the fumes of an intoxicating weed, "called *tobacco*," mingled with liquid-amber. While this soothing process of fumigation was going on, the emperor enjoyed the exhibitions of his mountebanks and jugglers, of whom a regular corps was attached to the palace. No people, not even those of China or Hindostan, surpassed the Aztecs in feats of agility and legerdemain.

Sometimes he amused himself with his jester; for the Indian monarch had his jesters, as well as his more refined brethren of Europe, at that day. Indeed, he used to say, that more instruction was to be gathered from them than from wiser men, for they dared to tell the truth. At other times, he witnessed the graceful dances of his women, or took delight in listening to music,—if the rude minstrelsy of the Mexicans deserve that name,—accompanied by a chant, in slow and solemn cadence, celebrating the heroic deeds of great Aztec warriors, or of his own princely line.

When he had sufficiently refreshed his spirits with these diversions, he composed himself to sleep, for in his *siesta* he was as regular as a Spaniard. On awaking, he gave audience to ambassadors from foreign states, or his own tributary cities, or to such caciques as had suits to prefer to him. They were introduced by the young nobles in attendance, and, whatever might be their rank, unless of the blood royal, they were obliged to submit to the humiliation of shrouding their rich dresses under the coarse mantle of *nequen*, and entering barefooted, with downcast eyes, into the presence. The emperor addressed few and brief remarks to the suitors, answering them generally by his secretaries; and the parties retired with the same reverential obeisance, taking care to keep their faces turned towards the monarch. Well might Cortés exclaim, that no court, whether of the Grand Seignior or any other infidel, ever displayed so pompous and elaborate a ceremonial!

Besides the crowd of retainers already noticed, the royal household was not complete without a host of artisans constantly employed in the erection or repair of buildings, besides a great number of jewelers and persons skilled in working metals, who found abundant demand for their trinkets among the dark-eyed beauties of the harem. The imperial mummers and jugglers were also very numerous, and the dancers belonging to the palace occupied a particular district of the city, appropriated exclusively to them.

The maintenance of this little host, amounting to some thousands of individuals, involved a heavy expenditure, requiring accounts of a complicated, and, to a simple people, it might well be, embarrassing nature. Everything, however, was conducted with perfect order; and all the various receipts and disbursements were set down in the picture-writing of the country. The arithmetical characters were of a more refined and conventional sort than those for narrative purposes; and a separate apartment was filled with hieroglyphical ledgers, exhibiting a complete view of the economy of the palace. The care of all this was intrusted to a treasurer, who acted as a sort of majordomo in the household, having a general superintendence over all its concerns. This responsible office, on the arrival of the Spaniards, was in the hands of a trusty cacique named Tapia.

Such is the picture of Montezuma's domestic establishment and way of living, as delineated by the Conquerors and their immediate followers, who had the best means of information; too highly colored, it may be, by the proneness to exaggerate, which was natural to those who first witnessed a spectacle so striking to the imagination, so new and unexpected. I have thought it best to present the full details, trivial though they may seem to the reader, as affording a curious picture of manners, so superior in point of refinement to those of the other Aboriginal tribes on the North American continent. Nor are they, in fact, so trivial, when we reflect, that, in these details of private life, we possess a surer measure of civilization, than in those of a public nature.

[INCA CIVILIZATION: CITY OF CUZCO]

From *The Conquest of Peru*, Bk. I, chap. i

[The introductory book, a view of the civilization of the Incas, includes an appreciation of their engineering achievement in building the fortress of Cuzco.]

The ancient city of Cuzco, meanwhile, had been gradually advancing in wealth and population, till it had become the worthy metropolis of a great and flourishing monarchy. It stood in a beautiful valley on an elevated region of the plateau, which, among the Alps, would have been buried in eternal snows, but which within the tropics enjoyed a genial and salubrious temperature. Towards the north it was defended by a lofty eminence, a spur of the great Cordillera; and the city was traversed by a river, or rather a small stream, over which bridges of timber, covered with heavy slabs of stone, furnished an easy means of communication with the opposite banks. The streets were long and narrow; the houses low, and those of the poorer sort built of clay and reeds. But Cuzco was the royal residence, and was adorned with the ample dwellings of the great nobility; and the massy fragments still incorporated in many of the modern edifices bear testimony to the size and solidity of the ancient.

The health of the city was promoted by spacious openings and squares, in which a numerous population from the capital and the distant country assembled to celebrate the high festivals of their religion. For Cuzco was the "Holy City"; and the great temple of the Sun, to which pilgrims resorted from the furthest borders of the empire, was the most magnificent structure in the New World, and unsurpassed, probably, in the costliness of its decorations by any building in the Old.

Towards the north, on the sierra or rugged eminence already

noticed, rose a strong fortress, the remains of which at the present day, by their vast size, excite the admiration of the traveler. It was defended by a single wall of great thickness, and twelve hundred feet long on the side facing the city, where the precipitous character of the ground was of itself almost sufficient for its defense. On the other quarter, where the approaches were less difficult, it was protected by two other semicircular walls of the same length as the preceding. They were separated, a considerable distance from one another and from the fortress; and the intervening ground was raised so that the walls afforded a breastwork for the troops stationed there in times of assault. The fortress consisted of three towers, detached from one another. One was appropriated to the Inca, and was garnished with the sumptuous decorations befitting a royal residence, rather than a military post. The other two were held by the garrison, drawn from the Peruvian nobles, and commanded by an officer of the blood royal; for the position was of too great importance to be intrusted to inferior hands. The hill was excavated below the towers, and several subterraneous galleries communicated with the city and the palaces of the Inca.

The fortress, the walls, and the galleries were all built of stone, the heavy blocks of which were not laid in regular courses, but so disposed that the small ones might fill up the interstices between the great. They formed a sort of rustic work, being roughhewn except towards the edges, which were finely wrought; and, though no cement was used, the several blocks were adjusted with so much exactness and united so closely, that it was impossible to introduce even the blade of a knife between them. Many of these stones were of vast size; some of them being full thirty-eight feet long, by eighteen broad, and six feet thick.

We are filled with astonishment, when we consider, that these enormous masses were hewn from their native bed and fashioned into shape, by a people ignorant of the use of iron; that they were brought from quarries, from four to fifteen leagues distant, without the aid of beasts of burden; were transported across rivers and ravines, raised to their elevated position on the sierra, and finally adjusted there with the nicest accuracy, without the knowledge of tools and machinery familiar to the European. Twenty thousand men are said to have been employed on this great structure, and fifty years consumed in the building. However this may be, we see in it the workings of a despotism which had the lives and fortunes of its vassals at its absolute disposal, and which, however mild in its general character, esteemed these vassals, when employed in its service, as lightly as the brute animals for which they served as a substitute.

[INCA CIVILIZATION: ARCHITECTURE]

From *The Conquest of Peru*, Bk. III, chap. viii

[Prescott continues his study of Inca civilization with an admiring picture of their architecture.]

It was late in the afternoon when the Conquerors came in sight of Cuzco. The descending sun was streaming his broad rays full on the imperial city, where many an altar was dedicated to his worship. The low ranges of buildings, showing in his beams like so many lines of silvery light, filled up the bosom of the valley and the lower slopes of the mountains, whose shadowy forms hung darkly over the fair city, as if to shield it from the menaced profanation. It was so late, that Pizarro resolved to defer his entrance till the following morning.

That night vigilant guard was kept in the camp, and the soldiers slept on their arms. But it passed away without annoyance from the enemy, and early on the following day, November 15, 1533, Pizarro prepared for his entrance into the Peruvian capital.

The little army was formed into three divisions, of which the center, or "battle," as it was called, was led by the general. The suburbs were thronged with a countless multitude of the natives, who had flocked from the city and the surrounding country to witness the showy, and, to them, startling pageant.

All looked with eager curiosity on the strangers, the fame of whose terrible exploits had spread to the remotest parts of the empire. They gazed with astonishment on their dazzling arms and fair complexions, which seemed to proclaim them the true Children of the Sun; and they listened with feelings of mysterious dread, as the trumpet sent forth its prolonged notes through the streets of the capital, and the solid ground shook under the heavy tramp of the cavalry.

The Spanish commander rode directly up the great square. It was surrounded by low piles of buildings, among which were several palaces of the Incas. One of these, erected by Huayna Capac, was surmounted by a tower, while the ground-floor was occupied by one or more immense halls, like those described in Caxamalca, where the Peruvian nobles held their *fêtes* in stormy weather. These buildings afforded convenient barracks for the troops, though, during the first few weeks, they remained under their tents in the open *plaza*, with their horses picketed by their side, ready to repulse any insurrection of the inhabitants.

The capital of the Incas, though falling short of the *El Dorado* which had engaged their credulous fancies, astonished the Spaniards by the beauty of its edifices, the length and regularity of its streets, and the good order and appearance of comfort, even luxury, visible in its numerous population. It far surpassed all they had yet seen in the New World. The population of the city is computed by one of the Conquerors at two hundred thousand inhabitants, and that of the suburbs at as many more. This account is not confirmed, as far as I have seen, by any other writer. But however it may be exaggerated, it is certain that Cuzco was the metropolis of a great empire, the residence of the Court and the chief nobility; frequented by the most skillful mechanics and artisans of every description, who found a demand for their ingenuity in the royal precincts; while the place was garrisoned by a numerous soldiery, and was the resort, finally, of emigrants from the most distant provinces. The quarters whence this motley population came were indicated by their peculiar dress, and especially their headgear, so rarely found at all on the American Indian, which, with its variegated colors, gave a picturesque effect to the groups and masses in the streets. The habitual order and decorum maintained in this multifarious assembly showed the excellent police of the capital, where the only sounds that disturbed the repose of the Spaniards were the noises of feasting and dancing, which the natives, with happy insensibility, constantly prolonged to a late hour of the night.

The edifices of the better sort—and they were very numerous —were of stone, or faced with stone. Among the principal were the royal residences; as each sovereign built a new palace for himself, covering, though low, a large extent of ground. The walls were sometimes stained or painted with gaudy tints, and the gates, we are assured, were sometimes of colored marble. "In the delicacy of the stonework," says another of the Conquerors, "the natives far excelled the Spaniards, though the roofs of their dwellings, instead of tiles, were only of thatch, but put together with the nicest art." The sunny climate of Cuzco did not require a very substantial material for defense against the weather.

The most important building was the fortress, planted on a solid rock, that rose boldly above the city. It was built of hewn stone, so finely wrought that it was impossible to detect the line of junction between the blocks; and the approaches to it were defended by three semicircular parapets, composed of such heavy masses of rock, that it bore resemblance to the kind of work known to architects as the Cyclopean. The fortress was raised to a height rare in Peruvian architecture; and from the summit of the tower the eye of the spectator ranged over a magnificent prospect; in which the wild features of the mountain scenery, rocks, woods, and waterfalls, were mingled with the rich verdure of the valley, and the shining city filling up the foreground,—all blended in sweet harmony under the deep azure of a tropical sky.

The streets were long and narrow. They were arranged with perfect regularity, crossing one another at right angles; and from the great square diverged four principal streets connecting with the high roads of the empire. The square itself, and many parts of the city, were paved with a fine pebble. Through the heart of the capital ran a river of pure water, if it might not be rather termed a canal, the banks or sides of which, for the distance of twenty leagues, were faced with stone. Across this stream, bridges, constructed of similar broad flags, were thrown, at intervals, so as to afford an easy communication between the different quarters of the capital.

The most sumptuous edifice in Cuzco, in the times of the Incas, was undoubtedly the great temple dedicated to the Sun, which, studded with gold plates, as already noticed, was surrounded by convents and dormitories for the priests, with their gardens and broad parterres sparkling with gold. The exterior ornaments had been already removed by the Conquerors, —all but the frieze of gold, which, imbedded in the stones, still encircled the principal building. It is probable that the tales of wealth, so greedily circulated among the Spaniards, greatly exceeded the truth. If they did not, the natives must have been very successful in concealing their treasures from the invaders. Yet much still remained, not only in the great House of the Sun, but in the inferior temples which swarmed in the capital. * * *

But the surest test of the civilization of a people—at least, as sure as any—afforded by mechanical art is to be found in their architecture, which presents so noble a field for the display of the grand and the beautiful, and which, at the same time, is so intimately connected with the essential comforts of life. There is no object on which the resources of the wealthy are more freely lavished, or which calls out more effectually the inventive talent of the artist. The painter and the sculptor may display their individual genius in creations of surpassing excellence, but it is the great monuments of architectural taste and magnificence that are stamped in a peculiar manner by the genius of the nation. The Greek, the Egyptian, the Saracen, the Gothic,—what a key do their respective styles afford to the character and condition of the people! The monuments of China, of Hindostan, and of Central America are all indicative of an immature period, in which the imagination has not been disciplined by study, and which, therefore, in its best results, betrays only the ill-regulated aspirations after the beautiful, that belong to a semicivilized people.

The Peruvian architecture, bearing also the general characteristics of an imperfect state of refinement, had still its peculiar character; and so uniform was that character, that the edifices throughout the country seem to have been all cast in the same mould. They were usually built of porphyry or granite; not unfrequently of brick. This, which was formed into blocks or squares of much larger dimensions than our brick, was made of a tenacious earth mixed up with reeds or tough grass, and acquired a degree of hardness with age that made it insensible alike to the storms and the more trying sun of the tropics. The walls were of great thickness, but low, seldom reaching to more than twelve or fourteen feet in height. It is rare to meet with accounts of a building that rose to a second story.

The apartments had no communication with one another, but usually opened into a court; and, as they were unprovided with windows, or apertures that served for them, the only light from without must have been admitted by the doorways. These were made with the sides approaching each other towards the top, so that the lintel was considerably narrower than the threshold, a peculiarity, also, in Egyptian architecture. The roofs have for the most part disappeared with time. Some few survive in the less ambitious edifices, of a singular bell-shape, and made of a composition of earth and pebbles. They are supposed, however, to have been generally formed of more perishable materials, of wood or straw. It is certain that some of the most considerable stone-buildings were thatched with straw. Many seem to have been constructed without the aid of cement; and writers have contended that the Peruvians were unacquainted with the use of mortar, or cement of any kind. But a close, tenacious mold, mixed with lime, may be discovered filling up the interstices of the granite in some buildings; and in others, where the well-fitted blocks leave no room for this coarser material, the eye of the antiquary has detected a fine bituminous glue, as hard as the rock itself.

The greatest simplicity is observed in the construction of the buildings, which are usually free from outward ornament; though in some the huge stones are shaped into a convex form with great regularity, and adjusted with such nice precision to one another, that it would be impossible, but for the flutings, to determine the line of junction. In others, the stone is rough, as it was taken from the quarry, in the most irregular forms, with the edges nicely wrought and fitted to each other. There is no appearance of columns or of arches; though there is some contradiction as to the latter point. But it is not to be doubted, that, although they may have made some approach to this mode of construction by the greater or less inclination of the walls, the Peruvian architects were wholly unacquainted with the true principle of the circular arch reposing on its keystone.

The architecture of the Incas is characterized, says an eminent traveler, "by simplicity, symmetry, and solidity." It may seem unphilosophical to condemn the peculiar fashion of a nation as indicating want of taste, because its standard of taste differs from our own. Yet there is an incongruity in the composition of the Peruvian buildings which argues a very imperfect acquaintance with the first principles of architecture. While they put together their bulky masses of porphyry and granite with the nicest art, they were incapable of mortising their timbers, and, in their ignorance of iron, knew no better way of holding the beams together than tying them with thongs of maguey. In the same incongruous spirit, the building that was thatched with straw, and unilluminated by a window, was glowing with tapestries of gold and silver! These are the inconsistencies of a rude people, among whom the arts are but partially developed. It might not be difficult to find examples of like inconsistency in the architecture and domestic arrangements of our Anglo-Saxon, and, at a still later period of our Norman ancestors.

Yet the buildings of the Incas were accommodated to the character of the climate, and were well fitted to resist those terrible convulsions which belong to the land of volcanoes. The wisdom of their plan is attested by the number which still survive, while the more modern constructions of the Conquerors have been buried in ruins. The hand of the Conquerors, indeed, has fallen heavily on these venerable monuments, and, in their blind and superstitious search for hidden treasure, has caused infinitely more ruin than time or the earthquake. Yet enough of these monuments still remain to invite the researches of the antiquary. Those only in the most conspicuous situations have been hitherto examined. But, by the testimony of travelers, many more are to be found in the less frequented parts of the country; and we may hope they will one day call forth a kindred spirit of enterprise to that which has so successfully explored the mysterious recesses of Central America and Yucatan.

[INCA CIVILIZATION: THE ROYAL FAMILY]

From *The Conquest of Peru*, Bk. I, chap. i

[The study of the physical environment is followed by a glowing description of the Inca ruler and his palaces.]

The Inca asserted his claims as a superior being by assuming a pomp in his manner of living well calculated to impose on his people. His dress was of the finest wool of the vicuña, richly dyed, and ornamented with a profusion of gold and precious stones. Round his head was wreathed a turban of many-colored folds, called the *llautu;* and a tasseled fringe, like that worn by the prince, but of a scarlet color, with two feathers of a rare and curious bird, called the *coraquenque*, placed upright in it, were the distinguishing insignia of royalty. The birds from which these feathers were obtained were found in a desert country among the mountains; and it was death to destroy or to take them, as they were reserved for the exclusive purpose of supplying the royal headgear. Every succeeding monarch was provided with a new pair of these plumes, and his credulous subjects fondly believed that only two individuals of the species had ever existed to furnish the simple ornament for the diadem of the Incas.

Although the Peruvian monarch was raised so far above the highest of his subjects, he condescended to mingle occasionally with them, and took great pains personally to inspect the condition of the humbler classes. He presided at some of the religious celebrations, and on these occasions entertained the great nobles at his table, when he complimented them, after the fashion of more civilized nations, by drinking the health of those whom he most delighted to honor.

But the most effectual means taken by the Incas for communicating with their people were their progresses through the empire. These were conducted, at intervals of several years, with great state and magnificence. The sedan, or litter, in which they traveled, richly emblazoned with gold and emeralds, was guarded by a numerous escort. The men who bore it on their shoulders were provided by two cities, specially appointed for the purpose. It was a post to be coveted by no one, if, as is asserted, a fall was punished by death. They traveled with ease and expedition, halting at the *tambos*, or inns, erected by government along the route, and occasionally at the royal palaces, which in the great towns afforded ample accommodations to the whole of the monarch's retinue. The noble roads which traversed the tableland were lined with people, who swept away the stones and stubble from their surface, strewing them with sweet-scented flowers, and vying with each other in carrying forward the baggage from one village to another. The monarch halted from time to time to listen to the grievances of his subjects, or to settle some points which had been referred to his decision by the regular tribunals. As the princely train wound its way along the mountain passes, every place was thronged with spectators eager to catch a glimpse of their sovereign; and, when he raised the curtains of his litter, and showed himself to their eyes, the air was rent with acclamations as they invoked blessings on his head. Tradition long commemorated the spots at which he halted, and the simple people of the country held them in reverence as places consecrated by the presence of an Inca.

The royal palaces were on a magnificent scale, and, far from being confined to the capital or a few principal towns, were scattered over all the provinces of their vast empire. The buildings were low, but covered a wide extent of ground. Some of the apartments were spacious, but they were generally small, and had no communication with one another, except that they opened into a common square or court. The walls were made of blocks of stone of various sizes, like those described in the fortress of Cuzco, roughhewn, but carefully wrought near the line of junction, which was scarcely visible to the eye. The roofs were of wood or rushes, which have perished under the rude touch of time, that has shown more respect for the walls of the edifices. The whole seems to have been characterized by solidity and strength, rather than by any attempt at architectural elegance.

But whatever want of elegance there may have been in the exterior of the imperial dwellings, it was amply compensated by the interior, in which all the opulence of the Peruvian princes was ostentatiously displayed. The sides of the apartments were thickly studded with gold and silver ornaments. Niches, prepared in the walls, were filled with images of animals and plants curiously wrought of the same costly materials; and even much of the domestic furniture, including the utensils devoted to the most ordinary menial services, displayed the like wanton magnificence! With these gorgeous decorations were mingled richly colored stuffs of the delicate manufacture of the Peruvian wool, which were of so beautiful a texture, that the Spanish sovereigns, with all the luxuries of Europe and Asia at their command, did not disdain to use them. The royal household consisted of a throng of menials, supplied by the neighboring towns and villages, which, as in Mexico, were bound to furnish the monarch with fuel and other necessaries for the consumption of the palace.

But the favorite residence of the Incas was at Yucay, about four leagues distant from the capital. In this delicious valley, locked up within the friendly arms of the sierra, which sheltered it from the rude breezes of the east, and refreshed by gushing fountains and streams of running water, they built the most beautiful of their palaces. Here, when wearied with the dust and toil of the city, they loved to retreat, and solace themselves with the society of their favorite concubines, wandering amidst groves and airy gardens, that shed around their soft, intoxicating odors, and lulled the senses to voluptuous repose. Here, too, they loved to indulge in the luxury of their baths, replenished by streams of crystal water which were conducted through subterraneous silver channels into basins of gold. The spacious gardens were stocked with numerous varieties of plants and flowers that grew without effort in this *temperate* region of the tropics, while parterres of a more extraordinary kind were planted by their side, glowing with the various forms of vegetable life skillfully imitated in gold and silver! Among them the Indian corn, the most beautiful of American grains, is particularly commemorated, and the curious workmanship is noticed with which the golden ear was half disclosed amidst the broad leaves of silver, and the light tassel of the same material that floated gracefully from its top.

If this dazzling picture staggers the faith of the reader, he may reflect that the Peruvian mountains teemed with gold; that the natives understood the art of working the mines, to a considerable extent; that none of the ore, as we shall see hereafter, was converted into coin, and that the whole of it passed into the hands of the sovereign for his own exclusive benefit, whether for purposes of utility or ornament. Certain it is that no fact is better attested by the Conquerors themselves, who had ample means of information, and no motive for misstatement.—The Italian poets, in their gorgeous pictures of the gardens of Alcina and Morgana, came nearer the truth than they imagined.

[INCA CIVILIZATION: REVENUES AND REGISTERS]

From *The Conquest of Peru*, Bk. I, chap. ii

[In his appreciative review of Inca culture, Prescott is particularly impressed with the governmental machinery for regulating community economic life—taking the census and collecting the taxes.]

The territory was cultivated wholly by the people. The lands belonging to the Sun were first attended to. They next tilled the lands of the old, of the sick, of the widow and the orphan, and of soldiers engaged in actual service; in short, of all that part of the community who, from bodily infirmity or any other cause, were unable to attend to their own concerns. The people were then allowed to work on their own ground, each man for himself, but with the general obligation to assist his neighbor, when any circumstance—the burden of a young and numerous family, for example—might demand it. Lastly, they cultivated the lands of the Inca. This was done, with great ceremony, by the whole population in a body. At break of day, they were summoned together by proclamation from some neighboring tower or eminence, and all the inhabitants of the district, men, women, and children, appeared dressed in their gayest apparel, bedecked with their little store of finery and ornaments, as if for some great jubilee. They went through the labors of the day with the same joyous spirit, chanting their popular ballads which commemorated the heroic deeds of the Incas, regulating their movements by the measure of the chant, and all mingling in the chorus, of which the word *hailli*, or "triumph," was usually the burden. These national airs had something soft and pleasing in their character, that recommended them to the Spaniards; and many a Peruvian song was set to music by them after the Conquest, and was listened to by the unfortunate natives with melancholy satisfaction, as it called up recollections of the past, when their days glided peacefully away under the scepter of the Incas.

A similar arrangement prevailed with respect to the different manufactures as to the agricultural products of the country.

The flocks of llamas, or Peruvian sheep, were appropriated exclusively to the Sun and to the Inca. Their number was immense. They were scattered over the different provinces, chiefly in the colder regions of the country, where they were intrusted to the care of experienced shepherds, who conducted them to different pastures according to the change of season. A large number was every year sent to the capital for the consumption of the Court, and for the religious festivals and sacrifices. But these were only the males, as no female was allowed to be killed. The regulations for the care and breeding of these flocks were prescribed with the greatest minuteness, and with a sagacity which excited the admiration of the Spaniards, who were familiar with the management of the great migratory flocks of merinos in their own country.

At the appointed season, they were all sheared, and the wool was deposited in the public magazines. It was then dealt out to each family in such quantities as sufficed for its wants, and was consigned to the female part of the household, who were well instructed in the business of spinning and weaving. When this labor was accomplished, and the family was provided with a coarse but warm covering, suited to the cold climate of the mountains,—for, in the lower country, cotton, furnished in like manner by the Crown, took the place, to a certain extent, of wool,—the people were required to labor for the Inca. The quantity of the cloth needed, as well as the peculiar kind and quality of the fabric, was first determined at Cuzco. The work was then apportioned among the different provinces. Officers, appointed for the purpose, superintended the distribution of the wool, so that the manufacture of the different articles should be intrusted to the most competent hands. They did not leave the matter here, but entered the dwellings, from time to time, and saw that the work was faithfully executed. This domestic inquisition was not confined to the labors for the Inca. It included, also, those for the several families; and care was taken that each household should employ the materials furnished for its own use in the manner that was intended, so that no one should be unprovided with necessary apparel. In this domestic labor all the female part of the establishment was expected to join. Occupation was found for all, from the child five years old to the aged matron not too infirm to hold a distaff. No one, at least none but the decrepit and the sick, was allowed to eat the bread of idleness in Peru. Idleness was a crime in the eye of the law, and, as such, severely punished; while industry was publicly commended and stimulated by rewards.

The like course was pursued with reference to the other requisitions of the government. All the mines in the kingdom belonged to the Inca. They were wrought exclusively for his benefit, by persons familiar with this service, and selected from the districts where the mines were situated. Every Peruvian of the lower class was a husbandman, and, with the exception of those already specified, was expected to provide for his own support by the cultivation of his land. A small portion of the community, however, was instructed in mechanical arts; some of them of the more elegant kind, subservient to the purposes of luxury and ornament. The demand for these was chiefly limited to the sovereign and his Court; but the labor of a larger number of hands was exacted for the execution of the great public works which covered the land. The nature and amount of the services required were all determined at Cuzco by commissioners well instructed in the resources of the country, and in the character of the inhabitants of different provinces.

This information was obtained by an admirable regulation, which has scarcely a counterpart in the annals of a semicivilized people. A register was kept of all the births and deaths throughout the country, and exact returns of the actual population were made to government every year, by means of the *quipus*, a curious invention, which will be explained hereafter. At certain intervals, also, a general survey of the country was made, exhibiting a complete view of the character of the soil, its fertility, the nature of its products, both agricultural and mineral,—in short, of all that constituted the physical resources of the empire. Furnished with these statistical details, it was easy for the government, after determining the amount of requisitions, to distribute the work among the respective provinces best qualified to execute it. The task of apportioning the labor was assigned to the local authorities, and great care was taken that it should be done in such a manner, that, while the most competent hands were selected, it should not fall disproportionately heavy on any.

The different provinces of the country furnished persons peculiarly suited to different employments, which, as we shall see hereafter, usually descended from father to son. Thus, one district supplied those most skilled in working the mines, another the most curious workers in metals, or in wood, and so on. The artisan was provided by government with the materials; and no one was required to give more than a stipulated portion of his time to the public service. He was then succeeded by another for the like term; and it should be observed, that all who were engaged in the employment of the government—and the remark applies equally to agricultural labor—were maintained, for the time, at the public expense. By this constant rotation of labor, it was intended that no one should be overburdened, and that each man should have time to provide for the demands of his own household. It was impossible—in the judgment of a high Spanish authority—to improve on the system of distribution, so carefully was it accommodated to the condition and comfort of the artisan. The security of the working classes seems to have been ever kept in view in the regulations of the government; and these were so discreetly arranged, that the most wearing and unwholesome labors, as those of the mines, occasioned no detriment to the health of the laborer; a striking contrast to his subsequent condition under the Spanish rule.

A part of the agricultural produce and manufactures was transported to Cuzco, to minister to the immediate demands of the Inca and his Court. But far the greater part was stored in magazines scattered over the different provinces. These spacious buildings, constructed of stone, were divided between the Sun and the Inca, though the greater share seems to have been appropriated by the monarch. By a wise regulation, any deficiency in the contributions of the Inca might be supplied from the granaries of the Sun. But such a necessity could rarely have happened; and the providence of the government usually left a large surplus in the royal depositories, which was removed to a third class of magazines, whose design was to supply the people in seasons of scarcity, and, occasionally, to furnish relief to individuals, whom sickness or misfortune had reduced to poverty; thus, in a manner, justifying the assertion of a Castilian document, that a large portion of the revenues of the Inca found its way back again, through one channel or another, into the hands of the people. These magazines were found by the Spaniards, on their arrival, stored with all the various products and manufactures of the country,—with maize, *coca*, *quinua*, woolen and cotton stuffs of the finest quality, with vases and utensils of gold, silver, and copper, in short, with every article of luxury or use within the compass of Peruvian skill. The magazines of grain, in particular, would frequently have sufficed for the consumption of the adjoining district for several years. An inventory of the various products of the country, and the quarters whence they were obtained, was every year taken by the royal officers, and recorded by the *quipucamayus* on their registers, with surprising regularity and precision. These registers were transmitted to the capital, and submitted to the Inca, who could thus at a glance, as it were, embrace the whole results of the national industry, and see how far they corresponded with the requisitions of government.

Such are some of the most remarkable features of the Peruvian institutions relating to property, as delineated by writers who, however contradictory in the details, have a general conformity of outline. These institutions are certainly so remarkable, that it is hardly credible they should ever have been enforced throughout a great empire, and for a long period of years. Yet we have the most unequivocal testimony to the fact from the Spaniards, who landed in Peru in time to witness their operation; some of whom, men of high judicial station and character, were commissioned by the government to make investigations into the state of the country under its ancient rulers.

[SPANISH–ARAB CULTURE]

From *Ferdinand and Isabella*, Vol. I, pt. i, chap. viii

[Part of a "Review of the Political and Intellectual Condition of the Spanish Arabs Previous to the War of Granada," in which they were subdued.]

The Saracens gave an entirely new face to pharmacy and chemistry. They introduced a great variety of salutary medicaments into Europe. The Spanish Arabs, in particular, are commended by Sprengel above their brethren for their observations on the practice of medicine. But whatever real knowledge they possessed was corrupted by their inveterate propensity for mystical and occult science. They too often exhausted both health and fortune in fruitless researches after the elixir of life and the philosopher's stone. Their medical prescriptions were regulated by the aspect of the stars. Their physics were debased by magic, their chemistry degenerated into alchemy, their astronomy into astrology.

In the fruitful field of history, their success was even more equivocal. They seem to have been wholly destitute of the philosophical spirit, which gives life to this kind of composition. They were the disciples of fatalism and the subjects of a despotic government. Man appeared to them only in the contrasted aspects of slave and master. What could they know of the finer moral relations, or of the higher energies of the soul, which are developed only under free and beneficent institutions? Even could they have formed conceptions of these, how would they have dared to express them? Hence their histories are too often mere barren chronological details, or fulsome panegyrics on their princes, unenlivened by a single spark of philosophy or criticism.

Although the Spanish Arabs are not entitled to the credit of having wrought any important revolution in intellectual or moral science, they are commended by a severe critic, as exhibiting in their writings "the germs of many theories, which have been reproduced as discoveries in later ages," and they silently perfected several of those useful arts, which have had a sensible influence on the happiness and improvement of mankind. Algebra, and the higher mathematics, were taught in their schools, and thence diffused over Europe. The manufacture of paper, which, since the invention of printing, has contributed so essentially to the rapid circulation of knowledge, was derived through them. Casiri has discovered several manuscripts of cotton paper in the Escurial as early as 1009, and of linen paper of the date of 1106; the origin of which latter fabric Tiraboschi has ascribed to an Italian of Trevigi, in the middle of the fourteenth century. Lastly, the application of gunpowder to military science, which has wrought an equally important revolution, though of a more doubtful complexion, in the condition of society, was derived through the same channel.

The influence of the Spanish Arabs, however, is discernible not so much in the amount of knowledge, as in the impulse, which they communicated to the long dormant energies of Europe. Their invasion was coeval with the commencement of that night of darkness, which divides the modern from the ancient world. The soil had been impoverished by long, assiduous cultivation. The Arabians came like a torrent, sweeping down and obliterating even the landmarks of former civilization, but bringing with it a fertilizing principle, which, as the waters receded, gave new life and loveliness to the landscape. The writings of the Saracens were translated and diffused throughout Europe. Their schools were visited by disciples, who, roused from their lethargy, caught somewhat of the generous enthusiasm of their masters; and a healthful action was given to the European intellect, which, however ill-directed at first, was thus prepared for the more judicious and successful efforts of later times.

It is comparatively easy to determine the value of the scientific labors of a people, for truth is the same in all languages; but the laws of taste differ so widely in different nations, that it requires a nicer discrimination to pronounce fairly upon such works as are regulated by them. Nothing is more common than to see the poetry of the East condemned as tumid, over-refined, infected with meretricious ornament and conceits, and, in short, as every way contravening the principles of good taste. Few of the critics, who thus peremptorily condemn, are capable of reading a line of the original. The merit of poetry, however, consists so much in its literary execution, that a person, to pronounce upon it, should be intimately acquainted with the whole import of the idiom in which it is written. The style of poetry, indeed of all ornamental writing, whether prose or verse, in order to produce a proper effect, must be raised or relieved, as it were, upon the prevailing style of social intercourse. Even where this is highly figurative and impassioned, as with the Arabians, whose ordinary language is made up of metaphor, that of the poet must be still more so. Hence the tone of elegant literature varies so widely in different countries, even in those of Europe, which approach the nearest to each other in their principles of taste, that it would be found extremely difficult to effect a close translation of the most admired specimens of eloquence from the language of one nation into that of any other. A page of Boccaccio or Bembo, for instance, done into literal English, would have an air of intolerable artifice and verbiage. The choicest morsels of Massillon, Bossuet, or the rhetorical Thomas, would savor marvelously of bombast; and how could we in any degree keep pace with the magnificent march of the Castilian! Yet surely we are not to impugn the taste of all those nations, who attach much more importance, and have paid (at least this is true of the French and Italian) much greater attention to the mere beauties of literary finish, than English writers.

Whatever may be the sins of the Arabians on this head, they are certainly not those of negligence. The Spanish Arabs, in particular, were noted for the purity and elegance of their idiom; insomuch that Casiri affects to determine the locality of an author by the superior refinement of his style. Their copious philological and rhetorical treatises, their arts of poetry, grammars, and rhyming dictionaries, show to what an excessive refinement they elaborated the art of composition.

Academies, far more numerous than those of Italy, to which they subsequently served for a model, invited by their premiums frequent competitions in poetry and eloquence. To poetry, indeed, especially of the tender kind, the Spanish Arabs seem to have been as indiscriminately addicted as the Italians in the time of Petrarch; and there was scarcely a doctor in church or state, but at some time or other offered up his amorous incense on the altar of the muse.

With all this poetic feeling, however, the Arabs never availed themselves of the treasures of Grecian eloquence, which lay open before them. Not a poet or orator of any eminence in that language seems to have been translated by them. The temperate tone of Attic composition appeared tame to the fervid conceptions of the East. Neither did they venture upon what in Europe are considered the higher walks of the art, the drama and the epic. None of their writers in prose or verse show much attention to the development or dissection of character. Their inspiration exhaled in lyrical effusions, in elegies, epigrams, and idyls. They sometimes, moreover, like the Italians, employed verse as the vehicle of instruction in the grave and recondite sciences. The general character of their poetry is bold, florid, impassioned, richly colored with imagery, sparkling with conceits and metaphors, and occasionally breathing a deep tone of moral sensibility, as in some of the plaintive effusions ascribed by Conde to the royal poets of Cordova. The compositions of the golden age of the Abasides, and of the preceding period, do not seem to have been infected with the taint of exaggeration, so offensive to a European, which distinguishes the later productions in the decay of the empire.

Whatever be thought of the influence of the Arabic on European literature in general, there can be no reasonable doubt that it has been considerable on the Provençal and the Castilian. In the latter especially, so far from being confined to the vocabulary, or to external forms of composition, it seems to have penetrated deep into its spirit, and is plainly discernible in that affectation of stateliness and oriental hyperbole, which characterizes Spanish writers even at the present day; in the subtilties and conceits with which the ancient Castilian verse is so liberally bespangled; and in the relish for proverbs and prudential maxims, which is so general that it may be considered national.

A decided effect has been produced on the romantic literature of Europe by those tales of fairy enchantment, so characteristic of oriental genius, and in which it seems to have reveled with uncontrolled delight. These tales, which furnished the principal diversion of the East, were imported by the Saracens into Spain; and we find the monarchs of Cordova solacing their leisure hours with listening to their *rawis*, or novelists, who sang to them

"Of ladye-love and war, romance, and knightly worth."

The same spirit, penetrating into France, stimulated the more sluggish inventions of the *trouvère*, and, at a later and more polished period, called forth the imperishable creations of the Italian muse.

It is unfortunate for the Arabians, that their literature should be locked up in a character and idiom so difficult of access to European scholars. Their wild, imaginative poetry, scarcely capable of transfusion into a foreign tongue, is made known to us only through the medium of bald prose translation; while their scientific treatises have been done into Latin with an inaccuracy, which, to make use of a pun of Casiri's, merits the name of perversions rather than versions of the originals. How obviously inadequate, then, are our means of forming any just estimate of their literary merits! It is unfortunate for them, moreover, that the Turks, the only nation, which, from an identity of religion and government with the Arabs, as well as from its political consequence, would seem to represent them on the theater of modern Europe, should be a race so degraded; one which, during the five centuries, that it has been in possession of the finest climate and monuments of antiquity, has so seldom been quickened into a display of genius, or added so little of positive value to the literary treasures descended from its ancient masters. Yet this people, so sensual and sluggish, we are apt to confound in imagination with the sprightly, intellectual Arab. Both indeed have been subjected to the influence of the same degrading political and religious institutions, which on the Turks have produced the results naturally to have been expected; while the Arabians, on the other hand, exhibit the extraordinary phenomenon of a nation, under all these embarrassments, rising to a high degree of elegance and intellectual culture.

The empire, which once embraced more than half of the ancient world, has now shrunk within its original limits; and the Bedouin wanders over his native desert as free, and almost as uncivilized, as before the coming of his apostle. The language, which was once spoken along the southern shores of the Mediterranean and the whole extent of the Indian ocean, is broken up into a variety of discordant dialects. Darkness has again settled over those regions of Africa, which were illumined by the light of learning. The elegant dialect of the Koran is studied as a dead language, even in the birthplace of the prophet. Not a printing press at this day is to be found throughout the whole Arabian Peninsula. Even in Spain, in Christian Spain, alas! the contrast is scarcely less degrading. A death-like torpor has succeeded to her former intellectual activity. Her cities are emptied of the population with which they teemed in the days of the Saracens. Her climate is as fair, but her fields no longer bloom with the same rich and variegated husbandry. Her most interesting monuments are those constructed by the Arabs; and the traveler, as he wanders amid their desolate, but beautiful ruins, ponders on the destinies of a people, whose very existence seems now to have been almost as fanciful as the magical creations in one of their own fairy tales.

[CASTILIAN LITERATURE AND LEARNING]

From *Ferdinand and Isabella*, Vol. II, pt. i, chaps. xix–xx

[Part of a long description of cultural developments under Ferdinand and Isabella.]

The scope of the present work precludes the possibility of a copious enumeration of the pioneers of ancient learning, to whom Spain owes so large a debt of gratitude. The Castilian scholars of the close of the fifteenth, and the beginning of the sixteenth century, may take rank with their illustrious contemporaries of Italy. They could not indeed achieve such brilliant results in the discovery of the remains of antiquity, for such remains had been long scattered and lost amid the centuries of exile and disastrous warfare consequent to the Saracen invasion. But they were unwearied in their illustrations, both oral and written, of the ancient authors; and their numerous commentaries, translations, dictionaries, grammars, and various works of criticism, many of which, though now obsolete, passed into repeated editions in their own day, bear ample testimony to the generous zeal, with which they conspired to raise their contemporaries to a proper level for contemplating the works of the great masters of antiquity; and well entitled them to the high eulogium of Erasmus, that "liberal studies were brought, in the course of a few years, in Spain to so flourishing a condition, as might not only excite the admiration, but serve as a model to the most cultivated nations of Europe."

The Spanish universities were the theater, on which this classical erudition was more especially displayed. Previous to Isabella's reign, there were but few schools in the kingdom; not one indeed of any note, except in Salamanca; and this did not escape the blight which fell on every generous study. But under the cheering patronage of the present government, they were soon filled, and widely multiplied. Academies of repute were to be found in Seville, Toledo, Salamanca, Granada, and Alcalá; and learned teachers were drawn from abroad by the most liberal emoluments. At the head of these establishments stood "the illustrious city of Salamanca," as Marineo fondly terms it, "mother of all liberal arts and virtues, alike renowned for noble cavaliers and learned men." Such was its reputation, that foreigners as well as natives were attracted to its schools, and at one time, according to the authority of the same professor, seven thousand students were assembled within its walls. A letter of Peter Martyr, to his patron the count of Tendilla, gives a whimsical picture of the literary enthusiasm of this place. The throng was so great to hear his introductory lecture on one of the Satires of Juvenal, that every avenue to the hall was blockaded, and the professor was borne in on the shoulders of the students. Professorships in every department of science then studied, as well as of polite letters, were established at the university, the "new Athens," as Martyr somewhere styles it. Before the close of Isabella's reign, however, its glories were rivaled, if not eclipsed, by those of Alcalá; which combined higher advantages for ecclesiastical with civil education, and which, under the splendid patronage of Cardinal Ximenes, executed the famous Polyglot version of the Scriptures, the most stupendous literary enterprise of that age.

This active cultivation was not confined to the dead languages, but spread more or less over every department of knowledge. Theological science, in particular, received a large share of attention. It had always formed a principal object of academic instruction, though suffered to languish under the universal corruption of the preceding reign. It was so common for the clergy to be ignorant of the most elementary knowledge, that the council of Aranda found it necessary to pass an ordinance, the year before Isabella's accession, that no person should be admitted to orders who was ignorant of Latin. The queen took the most effectual means for correcting this abuse, by raising only competent persons to ecclesiastical dignities. The highest stations in the church were reserved for those, who combined the highest intellectual endowments with unblemished piety. Cardinal Mendoza, whose acute and comprehensive mind entered with interest into every scheme for the promotion of science, was archbishop of Toledo; Talavera, whose hospitable mansion was itself an academy for men of letters, and whose princely revenues were liberally dispensed for their support, was raised to the see of Granada; and Ximenes, whose splendid literary projects will require more particular notice hereafter, succeeded Mendoza in the primacy of Spain. Under the protection of these enlightened patrons, theological studies were pursued with ardor, the Scriptures copiously illustrated, and sacred eloquence cultivated with success.

A similar impulse was felt in the other walks of science. Jurisprudence assumed a new aspect, under the learned labors of Montalvo. The mathematics formed a principal branch of education, and were successfully applied to astronomy and geography. Valuable treatises were produced on medicine, and on the more familiar practical arts, as husbandry, for example. History, which since the time of Alfonso the Tenth, had been held in higher honor and more widely cultivated in Castile than in any other European state, began to lay aside the garb of chronicle, and to be studied on more scientific principles. Charters and diplomas were consulted, manuscripts collated, coins and lapidary inscriptions deciphered, and collections made of these materials, the true basis of authentic history; and an office of public archives, like that now existing at Simancas, was established at Burgos, and placed under the care of Alonso de Mota, as keeper, with a liberal salary.

Nothing could have been more opportune for the enlightened purposes of Isabella, than the introduction of the art of printing into Spain, at the commencement, indeed in the very first year, of her reign. She saw, from the first moment, all the advantages which it promised for diffusing and perpetuating the discoveries of science. She encouraged its establishment, by large privileges to those who exercised it, whether natives or foreigners, and by causing many of the works, composed by her subjects, to be printed at her own charge.

Among the earlier printers we frequently find the names of Germans; a people, who to the original merits of the discovery may justly add that of its propagation among every nation of Europe. We meet with a *pragmática*, or royal ordinance, dated in 1477, exempting a German, named Theodoric, from taxation, on the ground of being "one of the principal persons in the discovery and practice of the art of printing books, which he had brought with him into Spain at great risk and expense, with the design of ennobling the libraries of the kingdom." Monopolies for printing and selling books for a limited period, answering to the modern copyright, were granted to certain persons, in consideration of their doing so at a reasonable rate. It seems to have been usual for the printers to be also the publishers and venders of books. These exclusive privileges, however, do not appear to have been carried to a mischievous extent. Foreign books, of every description, by a law of 1480, were allowed to be imported into the kingdom, free of all duty whatever; an enlightened provision, which might furnish a useful hint to legislators of the nineteenth century.

The first press appears to have been erected at Valencia, in 1474; although the glory of precedence is stoutly contested by several places, and especially by Barcelona. The first work printed was a collection of songs, composed for a poetical contest in honor of the Virgin, for the most part in the Limousin or Valencian dialect. In the following year the first ancient classic, being the works of Sallust, was printed; and in 1478 there appeared from the same press a translation of the Scriptures, in the Limousin, by father Boniface Ferrer, brother of the famous Dominican, St. Vincent Ferrer. Through the liberal patronage of the government, the art was widely diffused; and, before the end of the fifteenth century, presses were established and in active operation in the principal cities of the united kingdom; in Toledo, Seville, Ciudad Real, Granada, Valladolid, Burgos, Salamanca, Zamora, Saragossa, Valencia, Barcelona, Monte Rey, Lerida, Murcia, Tolosa, Tarragona, Alcalá de Henares, and Madrid.

It is painful to notice amidst the judicious provisions for the encouragement of science, one so entirely repugnant to their spirit as the establishment of the censorship. By an ordinance, dated at Toledo, July 8th, 1502, it was decreed, that, "as many of the books sold in the kingdom were defective, or false, or apocryphal, or pregnant with vain and superstitious novelties, it was therefore ordered that no book should hereafter be printed without special license from the king, or some person regularly commissioned by him for the purpose." The names of the commissioners then follow, consisting mostly of ecclesiastics, archbishops and bishops, with authority respectively over their several dioceses. This authority was devolved in later times, under Charles the Fifth and his successors, on the Council of the Supreme, over which the inquisitor general presided *ex officio*. The immediate agents employed in the examination were also drawn from the Inquisition, who exercised this important trust, as is well known, in a manner most fatal to the interests of letters and humanity. Thus a provision, destined in its origin for the advancement of science, by purifying it from the crudities and corruptions which naturally infect it in a primitive age, contributed more effectually to its discouragement, than any other which could have been devised, by interdicting the freedom of expression, so indispensable to freedom of inquiry.

While endeavoring to do justice to the progress of civilization in this reign, I should regret to present to the reader an over-colored picture of its results. Indeed, less emphasis should be laid on any actual results, than on the spirit of improvement, which they imply in the nation, and the liberal dispositions of the government. The fifteenth century was distinguished by a zeal for research and laborious acquisition, especially in ancient literature, throughout Europe, which showed itself in Italy in the beginning of the age, and in Spain, and some other countries, towards the close. It was natural that men should explore the long-buried treasures descended from their ancestors, before venturing on anything of their own creation. Their efforts were eminently successful; and, by opening an acquaintance with the immortal productions of ancient literature, they laid the best foundation for the cultivation of the modern.

In the sciences, their success was more equivocal. A blind reverence for authority, a habit of speculation, instead of experiment, so pernicious in physics, in short an ignorance of the true principles of philosophy, often led the scholars of that day in a wrong direction. Even when they took a right one, their attainments, under all these impediments, were necessarily so small, as to be scarcely perceptible, when viewed from the brilliant heights to which science has arrived in our own age. Unfortunately for Spain, its subsequent advancement has been so retarded, that a comparison of the fifteenth century with those which succeeded it, is by no means so humiliating to the former as in some other countries of Europe; and it is certain, that in general intellectual fermentation, no period has surpassed, if it can be said to have rivaled, the age of Isabella.

Ornamental or polite literature, which, emanating from the taste and sensibility of a nation, readily exhibits its various fluctuations of fashion and feeling, was stamped in Spain with the distinguishing characteristics of this revolutionary age. The Provençal, which reached such high perfection in Catalonia, and subsequently in Aragon, as noticed in an introductory chapter, expired with the union of this monarchy with Castile, and the dialect ceased to be applied to literary purposes altogether, after the Castilian became the language of the court in the united kingdoms. The poetry of Castile, which throughout the present reign continued to breathe the same patriotic spirit, and to exhibit the same national peculiarities that had distinguished it from the time of the Cid, submitted soon after Ferdinand's death to the influence of the more polished Tuscan, and henceforth, losing somewhat of its distinctive physiognomy, assumed many of the prevalent features of continental literature. Thus the reign of Ferdinand and Isabella becomes an epoch as memorable in literary, as in civil history.

The most copious vein of fancy, in that day, was turned in the direction of the prose romance of chivalry; now seldom disturbed, even in its own country, except by the antiquary. The circumstances of the age naturally led to its production.

The romantic Moorish wars, teeming with adventurous exploit and picturesque incident, carried on with the natural enemies of the Christian knight, and opening moreover all the legendary stores of oriental fable,—the stirring adventures by sea as well as land,—above all, the discovery of a world beyond the waters, whose unknown regions gave full scope to the play of the imagination, all contributed to stimulate the appetite for the incredible chimeras, the *magnanime menzogne*, of chivalry. The publication of "Amadis de Gaula" gave a decided impulse to this popular feeling. This romance, which seems now well ascertained to be the production of a Portuguese in the latter half of the fourteenth century, was first printed in a Spanish version, probably not far from 1490. Its editor, Garci Ordoñez de Montalvo, states, in his prologue, that "he corrected it from the ancient originals, pruning it of all superfluous phrases, and substituting others of a more polished and elegant style." How far its character was benefited by this work of purification may be doubted; although it is probable it did not suffer so much by such a process as it would have done in a later and more cultivated period. The simple beauties of this fine old romance, its bustling incidents, relieved by the delicate play of oriental machinery, its general truth of portraiture, above all, the knightly character of the hero, who graced the prowess of chivalry with a courtesy, modesty, and fidelity, unrivaled in the creations of romance, soon recommended it to popular favor and imitation. A continuation, bearing the title of "Las Sergas de Esplandian," was given to the world by Montalvo himself, and grafted on the original stock, as the fifth book of the Amadis, before 1510. A sixth, containing the adventures of his nephew, was printed at Salamanca in the course of the last-mentioned year; and thus the idle writers of the day continued to propagate dullness through a series of heavy tomes, amounting in all to four and twenty books, until the much abused public would no longer suffer the name of Amadis to cloak the manifold sins of his posterity. Other knights-errant were sent roving about the world at the same time, whose exploits would fill a library; but fortunately they have been permitted to pass into oblivion, from which a few of their names only have been rescued by the caustic criticism of the curate in Don Quixote; who, it will be remembered, after declaring that the virtues of the parent shall not avail his posterity, condemns them and their companions, with one or two exceptions only, to the fatal funeral pile.

These romances of chivalry must have undoubtedly contributed to nourish those exaggerated sentiments, which from a very early period entered into the Spanish character. Their evil influence, in a literary view, resulted less from their improbabilities of situation, which they possessed in common with the inimitable Italian epics, than from the false pictures which they presented of human character, familiarizing the eye of the reader with such models as debauched the taste, and rendered him incapable of relishing the chaste and sober productions of art. It is remarkable that the chivalrous romance, which was so copiously cultivated through the greater part of the sixteenth century, should not have assumed the poetic form, as in Italy, and indeed among our Norman ancestors; and that, in its prose dress, no name of note appears to raise it to a high degree of literary merit. Perhaps such a result might have been achieved, but for the sublime parody of Cervantes, which cut short the whole race of knights-errant, and by the fine irony, which it threw around the mock heroes of chivalry, extinguished them forever.

The most popular poetry of this period, that springing from the body of the people, and most intimately addressed to it, is the ballads, or *romances*, as they are termed in Spain. These indeed were familiar to the Peninsula as far back as the twelfth and thirteenth centuries; but in the present reign they received a fresh impulse from the war with Granada, and composed, under the name of the Moorish ballads, what may perhaps be regarded, without too high praise, as the most exquisite popular minstrelsy of any age or country.

The humble narrative lyrics making up the mass of ballad poetry, and forming the natural expression of a simple state of society, would seem to be most abundant in nations endowed with keen sensibilities, and placed in situations of excitement and powerful interest, fitted to develope them. The light and lively French have little to boast of in this way. The Italians, with a deeper poetic feeling, were too early absorbed in the gross business habits of trade, and their literature received too high a direction from its master spirits, at its very commencement, to allow any considerable deviation in this track. The countries where it has most thriven, are probably Great Britain and Spain. The English and the Scotch, whose constitutionally pensive and even melancholy temperament has been deepened by the sober complexion of the climate, were led to the cultivation of this poetry still further by the stirring scenes of feudal warfare in which they were engaged, especially along the borders. The Spaniards, to similar sources of excitement, added that of high religious feeling in their struggles with the Saracens, which gave a somewhat loftier character to their effusions. Fortunately for them, their early annals gave birth, in the Cid, to a hero, whose personal renown was identified with that of his country, round whose name might be concentrated all the scattered lights of song, thus enabling the nation to build up its poetry on the proudest historic recollections. The feats of many other heroes, fabulous as well as real, were permitted to swell the stream of traditionary verse; and thus a body of poetical annals, springing up as it were from the depths of the people, was bequeathed from sire to son, contributing, perhaps, more powerfully than any real history could have done, to infuse a common principle of patriotism into the scattered members of the nation. ✱ ✱ ✱

We have now surveyed the different kinds of poetic culture familiar to Spain under Ferdinand and Isabella. Their most conspicuous element is the national spirit which pervades them, and the exclusive attachment which they manifest to the primitive forms of versification peculiar to the Peninsula. The most remarkable portion of this body of poetry may doubtless be considered the Spanish *romances*, or ballads; that popular minstrelsy, which, commemorating the picturesque and chivalrous incidents of the age, reflects most faithfully the romantic genius of the people, who gave it utterance. The lyric efforts of the period were less successful. There were few elaborate attempts in this field, indeed, by men of decided genius. But the great obstacle may be found in the imperfection of the language and the deficiency of the more exact and finished metrical forms, indispensable to high poetic execution.

[THE ESCORIAL]

From *Philip the Second*, Bk. VI, chap. ii

[The final chapter of this work, part of an uncompleted discussion of the "Domestic Affairs of Spain." The chapter deals with Philip as a defender of the Faith.]

A few pages back, while touching on alienations in mortmain, I had occasion to allude to the Escorial, that "eighth wonder of the world," as it is proudly styled by the Spaniards. There can be no place more proper to give an account of this extraordinary edifice than the part of the narrative in which I have been desirous to throw as much light as possible on the character and occupations of Philip. The Escorial engrossed the leisure of more than thirty years of his life; it reflects in a peculiar manner his tastes and the austere character of his mind; and, whatever criticism may be passed on it as a work of art, it cannot be denied that, if every other vestige of his reign were to be swept away, that wonderful structure would of itself suffice to show the grandeur of his plans and the extent of his resources.

The common tradition that Philip built the Escorial in pursuance of a vow which he made at the time of the great battle of St. Quentin, the tenth of August, 1557, has been rejected by modern critics, on the ground that contemporary writers, and among them the historians of the convent, make no mention of the fact. But a recently discovered document leaves little doubt that such a vow was actually made. However this may have been, it is certain that the king designed to commemorate the event by this structure, as is intimated by its dedication to St. Lawrence, the martyr on whose day the victory was gained. The name given to the place was *El Sitio de San Lorenzo el Real*. But the monastery was better known from the hamlet near which it stood,—*El Escurial*, or *El Escorial*,—which latter soon became the orthography generally adopted by the Castilians.

The motives which, after all, operated probably most powerfully on Philip, had no connection with the battle of St. Quentin. His father the emperor had directed by his will that his bones should remain at Yuste until a more suitable place should be provided for them by his son. The building now to be erected was designed expressly as a mausoleum for Philip's parents, as well as for their descendants of the royal line of Austria. But the erection of a religious house on a magnificent scale, that would proclaim to the world his devotion to the Faith, was the predominant idea in the mind of Philip. It was, moreover, a part of his scheme to combine in the plan a palace for himself; for, with a taste which he may be said to have inherited from his father, he loved to live in the sacred shadows of the cloister. These ideas, somewhat incongruous as they may seem, were fully carried out by the erection of an edifice dedicated at once to the threefold purpose of a palace, a monastery, and a tomb.

Soon after the king's return to Spain, he set about carrying his plan into execution. The site which, after careful examination, he selected for the building, was among the mountains of the Guadarrama, on the borders of New Castile, about eight leagues northwest of Madrid. The healthiness of the place and its convenient distance from the capital combined with the stern and solitary character of the region, so congenial to his taste, to give it the preference over other spots which might have found more favor with persons of a different nature. Encompassed by rude and rocky hills, which sometimes soar to the gigantic elevation of mountains, it seemed to be shut out completely from the world. The vegetation was of a thin and stunted growth, seldom spreading out into the luxuriant foliage of the lower regions; and the winds swept down from the neighboring sierra with the violence of a hurricane. Yet the air was salubrious, and the soil was nourished by springs of the purest water. To add to its recommendations, a quarry, close at hand, of excellent stone somewhat resembling granite in appearance, readily supplied the materials for building,—a circumstance, considering the vastness of the work, of no little importance.

The architect who furnished the plans, and on whom the king relied for superintending their execution, was Juan Bautista de Toledo. He was born in Spain, and, early discovering uncommon talents for his profession, was sent to Italy. Here he studied the principles of his art, under the great masters who were then filling their native land with those monuments of genius that furnished the best study to the artist. Toledo imbibed their spirit, and under their tuition acquired that simple, indeed severe, taste which formed a contrast to the prevalent tone of Spanish architecture, but which, happily, found favor with his royal patron.

Before a stone of the new edifice was laid, Philip had taken care to provide himself with the tenants who were to occupy it. At a general chapter of the Jeronymite fraternity, a prior was chosen for the convent of the Escorial, which was to consist of fifty members, soon increased to double that number. Philip had been induced to give the preference to the Jeronymite order, partly from their general reputation for ascetic piety, and in part from the regard shown for them by his father, who had chosen a convent of that order as the place of his last retreat. The monks were speedily transferred to the village of the Escorial, where they continued to dwell until accommodations were prepared for them in the magnificent pile which they were thenceforth to occupy.

Their temporary habitation was of the meanest kind, like most of the buildings in the hamlet. It was without window or chimney, and the rain found its way through the dilapidated roof of the apartment which they used as a chapel, so that they were obliged to protect themselves by a coverlet stretched above their heads. A rude altar was raised at one end of the chapel, over which was scrawled on the wall with charcoal the figure of a crucifix.

The king, on his visits to the place, was lodged in the house of the curate, in not much better repair than the other dwellings in the hamlet. While there he was punctual in his attendance at mass, when a rude seat was prepared for him near the choir, consisting of a three-legged stool, defended from vulgar eyes by a screen of such old and tattered cloth that the inquisitive spectator might without difficulty see him through the holes in it. He was so near the choir that the monk who stood next to him could hardly avoid being brought into contact with the royal person. The Jeronymite who tells the story assures us that Brother Antonio used to weep as he declared that more than once, when he cast a furtive glance at the monarch, he saw his eyes filled with tears. "Such," says the good father, "were the devout and joyful feelings with which the king, as he gazed on the poverty around him, meditated his lofty plans for converting this poverty into a scene of grandeur more worthy of the worship to be performed there."

The brethren were much edified by the humility shown by Philip when attending the services in this wretched cabin. They often told the story of his one day coming late to matins, when, unwilling to interrupt the services, he quietly took his seat by the entrance, on a rude bench, at the upper end of which a peasant was sitting. He remained some time before his presence was observed, when the monks conducted him to his tribune.

On the twenty-third of April, 1563, the first stone of the monastery was laid. On the twentieth of August following, the cornerstone of the church was also laid, with still greater pomp and solemnity. The royal confessor, the bishop of Cuenca, arrayed in his pontificals, presided over the ceremonies. The king was present, and laid the stone with his own hands. The principal nobles of the court were in attendance, and there was a great concourse of spectators, both ecclesiastics and laymen; the solemn services were concluded by the brotherhood, who joined in an anthem of thanksgiving and praise to the Almighty, to whom so glorious a monument was to be reared in this mountain-wilderness.

The rude sierra now swarmed with life. The ground was

covered with tents and huts. The busy hum of labor mingled with the songs of the laborers, which, from their various dialects, betrayed the different, and oftentimes distant, provinces from which they had come. In this motley host the greatest order and decorum prevailed; nor were the peaceful occupations of the day interrupted by any indecent brawls.

As the work advanced, Philip's visits to the Escorial were longer and more frequent. He had always shown his love for the retirement of the cloister, by passing some days of every year in it. Indeed, he was in the habit of keeping Holy Week not far from the scene of his present labors, at the convent of Guisando. In his present monastic retreat he had the additional interest afforded by the contemplation of the great work, which seemed to engage as much of his thoughts as any of the concerns of government.

Philip had given a degree of attention to the study of the fine arts seldom found in persons of his condition. He was a connoisseur in painting, and, above all, in architecture, making a careful study of its principles, and occasionally furnishing designs with his own hand. No prince of his time left behind him so many proofs of his taste and magnificence in building. The royal mint at Segovia, the hunting-seat of the Pardo, the pleasant residence of Aranjuez, the alcazar of Madrid, the "Armeria Real," and other noble works which adorned his infant capital, were either built or greatly embellished by him. The land was covered with structures, both civil and religious, which rose under the royal patronage. Churches and convents —the latter in lamentable profusion—constantly met the eye of the traveler. The general style of their execution was simple in the extreme. Some, like the great cathedral of Valladolid, of more pretension, but still showing the same austere character in their designs, furnished excellent models of architecture to counteract the meretricious tendencies of the age. Structures of a different kind from these were planted by Philip along the frontiers in the north and on the southern coasts of the kingdom; and the voyager in the Mediterranean beheld fortress after fortress crowning the heights above the shore, for its defense against the Barbary corsair. Nor was the king's passion for building confined to Spain. Wherever his armies penetrated in the semicivilized regions of the New World, the march of the conqueror was sure to be traced by the ecclesiastical and military structures which rose in his rear.

Fortunately, similarity of taste led to the most perfect harmony between the monarch and his architect in their conferences on the great work which was to crown the architectural glories of Philip's reign. The king inspected the details, and watched over every step in the progress of the building, with as much care as Toledo himself. In order to judge of the effect from a distance, he was in the habit of climbing the mountains at a spot about half a league from the monastery, where a kind of natural chair was formed by the crags. Here, with his spyglass in his hand, he would sit for hours and gaze on the complicated structure growing up below. The place is still known as the "king's seat."

It was certainly no slight proof of the deep interest which Philip took in the work that he was content to exchange his palace at Madrid for a place that afforded him no better accommodations than the poverty-stricken village of the Escorial. In 1571 he made an important change in these accommodations, by erecting a chapel which might afford the monks a more decent house of worship than their old weather-beaten hovel; and with this he combined a comfortable apartment for himself. In these new quarters he passed still more of his time in cloistered seclusion than he had done before. Far from confining his attention to a supervision of the Escorial, he brought his secretaries and his papers along with him, read here his despatches from abroad, and kept up a busy correspondence with all parts of his dominions. He did four times the amount of work here, says a Jeronymite, that he did in the same number of days in the capital. He used to boast that, thus hidden from the world, with a little bit of paper, he ruled over both hemispheres. That he did not always wisely rule is proved by more than one of his despatches relating to the affairs of Flanders, which issued from this consecrated place. Here he received accounts of the proceedings of his heretic subjects in the Netherlands, and of the Morisco insurgents in Granada. And as he pondered on their demolition of church and convent, and their desecration of the most holy symbols of the Catholic faith, he doubtless felt a proud satisfaction in proving his own piety to the world by the erection of the most sumptuous edifice ever dedicated to the Cross.

In 1577 the Escorial was so far advanced towards completion as to afford accommodations not merely for Philip and his personal attendants, but for many of the court, who were in the habit of spending some time there with the king during the summer. On one of these occasions an accident occurred which had nearly been attended with most disastrous consequences to the building.

A violent thunderstorm was raging in the mountains, and the lightning struck one of the great towers of the monastery. In a short time the upper portion of the building was in a blaze. So much of it, fortunately, was of solid materials that the fire made slow progress. But the difficulty of bringing water to bear on it was extreme. It was eleven o'clock at night when the fire broke out, and in the orderly household of Philip all had retired to rest. They were soon roused by the noise. The king took his station on the opposite tower, and watched with deep anxiety the progress of the flames. The duke of Alva was one among the guests. Though sorely afflicted with the gout at the time, he wrapped his dressing-gown about him and climbed to a spot which afforded a still nearer view of the conflagration. Here the "good duke" at once assumed the command, and gave his orders with as much promptness and decision as on the field of battle.

All the workmen, as well as the neighboring peasantry, were assembled there. The men showed the same spirit of subordination which they had shown throughout the erection of the building. The duke's orders were implicitly obeyed; and more than one instance is recorded of daring self-devotion among the workmen, who toiled as if conscious they were under the eye of their sovereign. The tower trembled under the fury of the flames; and the upper portion of it threatened every moment to fall in ruins. Great fears were entertained that it would crush the hospital, situated in that part of the monastery. Fortunately, it fell in an opposite direction, carrying with it a splendid chime of bells that was lodged in it, but doing no injury to the spectators. The loss which bore most heavily on the royal heart was that of sundry inestimable relics which perished in the flames. But Philip's sorrow was mitigated when he learned that a bit of the true cross, and the right arm of St. Lawrence, the martyred patron of the Escorial, were rescued from the flames. At length, by incredible efforts, the fire, which had lasted till six in the morning, was happily extinguished, and Philip withdrew to his chamber, where his first act, we are told, was to return thanks to the Almighty for the preservation of the building consecrated to his service.

The king was desirous that as many of the materials as possible for the structure should be collected from his own dominions. These were so vast, and so various in their productions, that they furnished nearly every article required for the construction of the edifice, as well as for its interior decoration. The gray stone of which its walls were formed was drawn from a neighboring quarry. It was called *berroqueña*,—a stone bearing a resemblance to granite, though not so hard. The blocks hewn from the quarries, and dressed there, were of such magnitude as sometimes to require forty or fifty yoke of oxen to drag them. The jasper came from the neighborhood of Burgo de Osma. The more delicate marbles, of a great variety of colors, were furnished by the mountain ranges in the south of the Peninsula. The costly and elegant fabrics were many of them supplied by native artisans. Such were the damasks and velvets of Granada. Other cities, as Madrid, Toledo, and Saragossa, showed the proficiency of native art in curious manufactures of bronze and iron, and occasionally of the more precious metals.

Yet Philip was largely indebted to his foreign possessions, especially those in Italy and the Low Countries, for the embellishment of the interior of the edifice, which, in its sumptuous style of decoration, presented a contrast to the stern simplicity of its exterior. Milan, so renowned at that period for its fine workmanship in steel, gold, and precious stones, contributed many exquisite specimens of art. The walls were clothed with gorgeous tapestries from the Flemish looms. Spanish convents vied with each other in furnishing embroideries for the altars. Even the rude colonies in the New World had their part in the great work, and the American forests supplied their cedar and ebony and richly-tinted woods, which displayed all their magical brilliancy of color under the hands of the Castilian workman.

Though desirous as far as possible to employ the products of his own dominions and to encourage native art, in one particular he resorted almost exclusively to foreigners. The oil-paintings and frescoes which profusely decorated the walls and ceilings of the Escorial were executed by artists drawn chiefly from Italy, whose schools of design were still in their glory. But, of all living painters, Titian was the one whom Philip, like his father, most delighted to honor. To the king's generous patronage the world is indebted for some of that great master's noblest productions, which found a fitting place on the walls of the Escorial.

The prices which Philip paid enabled him to command the services of the most eminent artists. Many anecdotes are told of his munificence. He was, however, a severe critic. He did not prematurely disclose his opinion. But when the hour came, the painter had sometimes the mortification to find the work he had executed, it may be with greater confidence than skill, peremptorily rejected, or at best condemned to some obscure corner of the building. This was the fate of an Italian artist, of much more pretension than power, who, after repeated failures according to the judgment of the king,—which later critics have not reversed,—was dismissed to his own country. But even here Philip dealt in a magnanimous way with the unlucky painter. "It is not Zuccaro's fault," he said, "but that of the persons who brought him here"; and when he sent him back to Italy he gave him a considerable sum of money in addition to his large salary.

Before this magnificent pile, in a manner the creation of his own taste, Philip's nature appeared to expand, and to discover some approach to those generous sympathies for humanity which elsewhere seem to have been denied him. He would linger for hours while he watched the labors of the artist, making occasional criticisms, and laying his hand familiarly on his shoulder. He seemed to put off the coldness and reserve which formed so essential a part of his character. On one occasion, it is said, a stranger, having come into the Escorial when the king was there, mistook him for one of the officials, and asked him some questions about the pictures. Philip, without undeceiving the man, humored his mistake, and good-naturedly undertook the part of *cicerone*, by answering his inquiries and showing him some of the objects most worth seeing. Similar anecdotes have been told of others. What is strange is that Philip should have acted the part of the good-natured man.

In 1584 the masonry of the Escorial was completed. Twenty-one years had elapsed since the first stone of the monastery was laid. This certainly must be regarded as a short period for the erection of so stupendous a pile. St. Peter's church, with which one naturally compares it as the building nearest in size and magnificence, occupied more than a century in its erection, which spread over the reigns of at least eighteen popes. But the Escorial, with the exception of the subterraneous chapel constructed by Philip the Fourth for the burial-place of the Spanish princes, was executed in the reign of one monarch. That monarch held in his hands the revenues of both the Old World and the New; and, as he gave in some sort a personal supervision to the work, we may be sure that no one was allowed to sleep on his post.

Yet the architect who designed the building was not permitted to complete it. Long before it was finished, the hand of Toledo had mouldered in the dust. By his death it seemed that Philip had met with an irreparable loss. He felt it to be so himself, and with great distrust consigned the important task to Juan de Herrera, a young Asturian. But, though young, Herrera had been formed on the best models; for he was the favorite pupil of Toledo, and it soon appeared that he had not only imbibed the severe and elevated tastes of his master, but that his own genius fully enabled him to comprehend all Toledo's great conceptions, and to carry them out as perfectly as that artist could have done himself. Philip saw with satisfaction that he had made no mistake in his selection. He soon conferred as freely with the new architect as he had done with his predecessor. He even showed him greater favor, settling on him a salary of a thousand ducats a year and giving him an office in the royal household, and the cross of St. Iago. Herrera had the happiness to complete the Escorial. Indeed, he lived some six years after its completion. He left several works, both civil and ecclesiastical, which perpetuate his fame. But the Escorial is the monument by which his name, and that of his master, Toledo, have come down to posterity as those of the two greatest architects of whom Spain can boast.

This is not the place for criticism on the architectural merits of the Escorial. Such criticism more properly belongs to a treatise on art. It has been my object simply to lay before the reader such an account of the execution of this great work as would enable him to form some idea of the object to which Philip devoted so large a portion of his time, and which so eminently reflected his peculiar cast of mind.

Critics have greatly differed from each other in their judgments of the Escorial. Few foreigners have been found to acquiesce in the undiluted panegyric of those Castilians who pronounce it the eighth wonder of the world. Yet it cannot be denied that few foreigners are qualified to decide on the merits of a work, to judge of which correctly requires a perfect understanding of the character of the country in which it was built, and of the monarch who built it. The traveler who gazes on its long lines of cold gray stone, scarcely broken by an ornament, feels a dreary sensation creeping over him, while he contrasts it with the lighter and more graceful edifices to which his eye has been accustomed. But he may read in this the true expression of the founder's character. Philip did not aim at the beautiful, much less at the festive and cheerful. The feelings which he desired to raise in the spectator were of that solemn, indeed somber complexion which corresponded best with his own religious faith.

Whatever defects may be charged on the Escorial, it is impossible to view it from a distance, and see the mighty pile as it emerges from the gloomy depths of the mountains, without feeling how perfectly it conforms in its aspect to the wild and melancholy scenery of the sierra. Nor can one enter the consecrated precincts without confessing the genius of the place, and experiencing sensations of a mysterious awe as he wanders through the desolate halls, which fancy peoples with the solemn images of the past.

The architect of the building was embarrassed by more than one difficulty of a very peculiar kind. It was not simply a monastery that he was to build. The same edifice, as we have seen, was to comprehend at once a convent, a palace, and a tomb. It was no easy problem to reconcile objects so discordant and infuse into them a common principle of unity. It is no reproach to the builder that he did not perfectly succeed in this, and that the palace should impair the predominant tone of feeling raised by the other parts of the structure, looking in fact like an excrescence, rather than an integral portion of the edifice.

Another difficulty, of a more whimsical nature, imposed on the architect, was the necessity of accommodating the plan of the building to the form of a gridiron,—as typical of the kind of martyrdom suffered by the patron saint of the Escorial. Thus, the long lines of cloisters, with their intervening courts, served for the bars of the instrument; the four lofty spires at the corners of the monastery represented its legs inverted; and the palace, extending its slender length on the east, furnished the awkward handle.

It is impossible for language to convey any adequate idea of a work of art. Yet architecture has this advantage over the sister arts of design, that the mere statement of the dimensions helps us much in forming a conception of the work. A few of these dimensions will serve to give an idea of the magnitude of the edifice. They are reported to us by Los Santos, a Jerony-mite monk, who has left one of the best accounts of the Escorial.

The main building, or monastery, he estimates at seven hundred and forty Castilian feet in length by five hundred and eighty in breadth. Its greatest height, measured to the central cross above the dome of the great church, is three hundred and fifteen feet. The whole circumference of the Escorial, including the palace, he reckons at two thousand nine hundred and eighty feet, or near three-fifths of a mile. The patient inquirer tells us there were no less than twelve thousand doors and windows in the building; that the weight of the keys alone amounted to fifty *arrobas*, or twelve hundred and fifty pounds; and, finally, that there were sixty-eight fountains playing in the halls and courts of this enormous pile.

The cost of its construction and interior decoration, we are informed by Father Siguença, amounted to very near six millions of ducats. Siguença was prior of the monastery, and had access, of course, to the best sources of information. That he did not exaggerate, may be inferred from the fact that he was desirous to relieve the building from the imputation of any excessive expenditure incurred in its erection,—a common theme of complaint, it seems, and one that was urged with strong marks of discontent by contemporary writers. Probably no single edifice ever contained such an amount and variety of inestimable treasures as the Escorial,—so many paintings and sculptures by the greatest masters,—so many articles of exquisite workmanship, composed of the most precious ma-terials. It would be a mistake to suppose that when the build-ing was finished the labors of Philip were at an end. One might almost say they were but begun. The casket was com-pleted; but the remainder of his days was to be passed in filling it with the rarest and richest gems. This was a labor never to be completed. It was to be bequeathed to his successors, who, with more or less taste, but with the revenues of the Indies at their disposal, continued to lavish them on the embellishment of the Escorial.

Philip the Second set the example. He omitted nothing which

could give a value, real or imaginary, to his museum. He gathered at an immense cost several hundred cases of the bones of saints and martyrs, depositing them in rich silver shrines of elaborate workmanship. He collected four thousand volumes, in various languages, especially the Oriental, as the basis of the fine library of the Escorial.

The care of successive princes, who continued to spend there a part of every year, preserved the palace-monastery and its contents from the rude touch of Time. But what the hand of Time had spared the hand of violence destroyed. The French, who in the early part of the present century swept like a horde of Vandals over the Peninsula, did not overlook the Escorial. For in it they saw the monument designed to commemorate their own humiliating defeat. A body of dragoons under La Houssaye burst into the monastery in the winter of 1808; and the ravages of a few days demolished what it had cost years and the highest efforts of art to construct. The apprehension of similar violence from the Carlists, in 1837, led to the removal of the finest paintings to Madrid. The Escorial ceased to be a royal residence. Tenantless and unprotected, it was left to the fury of the blasts which swept down the hills of the Guadarrama.

The traveler who now visits the place will find its condition very different from what it was in the beginning of the century. The bare and mildewed walls no longer glow with the magical tints of Raphael and Titian and the sober pomp of the Castilian school. The exquisite specimens of art with which the halls were filled have been wantonly demolished, or more frequently pilfered for the sake of the rich materials. The monks, so long the guardians of the place, have shared the fate of their brethren elsewhere since the suppression of religious houses, and their venerable forms have disappeared. Silence and solitude reign throughout the courts, undisturbed by any sound save that of the ceaseless winds, which seem to be ever chanting their melancholy dirge over the faded glories of the Escorial. There is little now to remind one of the palace or of the monastery. Of the three great objects to which the edifice was devoted, one alone survives,—that of a mausoleum for the royal line of Castile. The spirit of the dead broods over the place,—of the sceptered dead, who lie in the same dark chamber where they have lain for centuries, unconscious of the changes that have been going on all around them.

V. WAR

[TECHNIQUE OF WAR]

From *Ferdinand and Isabella*, Vol. I, pt. i, chap. xi

[Part of a general view of the policy pursued in the conduct of the War of Granada. It is clear that later critics made too much of the romantic historians' devotion to war, but there can be no doubt of the "relish for gunpowder" revealed in Prescott's volumes. However, his interest in war was not exclusively in the carnage of battle but in the details of military technique as well.]

Notwithstanding the importance of the results in the war of Granada, a detail of the successive steps by which they were achieved would be most tedious and trifling. No siege or single military achievement of great moment occurred until nearly four years from this period, in 1487; although, in the intervening time, a large number of fortresses and petty towns, together with a very extensive tract of territory, were recovered from the enemy. Without pursuing the chronological order of events, it is probable that the end of history will be best attained by presenting a concise view of the general policy pursued by the sovereigns in the conduct of the war.

The Moorish wars under preceding monarchs had consisted of little else than *cavalgadas*, or inroads into the enemy's territory, which, pouring like a torrent over the land, swept away whatever was upon the surface, but left it in its essential resources wholly unimpaired. The bounty of nature soon repaired the ravages of man, and the ensuing harvest seemed to shoot up more abundantly from the soil, enriched by the blood of the husbandman. A more vigorous system of spoliation was now introduced. Instead of one campaign, the army took the field in spring and autumn, intermitting its efforts only during the intolerable heats of summer, so that the green crop had no time to ripen, ere it was trodden down under the iron heel of war.

The apparatus for devastation was also on a much greater scale than had ever before been witnessed. From the second year of the war, thirty thousand foragers were reserved for this service, which they effected by demolishing farmhouses, granaries, and mills, (which last were exceedingly numerous in a land watered by many small streams,) by eradicating the vines, and laying waste the olive-gardens and plantations of oranges, almonds, mulberries, and all the rich varieties that grew luxuriant in this highly favored region. This merciless devastation extended for more than two leagues on either side of the line of march. At the same time, the Mediterranean fleet cut off all supplies from the Barbary coast, so that the whole kingdom might be said to be in a state of perpetual blockade. Such and so general was the scarcity occasioned by this system, that the Moors were glad to exchange their Christian captives for provisions, until such ransom was interdicted by the sovereigns, as tending to defeat their own measures.

Still there was many a green and sheltered valley in Granada, which yielded its returns unmolested to the Moorish husbandman; while his granaries were occasionally enriched with the produce of a border foray. The Moors too, although naturally a luxurious people, were patient of suffering, and capable of enduring great privation. Other measures, therefore, of a still more formidable character, became necessary in conjunction with this rigorous system of blockade.

The Moorish towns were for the most part strongly defended, presenting within the limits of Granada, as has been said, more than ten times the number of fortified places that are now scattered over the whole extent of the Peninsula. They stood along the crest of some precipice, or bold sierra, whose natural strength was augmented by the solid masonry with which they were surrounded, and which, however insufficient to hold out against modern artillery, bade defiance to all the enginery of battering warfare known previously to the fifteenth century.

It was this strength of fortification, combined with that of their local position, which frequently enabled a slender garrison in these places to laugh to scorn all the efforts of the proudest Castilian armies.

The Spanish sovereigns were convinced, that they must look to their artillery as the only effectual means for the reduction of these strongholds. In this, they as well as the Moors were extremely deficient, although Spain appears to have furnished earlier examples of its use than any other country in Europe. Isabella, who seems to have had the particular control of this department, caused the most skillful engineers and artisans to be invited into the kingdom from France, Germany, and Italy. Forges were constructed in the camp, and all the requisite materials prepared for the manufacture of cannon, balls, and powder. Large quantities of the last were also imported from Sicily, Flanders, and Portugal. Commissaries were established over the various departments, with instructions to provide whatever might be necessary for the operatives; and the whole was intrusted to the supervision of Don Francisco Ramirez, an hidalgo of Madrid, a person of much experience, and extensive military science, for that day. By these efforts, unremittingly pursued during the whole of the war, Isabella assembled a train of artillery, such as was probably not possessed at that time by any other European potentate.

Still the clumsy construction of the ordnance betrayed the infancy of the art. More than twenty pieces of artillery used at the siege of Baza, during this war, are still to be seen in that city, where they long served as columns in the public market-place. The largest of the lombards, as the heavy ordnance was called, are about twelve feet in length, consisting of iron bars two inches in breadth, held together by bolts and rings of the same metal. These were firmly attached to their carriages, incapable either of horizontal or vertical movement. It was this clumsiness of construction, which led Machiavelli, some thirty years after, to doubt the expediency of bringing cannon into field engagements; and he particularly recommends in his treatise on the Art of War, that the enemy's fire should be evaded, by intervals in the ranks being left open opposite to his cannon.

The balls thrown from these engines were sometimes of iron, but more usually of marble. Several hundred of the latter have been picked up in the fields around Baza, many of which are fourteen inches in diameter, and weigh a hundred and seventy-five pounds. Yet this bulk, enormous as it appears, shows a considerable advance in the art since the beginning of the century, when the stone balls discharged, according to Zurita, at the siege of Balaguer, weighed not less than five hundred and fifty pounds. It was very long before the exact proportions requisite for obtaining the greatest effective force could be ascertained.

The awkwardness with which their artillery was served, corresponded with the rudeness of its manufacture. It is noticed as a remarkable circumstance by the chronicler, that two batteries, at the siege of Albahar, discharged one hundred and forty balls in the course of a day. Besides this more usual kind of ammunition, the Spaniards threw from their engines large globular masses, composed of certain inflammable ingredients mixed with gunpowder, "which, scattering long trains of light," says an eyewitness, "in their passage through the air, filled the beholders with dismay, and, descending on the roofs of the edifices, frequently occasioned extensive conflagration."

The transportation of their bulky engines was not the least of the difficulties which the Spaniards had to encounter in this war. The Moorish fortresses were frequently intrenched in the depths of some mountain labyrinth, whose rugged passes were scarcely accessible to cavalry. An immense body of pioneers, therefore, was constantly employed in constructing roads for the artillery across these sierras, by leveling the mountains, filling up the intervening valleys with rocks, or with cork trees and other timber that grew prolific in the wilderness, and throwing bridges across the torrents and precipitous *barrancos*. Pulgar had the curiosity to examine one of the causeways thus constructed, preparatory to the siege of Cambil, which, although six thousand pioneers were constantly employed in the work, was attended with such difficulty, that it advanced only three leagues in twelve days. It required, says the historian, the entire demolition of one of the most rugged parts of the sierra, which no one could have believed practicable by human industry.

The Moorish garrisons, perched on their mountain fastnesses, which, like the eyry of some bird of prey, seemed almost inaccessible to man, beheld with astonishment the heavy trains of artillery, emerging from the passes, where the foot of the hunter had scarcely been known to venture. The walls which encompassed their cities, although lofty, were not of sufficient thickness to withstand long the assaults of these formidable engines. The Moors were deficient in heavy ordnance. The weapons on which they chiefly relied for annoying the enemy at a distance were the arquebus and crossbow, with the last of which they were unerring marksmen, being trained to it from infancy. They adopted a custom, rarely met with in civilized nations of any age, of poisoning their arrows; distilling for this purpose the juice of aconite, or wolfsbane, which they found in the *Sierra Nevada*, or Snowy Mountains, near Granada. A piece of linen or cotton cloth steeped in this decoction was wrapped round the point of the weapon, and the wound inflicted by it, however trivial in appearance, was sure to be mortal. Indeed a Spanish writer, not content with this, imputes such malignity to the virus, that a drop of it, as he asserts, mingling with the blood oozing from a wound, would ascend the stream into the vein, and diffuse its fatal influence over the whole system!

Ferdinand, who appeared at the head of his armies throughout the whole of this war, pursued a sagacious policy in reference to the beleaguered cities. He was ever ready to meet the first overtures to surrender, in the most liberal spirit; granting protection of person, and such property as the besieged could transport with them, and assigning them a residence, if they preferred it, in his own dominions. Many, in consequence of this, migrated to Seville and other cities of Andalusia, where they were settled on estates which had been confiscated by the inquisitors; who looked forward, no doubt, with satisfaction to the time, when they should be permitted to thrust their sickle into the new crop of heresy, whose seeds were thus sown amid the ashes of the old one. Those who preferred to remain in the conquered Moorish territory, as Castilian subjects, were permitted the free enjoyment of personal rights and property, as well as of their religion; and, such was the fidelity with which Ferdinand redeemed his engagements during the war, by the punishment of the least infraction of them by his own people, that many, particularly of the Moorish peasantry, preferred abiding in their early homes to removing to Granada, or other places of the Moslem dominion. It was, perhaps a counterpart of the same policy, which led Ferdinand to chastise any attempt at revolt, on the part of his new Moorish subjects, the Mudejares, as they were called, with an unsparing rigor, which merits the reproach of cruelty. Such was the military execution inflicted on the rebellious town of Benemaquez, where he commanded one hundred and ten of the principal inhabitants to be hung above the walls, and, after consigning the rest of the population, men, women, and children, to slavery, caused the place to be razed to the ground. The humane policy, usually pursued by Ferdinand, seems to have had a more favorable effect on his enemies, who were exasperated, rather than intimidated, by this ferocious act of vengeance.

The magnitude of the other preparations corresponded with those for the ordnance department. The amount of forces assembled at Cordova, we find variously stated at ten or twelve thousand horse, and twenty, and even forty thousand foot, exclusive of foragers. On one occasion, the whole number, including men for the artillery service and the followers of the camp, is reckoned at eighty thousand. The same number of beasts of burden were employed in transporting the supplies required for this immense host, as well as for provisioning the conquered cities standing in the midst of a desolated country. The queen, who took this department under her special cognizance, moved along the frontier, stationing herself at points most contiguous to the scene of operations. There, by means of posts regularly established, she received hourly intelligence of the war. At the same time she transmitted the requisite munitions for the troops, by means of convoys sufficiently strong to secure them against the irruptions of the wily enemy.

Isabella, solicitous for everything that concerned the welfare of her people, sometimes visited the camp in person, encouraging the soldiers to endure the hardships of war, and relieving their necessities by liberal donations of clothes and money. She caused also a number of large tents, known as "the queen's hospitals," to be always reserved for the sick and wounded, and furnished them with the requisite attendants and medicines, at her own charge. This is considered the earliest attempt at the formation of a regular camp hospital, on record.

Isabella may be regarded as the soul of this war. She engaged in it with the most exalted views, less to acquire territory, than to re-establish the empire of the Cross over the ancient domain of Christendom. On this point, she concentrated all the energies of her powerful mind, never suffering herself to be diverted by any subordinate interest from this one great and glorious object. When the king, in 1484, would have paused a while from the Granadine war, in order to prosecute his claims to Roussillon against the French, on the demise of Louis the Eleventh, Isabella strongly objected to it; but, finding her remonstrance ineffectual, she left her husband in Aragon, and repaired to Cordova, where she placed the cardinal of Spain at the head of the army, and prepared to open the campaign in the usual vigorous manner. Here, however, she was soon joined by Ferdinand, who, on a cooler revision of the subject, deemed it prudent to postpone his projected enterprise.

On another occasion, in the same year, when the nobles, fatigued with the service, had persuaded the king to retire earlier than usual, the queen, dissatisfied with the proceeding, addressed a letter to her husband, in which, after representing the disproportion of the results to the preparations, she besought him to keep the field as long as the season should serve. The grandees, says Lebrija, mortified at being surpassed in zeal for the holy war by a woman, eagerly collected their forces, which had been partly disbanded, and returned across the borders to renew hostilities.

A circumstance, which had frequently frustrated the most magnificent military enterprises under former reigns, was the factions of these potent vassals, who, independent of each other, and almost of the crown, could rarely be brought to act in efficient concert for a length of time, and broke up the camp on the slightest personal jealousy. Ferdinand experienced something of this temper in the duke of Medina Celi, who, when he had received orders to detach a corps of his troops to the support of the count of Benavente, refused, replying to the messenger, "Tell your master, that I came here to serve him at the head of my household troops, and they go nowhere without me as their leader." The sovereigns managed this fiery spirit with the greatest address, and, instead of curbing it, endeavored to direct it in the path of honorable emulation. The queen, who as their hereditary sovereign received a more deferential homage from her Castilian subjects than Ferdinand, frequently wrote to her nobles in the camp, complimenting some on their achievements, and others less fortunate on their intentions, thus cheering the hearts of all, says the chronicler, and stimulating them to deeds of heroism. On the most deserving she freely lavished those honors which cost little to the sovereign, but are most grateful to the subject. The marquis of Cadiz, who was pre-eminent above every other captain in this war for sagacity and conduct, was rewarded after his brilliant surprise of Zahara, with the gift of that city, and the titles of Marquis of Zahara and Duke of Cadiz. The warrior, however, was unwilling to resign the ancient title under which he had won his laurels, and ever after subscribed himself, Marquis Duke of Cadiz. Still more emphatic honors were conferred on the Count de Cabra, after the capture of the king of Granada. When he presented himself before the sovereigns, who were at Vitoria, the clergy and cavaliers of the city marched out to receive him, and he entered in solemn procession on the right hand of the grand cardinal of Spain. As he advanced up the hall of audience in the royal palace, the king and queen came forward to welcome him, and then seated him by themselves at table, declaring that "the conqueror of kings should sit with kings." These honors were followed by the more substantial gratuity of a hundred thousand maravedies annual rent; "a fat donative," says an old chronicler, "for so lean a treasury." The young alcayde de los donzeles experienced a similar reception on the ensuing day. Such acts of royal condescension were especially grateful to the nobility of a court, circumscribed beyond every other in Europe by stately and ceremonious etiquette.

The duration of the war of Granada was such as to raise the militia throughout the kingdom nearly to a level with regular troops. Many of these levies, indeed, at the breaking out of the war, might pretend to this character. Such were those furnished by the Andalusian cities, which had been long accustomed to skirmishes with their Moslem neighbors. Such too was the well-appointed chivalry of the military orders, and the organized militia of the hermandad, which we find sometimes supplying a body of ten thousand men for the service. To these may be added the splendid throng of cavaliers and hidalgos, who swelled the retinues of the sovereigns and the great nobility. The king was attended in battle by a bodyguard of a thousand knights, one half light, and the other half heavy armed, all superbly equipped and mounted, and trained to arms from childhood, under the royal eye.

Although the burden of the war bore most heavily on Andalusia, from its contiguity to the scene of action, yet recruits were drawn in abundance from the most remote provinces, as Galicia, Biscay, and the Asturias, from Aragon, and even the transmarine dominions of Sicily. The sovereigns did not disdain to swell their ranks with levies of a humbler description, by promising an entire amnesty to those malefactors, who had left the country in great numbers of late years to escape justice, on condition of their serving in the Moorish war. Throughout this motley host the strictest discipline and decorum were maintained. The Spaniards have never been disposed to intemperance; but the passion for gaming, especially with dice, to which they seem to have been immoderately addicted at that day, was restrained by the severest penalties.

[GONSALVO AS GENERAL]

From *Ferdinand and Isabella*, Vol. III, pt. ii, chap. xv

[Gonsalvo was the Spanish commander in the Franco-Spanish wars over Italy. This selection is part of an analysis of the causes of the Spanish victory.]

His success, it is true, is imputable in part to the signal errors of his adversaries. The magnificent expedition of Charles the Eighth, failed to produce any permanent impression, chiefly in consequence of the precipitation with which it had been entered into, without sufficient concert with the Italian states, who became a formidable enemy when united in his rear. He did not even avail himself of his temporary acquisition of Naples to gather support from the attachment of his new subjects. Far from incorporating with them, he was regarded as a foreigner and an enemy, and, as such, expelled by the joint action of all Italy from its bosom, as soon as it had recovered sufficient strength to rally.

Louis the Twelfth profited by the errors of his predecessor. His acquisitions in the Milanese formed a basis for future operations; and by negotiation and otherwise he secured the alliance and the interests of the various Italian governments on his side. These preliminary arrangements were followed by preparations every way commensurate with his object. He failed in the first campaign, however, by intrusting the command to incompetent hands, consulting birth rather than talent or experience.

In the succeeding campaigns, his failure, though partly chargeable on himself, was less so than on circumstances beyond his control. The first of these was the long detention of the army before Rome by cardinal D'Amboise, and its consequent exposure to the unexampled severity of the ensuing winter. A second was the fraudulent conduct of the commissaries, implying, no doubt, some degree of negligence in the person who appointed them; and lastly, the want of a suitable commander-in-chief of the army. La Tremouille being ill, and D'Aubigny a prisoner in the hands of the enemy, there appeared no one among the French qualified to cope with the Spanish general. The marquis of Mantua, independently of the disadvantage of being a foreigner, was too timid in council, and dilatory in conduct, to be any way competent to this difficult task.

If his enemies, however, committed great errors, it is altogether owing to Gonsalvo that he was in a situation to take advantage of them. Nothing could be more unpromising than his position on first entering Calabria. Military operations had been conducted in Spain on principles totally different from those which prevailed in the rest of Europe. This was the case especially in the late Moorish wars, where the old tactics and the character of the ground brought light cavalry chiefly into use. This, indeed, constituted his principal strength at this period; for his infantry, though accustomed to irregular service, was indifferently armed and disciplined. An important revolution, however, had occurred in the other parts of Europe. The infantry had there regained the superiority which it maintained in the days of the Greeks and Romans. The experiment had been made on more than one bloody field; and it was found, that the solid columns of Swiss and German pikes not only bore down all opposition in their onward march, but presented an impregnable barrier, not to be shaken by the most desperate charges of the best heavy-armed cavalry. It was against these dreaded battalions that Gonsalvo was now called to measure for the first time the bold, but rudely armed and comparatively raw recruits from Galicia and the Asturias.

He lost his first battle, into which it should be remembered he was precipitated against his will. He proceeded afterwards with the greatest caution, gradually familiarizing his men with the aspect and usages of the enemy whom they held in such awe, before bringing them again to a direct encounter. He put himself to school during this whole campaign, carefully acquainting himself with the tactics, discipline, and novel arms of his adversaries, and borrowing just so much as he could incorporate into the ancient system of the Spaniards, without discarding the latter altogether. Thus, while he retained the short sword and buckler of his countrymen, he fortified his battalions with a large number of spearmen, after the German fashion. The arrangement is highly commended by the sagacious Machiavelli, who considers it as combining the advantages of both systems; since, while the long spear served all the purposes of resistance, or even of attack on level ground, the short swords and targets enabled their wearers, as already noticed, to cut in under the dense array of hostile pikes, and bring the enemy to close quarters, where his formidable weapon was of no avail.

While Gonsalvo made this innovation in the arms and tactics, he paid equal attention to the formation of a suitable character in his soldiery. The circumstances in which he was placed at Barleta, and on the Garigliano, imperatively demanded this. Without food, clothes, or pay, without the chance even of retrieving his desperate condition by venturing a blow at the enemy, the Spanish soldier was required to remain passive. To do this demanded patience, abstinence, strict subordination, and a degree of resolution far higher than that required to combat obstacles, however formidable in themselves, where active exertion, which tasks the utmost energies of the soldier, renews his spirits and raises them to a contempt of danger. It was calling on him, in short, to begin with achieving that most difficult of all victories, the victory over himself.

All this the Spanish commander effected. He infused into his men a portion of his own invincible energy. He inspired a love of his person, which led them to emulate his example, and a confidence in his genius and resources, which supported them under all their privations by a firm reliance on a fortunate issue. His manners were distinguished by a graceful courtesy, less encumbered with etiquette than was usual with persons of his high rank in Castile. He knew well the proud and independent feelings of the Spanish soldier; and, far from annoying him by unnecessary restraints, showed the most liberal indulgence at all times. But his kindness was tempered with severity, which displayed itself, on such occasions as required interposition, in a manner that rarely failed to repress everything like insubordination. The reader will readily recall an example of this in the mutiny before Tarento; and it was doubtless by the assertion of similar power, that he was so long able to keep in check his German mercenaries, distinguished above the troops of every other nation by their habitual license and contempt of authority.

While Gonsalvo relied so freely on the hardy constitution and patient habits of the Spaniards, he trusted no less to the deficiency of these qualities in the French, who, possessing little of the artificial character formed under the stern training of later times, resembled their Gaulish ancestors in the facility with which they were discouraged by unexpected obstacles, and the difficulty with which they could be brought to rally. In this he did not miscalculate. The French infantry, drawn from the militia of the country, hastily collected and soon to be disbanded, and the independent nobility and gentry who composed the cavalry service, were alike difficult to be brought within the strict curb of military rule. The severe trials, which steeled the souls, and gave sinewy strength to the constitutions, of the Spanish soldiers, impaired those of their enemies, introduced divisions into their councils, and relaxed the whole tone of discipline. Gonsalvo watched the operation of all this, and, coolly waiting the moment when his weary and disheartened adversary should be thrown off his guard, collected all his strength for a decisive blow, by which to terminate the action. Such was the history of those memorable campaigns, which closed with the brilliant victories of Cerignola and the Garigliano.

In a review of his military conduct, we must not overlook his politic deportment towards the Italians, altogether the reverse of the careless and insolent bearing of the French. He availed himself liberally of their superior science, showing great deference, and confiding the most important trusts, to their officers. Far from the reserve usually shown to foreigners, he appeared insensible to national distinctions, and ardently embraced them as companions in arms, embarked in a common cause with himself. In their tourney with the French before Barleta, to which the whole nation attached such importance as a vindication of national honor, they were entirely supported by Gonsalvo, who furnished them with arms, secured a fair field of fight, and shared the triumph of the victors as that of his own countrymen,—paying those delicate attentions, which cost far less, indeed, but to an honorable mind are of greater value, than more substantial benefits. He conciliated the good-will of the Italian states by various important services; of the Venetians, by his gallant defense of their possessions in the Levant; of the people of Rome, by delivering them from the pirates of Ostia; while he succeeded, notwithstanding the excesses of his soldiery, in captivating the giddy Neapolitans to such a degree, by his affable manners and splendid style of life, as seemed to efface from their minds every recollection of the last and most popular of their monarchs, the unfortunate Frederic.

The distance of Gonsalvo's theater of operations from his own country, apparently most discouraging, proved extremely favorable to his purposes. The troops, cut off from retreat by a wide sea and an impassable mountain barrier, had no alternative but to conquer, or to die. Their long continuance in the field without disbanding gave them all the stern, inflexible qualities of a standing army; and, as they served through so many successive campaigns under the banner of the same leader, they were drilled in a system of tactics far steadier and more uniform than could be acquired under a variety of commanders, however able. Under these circumstances, which so well fitted them for receiving impressions, the Spanish army was gradually moulded into the form determined by the will of its great chief.

When we look at the amount of forces at the disposal of Gonsalvo, it appears so paltry, especially compared with the gigantic apparatus of later wars, that it may well suggest disparaging ideas of the whole contest. To judge correctly, we must direct our eyes to the result. With this insignificant force, we shall then see the kingdom of Naples conquered, and the best generals and armies of France annihilated; an important innovation effected in military science; the art of mining, if not invented, carried to unprecedented perfection; a thorough reform introduced in the arms and discipline of the Spanish soldier; and the organization completed of that valiant infantry, which is honestly eulogized by a French writer, as irresistible in attack, and impossible to rout; and which carried the banners of Spain victorious, for more than a century, over the most distant parts of Europe.

[GREAT BATTLE WITH THE INDIANS]
From *The Conquest of Mexico*, Bk. II, chap. iv

[Cortés has just started his invasion of the continent and this vivid selection tells of the defeat of the Tabascans, who tried to bar the onward march of the Spaniards.]

At the first glimmering of light he mustered his army, and declared his purpose not to abide, cooped up in the town, the assault of the enemy, but to march at once against him. For he well knew that the spirits rise with action, and that the attacking party gathers a confidence from the very movement, which is not felt by the one who is passively, perhaps anxiously, awaiting the assault. The Indians were understood to be encamped on a level ground a few miles distant from the city, called the plain of Ceutla. The general commanded that Ordaz should march with the foot, including the artillery, directly across the country, and attack them in front, while he himself would fetch a circuit with the horse, and turn their flank when thus engaged, or fall upon their rear.

These dispositions being completed, the little army heard mass and then sallied forth from the wooden walls of Tabasco. It was Lady-day, the twenty-fifth of March,—long memorable in the annals of New Spain. The district around the town was chequered with patches of maize, and, on the lower level, with plantations of cacao,—supplying the beverage, and perhaps the coin of the country, as in Mexico. These plantations, requiring constant irrigation, were fed by numerous canals and reservoirs of water, so that the country could not be traversed without great toil and difficulty. It was, however, intersected by a narrow path or causeway, over which the cannon could be dragged.

The troops advanced more than a league on their laborious march, without descrying the enemy. The weather was sultry, but few of them were embarrassed by the heavy mail worn by the European cavaliers at that period. Their cotton jackets, thickly quilted, afforded a tolerable protection against the arrows of the Indian, and allowed room for the freedom and activity of movement essential to a life of rambling adventure in the wilderness.

At length they came in sight of the broad plains of Ceutla, and beheld the dusky lines of the enemy stretching, as far as the eye could reach, along the edge of the horizon. The Indians had shown some sagacity in the choice of their position; and, as the weary Spaniards came slowly on, floundering through the morass, the Tabascans set up their hideous battle-cries, and discharged volleys of arrows, stones, and other missiles, which rattled like hail on the shields and helmets of the assailants. Many were severely wounded before they could gain the firm ground, where they soon cleared a space for themselves, and opened a heavy fire of artillery and musketry on the dense columns of the enemy, which presented a fatal mark for the balls. Numbers were swept down at every discharge; but the bold barbarians, far from being dismayed, threw up dust and leaves to hide their losses, and, sounding their war instruments, shot off fresh flights of arrows in return.

They even pressed closer on the Spaniards, and, when driven off by a vigorous charge, soon turned again, and, rolling back like the waves of the ocean, seemed ready to overwhelm the little band by weight of numbers. Thus cramped, the latter had scarcely room to perform their necessary evolutions, or even to work their guns with effect.

The engagement had now lasted more than an hour, and

the Spaniards, sorely pressed, looked with great anxiety for the arrival of the horse,—which some unaccountable impediments must have detained,—to relieve them from their perilous position. At this crisis, the furthest columns of the Indian army were seen to be agitated and thrown into a disorder that rapidly spread through the whole mass. It was not long before the ears of the Christians were saluted with the cheering war-cry of "San Jago and San Pedro!" and they beheld the bright helmets and swords of the Castilian chivalry flashing back the rays of the morning sun, as they dashed through the ranks of the enemy, striking to the right and left, and scattering dismay around them. The eye of faith, indeed, could discern the patron Saint of Spain, himself, mounted on his gray war-horse, heading the rescue and trampling over the bodies of the fallen infidels!

The approach of Cortés had been greatly retarded by the broken nature of the ground. When he came up, the Indians were so hotly engaged, that he was upon them before they observed his approach. He ordered his men to direct their lances at the faces of their opponents, who, terrified at the monstrous apparition,—for they supposed the rider and the horse, which they had never before seen, to be one and the same,—were seized with a panic. Ordaz availed himself of it to command a general charge along the line, and the Indians, many of them throwing away their arms, fled without attempting further resistance.

Cortés was too content with the victory, to care to follow it up by dipping his sword in the blood of the fugitives. He drew off his men to a copse of palms which skirted the place, and under their broad canopy the soldiers offered up thanksgivings to the Almighty for the victory vouchsafed them. The field of battle was made the site of a town, called, in honor of the day on which the action took place, *Santa María de la Vitoria*, long afterwards the capital of the Province. The number of those who fought or fell in the engagement is altogether doubtful. Nothing, indeed, is more uncertain than numerical estimates of barbarians. And they gain nothing in probability, when they come, as in the present instance, from the reports of their enemies. Most accounts, however, agree that the Indian force consisted of five squadrons of eight thousand men each. There is more discrepancy as to the number of slain, varying from one to thirty thousand! In the monstrous discordance, the common disposition to exaggerate may lead us to look for truth in the neighborhood of the smallest number. The loss of the Christians was inconsiderable; not exceeding—if we receive their own reports, probably, from the same causes, much diminishing the truth—two killed and less than a hundred wounded! We may readily comprehend the feelings of the Conquerors, when they declared, that "Heaven must have fought on their side, since their own strength could never have prevailed against such a multitude of enemies!"

[BATTLE WITH THE TLASCALANS]

From *The Conquest of Mexico*, Bk. iii, chap. ii

[Moving along toward the City of Mexico, Cortés had to clear from his path many peoples, some of whom fought with great ferocity; among them were the Tlascalans.]

Soon after, they came in sight of a body of Indians, about a thousand, apparently, all armed and brandishing their weapons, as the Christians approached, in token of defiance. Cortés, when he had come within hearing, ordered the interpreters to proclaim that he had no hostile intentions; but wished only to be allowed a passage through their country, which he had entered as a friend. This declaration he commanded the royal notary, Godoy, to record on the spot, that, if blood were shed, it might not be charged on the Spaniards. This pacific proclamation was met, as usual on such occasions, by a shower of darts, stones, and arrows, which fell like rain on the Spaniards, rattling on their stout harness, and in some instances penetrating to the skin. Galled by the smart of their wounds, they called on the general to lead them on, till he sounded the well known battle-cry, "St. Jago, and at them!"

The Indians maintained their ground for a while with spirit, when they retreated with precipitation, but not in disorder. The Spaniards, whose blood was heated by the encounter, followed up their advantage with more zeal than prudence, suffering the wily enemy to draw them into a narrow glen or defile, intersected by a little stream of water, where the broken ground was impracticable for artillery, as well as for the movements of cavalry. Pressing forward with eagerness, to extricate themselves from their perilous position, to their great dismay, on turning an abrupt angle of the pass, they came in presence of a numerous army, choking up the gorge of the valley, and stretching far over the plains beyond. To the astonished eyes of Cortés, they appeared a hundred thousand men, while no account estimates them at less than thirty thousand.

They presented a confused assemblage of helmets, weapons, and many-colored plumes, glancing bright in the morning sun, and mingled with banners, above which proudly floated one that bore as a device the heron on a rock. It was the well known ensign of the house of Titcala, and, as well as the white and yellow stripes on the bodies, and the like colors on the feather-mail of the Indians, showed that they were the warriors of Xicotencatl.

As the Spaniards came in sight, the Tlascalans set up a hideous war-cry, or rather whistle, piercing the ear with its shrillness, and which, with the beat of their melancholy drums, that could be heard for half a league or more, might well have filled the stoutest heart with dismay. This formidable host came rolling on towards the Christians, as if to overwhelm them by their very numbers. But the courageous band of warriors, closely serried together and sheltered under their strong panoplies, received the shock unshaken, while the broken masses of the enemy, chafing and heaving tumultuously around them, seemed to recede only to return with new and accumulated force.

Cortés, as usual, in the front of danger, in vain endeavored, at the head of the horse, to open a passage for the infantry. Still his men, both cavalry and foot, kept their array unbroken, offering no assailable point to their foe. A body of the Tlascalans, however, acting in concert, assaulted a soldier named Moran, one of the best riders in the troop. They succeeded in dragging him from his horse, which they despatched with a thousand blows. The Spaniards, on foot, made a desperate effort to rescue their comrade from the hands of the enemy,—and from the horrible doom of the captive. A fierce struggle now began over the body of the prostrate horse. Ten of the Spaniards were wounded, when they succeeded in retrieving the unfortunate cavalier from his assailants, but in so disastrous a plight that he died on the following day. The horse was borne off in triumph by the Indians, and his mangled remains were sent, a strange trophy, to the different towns of Tlascala. The circumstance troubled the Spanish commander, as it divested the animal of the supernatural terrors with which the superstition of the natives had usually surrounded it. To prevent such a consequence, he had caused the two horses, killed on the preceding day, to be secretly buried on the spot.

The enemy now began to give ground gradually, borne down by the riders, and trampled under the hoofs of their horses. Through the whole of this sharp encounter, the Indian allies were of great service to the Spaniards. They rushed into the water, and grappled their enemies, with the desperation of men who felt that "their own safety was in the despair of safety." "I see nothing but death for us," exclaimed a Cempoallan chief to Marina; "we shall never get through the pass alive." "The God of the Christians is with us," answered the intrepid woman; "and He will carry us safely through."

Amidst the din of battle, the voice of Cortés was heard, cheering on his soldiers. "If we fail now," he cried, "the cross of Christ can never be planted in the land. Forward, comrades! When was it ever known that a Castilian turned his back on a foe?" Animated by the words and heroic bearing of their general, the soldiers, with desperate efforts, at length succeeded in forcing a passage through the dark columns of the enemy, and emerged from the defile on the open plain beyond.

Here they quickly recovered their confidence with their

superiority. The horse soon opened a space for the manœuvres of the artillery. The close files of their antagonists presented a sure mark; and the thunders of the ordnance vomiting forth torrents of fire and sulphurous smoke, the wide desolation caused in their ranks, and the strangely mangled carcasses of the slain, filled the barbarians with consternation and horror. They had no weapons to cope with these terrible engines, and their clumsy missiles, discharged from uncertain hands, seemed to fall ineffectual on the charmed heads of the Christians. What added to their embarrassment was, the desire to carry off the dead and wounded from the field, a general practice among the people of Anahuac, but which necessarily exposed them, while thus employed, to still greater loss.

Eight of their principal chiefs had now fallen; and Xicotencatl, finding himself wholly unable to make head against the Spaniards in the open field, ordered a retreat. Far from the confusion of a panic-struck mob, so common among barbarians, the Tlascalan force moved off the ground with all the order of a well disciplined army. Cortés, as on the preceding day, was too well satisfied with his present advantage to desire to follow it up. It was within an hour of sunset, and he was anxious before nightfall to secure a good position, where he might refresh his wounded troops, and bivouac for the night.

[VICTORY OVER THE TLASCALANS]

From *The Conquest of Mexico*, Bk. III, chap. iii

[Final victory over the Tlascalans came only after almost superhuman efforts by the Spaniards, helped materially by dissensions among the commanders of the native defenders.]

As a battle was now inevitable, Cortés resolved to march out and meet the enemy in the field. This would have a show of confidence, that might serve the double purpose of intimidating the Tlascalans, and inspiriting his own men, whose enthusiasm might lose somewhat of its heat, if compelled to await the assault of their antagonists, inactive in their own intrenchments. The sun rose bright on the following morning, the 5th of September, 1519, an eventful day in the history of the Spanish Conquest. The general reviewed his army, and gave them, preparatory to marching, a few words of encouragement and advice. The infantry he instructed to rely on the point rather than the edge of their swords, and to endeavor to thrust their opponents through the body. The horsemen were to charge at half speed, with their lances aimed at the eyes of the Indians. The artillery, the arquebusiers, and crossbowmen, were to support one another, some loading while others discharged their pieces, that there should be an unintermitted firing kept up through the action. Above all, they were to maintain their ranks close and unbroken, as on this depended their preservation.

They had not advanced a quarter of a league, when they came in sight of the Tlascalan army. Its dense array stretched far and wide over a vast plain or meadow ground, about six miles square. Its appearance justified the report which had been given of its numbers. Nothing could be more picturesque than the aspect of these Indian battalions, with the naked bodies of the common soldiers gaudily painted, the fantastic helmets of the chiefs glittering with gold and precious stones, and the glowing panoplies of feather-work, which decorated their persons. Innumerable spears and darts tipped with points of transparent *itztli*, or fiery copper, sparkled bright in the morning sun, like the phosphoric gleams playing on the surface of a troubled sea, while the rear of the mighty host was dark with the shadows of banners, on which were emblazoned the armorial bearings of the great Tlascalan and Otomie chieftains. Among these, the white heron on the rock, the cognizance of the house of Xicotencatl, was conspicuous, and, still more, the golden eagle with outspread wings, in the fashion of a Roman *signum*, richly ornamented with emeralds and silver-work, the great standard of the republic of Tlascala.

The common file wore no covering except a girdle round the loins. Their bodies were painted with the appropriate colors of the chieftain whose banner they followed. The feather-mail of the higher class of warriors exhibited, also, a similar selection of colors for the like object, in the same manner as the color of the tartan indicates the peculiar clan of the Highlander. The caciques and principal warriors were clothed in a quilted cotton tunic, two inches thick, which, fitting close to the body, protected, also, the thighs and the shoulders. Over this the wealthier Indians wore cuirasses of thin gold plate, or silver. Their legs were defended by leathern boots or sandals, trimmed with gold. But the most brilliant part of their costume was a rich mantle of the *plumaje* or feather-work, embroidered with curious art, and furnishing some resemblance to the gorgeous surcoat worn by the European knight over his armor in the Middle Ages. This graceful and picturesque dress was surmounted by a fantastic headpiece made of wood or leather, representing the head of some wild animal, and frequently displaying a formidable array of teeth. With this covering the warrior's head was enveloped, producing a most grotesque and hideous effect. From the crown floated a splendid panache of the richly variegated plumage of the tropics, indicating, by its form and colors, the rank and family of the wearer. To complete their defensive armor, they carried shields or targets, made sometimes of wood covered with leather, but more usually of a light frame of reeds quilted with cotton, which were preferred, as tougher and less liable to fracture than the former. They had other bucklers, in which the cotton was covered with an elastic substance, enabling them to be shut up in a more compact form, like a fan or umbrella. These shields were decorated with showy ornaments, according to the taste or wealth of the wearer, and fringed with a beautiful pendant of feather-work.

Their weapons were slings, bows and arrows, javelins, and darts. They were accomplished archers, and would discharge two or even three arrows at a time. But they most excelled in throwing the javelin. One species of this, with a thong attached to it, which remained in the slinger's hand, that he might recall the weapon, was especially dreaded by the Spaniards.

These various weapons were pointed with bone, or the mineral *itztli*, (obsidian,) the hard vitreous substance, already noticed, as capable of taking an edge like a razor, though easily blunted. Their spears and arrows were also frequently headed with copper. Instead of a sword, they bore a two handed staff, about three feet and a half long, in which, at regular distances, were inserted, transversely, sharp blades of *itztli*,—a formidable weapon, which, an eyewitness assures us, he had seen fell a horse at a blow.

Such was the costume of the Tlascalan warrior, and, indeed, of that great family of nations generally, who occupied the plateau of Anahuac. Some parts of it, as the targets and the cotton mail or *escaupil*, as it was called in Castilian, were so excellent, that they were subsequently adopted by the Spaniards, as equally effectual in the way of protection, and superior, on the score of lightness and convenience, to their own. They were of sufficient strength to turn an arrow, or the stroke of a javelin, although impotent as a defense against firearms. But what armor is not? Yet it is probably no exaggeration to say, that, in convenience, gracefulness, and strength, the arms of the Indian warrior were not very inferior to those of the polished nations of antiquity.

As soon as the Castilians came in sight, the Tlascalans set up their yell of defiance, rising high above the wild barbaric minstrelsy of shell, atabal, and trumpet, with which they proclaimed their triumphant anticipations of victory over the paltry forces of the invaders. When the latter had come within bowshot, the Indians hurled a tempest of missiles, that darkened the sun for a moment as with a passing cloud, strewing the earth around with heaps of stones and arrows. Slowly and steadily the little band of Spaniards held on its way amidst their arrowy shower, until it reached what appeared the proper distance for delivering its fire with full effect. Cortés then halted, and, hastily forming his troops, opened a general well-directed fire along the whole line. Every shot bore its errand of death; and the ranks of the Indians were mowed down faster than their comrades in the rear could carry off their bodies, according to custom, from the field. The balls in their passage through the crowded files, bearing splinters of the broken harness, and mangled limbs of the warriors, scattered havoc and desolation in their path. The mob of barbarians stood petrified with dismay, till, at length, galled to desperation by their intolerable suffering, they poured forth simultaneously their hideous war-shriek, and rushed impetuously on the Christians.

On they came like an avalanche, or mountain torrent, shaking the solid earth, and sweeping away every obstacle in its path. The little army of Spaniards opposed a bold front to the over-whelming mass. But no strength could withstand it. They faltered, gave way, were borne along before it, and their ranks were broken and thrown into disorder. It was in vain, the general called on them to close again and rally. His voice was drowned by the din of fight and the fierce cries of the assailants. For a moment, it seemed that all was lost. The tide of battle had turned against them, and the fate of the Christians was sealed.

But every man had that within his bosom, which spoke louder than the voice of the general. Despair gave unnatural energy to his arm. The naked body of the Indian afforded no resistance to the sharp Toledo steel; and with their good swords, the Spanish infantry at length succeeded in staying the human torrent. The heavy guns from a distance thundered on the flank of the assailants, which, shaken by the iron tempest, was thrown into disorder. Their very numbers increased the confusion, as they were precipitated on the masses in front. The horses at the same moment, charging gallantly under Cortés, followed up the advantage, and at length compelled the tumultuous throng to fall back with greater precipitation and disorder than that with which they had advanced.

More than once in the course of the action, a similar assault was attempted by the Tlascalans, but each time with less spirit, and greater loss. They were too deficient in military science to profit by their vast superiority in numbers. They were distributed into companies, it is true, each serving under its own chieftain and banner. But they were not arranged by rank and file, and moved in a confused mass, promiscuously heaped together. They knew not how to concentrate numbers on a given point, or even how to sustain an assault, by employing successive detachments to support and relieve one another. A very small part only of their array could be brought into contact with an enemy inferior to them in amount of forces. The remainder of the army, inactive and worse than useless, in the rear, served only to press tumultuously on the advance, and embarrass its movements by mere weight of numbers, while, on the least alarm, they were seized with a panic and threw the whole body into inextricable confusion. It was, in short, the combat of the ancient Greeks and Persians over again.

Still, the great numerical superiority of the Indians might have enabled them, at a severe cost of their own lives, indeed, to wear out, in time, the constancy of the Spaniards, disabled by wounds and incessant fatigue. But, fortunately for the latter, dissensions arose among their enemies. A Tlascalan chieftain, commanding one of the great divisions, had taken umbrage at the haughty demeanor of Xicotencatl, who had charged him with misconduct or cowardice in the late action. The injured cacique challenged his rival to single combat. This did not take place. But, burning with resentment, he chose the present occasion to indulge it, by drawing off his forces, amounting to ten thousand men, from the field. He also persuaded another of the commanders to follow his example.

Thus reduced to about half his original strength, and that greatly crippled by the losses of the day, Xicotencatl could no longer maintain his ground against the Spaniards. After disputing the field with admirable courage for four hours, he retreated and resigned it to the enemy. The Spaniards were too much jaded, and too many were disabled by wounds, to allow them to pursue; and Cortés, satisfied with the decisive victory he had gained, returned in triumph to his position on the hill of Tzompach.

[BATTLE WITH THE AZTECS]

From *The Conquest of Mexico*, Bk. V, chap. i

[The Spaniards finally reached Mexico, and Prescott's spirited prose describes one of the many battles with the Aztecs, who fought with great bravery.]

The palace of Axayacatl, in which the Spaniards were quartered, was, as the reader may remember, a vast, irregular pile of stone buildings, having but one floor, except in the center, where another story was added, consisting of a suite of apartments which rose like turrets on the main building of the edifice. A vast area stretched around, encompassed by a stone wall of no great height. This was supported by towers or bulwarks at certain intervals, which gave it some degree of strength, not, indeed, as compared with European fortifications, but sufficient to resist the rude battering enginery of the Indians. The parapet had been pierced here and there with embrasures for the artillery, which consisted of thirteen guns; and smaller apertures were made in other parts for the convenience of the arquebusiers. The Spanish forces found accommodations within the great building; but the numerous body of Tlascalan auxiliaries could have had no other shelter than what was afforded by barracks or sheds hastily constructed for the purpose in the spacious courtyard. Most of them, probably, bivouacked under the open sky, in a climate milder than that to which they were accustomed among the rude hills of their native land. Thus crowded into a small and compact compass, the whole army could be assembled at a moment's notice; and, as the Spanish commander was careful to enforce the strictest discipline and vigilance, it was scarcely possible that he could be taken by surprise. No sooner, therefore, did the trumpet call to arms, as the approach of the enemy was announced, than every soldier was at his post, the cavalry mounted, the artillerymen at their guns, and the archers and arquebusiers stationed so as to give the assailants a warm reception.

On they came, with the companies, or irregular masses, into which the multitude was divided, rushing forward each in its own dense column, with many a gay banner displayed, and many a bright gleam of light reflected from helmet, arrow, and spearhead, as they were tossed about in their disorderly array. As they drew near the inclosure, the Aztecs set up a hideous yell, or rather that shrill whistle used in fight by the nations of Anahuac, which rose far above the sound of shell and atabal, and their other rude instruments of warlike melody. They followed this by a tempest of missiles,—stones, darts, and arrows,—which fell thick as rain on the besieged, while volleys of the same kind descended from the crowded terraces in the neighborhood.

The Spaniards waited until the foremost column had arrived within the best distance for giving effect to their fire, when a general discharge of artillery and arquebuses swept the ranks of the assailants, and mowed them down by hundreds. The Mexicans were familiar with the report of these formidable engines, as they had been harmlessly discharged on some holiday festival; but never till now had they witnessed their murderous power. They stood aghast for a moment, as with bewildered looks they staggered under the fury of the fire; but, soon rallying, the bold barbarians uttered a piercing cry, and rushed forward over the prostrate bodies of their comrades. A second and a third volley checked their career, and threw them into disorder, but still they pressed on, letting off clouds of arrows; while their comrades on the roofs of the houses took more deliberate aim at the combatants in the courtyard. The Mexicans were particularly expert in the use of the sling; and the stones which they hurled from their elevated positions on the heads of their enemies did even greater execution than the arrows. They glanced, indeed, from the mail-covered bodies of the cavaliers, and from those who were sheltered under the cotton panoply, or *escaupil.* But some of the soldiers, especially the veterans of Cortés, and many of their Indian allies, had but slight defenses, and suffered greatly under this stony tempest.

The Aztecs, meanwhile, had advanced close under the walls of the intrenchment; their ranks broken and disordered, and their limbs mangled by the unintermitting fire of the Christians. But they still pressed on, under the very muzzle of the guns. They endeavored to scale the parapet, which, from its moderate height, was in itself a work of no great difficulty. But the moment they showed their heads above the rampart, they were shot down by the unerring marksmen within, or stretched on the ground by a blow of a Tlascalan *maquahuitl*. Nothing daunted, others soon appeared to take the place of the fallen, and strove, by raising themselves on the writhing bodies of their dying comrades, or by fixing their spears in the crevices of the wall, to surmount the barrier. But the attempt proved equally vain.

Defeated here, they tried to effect a breach in the parapet by battering it with heavy pieces of timber. The works were not constructed on those scientific principles by which one part is made to overlook and protect another. The besiegers, therefore, might operate at their pleasure, with but little molestation from the garrison within, whose guns could not be brought into a position to bear on them, and who could mount no part of their own works for their defense, without exposing their persons to the missiles of the whole besieging army. The parapet, however, proved too strong for the efforts of the assailants. In their despair they endeavored to set the Christian quarters on fire, shooting burning arrows into them, and climbing up so as to dart their firebrands through the embrasures. The principal edifice was of stone. But the temporary defenses of the Indian allies, and other parts of the exterior works, were of wood. Several of these took fire, and the flame spread rapidly among the light, combustible materials. This was a disaster for which the besieged were wholly unprepared. They had little water, scarcely enough for their own consumption. They endeavored to extinguish the flames by heaping on earth. But in vain. Fortunately the great building was of materials which defied the destroying element. But the fire raged in some of the outworks, connected with the parapet, with a fury which could only be checked by throwing down a part of the wall itself, thus laying open a formidable breach. This, by the general's order, was speedily protected by a battery of heavy guns, and a file of arquebusiers, who kept up an incessant volley through the opening on the assailants.

The fight now raged with fury on both sides. The walls around the palace belched forth an unintermitting sheet of flame and smoke. The groans of the wounded and dying were lost in the fiercer battle-cries of the combatants, the roar of the artillery, the sharper rattle of the musketry, and the hissing sound of Indian missiles. It was the conflict of the European with the American; of civilized man with the barbarian; of the science of the one with the rude weapons and warfare of the other. And as the ancient walls of Tenochtitlan shook under the thunders of the artillery,—it announced that the white man, the destroyer, had set his foot within her precincts.

Night at length came, and drew her friendly mantle over the contest. The Aztec seldom fought by night. It brought little repose, however, to the Spaniards, in hourly expectation of an assault; and they found abundant occupation in restoring the breaches in their defenses, and in repairing their battered armor. The beleaguering host lay on their arms through the night, giving token of their presence, now and then, by sending a stone or shaft over the battlements, or by a solitary cry of defiance from some warrior more determined than the rest, till all other sounds were lost in the vague, indistinct murmurs which float upon the air in the neighborhood of a vast assembly.

The ferocity shown by the Mexicans seems to have been a thing for which Cortés was wholly unprepared. His past experience, his uninterrupted career of victory with a much feebler force at his command, had led him to underrate the military efficiency, if not the valor, of the Indians. The apparent facility, with which the Mexicans had acquiesced in the outrages on their sovereign and themselves, had led him to hold their courage, in particular, too lightly. He could not believe the present assault to be anything more than a temporary ebullition of the populace, which would soon waste itself by its own fury. And he proposed, on the following day, to sally out and inflict such chastisement on his foes as should bring them to their senses, and show who was master in the capital.

With early dawn, the Spaniards were up and under arms; but not before their enemies had given evidence of their hostility by the random missiles, which, from time to time, were sent into the inclosure. As the gray light of morning advanced, it showed the besieging army far from being diminished in numbers, filling up the great square and neighboring avenues in more dense array than on the preceding evening. Instead of a confused, disorderly rabble, it had the appearance of something like a regular force, with its battalions distributed under their respective banners, the devices of which showed a contribution from the principal cities and districts in the Valley. High above the rest was conspicuous the ancient standard of Mexico, with its well known cognizance, an eagle pouncing on an ocelot, emblazoned on a rich mantle of feather-work. Here and there priests might be seen mingling in the ranks of the besiegers, and, with frantic gestures, animating them to avenge their insulted deities.

The greater part of the enemy had little clothing save the *maxtlatl*, or sash round the loins. They were variously armed, with long spears tipped with copper, or flint, or sometimes merely pointed and hardened in the fire. Some were provided with slings, and others with darts having two or three points, with long strings attached to them, by which, when discharged, they could be torn away again from the body of the wounded. This was a formidable weapon, much dreaded by the Spaniards. Those of a higher order wielded the terrible *maquahuitl*, with its sharp and brittle blades of obsidian. Amidst the motley bands of warriors, were seen many whose showy dress and air of authority intimated persons of high military consequence. Their breasts were protected by plates of metal, over which was thrown the gay surcoat of feather-work. They wore casques resembling, in their form, the head of some wild and ferocious animal, crested with bristly hair, or overshadowed by tall and graceful plumes of many a brilliant color. Some few were decorated with the red fillet bound round the hair, having tufts of cotton attached to it, which denoted by their number that of the victories they had won, and their own pre-eminent rank among the warriors of the nation. The motley assembly plainly showed that priest, warrior, and citizen had all united to swell the tumult.

Before the sun had shot his beams into the Castilian quarters, the enemy were in motion, evidently preparing to renew the assault of the preceding day. The Spanish commander deter-mined to anticipate them by a vigorous sortie, for which he had already made the necessary dispositions. A general dis-charge of ordnance and musketry sent death far and wide into the enemy's ranks, and, before they had time to recover from their confusion, the gates were thrown open, and Cortés, sallying out at the head of his cavalry, supported by a large body of infantry and several thousand Tlascalans, rode at full gallop against them. Taken thus by surprise, it was scarcely possible to offer much resistance. Those who did were trampled down under the horses' feet, cut to pieces with the broadswords, or pierced with the lances of the riders. The infantry followed up the blow, and the rout for the moment was general.

But the Aztecs fled only to take refuge behind a barricade, or strong work of timber and earth, which had been thrown across the great street through which they were pursued. Rallying on the other side, they made a gallant stand, and poured in turn a volley of their light weapons on the Spaniards, who, saluted with a storm of missiles at the same time, from the terraces of the houses, were checked in their career, and thrown into some disorder.

Cortés, thus impeded, ordered up a few pieces of heavy ord-nance, which soon swept away the barricades, and cleared a passage for the army. But it had lost the momentum acquired in its rapid advance. The enemy had time to rally and to meet the Spaniards on more equal terms. They were attacked in flank, too, as they advanced, by fresh battalions, who swarmed in from the adjoining streets and lanes. The canals were alive with boats filled with warriors, who, with their formidable darts searched every crevice or weak place in the armor of proof, and made havoc on the unprotected bodies of the Tlascalans. By repeated and vigorous charges, the Spaniards succeeded in driving the Indians before them; though many, with a desperation which showed they loved vengeance better than life, sought to embarrass the movements of their horses by clinging to their legs, or, more successfully strove to pull the riders from their saddles. And woe to the unfortunate cavalier who was thus dismounted,—to be despatched by the brutal *maquahuitl*, or to be dragged on board a canoe to the bloody altar of sacrifice!

But the greatest annoyance which the Spaniards endured was from the missiles from the *azoteas*, consisting often of large stones, hurled with a force that would tumble the stoutest rider from his saddle. Galled in the extreme by these discharges, against which even their shields afforded no adequate protection, Cortés ordered fire to be set to the buildings. This was no very difficult matter, since, although chiefly of stone, they were filled with mats, cane-work, and other combustible materials, which were soon in a blaze. But the buildings stood separated from one another by canals and drawbridges, so that the flames did not easily communicate to the neighboring edifices. Hence, the labor of the Spaniards was incalculably increased, and their progress in the work of destruction—fortunately for the city—was comparatively slow. They did not relax their efforts, however, till several hundred houses had been consumed, and the miseries of a conflagration, in which the wretched inmates perished equally with the defenders, were added to the other horrors of the scene.

The day was now far spent. The Spaniards had been everywhere victorious. But the enemy, though driven back on every point, still kept the field. When broken by the furious charges of the cavalry, he soon rallied behind the temporary defenses, which, at different intervals, had been thrown across the streets, and, facing about, renewed the fight with undiminished courage, till the sweeping away of the barriers by the cannon of the assailants left a free passage for the movements of their horse.

Thus the action was a succession of rallying and retreating, in which both parties suffered much, although the loss inflicted on the Indians was probably tenfold greater than that of the Spaniards. But the Aztecs could better afford the loss of a hundred lives than their antagonists that of one. And, while the Spaniards showed an array broken, and obviously thinned in numbers, the Mexican army, swelled by the tributary levies which flowed in upon it from the neighboring streets, exhibited, with all its losses, no sign of diminution. At length, sated with carnage, and exhausted by toil and hunger, the Spanish commander drew off his men, and sounded a retreat.

On his way back to his quarters, he beheld his friend, the secretary Duero, in a street adjoining, unhorsed, and hotly engaged with a body of Mexicans, against whom he was desperately defending himself with his poniard. Cortés, roused at the sight, shouted his war-cry, and, dashing into the midst of the enemy, scattered them like chaff by the fury of his onset; then, recovering his friend's horse, he enabled him to remount, and the two cavaliers, striking their spurs into their steeds, burst through their opponents and joined the main body of the army. Such displays of generous gallantry were not uncommon in these engagements, which called forth more feats of personal adventure than battles with antagonists better skilled in the science of war. The chivalrous bearing of the general was emulated in full measure by Sandoval, De Leon, Olid, Alvarado, Ordaz, and his other brave companions, who won such glory under the eye of their leader, as prepared the way for the independent commands which afterwards placed provinces and kingdoms at their disposal.

The undaunted Aztecs hung on the rear of their retreating foes, annoying them at every step by fresh flights of stones and arrows; and, when the Spaniards had re-entered their fortress, the Indian host encamped around it, showing the same dogged resolution as on the preceding evening. Though true to their ancient habits of inaction during the night, they broke the stillness of the hour by insulting cries and menaces, which reached the ears of the besieged. "The gods have delivered you, at last, into our hands," they said; "Huitzilopotchli has long cried for his victims. The stone of sacrifice is ready. The knives are sharpened. The wild beasts in the palace are roaring for their offal. And the cages," they added, taunting the Tlascalans with their leanness, "are waiting for the false sons of Anahuac, who are to be fattened for the festival!" These dismal menaces, which sounded fearfully in the ears of the besieged, who understood too well their import, were mingled with piteous lamentations for their sovereign, whom they called on the Spaniards to deliver up to them.

[STORMING THE GREAT TEMPLE]

From *The Conquest of Mexico*, Bk. V, chap. ii

[There are many graphic battle scenes in Prescott's works, but the storming of the great temple is one of the best. Although victorious, the Spaniards won at great cost to their small army.]

Opposite to the Spanish quarters, at only a few rods' distance, stood the great *teocalli* of Huitzilopotchli. This pyramidal mound, with the sanctuaries that crowned it, rising altogether to the height of near a hundred and fifty feet, afforded an elevated position that completely commanded the palace of Axayacatl, occupied by the Christians. A body of five or six hundred Mexicans, many of them nobles and warriors of the highest rank, had got possession of the *teocalli*, whence they discharged such a tempest of arrows on the garrison, that no one could leave his defenses for a moment without imminent danger; while the Mexicans, under shelter of the sanctuaries, were entirely covered from the fire of the besieged. It was obviously necessary to dislodge the enemy, if the Spaniards would remain longer in their quarters.

Cortés assigned this service to his chamberlain, Escobar, giving him a hundred men for the purpose, with orders to storm the *teocalli*, and set fire to the sanctuaries. But that officer was thrice repulsed in the attempt, and, after the most desperate

efforts, was obliged to return with considerable loss, and
without accomplishing his object.

Cortés, who saw the immediate necessity of carrying the
place, determined to lead the storming party himself. He was
then suffering much from the wound in his left hand, which
had disabled it for the present. He made the arm serviceable,
however, by fastening his buckler to it, and, thus crippled,
sallied out at the head of three hundred chosen cavaliers, and
several thousand of his auxiliaries.

In the courtyard of the temple he found a numerous body of
Indians prepared to dispute his passage. He briskly charged
them, but the flat, smooth stones of the pavement were so
slippery, that the horses lost their footing, and many of them
fell. Hastily dismounting, they sent back the animals to their
quarters, and, renewing the assault, the Spaniards succeeded
without much difficulty in dispersing the Indian warriors, and
opening a free passage for themselves to the *teocalli*. This
building, as the reader may remember, was a huge pyramidal
structure, about three hundred feet square at the base. A
flight of stone steps on the outside, at one of the angles of the
mound, led to a platform, or terraced walk, which passed
round the building until it reached a similar flight of stairs
directly over the preceding, that conducted to another landing
as before. As there were five bodies or divisions of the *teocalli*,
it became necessary to pass round its whole extent four times,
or nearly a mile, in order to reach the summit, which, it may
be recollected, was an open area, crowned only by the two
sanctuaries dedicated to the Aztec deities.

Cortés, having cleared a way for the assault, sprang up the
lower stairway, followed by Alvarado, Sandoval, Ordaz, and
the other gallant cavaliers of his little band, leaving a file of
arquebusiers and a strong corps of Indian allies to hold the
enemy in check at the foot of the monument. On the first
landing, as well as on the several galleries above, and on the
summit, the Aztec warriors were drawn up to dispute his passage. From their elevated position they showered down volleys
of lighter missiles, together with heavy stones, beams, and

burning rafters, which, thundering along the stairway, overturned the ascending Spaniards, and carried desolation through
their ranks. The more fortunate, eluding or springing over
these obstacles, succeeded in gaining the first terrace; where,
throwing themselves on their enemies, they compelled them,
after a short resistance, to fall back. The assailants pressed on,
effectually supported by a brisk fire of the musketeers from
below, which so much galled the Mexicans in their exposed
situation, that they were glad to take shelter on the broad
summit of the *teocalli*.

Cortés and his comrades were close upon their rear, and the
two parties soon found themselves face to face on this aerial
battlefield, engaged in mortal combat in presence of the whole
city, as well as of the troops in the courtyard, who paused,
as if by mutual consent, from their own hostilities, gazing in
silent expectation on the issue of those above. The area,
though somewhat smaller than the base of the *teocalli*, was large
enough to afford a fair field of fight for a thousand combatants.
It was paved with broad, flat stones. No impediment occurred
over its surface, except the huge sacrificial block, and the temples
of stone which rose to the height of forty feet, at the further
extremity of the arena. One of these had been consecrated
to the Cross. The other was still occupied by the Mexican
war-god. The Christian and the Aztec contended for their
religions under the very shadow of their respective shrines;
while the Indian priests, running to and fro, with their hair
wildly streaming over their sable mantles, seemed hovering in
mid air, like so many demons of darkness urging on the work
of slaughter!

The parties closed with the desperate fury of men who had
no hope but in victory. Quarter was neither asked nor given;
and to fly was impossible. The edge of the area was unprotected by parapet or battlement. The least slip would be fatal;
and the combatants, as they struggled in mortal agony, were
sometimes seen to roll over the sheer sides of the precipice
together. Cortés himself is said to have had a narrow escape
from this dreadful fate. Two warriors, of strong, muscular

frames, seized on him, and were dragging him violently towards the brink of the pyramid. Aware of their intention, he struggled with all his force, and, before they could accomplish their purpose, succeeded in tearing himself from their grasp, and hurling one of them over the walls with his own arm! The story is not improbable in itself, for Cortés was a man of uncommon agility and strength. It has been often repeated; but not by contemporary history.

The battle lasted with unintermitting fury for three hours. The number of the enemy was double that of the Christians; and it seemed as if it were a contest which must be determined by numbers and brute force, rather than by superior science. But it was not so. The invulnerable armor of the Spaniard, his sword of matchless temper, and his skill in the use of it, gave him advantages which far outweighed the odds of physical strength and numbers. After doing all that the courage of despair could enable men to do, resistance grew fainter and fainter on the side of the Aztecs. One after another they had fallen. Two or three priests only survived to be led away in triumph by the victors. Every other combatant was stretched a corpse on the bloody arena, or had been hurled from the giddy heights. Yet the loss of the Spaniards was not inconsiderable. It amounted to forty-five of their best men, and nearly all the remainder were more or less injured in the desperate conflict.

The victorious cavaliers now rushed towards the sanctuaries. The lower story was of stone; the two upper were of wood. Penetrating into their recesses, they had the mortification to find the image of the Virgin and the Cross removed. But in the other edifice they still beheld the grim figure of Huitzilopotchli, with his censer of smoking hearts, and the walls of his oratory reeking with gore,—not improbably of their own countrymen! With shouts of triumph the Christians tore the uncouth monster from his niche, and tumbled him, in the presence of the horror-struck Aztecs, down the steps of the *teocalli.* They then set fire to the accursed building. The flames speedily ran up the slender towers, sending forth an ominous light over city, lake, and valley, to the remotest hut among the mountains. It was the funeral pyre of Paganism, and proclaimed the fall of that sanguinary religion which had so long hung like a dark cloud over the fair regions of Anahuac!

Having accomplished this good work, the Spaniards descended the winding slopes of the *teocalli* with more free and buoyant step, as if conscious that the blessing of Heaven now rested on their arms. They passed through the dusky files of Indian warriors in the courtyard, too much dismayed by the appalling scenes they had witnessed to offer resistance; and reached their own quarters in safety. That very night they followed up the blow by a sortie on the sleeping town, and burned three hundred houses, the horrors of conflagration being made still more impressive by occurring at the hour when the Aztecs, from their own system of warfare, were least prepared for them.

["NOCHE TRISTE": ESCAPE OF THE SPANIARDS]

From *The Conquest of Mexico*, Bk. V, chap. iii

[So critical was the situation of the Spaniards that Cortés decided to evacuate the capital. This action marked one of the low points in the fortunes of the Spanish invaders.]

The night was cloudy, and a drizzling rain, which fell without intermission, added to the obscurity. The great square before the palace was deserted, as, indeed, it had been since the fall of Montezuma. Steadily, and as noiselessly as possible, the Spaniards held their way along the great street of Tlacopan, which so lately had resounded to the tumult of battle. All was now hushed in silence; and they were only reminded of the past by the occasional presence of some solitary corpse, or a dark heap of the slain, which too plainly told where the strife had been hottest. As they passed along the lanes and alleys which opened into the great street, or looked down the canals, whose polished surface gleamed with a sort of ebon luster through the obscurity of night, they easily fancied that they discerned the shadowy forms of their foe lurking in ambush, and ready to spring on them. But it was only fancy; and the city slept undisturbed even by the prolonged echoes of the tramp of the horses, and the hoarse rumbling of the artillery and baggage trains. At length, a lighter space beyond the dusky line of buildings showed the van of the army that it was emerging on the open causeway. They might well have congratulated themselves on having thus escaped the dangers of an assault in the city itself, and that a brief time would place them in comparative safety on the opposite shore.—But the Mexicans were not all asleep.

As the Spaniards drew near the spot where the street opened on the causeway, and were preparing to lay the portable bridge across the uncovered breach, which now met their eyes, several Indian sentinels, who had been stationed at this, as at the other approaches to the city, took the alarm, and fled, rousing their countrymen by their cries. The priests, keeping their night watch on the summit of the *teocallis*, instantly caught the tidings and sounded their shells, while the huge drum in the desolate temple of the war-god sent forth those solemn tones, which, heard only in seasons of calamity, vibrated through every corner of the capital. The Spaniards saw that no time was to be lost. The bridge was brought forward and fitted with all possible expedition. Sandoval was the first to try its strength, and, riding across, was followed by his little body of chivalry, his infantry, and Tlascalan allies, who formed the first division of the army. Then came Cortés and his squadrons, with the baggage, ammunition wagons, and a part of the artillery. But before they had time to defile across the narrow passage, a gathering sound was heard, like that of a mighty forest agitated by the winds. It grew louder and louder, while on the dark waters of the lake was heard a plashing noise, as of many oars. Then came a few stones and arrows striking at random among the hurrying troops. They fell every moment faster and more furious, till they thickened into a terrible tempest, while the very heavens were rent with the yells and war-cries of myriads of combatants, who seemed all at once to be swarming over land and lake!

The Spaniards pushed steadily on through this arrowy sleet, though the barbarians, dashing their canoes against the sides of the causeway, clambered up and broke in upon their ranks. But the Christians, anxious only to make their escape, declined all combat except for self-preservation. The cavaliers, spurring forward their steeds, shook off their assailants, and rode over their prostrate bodies, while the men on foot with their good swords or the butts of their pieces drove them headlong again down the sides of the dike.

But the advance of several thousand men, marching, probably, on a front of not more than fifteen or twenty abreast, necessarily required much time, and the leading files had already reached the second breach in the causeway before those in the rear had entirely traversed the first. Here they halted; as they had no means of effecting a passage, smarting all the while under unintermitting volleys from the enemy, who were clustered thick on the waters around this second opening. Sorely distressed, the vanguard sent repeated messages to the rear to demand the portable bridge. At length the last of the army had crossed, and Magarino and his sturdy followers endeavored to raise the ponderous framework. But it stuck fast in the sides of the dike. In vain they strained every nerve. The weight of so many men and horses, and above all of the heavy artillery, had wedged the timbers so firmly in the stones and earth, that it was beyond their power to dislodge them. Still they labored amidst a torrent of missiles, until, many of them slain, and all wounded, they were obliged to abandon the attempt.

The tidings soon spread from man to man, and no sooner was their dreadful import comprehended, than a cry of despair arose, which for a moment drowned all the noise of conflict. All means of retreat were cut off. Scarcely hope was left. The only hope was in such desperate exertions as each could make for himself. Order and subordination were at an end. Intense danger produced intense selfishness. Each thought only of his own life. Pressing forward, he trampled down the weak and the wounded, heedless whether it were friend or foe. The leading files, urged on by the rear, were crowded on the brink of the gulf. Sandoval, Ordaz, and the other cavaliers dashed into the water. Some succeeded in swimming their horses across. Others failed, and some, who reached the opposite bank, being overturned in the ascent, rolled headlong with their steeds into the lake. The infantry followed pellmell, heaped promiscuously on one another, frequently pierced by the shafts, or struck down by the war-clubs of the Aztecs; while many an unfortunate victim was dragged half-stunned on board their canoes, to be reserved for a protracted, but more dreadful death.

The carnage raged fearfully along the length of the causeway. Its shadowy bulk presented a mark of sufficient distinctness for the enemy's missiles, which often prostrated their own countrymen in the blind fury of the tempest. Those nearest the dike, running their canoes alongside, with a force that shattered them to pieces, leaped on the land, and grappled with the Christians, until both came rolling down the side of the causeway together. But the Aztec fell among his friends, while his antagonist was borne away in triumph to the sacrifice. The struggle was long and deadly. The Mexicans were recognized by their white cotton tunics, which showed faint through the darkness. Above the combatants rose a wild and discordant clamor, in which horrid shouts of vengeance were mingled with groans of agony, with invocations of the saints and the blessed Virgin, and with the screams of women; for there were several women, both natives and Spaniards, who had accompanied the Christian camp. Among these, one named María de Estrada is particularly noticed for the courage she displayed, battling with broadsword and target like the stanchest of the warriors.

The opening in the causeway, meanwhile, was filled up with the wreck of matter which had been forced into it, ammunition wagons, heavy guns, bales of rich stuffs scattered over the waters, chests of solid ingots, and bodies of men and horses, till over this dismal ruin a passage was gradually formed, by which those in the rear were enabled to clamber to the other side. Cortés, it is said, found a place that was fordable, where, halting, with the water up to his saddle-girths, he endeavored to check the confusion, and lead his followers by a safer path to the opposite bank. But his voice was lost in the wild uproar, and finally, hurrying on with the tide, he pressed forwards with a few trusty cavaliers, who remained near his person, to the van; but not before he had seen his favorite page, Juan de Salazar, struck down, a corpse, by his side. Here he found Sandoval and his companions, halting before the third and last breach, endeavoring to cheer on their followers to surmount it. But their resolution faltered. It was wide and deep; though the passage was not so closely beset by the enemy as the preceding ones. The cavaliers again set the example by plunging into the water. Horse and foot followed as they could, some swimming, others with dying grasp clinging to the manes and tails of the struggling animals. Those fared best, as the general had predicted, who traveled lightest; and many were the unfortunate wretches, who, weighed down by the fatal gold which they loved so well, were buried with it in the salt floods of the lake. Cortés, with his gallant comrades, Olid, Morla, Sandoval, and some few others, still kept in the advance, leading his broken remnant off the fatal causeway. The din of battle lessened in the distance; when the rumor reached them, that the rear-guard would be wholly overwhelmed without speedy relief. It seemed almost an act of desperation; but the generous hearts of the Spanish cavaliers did not stop to calculate danger, when the cry for succor reached them. Turning their horses' bridles, they galloped back to the theater of action, worked their way through the press, swam the canal, and placed themselves in the thick of the mêlée on the opposite bank.

The first gray of the morning was now coming over the waters. It showed the hideous confusion of the scene which had been shrouded in the obscurity of night. The dark masses of combatants, stretching along the dike, were seen struggling for mastery, until the very causeway on which they stood appeared to tremble, and reel to and fro, as if shaken by an earthquake; while the bosom of the lake, as far as the eye could reach, was darkened by canoes crowded with warriors, whose spears and bludgeons, armed with blades of "volcanic glass," gleamed in the morning light.

The cavaliers found Alvarado unhorsed, and defending himself with a poor handful of followers against an overwhelming tide of the enemy. His good steed, which had borne him through many a hard fight, had fallen under him. He was himself wounded in several places, and was striving in vain to rally his scattered column, which was driven to the verge of the canal by the fury of the enemy, then in possession of the whole rear of the causeway, where they were reinforced every hour by fresh combatants from the city. The artillery in the earlier part of the engagement had not been idle, and its iron shower, sweeping along the dike, had mowed down the assailants by hundreds. But nothing could resist their impetuosity. The front ranks, pushed on by those behind, were at length forced up to the pieces, and, pouring over them like a torrent, overthrew men and guns in one general ruin. The resolute charge of the Spanish cavaliers, who had now arrived, created a temporary check, and gave time for their countrymen to make a feeble rally. But they were speedily borne down by the returning flood. Cortés and his companions were compelled to plunge again into the lake,—though all did not escape. Alvarado stood on the brink for a moment, hesitating what to do. Unhorsed as he was, to throw himself into the water, in the face of the hostile canoes that now swarmed around the opening, afforded but a desperate chance of safety. He had but a second for thought. He was a man of powerful frame, and despair gave him unnatural energy. Setting his long lance firmly on the wreck which strewed the bottom of the lake, he sprung forward with all his might, and cleared the wide gap at a leap! Aztecs and Tlascalans gazed in stupid amazement, exclaiming, as they beheld the incredible feat, "This is truly the *Tonatiuh*,—the child of the Sun!"—The breadth of the opening is not given. But it was so great, that the valorous captain Diaz, who well remembered the place, says the leap was impossible to any man. Other contemporaries, however, do not discredit the story. It was, beyond doubt, matter of popular belief at the time; it is to this day familiarly known to every inhabitant of the capital; and the name of the *Salto de Alvarado*, "Alvarado's Leap," given to the spot, still commemorates an exploit which rivaled those of the demigods of Grecian fable.

Cortés and his companions now rode forward to the front, where the troops, in a loose, disorderly manner, were marching off the fatal causeway. A few only of the enemy hung on their rear, or annoyed them by occasional flights of arrows from the lake. The attention of the Aztecs was diverted to the rich spoil that strewed the battleground; fortunately for the Spaniards, who, had their enemy pursued with the same ferocity with which he had fought, would, in their crippled condition, have been cut off, probably, to a man. But little molested, therefore, they were allowed to defile through the adjacent village, or suburbs, it might be called, of Popotla.

[DEFEAT OF THE SPANIARDS]

From *The Conquest of Mexico*, Bk. VI, chap. vi

[The Spaniards besieged the Aztec capital, but before its final capitulation the conquerors more than once suffered terrible blows.]

Famine was now gradually working its way into the heart of the beleaguered city. It seemed certain, that, with this strict blockade, the crowded population must in the end be driven to capitulate, though no arm should be raised against them. But it required time; and the Spaniards, though constant and enduring by nature, began to be impatient of hardships scarcely inferior to those experienced by the besieged. In some respects their condition was even worse, exposed, as they were, to the cold, drenching rains, which fell with little intermission, rendering their situation dreary and disastrous in the extreme.

In this state of things, there were many who would willingly have shortened their sufferings, and taken the chance of carrying the place by a *coup de main*. Others thought it would be best to get possession of the great market of Tlatelolco, which, from its situation in the northwestern part of the city, might afford the means of communication with the camps of both Alvarado and Sandoval. This place, encompassed by spacious porticos, would furnish accommodations for a numerous host; and, once established in the capital, the Spaniards would be in a position to follow up the blow with far more effect than at a distance.

These arguments were pressed by several of the officers, particularly by Alderete, the royal treasurer, a person of much consideration, not only from his rank, but from the capacity and zeal he had shown in the service. In deference to their wishes, Cortés summoned a council of war, and laid the matter before it. The treasurer's views were espoused by most of the high-mettled cavaliers, who looked with eagerness to any change of their present forlorn and wearisome life; and Cortés, thinking it, probably, more prudent to adopt the less expedient course, than to enforce a cold and reluctant obedience to his own opinion, suffered himself to be overruled.

A day was fixed for the assault, which was to be made simultaneously by the two divisions under Alvarado and the commander-in-chief. Sandoval was instructed to draw off the greater part of his forces from the northern causeway, and to unite himself with Alvarado, while seventy picked soldiers were to be detached to the support of Cortés.

On the appointed morning, the two armies, after the usual celebration of mass, advanced along their respective causeways against the city. They were supported, in addition to the brigantines, by a numerous fleet of Indian boats, which were to force a passage up the canals, and by a countless multitude of allies, whose very numbers served in the end to embarrass their operations. After clearing the suburbs, three avenues presented themselves, which all terminated in the square of Tlatelolco.

The principal one, being of much greater width than the other two, might rather be called a causeway than a street, since it was flanked by deep canals on either side. Cortés divided his force into three bodies. One of them he placed under Alderete, with orders to occupy the principal street. A second he gave in charge to Andres de Tapia and Jorge de Alvarado; the former a cavalier of courage and capacity, the latter, a younger brother of Don Pedro, and possessed of the intrepid spirit which belonged to that chivalrous family. These were to penetrate by one of the parallel streets, while the general himself, at the head of the third division, was to occupy the other. A small body of cavalry, with two or three field-pieces, was stationed as a reserve in front of the great street of Tacuba, which was designated as the rallying point for the different divisions.

Cortés gave the most positive instructions to his captains, not to advance a step without securing the means of retreat, by carefully filling up the ditches, and the openings in the causeway. The neglect of this precaution by Alvarado, in an assault which he had made on the city but a few days before, had been attended with such serious consequences to his army, that Cortés rode over, himself, to his officer's quarters, for the purpose of publicly reprimanding him for his disobedience of orders. On his arrival at the camp, however, he found that his offending captain had conducted the affair with so much gallantry, that the intended reprimand—though well deserved—subsided into a mild rebuke.

The arrangements being completed, the three divisions marched at once up the several streets. Cortés, dismounting, took the van of his own squadron, at the head of his infantry. The Mexicans fell back as he advanced, making less resistance than usual. The Spaniards pushed on, carrying one barricade after another, and carefully filling up the gaps with rubbish, so as to secure themselves a footing. The canoes supported the attack, by moving along the canals, and grappling with those of the enemy; while numbers of the nimble-footed Tlascalans, scaling the terraces, passed on from one house to another, where they were connected, hurling the defenders into the streets below. The enemy, taken apparently by surprise, seemed incapable of withstanding for a moment the fury of the assault; and the victorious Christians, cheered on by the shouts of triumph which arose from their companions in the adjoining streets, were only the more eager to be first at the destined goal.

Indeed, the facility of his success led the general to suspect that he might be advancing too fast; that it might be a device of the enemy to draw them into the heart of the city, and then surround or attack them in the rear. He had some misgivings, moreover, lest his too ardent officers, in the heat of the chase, should, notwithstanding his commands, have overlooked the necessary precaution of filling up the breaches. He, accordingly, brought his squadron to a halt, prepared to baffle any insidious movement of his adversary. Meanwhile he received more than one message from Alderete, informing him that he had nearly gained the market. This only increased the general's apprehension, that, in the rapidity of his advance, he might have neglected to secure the ground. He determined to trust no eyes but his own, and, taking a small body of troops, proceeded at once to reconnoitre the route followed by the treasurer.

He had not proceeded far along the great street, or causeway, when his progress was arrested by an opening ten or twelve paces wide, and filled with water, at least two fathoms deep, by which a communication was formed between the canals on the opposite sides. A feeble attempt had been made to stop the gap with the rubbish of the causeway, but in too careless a manner to be of the least service; and a few straggling stones and pieces of timber only showed that the work had been abandoned almost as soon as begun. To add to his consternation, the general observed that the sides of the causeway in this neighborhood had been pared off, and, as was evident, very recently. He saw in all this the artifice of the cunning enemy; and had little doubt that his hotheaded officer had rushed into a snare deliberately laid for him. Deeply alarmed, he set about repairing the mischief as fast as possible, by ordering his men to fill up the yawning chasm.

But they had scarcely begun their labors, when the hoarse

echoes of conflict in the distance were succeeded by a hideous sound of mingled yells and war-whoops, that seemed to rend the very heavens. This was followed by a rushing noise, as of the tread of thronging multitudes, showing that the tide of battle was turned back from its former course, and was rolling on towards the spot where Cortés and his little band of cavaliers were planted.

His conjecture proved too true. Alderete had followed the retreating Aztecs with an eagerness which increased with every step of his advance. He had carried the barricades, which had defended the breach, without much difficulty, and, as he swept on, gave orders that the opening should be stopped. But the blood of the high-spirited cavaliers was warmed by the chase, and no one cared to be detained by the ignoble occupation of filling up the ditches, while he could gather laurels so easily in the fight; and they all pressed on, exhorting and cheering one another with the assurance of being the first to reach the square of Tlatelolco. In this way they suffered themselves to be decoyed into the heart of the city; when suddenly the horn of Guatemozin—the sacred symbol, heard only in seasons of extraordinary peril—sent forth a long and piercing note from the summit of a neighboring *teocalli*. In an instant, the flying Aztecs, as if maddened by the blast, wheeled about, and turned on their pursuers. At the same time, countless swarms of warriors from the adjoining streets and lanes poured in upon the flanks of the assailants, filling the air with the fierce, unearthly cries which had reached the ears of Cortés, and drowning, for a moment, the wild dissonance which reigned in the other quarters of the capital.

The army, taken by surprise, and shaken by the fury of the assault, were thrown into the utmost disorder. Friends and foes, white men and Indians, were mingled together in one promiscuous mass. Spears, swords, and war-clubs were brandished together in the air. Blows fell at random. In their eagerness to escape, they trod down one another. Blinded by the missiles, which now rained on them from the *azoteas*, they staggered on, scarcely knowing in what direction, or fell, struck down by hands which they could not see. On they came like a rushing torrent sweeping along some steep declivity, and rolling in one confused tide towards the open breach, on the further side of which stood Cortés and his companions, horror-struck at the sight of the approaching ruin. The foremost files soon plunged into the gulf, treading one another under the flood, some striving ineffectually to swim, others, with more success, to clamber over the heaps of their suffocated comrades. Many, as they attempted to scale the opposite sides of the slippery dike, fell into the water, or were hurried off by the warriors in the canoes, who added to the horrors of the rout by the fresh storm of darts and javelins, which they poured on the fugitives.

Cortés, meanwhile, with his brave followers, kept his station undaunted on the other side of the breach. "I had made up my mind," he says, "to die, rather than desert my poor followers in their extremity!" With outstretched hands he endeavored to rescue as many as he could from the watery grave, and from the more appalling fate of captivity. He as vainly tried to restore something like presence of mind and order among the distracted fugitives. His person was too well known to the Aztecs, and his position now made him a conspicuous mark for their weapons. Darts, stones, and arrows fell around him thick as hail, but glanced harmless from his steel helmet and armor of proof. At length a cry of "Malinche," "Malinche," arose among the enemy; and six of their number, strong and athletic warriors, rushing on him at once, made a violent effort to drag him on board their boat. In the struggle he received a severe wound in the leg, which, for the time, disabled it. There seemed to be no hope for him; when a faithful follower, Christóval de Olea, perceiving his general's extremity, threw himself on the Aztecs, and with a blow cut off the arm of one savage, and then plunged his sword in the body of another. He was quickly supported by a comrade named Lerma, and by a Tlascalan chief, who, fighting over the prostrate body of Cortés, despatched three more of the assailants, though the heroic Olea paid dearly for his self-devotion, as he fell mortally wounded by the side of his general.

The report soon spread among the soldiers, that their commander was taken; and Quiñones, the captain of his guard, with several others, pouring in to the rescue, succeeded in disentangling Cortés from the grasp of his enemies who were struggling with him in the water, and, raising him in their arms, placed him again on the causeway. One of his pages, meanwhile, had advanced some way through the press, leading a horse for his master to mount. But the youth received a wound in the throat from a javelin, which prevented him from effecting his object. Another of his attendants was more successful. It was Guzman, his chamberlain; but, as he held the bridle, while Cortés was assisted into the saddle, he was snatched away by the Aztecs, and, with the swiftness of thought, hurried off by their canoes. The general still lingered, unwilling to leave the spot, while his presence could be of the least service. But the faithful Quiñones, taking his horse by the bridle, turned his head from the breach, exclaiming, at the same time, that "his master's life was too important to the army to be thrown away there."

Yet it was no easy matter to force a passage through the press. The surface of the causeway, cut up by the feet of men and horses, was knee-deep in mud, and in some parts was so much broken, that the water from the canals flowed over it. The crowded mass, in their efforts to extricate themselves from their perilous position, staggered to and fro like a drunken man. Those on the flanks were often forced by the lateral pressure of their comrades down the slippery sides of the dike, where they were picked up by the canoes of the enemy, whose shouts of triumph proclaimed the savage joy with which they gathered in every new victim for the sacrifice. Two cavaliers, riding by the general's side, lost their footing, and rolled down the declivity into the water. One was taken and his horse killed. The other was happy enough to escape. The valiant ensign, Corral, had a similar piece of good fortune. He slipped into the canal, and the enemy felt sure of their prize, when he again succeeded in recovering the causeway with the tattered banner of Castile still flying above his head. The barbarians set up a cry of disappointed rage, as they lost possession of a trophy, to which the people of Anahuac attached, as we have seen, the highest importance, hardly inferior in their eyes to the capture of the commander-in-chief himself.

Cortés at length succeeded in regaining the firm ground, and reaching the open place before the great street of Tacuba. Here, under a sharp fire of the artillery, he rallied his broken squadrons, and, charging at the head of the little body of horses, which, not having been brought into action, were still fresh, he beat off the enemy. He then commanded the retreat of the two other divisions. The scattered forces again united; and the general, sending forward his Indian confederates, took the rear with a chosen body of cavalry to cover the retreat of the army, which was effected with but little additional loss.

Andres de Tapia was despatched to the western causeway to acquaint Alvarado and Sandoval with the failure of the enterprise. Meanwhile the two captains had penetrated far into the city. Cheered by the triumphant shouts of their countrymen in the adjacent streets, they had pushed on with extraordinary vigor, that they might not be outstripped in the race of glory. They had almost reached the market-place, which lay nearer to their quarters than to the general's, when they heard the blast from the dread horn of Guatemozin, followed by the over-powering yell of the barbarians, which had so startled the ears of Cortés; till at length the sounds of the receding conflict died away in the distance. The two captains now understood that the day must have gone hard with their countrymen. They soon had further proof of it, when the victorious Aztecs, returning from the pursuit of Cortés, joined their forces to those engaged with Sandoval and Alvarado, and fell on them with redoubled fury. At the same time they rolled on the ground two or three of the bloody heads of the Spaniards, shouting the name of "Malinche." The captains, struck with horror at the spectacle,—though they gave little credit to the words of the enemy,—instantly ordered a retreat. Indeed, it was not in their power to maintain their ground against the furious assaults of the besieged, who poured on them, swarm after swarm, with a desperation, of which, says one who was there, "although it seems as if it were now present to my eyes, I can give but a faint idea to the reader, God alone could have brought us off safe from the perils of that day." The fierce barbarians followed up the Spaniards to their very intrenchments. But here they were met, first by the cross fire of the brigantines, which, dashing through the palisades planted to obstruct their movements, completely enfiladed the causeway, and next by that of the small battery erected in front of the camp, which, under the management of a skillful engineer, named Medrano, swept the whole length of the defile. Thus galled in front and on flank, the shattered columns of the Aztecs were compelled to give way and take shelter under the defenses of the city.

The greatest anxiety now prevailed in the camp, regarding the fate of Cortés; for Tapia had been detained on the road by scattered parties of the enemy, whom Guatemozin had stationed there to interrupt the communications between the camps. He arrived, at length, however, though bleeding from several wounds. His intelligence, while it reassured the Spaniards as to the general's personal safety, was not calculated to allay their uneasiness in other respects.

[FINAL VICTORY OVER THE AZTECS]
From *The Conquest of Mexico*, Bk. VI, chap. viii

[The Aztecs were gradually worn down and finally, half-starved, they could not stay the climactic assault of Cortés.]

It was the memorable 13th of August, 1521, the day of St. Hypolito,—from this circumstance selected as the patron saint of modern Mexico,—that Cortés led his warlike array for the last time across the black and blasted environs which lay around the Indian capital. On entering the Aztec precincts, he paused, willing to afford its wretched inmates one more chance of escape, before striking the fatal blow. He obtained an interview with some of the principal chiefs, and expostulated with them on the conduct of their prince. "He surely will not," said the general, "see you all perish, when he can so easily save you." He then urged them to prevail on Guatemozin to hold a conference with him, repeating the assurances of his personal safety.

The messengers went on their mission, and soon returned with the *cihuacoatl* at their head, a magistrate of high authority among the Mexicans. He said, with a melancholy air, in which his own disappointment was visible, that "Guatemozin was ready to die where he was, but would hold no interview with the Spanish commander"; adding, in a tone of resignation, "it is for you to work your pleasure." "Go, then," replied the stern Conqueror, "and prepare your countrymen for death. Their hour is come."

He still postponed the assault for several hours. But the impatience of his troops at this delay was heightened by the rumor, that Guatemozin and his nobles were preparing to escape with their effects in the *piraguas* and canoes which were moored on the margin of the lake. Convinced of the fruitlessness and impolicy of further procrastination, Cortés made his final dispositions for the attack, and took his own station on an *azotea*, which commanded the theater of operations.

When the assailants came into presence of the enemy, they found them huddled together in the utmost confusion, all ages and sexes, in masses so dense that they nearly forced one another over the brink of the causeways into the water below. Some had climbed on the terraces, others feebly supported themselves against the walls of the buildings. Their squalid and tattered garments gave a wildness to their appearance, which still further heightened the ferocity of their expression, as they glared on their enemy with eyes in which hate was mingled with despair. When the Spaniards had approached within bowshot, the Aztecs let off a flight of impotent missiles, showing, to the last, the resolute spirit, though they had lost the strength, of their better days. The fatal signal was then given by the discharge of an arquebus,—speedily followed by peals of heavy ordnance, the rattle of firearms, and the hellish shouts of the confederates, as they sprang upon their victims. It is unnecessary to stain the page with a repetition of the horrors of the preceding day. Some of the wretched Aztecs threw themselves into the water, and were picked up by the canoes. Others sunk and were suffocated in the canals. The number of these became so great, that a bridge was made of their dead bodies, over which the assailants could climb to the opposite banks. Others again, especially the women, begged for mercy, which, as the chroniclers assure us, was everywhere granted by the Spaniards, and, contrary to the instructions and entreaties of Cortés, everywhere refused by the confederates.

While this work of butchery was going on, numbers were observed pushing off in the barks that lined the shore, and making the best of their way across the lake. They were constantly intercepted by the brigantines, which broke through the flimsy array of boats; sending off their volleys to the right and left, as the crews of the latter hotly assailed them. The battle raged as fiercely on the lake as on the land. Many of the Indian vessels were shattered and overturned. Some few, however, under cover of the smoke, which rolled darkly over the waters, succeeded in clearing themselves of the turmoil, and were fast nearing the opposite shore.

Sandoval had particularly charged his captains to keep an eye on the movements of any vessel in which it was at all probable that Guatemozin might be concealed. At this crisis, three or four of the largest *piraguas* were seen skimming over the water, and making their way rapidly across the lake. A captain, named Garci Holguin, who had command of one of the best sailers in the fleet, instantly gave them chase. The wind was favorable, and, every moment, he gained on the fugitives, who pulled their oars with a vigor that despair alone could have given. But it was in vain; and, after a short race, Holguin, coming alongside of one of the *piraguas*, which, whether from its appearance, or from information he had received, he conjectured might bear the Indian emperor, ordered his men to level their crossbows at the boat. But, before they could discharge them, a cry arose from those in it, that their lord was on board. At the same moment, a young warrior, armed with buckler and *maquahuitl*, rose up, as if to beat off the assailants. But, as the Spanish captain ordered his men not to shoot, he dropped his weapons, and exclaimed, "I am Guatemozin; lead me to Malinche, I am his prisoner; but let no harm come to my wife and my followers."

Holguin assured him, that his wishes should be respected, and assisted him to get on board the brigantine, followed by his wife and attendants. These were twenty in number, consisting of Coanaco, the deposed lord of Tezcuco, the lord of Tlacopan, and several other caciques and dignitaries, whose rank, probably, had secured them some exemption from the general calamities of the siege. When the captives were seated on the deck of his vessel, Holguin requested the Aztec prince to put an end to the combat by commanding his people in the other canoes to surrender. But, with a dejected air, he replied, "It is not necessary. They will fight no longer, when they see that their prince is taken." He spoke truth. The news of Guatemozin's capture spread rapidly through the fleet, and on shore, where the Mexicans were still engaged in conflict with their enemies. It ceased, however, at once. They made no further resistance; and those on the water quickly followed the brigantines, which conveyed their captive monarch to land. It seemed as if the fight had been maintained thus long, the better to divert the enemy's attention, and cover their master's retreat.

Meanwhile Sandoval, on receiving tidings of the capture, brought his own brigantine alongside of Holguin's, and demanded the royal prisoner to be surrendered to him. But his captain claimed him as his prize. A dispute arose between the parties, each anxious to have the glory of the deed, and perhaps the privilege of commemorating it on his escutcheon. The controversy continued so long that it reached the ears of Cortés, who, in his station on the *azotea*, had learned, with no little satisfaction, of the capture of his enemy. He instantly sent orders to his wrangling officers, to bring Guatemozin before him, that he might adjust the difference between them. He charged them, at the same time, to treat their prisoner with respect. He then made preparations for the interview; caused the terrace to be carpeted with crimson cloth and matting, and a table to be spread with provisions, of which the unhappy Aztecs stood so much in need. His lovely Indian mistress, Doña Marina, was present to act as interpreter. She had stood by his side through all the troubled scenes of the Conquest, and she was there now to witness its triumphant termination.

Guatemozin, on landing, was escorted by a company of infantry to the presence of the Spanish commander. He mounted the *azotea* with a calm and steady step, and was easily to be distinguished from his attendant nobles, though his full, dark eye was no longer lighted up with its accustomed fire, and his features wore an expression of passive resignation, that told little of the fierce and fiery spirit that burned within. His head was large, his limbs well proportioned, his complexion fairer than those of his bronze-colored nation, and his whole deportment singularly mild and engaging.

Cortés came forward with a dignified and studied courtesy to receive him. The Aztec monarch probably knew the person of his conqueror, for he first broke silence by saying; "I have done all that I could, to defend myself and my people. I am now reduced to this state. You will deal with me, Malinche, as you list." Then, laying his hand on the hilt of a poniard, stuck in the general's belt, he added, with vehemence, "Better despatch me with this, and rid me of life at once." Cortés was filled with admiration at the proud bearing of the young barbarian, showing in his reverses a spirit worthy of an ancient Roman. "Fear not," he replied, "you shall be treated with all honor. You have defended your capital like a brave warrior. A Spaniard knows how to respect valor even in an enemy." He then inquired of him, where he had left the princess, his wife; and, being informed that she still remained under protection of a Spanish guard on board the brigantine, the general sent to have her escorted to his presence.

[SPANIARD VS. SPANIARD: BATTLE OF LAS SALINAS]

From *The Conquest of Peru*, Bk. IV, chap. ii

[The conquerors fell out among themselves in Peru and a bitter struggle developed between Almagro and the Pizarros.]

It was not long before the bright arms and banners of the Spaniards under Hernando Pizarro were seen emerging from the mountain passes. The troops came forward in good order, and like men whose steady step showed that they had been spared in the march, and were now fresh for action. They advanced slowly across the plain, and halted on the opposite border of the little stream which covered the front of Orgoñez. Here Hernando, as the sun had set, took up his quarters for the night, proposing to defer the engagement till daylight.

The rumors of the approaching battle had spread far and wide over the country; and the mountains and rocky heights around were thronged with multitudes of natives, eager to feast their eyes on a spectacle, where, whichever side were victorious, the defeat would fall on their enemies. The Castilian women and children, too, with still deeper anxiety, had thronged out from Cuzco to witness the deadly strife in which brethren and kindred were to contend for mastery. The whole number of the combatants was insignificant; though not as compared with those usually engaged in these American wars. It is not, however, the number of the players, but the magnitude of the stake, that gives importance and interest to the game; and in this bloody game, they were to play for the possession of an empire.

The night passed away in silence, unbroken by the vast assembly which covered the surrounding hilltops. Nor did the soldiers of the hostile camps, although keeping watch within hearing of one another, and with the same blood flowing in their veins, attempt any communication. So deadly was the hate in their bosoms!

The sun rose bright, as usual in this beautiful climate, on Saturday, the twenty-sixth day of April, 1538. But long before his beams were on the plain, the trumpet of Hernando Pizarro had called his men to arms. His forces amounted in all to about seven hundred. They were drawn from various quarters, the veterans of Pizarro, the followers of Alonso de Alvarado,— many of whom, since their defeat, had found their way back to Lima,—and the late reinforcement from the isles, most of them seasoned by many a toilsome march in the Indian campaigns, and many a hard-fought field. His mounted troops were inferior to those of Almagro; but this was more than compensated by the strength of his infantry, comprehending a well-trained corps of arquebusiers, sent from St. Domingo, whose weapons were of the improved construction recently introduced from Flanders. They were of a large caliber, and threw double-headed shot, consisting of bullets linked together by an iron chain. It was doubtless a clumsy weapon compared with modern firearms, but, in hands accustomed to wield it, proved a destructive instrument.

Hernando Pizarro drew up his men in the same order of battle as that presented by the enemy,—throwing his infantry into the center, and disposing his horse on the flanks; one corps of which he placed under command of Alonso de Alvarado, and took charge of the other himself. The infantry was headed by his brother Gonzalo, supported by Pedro de Valdivia, the future hero of Arauco, whose disastrous story forms the burden of romance as well as of chronicle.

Mass was said, as if the Spaniards were about to fight what they deemed the good fight of the faith, instead of imbruing their hands in the blood of their countrymen. Hernando Pizarro then made a brief address to his soldiers. He touched on the personal injuries he and his family had received from Almagro; reminded his brother's veterans that Cuzco had been wrested from their possession; called up the glow of shame on the brows of Alvarado's men as he talked of the rout of Abancay, and, pointing out the Inca metropolis that sparkled in the morning sunshine, he told them that there was the prize of the victor. They answered his appeal with acclamations;

and the signal being given, Gonzalo Pizarro, heading his battalion of infantry, led it straight across the river. The water was neither broad nor deep, and the soldiers found no difficulty in gaining a landing, as the enemy's horse was prevented by the marshy ground from approaching the borders. But, as they worked their way across the morass, the heavy guns of Orgoñez played with effect on the leading files, and threw them into disorder. Gonzalo and Valdivia threw themselves into the midst of their followers, menacing some, encouraging others, and at length led them gallantly forward to the firm ground. Here the arquebusiers, detaching themselves from the rest of the infantry, gained a small eminence, whence, in their turn, they opened a galling fire on Orgoñez, scattering his array of spearmen, and sorely annoying the cavalry on the flanks.

Meanwhile, Hernando, forming his two squadrons of horse into one column, crossed under cover of this well-sustained fire, and, reaching the firm ground, rode at once against the enemy. Orgoñez, whose infantry was already much crippled, advancing his horse, formed the two squadrons into one body, like his antagonist, and spurred at full gallop against the assailants. The shock was terrible; and it was hailed by the swarms of Indian spectators on the surrounding heights with a fiendish yell of triumph, that rose far above the din of battle, till it was lost in distant echoes among the mountains.

The struggle was desperate. For it was not that of the white man against the defenseless Indian, but of Spaniard against Spaniard; both parties cheering on their comrades with their battlecries of "*El Rey y Almagro*," or "*El Rey y Pizarro*," —while they fought with a hate, to which national antipathy was as nothing; a hate strong in proportion to the strength of the ties that had been rent asunder.

In this bloody field well did Orgoñez do his duty, fighting like one to whom battle was the natural element. Singling out a cavalier, whom, from the color of the sobre-vest on his armor, he erroneously supposed to be Hernando Pizarro, he charged him in full career, and overthrew him with his lance.

Another he ran through in like manner, and a third he struck down with his sword, as he was prematurely shouting "Victory!" But while thus doing the deeds of a paladin of romance, he was hit by a chain-shot from an arquebus, which, penetrating the bars of his visor, grazed his forehead, and deprived him for a moment of reason. Before he had fully recovered, his horse was killed under him, and though the fallen cavalier succeeded in extricating himself from the stirrups, he was surrounded, and soon overpowered by numbers. Still refusing to deliver up his sword, he asked "if there was no knight to whom he could surrender." One Fuentes, a menial of Pizarro, presenting himself as such, Orgoñez gave his sword into his hands,—and the dastard, drawing his dagger, stabbed his defenseless prisoner to the heart! His head, then struck off, was stuck on a pike, and displayed, a bloody trophy, in the great square of Cuzco, as the head of a traitor. Thus perished as loyal a cavalier, as decided in council, and as bold in action, as ever crossed to the shores of America.

The fight had now lasted more than an hour, and the fortune of the day was turning against the followers of Almagro. Orgoñez being down, their confusion increased. The infantry, unable to endure the fire of the arquebusiers, scattered and took refuge behind the stone-walls, that here and there straggled across the country. Pedro de Lerma, vainly striving to rally the cavalry, spurred his horse against Hernando Pizarro, with whom he had a personal feud. Pizarro did not shrink from the encounter. The lances of both the knights took effect. That of Hernando penetrated the thigh of his opponent, while Lerma's weapon, glancing by his adversary's saddlebow, struck him with such force above the groin, that it pierced the joints of his mail, slightly wounding the cavalier, and forcing his horse back on his haunches. But the press of the fight soon parted the combatants, and, in the turmoil that ensued, Lerma was unhorsed, and left on the field covered with wounds.

There was no longer order, and scarcely resistance, among the followers of Almagro. They fled, making the best of their way to Cuzco, and happy was the man who obtained quarter when he asked it. Almagro himself, too feeble to sit so long on his horse, reclined on a litter, and from a neighboring eminence surveyed the battle, watching its fluctuations with all the interest of one who felt that honor, fortune, life itself, hung on the issue. With agony not to be described, he had seen his faithful followers, after their hard struggle, borne down by their opponents, till, convinced that all was lost, he succeeded in mounting a mule, and rode off for a temporary refuge to the fortress of Cuzco. Thither he was speedily followed, taken, and brought in triumph to the capital, where, ill as he was, he was thrown into irons, and confined in the same apartment of the stone building in which he had imprisoned the Pizarros.

[MASSACRE OF THE INCAS—CAPTURE OF THE INCA]

From *The Conquest of Peru*, Bk. III, chap. v

[Francisco Pizarro, with great duplicity, engages to treat peacefully with the Incas and then orders an attack upon them.]

The clouds of the evening had passed away, and the sun rose bright on the following morning, the most memorable epoch in the annals of Peru. It was Saturday, the sixteenth of November, 1532. The loud cry of the trumpet called the Spaniards to arms with the first streak of dawn; and Pizarro, briefly acquainting them with the plan of the assault, made the necessary dispositions.

The *plaza*, as mentioned in the preceding chapter, was defended on its three sides by low ranges of buildings, consisting of spacious halls with wide doors or vomitories opening into the square. In these halls he stationed his cavalry in two divisions, one under his brother Hernando, the other under De Soto. The infantry he placed in another of the buildings, reserving twenty chosen men to act with himself as occasion might require. Pedro de Candia, with a few soldiers and the artillery,—comprehending under this imposing name two small pieces of ordnance, called falconets,—he established in the fortress. All received orders to wait at their posts till the arrival of the Inca. After his entrance into the great square, they were still to remain under cover, withdrawn from observation, till the signal was given by the discharge of a gun, when they were to cry their war-cries, to rush out in a body from their covert, and, putting the Peruvians to the sword, bear off the person of the Inca. The arrangement of the immense halls, opening on a level with the *plaza*, seemed to be contrived on purpose for a *coup de théatre*. Pizarro particularly inculcated order and implicit obedience, that in the hurry of the moment there should be no confusion. Everything depended on their acting with concert, coolness, and celerity.

The chief next saw that their arms were in good order; and that the breastplates of their horses were garnished with bells, to add by their noise to the consternation of the Indians. Refreshments were, also, liberally provided, that the troops should be in condition for the conflict. These arrangements being completed, mass was performed with great solemnity by the ecclesiastics who attended the expedition; the God of battles was invoked to spread his shield over the soldiers who were fighting to extend the empire of the Cross; and all joined with enthusiasm in the chant, *"Exsurge, Domine,"* "Rise, O Lord! and judge thine own cause." One might have supposed them a company of martyrs, about to lay down their lives in defense of their faith, instead of a licentious band of adventurers, meditating one of the most atrocious acts of perfidy on the record of history! Yet, whatever were the vices of the Castilian cavalier, hypocrisy was not among the number. He felt that he was battling for the Cross, and under this conviction, exalted as it was at such a moment as this into the predominant impulse, he was blind to the baser motives which mingled with the enterprise. With feelings thus kindled to a flame of religious ardor, the soldiers of Pizarro looked forward with renovated spirits to the coming conflict; and the chieftain saw with satisfaction, that in the hour of trial his men would be true to their leader and themselves. * * *

Pizarro saw that the hour had come. He waved a white scarf in the air, the appointed signal. The fatal gun was fired from the fortress. Then, springing into the square, the Spanish captain and his followers shouted the old war-cry of "St. Jago and at them." It was answered by the battle-cry of every Spaniard in the city, as, rushing from the avenues of the great halls in which they were concealed, they poured into the *plaza*, horse and foot, each in his own dark column, and threw themselves into the midst of the Indian crowd. The latter, taken by surprise, stunned by the report of artillery and muskets, the echoes of which reverberated like thunder from the surrounding buildings, and blinded by the smoke which rolled in sulphurous volumes along the square, were seized with a panic. They knew not whither to fly for refuge from the coming ruin. Nobles and commoners,—all were trampled down under the fierce charge of the cavalry, who dealt their blows, right and left, without sparing; while their swords, flashing through the thick gloom, carried dismay into the hearts of the wretched natives, who now, for the first time, saw the horse and his rider in all their terrors. They made no resistance,—as, indeed, they had no weapons with which to make it. Every avenue to escape was closed, for the entrance to the square was choked up with the dead bodies of men who had perished in vain efforts to fly; and, such was the agony of the survivors under the terrible pressure of their assailants, that a large body of Indians, by their convulsive struggles, burst through the wall of stone and dried clay which formed part of the boundary of the *plaza!* It fell, leaving an opening of more than a hundred paces, through which multitudes now found their way into the country, still hotly pursued by the cavalry, who, leaping the fallen rubbish, hung on the rear of the fugitives, striking them down in all directions.

Meanwhile the fight, or rather massacre, continued hot around the Inca, whose person was the great object of the assault. His faithful nobles, rallying about him, threw themselves in the way of the assailants, and strove, by tearing them from their saddles, or, at least, by offering their own bosoms as a mark for their vengeance, to shield their beloved master. It is said by some authorities, that they carried weapons concealed under their clothes. If so, it availed them little, as it is not pretended that they used them. But the most timid animal will defend itself when at bay. That they did not so in the present instance is proof that they had no weapons to use. Yet they still continued to force back the cavaliers, clinging to their horses with dying grasp, and, as one was cut down, another taking the place of his fallen comrade with a loyalty truly affecting.

The Indian monarch, stunned and bewildered, saw his faithful subjects falling round him without fully comprehending his situation. The litter on which he rode heaved to and fro, as the mighty press swayed backwards and forwards; and he gazed on the overwhelming ruin, like some forlorn mariner, who, tossed about in his bark by the furious elements, sees the lightning's flash and hears the thunder bursting around him with the consciousness that he can do nothing to avert his fate. At length, weary with the work of destruction, the Spaniards, as the shades of evening grew deeper, felt afraid that the royal prize might, after all, elude them; and some of the cavaliers made a desperate attempt to end the affray at once by taking Atahuallpa's life. But Pizarro, who was nearest his person, called out with stentorian voice, "Let no one, who values his life, strike at the Inca"; and, stretching out his arm to shield him, received a wound on the hand from one of his own men,— the only wound received by a Spaniard in the action.

The struggle now became fiercer than ever round the royal litter. It reeled more and more, and at length, several of the nobles who supported it having been slain, it was overturned, and the Indian prince would have come with violence to the ground, had not his fall been broken by the efforts of Pizarro and some other of the cavaliers, who caught him in their arms. The imperial *borla* was instantly snatched from his temples by a soldier named Estete, and the unhappy monarch, strongly secured, was removed to a neighboring building, where he was carefully guarded.

All attempt at resistance now ceased. The fate of the Inca soon spread over town and country. The charm which might have held the Peruvians together was dissolved. Every man thought only of his own safety. Even the soldiery encamped on the adjacent fields took the alarm, and, learning the fatal tidings, were seen flying in every direction before their pursuers, who in the heat of triumph showed no touch of mercy. At length night, more pitiful than man, threw her friendly mantle over the fugitives, and the scattered troops of Pizarro rallied once more at the sound of the trumpet in the bloody square of Caxamalca.

[THE BATTLE OF LEPANTO]

From *Philip the Second*, Bk. V, chap. x

[This battle, which has been called the greatest naval battle since Actium, was the outstanding event in the long naval duel between the Spaniards and the Turks. The Spanish commander, Don John of Austria, was the natural brother of Philip.]

On the third of October, Don John, without waiting longer for the missing vessels, again put to sea, and stood for the gulf of Lepanto. As the fleet swept down the Ionian Sea, it passed many a spot famous in ancient story. None, we may imagine, would be so likely to excite an interest at this time as Actium, on whose waters was fought the greatest naval battle of antiquity. But the mariner, probably, gave little thought to the past, as he dwelt on the conflict that awaited him at Lepanto. On the fifth, a thick fog enveloped the armada and shut out every object from sight. Fortunately, the vessels met with no injury, and, passing by Ithaca, the ancient home of Ulysses, they safely anchored off the eastern coast of Cephalonia. For two days their progress was thwarted by head-winds. But on the seventh, Don John, impatient of delay, again put to sea, though wind and weather were still unfavorable.

While lying off Cephalonia he had received tidings that

Famagosta, the second city of Cyprus, had fallen into the hands of the enemy, and this under circumstances of unparalleled perfidy and cruelty. The place, after a defense that had cost hecatombs of lives to the besiegers, was allowed to capitulate on honorable terms. Mustapha, the Moslem commander, the same fierce chief who had conducted the siege of Malta, requested an interview at his quarters with four of the principal Venetian captains. After a short and angry conference, he ordered them all to execution. Three were beheaded. The other, a noble named Bragadino, who had held the supreme command, he caused to be flayed alive in the market-place of the city. The skin of the wretched victim was then stuffed; and with this ghastly trophy dangling from the yardarm of his galley, the brutal monster sailed back to Constantinople, to receive the reward of his services from Selim. These services were great. The fall of Famagosta secured the fall of Cyprus, which thus became permanently incorporated in the Ottoman empire.

The tidings of these shocking events filled the breast of every Venetian with an inextinguishable thirst for vengeance. The confederates entered heartily into these feelings; and all on board of the armada were impatient for the hour that was to bring them hand to hand with the enemies of the Faith.

It was two hours before dawn, on Sunday, the memorable seventh of October, when the fleet weighed anchor. The wind had become lighter; but it was still contrary, and the galleys were indebted for their progress much more to their oars than their sails. By sunrise they were abreast of the Curzolari, a cluster of huge rocks, or rocky islets, which on the north defends the entrance of the gulf of Lepanto. The fleet moved laboriously along, while every eye was strained to catch the first glimpse of the hostile navy. At length the watch on the foretop of the *Real* called out, "A sail!" and soon after declared that the whole Ottoman fleet was in sight. Several others, climbing up the rigging, confirmed his report; and in a few moments more, word was sent to the same effect by Andrew Doria, who commanded on the right. There was no longer any doubt; and Don John, ordering his pennon to be displayed at the mizzen-peak, unfurled the great standard of the League, given by the Pope, and directed a gun to be fired, the signal for battle. The report, as it ran along the rocky shores, fell cheerily on the ears of the confederates, who, raising their eyes towards the consecrated banner, filled the air with their shouts.

The principal captains now came on board the *Real*, to receive the last orders of the commander-in-chief. Even at this late hour there were some who ventured to intimate their doubts of the expediency of engaging the enemy in a position where he had a decided advantage. But Don John cut short the discussion. "Gentlemen," he said, "this is the time for combat, not for counsel." He then continued the dispositions he was making for the attack.

He had already given to each commander of a galley written instructions as to the manner in which the line of battle was to be formed in case of meeting the enemy. The armada was now disposed in that order. It extended on a front of three miles. Far on the right, a squadron of sixty-four galleys was commanded by the Genoese admiral, Andrew Doria,—a name of terror to the Moslems. The center, or *battle*, as it was called, consisting of sixty-three galleys, was led by John of Austria, who was supported on the one side by Colonna, the captain-general of the Pope, and on the other by the Venetian captain-general, Veniero. Immediately in the rear was the galley of the Grand Commander Requesens, who still remained near the person of his former pupil; though a difference which arose between them on the voyage, fortunately now healed, showed that the young commander-in-chief was wholly independent of his teacher in the art of war.

The left wing was commanded by the noble Venetian, Barbarigo, whose vessels stretched along the Ætolian shore, to which he approached as near as, in his ignorance of the coast, he dared to venture, so as to prevent his being turned by the enemy. Finally, the reserve, consisting of thirty-five galleys, was given to the brave marquis of Santa Cruz, with directions to act in any quarter where he thought his presence most needed. The smaller craft, some of which had now arrived, seem to have taken little part in the action, which was thus left to the galleys.

Each commander was to occupy so much space with his galley as to allow room for manœuvring it to advantage, and yet not enough to allow the enemy to break the line. He was directed to single out his adversary, to close with him at once, and board as soon as possible. The beaks of the galleys were pronounced to be a hinderance rather than a help in action. They were rarely strong enough to resist a shock from an antagonist, and they much interfered with the working and firing of the guns. Don John had the beak of his vessel cut away. The example was followed throughout the fleet, and, as it is said, with eminently good effect. It may seem strange that this discovery should have been reserved for the crisis of a battle.

When the officers had received their last instructions, they returned to their respective vessels; and Don John, going on board of a light frigate, passed rapidly through the part of the armada lying on his right, while he commanded Requesens to do the same with the vessels on his left. His object was to feel the temper of his men, and to rouse their mettle by a few words of encouragement. The Venetians he reminded of their recent injuries. The hour for vengeance, he told them, had arrived. To the Spaniards and other confederates he said, "You have come to fight the battle of the Cross; to conquer or to die. But, whether you are to die or conquer, do your duty this day, and you will secure a glorious immortality." His words were received with a burst of enthusiasm which went to the heart of the commander and assured him that he could rely on his men in the hour of trial. On returning to his vessel, he saw Veniero on his quarter-deck; and they exchanged salutations in as friendly a manner as if no difference had existed between them. At this solemn hour both these brave men were willing to forget all personal animosity in a common feeling of devotion to the great cause in which they were engaged.

The Ottoman fleet came on slowly and with difficulty. For,

strange to say, the wind, which had hitherto been adverse to the Christians, after lulling for a time, suddenly shifted to the opposite quarter and blew in the face of the enemy. As the day advanced, moroever, the sun, which had shone in the eyes of the confederates, gradually shot its rays into those of the Moslems. Both circumstances were of good omen to the Christians, and the first was regarded as nothing short of a direct interposition of Heaven. Thus ploughing its way along, the Turkish armament, as it came more into view, showed itself in greater strength than had been anticipated by the allies. It consisted of nearly two hundred and fifty royal galleys, most of them of the largest class, besides a number of smaller vessels in the rear, which, like those of the allies, appear scarcely to have come into action. The men on board, of every description, were computed at not less than a hundred and twenty thousand. The galleys spread out, as usual with the Turks, in the form of a regular half moon, covering a wider extent of surface than the combined fleets, which they somewhat exceeded in number. They presented, indeed, as they drew nearer, a magnificent array, with their gilded and gaudily-painted prows, and their myriads of pennons and streamers fluttering gayly in the breeze; while the rays of the morning sun glanced on the polished scimitars of Damascus, and on the superb aigrettes of jewels which sparkled in the turbans of the Ottoman chiefs.

In the center of the extended line, and directly opposite to the station occupied by the captain-general of the League, was the huge galley of Ali Pasha. The right of the armada was commanded by Mahomet Sirocco, viceroy of Egypt, a circumspect as well as courageous leader; the left, by Uluch Ali, dey of Algiers, the redoubtable corsair of the Mediterranean. Ali Pasha had experienced a difficulty like that of Don John, as several of his officers had strongly urged the inexpediency of engaging so formidable an armament as that of the allies. But Ali, like his rival, was young and ambitious. He had been sent by his master to fight the enemy; and no remonstrances, not even those of Mahomet Sirocco, for whom he had great respect, could turn him from his purpose.

He had, moreover, received intelligence that the allied fleet was much inferior in strength to what it proved. In this error he was fortified by the first appearance of the Christians; for the extremity of their left wing, commanded by Barbarigo, stretching behind the Ætolian shore, was hidden from his view. As he drew nearer and saw the whole extent of the Christian lines, it is said his countenance fell. If so, he still did not abate one jot of his resolution. He spoke to those around him with the same confidence as before, of the result of the battle. He urged his rowers to strain every nerve. Ali was a man of more humanity in his nature than often belonged to his nation. His galley-slaves were all, or nearly all, Christian captives; and he addressed them in this brief and pithy manner: "If your countrymen are to win this day, Allah give you the benefit of it; yet if I win it, you shall certainly have your freedom. If you feel that I do well by you, do then the like by me."

As the Turkish admiral drew nearer, he made a change in his order of battle, by separating his wings farther from his center, thus conforming to the dispositions of the allies. Before he had come within cannon-shot, he fired a gun by way of challenge to his enemy. It was answered by another from the galley of John of Austria. A second gun discharged by Ali was as promptly replied to by the Christian commander. The distance between the two fleets was now rapidly diminishing. At this solemn moment a death-like silence reigned throughout the armament of the confederates. Men seemed to hold their breath, as if absorbed in the expectation of some great catastrophe. The day was magnificent. A light breeze, still adverse to the Turks, played on the waters, somewhat fretted by the contrary winds. It was nearly noon; and as the sun, mounting through a cloudless sky, rose to the zenith, he seemed to pause, as if to look down on the beautiful scene, where the multitude of galleys, moving over the water, showed like a holiday spectacle rather than a preparation for mortal combat.

The illusion was soon dispelled by the fierce yells which rose on the air from the Turkish armada. It was the customary war-cry with which the Moslems entered into battle. Very different was the scene on board of the Christian galleys. Don John might be there seen, armed *cap-à-pie*, standing on the prow of the *Real*, anxiously awaiting the conflict. In this conspicuous position, kneeling down, he raised his eyes to heaven, and humbly prayed that the Almighty would be with his people on that day. His example was followed by the whole fleet. Officers and men, all prostrating themselves on their knees and turning their eyes to the consecrated banner which floated from the *Real*, put up a petition like that of their commander. They then received absolution from the priests, of whom there were some in every vessel; and each man, as he rose to his feet, gathered new strength, as he felt assured that the Lord of Hosts would fight on his side.

When the foremost vessels of the Turks had come within cannon-shot, they opened their fire on the Christians. The firing soon ran along the whole of the Turkish line, and was kept up without interruption as it advanced. Don John gave orders for trumpet and atabal to sound the signal for action; which was followed by the simultaneous discharge of such of the guns in the combined fleet as could be brought to bear on the enemy. The Spanish commander had caused the *galeazzas*, those mammoth warships of which some account has been already given, to be towed half a mile ahead of the fleet, where they might intercept the advance of the Turks. As the latter came abreast of them, the huge galleys delivered their broadsides right and left, and their heavy ordnance produced a startling effect. Ali Pasha gave orders for his galleys to open their line and pass on either side, without engaging these monsters of the deep, of which he had had no experience. Even so their heavy guns did considerable damage to several of the nearest vessels, and created some confusion in the pacha's line of battle. They were, however, but unwieldy craft, and, having accomplished their object, seem to have taken no further part in the combat.

The action began on the left wing of the allies, which Mahomet Sirocco was desirous of turning. This had been anticipated by Barbarigo, the Venetian admiral, who commanded in that quarter. To prevent it, as we have seen, he lay with his vessels as near the coast as he dared. Sirocco, better acquainted with the soundings, saw there was space enough for him to pass, and, darting by with all the speed that oars could give him, he succeeded in doubling on his enemy. Thus placed between two fires, the extreme of the Christian left fought at terrible disadvantage. No less than eight galleys went to the bottom, and several others were captured. The brave Barbarigo, throwing himself into the heat of the fight, without availing himself of his defensive armor, was pierced in the eye by an arrow, and, reluctant to leave the glory of the field to another, was borne to his cabin. The combat still continued with unabated fury on the part of the Venetians. They fought like men who felt that the war was theirs, and who were animated not only by their thirst for glory, but for revenge.

Far on the Christian right a manœuvre similar to that so successfully executed by Sirocco was attempted by Uluch Ali, the dey of Algiers. Profiting by his superiority in numbers, he endeavored to turn the ring wing of the confederates. It was in this quarter that Andrew Doria commanded. He had foreseen this movement of his enemy, and he succeeded in foiling it. It was a trial of skill between the two most accomplished seamen in the Mediterranean. Doria extended his line so far to the right, indeed, to prevent being surrounded, that Don John was obliged to remind him that he left the center too much exposed. His dispositions were so unfortunate for himself that his own line was thus weakened and afforded some vulnerable points to his assailant. These were soon detected by the eagle eye of Uluch Ali; and, like the king of birds swooping on his prey, he fell on some galleys separated by a considerable interval from their companions, and, sinking more than one, carried off the great *Capitana* of Malta in triumph as his prize.

While the combat opened thus disastrously to the allies both on the right and on the left, in the center they may be said to have fought with doubtful fortune. Don John had led his division gallantly forward. But the object on which he was intent was an encounter with Ali Pasha, the foe most worthy of his sword. The Turkish commander had the same combat no less at heart. The galleys of both were easily recognized, not only from their position, but from their superior size and richer decoration. The one, moreover, displayed the holy banner of the League; the other the great Ottoman standard. This, like the ancient standard of the caliphs, was held sacred in its character. It was covered with texts from the Koran, emblazoned in letters of gold, and had the name of Allah inscribed upon it no less than twenty-eight thousand nine hundred times. It was the banner of the sultan, having passed from father to son since the foundation of the imperial dynasty, and was never seen in the field unless the grand seigneur or his lieutenant was there in person.

Both the chiefs urged on their rowers to the top of their speed. Their galleys soon shot ahead of the rest of the line, driven through the boiling surges as by the force of a tornado, and closed with a shock that made every timber crack and the two vessels quiver to their very keels. So powerful, indeed, was the impetus they received that the pacha's galley, which was considerably the larger and loftier of the two, was thrown so far upon its opponent that the prow reached the fourth bench of rowers. As soon as the vessels were disengaged from each other, and those on board had recovered from the shock, the work of death began. Don John's chief strength consisted in some three hundred Spanish arquebusiers, culled from the flower of his infantry. Ali, on the other hand, was provided with an equal number of janizaries. He was followed by a smaller vessel, in which two hundred more were stationed as a *corps de réserve*. He had, moreover, a hundred archers on board. The bow was still as much in use with the Turks as with the other Moslems.

The pacha opened at once on his enemy a terrible fire of cannon and musketry. It was returned with equal spirit and much more effect; for the Turks were observed to shoot over the heads of their adversaries. The Moslem galley was unprovided with the defenses which protected the sides of the Spanish vessels; and the troops, crowded together on the lofty prow, presented an easy mark to their enemy's balls. But, though numbers of them fell at every discharge, their places were soon supplied by those in reserve. They were enabled, therefore, to keep up an incessant fire, which wasted the strength of the Spaniards; and, as both Christian and Mussulman fought with indomitable spirit, it seemed doubtful to which side victory would incline.

The affair was made more complicated by the entrance of other parties into the conflict. Both Ali and Don John were supported by some of the most valiant captains in their fleets. Next to the Spanish commander, as we have seen, were Colonna and the veteran Veniero, who, at the age of seventy-six, performed feats of arms worthy of a paladin of romance. In this way a little squadron of combatants gathered round the principal leaders, who sometimes found themselves assailed by several enemies at the same time. Still the chiefs did not lose sight of one another; but, beating off their inferior foes as well as they could, each, refusing to loosen his hold, clung with mortal grasp to his antagonist.

Thus the fight raged along the whole extent of the entrance to the gulf of Lepanto. The volumes of vapor rolling heavily over the waters effectually shut out from sight whatever was passing at any considerable distance, unless when a fresher breeze dispelled the smoke for a moment, or the flashes of the heavy guns threw a transient gleam on the dark canopy of battle. If the eye of the spectator could have penetrated the cloud of smoke that enveloped the combatants, and have embraced the whole scene at a glance, he would have perceived them broken up into small detachments, separately engaged one with another, independently of the rest, and indeed ignorant of all that was doing in other quarters. The contest exhibited few of those large combinations and skillful manœuvres to be expected in a great naval encounter. It was rather an assemblage of petty actions, resembling those on land. The galleys, grappling together, presented a level arena, on which soldier and galley-slave fought hand to hand, and the fate of the engagement was generally decided by boarding. As in most hand-to-hand contests, there was an enormous waste of life. The decks were loaded with corpses, Christian and Moslem lying promiscuously together in the embrace of death. Instances are recorded where every man on board was slain or wounded. It was a ghastly spectacle, where blood flowed in rivulets down the sides of the vessels, staining the waters of the gulf for miles around.

It seemed as if a hurricane had swept over the sea and covered it with the wreck of the noble armaments which a moment before were so proudly riding on its bosom. Little had they now to remind one of their late magnificent array, with their hulls battered, their masts and spars gone or splintered by the shot, their canvas cut into shreds and floating wildly on the breeze, while thousands of wounded and drowning men were clinging to the floating fragments and calling piteously for help. Such was the wild uproar which succeeded the Sabbath-like stillness that two hours before had reigned over these beautiful solitudes.

The left wing of the confederates, commanded by Barbarigo, had been sorely pressed by the Turks, as we have seen, at the beginning of the fight. Barbarigo himself had been mortally wounded. His line had been turned. Several of his galleys had been sunk. But the Venetians gathered courage from despair. By incredible efforts, they succeeded in beating off their enemies. They became the assailants in their turn. Sword in hand, they carried one vessel after another. The Capuchin was seen in the thickest of the fight, waving aloft his crucifix and leading the boarders to the assault. The Christian galley-slaves, in some instances, broke their fetters and joined their countrymen against their masters. Fortunately, the vessel of Mahomet Sirocco, the Moslem admiral, was sunk; and though extricated from the water himself, it was only to perish by the sword of his conqueror, Giovanni Contarini. The Venetian could find in his heart no mercy for the Turk.

The fall of their commander gave the final blow to his followers. Without further attempt to prolong the fight, they fled before the avenging swords of the Venetians. Those nearest the land endeavored to escape by running their vessels ashore, where they abandoned them as prizes to the Christians. Yet many of the fugitives, before gaining the land, perished miserably in the waves. Barbarigo, the Venetian admiral, who was still lingering in agony, heard the tidings of the enemy's defeat, and, uttering a few words expressive of his gratitude to Heaven, which had permitted him to see this hour, he breathed his last.

During this time the combat had been going forward in the center between the two commanders-in-chief, Don John and Ali Pasha, whose galleys blazed with an incessant fire of artillery and musketry, that enveloped them like "a martyr's robe of flames." The parties fought with equal spirit, though not with equal fortune. Twice the Spaniards had boarded their enemy, and both times they had been repulsed with loss. Still, their superiority in the use of firearms would have given them a decided advantage over their opponents if the loss they had inflicted had not been speedily repaired by fresh reinforcements. More than once the contest between the two chieftains was interrupted by the arrival of others to take part in the fray. They soon, however, returned to each other, as if unwilling to waste their strength on a meaner enemy. Through the whole engagement both commanders exposed themselves to danger as freely as any common soldier. In such a contest even Philip must have admitted that it would be difficult for his brother to find, with honor, a place of safety. Don John received a wound in the foot. It was a slight one, however, and he would not allow it to be dressed till the action was over.

Again his men were mustered, and a third time the trumpets sounded to the attack. It was more successful than the preceding. The Spaniards threw themselves boldly into the Turkish galley. They were met with the same spirit as before by the janizaries. Ali Pasha led them on. Unfortunately, at this moment he was struck in the head by a musket-ball and stretched senseless in the gangway. His men fought worthily of their ancient renown. But they missed the accustomed voice of their commander. After a short but ineffectual struggle against the fiery impetuosity of the Spaniards, they were overpowered and threw down their arms. The decks were loaded with the bodies of the dead and the dying. Beneath these was discovered the Turkish commander-in-chief, severely wounded, but perhaps not mortally. He was drawn forth by some Castilian soldiers, who, recognizing his person, would at once have despatched him. But the disabled chief, having rallied from the first effects of his wound, had sufficient presence of mind to divert them from their purpose by pointing out the place below where he had deposited his money and jewels; and they hastened to profit by the disclosure before the treasure should fall into the hands of their comrades.

Ali was not so successful with another soldier, who came up soon after, brandishing his sword and preparing to plunge it into the body of the prostrate commander. It was in vain that the latter endeavored to turn the ruffian from his purpose. He was a convict, one of those galley-slaves whom Don John had caused to be unchained from the oar and furnished with arms. He could not believe that any treasure would be worth so much as the head of the pacha. Without further hesitation, he dealt him a blow which severed it from his shoulders. Then, returning to his galley, he laid the bloody trophy before Don John. But he had miscalculated on his recompense. His commander gazed on it with a look of pity mingled with horror. He may have thought of the generous conduct of Ali to his Christian captives, and have felt that he deserved a better fate. He coldly inquired "of what use such a present could be to him," and then ordered it to be thrown into the sea. Far from the order being obeyed, it is said the head was stuck on a pike and raised aloft on board of the captured galley. At the same time the banner of the Crescent was pulled down; while that of the Cross, run up in its place, proclaimed the downfall of the pacha.

The sight of the sacred ensign was welcomed by the Christians with a shout of "Victory!" which rose high above the din of battle. The tidings of the death of Ali soon passed from mouth to mouth, giving fresh heart to the confederates, but falling like a knell on the ears of the Moslems. Their confidence was gone. Their fire slackened. Their efforts grew weaker and weaker. They were too far from shore to seek an asylum there, like their comrades on the right. They had no resource but to prolong the combat or to surrender. Most preferred the latter. Many vessels were carried by boarding, others were sunk by the victorious Christians. Ere four hours had elapsed, the center, like the right wing, of the Moslems might be said to be annihilated.

Still the fight was lingering on the right of the confederates, where, it will be remembered, Uluch Ali, the Algerine chief, had profited by Doria's error in extending his line so far as greatly to weaken it. Uluch Ali, attacking it on its most vulnerable quarter, had succeeded, as we have seen, in capturing and destroying several vessels, and would have inflicted still heavier losses on his enemy had it not been for the seasonable succor received from the marquis of Santa Cruz. This brave officer, who commanded the reserve, had already been of much service to Don John when the *Real* was assailed by several Turkish galleys at once during his combat with Ali Pasha; for at this juncture the marquis of Santa Cruz arriving, and beating off the assailants, one of whom he afterwards captured, enabled the commander-in-chief to resume his engagement with the pacha.

No sooner did Santa Cruz learn the critical situation of Doria than, supported by Cardona, "general" of the Sicilian squadron, he pushed forward to his relief. Dashing into the midst of the mêlée, the two commanders fell like a thunderbolt on the Algerine galleys. Few attempted to withstand the shock. But in their haste to avoid it they were encountered by Doria and his Genoese galleys. Thus beset on all sides, Uluch Ali was compelled to abandon his prizes and provide for his own safety by flight. He cut adrift the Maltese *Capitana*, which he had lashed to his stern, and on which three hundred corpses attested the desperate character of her defense. As tidings reached him of the discomfiture of the center and of the death of Ali Pasha, he felt that nothing remained but to make the best of his way from the fatal scene of action and save as many of his own ships as he could. And there were no ships in the

Turkish fleet superior to his, or manned by men under more perfect discipline. For they were the famous corsairs of the Mediterranean, who had been rocked from infancy on its waters.

Throwing out his signals for retreat, the Algerine was soon to be seen, at the head of his squadron, standing towards the north, under as much canvas as remained to him after the battle, and urged forward through the deep by the whole strength of his oarsmen. Doria and Santa Cruz followed quickly in his wake. But he was borne on the wings of the wind, and soon distanced his pursuers. Don John, having disposed of his own assailants, was coming to the support of Doria, and now joined in the pursuit of the viceroy. A rocky headland, stretching far into the sea, lay in the path of the fugitive; and his enemies hoped to intercept him there. Some few of his vessels were stranded on the rocks. But the rest, near forty in number, standing more boldly out to sea, safely doubled the promontory. Then, quickening their flight, they gradually faded from the horizon, their white sails, the last thing visible, showing in the distance like a flock of Arctic sea-fowl on their way to their native homes. The confederates explained the inferior sailing of their own galleys on this occasion by the circumstance of their rowers, who had been allowed to bear arms in the fight, being crippled by their wounds.

The battle had lasted more than four hours. The sky, which had been almost without a cloud through the day, began now to be overcast, and showed signs of a coming storm. Before seeking a place of shelter for himself and his prizes, Don John reconnoitered the scene of action. He met with several vessels too much damaged for further service. These, mostly belonging to the enemy, after saving what was of any value on board, he ordered to be burnt. He selected the neighboring port of Petala, as affording the most secure and accessible harbor for the night. Before he had arrived there, the tempest began to mutter and darkness was on the water. Yet the darkness rendered only more visible the blazing wrecks, which, sending up streams of fire mingled with showers of sparks, looked like volcanoes on the deep.

VI. DRAMATIC SCENES

[The Romantic historians welcomed eagerly any opportunity to describe a dramatic episode. Memorable scenes such as Cortés' speech to his faltering companions after he had burned his fleet, Pizarro's challenge to his confederates, the seizure of Montezuma, and the Inca's ransom have become high spots in history partly because Prescott gave them full dramatic value when he described them. It should be noted, however, that he used the sources for these episodes critically and, sometimes, skeptically.]

[THE AZTECS SENSE THE COMING OF THE CONQUERORS]

From *The Conquest of Mexico*, Bk. II, chap. vi

[Prescott turns aside for a moment from his narrative of Cortés' progress to Mexico to note the evil tidings that had preceded him.]

Such was the condition of the Aztec monarchy, on the arrival of Cortés;—the people disgusted with the arrogance of the sovereign; the provinces and distant cities outraged by fiscal exactions; while potent enemies in the neighborhood lay watching the hour when they might assail their formidable rival with advantage. Still the kingdom was strong in its internal resources, in the will of its monarch, in the long habitual deference to his authority,—in short, in the terror of his name, and in the valor and discipline of his armies, grown gray in active service, and well drilled in all the tactics of Indian warfare. The time had now come, when these imperfect tactics and rude weapons of the barbarian were to be brought into collision with the science and enginery of the most civilized nations of the globe.

During the latter years of his reign, Montezuma had rarely taken part in his military expeditions, which he left to his captains, occupying himself chiefly with his sacerdotal functions. Under no prince had the priesthood enjoyed greater consideration and immunities. The religious festivals and rites were celebrated with unprecedented pomp. The oracles were consulted on the most trivial occasions; and the sanguinary deities were propitiated by hecatombs of victims dragged in triumph to the capital from the conquered or rebellious provinces. The religion, or, to speak correctly, the superstition of Montezuma proved a principal cause of his calamities.

In a preceding chapter I have noticed the popular traditions respecting Quetzalcoatl, that deity with a fair complexion and flowing beard, so unlike the Indian physiognomy, who, after fulfilling his mission of benevolence among the Aztecs, embarked on the Atlantic Sea for the mysterious shores of Tlapallan. He promised, on his departure, to return at some future day with his posterity, and resume the possession of his empire. That day was looked forward to with hope or with apprehension, according to the interest of the believer, but with general confidence throughout the wide borders of Anahuac. Even after the Conquest, it still lingered among the Indian races, by whom it was as fondly cherished, as the advent of their king Sebastian continued to be by the Portuguese, or that of the Messiah by the Jews.

A general feeling seems to have prevailed in the time of Montezuma, that the period for the return of the deity, and the full accomplishment of his promise, was near at hand. This conviction is said to have gained ground from various preternatural occurrences, reported with more or less detail by all the most ancient historians. In 1510, the great lake of Tezcuco, without the occurrence of a tempest, or earthquake, or any other visible cause, became violently agitated, overflowed its banks, and, pouring into the streets of Mexico, swept off many of the buildings by the fury of the waters. In 1511, one of the turrets of the great temple took fire, equally without any apparent cause, and continued to burn in defiance of all attempts to extinguish it. In the following years, three comets were seen; and not long before the coming of the Spaniards a strange light broke forth in the east. It spread broad at its base on the horizon, and rising in a pyramidal form tapered off as it approached the zenith. It resembled a vast sheet or flood of fire, emitting sparkles, or, as an old writer expresses it, "seemed thickly powdered with stars." At the same time, low voices were heard in the air, and doleful wailings, as if to announce some strange, mysterious calamity! The Aztec monarch, terrified at the apparitions in the heavens, took counsel of Nezahualpilli, who was a great proficient in the subtle science of astrology. But the royal sage cast a deeper cloud over his spirit, by reading in these prodigies the speedy downfall of the empire.

Such are the strange stories reported by the chroniclers, in which it is not impossible to detect the glimmerings of truth. Nearly thirty years had elapsed since the discovery of the Islands by Columbus, and more than twenty since his visit to the American continent. Rumors, more or less distinct, of this wonderful appearance of the white men, bearing in their hands the thunder and the lightning, so like in many respects to the traditions of Quetzalcoatl, would naturally spread far and wide among the Indian nations. Such rumors, doubtless, long before the landing of the Spaniards in Mexico, found their way up the grand plateau, filling the minds of men with anticipations of the near coming of the period when the great deity was to return and receive his own again.

In the excited state of their imaginations, prodigies became a familiar occurrence. Or rather, events not very uncommon in themselves, seen through the discolored medium of fear, were easily magnified into prodigies; and the accidental swell of the lake, the appearance of a comet, and the conflagration of a building were all interpreted as the special annunciations of Heaven. Thus it happens in those great political convulsions which shake the foundations of society,—the mighty events that cast their shadows before them in their coming. Then it is that the atmosphere is agitated with the low, prophetic murmurs, with which Nature, in the moral as in the physical world, announces the march of the hurricane;

> "When from the shores
> And forest-rustling mountains comes a voice,
> That, solemn sounding, bids the world prepare!"

When tidings were brought to the capital, of the landing of Grijalva on the coast, in the preceding year, the heart of Montezuma was filled with dismay. He felt as if the destinies which had so long brooded over the royal line of Mexico were to be accomplished, and the scepter was to pass away from his house forever. Though somewhat relieved by the departure of the Spaniards, he caused sentinels to be stationed on the heights; and, when the Europeans returned under Cortés, he doubtless received the earliest notice of the unwelcome event. It was by his orders, however, that the provincial governor had prepared so hospitable a reception for them. The hieroglyphical report of these strange visitors, now forwarded to the capital, revived all his apprehensions. He called, without delay, a meeting of his principal counselors, including the kings of Tezcuco and Tlacopan, and laid the matter before them.

[CORTÉS SINKS HIS FLEET]

From *The Conquest of Mexico*, Bk. II, chap. viii

[Cortés had made up his mind to march to the Aztec capital, but he wanted to make it impossible for his soldiers to think of retreat. He therefore ordered the fleet sunk.]

Shortly after the departure of the commissioners, an affair occurred of a most unpleasant nature. A number of persons, with the priest Juan Diaz at their head, ill-affected, from some cause or other, towards the administration of Cortés, or not relishing the hazardous expedition before them, laid a plan to seize one of the vessels, make the best of their way to Cuba, and report to the governor the fate of the armament. It was conducted with so much secrecy, that the party had got their provisions, water, and everything necessary for the voyage, on board, without detection; when the conspiracy was betrayed, on the very night they were to sail, by one of their own number, who repented the part he had taken in it. The general caused the persons implicated to be instantly apprehended. An examination was instituted. The guilt of the parties was placed beyond a doubt. Sentence of death was passed on two of the ringleaders; another, the pilot, was condemned to lose his feet, and several others to be whipped. The priest, probably the most guilty of the whole, claiming the usual benefit of clergy, was permitted to escape. One of those condemned to the gallows was named Escudero, the very alguacil who, the reader may remember, so stealthily apprehended Cortés before the sanctuary in Cuba. The general, in signing the death-warrants, was heard to exclaim, "Would that I had never learned to write!" It was not the first time, it was remarked, that the exclamation had been uttered in similar circumstances.

The arrangements being now finally settled at the Villa Rica, Cortés sent forward Alvarado, with a large part of the army, to Cempoalla, where he soon after joined them with the remainder. The late affair of the conspiracy seems to have made a deep impression on his mind. It showed him, that there were timid spirits in the camp on whom he could not rely, and who, he feared, might spread the seeds of disaffection among their companions. Even the more resolute, on any occasion of disgust or disappointment hereafter, might falter in purpose, and, getting possession of the vessels, abandon the enterprise. This was already too vast, and the odds were too formidable, to authorize expectation of success with diminution of numbers. Experience showed that this was always to be apprehended, while means of escape were at hand. The best chance for success was to cut off these means.—He came to the daring resolution to destroy the fleet, without the knowledge of his army.

When arrived at Cempoalla, he communicated his design to a few of his devoted adherents, who entered warmly into his views. Through them he readily persuaded the pilots, by means of those golden arguments which weigh more than any other with ordinary minds, to make such a report of the condition of the fleet as suited his purpose. The ships, they said, were grievously racked by the heavy gales they had encountered, and, what was worse, the worms had eaten into their sides and bottoms until most of them were not seaworthy, and some, indeed, could scarcely now be kept afloat.

Cortés received the communication with surprise; "for he could well dissemble," observes Las Casas, with his usual friendly comment, "when it suited his interests." "If it be so," he exclaimed, "we must make the best of it! Heaven's will be done!" He then ordered five of the worst conditioned to be dismantled, their cordage, sails, iron, and whatever was movable, to be brought on shore, and the ships to be sunk. A survey was made of the others, and, on a similar report, four more were condemned in the same manner. Only one small vessel remained!

When the intelligence reached the troops in Cempoalla, it caused the deepest consternation. They saw themselves cut off by a single blow from friends, family, country! The stoutest hearts quailed before the prospect of being thus abandoned on a hostile shore, a handful of men arrayed against a formidable empire. When the news arrived of the destruction of the five vessels first condemned, they had acquiesced in it as a necessary measure, knowing the mischievous activity of the insects in these tropical seas. But, when this was followed by the loss of the remaining four, suspicions of the truth flashed on their minds. They felt they were betrayed. Murmurs, at first deep, swelled louder and louder, menacing open mutiny. "Their general," they said, "had led them like cattle to be butchered in the shambles!" The affair wore a most alarming aspect. In no situation was Cortés ever exposed to greater danger from his soldiers.

His presence of mind did not desert him at this crisis. He called his men together, and, employing the tones of persuasion rather than authority, assured them, that a survey of the ships showed they were not fit for service. If he had ordered them to be destroyed, they should consider, also, that his was the greatest sacrifice, for they were his property,—all, indeed, he possessed in the world. The troops, on the other hand, would derive one great advantage from it, by the addition of a hundred able-bodied recruits, before required to man the vessels. But, even if the fleet had been saved, it could have been of little service in their present expedition; since they would not need it if they succeeded, while they would be too far in the interior to profit by it if they failed. He besought them to turn their thoughts in another direction. To be thus calculating chances and means of escape was unworthy of brave souls. They had set their hands to the work; to look back, as they advanced, would be their ruin. They had only to resume their former confidence in themselves and their general, and success was certain. "As for me," he concluded, "I have chosen my part. I will remain here, while there is one to bear me company. If there be any so craven, as to shrink from sharing the dangers of our glorious enterprise, let them go home, in God's name. There is still one vessel left. Let them take that and return to Cuba. They can tell there, how they have deserted their commander and their comrades, and patiently wait till we return loaded with the spoils of the Aztecs."

The politic orator had touched the right chord in the bosoms of the soldiers. As he spoke, their resentment gradually died away. The faded visions of future riches and glory, rekindled by his eloquence, again floated before their imaginations. The first shock over, they felt ashamed of their temporary distrust. The enthusiasm for their leader revived, for they felt that under his banner only they could hope for victory; and, as he concluded, they testified the revulsion of their feelings by making the air ring with their shouts, "To Mexico! to Mexico!"

The destruction of his fleet by Cortés is, perhaps, the most remarkable passage in the life of this remarkable man. History, indeed, affords examples of a similar expedient in emergencies somewhat similar; but none where the chances of success were so precarious, and defeat would be so disastrous. Had he failed, it might well seem an act of madness. Yet it was the fruit of deliberate calculation. He had set fortune, fame, life itself, all upon the cast, and must abide the issue. There was no alternative in his mind but to succeed or perish.

The measure he adopted greatly increased the chance of success. But to carry it into execution, in the face of an incensed and desperate soldiery, was an act of resolution that has few parallels in history.

[A CONSPIRACY DETECTED]

From *The Conquest of Mexico*, Bk. III, chap. vi

[Doña Marina was a beautiful native girl who became Cortés's mistress and a loyal ally of the Conquerors. One of the obstacles on the way to Mexico were the Cholulans who, under the guise of friendship, planned to entrap the Spaniards.]

From this time, the deportment of their Cholulan hosts underwent a visible alteration. They did not visit the quarters as before, and, when invited to do so, excused themselves on pretense of illness. The supply of provisions was stinted, on the ground that they were short of maize. These symptoms of alienation, independently of temporary embarrassment, caused serious alarm in the breast of Cortés, for the future. His apprehensions were not allayed by the reports of the Cempoallans, who told him, that in wandering round the city, they had seen several streets barricaded, the *azoteas*, or flat roofs of the houses, loaded with huge stones and other missiles, as if preparatory to an assault, and in some places they had found holes covered over with branches, and upright stakes planted within, as if to embarrass the movements of the cavalry. Some Tlascalans coming in, also, from their camp, informed the general, that a great sacrifice, mostly of children, had been offered up in a distant quarter of the town, to propitiate the favor of the gods, apparently for some intended enterprise. They added, that they had seen numbers of the citizens leaving the city with their women and children, as if to remove them to a place of safety. These tidings confirmed the worst suspicions of Cortés, who had no doubt that some hostile scheme was in agitation. If he had felt any, a discovery by Marina, the good angel of the expedition, would have turned these doubts into certainty.

The amiable manners of the Indian girl had won her the regard of the wife of one of the caciques, who repeatedly urged Marina to visit her house, darkly intimating that in this way she would escape the fate that awaited the Spaniards. The interpreter, seeing the importance of obtaining further intelligence at once, pretended to be pleased with the proposal, and affected, at the same time, great discontent with the white men, by whom she was detained in captivity. Thus throwing the credulous Cholulan off her guard, Marina gradually insinuated herself into her confidence, so far as to draw from her a full account of the conspiracy.

It originated, she said, with the Aztec emperor, who had sent rich bribes to the great caciques, and to her husband among others, to secure them in his views. The Spaniards were to be assaulted as they marched out of the capital, when entangled in its streets, in which numerous impediments had been placed to throw the cavalry into disorder. A force of twenty thousand Mexicans was already quartered at no great distance from the city, to support the Cholulans in the assault. It was confidently expected that the Spaniards, thus embarrassed in their movements, would fall an easy prey to the superior strength of their enemy. A sufficient number of prisoners was to be reserved to grace the sacrifices of Cholula; the rest were to be led in fetters to the capital of Montezuma.

While this conversation was going on, Marina occupied herself with putting up such articles of value and wearing apparel as she proposed to take with her in the evening, when she could escape unnoticed from the Spanish quarters to the house of her Cholulan friend, who assisted her in the operation. Leaving her visitor thus employed, Marina found an opportunity to steal away for a few moments, and, going to the general's apartment, disclosed to him her discoveries. He immediately caused the cacique's wife to be seized, and, on examination, she fully confirmed the statement of her Indian mistress.

The intelligence thus gathered by Cortés filled him with the deepest alarm. He was fairly taken in the snare. To fight or to fly seemed equally difficult. He was in a city of enemies, where every house might be converted into a fortress, and where such embarrassments were thrown in the way, as might render the manœuvres of his artillery and horse nearly impracticable. In addition to the wily Cholulans, he must cope, under all these disadvantages, with the redoubtable warriors of Mexico. He was like a traveler who has lost his way in the darkness among precipices, where any step may dash him to pieces, and where to retreat or to advance is equally perilous.

He was desirous to obtain still further confirmation and particulars of the conspiracy. He accordingly induced two of the priests in the neighborhood, one of them a person of much influence in the place, to visit his quarters. By courteous treatment, and liberal largesses of the rich presents he had received from Montezuma,—thus turning his own gifts against the giver,—he drew from them a full confirmation of the previous report. The emperor had been in a state of pitiable vacillation since the arrival of the Spaniards. His first orders to the Cholulans were, to receive the strangers kindly. He had recently consulted his oracles anew, and obtained for answer, that Cholula would be the grave of his enemies; for the gods would be sure to support him in avenging the sacrilege offered to the Holy City. So confident were the Aztecs of success, that numerous manacles, or poles with thongs which served as such, were already in the place to secure the prisoners.

Cortés, now feeling himself fully possessed of the facts, dismissed the priests, with injunctions of secrecy, scarcely necessary. He told them it was his purpose to leave the city on the following morning, and requested that they would induce some of the principal caciques to grant him an interview in his quarters. He then summoned a council of his officers, though, as it seems, already determined as to the course he was to take.

The members of the council were differently affected by the startling intelligence, according to their different characters. The more timid, disheartened by the prospect of obstacles which seemed to multiply as they drew nearer the Mexican capital, were for retracing their steps, and seeking shelter in the friendly city of Tlascala. Others, more persevering, but prudent, were for taking the more northerly route, originally recommended by their allies. The greater part supported the general, who was ever of opinion that they had no alternative but to advance. Retreat would be ruin. Halfway measures were scarcely better; and would infer a timidity which must discredit them with both friend and foe. Their true policy was to rely on themselves; to strike such a blow, as should intimidate their enemies, and show them that the Spaniards were as incapable of being circumvented by artifice, as of being crushed by weight of numbers and courage in the open field.

When the caciques, persuaded by the priests, appeared before Cortés, he contented himself with gently rebuking their want of hospitality, and assured them the Spaniards would be no longer a burden to their city, as he proposed to leave it early on the following morning. He requested, moreover, that they would furnish a reinforcement of two thousand men to transport his artillery and baggage. The chiefs, after some consultation, acquiesced in a demand which might in some measure favor their own designs.

On their departure, the general summoned the Aztec ambassadors before him. He briefly acquainted them with his detection of the treacherous plot to destroy his army, the contrivance of which he said, was imputed to their master, Montezuma. It grieved him much, he added, to find the emperor implicated in so nefarious a scheme, and that the Spaniards must now march as enemies against the prince, whom they had hoped to visit as a friend.

The ambassadors, with earnest protestations, asserted their entire ignorance of the conspiracy; and their belief that Montezuma was equally innocent of a crime, which they charged wholly on the Cholulans. It was clearly the policy of Cortés to keep on good terms with the Indian monarch; to profit as long as possible by his good offices; and to avail himself of his fancied security—such feelings of security as the general could inspire him with—to cover his own future operations. He affected to give credit, therefore, to the assertion of the envoys, and declared his unwillingness to believe, that a monarch, who had rendered the Spaniards so many friendly offices, would now consummate the whole by a deed of such unparalleled baseness. The discovery of their twofold duplicity, he added, sharpened his resentment against the Cholulans, on whom he would take such vengeance as should amply requite the injuries done both to Montezuma and the Spaniards. He then dismissed the ambassadors, taking care, notwithstanding this show of confidence, to place a strong guard over them, to prevent communication with the citizens.

That night was one of deep anxiety to the army. The ground they stood on seemed loosening beneath their feet, and any moment might be the one marked for their destruction. Their vigilant general took all possible precautions for their safety, increasing the number of the sentinels, and posting his guns in such a manner as to protect the approaches to the camp. His eyes, it may well be believed, did not close during the night. Indeed, every Spaniard lay down in his arms, and every horse stood saddled and bridled, ready for instant service. But no assault was meditated by the Indians, and the stillness of the hour was undisturbed except by the occasional sounds heard in a populous city, even when buried in slumber, and by the hoarse cries of the priests from the turrets of the *teocallis*, proclaiming through their trumpets the watches of the night.

[THE MASSACRE OF THE CHOLULANS]

From *The Conquest of Mexico*, Bk. III, chap. vii

[The discovery of the Cholulan plot enabled the Spaniards to crush completely the opposition.]

With the first streak of morning light, Cortés was seen on horseback, directing the movements of his little band. The strength of his forces he drew up in the great square or court, surrounded partly by buildings, as before noticed, and in part by a high wall. There were three gates of entrance, at each of which he placed a strong guard. The rest of his troops, with his great guns, he posted without the inclosure, in such a manner as to command the avenues and secure those within from interruption in their bloody work. Orders had been sent the night before to the Tlascalan chiefs to hold themselves ready, at a concerted signal, to march into the city and join the Spaniards.

The arrangements were hardly completed, before the Cholulan caciques appeared, leading a body of levies, *tamanes*, even more numerous than had been demanded. They were marched, at once, into the square, commanded, as we have seen, by the Spanish infantry which was drawn up under the walls. Cortés then took some of the caciques aside. With a stern air, he bluntly charged them with the conspiracy, showing that he was well acquainted with all the particulars. He had visited their city, he said, at the invitation of their emperor; had come as a friend; had respected the inhabitants and their property; and, to avoid all cause of umbrage, had left a great part of his forces without the walls. They had received him with a show of kindness and hospitality, and, reposing on this, he had been decoyed into the snare, and found this kindness only a mask to cover the blackest perfidy.

The Cholulans were thunderstruck at the accusation. An undefined awe crept over them, as they gazed on the mysterious strangers, and felt themselves in the presence of beings who seemed to have the power of reading the thoughts scarcely formed in their bosoms. There was no use in prevarication or denial before such judges. They confessed the whole, and endeavored to excuse themselves by throwing the blame on Montezuma. Cortés, assuming an air of higher indignation at this, assured them that the pretense should not serve, since, even if well founded, it would be no justification; and he would now make such an example of them for their treachery, that the report of it should ring throughout the wide borders of Anahuac!

The fatal signal, the discharge of an arquebus, was then given. In an instant every musket and crossbow was leveled at the unfortunate Cholulans in the courtyard, and a frightful volley poured into them as they stood crowded together like a herd of deer in the center. They were taken by surprise, for they had not heard the preceding dialogue with the chiefs. They made scarcely any resistance to the Spaniards, who followed up the discharge of their pieces by rushing on them with their swords; and, as the half-naked bodies of the natives afforded no protection, they hewed them down with as much ease as the reaper mows down the ripe corn in harvest time. Some endeavored to scale the walls, but only afforded a surer mark to the arquebusiers and archers. Others threw themselves into the gateways, but were received on the long pikes of the soldiers who guarded them. Some few had better luck in hiding themselves under the heaps of slain with which the ground was soon loaded.

While this work of death was going on, the countrymen of the slaughtered Indians, drawn together by the noise of the massacre, had commenced a furious assault on the Spaniards from without. But Cortés had placed his battery of heavy guns in a position that commanded the avenues, and swept off the files of the assailants as they rushed on. In the intervals between the discharges, which, in the imperfect state of the science in that day, were much longer than in ours, he forced back the press by charging with the horse into the midst. The steeds, the guns, the weapons of the Spaniards were all new to the Cholulans. Notwithstanding the novelty of the terrific spectacle, the flash of firearms mingling with the deafening roar of the artillery as its thunders reverberated among the buildings, the despairing Indians pushed on to take the places of their fallen comrades.

While this fierce struggle was going forward, the Tlascalans, hearing the concerted signal, had advanced with quick pace into the city. They had bound, by order of Cortés, wreaths of sedge round their heads, that they might the more surely be distinguished from the Cholulans. Coming up in the very heat of the engagement, they fell on the defenseless rear of the townsmen, who, trampled down under the heels of the Castilian cavalry on one side, and galled by their vindictive enemies on the other, could no longer maintain their ground. They gave way, some taking refuge in the nearest buildings, which, being partly of wood, were speedily set on fire. Others fled to the temples. One strong party, with a number of priests at its head, got possession of the great *teocalli*. There was a vulgar tradition, already alluded to, that, on removal of part of the walls, the god would send forth an inundation to overwhelm his enemies. The superstitious Cholulans with great difficulty succeeded in wrenching away some of the stones in the walls of the edifice. But dust, not water, followed. Their false god deserted them in the hour of need. In despair they flung themselves into the wooden turrets that crowned the temple, and pouring down stones, javelins, and burning arrows on the Spaniards, as they climbed the great staircase, which, by a flight of one hundred and twenty steps, scaled the face of the pyramid. But the fiery shower fell harmless on the steel bonnets of the Christians, while they availed themselves of the burning shafts to set fire to the wooden citadel, which was speedily wrapt in flames. Still the garrison held out, and though quarter, *it is said*, was offered, only one Cholulan availed himself of it. The rest threw themselves headlong from the parapet, or perished miserably in the flames.

All was now confusion and uproar in the fair city which had so lately reposed in security and peace. The groans of the dying, the frantic supplications of the vanquished for mercy, were mingled with the loud battle-cries of the Spaniards as they rode down their enemy, and with the shrill whistle of the Tlascalans, who gave full scope to the long cherished rancor of ancient rivalry. The tumult was still further swelled by the incessant rattle of musketry, and the crash of falling timbers, which sent up a volume of flame that outshone the ruddy light of morning, making all together a hideous confusion of sights and sounds, that converted the Holy City into a Pandemonium. As resistance slackened, the victors broke into the houses and sacred places, plundering them of whatever valuables they contained, plate, jewels, which were found in some quantity, wearing apparel and provisions, the two last coveted even more than the former by the simple Tlascalans, thus facilitating a division of the spoil much to the satisfaction of their Christian confederates. Amidst this universal license, it is worthy of remark, the commands of Cortés were so far respected that no violence was offered to women or children, though these, as well as numbers of the men, were made prisoners to be swept into slavery by the Tlascalans. These scenes of violence had lasted some hours, when Cortés, moved by the entreaties of some Cholulan chiefs, who had been reserved from the massacre, backed by the prayers of the Mexican envoys, consented, out of regard, as he said, to the latter, the representatives of Montezuma, to call off the soldiers, and put a stop, as well as he could, to further outrage. Two of the caciques were, also, permitted to go to their countrymen with assurances of pardon and protection to all who would return to their obedience.

These measures had their effect. By the joint efforts of Cortés and the caciques, the tumult was with much difficulty appeased. The assailants, Spaniards and Indians, gathered under their respective banners, and the Cholulans, relying on the assurance of their chiefs, gradually returned to their homes.

[THE SEIZURE OF MONTEZUMA]
From *The Conquest of Mexico*, Bk. IV, chap. iii

[Never too secure because of the great disparity in numbers, Cortés thought that by boldly seizing Montezuma, while parleying with him, he could paralyze the Aztecs.]

That night, Cortés was heard pacing his apartment to and fro, like a man oppressed by thought, or agitated by strong emotion. He may have been ripening in his mind the daring scheme for the morrow. In the morning the soldiers heard mass as usual, and father Olmedo invoked the blessing of

Heaven on their hazardous enterprise. Whatever might be the cause in which he was embarked, the heart of the Spaniard was cheered with the conviction that the Saints were on his side!

Having asked an audience from Montezuma, which was readily granted, the general made the necessary arrangements for his enterprise. The principal part of his force was drawn up in the courtyard, and he stationed a considerable detachment in the avenues leading to the palace, to check any attempt at rescue by the populace. He ordered twenty-five or thirty of the soldiers to drop in at the palace, as if by accident, in groups of three or four at a time, while the conference was going on with Montezuma. He selected five cavaliers, in whose courage and coolness he placed the most trust, to bear him company; Pedro de Alvarado, Gonzalo de Sandoval, Francisco de Lujo, Velasquez de Leon, and Alonso de Avila,—brilliant names in the annals of the Conquest. All were clad, as well as the common soldiers, in complete armor, a circumstance of too familiar occurrence to excite suspicion.

The little party were graciously received by the emperor, who soon, with the aid of the interpreters, became interested in a sportive conversation with the Spaniards, while he indulged his natural munificence by giving them presents of gold and jewels. He paid the Spanish general the particular compliment of offering him one of his daughters as his wife; an honor which the latter respectfully declined, on the ground that he was already accommodated with one in Cuba, and that his religion forbade a plurality.

When Cortés perceived that a sufficient number of his soldiers were assembled, he changed his playful manner, and with a serious tone briefly acquainted Montezuma with the treacherous proceedings in the *tierra caliente*, and the accusation of him as their author. The emperor listened to the charge with surprise; and disavowed the act, which he said could only have been imputed to him by his enemies. Cortés expressed his belief in his declaration, but added, that, to prove it true, it would be necessary to send for Quauhpopoca and his accomplices, that they might be examined and dealt with according to their deserts. To this Montezuma made no objection. Taking from his wrist, to which it was attached, a precious stone, the royal signet, on which was cut the figure of the War-god, he gave it to one of his nobles, with orders to show it to the Aztec governor, and require his instant presence in the capital, together with all those who had been accessory to the murder of the Spaniards. If he resisted, the officer was empowered to call in the aid of the neighboring towns, to enforce the mandate.

When the messenger had gone, Cortés assured the monarch that this prompt compliance with his request convinced him of his innocence. But it was important that his own sovereign should be equally convinced of it. Nothing would promote this so much as for Montezuma to transfer his residence to the palace occupied by the Spaniards, till on the arrival of Quauhpopoca the affair could be fully investigated. Such an act of condescension would, of itself, show a personal regard for the Spaniards, incompatible with the base conduct alleged against him, and would fully absolve him from all suspicion!

Montezuma listened to this proposal, and the flimsy reasoning with which it was covered, with looks of profound amazement. He became pale as death; but in a moment, his face flushed with resentment, as, with the pride of offended dignity, he exclaimed, "When was it ever heard that a great prince, like myself, voluntarily left his own palace to become a prisoner in the hands of strangers!"

Cortés assured him he would not go as a prisoner. He would experience nothing but respectful treatment from the Spaniards; would be surrounded by his own household, and hold intercourse with his people as usual. In short, it would be but a change of residence, from one of his palaces to another, a circumstance of frequent occurrence with him.—It was in vain. "If I should consent to such a degradation," he answered, "my subjects never would!" When further pressed, he offered to give up one of his sons and of his daughters to remain as hostages with the Spaniards, so that he might be spared this disgrace.

Two hours passed in this fruitless discussion, till a high-mettled cavalier, Velasquez de Leon, impatient of the long delay, and seeing that the attempt, if not the deed, must ruin them, cried out, "Why do we waste words on this barbarian? We have gone too far to recede now. Let us seize him, and, if he resists, plunge our swords into his body!" The fierce tone and menacing gestures, with which this was uttered, alarmed the monarch, who inquired of Marina what the angry Spaniard said. The interpreter explained it in as gentle a manner as she could, beseeching him "to accompany the white men to their quarters, where he would be treated with all respect and kindness, while to refuse them would but expose himself to violence, perhaps to death." Marina, doubtless, spoke to her sovereign as she thought, and no one had better opportunity of knowing the truth than herself.

This last appeal shook the resolution of Montezuma. It was in vain that the unhappy prince looked around for sympathy or support. As his eyes wandered over the stern visages and iron forms of the Spaniards, he felt that his hour was indeed come; and, with a voice scarcely audible from emotion, he consented to accompany the strangers,—to quit the palace, whither he was never more to return. Had he possessed the spirit of the first Montezuma, he would have called his guards around him, and left his lifeblood on the threshold, sooner than have been dragged a dishonored captive across it. But his courage sunk under circumstances. He felt he was the instrument of an irresistible Fate!

No sooner had the Spaniards got his consent, than orders were given for the royal litter. The nobles, who bore and attended it, could scarcely believe their senses, when they learned their master's purpose. But pride now came to Montezuma's aid, and, since he must go, he preferred that it should appear to be with his own free will. As the royal retinue, escorted by the Spaniards, marched through the street with downcast eyes and dejected mien, the people assembled in crowds, and a rumor ran among them, that the emperor was carried off by force to the quarters of the white men. A tumult would have soon arisen but for the intervention of Montezuma himself, who called out to the people to disperse, as he was visiting his friends of his own accord; thus sealing his ignominy by a declaration which deprived his subjects of the only excuse for resistance. On reaching the quarters, he sent out his nobles with similar assurances to the mob, and renewed orders to return to their homes.

He was received with ostentatious respect by the Spaniards, and selected the suite of apartments which best pleased him. They were soon furnished with fine cotton tapestries, featherwork, and all the elegancies of Indian upholstery. He was attended by such of his household as he chose, his wives and his pages, and was served with his usual pomp and luxury at his meals. He gave audience, as in his own palace, to his subjects, who were admitted to his presence, few, indeed, at a time, under the pretext of greater order and decorum. From the Spaniards themselves he met with a formal deference. No one, not even the general himself, approached him without doffing his casque, and rendering the obeisance due to his rank. Nor did they ever sit in his presence, without being invited by him to do so.

With all this studied ceremony and show of homage, there was one circumstance which too clearly proclaimed to his people that their sovereign was a prisoner. In the front of the palace a patrol of sixty men was established, and the same number in the rear. Twenty of each corps mounted guard at once, maintaining a careful watch, day and night. Another body, under command of Velasquez de Leon, was stationed in the royal antechamber. Cortés punished any departure from duty, or relaxation of vigilance, in these sentinels, with the utmost severity. He felt, as, indeed, every Spaniard must have felt, that the escape of the emperor now would be their ruin. Yet the task of this unintermitting watch sorely added to their fatigues. "Better this dog of a king should die," cried a soldier one day, "than that we should wear out our lives in this manner." The words were uttered in the hearing of Montezuma, who gathered something of their import, and the offender was severely chastised by order of the general. Such instances of disrespect, however, were very rare. Indeed, the amiable deportment of the monarch, who seemed to take pleasure in the society of his jailers, and who never allowed a favor or attention from the meanest soldier to go unrequited, inspired the Spaniards with as much attachment as they were capable of feeling—for a barbarian.

[THE STERN RESOLUTION OF PIZARRO]

From *The Conquest of Peru*, Bk. II, chap. iv

[Pizarro disobeyed the orders of his superior and, joined by a handful of followers, decided upon the conquest of Peru.]

But by the same vessel letters came to Pizarro from his two confederates, Luque and Almagro, beseeching him not to despair in his present extremity, but to hold fast to his original purpose. To return under the present circumstances would be to seal the fate of the expedition; and they solemnly engaged, if he would remain firm at his post, to furnish him in a short time with the necessary means for going forward.

A ray of hope was enough for the courageous spirit of Pizarro. It does not appear that he himself had entertained, at any time, thoughts of returning. If he had, these words of encouragement entirely banished them from his bosom, and he prepared to stand the fortune of the cast on which he had so desperately ventured. He knew, however, that solicitations or remonstrances would avail little with the companions of his enterprise; and he probably did not care to win over the more timid spirits who, by perpetually looking back, would only be a clog on his future movements. He announced his own purpose, however, in a laconic but decided manner, characteristic of a man more accustomed to act than to talk, and well calculated to make an impression on his rough followers.

Drawing his sword, he traced a line with it on the sand from east to west. Then turning towards the south, "Friends and comrades!" he said, "on that side are toil, hunger, nakedness, the drenching storm, desertion, and death; on this side, ease and pleasure. There lies Peru with its riches; here, Panamá and its poverty. Choose, each man, what best becomes a brave Castilian. For my part, I go to the south." So saying, he stepped across the line. He was followed by the brave pilot Ruiz; next by Pedro de Candia, a cavalier, born, as his name imports, in one of the isles of Greece. Eleven others successively crossed the line, thus intimating their willingness to abide the fortunes of their leader, for good or for evil. Fame, to quote the enthusiastic language of an ancient chronicler, has commemorated the names of this little band, "who thus, in the face of difficulties unexampled in history, with death rather than riches for their reward, preferred it all to abandoning their honor, and stood firm by their leader as an example of loyalty to future ages."

But the act excited no such admiration in the mind of Tafur, who looked on it as one of gross disobedience to the commands of the governor, and as little better than madness, involving the certain destruction of the parties engaged in it. He refused to give any sanction to it himself by leaving one of his vessels with the adventurers to prosecute their voyage, and it was with great difficulty that he could be persuaded even to allow them a part of the stores which he had brought for their support. This had no influence on their determination, and the little party, bidding adieu to their returning comrades, remained unshaken in their purpose of abiding the fortunes of their commander.

There is something striking to the imagination in the spectacle of these few brave spirits, thus consecrating themselves to a daring enterprise, which seemed as far above their strength as any recorded in the fabulous annals of knight-errantry. A handful of men, without food, without clothing, almost without arms, without knowledge of the land to which they were bound, without vessel to transport them, were here left on a lonely rock in the ocean with the avowed purpose of carrying on a crusade against a powerful empire, staking their lives on its success. What is there in the legends of chivalry that surpasses it? This was the crisis of Pizarro's fate. There are moments in the lives of men, which, as they are seized or neglected, decide their future destiny. Had Pizarro faltered from his strong purpose, and yielded to the occasion, now so temptingly presented, for extricating himself and his broken band from their desperate position, his name would have been buried with his fortunes, and the conquest of Peru would have been left for other and more successful adventurers. But his constancy was equal to the occasion, and his conduct here proved him competent to the perilous post he had assumed, and inspired others with a confidence in him which was the best assurance of success.

[THE INCA'S RANSOM]
From *The Conquest of Peru*, Bk. III, chap. v

[The capture of the Inca was followed by the famous parley for his freedom, and by his promise to give, as a ransom, a fabulous treasure of gold and silver.]

It was not long before Atahuallpa discovered, amidst all the show of religious zeal in his Conquerors, a lurking appetite more potent in most of their bosoms than either religion or ambition. This was the love of gold. He determined to avail himself of it to procure his own freedom. The critical posture of his affairs made it important that this should not be long delayed. His brother, Huascar, ever since his defeat, had been detained as a prisoner, subject to the victor's orders. He was now at Andamarca, at no great distance from Caxamalca; and Atahuallpa feared, with good reason, that, when his own imprisonment was known, Huascar would find it easy to corrupt his guards, make his escape, and put himself at the head of the contested empire, without a rival to dispute it.

In the hope, therefore, to effect his purpose by appealing

to the avarice of his keepers, he one day told Pizarro, that, if he would set him free, he would engage to cover the floor of the apartment on which they stood with gold. Those present listened with an incredulous smile; and, as the Inca received no answer, he said, with some emphasis, that "he would not merely cover the floor, but would fill the room with gold as high as he could reach"; and, standing on tiptoe, he stretched out his hand against the wall. All stared with amazement; while they regarded it as the insane boast of a man too eager to procure his liberty to weigh the meaning of his words. Yet Pizarro was sorely perplexed. As he had advanced into the country, much that he had seen, and all that he had heard, had confirmed the dazzling reports first received of the riches of Peru. Atahuallpa himself had given him the most glowing picture of the wealth of the capital, where the roofs of the temples were plated with gold, while the walls were hung with tapestry and the floors inlaid with tiles of the same precious metal. There must be some foundation for all this. At all events, it was safe to accede to the Inca's proposition; since, by so doing, he could collect, at once, all the gold at his disposal, and thus prevent its being purloined or secreted by the natives. He therefore acquiesced in Atahuallpa's offer, and, drawing a red line along the wall at the height which the Inca had indicated, he caused the terms of the proposal to be duly recorded by the notary. The apartment was about seventeen feet broad, by twenty-two feet long, and the line round the walls was nine feet from the floor. This space was to be filled with gold; but it was understood that the gold was not to be melted down into ingots, but to retain the original form of the articles into which it was manufactured, that the Inca might have the benefit of the space which they occupied. He further agreed to fill an adjoining room of smaller dimensions twice full with silver, in like manner; and he demanded two months to accomplish all this.

[THE DIVISION OF THE INCA'S RANSOM]

From *The Conquest of Peru*, Bk. III, chap. vii

[The impatience of the soldiers, as well as other considerations, caused an early division of the spoil. The difficulties involved in this division and the ways in which they were solved are now set forth.]

The arrival of Almagro produced a considerable change in Pizarro's prospects, since it enabled him to resume active operations, and push forward his conquests in the interior. The only obstacle in his way was the Inca's ransom, and the Spaniards had patiently waited, till the return of the emissaries from Cuzco swelled the treasure to a large amount, though still below the stipulated limit. But now their avarice got the better of their forbearance, and they called loudly for the immediate division of the gold. To wait longer would only be to invite the assault of their enemies, allured by a bait so attractive. While the treasure remained uncounted, no man knew its value, nor what was to be his own portion. It was better to distribute it at once, and let every one possess and defend his own. Several, moreover, were now disposed to return home, and take their share of the gold with them, where they could place it in safety. But these were few, while much the larger part were only anxious to leave their present quarters, and march at once to Cuzco. More gold, they thought, awaited them in that capital, than they could get here by prolonging their stay; while every hour was precious, to prevent the inhabitants from secreting their treasures, of which design they had already given indication.

Pizarro was especially moved by the last consideration; and he felt, that, without the capital, he could not hope to become master of the empire. Without further delay, the division of the treasure was agreed upon.

Yet, before making this, it was necessary to reduce the whole to ingots of a uniform standard, for the spoil was composed of an infinite variety of articles, in which the gold was of very different degrees of purity. These articles consisted of goblets, ewers, salvers, vases of every shape and size, ornaments and utensils for the temples and the royal palaces, tiles and plates for the decoration of the public edifices, curious imitations of different plants and animals. Among the plants, the most beautiful was the Indian corn, in which the golden ear was sheathed in its broad leaves of silver, from which hung a rich tassel of threads of the same precious metal. A fountain was also much admired, which sent up a sparkling jet of gold, while birds and animals of the same material played in the waters at its base. The delicacy of the workmanship of some of these, and the beauty and ingenuity of the design, attracted the admiration of better judges than the rude Conquerors of Peru.

Before breaking up these specimens of Indian art, it was determined to send a quantity, which should be deducted from the royal fifth, to the Emperor. It would serve as a sample of the ingenuity of the natives, and would show him the value of his conquests. A number of the most beautiful articles was selected, to the amount of a hundred thousand ducats, and Hernando Pizarro was appointed to be the bearer of them to Spain. He was to obtain an audience of Charles, and, at the same time that he laid the treasures before him, he was to give an account of the proceedings of the Conquerors, and to seek a further augmentation of their powers and dignities.

No man in the army was better qualified for this mission, by his address and knowledge of affairs, than Hernando Pizarro; no one would be so likely to urge his suit with effect at the haughty Castilian court. But other reasons influenced the selection of him at the present juncture.

His former jealousy of Almagro still rankled in his bosom, and he had beheld that chief's arrival at the camp with feelings of disgust, which he did not care to conceal. He looked on him as coming to share the spoils of victory, and defraud his brother of his legitimate honors. Instead of exchanging the cordial greeting proffered by Almagro at their first interview, the arrogant cavalier held back in sullen silence. His brother Francis was greatly displeased at a conduct which threatened to renew their ancient feud, and he induced Hernando to accompany him to Almagro's quarters, and make some acknowledgment for his uncourteous behavior. But, notwithstanding this show of reconciliation, the general thought the present a favorable opportunity to remove his brother from the scene of operations, where his factious spirit more than counterbalanced his eminent services.

The business of melting down the plate was intrusted to the Indian goldsmiths, who were thus required to undo the work of their own hands. They toiled day and night, but such was the quantity to be recast, that it consumed a full month. When the whole was reduced to bars of a uniform standard, they were nicely weighed, under the superintendence of the royal inspectors. The total amount of the gold was found to be one million, three hundred and twenty-six thousand, five hundred and thirty-nine *pesos de oro*, which, allowing for the greater value of money in the sixteenth century, would be equivalent, probably, at the present time, to near *three millions and a half of pounds sterling*, or somewhat less than *fifteen millions and a half of dollars*. The quantity of silver was estimated at fifty-one thousand six hundred and ten marks. History affords no parallel of such a booty—and that, too, in the most convertible form, in ready money, as it were—having fallen to the lot of a little band of military adventurers, like the Conquerors of Peru. The great object of the Spanish expeditions in the New World was gold. It is remarkable that their success should have been so complete. Had they taken the track of the English, the French, or the Dutch, on the shores of the northern continent, how different would have been the result! It is equally worthy of remark, that the wealth thus suddenly acquired, by diverting them from the slow but surer and more permanent sources of national prosperity, has in the end glided from their grasp, and left them among the poorest of the nations of Christendom.

A new difficulty now arose in respect to the division of the treasure. Almagro's followers claimed to be admitted to a share of it; which, as they equalled, and indeed, somewhat exceeded in number Pizarro's company, would reduce the gains of these last very materially. "We were not here, it is true," said Almagro's soldiers to their comrades, "at the seizure of the Inca, but we have taken our turn in mounting guard over him since his capture, have helped you to defend your treasures, and now give you the means of going forward and securing your conquests. It is a common cause," they urged, "in which all are equally embarked, and the gains should be shared equally between us."

But this way of viewing the matter was not at all palatable to Pizarro's company, who alleged that Atahuallpa's contract had been made exclusively with them; that they had seized the Inca, had secured the ransom, had incurred, in short, all the risk of the enterprise, and were not now disposed to share the fruits of it with every one who came after them.—There was much force, it could not be denied, in this reasoning, and it was finally settled between the leaders, that Almagro's followers should resign their pretensions for a stipulated sum of no great amount, and look to the career now opened to them for carving out their fortunes for themselves.

This delicate affair being thus harmoniously adjusted, Pizarro prepared, with all solemnity, for a division of the imperial spoil. The troops were called together in the great square, and the Spanish commander, "with the fear of God before his eyes," says the record, "invoked the assistance of Heaven to do the work before him conscientiously and justly." The appeal may seem somewhat out of place at the distribution of spoil so unrighteously acquired; yet, in truth, considering the magnitude of the treasure, and the power assumed by Pizarro to distribute it according to the respective deserts of the individuals, there were few acts of his life involving a heavier responsibility. On his present decision might be said to hang the future fortunes of each one of his followers,—poverty or independence during the remainder of his days.

The royal fifth was first deducted, including the remittance already sent to Spain. The share appropriated by Pizarro amounted to fifty-seven thousand two hundred and twenty-two pesos of gold, and two thousand three hundred and fifty marks of silver. He had besides this the great chair or throne of the Inca, of solid gold, and valued at twenty-five thousand *pesos de oro*. To his brother Hernando were paid thirty-one thousand and eighty pesos of gold, and two thousand three hundred and fifty marks of silver. De Soto received seventeen thousand seven hundred and forty pesos of gold, and seven hundred and twenty-four marks of silver. Most of the remaining cavalry, sixty in number, received each eight thousand eight hundred and eighty pesos of gold, and three hundred and sixty-two marks of silver, though some had more, and a few considerably less. The infantry mustered in all one hundred and five men. Almost one fifth of them were allowed, each, four thousand four hundred and forty pesos of gold, and one hundred and eighty marks of silver, half of the compensation of the troopers. The remainder received one fourth part less; though here again there were exceptions, and some were obliged to content themselves with a much smaller share of the spoil.

The new church of San Francisco, the first Christian temple in Peru, was endowed with two thousand two hundred and twenty pesos of gold. The amount assigned to Almagro's company was not excessive, if it was not more than twenty thousand pesos; and that reserved for the colonists of San Miguel, which amounted only to fifteen thousand pesos, was unaccountably small. There were among them certain soldiers, who at an early period of the expedition, as the reader may remember, abandoned the march, and returned to San Miguel. These, certainly, had little claim to be remembered in the division of booty. But the greater part of the colony consisted of invalids, men whose health had been broken by their previous hardships, but who still, with a stout and willing heart, did good service in their military post on the seacoast. On what grounds they had forfeited their claims to a more ample remuneration, it is not easy to explain.

[THE TERRIBLE MARCH OF ALVARADO]

From *The Conquest of Peru*, Bk. III, chap. ix

[Pizarro was challenged by several rivals, among them Alvarado, who sought to invade Pizarro's territory. Alvarado's experiences in the mountains illustrate the almost incredible difficulties faced by the adventurers.]

Some time before this occurrence, the Spanish governor, while in Cuzco, received tidings of an event much more alarming to him than any Indian hostilities. This was the arrival on the coast of a strong Spanish force, under command of Don Pedro de Alvarado, the gallant officer who had served under Cortés with such renown in the war of Mexico. That cavalier, after forming a brilliant alliance in Spain, to which he was entitled by his birth and military rank, had returned to his government of Guatemala, where his avarice had been roused by the magnificent reports he daily received of Pizarro's conquests. These conquests, he learned, had been confined to Peru; while the northern kingdom of Quito, the ancient residence of Atahuallpa, and, no doubt, the principal depository of his treasures, yet remained untouched. Affecting to consider this country as falling without the governor's jurisdiction, he immediately turned a large fleet, which he had intended for the Spice Islands, in the direction of South America; and in March, 1534, he landed in the bay of Caraques, with five hundred followers, of whom half were mounted, and all admirably provided with arms and ammunition. It was the best equipped and the most formidable array that had yet appeared in the southern seas.

Although manifestly an invasion of the territory conceded to Pizarro by the Crown, the reckless cavalier determined to march at once on Quito. With the assistance of an Indian guide, he proposed to take the direct route across the mountains, a passage of exceeding difficulty, even at the most favorable season.

After crossing the Rio Dable, Alvarado's guide deserted him, so that he was soon entangled in the intricate mazes of the sierra; and, as he rose higher and higher into the regions of winter, he became surrounded with ice and snow, for which his men, taken from the warm countries of Guatemala, were but ill prepared. As the cold grew more intense, many of them were so benumbed, that it was with difficulty they could proceed. The infantry, compelled to make exertions, fared best. Many of the troopers were frozen stiff in their saddles. The Indians, still more sensible to the cold, perished by hundreds. As the Spaniards huddled round their wretched bivouacs, with such scanty fuel as they could glean, and almost without food, they waited in gloomy silence the approach of morning. Yet the morning light, which gleamed coldly on the cheerless waste, brought no joy to them. It only revealed more clearly the extent of their wretchedness. Still struggling on through the winding Puertos Nevados, or Snowy Passes, their track was dismally marked by fragments of dress, broken harness, golden ornaments, and other valuables plundered on their march,— by the dead bodies of men, or by those less fortunate, who were left to die alone in the wilderness. As for the horses, their carcasses were not suffered long to cumber the ground, as they were quickly seized and devoured half raw by the starving soldiers, who, like the famished condors, now hovering in troops above their heads, greedily banqueted on the most offensive offal to satisfy the gnawings of hunger.

Alvarado, anxious to secure the booty which had fallen into his hands at an earlier part of his march, encouraged every man to take what gold he wanted from the common heap, reserving only the royal fifth. But they only answered, with a ghastly smile of derision, "that food was the only gold for them." Yet in this extremity, which might seem to have dissolved the very ties of nature, there are some affecting instances recorded of self-devotion; of comrades who lost their lives in assisting others, and of parents and husbands (for some of the cavaliers were accompanied by their wives) who, instead of seeking their own safety, chose to remain and perish in the snows with the objects of their love.

To add to their distress, the air was filled for several days with thick clouds of earthy particles and cinders, which blinded the men, and made respiration exceedingly difficult. This phenomenon, it seems probable, was caused by an eruption of the distant Cotopaxi, which, about twelve leagues southeast of Quito, rears up its colossal and perfectly symmetrical cone far above the limits of eternal snow,—the most beautiful and the most terrible of the American volcanoes. At the time of Alvarado's expedition, it was in a state of eruption, the earliest instance of the kind on record, though doubtless not the earliest. Since that period, it has been in frequent commotion, sending up its sheets of flame to the height of half a mile, spouting forth cataracts of lava that have overwhelmed towns and villages in their career, and shaking the earth with subterraneous thunders, that, at the distance of more than a hundred leagues, sounded like the reports of artillery! Alvarado's followers, unacquainted with the cause of the phenomenon, as they wandered over tracts buried in snow,—the sight of which was strange to them,—in an atmosphere laden with ashes, became bewildered by this confusion of the elements, which Nature seemed to have contrived purposely for their destruction. Some of these men were the soldiers of Cortés, steeled by many a painful march, and many a sharp encounter with the Aztecs. But this war of the elements, they now confessed, was mightier than all.

At length, Alvarado, after sufferings, which even the most hardy, probably, could have endured but a few days longer, emerged from the Snowy Pass, and came on the elevated tableland, which spreads out, at the height of more than nine thousand feet above the ocean, in the neighborhood of Riobamba. But one fourth of his gallant army had been left to feed the condor in the wilderness, besides the greater part, at least two thousand, of his Indian auxiliaries. A great number of his horses, too, had perished; and the men and horses that escaped were all of them more or less injured by the cold and the extremity of suffering.—Such was the terrible passage of the Puertos Nevados, which I have only briefly noticed as an episode to the Peruvian conquest, but the account of which, in all its details, though it occupied but a few weeks in duration, would give one a better idea of the difficulties encountered by the Spanish cavaliers, than volumes of ordinary narrative.

[AN AUTO DE FÉ]

From *Philip the Second*, Bk. II, chap. iii

[Part of a narrative of the Inquisition in Spain, detailing one of the most terrible features of that institution.]

At length, the preliminary information having been obtained, the proscribed having been marked out, the plan of attack settled, an order was given for the simultaneous arrest of all persons suspected of heresy, throughout the kingdom. It fell like a thunderbolt on the unhappy victims, who had gone on with their secret associations, little suspecting the ruin that hung over them. No resistance was attempted. Men and women, churchmen and laymen, persons of all ranks and professions, were hurried from their homes and lodged in the secret chambers of the Inquisition. Yet these could not furnish accommodations for the number, and many were removed to the ordinary prisons, and even to convents and private dwellings. In Seville alone eight hundred were arrested on the first day. Fears were entertained of an attempt at rescue, and an additional guard was stationed over the places of confinement. The inquisitors were in the condition of a fisherman whose cast has been so successful that the draught of fishes seems likely to prove too heavy for his net.

The arrest of one party gradually led to the detection of others. Dragged from his solitary dungeon before the secret tribunal of the Inquisition, alone, without counsel to aid or one friendly face to cheer him, without knowing the name of his accuser, without being allowed to confront the witnesses who were there to swear away his life, without even a sight of his own process, except such garbled extracts as the wily judges thought fit to communicate, is it strange that the unhappy victim, in his perplexity and distress, should have been drawn into disclosures fatal to his associates and himself? If these disclosures were not to the mind of his judges, they had only to try the efficacy of the torture,—the rack, the cord, and the pulley,—until, when every joint had been wrenched from its socket, the barbarous tribunal was compelled to suspend, not terminate, the application, from the inability of the sufferer to endure it. Such were the dismal scenes enacted in the name of religion, and by the ministers of religion, as well as of the Inquisition,—scenes to which few of those who had once witnessed them, and escaped with life, dared ever to allude. For to reveal the secrets of the Inquisition was death.

At the expiration of eighteen months from the period of the first arrests, many of the trials had been concluded, the doom of the prisoners was sealed, and it was thought time that the prisons should disgorge their superfluous inmates. Valladolid was selected as the theater of the first *auto de fé*, both from the importance of the capital and the presence of the court, which would thus sanction and give greater dignity to the celebration. This event took place in May, 1559. The Regent Joanna, the young prince of Asturias, Don Carlos, and the principal grandees of the court, were there to witness the spectacle. By rendering the heir of the crown thus early familiar with the tender mercies of the Holy Office, it may have been intended to conciliate his favor to that institution. If such was the object, according to the report it signally failed, since the woeful spectacle left no other impressions on the mind of the prince than those of indignation and disgust.

The example of Valladolid was soon followed by *autos de fé* in Granada, Toledo, Seville, Barcelona,—in short, in the twelve capitals in which tribunals of the Holy Office were established. A second celebration at Valladolid was reserved for the eighth of October in the same year, when it would be graced by the presence of the sovereign himself. Indeed, as several of the processes had been concluded some months before this period, there is reason to believe that the sacrifice of more than one of the victims had been postponed in order to give greater effect to the spectacle.

The *auto de fé*—"act of faith"—was the most imposing, as it was the most awful, of the solemnities authorized by the Roman Catholic Church. It was intended, somewhat profanely, as has been intimated, to combine the pomp of the Roman triumph with the terrors of the day of judgment. It may remind one quite as much of those bloody festivals prepared for the entertainment of the Cæsars in the Coliseum. The religious import of the *auto de fé* was intimated by the circumstance of its being celebrated on a Sunday, or some other holiday of the Church. An indulgence for forty days was granted by his holiness to all who should be present at the spectacle; as if the appetite for witnessing the scenes of human suffering required to be stimulated by a bounty,—that, too, in Spain, where the amusements were, and still are, of the most sanguinary character.

The scene for this second *auto de fé* at Valladolid was the great square in front of the church of St. Francis. At one end a platform was raised, covered with rich carpeting, on which were ranged the seats of the inquisitors, emblazoned with the arms of the Holy Office. Near to this was the royal gallery, a private entrance to which secured the inmates from molestation by the crowd. Opposite to this gallery a large scaffold was erected, so as to be visible from all parts of the arena, and was appropriated to the unhappy martyrs who were to suffer in the *auto*.

At six in the morning all the bells in the capital began to toll, and a solemn procession was seen to move from the dismal fortress of the Inquisition. In the van marched a body of troops, to secure a free passage for the procession. Then came the condemned, each attended by two familiars of the Holy Office, and those who were to suffer at the stake by two friars, in addition, exhorting the heretic to abjure his errors. Those admitted to penitence wore a sable dress; while the unfortunate martyr was enveloped in a loose sack of yellow cloth, —the *san benito*,—with his head surmounted by a cap of pasteboard of a conical form, which, together with the cloak, was embroidered with figures of flames and of devils fanning and feeding them; all emblematical of the destiny of the heretic's soul in the world to come, as well as of his body in the present. Then came the magistrates of the city, the judges of the courts, the ecclesiastical orders, and the nobles of the land, on horseback. These were followed by the members of the dread tribunal, and the fiscal, bearing a standard of crimson damask, on one side of which were displayed the arms of the Inquisition, and on the other the insignia of its founders, Sixtus the Fifth and Ferdinand the Catholic. Next came a numerous train of familiars, well mounted, among whom were many of the gentry of the province, proud to act as the bodyguard of the Holy Office. The rear was brought up by an immense concourse of the common people, stimulated on the present occasion, no doubt, by the loyal desire to see their new sovereign, as well as by the ambition to share in the triumphs of the *auto de fé*. The number thus drawn together from the capital and the country, far exceeding what was usual on such occasions, is estimated by one present at full two hundred thousand.

As the multitude defiled into the square, the inquisitors took their place on the seats prepared for their reception. The condemned were conducted to the scaffold, and the royal station was occupied by Philip, with the different members of his household. At his side sat his sister, the late regent, his son, Don Carlos, his nephew, Alexander Farnese, several foreign ambassadors, and the principal grandees and higher ecclesiastics in attendance on the court. It was an august assembly of the greatest and the proudest in the land. But the most indifferent spectator, who had a spark of humanity in his bosom, might have turned with feelings of admiration from this array of worldly power, to the poor martyr, who, with no support but what he drew from within, was prepared to defy this power and to lay down his life in vindication of the rights of conscience. Some there may have been, in that large concourse, who shared in these sentiments. But their number was small indeed in comparison with those who looked on the wretched victim as the enemy of God, and his approaching sacrifice as the most glorious triumph of the Cross.

The ceremonies began with a sermon, "the sermon of the faith," by the bishop of Zamora. The subject of it may well be guessed, from the occasion. It was no doubt plentifully larded with texts of Scripture, and, unless the preacher departed from the fashion of the time, with passages from the heathen writers, however much out of place they may seem in an orthodox discourse.

When the bishop had concluded, the grand inquisitor administered an oath to the assembled multitude, who on their knees solemnly swore to defend the Inquisition, to maintain the purity of the faith, and to inform against anyone who should swerve from it. As Philip repeated an oath of similar import, he suited the action to the word, and, rising from his seat, drew his sword from its scabbard, as if to announce himself the determined champion of the Holy Office. In the earlier *autos* of the Moorish and Jewish infidels, so humiliating an oath had never been exacted from the sovereign.

After this, the secretary of the tribunal read aloud an instrument reciting the grounds for the conviction of the prisoners, and the respective sentences pronounced against them. Those who were to be admitted to penitence, each, as his sentence was proclaimed, knelt down, and, with his hands on the missal, solemnly abjured his errors, and was absolved by the grand inquisitor. The absolution, however, was not so entire as to relieve the offender from the penalty of his transgressions in this world. Some were doomed to perpetual imprisonment in the cells of the Inquisition, others to lighter penances. All were doomed to the confiscation of their property,—a point of too great moment to the welfare of the tribunal ever to be omitted. Besides this, in many cases the offender, and, by a glaring perversion of justice, his immediate descendants, were rendered forever ineligible to public office of any kind, and their names branded with perpetual infamy. Thus blighted in fortune and in character, they were said, in the soft language of the Inquisition, to be *reconciled*.

As these unfortunate persons were remanded, under a strong guard, to their prisons, all eyes were turned on the little company of martyrs, who, clothed in the ignominious garb of the *san benito*, stood awaiting the sentence of their judges, with cords round their necks, and in their hands a cross, or sometimes an inverted torch, typical of their own speedy dissolution. The interest of the spectators was still further excited, in the present instance, by the fact that several of these victims were not only illustrious for their rank, but yet more so for their talents and virtues. In their haggard looks, their emaciated forms, and too often, alas! their distorted limbs, it was easy to read the story of their sufferings in their long imprisonment, for some of them had been confined in the dark cells of the Inquisition much more than a year. Yet their countenances, though haggard, far from showing any sign of weakness or fear, were lighted up with the glow of holy enthusiasm, as of men prepared to seal their testimony with their blood.

[THE EXECUTION OF EGMONT AND HOORNE]

From *Philip the Second*, Bk. III, chap. v

[Part of the section on Philip's conquest of the Netherlands. Egmont and Hoorne were nobles who, though good Catholics, opposed the Inquisition and Philip's attempts to make the Netherlands a Spanish dependency. They were condemned by Alva's "Council of Blood."]

On the afternoon of the fourth, the duke of Alva had sent for Martin Rithovius, bishop of Ypres; and, communicating to him the sentence of the nobles, he requested the prelate to visit the prisoners, acquaint them with their fate, and prepare them for their execution on the following day. The bishop, an excellent man, and the personal friend of Egmont, was astounded by the tidings. He threw himself at Alva's feet, imploring mercy for the prisoners, and, if he could not spare their lives, beseeching him at least to grant them more time for preparation. But Alva sternly rebuked the prelate, saying that he had been summoned, not to thwart the execution of the law, but to console the prisoners and enable them to die like Christians. The bishop, finding his entreaties useless, rose and addressed himself to his melancholy mission.

It was near midnight when he entered Egmont's apartment, where he found the poor nobleman, whose strength had been already reduced by confinement, and who was wearied by the fatigue of the journey, buried in slumber. It is said that the two lords, when summoned to Brussels, had indulged the vain hope that it was to inform them of the conclusion of their trial and their acquittal! However this may be, Egmont seems to have been but ill prepared for the dreadful tidings he received. He turned deadly pale as he listened to the bishop, and exclaimed, with deep emotion, "It is a terrible sentence. Little did I imagine that any offense I had committed against God or the king could merit such a punishment. It is not death that I fear. Death is the common lot of all. But I shrink from dishonor. Yet I may hope that my sufferings will so far expiate my offenses that my innocent family will not be involved in my ruin by the confiscation of my property. Thus much, at least, I think I may claim in consideration of my past services." Then, after a pause, he added, "Since my death is the will of God and his majesty, I will try to meet it with patience." He asked the bishop if there were no hope. On being answered, "None whatever," he resolved to devote himself at once to preparing for the solemn change.

He rose from his couch, and hastily dressed himself. He then made his confession to the prelate, and desired that mass might be said, and the sacrament administered to him. This was done with great solemnity, and Egmont received the communion in the most devout manner, manifesting the greatest contrition for his sins. He next inquired of the bishop to what prayer he could best have recourse to sustain him in this trying hour. The prelate recommended to him that prayer which our Saviour had commended to his disciples. The advice pleased the count, who earnestly engaged in his devotions. But a host of tender recollections crowded on his mind, and the images of his wife and children drew his thoughts in another direction, till the kind expostulations of the prelate again restored him to himself.

Egmont asked whether it would be well to say anything on the scaffold for the edification of the people. But the bishop discouraged him, saying that he would be imperfectly heard, and that the people, in their present excitement, would be apt to misinterpret what he said to their own prejudice.

Having attended to his spiritual concerns, Egmont called for writing materials, and wrote a letter to his wife, whom he had not seen during his long confinement; and to her he now bade a tender farewell. He then addressed another letter, written in French, in a few brief and touching sentences, to the king,— which fortunately has been preserved to us. "This morning," he says, "I have been made acquainted with the sentence which it has pleased your majesty to pass upon me. And although it has never been my intent to do aught against the person or the the service of your majesty, or against our true, ancient, and Catholic faith, yet I receive in patience what it has pleased God to send me. If during these troubles I have counseled or permitted aught which might seem otherwise, I have done so from a sincere regard for the service of God and your majesty, and from what I believed the necessity of the times. Wherefore I pray your majesty to pardon it, and for the sake of my past services to take pity on my poor wife, my children, and my servants. In this trust, I commend myself to the mercy of God." The letter is dated Brussels, "on the point of death," June 5th, 1568.

Having time still left, the count made a fair copy of the two letters, and gave them to the bishop, entreating him to deliver them according to their destination. He accompanied that to Philip with a ring, to be given at the same time to the monarch. It was of great value, and, as it had been the gift of Philip himself during the count's late visit to Madrid, it might soften the heart of the king by reminding him of happier days, when he had looked with an eye of favor on his unhappy vassal.

Having completed all his arrangements, Egmont became impatient for the hour of his departure; and he expressed the hope that there would be no unnecessary delay. At ten in the morning the soldiers appeared who were to conduct him to the scaffold. They brought with them cords, as usual, to bind the prisoner's hands. But Egmont remonstrated, and showed that he had, himself, cut off the collar of his doublet and shirt, in order to facilitate the stroke of the executioner. This he did to convince them that he meditated no resistance; and on his promising that he would attempt none, they consented to his remaining with his hands unbound.

Egmont was dressed in a crimson damask robe, over which was a Spanish mantle fringed with gold. His breeches were of black silk, and his hat, of the same material, was garnished with white and sable plumes. In his hand, which, as we have seen, remained free, he held a white handkerchief. On his way to the place of execution he was accompanied by Julian de Romero, *maître de camp*, by the captain, Salinas, who had charge of the fortress of Ghent, and by the bishop of Ypres. As the procession moved slowly forward, the count repeated some portion of the fifty-first Psalm,—"Have mercy on me, O God!"—in which the good prelate joined with him. In the center of the square, on the spot where so much of the best blood of the Netherlands has been shed, stood the scaffold, covered with black cloth. On it were two velvet cushions with a small table, shrouded likewise in black, and supporting a silver crucifix. At the corners of the platform were two poles, pointed at the end with steel, intimating the purpose for which they were intended.

In front of the scaffold was the provost of the court, mounted on horseback, and bearing the red wand of office in his hand. The executioner remained, as usual, below the platform, screened from view, that he might not, by his presence before it was necessary, outrage the feelings of the prisoners. The troops, who had been under arms all night, were drawn up around in order of battle; and strong bodies of arquebusiers were posted in the great avenues which led to the square. The space left open by the soldiery was speedily occupied by a crowd of eager spectators. Others thronged the roofs and windows of the buildings that surrounded the market-place, some of which, still standing at the present day, show, by their quaint and venerable architecture, that they must have looked down on the tragic scene we are now depicting.

It was indeed a gloomy day for Brussels,—so long the residence of the two nobles, where their forms were as familiar and where they were held in as much love and honor as in any of their own provinces. All business was suspended. The shops were closed. The bells tolled in all the churches. An air of gloom, as of some impending calamity, settled on the city. "It seemed," says one residing there at the time, "as if the day of judgment were at hand!"

As the procession slowly passed through the ranks of the soldiers, Egmont saluted the officers—some of them his ancient companions—with such a sweet and dignified composure in his manner as was long remembered by those who saw it. And few even of the Spaniards could refrain from tears as they took their last look at the gallant noble who was to perish by so miserable an end.

With a steady step he mounted the scaffold, and, as he crossed it, gave utterance to the vain wish that, instead of meeting such a fate, he had been allowed to die in the service of his king and country. He quickly, however, turned to other thoughts, and, kneeling on one of the cushions, with the bishop beside him on the other, he was soon engaged earnestly in prayer. With his eyes raised towards heaven with a look of unutterable sadness, he prayed so fervently and loud as to be distinctly heard by the spectators. The prelate, much affected, put into his hands the silver crucifix, which Egmont repeatedly kissed; after which, having received absolution for the last time, he rose and made a sign to the bishop to retire. He then stripped off his mantle and robe; and, again kneeling, he drew a silk cap, which he had brought for the purpose, over his eyes, and, re-peating the words, "Into thy hands, O Lord, I commend my spirit," he calmly awaited the stroke of the executioner.

The low sounds of lamentation which from time to time

had been heard among the populace were now hushed into silence, as the minister of justice, appearing on the platform, approached his victim and with a single blow of the sword severed the head from the body. A cry of horror rose from the multitude, and some, frantic with grief, broke through the ranks of the soldiers and wildly dipped their handkerchiefs in the blood that streamed from the scaffold, treasuring them up, says the chronicler, as precious memorials of love and incitements to vengeance. The head was then set on one of the poles at the end of the platform, while a mantle thrown over the mutilated trunk hid it from the public gaze.

It was near noon when orders were sent to lead forth the remaining prisoner to execution. It had been assigned to the curate of La Chapelle to acquaint Count Hoorne with his fate. That nobleman received the awful tidings with less patience than was shown by his friend. He gave way to a burst of indignation at the cruelty and injustice of the sentence. It was a poor requital, he said, for eight-and-twenty years of faithful service to his sovereign. Yet, he added, he was not sorry to be released from a life of such incessant fatigue. For some time he refused to confess, saying he had done enough in the way of confession. When urged not to throw away the few precious moments that were left to him, he at length consented.

The count was dressed in a plain suit of black, and wore a Milanese cap upon his head. He was, at this time, about fifty years of age. He was tall, with handsome features, and altogether of a commanding presence. His form was erect, and as he passed with a steady step through the files of soldiers, on his way to the place of execution, he frankly saluted those of his acquaintance whom he saw among the spectators. His look had in it less of sorrow than of indignation, like that of one conscious of enduring wrong. He was spared one pang, in his last hour, which had filled Egmont's cup with bitterness: though, like him, he had a wife, he was to leave no orphan family to mourn him.

As he trod the scaffold, the apparatus of death seemed to have no power to move him. He still repeated the declaration that, "often as he had offended his Maker, he had never, to his knowledge, committed any offense against the king." When his eyes fell on the bloody shroud that enveloped the remains of Egmont, he inquired if it were the body of his friend. Being answered in the affirmative, he made some remark in Castilian, not understood. He then prayed for a few moments, but in so low a tone that the words were not caught by the bystanders, and, rising, he asked pardon of those around if he had ever offended any of them, and earnestly besought their prayers. Then, without further delay, he knelt down, and, repeating the words, "*In manus tuas, Domine*," he submitted himself to his fate.

His bloody head was set up opposite to that of his fellow-sufferer. For three hours these ghastly trophies remained exposed to the gaze of the multitude. They were then taken down, and, with the bodies, placed in leaden coffins, which were straightway removed,—that containing the remains of Egmont to the convent of Santa Clara, and that of Hoorne to the ancient church of Ste. Gudule. To these places, especially to Santa Clara, the people now flocked, as to the shrine of a martyr. They threw themselves on the coffin, kissing it and bedewing it with their tears, as if it had contained the relics of some murdered saint; while many of them, taking little heed of the presence of informers, breathed vows of vengeance, some even swearing not to trim either hair or beard till these vows were executed. The government seems to have thought it prudent to take no notice of this burst of popular feeling. But a funeral hatchment, blazoned with the arms of Egmont, which, as usual after the master's death, had been fixed by his domestics on the gates of his mansion, was ordered to be instantly removed,— no doubt, as tending to keep alive the popular excitement. The bodies were not allowed to remain long in their temporary places of deposit, but were transported to the family residences of the two lords in the country, and laid in the vaults of their ancestors.

VII. DESCRIPTIONS

[One of the reasons for Prescott's popularity has been his ability to describe graphically the settings of events. The Romantic historian knew how, as the modern historian usually does not, to make the reader visualize places and episodes. Unlike Parkman, Prescott could not base his descriptions of places on notes taken on the spot. It must not be assumed, however, that for that reason he had to depend entirely on his imagination. As a matter of fact, he sought specific descriptive detail not only in the early Spanish chroniclers but in the works of modern travelers, such as Humboldt and William Tudor, who had been over the same ground.]

[THE SPANIARDS CLIMB THE TABLELAND]

From *The Conquest of Mexico*, Bk. III, chap. i

[After Cortés sank his little fleet, he and his soldiers set off for the Mexican capital. On the way they met with interesting scenes and heard intriguing tales of the Aztec power.]

He now made arrangements for his speedy departure from the Totonac capital. The forces reserved for the expedition amounted to about four hundred foot and fifteen horse, with seven pieces of artillery. He obtained, also, thirteen hundred Indian warriors, and a thousand *tamanes*, or porters, from the cacique of Cempoalla, to drag the guns, and transport the baggage. He took forty more of their principal men as hostages, as well as to guide him on the way, and serve him by their counsels among the strange tribes he was to visit. They were, in fact, of essential service to him throughout the march.

The remainder of his Spanish force he left in garrison at Villa Rica de Vera Cruz, the command of which he had intrusted to the alguacil, Juan de Escalante, an officer devoted to his interests. The selection was judicious. It was important to place there a man who would resist any hostile interference from his

European rivals, on the one hand, and maintain the present friendly relations with the natives, on the other. Cortés recommended the Totonac chiefs to apply to this officer, in case of any difficulty, assuring them, that, so long as they remained faithful to their new sovereign and religion, they should find a sure protection in the Spaniards.

Before marching, the general spoke a few words of encouragement to his own men. He told them, they were now to embark, in earnest, on an enterprise which had been the great object of their desires; and that the blessed Saviour would carry them victorious through every battle with their enemies. "Indeed," he added, "this assurance must be our stay, for every other refuge is now cut off, but that afforded by the Providence of God, and your own stout hearts." He ended by comparing their achievements to those of the ancient Romans, "in phrases of honeyed eloquence far beyond any thing I can repeat," says the brave and simple-hearted chronicler who heard them. Cortés was, indeed, master of that eloquence which went to the soldiers' hearts. For their sympathies were his, and he shared in that romantic spirit of adventure which belonged to them. "We are ready to obey you," they cried as with one voice. "Our fortunes, for better or worse, are cast with yours." Taking leave, therefore, of their hospitable Indian friends, the little army, buoyant with high hopes and lofty plans of conquest, set forward on the march to Mexico.

It was the sixteenth of August, 1519. During the first day, their road lay through the *tierra caliente*, the beautiful land where they had been so long lingering; the land of the vanilla, cochineal, cacao, (not till later days of the orange and the sugar-cane,) products which, indigenous to Mexico, have now become the luxuries of Europe; the land where the fruits and the flowers chase one another in unbroken circle through the year; where the gales are loaded with perfumes till the sense aches at their sweetness; and the groves are filled with many-colored birds, and insects whose enameled wings glisten like diamonds in the bright sun of the tropics. Such are the magical splendors of this paradise of the senses. Yet Nature, who generally works in a spirit of compensation, has provided one here; since the same burning sun, which quickens into life these glories of the vegetable and animal kingdoms, calls forth the pestilent *malaria*, with its train of bilious disorders, unknown to the cold skies of the North. The season in which the Spaniards were there, the rainy months of summer, was precisely that in which the *vómito* rages with greatest fury; when the European stranger hardly ventures to set his foot on shore, still less to linger there a day. We find no mention made of it in the records of the Conquerors, nor any notice, indeed, of an uncommon mortality. The fact doubtless corroborates the theory of those who postpone the appearance of the yellow fever till long after the occupation of the country by the whites. It proves, at least, that, if existing before, it must have been in a very much mitigated form.

After some leagues of travel over roads made nearly impassable by the summer rains, the troops began the gradual ascent—more gradual on the eastern than the western declivities of the Cordilleras—which leads up to the tableland of Mexico. At the close of the second day, they reached Xalapa, a place still retaining the same Aztec name, that it has communicated to the drug raised in its environs, the medicinal virtues of which are now known throughout the world. This town stands midway up the long ascent, at an elevation where the vapors from the ocean, touching in their westerly progress, maintain a rich verdure throughout the year. Though somewhat infected with these marine fogs, the air is usually bland and salubrious. The wealthy resident of the lower regions retires here for safety in the heats of summer, and the traveler hails its groves of oak with delight, as announcing that he is above the deadly influence of the *vómito*. From this delicious spot, the Spaniards enjoyed one of the grandest prospects in nature. Before them was the steep ascent,—much steeper after this point,—which they were to climb. On the right rose the *Sierra Madre*, girt with its dark belt of pines, and its long lines of shadowy hills stretching away in the distance. To the south, in brilliant contrast, stood the mighty Orizaba, with his white robe of snow descending far down his sides, towering in solitary grandeur, the giant specter of the Andes. Behind them, they beheld, unrolled at their feet, the magnificent *tierra caliente*, with its gay confusion of meadows, streams, and flowering forests, sprinkled over with shining Indian villages, while a faint line of light on the edge of the horizon told them that there was the ocean, beyond which were the kindred and country—they were many of them never more to see.

Still winding their way upward, amidst scenery as different as was the temperature from that of the regions below, the army passed through settlements containing some hundreds of inhabitants each, and on the fourth day reached a "strong town," as Cortés terms it, standing on a rocky eminence, supposed to be that now known by the Mexican name of Naulinco. Here they were hospitably entertained by the inhabitants, who were friends of the Totonacs. Cortés endeavored, through father Olmedo, to impart to them some knowledge of Christian truths, which were kindly received, and the Spaniards were allowed to erect a cross in the place, for the future adoration of the natives. Indeed, the route of the army might be tracked by these emblems of man's salvation, raised wherever a willing population of Indians invited it, suggesting a very different idea from what the same memorials intimate to the traveler in these mountains solitudes in our day.

The troops now entered a rugged defile, the Bishop's Pass, as it is called, capable of easy defense against an army. Very soon they experienced a most unwelcome change of climate. Cold winds from the mountains, mingled with rain, and, as they rose still higher, with driving sleet and hail, drenched their garments, and seemed to penetrate to their very bones. The Spaniards, indeed, partially covered by their armor and thick jackets of quilted cotton, were better able to resist the weather, though their long residence in the sultry regions of the valley made them still keenly sensible to the annoyance. But the poor Indians, natives of the *tierra caliente*, with little protection in the way of covering, sunk under the rude assault of the elements, and several of them perished on the road.

The aspect of the country was as wild and dreary as the climate. Their route wound along the spur of the huge Cofre de Perote, which borrows its name, both in Mexican and Castilian, from the coffer-like rock on its summit. It is one of the great volcanoes of New Spain. It exhibits now, indeed, no vestige of a crater on its top, but abundant traces of volcanic action at its base, where acres of lava, blackened scoriæ, and cinders, proclaim the convulsions of nature, while numerous shrubs and mouldering trunks of enormous trees, among the crevices, attest the antiquity of these events. Working their toilsome way across this scene of desolation, the path often led them along the borders of precipices, down whose sheer depths of two or three thousand feet the shrinking eye might behold another climate, and see all the glowing vegetation of the tropics choking up the bottom of the ravines.

After three days of this fatiguing travel, the wayworn army emerged through another defile, the *Sierra del Agua.* They soon came upon an open reach of country, with a genial climate, such as belongs to the temperate latitudes of southern Europe. They had reached the level of more than seven thousand feet above the ocean, where the great sheet of tableland spreads out for hundreds of miles along the crests of the Cordilleras. The country showed signs of careful cultivation, but the products were, for the most part, not familiar to the eyes of the Spaniards. Fields and hedges of the various tribes of the cactus, the towering organum, and plantations of aloes with rich yellow clusters of flowers on their tall stems, affording drink and clothing to the Aztec, were everywhere seen. The plants of the torrid and temperate zones had disappeared, one after another, with the ascent into these elevated regions. The glossy and dark-leaved banana, the chief, as it is the cheapest, aliment of the countries below, had long since faded from the landscape. The hardy maize, however, still shone with its golden harvests in all the pride of cultivation, the great staple of the higher, equally with the lower terraces of the plateau.

Suddenly the troops came upon what seemed the environs of a populous city, which, as they entered it, appeared to surpass even that of Cempoalla in the size and solidity of its structures. These were of stone and lime, many of them spacious and tolerably high. There were thirteen *teocallis* in the place; and in the suburbs they had seen a receptacle, in which, according to Bernal Diaz, were stored a hundred thousand skulls of human victims, all piled and ranged in order! He reports the number as one he had ascertained by counting them himself. Whatever faith we may attach to the precise accuracy of his figures, the result is almost equally startling. The Spaniards were destined to become familiar with this appalling spectacle, as they approached nearer to the Aztec capital.

The lord of the town ruled over twenty thousand vassals. He was tributary to Montezuma, and a strong Mexican garrison was quartered in the place. He had probably been advised of the approach of the Spaniards, and doubted how far it would be welcome to his sovereign. At all events, he gave them a cold reception, the more unpalatable after the extraordinary sufferings of the last few days. To the inquiry of Cortés, whether he were subject to Montezuma, he answered, with real or affected surprise, "Who is there that is not a vassal to Montezuma?" The general told him, with some emphasis, that he was not. He then explained whence and why he came, assuring him that he served a monarch who had princes for his vassals as powerful as the Aztec monarch himself.

The cacique in turn fell nothing short of the Spaniard, in the pompous display of the grandeur and resources of the Indian emperor. He told his guest that Montezuma could muster thirty great vassals, each master of a hundred thousand men! His revenues were immense, as every subject, however poor, paid something. They were all expended on his magnificent state, and in support of his armies. These were continually in the field, while garrisons were maintained in most of the large cities of the empire. More than twenty thousand victims, the fruit of his wars, were annually sacrificed on the altars of his gods! His capital, the cacique said, stood in a lake, in the center of a spacious valley. The lake was commanded by the emperor's vessels, and the approach to the city was by means of causeways, several miles long, connected in parts by wooden bridges, which, when raised, cut off all communication with the country. Some other things he added, in answer to queries of his guest, in which, as the reader may imagine, the crafty, or credulous cacique varnished over the truth with a lively coloring of romance. Whether romance, or reality, the Spaniards could not determine. The particulars they gleaned were not of a kind to tranquillize their minds, and might well have made bolder hearts than theirs pause, ere they advanced. But far from it. "The words which we heard," says the stout old cavalier, so often quoted, "however they may have filled us with wonder, made us—such is the temper of the Spaniard— only the more earnest to prove the adventure, desperate as it might appear."

In a further conversation Cortés inquired of the chief, whether his country abounded in gold, and intimated a desire to take home some, as specimens to his sovereign. But the Indian lord declined to give him any, saying it might displease Montezuma. "Should he command it," he added, "my gold, my person, and all I possess, shall be at your disposal." The general did not press the matter further.

[FIRST VIEW OF THE VALLEY OF MEXICO]

From *The Conquest of Mexico*, Bk. III, chap. viii

[The Spaniards resumed their march to the Aztec capital after the massacre of the Cholulans. They were deeply impressed with the view of the valley where lay the chief city.]

They had not advanced far, when, turning an angle of the sierra, they suddenly came on a view which more than compensated the toils of the preceding day. It was that of the Valley of Mexico, or Tenochtitlan, as more commonly called by the natives; which, with its picturesque assemblage of water, woodland, and cultivated plains, its shining cities and shadowy hills, was spread out like some gay and gorgeous panorama before them. In the highly rarefied atmosphere of these upper regions, even remote objects have a brilliancy of coloring and a distinctness of outline which seem to annihilate distance. Stretching far away at their feet, were seen noble forests of oak, sycamore, and cedar, and beyond, yellow fields of maize and the towering maguey, intermingled with orchards and blooming gardens; for flowers, in such demand for their religious festivals, were even more abundant in this populous valley than in other parts of Anahuac. In the center of the great basin were beheld the lakes, occupying then a much larger portion of its surface than at present; their borders thickly studded with towns and hamlets, and, in the midst,—like some Indian empress with her coronal of pearls,—the fair city of Mexico, with her white towers and pyramidal temples, reposing, as it were, on the bosom of the waters,—the far-famed "Venice of the Aztecs." High over all rose the royal hill of Chapoltepec, the residence of the Mexican monarchs, crowned with the same grove of gigantic cypresses, which at this day fling their broad shadows over the land. In the distance beyond the blue waters of the lake, and nearly screened by intervening foliage, was seen a shining speck, the rival capital of Tezcuco, and, still further on, the dark belt of porphyry, girdling the Valley around, like a rich setting which Nature had devised for the fairest of her jewels.

Such was the beautiful vision which broke on the eyes of the Conquerors. And even now, when so sad a change has come over the scene; when the stately forests have been laid low, and the soil, unsheltered from the fierce radiance of a tropical sun, is in many places abandoned to sterility; when the waters have retired, leaving a broad and ghastly margin white with the incrustation of salts, while the cities and hamlets on their borders have mouldered into ruins;—even now that desolation broods over the landscape, so indestructible are the lines of beauty which Nature has traced on its features, that no traveler, however cold, can gaze on them with any other emotions than those of astonishment and rapture.

What, then, must have been the emotions of the Spaniards, when, after working their toilsome way into the upper air, the cloudy tabernacle parted before their eyes, and they beheld these fair scenes in all their pristine magnificence and beauty! It was like the spectacle which greeted the eyes of Moses from the summit of Pisgah, and, in the warm glow of their feelings, they cried out, "It is the promised land!"

[THE CONQUERORS ENTER THE CAPITAL]

From *The Conquest of Mexico*, Bk. III, chap. ix

[With little delay, Cortés and his companions entered the capital. Its people, buildings, and public works were a great wonder to the incredulous Spaniards.]

Everywhere the Conquerors beheld the evidence of a crowded and thriving population, exceeding all they had yet seen. The temples and principal buildings of the cities were covered with a hard white stucco, which glistened like enamel in the level beams of the morning. The margin of the great basin was more thickly gemmed, than that of Chalco, with towns and hamlets. The water was darkened by swarms of canoes filled with Indians, who clambered up the sides of the causeway, and gazed with curious astonishment on the strangers. And here, also, they beheld those fairy islands of flowers, over-shadowed occasionally by trees of considerable size, rising and falling with the gentle undulation of the billows. At the distance of half a league from the capital, they encountered a solid work or curtain of stone, which traversed the dike. It was twelve feet high, was strengthened by towers at the extremities, and in the center was a battlemented gateway, which opened a passage to the troops. It was called the Fort of Xoloc, and became memorable in aftertimes as the position occupied by Cortés in the famous siege of Mexico.

Here they were met by several hundred Aztec chiefs, who came out to announce the approach of Montezuma, and to welcome the Spaniards to his capital. They were dressed in the fanciful gala costume of the country, with the *maxtlatl*, or cotton sash, around their loins, and a broad mantle of the same material, or of the brilliant feather-embroidery, flowing gracefully down their shoulders. On their necks and arms they displayed collars and bracelets of turquoise mosaic, with which delicate plumage was curiously mingled, while their ears, under-lips, and occasionally their noses, were garnished with pendants formed of precious stones, or crescents of fine gold. As each cacique made the usual formal salutation of the country separately to the general, the tedious ceremony delayed the march more than an hour. After this, the army experienced no further interruption till it reached a bridge near the gates of the city. It was built of wood, since replaced by one of stone, and was thrown across an opening of the dike, which furnished an outlet to the waters, when agitated by the winds, or swollen by a sudden influx in the rainy season. It was a drawbridge; and the Spaniards, as they crossed it, felt how truly they were committing themselves to the mercy of Montezuma, who, by thus cutting off their communications with the country, might hold them prisoners in his capital.

In the midst of these unpleasant reflections, they beheld the glittering retinue of the emperor emerging from the great street which led then, as it still does, through the heart of the city. Amidst a crowd of Indian nobles, preceded by three officers of state, bearing golden wands, they saw the royal palanquin blazing with burnished gold. It was borne on the shoulders of nobles, and over it a canopy of gaudy feather-work, powdered with jewels, and fringed with silver, was supported by four attendants of the same rank. They were barefooted, and walked with a slow, measured pace, and with eyes bent on the ground. When the train had come within a convenient distance, it halted, and Montezuma, descending from his litter, came forward leaning on the arms of the lords of Tezcuco and Iztapalapan, his nephew and brother, both of whom, as we have seen, had already been made known to the Spaniards. As the monarch advanced under the canopy, the obsequious attendants strewed the ground with cotton tapestry, that his imperial feet might not be contaminated by the rude soil. His subjects of high and low degree, who lined the sides of the causeway, bent forward with their eyes fastened on the ground as he passed, and some of the humbler class prostrated themselves before him. Such was the homage paid to the Indian despot, showing that the slavish forms of oriental adulation were to be found among the rude inhabitants of the Western World.

Montezuma wore the girdle and ample square cloak, *tilmatli*, of his nation. It was made of the finest cotton, with the embroidered ends gathered in a knot round his neck. His feet were defended by sandals having soles of gold, and the leathern thongs which bound them to his ankles were embossed with the same metal. Both the cloak and sandals were sprinkled with pearls and precious stones, among which the emerald and the *chalchivitl*—a green stone of higher estimation than any other among the Aztecs—were conspicuous. On his head he wore no other ornament than a *panache* of plumes of the royal green which floated down his back, the badge of military, rather than of regal, rank.

He was at this time about forty years of age. His person was tall and thin, but not ill-made. His hair, which was black and straight, was not very long; to wear it short was considered unbecoming persons of rank. His beard was thin; his complexion somewhat paler than is often found in his dusky, or rather copper-colored race. His features, though serious in their expression, did not wear the look of melancholy, indeed, of dejection, which characterizes his portrait, and which may well have settled on them at a later period. He moved with dignity, and his whole demeanor, tempered by an expression of benignity not to have been anticipated from the reports circulated of his character, was worthy of a great prince.—Such is the portrait left to us of the celebrated Indian emperor, in this his first interview with the white men.

The army halted as he drew near. Cortés, dismounting, threw his reins to a page, and, supported by a few of the principal cavaliers, advanced to meet him. The interview must have been one of uncommon interest to both. In Montezuma, Cortés beheld the lord of the broad realms he had traversed, whose magnificence and power had been the burden of every tongue. In the Spaniard, on the other hand, the Aztec prince saw the strange being whose history seemed to be so mysteriously connected with his own; the predicted one of his oracles; whose achievements proclaimed him something more than human. But, whatever may have been the monarch's feelings, he so far suppressed them as to receive his guest with princely courtesy, and to express his satisfaction at personally seeing him in his capital. Cortés responded by the most profound expressions of respect, while he made ample acknowledgments for the substantial proofs which the emperor had given the Spaniards of his munificence. He then hung round Montezuma's neck a sparkling chain of colored crystal, accompanying this with a movement as if to embrace him, when he was restrained by the two Aztecs lords, shocked at the menaced profanation of the sacred person of their master. After the interchange of these civilities, Montezuma appointed his brother to conduct the Spaniards to their residence in the capital, and again entering his litter was borne off amidst prostrate crowds in the same state in which he had come. The Spaniards quickly followed, and with colors flying and music playing soon made their entrance into the southern quarter of Tenochtitlan.

Here, again, they found fresh cause for admiration in the grandeur of the city, and the superior style of its architecture. The dwellings of the poorer class were, indeed, chiefly of reeds and mud. But the great avenue through which they were now marching was lined with the houses of the nobles, who were encouraged by the emperor to make the capital their residence. They were built of a red porous stone drawn from quarries in the neighborhood, and, though they rarely rose to a second story, often covered a large space of ground. The flat roofs, *azoteas*, were protected by stone parapets, so that every house was a fortress. Sometimes these roofs resembled parterres of flowers, so thickly were they covered with them, but more frequently these were cultivated in broad terraced gardens, laid out between the edifices. Occasionally a great square or market-place intervened, surrounded by its porticos of stone and stucco;

or a pyramidal temple reared its colossal bulk, crowned with its tapering sanctuaries, and altars blazing with inextinguishable fires. The great street facing the southern causeway, unlike most others in the place, was wide, and extended some miles in nearly a straight line, as before noticed, through the center of the city. A spectator standing at one end of it, as his eye ranged along the deep vista of temples, terraces, and gardens, might clearly discern the other, with the blue mountains in the distance, which, in the transparent atmosphere of the tableland, seemed almost in contact with the buildings.

But what most impressed the Spaniards was the throngs of people who swarmed through the streets and on the canals, filling every doorway and window, and clustering on the roofs of the buildings. "I well rememer the spectacle," exclaims Bernal Diaz; "it seems now, after so many years, as present to my mind, as if it were but yesterday." But what must have been the sensations of the Aztecs themselves, as they looked on the portentous pageant! as they heard, now for the first time, the well-cemented pavement ring under the iron tramp of the horses,—the strange animals which fear had clothed in such supernatural terrors; as they gazed on the children of the East, revealing their celestial origin in their fair complexions; saw the bright falchions and bonnets of steel, a metal to them unknown, glancing like meteors in the sun, while sounds of unearthly music—at least, such as their rude instruments had never wakened—floated in the air! But every other emotion was lost in that of deadly hatred, when they beheld their detested enemy, the Tlascalan, stalking, in defiance, as it were, through their streets, and staring around with looks of ferocity and wonder, like some wild animal of the forest, who had strayed by chance from his native fastnesses into the haunts of civilization.

[GONZALO PIZARRO DISCOVERS THE NAPO RIVER]

From *The Conquest of Peru*, Bk. IV, chap. iv

[Gonzalo Pizarro had been assigned to rule over the government of Quito, with instructions to explore the country farther east. Discovery of cinnamon as well as land was the objective.]

Gonzalo Pizarro received the news of his appointment to the government of Quito with undisguised pleasure; not so much for the possession that it gave him of this ancient Indian province, as for the field that it opened for discovery towards the east,—the fabled land of oriental spices, which had long captivated the imagination of the Conquerors. He repaired to his government without delay, and found no difficulty in awakening a kindred enthusiasm to his own in the bosoms of his followers. In a short time, he mustered three hundred and fifty Spaniards, and four thousand Indians. One hundred and fifty of his company were mounted, and all were equipped in the most thorough manner for the undertaking. He provided moreover, against famine by a large stock of provisions, and an immense drove of swine which followed in the rear.

It was the beginning of 1540, when he set out on this celebrated expedition. The first part of the journey was attended with comparatively little difficulty, while the Spaniards were yet in the land of the Incas; for the distractions of Peru had not been felt in this distant province, where the simple people still lived as under the primitive sway of the Children of the Sun. But the scene changed as they entered the territory of Quixos, where the character of the inhabitants, as well as of the climate, seemed to be of another description. The country was traversed by lofty ranges of the Andes, and the adventurers were soon entangled in their deep and intricate passes. As they rose into the more elevated regions, the icy winds that swept down the sides of the Cordilleras benumbed their limbs, and many of the natives found a wintry grave in the wilderness. While crossing this formidable barrier, they experienced one of those tremendous earthquakes which, in these volcanic regions, so often shake the mountains to their base. In one place, the earth was rent asunder by the terrible throes of Nature, while streams of sulphurous vapor issued from the cavity, and a village with some hundreds of houses was precipitated into the frightful abyss!

On descending the eastern slopes, the climate changed; and, as they came on the lower level, the fierce cold was succeeded by a suffocating heat, while tempests of thunder and lightning, rushing from out the gorges of the sierra, poured on their heads with scarcely any intermission day or night, as if the offended deities of the place were willing to take vengeance on the invaders of their mountain solitudes. For more than six weeks the deluge continued unabated, and the forlorn wanderers, wet, and weary with incessant toil, were scarcely able to drag their limbs along the soil broken up and saturated with the moisture. After some months of toilsome travel, in which they had to cross many a morass and mountain stream, they at length reached *Canelas*, the Land of Cinnamon. They saw the trees bearing the precious bark, spreading out into broad forests; yet, however valuable an article for commerce it might have proved in accessible situations, in these remote regions it was of little worth to them. But, from the wandering tribes of savages whom they occasionally met in their path, they learned that at ten days' distance was a rich and fruitful land abounding with gold, and inhabited by populous nations. Gonzalo Pizarro had already reached the limits originally proposed for the expedition. But this intelligence renewed his hopes, and he resolved to push the adventure farther. It would have been well for him and his followers, had they been content to return on their footsteps.

Continuing their march, the country now spread out into broad savannas terminated by forests, which, as they drew near, seemed to stretch on every side to the very verge of the horizon. Here they beheld trees of that stupendous growth seen only in the equinoctial regions. Some were so large, that sixteen men could hardly encompass them with extended arms! The wood was thickly matted with creepers and parasitical vines, which hung in gaudy-colored festoons from tree to tree, clothing them in a drapery beautiful to the eye, but forming an impenetrable network. At every step of their way, they were obliged to hew open a passage with their axes, while their garments, rotting from the effects of the drenching rains to which they had been exposed, caught in every bush and bramble, and hung about them in shreds. Their provisions, spoiled by the weather, had long since failed, and the livestock which they had taken with them had either been consumed or made their escape in the woods and mountain passes. They had set out with nearly a thousand dogs, many of them of the ferocious breed used in hunting down the unfortunate natives. These they now gladly killed, but their miserable carcasses furnished a lean banquet for the famishing travelers; and, when these were gone, they had only such herbs and dangerous roots as they could gather in the forest.

At length the wayworn company came on a broad expanse of water formed by the Napo, one of the great tributaries of the Amazon, and which, though only a third or fourth rate river in America, would pass for one of the first magnitude in the Old World. The sight gladdened their hearts, as, by winding along its banks, they hoped to find a safer and more practicable route. After traversing its borders for a considerable distance, closely beset with thickets which it taxed their strength to the utmost to overcome, Gonzalo and his party came within hearing of a rushing noise that sounded like subterranean thunder. The river, lashed into fury, tumbled along over rapids with frightful velocity, and conducted them to the brink of a magnificent cataract, which, to their wondering fancies, rushed down in one vast volume of foam to the depth of twelve hundred feet! The appalling sounds which they had heard for the distance of six leagues were rendered yet more oppressive to the spirits by the gloomy stillness of the surrounding forests. The rude warriors were filled with sentiments of awe. Not a bark dimpled the waters. No living thing was to be seen but the wild tenants of the wilderness, the unwieldy boa, and the loathsome alligator basking on the borders of the stream. The trees towering in widespread magnificence towards the heavens, the river rolling on in its rocky bed as it had rolled for ages, the solitude and silence of the scene, broken only by the hoarse fall of waters, or the faint rustling of the woods,—all seemed to spread out around them in the same wild and primitive state as when they came from the hands of the Creator.

For some distance above and below the falls, the bed of the river contracted so that its width did not exceed twenty feet. Sorely pressed by hunger, the adventurers determined, at all hazards, to cross to the opposite side, in hopes of finding a country that might afford them sustenance. A frail bridge was constructed by throwing the huge trunks of trees across the chasm, where the cliffs, as if split asunder by some convulsion of nature, descended sheer down a perpendicular depth of several hundred feet. Over this airy causeway the men and horses succeeded in effecting their passage with the loss of a single Spaniard, who, made giddy by heedlessly looking down, lost his footing and fell into the boiling surges below.

Yet they gained little by the exchange. The country wore the same unpromising aspect, and the riverbanks were studded with gigantic trees, or fringed with impenetrable thickets. The tribes of Indians, whom they occasionally met in the pathless wilderness, were fierce and unfriendly, and they were engaged in perpetual skirmishes with them. From these they learned that a fruitful country was to be found down the river at the distance of only a few days' journey, and the Spaniards held on their weary way, still hoping and still deceived, as the promised land flitted before them, like the rainbow, receding as they advanced.

VIII. PORTRAITS

[Although Prescott had no theory of the role of the individual in historical causation, the biographical element in his work is large. He attempted to analyze each major figure thoroughly and impartially, cataloguing rather mechanically his physical, mental, and moral traits, and, as in the case of Isabella and Ximenes, comparing his subject with a similar personage in some other era or country. It is important to remember in this connection Prescott's principle of historic judgment: that though the morality of an age or civilization must be judged by absolute standards, individuals may be fairly tried only by the standards appropriate to their time.]

[QUEEN ISABELLA]

From *Ferdinand and Isabella*, Vol. III, pt. ii, chap. xvi

[This character sketch follows a description of Isabella's last illness and death.]

Her person, as mentioned in the early part of the narrative, was of the middle height, and well proportioned. She had a clear, fresh complexion, with light blue eyes and auburn hair,— a style of beauty exceedingly rare in Spain. Her features were regular, and universally allowed to be uncommonly handsome. The illusion which attaches to rank, more especially when united with engaging manners, might lead us to suspect some exaggeration in the encomiums so liberally lavished on her. But they would seem to be in a great measure justified by the portraits that remain of her, which combine a faultless symmetry of features with singular sweetness and intelligence of expression.

Her manners were most gracious and pleasing. They were marked by natural dignity and modest reserve, tempered by an affability which flowed from the kindliness of her disposition. She was the last person to be approached with undue familiarity; yet the respect which she imposed was mingled with the strongest feelings of devotion and love. She showed great tact in accommodating herself to the peculiar situation and character of those around her. She appeared in arms at the head of her troops, and shrunk from none of the hardships of war. During the reforms introduced into the religious houses, she visited the nunneries in person, taking her needlework with her, and passing the day in the society of the inmates. When traveling in Galicia, she attired herself in the costume of the country, borrowing for that purpose the jewels and other ornaments of the ladies there, and returning them with liberal additions. By this condescending and captivating deportment, as well as by her higher qualities, she gained an ascendency over her turbulent subjects, which no king of Spain could ever boast.

She spoke the Castilian with much elegance and correctness. She had an easy fluency of discourse, which, though generally of a serious complexion, was occasionally seasoned with agreeable sallies, some of which have passed into proverbs. She was temperate even to abstemiousness in her diet, seldom or never tasting wine; and so frugal in her table, that the daily expenses for herself and family did not exceed the moderate sum of forty ducats. She was equally simple and economical in her apparel. On all public occasions, indeed, she displayed a royal magnificence; but she had no relish for it in private, and she freely gave away her clothes and jewels, as presents to her friends. Naturally of a sedate, though cheerful temper, she had little taste for the frivolous amusements, which make up so much of a court life; and, if she encouraged the presence of minstrels and musicians in her palace, it was to wean her young nobility from the coarser and less intellectual pleasures to which they were addicted.

Among her moral qualities, the most conspicuous, perhaps, was her magnanimity. She betrayed nothing little or selfish, in thought or action. Her schemes were vast, and executed in the same noble spirit, in which they were conceived. She never employed doubtful agents or sinister measures, but the most direct and open policy. She scorned to avail herself of advantages offered by the perfidy of others. Where she had once given her confidence, she gave her hearty and steady support; and she was scrupulous to redeem any pledge she had made to those who ventured in her cause, however unpopular. She sustained Ximenes in all his obnoxious, but salutary reforms. She seconded Columbus in the prosecution of his arduous enterprise, and shielded him from the calumny of his enemies. She did the same good service to her favorite, Gonsalvo de Cordova; and the day of her death was felt, and, as it proved, truly felt by both, as the last of their good fortune. Artifice and duplicity were so abhorrent to her character, and so averse from her domestic policy, that when they appear in the foreign relations of Spain, it is certainly not imputable to her. She was incapable of harboring any petty distrust, or latent malice; and, although stern in the execution and exaction of public justice, she made the most generous allowance, and even sometimes advances, to those who had personally injured her.

But the principle, which gave a peculiar coloring to every feature of Isabella's mind, was piety. It shone forth from the very depths of her soul with a heavenly radiance, which illuminated her whole character. Fortunately, her earliest years had been passed in the rugged school of adversity, under the eye of a mother, who implanted in her serious mind such strong principles of religion as nothing in after life had power to shake. At an early age, in the flower of youth and beauty, she was introduced to her brother's court; but its blandishments, so dazzling to a young imagination, had no power over hers; for she was surrounded by a moral atmosphere of purity,

"Driving far off each thing of sin and guilt."

Such was the decorum of her manners, that, though encompassed by false friends and open enemies, not the slightest reproach was breathed on her fair name in this corrupt and calumnious court.

She gave a liberal portion of her time to private devotions, as well as to the public exercises of religion. She expended large sums in useful charities, especially in the erection of hospitals, and churches, and the more doubtful endowments of monasteries. Her piety was strikingly exhibited in that unfeigned humility, which, although the very essence of our faith, is so rarely found; and most rarely in those, whose great powers and exalted stations seem to raise them above the level of ordinary mortals. A remarkable illustration of this is afforded in the queen's correspondence with Talavera, in which her meek and docile spirit is strikingly contrasted with the Puritanical intolerance of her confessor. Yet Talavera, as we have seen, was sincere, and benevolent at heart. Unfortunately, the royal conscience was at times committed to very different keeping; and that humility which, as we have repeatedly had occasion to notice, made her defer so reverentially to her ghostly advisers, led, under the fanatic Torquemada, the confessor of her early youth, to those deep blemishes on her administration, the establishment of the Inquisition, and the exile of the Jews.

But, though blemishes of the deepest dye on her administration, they are certainly not to be regarded as such on her moral character. It will be difficult to condemn her, indeed, without condemning the age; for these very acts are not only excused, but extolled by her contemporaries, as constituting her strongest claims to renown, and to the gratitude of her country. They proceeded from the principle, openly avowed by the court of Rome, that zeal for the purity of the faith could atone for every crime. This immoral maxim, flowing from the head of the church, was echoed in a thousand different forms by the subordinate clergy, and greedily received by a superstitious people. It was not to be expected, that a solitary woman, filled with natural diffidence of her own capacity on such subjects, should array herself against those venerated counselors, whom she had been taught from her cradle to look to as the guides and guardians of her conscience.

However mischievous the operations of the Inquisition may have been in Spain, its establishment, in point of principle, was not worse than many other measures, which have passed with far less censure, though in a much more advanced and civilized age. Where, indeed, during the sixteenth, and the greater part of the seventeenth century, was the principle of persecution abandoned by the dominant party, whether Catholic or Protestant? And where that of toleration asserted, except by the weaker? It is true, to borrow Isabella's own expression, in her letter to Talavera, the prevalence of a bad custom cannot constitute its apology. But it should serve much to mitigate our condemnation of the queen, that she fell into no greater error, in the imperfect light in which she lived, than was common to the greatest minds in a later and far riper period.

Isabella's actions, indeed, were habitually based on principle. Whatever errors of judgment be imputed to her, she most anxiously sought in all situations to discern and discharge her duty. Faithful in the dispensation of justice, no bribe was large enough to ward off the execution of the law. No motive, not even conjugal affection, could induce her to make an unsuitable appointment to public office. No reverence for the ministers of religion could lead her to wink at their misconduct; nor could the deference she entertained for the head of the church, allow her to tolerate his encroachments on the rights of her crown. She seemed to consider herself especially bound to preserve entire the peculiar claims and privileges of Castile, after its union under the same sovereign with Aragon. And although, "while her own will was law," says Peter Martyr, "she governed in such a manner that it might appear the joint action of both Ferdinand and herself," yet she was careful never to surrender into his hands one of those prerogatives, which belonged to her as queen proprietor of the kingdom.

Isabella's measures were characterized by that practical good sense, without which the most brilliant parts may work more to the woe, than to the weal of mankind. Though engaged all her life in reforms, she had none of the failings so common in reformers. Her plans, though vast, were never visionary. The best proof of this is, that she lived to see most of them realized.

She was quick to discern objects of real utility. She saw

the importance of the new discovery of printing, and liberally patronized it, from the first moment it appeared. She had none of the exclusive, local prejudices, too common with her countrymen. She drew talent from the most remote quarters to her dominions, by munificent rewards. She imported foreign artisans for her manufactures; foreign engineers and officers for the discipline of her army; and foreign scholars to imbue her martial subjects with more cultivated tastes. She consulted the useful, in all her subordinate regulations; in her sumptuary laws, for instance, directed against the fashionable extravagances of dress, and the ruinous ostentation, so much affected by the Castilians in their weddings and funerals. Lastly, she showed the same perspicacity in the selection of her agents; well knowing that the best measures become bad in incompetent hands.

But, although the skillful selection of her agents was an obvious cause of Isabella's success, yet another, even more important, is to be found in her own vigilance and untiring exertions. During the first busy and bustling years of her reign, these exertions were of incredible magnitude. She was almost always in the saddle, for she made all her journeys on horseback; and she travelled with a rapidity, which made her always present on the spot where her presence was needed. She was never intimidated by the weather, or the state of her own health; and this reckless exposure undoubtedly contributed much to impair her excellent constitution.

She was equally indefatigable in her mental application. After assiduous attention to business through the day, she was often known to sit up all night, dictating despatches to her secretaries. In the midst of these overwhelming cares, she found time to supply the defects of early education by learning Latin, so as to understand it without difficulty, whether written or spoken; and indeed, in the opinion of a competent judge, to attain a critical accuracy in it. As she had little turn for light amusements, she sought relief from graver cares by some useful occupation appropriate to her sex; and she left ample evidence of her skill in this way, in the rich specimens of embroidery, wrought with her own fair hands, with which she decorated the churches. She was careful to instruct her daughters in these more humble departments of domestic duty; for she thought nothing too humble to learn, which was useful.

With all her high qualifications, Isabella would have been still unequal to the achievement of her grand designs, without possessing a degree of fortitude rare in either sex; not the courage, which implies contempt of personal danger,—though of this she had a larger share than falls to most men; nor that, which supports its possessor under the extremities of bodily pain,—though of this she gave ample evidence, since she endured the greatest suffering her sex is called to bear, without a groan; but that moral courage, which sustains the spirit in the dark hour of adversity, and, gathering light from within to dispel the darkness, imparts its own cheering influence to all around. This was shown remarkably in the stormy season which ushered in her accession, as well as through the whole of the Moorish war. It was her voice that decided never to abandon Alhama. Her remonstrances compelled the king and nobles to return to the field, when they had quitted it, after an ineffectual campaign. As dangers and difficulties multiplied, she multiplied resources to meet them; and, when her soldiers lay drooping under the evils of some protracted siege, she appeared in the midst, mounted on her war-horse, with her delicate limbs cased in knightly mail; and, riding through their ranks, breathed new courage into their hearts by her own intrepid bearing. To her personal efforts, indeed, as well as counsels, the success of this glorious war may be mainly imputed; and the unsuspicious testimony of the Venetian minister, Navagiero, a few years later, shows that the nation so considered it. "Queen Isabel," says he, "by her singular genius, masculine strength of mind, and other virtues most unusual in our own sex, as well as hers, was not merely of great assistance in, but the chief cause of the conquest of Granada. She was, indeed, a most rare and virtuous lady, one of whom the Spaniards talk far more than of the king, sagacious as he was and uncommon for his time."

Happily these masculine qualities in Isabella did not extinguish the softer ones which constitute the charm of her sex. Her heart overflowed with affectionate sensibility to her family and friends. She watched over the declining days of her aged mother, and ministered to her sad infirmities with all the delicacy of filial tenderness. We have seen abundant proofs how fondly and faithfully she loved her husband to the last, though this love was not always as faithfully requited. For her children she lived more than for herself; and for them too she died, for it was their loss and their afflictions which froze the current of her blood, before age had time to chill it. Her exalted state did not remove her above the sympathies of friendship. With her friends she forgot the usual distinctions of rank, sharing in their joys, visiting and consoling them in sorrow and sickness, and condescending in more than one instance to assume the office of executrix on their decease. Her heart, indeed, was filled with benevolence to all mankind. In the most fiery heat of war, she was engaged in devising means for mitigating its horrors. She is said to have been the first to introduce the benevolent institution of camp hospitals; and we have seen, more than once, her lively solicitude to spare the effusion of blood even of her enemies. But it is needless to multiply examples of this beautiful, but familiar trait in her character.

It is in these more amiable qualities of her sex, that Isabella's superiority becomes most apparent over her illustrious namesake, Elizabeth of England, whose history presents some features parallel to her own. Both were disciplined in early life by the teachings of that stern nurse of wisdom, adversity. Both were made to experience the deepest humiliation at the hands of their nearest relative, who should have cherished and protected them. Both succeeded in establishing themselves on the throne after the most precarious vicissitudes. Each conducted her kingdom, through a long and triumphant reign, to a height of glory, which it had never before reached. Both lived to see the vanity of all earthly grandeur, and to fall the victims of an inconsolable melancholy; and both left behind an illustrious name, unrivaled in the subsequent annals of their country.

But, with these few circumstances of their history, the resemblance ceases. Their characters afford scarcely a point of contact. Elizabeth, inheriting a large share of the bold and bluff King Harry's temperament, was haughty, arrogant, coarse, and irascible; while with these fiercer qualities she mingled deep dissimulation and strange irresolution. Isabella, on the other hand, tempered the dignity of royal station with the most bland and courteous manners. Once resolved, she was constant in her purposes, and her conduct in public and private life was characterized by candor and integrity. Both may be said to have shown that magnanimity, which is implied by the accomplishment of great objects in the face of great obstacles. But Elizabeth was desperately selfish; she was incapable of forgiving, not merely a real injury, but the slightest affront to her vanity; and she was merciless in exacting retribution. Isabella, on the other hand, lived only for others,—was ready at all times to sacrifice self to considerations of public duty; and, far from personal resentments, showed the greatest condescension and kindness to those who had most sensibly injured her; while her benevolent heart sought every means to mitigate the authorized severities of the law, even towards the guilty.

Both possessed rare fortitude. Isabella, indeed, was placed in situations, which demanded more frequent and higher displays of it than her rival; but no one will doubt a full measure of this quality in the daughter of Henry the Eighth. Elizabeth was better educated, and every way more highly accomplished than Isabella. But the latter knew enough to maintain her station with dignity; and she encouraged learning by a munificent patronage. The masculine powers and passions of Elizabeth seemed to divorce her in a great measure from the peculiar attributes of her sex; at least from those which constitute its peculiar charm; for she had abundance of its foibles,—a coquetry and love of admiration, which age could not chill; a levity, most careless, if not criminal; and a fondness for dress and tawdry magnificence of ornament, which was ridiculous, or disgusting, according to the different periods of life in which it was indulged. Isabella, on the other hand, distinguished through life for decorum of manners, and purity beyond the breath of calumny, was content with the legitimate affection which she could inspire within the range of her domestic circle. Far from a frivolous affectation of ornament or dress, she was most simple in her own attire, and seemed to set no value on her jewels, but as they could serve the necessities of the state; when they could be no longer useful in this way, she gave them away, as we have seen, to her friends.

Both were uncommonly sagacious in the selection of their ministers; though Elizabeth was drawn into some errors in this particular, by her levity, as was Isabella by religious feeling. It was this, combined with her excessive humility, which led to the only grave errors in the administration of the latter. Her rival fell into no such errors; and she was a stranger to the amiable qualities which led to them. Her conduct was certainly not controlled by religious principle; and, though the bulwark of the Protestant faith, it might be difficult to say whether she were at heart most a Protestant or a Catholic. She viewed religion in its connection with the state, in other words, with herself; and she took measures for enforcing conformity to her own views, not a whit less despotic, and scarcely less sanguinary, than those countenanced for conscience' sake by her more bigoted rival.

This feature of bigotry, which has thrown a shade over Isabella's otherwise beautiful character, might lead to a disparagement of her intellectual power compared with that of the English queen. To estimate this aright, we must contemplate the results of their respective reigns. Elizabeth found all the materials of prosperity at hand, and availed herself of them most ably to build up a solid fabric of national grandeur. Isabella created these materials. She saw the faculties of her people locked up in a deathlike lethargy, and she breathed into them the breath of life for those great and heroic enterprises, which terminated in such glorious consequences to the monarchy. It is when viewed from the depressed position of her early days, that the achievements of her reign seem scarcely less than miraculous. The masculine genius of the English queen stands out relieved beyond its natural dimensions by its separation from the softer qualities of her sex. While her rival's, like some vast, but symmetrical edifice, loses in appearance somewhat of its actual grandeur from the perfect harmony of its proportions.

The circumstances of their deaths, which were somewhat similar, displayed the great dissimilarity of their characters. Both pined amidst their royal state, a prey to incurable despondency, rather than any marked bodily distemper. In Elizabeth it sprung from wounded vanity, a sullen conviction, that she had outlived the admiration on which she had so long fed,—and even the solace of friendship, and the attachment of her subjects. Nor did she seek consolation, where alone it was to be found, in that sad hour. Isabella, on the other hand, sunk under a too acute sensibility to the sufferings of others. But, amidst the gloom, which gathered around her, she looked with the eye of faith to the brighter prospects which unfolded of the future; and, when she resigned her last breath, it was amidst the tears and universal lamentations of her people.

It is in this undying, unabated attachment of the nation, indeed, that we see the most unequivocal testimony to the virtues of Isabella. In the downward progress of things in Spain, some of the most ill-advised measures of her administration have found favor and been perpetuated, while the more salutary have been forgotten. This may lead to a misconception of her real merits. In order to estimate these, we must listen to the voice of her contemporaries, the eyewitnesses of the condition in which she found the state, and in which she left it. We shall then see but one judgment formed of her, whether by foreigners or natives. The French and Italian writers equally join in celebrating the triumphant glories of her reign, and her magnanimity, wisdom, and purity of character. Her own subjects extol her as "the most brilliant exemplar of every virtue," and mourn over the day of her death as "the last of the prosperity and happiness of their country." While those, who had nearer access to her person, are unbounded in their admiration of those amiable qualities, whose full power is revealed only in the un-

restrained intimacies of domestic life. The judgment of posterity has ratified the sentence of her own age. The most
enlightened Spaniards of the present day, by no means insensible to the errors of her government, but more capable of appreciating its merits, than those of a less instructed age, bear
honorable testimony to her deserts; and, while they pass over
the bloated magnificence of succeeding monarchs, who arrest
the popular eye, dwell with enthusiasm on Isabella's character,
as the most truly great in their line of princes.

[CARDINAL XIMENES]

From *Ferdinand and Isabella*, Vol. III, pt. ii, chap. xxv

[Cardinal Ximenes (Francisco Jiménez de Cisneros, 1436–
1517) was Confessor to Queen Isabella, Archbishop of Toledo,
Regent of Castile (1506–1507 and 1516–1517), and Inquisitor
General from 1507.]

Such was the end of this remarkable man; the most remarkable, in many respects, of his time. His character was of that
stern and lofty cast, which seems to rise above the ordinary
wants and weaknesses of humanity; his genius, of the severest
order, like Dante's or Michael Angelo's in the regions of fancy,
impresses us with ideas of power, that excite admiration akin to
terror. His enterprises, as we have seen, were of the boldest
character. His execution of them equally bold. He disdained
to woo fortune by any of those soft and pliant arts, which are
often the most effectual. He pursued his ends by the most
direct means. In this way he frequently multiplied difficulties;
but difficulties seemed to have a charm for him, by the opportunity they afforded of displaying the energies of his soul. ·
With these qualities he combined a versatility of talent,
usually found only in softer and more flexible characters.
Though bred in the cloister, he distinguished himself both in the
cabinet and the camp. For the latter, indeed, so repugnant to
his regular profession, he had a natural genius, according to the
testimony of his biographer; and he evinced his relish for it by

declaring, that "the smell of gunpowder was more grateful to him than the sweetest perfume of Arabia!" In every situation, however, he exhibited the stamp of his peculiar calling; and the stern lineaments of the monk were never wholly concealed under the mask of the statesman, or the visor of the warrior. He had a full measure of the religious bigotry which belonged to the age; and he had melancholy scope for displaying it, as chief of that dread tribunal, over which he presided during the last ten years of his life.

He carried the arbitrary ideas of his profession into political life. His regency was conducted on the principles of a military despotism. It was his maxim, that "a prince must rely mainly on his army for securing the respect and obedience of his subjects." It is true he had to deal with a martial and factious nobility, and the end which he proposed was to curb their licentiousness, and enforce the equitable administration of justice; but, in accomplishing this, he showed little regard to the constitution, or to private rights. His first act, the proclaiming of Charles king, was in open contempt of the usages and rights of the nation. He evaded the urgent demands of the Castilians for a convocation of cortes; for it was his opinion, "that freedom of speech, especially in regard to their own grievances, made the people insolent and irreverent to their rulers." The people, of course, had no voice in the measures which involved their most important interests. His whole policy, indeed, was to exalt the royal prerogative, at the expense of the inferior orders of the state. And his regency, short as it was, and highly beneficial to the country in many respects, must be considered as opening the way to that career of despotism, which the Austrian family followed up with such hard-hearted constancy.

But, while we condemn the politics, we cannot but respect the principles, of the man. However erroneous his conduct in our eyes, he was guided by his sense of duty. It was this, and the conviction of it in the minds of others, which constituted the secret of his great power. It made him reckless of difficulties, and fearless of all personal consequences. The consciousness of the integrity of his purposes rendered him, indeed, too unscrupulous as to the means of attaining them. He held his own life cheap, in comparison with the great reforms that he had at heart. Was it surprising, that he should hold as lightly the convenience and interests of others, when they thwarted their execution?

His views were raised far above considerations of self. As a statesman, he identified himself with the state; as a churchman, with the interests of his religion. He severely punished every offense against these. He as freely forgave every personal injury. He had many remarkable opportunities of showing this. His administration provoked numerous lampoons and libels. He despised them, as the miserable solace of spleen and discontent, and never persecuted their authors. In this he formed an honorable contrast to Cardinal Richelieu, whose character and condition suggest many points of resemblance with his own.

His disinterestedness was further shown by his mode of dispensing his large revenues. It was among the poor, and on great public objects. He built up no family. He had brothers and nephews; but he contented himself with making their condition comfortable, without diverting to their benefit the great trusts confided to him for the public. The greater part of the funds which he left at his death was settled on the university of Alcalá.

He had, however, none of that pride, which would make him ashamed of his poor and humble relatives. He had, indeed, a confidence in his own powers, approaching to arrogance, which led him to undervalue the abilities of others, and to look on them as his instruments rather than his equals. But he had none of the vulgar pride founded on wealth or station. He frequently alluded to his lowly condition in early life, with great humility, thanking Heaven, with tears in his eyes, for its extraordinary goodness to him. He not only remembered, but did many acts of kindness to his early friends, of which more than one touching anecdote is related. Such traits of sensibility, gleaming through the natural austerity and sternness of a disposition like his, like light breaking through a dark cloud, affect us the more sensibly by contrast.

He was irreproachable in his morals, and conformed literally to all the rigid exactions of his severe order, in the court as faithfully as in the cloister. He was sober, abstemious, chaste. In the latter particular, he was careful that no suspicion of the license which so often soiled the clergy of the period, should attach to him. On one occasion, while on a journey, he was invited to pass the night at the house of the duchess of Maqueda, being informed that she was absent. The duchess was at home, however, and entered the apartment before he retired to rest. "You have deceived me, lady," said Ximenes, rising in anger; "if you have any business with me, you will find me tomorrow at the confessional." So saying, he abruptly left the palace.

He carried his austerities and mortifications so far, as to endanger his health. There is a curious brief extant of Pope Leo the Tenth, dated the last year of the cardinal's life, enjoining him to abate his severe penance, to eat meat and eggs on the ordinary fasts, to take off his Franciscan frock, and sleep in linen and on a bed. He would never consent, however, to divest himself of his monastic weeds. "Even laymen," said he, alluding to the custom of the Roman Catholics, "put these on when they are dying; and shall I, who have worn them all my life, take them off at that time!"

Another anecdote is told in relation to his dress. Over his coarse woolen frock, he wore the costly apparel suited to his rank. An impertinent Franciscan preacher took occasion one day before him to launch out against the luxuries of the time, especially in dress, obviously alluding to the cardinal, who was attired in a superb suit of ermine, which had been presented to him. He heard the sermon patiently to the end, and after the services were concluded, took the preacher into the sacristy, and, having commended the general tenor of his discourse, showed under his furs and fine linen the coarse frock of his order, next his skin. Some accounts add, that the friar, on the other hand, wore fine linen under his monkish frock. After the cardinal's death, a little box was found in his apartment, containing the implements with which he used to mend the rents of his threadbare garment, with his own hands.

With so much to do, it may well be believed, that Ximenes was avaricious of time. He seldom slept more than four, or at most four hours and a half. He was shaved in the night, hearing at the same time some edifying reading. He followed the same practice at his meals, or varied it with listening to the arguments of some of his theological brethren, generally on some subtle question of school divinity. This was his only recreation. He had as little taste as time for lighter and more elegant amusements. He spoke briefly, and always to the point. He was no friend of idle ceremonies, and useless visits; though his situation exposed him more or less to both. He frequently had a volume lying open on the table before him, and when his visitor stayed too long, or took up his time with light and frivolous conversation, he intimated his dissatisfaction by resuming his reading. The cardinal's book must have been as fatal to a reputation as Fontenelle's ear trumpet.

I will close this sketch of Ximenes de Cisneros with a brief outline of his person. His complexion was sallow; his countenance sharp and emaciated, his nose aquiline; his upper lip projected far over the lower. His eyes were small, deep set in his head, dark, vivid, and penetrating. His forehead ample, and, what was remarkable, without a wrinkle, though the expression of his features was somewhat severe. His voice was clear, but not agreeable; his enunciation measured and precise. His demeanor was grave, his carriage firm and erect, he was tall in stature, and his whole presence commanding. His constitution, naturally robust, was impaired by his severe austerities and severer cares, and, in the latter years of his life, was so delicate as to be extremely sensible to the vicissitudes and inclemency of the weather.

I have noticed the resemblance which Ximenes bore to the great French minister, Cardinal Richelieu. It was, after all, however, more in the circumstances of situation, than in their characters; though the most prominent traits of these were not dissimilar. Both, though bred ecclesiastics, reached the highest honors of the state, and, indeed, may be said to have directed the destinies of their countries. Richelieu's authority, however, was more absolute than that of Ximenes, for he was screened by the shadow of royalty; while the latter was exposed, by his insulated and unsheltered position, to the full blaze of envy, and, of course, opposition. Both were ambitious of military glory and showed capacity for attaining it. Both achieved their great results by that rare union of high mental endowments and great efficiency in action, which is always irresistible.

The moral basis of their characters was entirely different. The French cardinal's was selfishness, pure and unmitigated. His religion, politics, his principles in short, in every sense, were subservient to this. Offenses against the state he could forgive; those against himself he pursued with implacable rancor. His authority was literally cemented with blood. His immense powers and patronage were perverted to the aggrandizement of his family. Though bold to temerity in his plans, he betrayed more than once a want of true courage in their execution. Though violent and impetuous, he could stoop to be a dissembler. Though arrogant in the extreme, he courted the soft incense of flattery. In his manners he had the advantage over the Spanish prelate. He could be a courtier in courts, and had a more refined and cultivated taste. In one respect, he had the advantage over Ximenes in morals. He was not, like him, a bigot. He had not the religious basis in his composition, which is the foundation of bigotry.—Their deaths were typical of their characters. Richelieu died, as he had lived, so deeply execrated, that the enraged populace would scarcely allow his remains to be laid quietly in the grave. Ximenes, on the contrary, was buried amid the tears and lamentations of the people; his memory was honored even by his enemies, and his name is reverenced by his countrymen, to this day, as that of a Saint.

[HERNANDO CORTÉS]

From *The Conquest of Mexico*, Bk. VII, chap. v

[At the end of his account of the career of a major character, Prescott usually summed up by presenting a moral balance sheet.]

The personal history of Cortés has been so minutely detailed in the preceding narrative, that it will be only necessary to touch on the more prominent features of his character. Indeed, the history of the Conquest, as I have already had occasion to remark, is necessarily that of Cortés, who is, if I may so say, not merely the soul, but the body, of the enterprise, present everywhere in person, in the thick of the fight, or in the building of the works, with his sword or with his musket, sometimes leading his soldiers, and sometimes directing his little navy. The negotiations, intrigues, correspondence, are all conducted by him; and, like Cæsar, he wrote his own Commentaries in the heat of the stirring scenes which form the subject of them. His character is marked with the most opposite traits, embracing qualities apparently the most incompatible. He was avaricious, yet liberal; bold to desperation, yet cautious and calculating in his plans; magnanimous, yet very cunning; courteous and affable in his deportment, yet inexorably stern; lax in his notions of morality, yet (not uncommon) a sad bigot. The great feature in his character was constancy of purpose; a constancy not to be daunted by danger, nor baffled by disappointment, nor wearied out by impediments and delays.

He was a knight-errant, in the literal sense of the word. Of all the band of adventurous cavaliers, whom Spain, in the sixteenth century, sent forth on the career of discovery and conquest, there was none more deeply filled with the spirit of romantic enterprise than Hernando Cortés. Dangers and difficulties, instead of deterring, seemed to have a charm in his eyes. They were necessary to rouse him to a full consciousness of his powers. He grappled with them at the outset, and, if I may so express mayself, seemed to prefer to take his enterprises by the most difficult side. He conceived, at the first moment of his landing in Mexico, the design of its conquest. When he saw the strength of its civilization, he was not turned from his purpose. When he was assailed by the superior force of Narvaez, he still persisted in it; and, when he was driven in ruin from the capital, he still cherished his original idea. How successfully he carried it into execution, we have seen. After the few years of repose which succeeded the Conquest, his adventurous spirit impelled him to that dreary march across the marshes of Chiapa; and, after another interval, to seek his fortunes on the stormy Californian Gulf. When he found that no other continent remained for him to conquer, he made serious proposals to the emperor to equip a fleet at his own expense, with which he would sail to the Moluccas, and subdue the Spice-Islands for the Crown of Castile!

This spirit of knight-errantry might lead us to undervalue his talents as a general, and to regard him merely in the light of a lucky adventurer. But this would be doing him injustice; for Cortés was certainly a great general, if that man be one, who performs great achievements with the resources which his own genius has created. There is probably no instance in history, where so vast an enterprise has been achieved by means apparently so inadequate. He may be truly said to have effected the Conquest by his own resources. If he was indebted for his success to the co-operation of the Indian tribes, it was the force of his genius that obtained command of such materials. He arrested the arm that was lifted to smite him, and made it do battle in his behalf. He beat the Tlascalans, and made them his stanch allies. He beat the soldiers of Narvaez, and doubled his effective force by it. When his own men deserted him, he did not desert himself. He drew them back by degrees, and compelled them to act by his will, till they were all as one man. He brought together the most miscellaneous collection of mercenaries who ever fought under one standard; adventurers from Cuba and the Isles, craving for gold; hidalgos, who came from the old country to win laurels; broken-down cavaliers, who hoped to mend their fortunes in the New World; vagabonds flying from justice; the grasping followers of Narvaez, and his own reckless veterans,—men with hardly a common tie, and burning with the spirit of jealousy and faction; wild tribes of the natives from all parts of the country, who had been sworn enemies from their cradles, and who had met only to cut one another's throats, and to procure victims for sacrifice; men, in short, differing in race, in language, and in interests, with scarcely anything in common among them. Yet this motley congregation was assembled in one camp, compelled to bend to the will of one man, to consort together in harmony, to breathe, as it were, one spirit, and to move on a common principle of action! It is in this wonderful power over the discordant masses thus gathered under his banner, that we recognize the genius of the great commander, no less than in the skill of his military operations.

His power over the minds of his soldiers was a natural result of their confidence in his abilities. But it is also to be attributed to his popular manners,—that happy union of authority and companionship, which fitted him for the command of a band of roving adventurers. It would not have done for him to have fenced himself round with the stately reserve of a commander of regular forces. He was embarked with his men in a common adventure, and nearly on terms of equality, since he held his commission by no legal warrant. But, while he indulged this freedom and familiarity with his soldiers, he never allowed it to interfere with their strict obedience, nor to impair the severity of discipline. When he had risen to higher consideration, although he affected more state, he still admitted his veterans to the same intimacy. "He preferred," says Diaz, "to be called 'Cortés' by us, to being called by any title; and with good reason," continues the enthusiastic old cavalier, "for the name of Cortés is as famous in our day as was that of Cæsar among the Romans, or of Hannibal among the Carthaginians." He showed the same kind regard towards his ancient comrades in the very last act of his life. For he appropriated a sum by his will for the celebration of two thousand masses for the souls of those who had fought with him in the campaigns of Mexico.

His character has been unconsciously traced by the hand of a master.

> "And oft *the chieftain* deigned to aid
> And mingle in the mirth they made;
> For, though, with men of high degree,
> The proudest of the proud was he,
> Yet, trained in camps, he knew the art
> To win the soldiers' hardy heart.
> They love a captain to obey,
> Boisterous as March, yet fresh as May;
> With open hand, and brow as free,
> Lover of wine, and minstrelsy;
> Ever the first to scale a tower,
> As venturous in a lady's bower;—
> Such buxom chief shall lead his host
> From India's fires to Zembla's frost."

Cortés, without much violence, might have sat for this portrait of Marmion.

Cortés was not a vulgar conqueror. He did not conquer from the mere ambition of conquest. If he destroyed the ancient capital of the Aztecs, it was to build up a more magnificent capital on its ruins. If he desolated the land, and broke up its existing institutions, he employed the short period of his administration in digesting schemes for introducing there a more improved culture and a higher civilization. In all his expeditions he was careful to study the resources of the country, its social organization, and its physical capacities. He enjoined it on his captains to attend particularly to these objects. If he was greedy of gold, like most of the Spanish cavaliers in the New World, it was not to hoard it, nor merely to lavish it in the support of a princely establishment, but to secure funds for prosecuting his glorious discoveries. Witness his costly expeditions to the Gulf of California. His enterprises were not undertaken solely for mercenary objects; as is shown by the various expeditions he set on foot for the discovery of a communication between the Atlantic and the Pacific. In his schemes of ambition he showed a respect for the interests of science, to be referred partly to the natural superiority of his mind, but partly, no doubt, to the influence of early education. It is, indeed, hardly possible, that a person of his wayward and mercurial temper should have improved his advantages at the University, but he brought away from it a tincture of scholarship, seldom found among the cavaliers of the period, and which had its influence in enlarging his own conceptions. His celebrated Letters are written with a simple elegance, that, as I have already had occasion to remark, have caused them to be compared to the military narrative of Cæsar. It will not be easy to find in the chronicles of the period a more concise, yet comprehensive, statement, not only of the events of his campaigns, but of the circumstances most worthy of notice in the character of the conquered countries.

Cortés was not cruel; at least, not cruel as compared with most of those who followed his iron trade. The path of the conqueror is necessarily marked with blood. He was not too scrupulous, indeed, in the execution of his plans. He swept away the obstacles which lay in his track; and his fame is darkened by the commission of more than one act which his boldest apologists will find it hard to vindicate. But he was not wantonly cruel. He allowed no outrage on his unresisting foes. This may seem small praise, but it is an exception to the usual conduct of his countrymen in their conquests, and it is something to be in advance of one's time. He was severe, it may be added, in enforcing obedience to his orders for protecting their persons and their property. With his licentious crew, it was, sometimes, not without hazard that he was so. After the Conquest, he sanctioned the system of *repartimientos;* but so did Columbus. He endeavored to regulate it by the most humane laws, and continued to suggest many important changes for ameliorating the condition of the natives. The best commentary on his conduct, in this respect, is the deference that was shown him by the Indians, and the confidence with which they appealed to him for protection in all their subsequent distresses.

In private life he seems to have had the power of attaching to himself, warmly, those who were near his person. The influence of this attachment is shown in every page of Bernal Diaz, though his work was written to vindicate the claims of the soldiers, in opposition to those of the general. He seems to have led a happy life with his first wife, in their humble retirement in Cuba; and regarded the second, to judge from the expressions in his testament, with confidence and love. Yet he cannot be acquitted from the charge of those licentious gallantries which entered too generally into the character of the military adventurer of that day. He would seem also, by the frequent suits in which he was involved, to have been of an irritable and contentious spirit. But much allowance must be made for the irritability of a man who had been too long accustomed to independent sway, patiently to endure the checks and control of the petty spirits who were incapable of comprehending the noble character of his enterprises. "He thought," says an eminent writer, "to silence his enemies by the brilliancy of the new career on which he had entered. He did not reflect, that these enemies had been raised by the very grandeur and rapidity of his success." He was rewarded for his efforts by the misinterpretation of his motives; by the calumnious charges of squandering the public revenues and of aspiring to independent sovereignty. But, although we may admit the foundation of many of the grievances alleged by Cortés, yet when we consider the querulous tone of his correspondence and the frequency of his litigation, we may feel a natural suspicion that his proud spirit was too sensitive to petty slights, and too jealous of imaginary wrongs.

One trait more remains to be noticed in the character of this remarkable man; that is, his bigotry, the failing of the age,—for, surely, it should be termed only a failing. When we see the hand, red with the blood of the wretched native, raised to invoke the blessing of Heaven on the cause which it maintains, we experience something like a sensation of disgust at the act, and a doubt of its sincerity. But this is unjust. We should throw ourselves back (it cannot be too often repeated) into the age; the age of the Crusades. For every Spanish cavalier, however sordid and selfish might be his private motives, felt himself to be the soldier of the Cross. Many of them would have died in defense of it. Whoever has read the correspondence of Cortés, or, still more, has attended to the circumstances of his career, will hardly doubt that he would have been among the first to lay down his life for the Faith. He more than once periled life, and fortune, and the success of his whole enterprise, by the premature and most impolitic manner in which he would have forced conversion on the natives. To the more rational spirit of the present day, enlightened by a purer Christianity, it may seem difficult to reconcile gross deviations from morals with such devotion to the cause of religion. But the religion taught in that day was one of form and elaborate ceremony. In the punctilious attention to discipline, the spirit of Christianity was permitted to evaporate. The mind, occupied with forms, thinks little of substance. In a worship that is addressed too exclusively to the senses, it is often the case, that morality becomes divorced from religion, and the measure of righteousness is determined by the creed rather than by the conduct.

In the earlier part of the History, I have given a description of the person of Cortés. It may be well to close this review of his character by the account of his manners and personal habits left us by Bernal Diaz, the old chronicler, who has accompanied us through the whole course of our narrative, and who may now fitly furnish the conclusion of it. No man knew his commander better; and, if the avowed object of his work might naturally lead to a disparagement of Cortés, this is more than counterbalanced by the warmth of his personal attachment, and by that *esprit de corps* which leads him to take a pride in the renown of his general.

"In his whole appearance and presence," says Diaz, "in his discourse, his table, his dress, in everything, in short, he had the air of a great lord. His clothes were in the fashion of the time; he set little value on silk, damask, or velvet, but dressed plainly and exceedingly neat; nor did he wear massy chains of gold, but simply a fine one, of exquisite workmanship, from which was suspended a jewel having the figure of our Lady the Virgin and her precious Son, with a Latin motto cut upon it. On his finger he wore a splendid diamond ring; and from his cap which, according to the fashion of that day, was of velvet, hung a medal, the device of which I do not remember. He was magnificently attended, as became a man of his rank, with chamberlains and major-domos and many pages; and the service of his table was splendid, with a quantity of both gold and silver plate. At noon he dined heartily, drinking about a pint of wine mixed with water. He supped well, though he was not dainty in regard to his food, caring little for the delicacies of the table, unless, indeed, on such occasions as made attention to these matters of some consequence.

"He was acquainted with Latin, and, as I have understood, was made Bachelor of Laws; and, when he conversed with learned men who addressed him in Latin, he answered them in the same language. He was also something of a poet; his conversation was agreeable, and he had a pleasant elocution. In his attendance on the services of the Church he was most punctual, devout in his manner, and charitable to the poor.

"When he swore, he used to say, 'On my conscience'; and when he was vexed with anyone, 'Evil betide you.' With his men he was very patient; and they were sometimes impertinent and even insolent. When very angry, the veins in his throat and forehead would swell, but he uttered no reproaches against either officer or soldier.

"He was fond of cards and dice, and, when he played, was always in good humor, indulging freely in jests and repartees. He was affable with his followers, especially with those who came over with him from Cuba. In his campaigns he paid strict attention to discipline, frequently going the rounds himself during the night, and seeing that the sentinels did their duty. He entered the quarters of his soldiers without ceremony, and chided those whom he found without their arms and accoutrements, saying, 'It was a bad sheep that could not carry its own wool.' On the expedition to Honduras he acquired the habit of sleeping after his meals, feeling unwell if he omitted it; and, however sultry or stormy the weather, he caused a carpet or his cloak to be thrown under a tree, and slept soundly for some time. He was frank and exceedingly liberal in his disposition, until the last few years of his life, when he was accused of parsimony. But we should consider that his funds were employed on great and costly enterprises; and that none of these, after the Conquest, neither his expedition to Honduras, nor his voyages to California, were crowned with success. It was perhaps intended that he should receive his recompense in a better world; and I fully believe it; for he was a good cavalier, most true in his devotions to the Virgin, to the Apostle St. Peter, and to all the other Saints."

Such is the portrait, which has been left to us by the faithful hand most competent to trace it, of Hernando Cortés, the Conqueror of Mexico.

[CHARLES THE FIFTH]

From *Philip the Second*, Bk. I, chap. ix

[Charles V (1500–1558), father of Philip II and grandson of Ferdinand and Isabella, turned his throne over to his son and spent the last two years of his life in the Monastery of St. Just.]

I have gone somewhat into detail in regard to the latter days of Charles the Fifth, who exercised in his retirement too important an influence on public affairs for such an account of him to be deemed an impertinent episode to the history of Philip the Second. Before parting from him forever, I will take a brief view of some peculiarities in his personal rather than his political character, which has long since been indelibly traced by a hand abler than mine.

Charles, at the time of his death, was in the fifty-eighth year of his age. He was older in constitution than in years. So much shaken had he been, indeed, in mind as well as body, that he may be said to have died of premature old age. Yet his physical development had been very slow. He was nearly twenty-one years old before any beard was to be seen on his chin. Yet by the time he was thirty-six, gray hairs began to make their appearance on his temples. At forty the gout had made severe inroads on a constitution originally strong; and before he was fifty, the man who could keep the saddle day and night in his campaigns, who seemed to be insensible to fatigue as he followed the chase among the wild passes of the Alpujarras, was obliged to be carried in a litter, like a poor cripple, at the head of his armies.

His mental development was equally tardy with his bodily. So long as Chièvres lived,—the Flemish noble who had the care of his early life,—Charles seemed to have no will of his own. During his first visit to Spain, where he came when seventeen years old, he gave so little promise that those who approached him nearest could discern no signs of his future greatness. Yet the young prince seems to have been conscious that he had the elements of greatness within him, and he patiently bided his time. "*Nondum*"—"Not yet"—was the motto which he adopted for his maiden shield, when but eighteen years old, at a tournament at Valladolid.

But when the death of the Flemish minister had released the young monarch from this state of dependence, he took the reins into his own hands, as Louis the Fourteenth did on the death of Mazarin. He now showed himself in an entirely new aspect. He even displayed greater independence than his predecessors had done. He no longer trusted everything, like them, to a council of state. He trusted only to himself; and if he freely communicated with some one favorite minister, like the elder Granvelle, and the cardinal, his son, it was in order to be counseled, not to be controlled by their judgments. He patiently informed himself of public affairs; and when foreign envoys had their audiences of him, they were surprised to find him possessed of everything relating to their own courts and the objects of their mission.

Yet he did not seem to be quick of apprehension, or, to speak more correctly, he was slow at arriving at his results. He would keep the courier waiting for days before he could come to a decision. When he did come to it, no person on earth could shake it. Talking one day with the Venetian Contarini about this habit of his mind, the courtly minister remarked that "it was not obstinacy to adhere to sound opinions." "True," said Charles, "but I sometimes adhere to those that are unsound."

His indefatigable activity both of mind and body formed a strong contrast to the lethargy of early years. His widely scattered empire, spreading over the Low Countries, Spain, Germany, and the New World, presented embarrassments which most princes would have found it impossible to overcome. At least, they would have been compelled to govern, in a great measure, by deputy,—to transact their business by agents. But Charles chose to do everything himself,—to devise his own plans and to execute them in person. The number of his journeys by land and by water, as noticed in his farewell address, is truly wonderful; for that was not the day of steamboats and railways. He seemed to lead the life of a courier. But it was for no trivial object that he made these expeditions. He knew where his presence was needed; and his promptness and punctuality brought him at the right time on the right spot. No spot in his broad empire was far removed from him. He seemed to possess the power of ubiquity.

The consciousness of his own strength roused to a flame the spark of ambition which had hitherto slept in his bosom. His schemes were so vast that it was a common opinion he aspired to universal monarchy. Like his grandfather, Ferdinand, and his own son, Philip, he threw over his schemes the cloak of religion. Or, to deal with him more fairly, religious principle probably combined with personal policy to determine his career. He seemed always ready to do battle for the Cross. He affected to identify the cause of Spain with the cause of Christendom. He marched against the Turks, and stayed the tide of Ottoman inroad in Hungary. He marched against the Protestants, and discomfited their armies in the heart of Germany. He crossed the Mediterranean, and humbled the Crescent at Algiers. He threw himself on the honor of Francis, and traveled through France to take vengeance on the rebels of Flanders. He twice entered France as an enemy and marched up to the gates of

Paris. Instead of the modest legend on his maiden shield, he now assumed the proud motto, "*Plus ultra*"; and he vindicated his right to it by sending his fleets across the ocean and by planting the banner of Castile on the distant shores of the Pacific. In these enterprises he was generally successful. His success led him to rely still more on himself. "Myself, and the lucky moment," was his favorite saying. The "star of Austria" was still a proverb. It was not till the evening of life that he complained of the fickleness of fortune,—that his star, as it descended to the horizon, was obscured by clouds and darkness.

Thus Charles's nerves were kept in a state of perpetual excitement. No wonder that his health should have sunk under it, like a plant forced by extraordinary stimulants to an unnatural production at the expense of its own vitality.

His habits were not all of them the most conducive to health. He slept usually only four hours; too short a time to repair the waste caused by incessant toil. His phlegmatic temperament did not incline him to excess. Yet there was one excess of which he was guilty,—the indulgence of his appetite to a degree most pernicious to his health. A Venetian contemporary tells us that, before rising in the morning, potted capon was usually served to him, dressed with sugar, milk, and spices. At noon he dined on a variety of dishes. Soon after vespers he took another meal, and later in the evening supped heartily on anchovies, or some other gross and savory food of which he was particularly fond. On one occasion complaining to his *maître-d'-hôtel* that the cook sent him nothing but dishes too insipid and tasteless to be eaten, the perplexed functionary, knowing Charles's passion for timepieces, replied that "he did not know what he could do, unless it were to serve his majesty a ragout of watches!" The witticism had one good effect, that of provoking a hearty laugh from the emperor,—a thing rarely witnessed in his latter days.

It was in vain that Cardinal Loaysa, his confessor, remonstrated, with an independence that does him credit, against his master's indulgence of his appetite, assuring him that resistance here would do more for his soul than any penance with the

scourge. It seems a pity that Charles, considering his propensi-
ties, should have so easily obtained absolution from fasts, and
that he should not, on the contrary, have transferred some of
the penance which he inflicted on his back to the offending part.
Even in the monastery of Yuste he still persevered in the same
pernicious taste. Anchovies, frogs' legs, and eel-pasties were
the dainty morsels with which he chose to be regaled, even
before the eyes of his physician. It would not have been amiss
for him to have exchanged his solitary repast more frequently
for the simpler fare of the refectory.

With these coarser tastes Charles combined many others of a
refined and intellectual character. We have seen his fondness for
music, and the delight he took in the sister art of design,—
especially in the works of Titian. He was painted several times
by this great master, and it was by his hand, as we have seen,
that he desired to go down to posterity. The emperor had,
moreover, another taste, perhaps talent, which, with a different
training and in a different sphere of life, might have led him to
the craft of authorship.

A curious conversation is reported as having been held by
him with Borja, the future saint, during one of the visits paid
by the Jesuit to Yuste. Charles inquired of his friend whether
it were wrong for a man to write his autobiography, provided
he did so honestly and with no motive of vanity. He said
that he had written his own memoirs, not from the desire of
self-glorification, but to correct manifold mistakes which had
been circulated of his doings, and to set his conduct in a true
light. One might be curious to know the answer, which is not
given, of the good father to this question. It is to be hoped that
it was not of a kind to induce the emperor to destroy the manuscript, which has never come to light.

However this may be, there is no reason to doubt that at one
period of his life he had compiled a portion of his autobiography.
In the imperial household, as I have already noticed, was a
Flemish scholar, William Van Male, or Malinæus, as he is called
in Latin, who, under the title of gentleman of the chamber,
wrote many a long letter for Charles, while standing by his

bedside, and read many a weary hour to him after the monarch had gone to rest,—not, as it would seem, to sleep. This personage tells us that Charles, when sailing on the Rhine, wrote an account of his expeditions to as late a date as 1550. This is not very definite. Any account written under such circumstances and in so short a time could be nothing but a sketch of the most general kind. Yet Van Male assures us that he had read the manuscript, which he commends for its terse and elegant diction; and he proposes to make a Latin version of it, the style of which should combine the separate merits of Tacitus, Livy, Suetonius, and Cæsar! The admiring chamberlain laments that, instead of giving it to the world, Charles should keep it jealously secured under lock and key.

The emperor's taste for authorship showed itself also in another form. This was by the translation of the "*Chevalier Delibéré*," a French poem then popular, celebrating the court of his ancestor, Charles the Bold of Burgundy. Van Male, who seems to have done for Charles the Fifth what Voltaire did for Frederick when he spoke of himself as washing the king's dirty linen, was employed also to overlook this translation, which he pronounces to have possessed great merit in regard to idiom and selection of language. The emperor then gave it to Acuña, a good poet of the court, to be done into Castilian verse. Thus metamorphosed, he proposed to give the copy to Van Male. A mischievous wag, Avila the historian, assured the emperor that it could not be worth less than five hundred gold crowns to that functionary. "And William is well entitled to them," said the monarch, "for he has sweat much over the work." Two thousand copies were forthwith ordered to be printed of the poem, which was to come out anonymously. Poor Van Male, who took a very different view of the profits, and thought that nothing was certain but the cost of the edition, would have excused himself from this proof of this master's liberality. It was all in vain; Charles was not to be balked in his generous purpose; and, without a line to propitiate the public favor by stating in the preface the share of the royal hand in the composition, it was ushered into the world.

Whatever Charles may have done in the way of an auto-biography, he was certainly not indifferent to posthumous fame. He knew that the greatest name must soon pass into oblivion, unless embalmed in the song of the bard or the page of the chronicler. He looked for a chronicler to do for him with his pen what Titian had done for him with his pencil,—exhibit him in his true proportions, and in a permanent form, to the eye of posterity. In this he does not seem to have been so much under the influence of vanity as of a natural desire to have his character and conduct placed in a fair point of view—what seemed to him to be such—for the contemplation or criticism of mankind.

The person whom the emperor selected for this delicate office was the learned Sepulveda. Sleidan he condemned as a slanderer; and Giovio, who had taken the other extreme and written of him with what he called the "golden pen" of history, he no less condemned as a flatterer. Charles encouraged Sepulveda to apply to him for information on matters relating to his government. But when requested by the historian to listen to what he had written, the emperor refused. "I will neither hear nor read," he replied, "what you have said of me. Others may do this when I am gone. But if you wish for any information on any point, I shall be always ready to give it to you." A history thus compiled was of the nature of an autobiography, and must be considered, therefore, as entitled to much the same confidence, and open to the same objections, as that kind of writing. Sepulveda was one of the few who had repeated access to Charles in his retirement at Yuste; and the monarch testified his regard for him by directing that particular care be taken that no harm should come to the historian's manuscript before it was committed to the press.

Such are some of the most interesting traits and personal anecdotes I have been able to collect of the man who for nearly forty years ruled over an empire more vast, with an authority more absolute, than any monarch since the days of Charlemagne. It may be thought strange that I should have omitted to notice one feature in his character, the most prominent in the line from which he was descended, at least on the mother's side,—his bigotry. But in Charles this was less conspicuous than in many others of his house; and while he sat upon the throne, the extent to which his religious principles were held in subordination by his political suggests a much closer parallel to the policy of his grandfather, Ferdinand the Catholic, than to that of his son, Philip the Second, or of his imbecile grandson, Philip the Third.

But the religious gloom which hung over Charles's mind took the deeper tinge of fanaticism after he had withdrawn to the monastery of Yuste. With his dying words, as we have seen, he bequeathed the Inquisition as a precious legacy to his son. In like manner, he endeavored to cherish in the Regent Joanna's bosom the spirit of persecution. And if it be true, as his biographer assures us, that Charles expressed a regret that he had respected the safe-conduct of Luther, the world had little reason to mourn that he exchanged the sword and the scepter for the breviary of the friar,—the throne of the Cæsars for his monastic retreat among the wilds of Estremadura.

IX. LITERARY CRITICISM

[WHAT IS POETICAL?]
From "Byron's Letter on Pope"

["Byron's Letter on Pope" was Prescott's first review, in the *North American Review*, XIII, 4, 445–473 (October, 1821). The selection is typical of the "associational" æsthetics which conservative critics borrowed from Scotland in the first third of the century. The article as a whole is a review of the Bowles-Byron controversy over the respective merits of art and nature as materials for poetry.]

It would be well to understand what is meant by the terms poetry, and poetical. We will not attempt to circumscribe poetry, by an exclusive definition, which, if we may judge from similar attempts, may after all be very defective; but we may safely point out what by universal consent are esteemed suitable topics for poetry.

All will admit that a star, a rose bud, a sunny cloud are poetical; and why? because they delight the soul with emotions of beauty. All will allow a mountain, a desert, a whirlwind, to be poetical;—why? because they animate us with consciousness of power, immensity,—all that is sublime. Everyone feels that tales of love, of revenge, of pining melancholy, in short whatever is built on the passions of the human heart, are highly poetical: and thence we infer that whatever suggests to us sentiments of grandeur, or beauty, and whatever moves the affections, is poetical in that degree. If natural objects, therefore, are more sublime, more beautiful, or more affecting than artificial, they are more poetical; and that they are so, we think it not difficult to prove.

What, for instance, in the material world can furnish us with more beautiful images than those which nature displays on a fine spring morning, when all is quick with joy and life; the landscape glowing in the brightness of a rising sun; the foliage, the spires of grass glittering with dew-drops; the playful rivulet now sparkling in the ray, now hiding itself in the covert; the song of birds; the bleating of sheep on the uplands; the lowing of cattle in the valley; "the living fragrance of flowers, yet fresh with childhood"; or the same landscape softened in the gray of twilight; when the glare of day is gone,—when a faint light only hovers on the waters; when no noise is heard save the chirping of the cricket, the sad moan of the whippoorwill, or the indistinct whisper, that seems to float on the distant hills;—when the voice of merriment and of labor have alike ceased; when all is hushed in profound repose, and the soul drinks in the sense of beauty?

What can art add that shall chime in with the spirit of these scenes and improve their character?

The white cottage, the tapering spire, the tinkling sheepbell, the cheerful sound of the village flute, the brisk motion of the mill-wheel scattering drops of liquid light, are artificial sounds and sights, and beautiful as they accord with the expression of the morning. At the close of day, the ruined abbey, the chime of distant bells, the slow beat of oars, heard at intervals, are no less beautiful, and in perfect harmony with the temper of the hour, which naturally leads to quiet, soothing meditation. They owe most of their beauty, however, to *natural associations*. The cottage is the abode of rustic simplicity, and tells us of man. The blithe strains of the minstrel speak of buoyant youth and heartfelt happiness; and the busy wheel reminds us also of plenty and healthful labor. The ruined abbey speaks to the heart of other times, and the music of village bells touches some chord in unison with the hour, till the "soul runs o'er with silent worship." It is to nature that these objects are primarily indebted for their beauty, and even these are beautiful in the landscape only as *auxiliaries*. Nature is the groundwork; they but swell the tide of feeling which she had first stirred within our bosoms. Nature would of herself have been all-sufficient to have excited these feelings; *they* could have done little without her; it is

"The gush of springs,
    The fall of lofty fountains, and the bend
    Of stirring branches, and the bud which brings
    The swiftest thought of beauty."

It is in a word images borrowed from nature, that excite in us perceptions of beauty. On these the poet dwells when he would impart a kindred glow to others; and heightens it by happy allusions to art;—but nature gives a tone to the whole, and the images she furnishes are therefore most poetical.

It will be less difficult, we imagine, to show the comparative inferiority of artificial to natural objects in raising emotions of power. Would you call up these feelings, go forth in the dead of night, contemplate the magnificence of heaven, the moon, "the stars in their development"; go to the sea-side, listen to the sad and solemn voice of the ocean, watch the gathering tempest, hear the night-winds sigh over the interminable waste; or gaze upon the hills, "whose scalps are pinnacled in clouds"; meditate on the might, which cast their dark foundations deep, and the generations of men that have been swept away at their feet. What works of man can compare with these? How far can they even add to the effect of such a spectacle?

The explosion of cannon in the hour of battle, the sound of a funeral bell at midnight are sublime; a ship would no doubt add to the sublimity of a storm, but here it is not the vessel, but the men within her that excite the terrible interest in our bosoms. The pyramids are perhaps the most sublime of human monuments; their age, their magnitude, their situation, all conspire to render them so; but what are the pyramids, with all the notions they suggest to us of power and duration, in comparison with the mountains, whose foundations were from the first. Place them at the foot of the Alps or of the Andes, and let one born in a sandy desert, who has seen neither hills nor pyramids, tell you which fills him with the strongest emotion. We are grown familiar with mountain scenery, and a pyramid produces a disproportionate effect on our imaginations. Yet nature will still maintain her sway over us, "tamen usque recurrit," and if we would lift the souls of our readers to the loftiest tone of enthusiasm, we borrow our images from nature. No one has done this more frequently and more successfully than Lord Byron.

Lastly, we think there can be no dispute that an exhibition of passions founded in nature must move us more forcibly than the manners and forms of artificial life, and that the former are consequently more poetical than the latter.

[THE DEVELOPMENT OF ENGLISH PROSE STYLE]

From "Essay Writing"

[This is one of the uncollected reviews, published in the *North American Review*, XIV, 319–350 (April, 1822). This important essay is evidence of Prescott's careful study of English prose in the period when he was forming his own style. Note that it reflects the contemporary American reaction against Latinity in diction. The concluding remarks on Irving's *Sketch Book* constitute one of the earliest recognitions of the historical importance of that work. Prescott acknowledged indebtedness for the materials of the first half of the article to Nathan Drake, an eighteenth-century historian and anthologist of the English essay.]

In our preceding remarks we have considered these essays, in reference to their value, as samples of *literature;* we will now, under favor of our readers, subjoin a few reflections on the influence which some of them have exerted over the English *language;* an influence perfectly accountable, as many of them were written with the avowed purpose of forming a polite taste in letters, and most of them claimed to be specimens of classical composition.

The English language was long in arrear of its literature; and has been gradually matured under a slow assiduous cultivation. Intellectual excellence may exist at any period; but excellence of language can only be obtained by labor and experience. It must be purified from terms merely synonymous, barren expletives, exotic idioms, before it can become vigorous and precise; and there must be many examples of false taste and barbarous jargon, before there can be created a high acknowledged standard of refinement and harmony. From these causes, English prose ripened slowly into perfection, and did not attain its ultimate polish until nearly two centuries after its literature had reached an elevation, which perhaps no subsequent age has surpassed. The first of those writers in English prose, whose works still continue to be the manual of every good scholar, were enabled to create them at that early period, by an unprecedented *vigor* of original genius. They were adventurers where man had never trod before, and strength was more serviceable than either delicacy or grace, in overcoming the numerous obstacles of an untraveled literature. Of course it was on their strength that they chiefly relied. They thought what they should say, not how they should say it. The vocabulary was, it is true, sufficiently copious for all the purposes of an elegant literature; but they were laying the foundation stones of that literature, and in the selection, they thought only of solidity and strength, and wisely left the study of grace and proportion to those who should come after them.

Indeed, where they aimed at a display of taste, they generally failed. Good taste must grow out of long cultivation. It is by comparison only that one thing is pronounced beautiful, another not. They had no standard of comparison;—they wrote in a new tongue, compounded of many others it is true, but entirely like none. As was natural, however, they endeavored to fashion it, as closely as possible, after the manner of the most polished language to which it bore any resemblance. The Latin accordingly was the model, by which all the writers of that day more or less governed themselves. In doing this, much violence was offered to the Saxon idiom; and this exclusive introduction of a Latin manner into a language, in which a great proportion of words was of Teutonic origin, made it at once formal, intricate, and ungraceful. The following remark of Sir Thomas Browne, who, in the succeeding age, both inculcated and exemplified to the most absurd extent this adoption of a foreign idiom, will show how generally the same design had been pursued by men of letters. "If elegancy still proceedeth," says he, in his Enquiries into Vulgar Errors, "and English pens maintain that stream we have of late observed to flow from many, we shall, within a few years, be fain to learn Latin to understand English, and a work will prove of equal facility in either." This excessive infusion of the Latin, however, although unfortunate in other respects, much invigorated our language by the magnificence of its vocabulary, and the sententious structure of its periods. We have said, that where the early writers aimed at a show of taste, they generally failed. They were taken with gaudy images and foolish conceits, as barbarians are captivated by glaring colors and glittering tinsel; finery they mistook for beauty. Sir Philip Sidney's Arcadia is an example in point, which, in spite of its wild romantic sweetness, is going fast into oblivion from this insufferable affectation. The euphuisms and the quibbles which found their way into the most serious discourses in the reign of James I, (that monarch of punning memory,) are a still more melancholy exemplification of perverted taste.

The violence of party spirit during the civil wars, and the acrimonious topics upon which the pen was chiefly employed, were unfavorable to the development or the cultivation of grace in composition. Milton, the most distinguished writer of the day, who, as Wordsworth has remarked, "though a Hebrew in soul, was deeply imbued with classical literature," constrained his rich and glorious imagination into the rigid inversions of the Latin idiom; and it was not until the Restoration, that this preposterous accommodation of a living language, to the genius of a dead one, was entirely laid aside. There was still, however, a lingering of the pedantry of the former age, which threw a shade over the glowing compositions of some of the finest geniuses of any age or country; but this wore off by degrees, under the influence of the social, though licentious manners of the court of Charles II, which naturally introduced a less stately, and a more free and familiar style, both of thinking and writing. This was bringing the language nearer to the tone of ordinary life; and, notwithstanding what may be said of "wells of old English undefiled," there is much more of the genuine raciness of its native soil in it thus improved, than in the stiff and latinized phraseology of older writers. Dryden, by the variety and flow of his periods, was the first to bring into disrepute the staid formalities of his predecessors. But Cowley, who is perhaps never more a poet than in his prose compositions, set the first example in his essays, (as has been sagaciously remarked by Murphy,[1]) of that sweet, easy, and perfectly natural manner, which was afterwards still farther recommended by the pure taste of Tillotson and Temple, and finally brought to a high polish under the graceful genius of Addison. Indeed, Addison professed to have modelled his style almost exclusively upon Tillotson; but he is neither so feeble nor so prolix, and it is easy to discover in him a much nearer resemblance to the naïveté and elegant simplicity of Sir William Temple.

The English language has received its greatest impulses under the patronage of female sovereigns. Under Elizabeth it was subdued, and under Anne, if not perfected, was at least put in the right road to perfection. Many coexisting circumstances united to produce such a refinement of language at this latter period. The intimacy into which the higher ranks had been thrown of late years with the French nation, and consequently with its literature, by their own domestic convulsions, had, as has been often remarked, an unfavorable effect upon English verse. It introduced that cold mechanical structure, to which the English heroic measure was almost equally well adapted with the French. But it was otherwise in prose, and the gay colloquial graces of the French tongue had a favorable influence upon the cumbrous pedantry of the English. In the further advancement of letters, criticism came now to be studied. Men had already seen a sufficient number of examples in every kind of writing, to form a high standard

[1] Vide Murphy's Essay on the Genius of Dr. Johnson. [Prescott's note.]

of excellence. The men in office, too, under queen Anne, were (as has been well observed by Drake) more or less imbued with a taste for letters, and were thus enabled, by authority as well as by inclination, to inculcate their literary partialities.

But a principal cause of the refinement of style at this period is to be attributed to the peculiar intellectual character of the existing writers, and of Addison more than all the rest. This character was not marked by the exuberant imagination, or intense feeling, or bold hardy energy of the preceding age; but by a subtle and ingenious wit, shrewd observation, and acute delicacy of taste. The turn of thought, induced by this constitution of mind, naturally disclosed itself in a style best suited to the exhibition of its peculiar beauties; a style which by its simple, conversational, and idiomatic character, was well adapted to light familiar topics, or to calm, philosophical reflection, or to sober, dispassionate reasoning; which, although not powerful or adventurous, and exceedingly loose and incorrect, might yet rise by an easy flow into a high pitch of graceful eloquence, and which, free from inversion, pedantry and art of any kind, might win its way to the heart by the expression of natural sentiment in the most natural manner. These qualities constitute the *substratum*, the primitive basis on which the style of queen Anne's day was formed; and it is curious to observe the different effect produced by the action of different individual tastes on this general basis. In Swift, for instance, we see the most homely and even vulgar images, connected by the general tenor of this pure and perspicuous style; and the gaudy and studied fancies which abound in most of the prose writings of Pope, sparkle only on the surface of the same sweet natural diction. But it was most happily suited to the simple genius of Addison. Indeed he recommended it no less by the critical precepts, than by the example of his periodical writings; and to these, more than to any other cause, must be referred the introduction of a polite taste in English composition, at the commencement of the last century.

Still much remained to be done, to a perfect organization

even of this pure style of composition, which was often loose, feeble, and ungrammatical. The successive labor of many fine writers gradually supplied these defects, and made it both vigorous and correct; and before the appearance of the Rambler in 1750, it had been carried to a point which it cannot hope to surpass in the gracefulness of Melmoth, and the Attic simplicity of Hume.

The publication of the Rambler forms an important era in the history of English style. Johnson would have been fitted by his giant strength to have grappled with all the obstacles that impeded the first adventurers in our language. He was therefore well fitted for the mighty task which he assumed in a riper period of that language of reclaiming the ἔπεα πτερόεντα, those fleeting beauties which had already escaped in the lapse of years, and of preventing their future progress to oblivion, by chaining them down to a permanent standard of accurate definition. His researches as a lexicographer no doubt much contributed to the elaborate pomp of his diction, by storing it with all the obsolete terms of a copious vocabulary. But he was still farther led to it by the natural complexion of his mind. He wanted a language that would afford scope for the free play of a grand and vigorous intellect; he would have broken through the fine and delicate texture of the style of Addison. He accordingly preferred the sententiousness of a Latin idiom; he was a great admirer of Browne, who, as we before remarked, was more distinguished than any of the elder writers for antiquated, latinized phraseology; Johnson would, in all probability, therefore, have attempted to reintroduce the old fashioned dialect, but happily the taste of the age was too far advanced to admit of it, and he substituted a measured an-tithetical construction of sentence, which although in the highest degree artificial, was both more elegant and more conformable to the idiom of his native tongue, than the awkward inversions of the old school. He still farther invigorated his language with a great number of Latin derivatives, and technical terms of science. By these expedients he built up a grand and im-posing style, well fitted for the exhibition of brilliant fancy and powerful thought, but very ill adapted to the common purposes and every day business of life.

These two peculiar manners of Addison and of Johnson may be looked upon as the extreme and opposite points in English composition, which no writer can go beyond without feebleness on the one hand, or bombast on the other. Indeed these are the faults to which their respective styles have a natural tendency; where extraordinary efforts are demanded, the former manner seems tame and cold, while in the familiar topics of common life, the latter has a truly ridiculous air of ostentatious formality. Many examples of these failures may be found both in the Spectator and the Rambler, and still more in the productions of their countless imitators.

The Rambler was not in great demand at the time of its publication; but it made a permanent impression on the character of English style, and by presenting a captivating model of vigorous composition, has done much to preserve the energies of the language, from being frittered away under the servile and humble followers of Addison. New beauties constantly developed themselves under these mutual influences; and as philological criticism soon advanced the grammar of the tongue to a high degree of accuracy, we may look upon the last half of the last century, a period embellished by the pens of Hume, Johnson, Hawkesworth, Goldsmith, Burke, Robertson, Gibbon, Junius, and Mackenzie, as the Augustan age of English fine writing; (our remarks will be understood as applying to language, and not to literature;) a period in which precision, perspicuity, copiousness, grace and vigor, in short whatever constitutes the perfection of style, were carried to a height which has not since been surpassed, and seldom been equaled.

English composition, then, may be said to have reached its meridian during the last half of the eighteenth century; what its tendencies have since been, and what they are now, forms an interesting subject of inquiry; and we trust our readers will pardon us, if we make a few general reflections upon it, although we fear we have already trespassed upon their patience, by the length of our remarks on the influence of periodical writings.

Language, no less than literature, has a constant tendency to change; what is capable of being made more perfect, is also capable of becoming less so, and with this principle of revolution within it, having once reached its *acme* of perfection, its next tendency must obviously be to decay. Both reflection and the experience of past ages will suggest to us several causes perpetually acting to produce such a revolution, and will enable us to determine with some degree of accuracy, its probable symptoms. The art of printing, a cause unknown to the ancients, is extremely unfavorable to the general preservation of a pure standard of composition, since by the increased relish, and consequently the increased demand for books, which it creates, it induces the ignorant to write, and the learned to write rapidly, and of course negligently. Thus the language becomes debased alike in the hands of dunces, and of men of genius; and we think we may see examples of this, every day of our lives.

Another cause of depreciation is the tendency to abstract speculation, which seems to prevail most in the advanced age of a nation. Philosophy shines brightest in the last page of Grecian literature: it cheered the decline of the Roman; and in Great Britain, the fondness for metaphysical science seems to have grown with the growth of the people, and, so far from being confined to prose, at the present day enters deeply into the very spirit of her poetry. Now the influence of all this upon language is decidedly bad, inasmuch as it tends to substitute the complex abstract phraseology of science, for the simple intelligible dialect, which naturally grows out of the habit among the earliest writers of directing their attention to the visible objects of external nature.

A third source of this adulteration (paradoxical as it may appear) is the tendency to excessive refinement. Language in time gets to be cultivated as a luxury; sound is preferred to sense; and even good writers, infected with the same effeminacy, grow dissatisfied with the simple familiar forms of antiquity, and superadd the embellishments of their own more luxurious taste.

A fourth and a last cause, and which is most operative on feeble minds, is that indiscriminate passion for notoriety, which prompts them, in the despair of obtaining it by surpassing their predecessors in the right way, to deviate into all sorts of affectation and conceit.

With these causes at work to undermine the purity of a language, it requires the utmost vigilance to preserve it long in a healthful and vigorous state. The symptoms above enumerated indicated the corruption of the Latin tongue; and perhaps a curious observer might fancy, that he already discerned something like these symptoms of degeneracy in the style of the popular English compositions of the present day. A few examples must suffice to explain our meaning.

A favorite manner with some, even of the best writers of our time, is that ornamented and highly artificial style, which is well illustrated by the philosophical writings of Stewart. No model of fine writing enjoys greater celebrity. Now we cannot but think, that for the severe subjects upon which it is employed, this manner is the very worst possible, and every way inferior to the chaste and simple diction of his learned predecessor, Dr. Reid; indeed, whatever may be the subject, we think such a fastidious selection of melodious epithets, such a copious expansion both of imagery and illustration, inconsistent with directness, manly vigor, or simplicity of thought.

Although this effeminate taste has prevailed to excess of late years, among the Scottish writers more particularly, yet we think it is not so prevalent, nor half so pernicious, as that mystical, fine spun, indefinite phraseology, whose object seems to be, rather to conceal thought, than to express it. Coleridge's Auto-Biography, Peter's Letters to his Kinsfolk, (both of which have gone into American editions,) are two examples among others that occur of this popular species of writing. It seems to have been borrowed from the very worst manner of the German mystics. Writers of this class never talk directly to the purpose. They explain to you what a thing is, by enumerating all that it is not, and, in the management of their ideas, remind us of the manner in which our Indians are said to have treated their captives, setting them up as marks for their arrows, not to hit, but to come as near to them as possible without hitting. They have also great proneness to abstract speculation, to which their mystical dialect is admirably fitted; and should the reader escape from this double darkness, without being utterly confounded, he will carry off such cloudy indistinct notions of things, as will be of very little service to him in his intercourse with the world.

A third, perhaps the most numerous, and certainly the most contemptible class of writers, consists of those, who, from corrupt taste, or a greedy appetite for notoriety, wander from the plain and beaten track into all kinds of affectation. The most current of these affectations is an uncommon familiarity, even homeliness of manner, and a forced, foolish sensibility, which claims to be extreme naturalness. All this is very pitiable, and, if widely cultivated, would in a short time melt down the very marrow of our language into the insipid prattle of a nursery dialect. The best sample in this way is found in the productions of a body, who (as we have somewhere remarked in a previous number) have obtained a niche for themselves in the temple of contemporary fame, as the Cockney school; and who, first in poetry and afterwards in prose, established their claim to this title, no less by the smart city air of their sentiments, than by the seat of their peculiar jurisdiction. We regret that the influence of these writers should not have been circumscribed by their own Cockney land; and still more deeply, that they should have found some men of unquestionable genius on this side of the Atlantic, who have condescended to adopt their puerile affectations.

From what we have said, we would not have it understood as our opinion, that English style has suffered any material or general debasement, or that it is in any immediate danger; on the contrary, when we consider the unprecedented fertility of the press of late years, we are astonished at its purity, and we could select many fine writers of the present day, whose chaste and eloquent diction would adorn the most flourishing period of the English language, no less than of its literature. But we do think, that we should always be solicitous for the preservation of beauties so delicate and perishable in their nature, as forms of expression, and that we should not only expose, and guard against corruption, but against the least tendency to corruption. We are the more solicitous, from the peculiar relation in which we stand to England, in this respect, a new people with an old language. Our own streams are fed from the more copious fountains of her literature; and if these are in the least degree contaminated, how shall ours escape the pollution?

The style hitherto predominating in the compositions of men of education in our own country, has been for the most part that plain, unvarnished style, better fitted to give information than delight; well suited to an intelligible disclosure of facts, but foreign to all the ambitious purposes of fine writing. Still we have had examples of this in more than one name, that will be remembered with gratitude by posterity. Franklin, Dennie, Ames, and Buckminster, to mention no others, have left us evidence of the distinctive physiognomy of their minds, no less in the peculiar merits of their style, than of their sentiments; and many more, were it not invidious, might be enumerated, who, in the present increasing appetite for letters, are cultivating with success the most refined beauties of English composition. The Sketch Book, however, is the only one pertinent to our purpose, as developing a new form, and constituting the last link in the series of periodical essay writing.

We ought not, however, to omit the fashion, which essay writing assumed, under the auspices of a confederacy of men of wit and learning, first in Scotland, and not long after in England, at the commencement of the present century. We allude to the Edinburgh, and the Quarterly Reviews, which (very different from anything that had before passed under the same title) may be considered as a miscellany of independent essays on every possible variety of topic, suggested and illustrated by the most recent publications. The extreme popularity soon acquired amongst all classes by this new kind of writing, treating as it did of matters in abstruse science and solid literature, no less than of polite taste and superficial criticism, is a powerful evidence of a far more extended and a deeper cultivation in the mass of good society, than existed in the days of the Spectator. What has been the influence of these Reviews, or of this kind of writing in general, for it has been liberally imitated, is an interesting subject of discussion, but this is not the place for it. We will only add, that it may be considered fortunate for the cause of truth and of good taste, that every subject, whether religious, political, or literary, has been discussed upon opposite principles in these two leading Reviews; and that whatever, in other respects, may be their individual merits or demerits, we must always remain grateful to the one, for the diligence and the discrimination it has manifested in bringing before the public the long neglected beauties of old English literature; and to the other, both for the accuracy of that geographical research, which has enabled it to make an important addition to the sum of human knowledge, and for its solicitude in preserving the English tongue, by precept and example, in the perfection of its classical purity.

That species of periodical essay writing, which had continued in Great Britain,[1] with little intermission, from the first appearance of the Tatler, disappeared under this extreme popularity of reviews and magazines. It has, however, arisen within a few years in our own country, with new and very different attractions. The Sketch Book certainly forms an epoch in the history of this kind of literature; for although of the same generic character with the British essayists, it has many important specific peculiarities. The former were written, as we

[1] Had we space, it would be an interesting occupation to trace the development of periodical composition, in our own country, through a series of magazines and literary journals, some of them of great merit, and of miscellaneous essays, bearing too near a resemblance to the general design of the British essayists, to admit here of a particular specification: in which latter class, the Old Bachelor and the Salmagundi may be cited as productions of the greatest merit. [Prescott's note.]

have before remarked, with a direct moral tendency, to expose and to reform the ignorance and the follies of the age. The Sketch Book, on the other hand, has no direct moral purpose, but is founded on sentiment and deep feeling. In its comic scenes (which by the bye we think its best) we have the broad caricature of a truly original humor, but not a faithful delineation of the state of society in any age or place. Neither do the beautiful pictures of English life hold out any direct moral aim, but are distinguished by the same rich coloring of sentiment that pervades, and, in fact, gives a character to the whole work. In one word, as the principal object of the British essayists was to instruct, so they have for the most part given a picture of common life, in simple language; while the principal object of the Sketch Book, being to delight, scenes only of exquisite emotion are selected, and painted in the most exquisite, but artificial language.

We confess, that we are somewhat apprehensive of the influence of a work, uniting such uncommon richness of thought and expression, upon our general taste, and doubt it may give younger readers, at least, a disrelish for the more simple and less stimulating compositions of Goldsmith and of Addison. Of one thing we are positive, that it is the very worst model in the world for the imitation of writers, especially of young writers, who, wanting genuine sensibility, will only expose the beggarly condition of their thoughts the more, by arraying them in this gorgeous apparel.

[IS ITALIAN POETRY AMORAL?]
From *Miscellanies*, pp. 478–484

[From "Italian Narrative Poetry," a review in the *North American Review*, XIX, 337–389 (October, 1824). Reprinted in *Miscellanies*, 410–485. This selection illustrates (1) Prescott's wide knowledge of European literature; (2) his more or less constant quarrel with the German school of critics (of which Madame de Staël was a member); (3) his Anglo-Saxon insistence on moral values in literature.]

In glancing over the long range of Italian narrative poems, one may be naturally led to the reflection that the most prolific branch of the national literature is devoted *exclusively* to purposes of mere amusement. Brilliant inventions, delicate humor, and a beautiful coloring of language are lavished upon all; but with the exception of the "Jerusalem," we rarely meet with sublime or ennobling sentiment, and very rarely with anything like a moral or philosophical purpose. Madame de Staël has attempted to fasten a reproach on the whole body of Italian letters, "that, with the exception of their works on physical science, they have never been directed to *utility*." The imputation applied in this almost unqualified manner is unjust. The language has been enriched by the valuable reflections of too many historians, the solid labors of too many antiquaries and critics, to be thus lightly designated. The learned lady may have found a model for her own comprehensive manner of philosophizing, and an ample refutation of her assertion in Machiavelli alone.[1] In their works of imagination, however, such an imputation appears to be well merited. The Italians seemed to demand from these nothing farther than from a fine piece of music, where the heart is stirred, the ear soothed, but the understanding not a whit refreshed. The splendid apparitions of their poet's fancy fade away from the mind of the reader, and, like the enchanted fabrics described in their romances, leave not a trace behind them.

In the works of fancy in our language, fiction is almost

[1] We say *manner*, not spirit. The "Discors isopra T. Livio," however, require less qualification on the score of their principles. They obviously furnished the model to the "Grandeur et Décadence des Romains," and the same extended philosophy which Montesquieu imitated in civil history, Madame de Staël has carried into literary.

Among the historians, antiquaries, &c., whose names are known where the language is not read, we might cite Guicciardini, Bembo, Sarpi, Giannone, Nardi, Davila, Denina, Muratori, Tiraboschi, Gravina, Bettinelli, Algarotti, Beccaria, Filanghieri, Cesarotti, Pignotti, and many others; a hollow muster-roll of names that it would be somewhat ridiculous to run over, did not their wide celebrity expose, in a stronger light, Madame de Staël's sweeping assertion. [Prescott's note.]

universally made subservient to more important and nobler purposes. The ancient drama, and novels, the modern prose drama, exhibit historical pictures of manners and accurate delineations of character. Most of the English poets in other walks, from the "moral Gower" to Cowper, Crabbe, and Wordsworth, have made their verses the elegant vehicles of religious or practical truth. Even descriptive poetry in England interprets the silence of external nature into a language of sentiment and devotion. It is characteristic of this spirit in the nation that Spenser, the only one of their classic writers who has repeated the fantastic legends of chivalry, deemed it necessary to veil his Italian fancy in a cloud of allegory, which, however it may be thought to affect the poem, shows unequivocally the didactic intention of the poet.

These grave and extended views are seldom visible in the ornamental writing of the Italians. It rarely conveys useful information, or inculcates moral or practical truth; but it is too commonly an elegant, unprofitable pastime. Novelle, lyrical, and epic poetry may be considered as constituting three principal streams of their lighter literature. These have continued to flow, with little interruption, the two first from the "golden urns" of Petrarch and Boccaccio, the last from the early sources we have already traced down to the present day. Their multitudinous novelle, with all their varieties of tragic and comic incident, the last by far the most frequent, present few just portraitures of character, still fewer examples of sound ethics or wise philosophy.[1] In the exuberance of their sonnets and canzone, we find some, it is true, animated by an efficient spirit of religion or patriotism; but too frequently they are of a purely amatory nature, the unsubstantial though brilliant exhalations of a heated fancy. The pastoral drama, the opera, and other beautiful varieties of invention, which, under the titles of

[1] The heavier charge of indecency lies upon many. The Novelle of Casti, published as late as 1804, make the foulest tales of Boccaccio appear fair beside them. They have run through several editions since their first appearance, and it tells not well for the land that a numerous class of readers can be found in it who take delight in banqueting upon such abominable offal. [Prescott's note.]

Bernesco, Burlesco, Maccherónico, and the like, have been nicely classed according to their different modifications of style and humor, while they manifest the mercurial temper and the originality of the nation, confirm the justice of our position.

The native melody of the Italian tongue, by seducing their writers into an overweening attention to sound, has doubtless been in one sense prejudicial to their literature. We do not mean to imply, in conformity with a vulgar opinion, that the language is deficient in energy or compactness. Its harmony is no proof of its weakness. It allows more licenses of contraction than any other European tongue, and retains more than any other the vigorous inversions of its Latin original. Dante is the most concise of early moderns, and we know none superior to Alfieri in this respect among those of our own age. Davanzati's literal translation of Tacitus is condensed into a smaller compass than its original, the most sententious of ancient histories; but still the silver tones of a language that almost sets itself to music as it is spoken, must have an undue attraction for the harmonious ear of an Italian. Their very first classical model of prose composition is an obvious example of it.

The frequency of *improvisation* is another circumstance that has naturally tended to introduce a less serious and thoughtful habit of composition. Above all, the natural perceptions of an Italian seem to be peculiarly sensible to *beauty*, independent of every other quality. Any one who has been in Italy must have recognized the glimpses of a pure taste through the rags of the meanest beggar. The musical pieces, when first exhibited at the theater of St. Carlos, are correctly pronounced upon by the Lazzaroni of Naples, and the mob of Florence decide with equal accuracy upon the productions of their immortal school. Cellini tells us that he exposed his celebrated statue of Perseus in the public square by order of his patron, Duke Cosmo First, who declared himself perfectly satisfied with it on learning the commendations of the people. It is not extraordinary that this exquisite sensibility to the beautiful should have also influenced them in literary art, and have led them astray sometimes from the substantial and the useful. Who but an Italian historian would, in this practical age, so far blend fact and fiction as, for the sake of rhetorical effect, to introduce into the mouths of his personages sentiments and speeches never uttered by them, as Botta has lately done in his history of the American War?

In justice, however, to the Italians, we must admit, that the reproach incurred by too concentrated an attention to beauty, to the exclusion of more enlarged and useful views in their lighter compositions, does not fall upon this or the last century. They have imbibed a graver and more philosophical cast of reflection, for which they seem partly indebted to the influence of English literature. Several of their most eminent authors have either visited or resided in Great Britain, and the genius of the language has been made known through the medium of skillful translations. Alfieri has transported into his tragedies the solemn spirit and vigorous characterization peculiar to the English. He somewhere remarks that "he could not read the language"; but we are persuaded his stern pen would never have traced the dying scene of Saul, had he not witnessed a representation of Macbeth. Ippolito Pindemonte, in his descriptive pieces, has deepened the tones of his native idiom with the moral melancholy of Gray and Cowper. Monti's compositions, both dramatic and miscellaneous, bear frequent testimony to his avowed admiration for Shakspeare; and Cesarotti, Foscolo, and Pignotti have introduced the "severer muses" of the north to a still wider and more familiar acquaintance with their countrymen.[1] Lastly, among the works of fancy which attest the practical scope of Italian letters in the last century, we must not omit the "Giorno" of Parini, the most curious and nicely-elaborated specimen of *didactic* satire pro-

[1] Both the prose and poetry of Foscolo are pregnant with more serious meditation and warmer patriotism than is usual in the works of the Italians. Pignotti, although his own national manner has been but little affected by his foreign erudition, has contributed more than any other to extend the influence of English letters among his countrymen. His works abound in allusions to them, and two of his principal poems are dedicated to the memory of Shakspeare and of Pope. [Prescott's note.]

duced in any age or country. Its polished irony, pointed at the domestic vices of the Italian nobility, indicates both the profligacy of the nation and the moral independence of the poet.

The Italian language, the firstborn of those descended from the Latin, is also the most beautiful. It is not surprising that a people endowed with an exquisite sensibility to beauty should have been often led to regard this language rather as a means of pleasure than of utility. We must not, however, so far yield to the unqualified imputation of Madame de Staël as to forget that they have other claims to our admiration than what arise from the inventions of the poet, or from the ideal beauties which they have revived of Grecian art; that the light of *genius* shed upon the world in the fourteenth, and that of *learning* in the fifteenth century, was all derived from Italy; that her writers first unfolded the sublimity of Christian doctrines as applied to modern literature, and by their patient, philological labors restored to life the buried literature of antiquity; that her schools revived and expounded the ancient code of law, since become the basis of so important a branch of jurisprudence both in Europe and our own country; that she *originated* literary, and brought to a perfection unequaled in any other language, unless it be our own, civil and political history; that she led the way in physical science and in that of political philosophy; and, finally, that of the two enlightened navigators who divide the glory of adding a new quarter to the globe, the one was a Genoese and the other a Florentine.

[SHAKESPEARE AND SCOTT]

[From "Novel Writing," a review in the *North American Review*, XXV, 183–302 (July, 1827).]

This department of fiction has been a favorite with the English, the last half century; and it now seems, equally whether we consider its philosophical spirit, or its execution as a work of art, to have reached as high a point of perfection as it can reasonably be expected to attain. In this improved state,

it has been purified from most of those frequent violations
of taste and morals, which formerly disfigured it; from the
licentiousness of Fielding and Smollet, the sentimentality of
Burney and Radcliffe, and the painful elaboration of Richardson. It is now characterized by a pure and manly tone of
sentiment, by a familiar acquaintance with the world, by an
extensive erudition, and by no ordinary beauties of eloquence.
Scott must of course be considered to have been the most efficient agent in producing this revolution; and from this circumstance he may, like Shakspeare, be taken for the representative
of his age. Like him, he has embraced, within his comprehensive glance, every variety of rank, profession, and party;
the principal object of both seems to have been the development of character, without any concern for the disposition of
incident, except as far as, by affording new points of view, it
may be made subservient to the main purpose. Hence probabilities are frequently violated, and the legitimate limits of the
play or novel having been attained, the narration is brought
up by a sort of apoplectic termination of the whole *dramatis
personæ*. Witness the historical plays of the one, and the
novels of the other, *passim*. Another deficiency, peculiar to
both these writers, is that of any avowed or implied moral purpose, in most of their fictions. They content themselves with
imitating the ordinary course of events in real life; with scarcely
any more equity, than is observed here, in the ultimate distribution of rewards and punishments. Take, for obvious examples,
the *dénouement* of Hamlet, or King Lear, of the Bride of Lam-
mermoor, or St. Ronan's Well,—where the same dreadful
catastrophe overwhelms alike the innocent and the guilty.
Perhaps, however, the influence of their writings has not been
less salutary on this account. An exhibition of the misery, the
mental disquietude inseparable from guilt, may be sufficiently
impressive. A moral, on the other hand, sturdily inculcated or
illustrated in every page, as is the case with Miss Edgeworth,
or which in any degree diverts the current of events from their
natural course, occasions a violence to probability, revolting
both to the taste and conviction of the reader. Both seem to

have possessed the remarkable faculty of abstracting themselves from self, if we may so say. Each one of their dramatic entities seems to possess a sort of conscious individuality, as in real life, and the whole of the complicated mechanism moves on, without ever betraying the invisible hand of the master. If anywhere the spirit of the author breaks forth, it is in a good-humored philosophy, which smiles at the vanities of life, which regards the world as a farce, and the men and women in it as players.

Scott, like his great predecessor, has called in the preternatural, not for vulgar purposes of poetical interest only, but for the illustration of popular superstition, and like him, he has made fiction the vehicle of historic truth; the form of his work has obviously given him greater scope for the exposition of his national antiquities; and the superior opulence of his literary acquirements has enabled him to enrich his compositions with a much greater variety of information.

Both are profound in the knowledge of men, but Shakspeare seems to have been endowed with a finer perception of the character of women; at least he has far surpassed his rival in the exhibition of tender and romantic passion. In everything relating to the sex, indeed, he is a warmer colorist than Scott. We will pursue the parallel no farther, and only remark in conclusion, that as the one is the greatest poetic, so the other is the greatest prose dramatist of any age or country; an eulogium which will not appear unmerited, if we consider the essence of the drama to consist in development of character.

[FICTION AS HISTORY]

[A second passage from "Novel Writing."]

The expense of talent, which of late years has been lavished on works of fiction, is matter of regret with some, who regard it as so much diverted from the service of truth and genuine knowledge. Such is not our view of it; and we cannot help thinking, that novels, as they are now conducted, might admit of some very plausible arguments in their favor, even on the ground of the *cui bono*, as compared with history. The moral and social organization of a people, is certainly not less interesting to the philosophical student, than the deeds of violence and intrigue, which chequer the page of history. The poems of Homer have done more to acquaint us with the domestic constitution of the Greeks, than all their histories put together; and where are future generations to obtain so clear a conception of the peculiarities of Scottish character as from the Waverley novels? What a flood of light would one such fiction as Old Mortality throw on the dark features of Roman story, even where it is most illuminated by the prolix pen of Livy, or the brief but effectual touches of Tacitus? History has to do with the outward appearances of things; with actors in masquerade. How often may even an eyewitness be deceived! De Retz has somewhere remarked on the impertinence of writers, "who in the seclusion of their closets, pretend to suggest the motives of conduct, which he, who was the focus of intrigue, was altogether unable to explain." On the other hand, fiction has no concern with actions of individuals, but with passions in the abstract, with the moral constitution of man, a subject, from obvious reasons, much less liable to misconception. In a word, history represents events as they are, and men as they appear; while fiction represents events as they appear probable, and men as they are. "The only difference between me and professed historians," says the lively Fielding, "is, that with me everything is true, save the names and the dates, while with them nothing is true but names and dates."

[THE ROMANTIC PERIOD IN ENGLISH POETRY]

[From "English Literature of the Nineteenth Century," a review in the *North American Review*, XXXV, 165–195 (July, 1832). This selection helps to reveal the quality of Prescott's romanticism through his taste in the English romantic poets. The remarks on Wordsworth represent the average level of American opinion of that poet in the 1830's.]

The sluggish calm in which the minds of men seemed to repose during the greater part of the eighteenth century, was at length dispelled by one of those tempests, which are occasionally sent to clear the moral atmosphere, and renovate the face of society. We allude to the American Revolution, an event of similar importance in the political, with the Reformation in the religious world, and which opened that contest between the principles of freedom and arbitrary power, that still continues, and is probably to form the history of the present century. The French Revolution soon followed, and the lively concussion given to men's minds, not only in the immediate theater of operation, but in the contiguous countries, especially Great Britain, was visible in the most important consequences. Men pushed their inquiries with reckless hardihood into the regions of science and speculation. Deep-rooted prejudices were torn up. Systems, which had been piled up by the diligence of ages, were brought to the ground, as it were, in a moment. The ancient schemes of education began now to be assailed, and more popular ones devised. It came to be understood, that knowledge was not intended for a few initiated alone, but for the mass of mankind. Utility was the avowed principle of action, and the sciences, especially those susceptible of most familiar practical application, were diligently cultivated. In the improved civilization of the lower ranks, a wide market was opened for literary products, and such substantial encouragement afforded, as brought the highest talent into the field of competition. The popular tribunal, thus erected, decided less on any principles of factitious taste, than on natural sentiment. Human character was required to be more justly delineated, human feelings to be more deeply sounded. The cold precepts of the preceding age were trampled down under the spontaneous movements of passion. The extraordinary character of passing events seemed to beget, indeed, an inordinate passion for novelty and excitement. Instead of the tameness of ordinary life, the poet carried his reader back to the stirring days of chivalry and romance, animating his verse with thrilling patriotic recollections, or agitating the depths of the soul with wild emotion. Indeed, the disjointed character of the times led to the most conflicting results; the cynical sneer of infidelity, and the steady assurance of religious trust. And one may recognize the influence of the present revolutionary age, no less in the devout poetry of Wordsworth, as any one who has read the Excursion will readily admit, than in the skepticism of Byron's.

But without dwelling longer on the general characteristics of the literature of the present age, it may be well to examine the several varieties which have been brought into most successful cultivation; and perhaps the most effectual mode of doing this will be by a brief survey of the writers, who have impressed them with their peculiar genius.

It is unnecessary to expatiate on the merits of Cowper, the morning star of our modern poetry, which shed a tranquil light over the stormy period that closed the eighteenth century. We shall probably not err in selecting Scott, Wordsworth and Byron, as the most fitting representatives of contemporary poetry, on account of their positive rank, or their success in the introduction of their respective systems. Some others, especially Crabbe, might be adduced as instinct with the spirit of the age, but none will be found on the whole so decidedly to have stamped, in a greater or less degree, their own features upon it.

Scott's verse is a prolific shoot from the ancient and long-neglected stock of English minstrelsy, which Percy attempted to bring into favorable notice about the middle of the last century. The attempt was stifled in its birth by Dr. Johnson, who found nothing attractive in the artlessness of the old ballad, and who, by a ridiculous parody on the style, succeeded, according to his admiring biographer, in rendering "Bishop Percy contemptible." It indeed brought some contempt on his performance, for, although nothing is so easy to make as a sneer, nothing is more difficult to answer. But, although the seed fell on stony ground in that day, it found soil in which to take deep root in our own. "I well remember," says Scott, in his agreeable auto-biography, "the tree under which I lay when I first entered on the enchanting perusal of Percy's Reliques of Ancient Poetry." With a congenial antiquarian spirit, he compiled the remains and imitations of Border minstrelsy, and sent them into the world, in order to ascertain the direction of the popular current. Finding that it set in his favor, he speedily launched forth his more formidable epics, which were drawn from similar sources, as the ballads of primitive English feeling and feudal exploit.

All who lived in that day will recollect the enthusiasm with which the public, wearied out with the monotonous commonplaces of later times, welcomed these delightful works, whose pages glowed with such vivid portraiture of character as had not been seen since the time of Shakspeare, or indeed in the narrative form, since that of Chaucer, while fancy shed over the whole the rich coloring of a romantic age, hitherto faintly seen through the dim veil of tradition.

> "The *first* of all the bards was he,
> That sung of Border chivalry."

The dialect adopted by Scott was in extremely good taste; not so obsolete as to require a glossary, like Chatterton's, and thus to give his pieces the fantastic appearance of a modern antique, but just antiquated enough to throw over them a picturesque costume, in perfect keeping with the age. The octosyllabic measure, borrowed from the old ballad, moreover, was admirably suited by its facile flexibility to the various, yet always simple, expression of his animated narrative, into which he seems to have transplanted all those natural wild flowers of poetry, which of late years had been left to linger unnoticed in the shade.

All this was manifestly in violation of the rules. The critics stared, shook their heads, and as Rochester somewhat irreverently observed of Cowley's poetry, "that not being of God, it could not stand," so they predicted that Scott's, "not being of the rules," could not. The poet, however, felt the strength of his hand, and so went on writing, while the public went on buying. More than thirty thousand copies of the first work, an amount altogether unprecedented, were readily disposed of, and succeeding efforts maintained the author's reputation. This blaze of popularity of course could not last long. The very peculiarities of the poet, at first so attractive, made him obnoxious to easy imitation, and the public became surfeited *ad nauseam* with spiritless copies of an original, whose mannerism, moreover, laid him open to ridiculous parody. The humblest mimic, by seizing on eccentricities of tone or gesture, may throw some degree of ridicule on his model, however exalted.

From these and some other causes, especially the increasing appetite for stimulating and passionate poetry, Scott's declined somewhat below the level, which in all probability it will hold with posterity; for no one surely at this time of day, who is sensible to the vigorous touches of character and nature which it exhibits, independently of its literary finish, can doubt, that it contains within itself the principle of immortality.

A poet, with little of the active and worldly temperament of Scott, appeared in Wordsworth, whose naturally grave and contemplative mood was nourished amid the romantic recesses of his native hills. But although by his position standing aloof, as it were, from man, he had nothing in him foreign to humanity. His contemplative habits led him to scrutinize his species with a philosophic eye, and by leveling in his own mind the artificial distinctions of society, extended his sympathies to the humblest of his fellow-creatures. A holy calm is shed over his writings, whose general purpose seems to be to reconcile man with himself and his destiny, by furnishing him with a key to the mysteries of his present condition. Wordsworth's soul is instinct with such a pure love of nature, so much simplicity, or as the French call it, loyalty of purpose, that had he not entangled himself in an unlucky theory, he might have shared the popularity of Cowper, whom he must be admitted to surpass in the general elevation, as well as the benevolence of his sentiments. As it is, there are few who read, and fewer still who relish him.

It may not be amiss to notice in passing, some points of the theory on which Mr. Wordsworth's muse, has been shipwrecked. According to him, low rustic life affords the best subjects for poetry, because the elementary feelings and essential passions of our nature are least under restraint, and best developed in it; while its language, purified indeed from acknowledged vulgarities, is best suited to the poet, as more simple and unelaborated than any other. These in brief are nearly his own words.

Now whatever may be thought of the situations, the feelings growing out of those situations are quite as natural and fully developed by men in society, as in the retirement of rustic life. Even in this last, it is difficult to understand why the poet's eye should be closed on all but the humbler orders, and not find fitting subjects of contemplation in persons of superior mental culture, and it may be, moral sensibility. In regard to diction, Mr. Wordsworth's practice is by no means comfortable to his theory. His language, so far from being that of rustic simplicity, is not to be compared in this respect with that of some other writers, as Burns, for example. Indeed, the elevated and frequently recondite character of his topics necessarily precludes this; while the perpetual struggle to accommodate himself to his theory frequently involves him in a dialect belonging neither to poetry nor common life, and which the intercalation now and then of a homely epithet or name, serves only, (we say it with all deference) to make supremely ridiculous.

In truth, expressions that may be natural in an early age, become affected in a later one. Wordsworth's writings show, moreover, that simple words do not necessarily constitute simplicity of expression; for there is scarcely any writer whose meaning is involved in greater mysticism, a circumstance apparently owing to his not accurately distinguishing between the results of his reason and his feelings.

The best proof of Wordsworth's failure is his want of popularity. The true tendency of his theory, is to level poetry to the comprehension and relish of the most untutored minds. Had he succeeded, he might have expected an almost unlimited currency,—the tavern-parlor popularity, which Cowper, and Burns, and Scott, *et tutti quanti*, are in possession of. Instead of this, the perusal of him is confined to the few, and those few the most cultivated persons, and not unfrequently of similar reserved tastes with his own. Perhaps, however, he may find some amends for the paucity of his admirers, in the sincerity of their admiration.

Mr. Wordsworth's poetical principles have been distorted into an apology for a sickly race of versifiers, branded as the cockney school, from the scene of their principal haunts, as well as the pert city air of their productions. These persons have aggravated Wordsworth's poetical defects into absolute vices, converting his homeliness into vulgarity, and his simplicity into the most infantine inanity. Indeed the chief characteristic of their manner may be found in what Scriblerus denominates the *infantine style;* "wherein a poet grows so very simple, as to think and talk like a child." Had they flourished in the time of this sagacious critic, their writings would have been invaluable to him, for the illustrations which they afford of every variety of the bathos. With these puerilities of style are combined a much more reprehensible laxity, or rather licentiousness of thought, on almost every topic. It would seem that the cheering warmth of popular patronage, which ripens so many of the nobler productions of nature, is apt to call into being also, swarms of pestilent insects, who defile for a season the hem of the muse's garment, but who, if some avenging Pope or Gifford do not arise to "break them on the wheel," are sure to be blown away sooner or later by the breath of public opinion.

[POETRY IN AMERICA]

[A second passage from "English Literature of the Nineteenth Century." The last paragraph combines a hackneyed cliché of the day (America's regrettable lack of romantic associations) with a prophecy for American literature which would have been worthy of Whitman.]

Poetry in our own country, during the present century, has felt a similar impulse with that communicated to it on the other side of the water. Indeed, nourished as we are, from similar sources, and subjected to a common discipline with English writers, our literature can only be a new variety of theirs. It may appear at first view, that poetic talent has been somewhat tardy in unfolding itself among us. But when did art or science ever first take root under a dependent colonial Government, as was ours till the latter part of the last century? Or, in a season of political agitation, which was our situation during the remainder of the age? They may, indeed, continue to flourish through such periods, from the impulse given at a preceding one. We do not mean, however, that the Muse was absolutely and invariably dumb during all this time, but she certainly never raised her voice to a lofty key, and by far the greater part of her productions is of that *mediocre* sort, which, in honest Dogberry's phrase, is "very tolerable and altogether not to be endured."

Since the establishment, however, of political independence and tranquillity, poetic talent has been developed among us in a considerable variety of beautiful forms, though in none of them, perhaps, on a very extended or elaborate scale. New-England has been hitherto the quarter of the country where it has been most successfully cultivated, whether owing to the severer character of the climate, or the more sedate and thoughtful temper of the people, or a more careful education than is to be found in other parts of the Union; circumstances which have all of them been found more or less favorable to the nurture of poetic sensibility.

The general complexion of this poetry is serious and contemplative, with a pretty uniform tinge of religious sentiment, austere sometimes and even gloomy, with many delicate touches of natural tenderness and a strong relish for the beauties of external nature. It must be admitted to be somewhat deficient in masculine strength and invention, and might be relieved by a larger infusion of the sportive sallies of wit and fancy.

Bryant is, by very general consent, placed at the head of our poetic department. His writings are distinguished by those graces which belong to naturally fine perceptions and a chastised taste. A deep moral feeling, serious but not sad, tinctures most of his views of man and nature, and insensibly raises thought from the contemplation of these lower objects, to that of the Mind who formed them.

Bryant has proved, beyond any other writer, the fruitfulness of our country in poetic topics and illustrations. This is indeed the proper theater for the American artist, the only one on which he can aspire to the praise of originality. Our inferiority to the old world, England, for example, in poetic material, has been often insisted on. It is true we have none of the stirring associations belonging to an illustrious body of ancient annals, and our soil is not strewed with the lingering monuments of architecture, beautiful though in ruins, which connect the present race with the age of feudal heroism; but then we have nature unfolded around us under a new aspect, and one every way as grand and as lovely as any in the old world; and we have man also, as exhibited under the influence of new institutions, and those better suited to the free expansion of his intellectual and moral faculties, than any hitherto known. If all this be not sufficient to warm the poet's visions, the fault must lie with him.

[CRITICAL PERIODICALS IN ENGLAND AND AMERICA]

[A third passage from "English Literature of the Nineteenth Century." This selection is interesting evidence of Prescott's growing distaste for criticism, particularly of the Scottish school.]

From poets we naturally pass to criticism, which, in the present age, has experienced a modification, that may be almost reckoned an invention. The old-fashioned periodical essays, the legitimate progeny of the Tatler and Spectator, had been gradually supplanted, after a run of nearly a century, by critical journals, devoted to the analysis of modern publications, but on the most frigid and spiritless principle, unenlivened by a single spark of philosophy or liberal speculation. In order to supply these manifold defects, an association was formed in Edinburgh, in the year 1805, by a number of gentlemen, among whom were Messrs. Jeffrey, Brougham, Smith, and some others, whose names, then just rising into notoriety, have since shed so bright an illumination over the various walks of politics and letters. This, as is well known, was the origin of the celebrated Edinburgh Review. The entirely novel principle on which the work was conducted, made the experiment a bold one. The public scarcely knew what to think of reviews, that seemed to have as little relation to the work reviewed, as Mr. Bayes's tragedy to his prologue, "which might stand for any other play as well as his." They stood aghast, moreover, at the intrepidity with which the new adventurers, fighting under their sanguinary motto, *judex damnatur cum nocens absolvitur*, waged indiscriminate hostility, not merely against the smaller craft that infest the seas of literature, but those of the heaviest metal.

There was some lack of closet erudition in the confederacy, but this was more than compensated by knowledge of the world, a surprising tact as to the management of their resources, and a happy confidence, which converted the reviewer into a sort of Dr. Pancrace, "homme de suffisance, homme de capacité, homme consommé dans toutes les sciences naturelles, morales, et politiques; homme savant, savantissime per omnes modos et casus, &c. &c." The public in short was fairly taken by surprise. The journal spread at once into an unprecedented circulation, and men seemed willing for a time to resign their judgments, even their old established prejudices, to these invisible self-constituted aristarchs.

In the meantime, the tories of the south saw with dismay this powerful engine in the hands of their adversaries, scattering doctrines savoring of little less than heresy in their estimation, whether in politics, religion, or letters. They accordingly provided an antidote in the London Quarterly, for the purpose of neutralizing the revolutionary principles of the whigs, both in politics and religion; understanding by the latter term, much the same with parson Thwackum, when he says, "by religion

I mean the Christian religion, and not only the Christian religion, but the Protestant religion, and not only the Protestant religion, but the church of England." The conduct of the war was intrusted to Mr. Gifford, a gentleman of indisputable erudition, and who, if less vivacious and less cunning of fence than his northern rival, had given sufficient proofs of his powers of flagellation, on the backs of the luckless Della Cruscans.

Between these opposite forces, collision soon occurred on all topics of general interest or importance, and the public, bewildered with the conflicting pretensions to infallibility, seemed now, for the first time, to comprehend that there might be two sides to every question. The deference to the primitive journal of course gradually subsided, and this decline of favor was accelerated by the evidence which every day unfolded of the inaccurracy of its predictions, not merely in the doubtful element of politics, but in literature, where more than one individual, whom the northern critics would have stifled at his birth, subsequently rose to a gigantic height, which entirely overshadowed their own comparatively puny dimensions. Witness, for example, Byron, Wordsworth, Madame de Staël, and the like, whose genius might well have been chilled by the early criticism they experienced, if genius like theirs could be chilled by criticism, or, as Byron somewhere expresses it, if

> "The sublime etherial particle
> Could be extinguished by an article."

These egregious blunders occasioned no slight distrust of the capacity of the critics, while the spirit of faction, which swayed the opinions, more or less, of both journals, brought equal discredit on their integrity; and thus the despotic authority, which in their corporate capacity and incognito condition they at first assumed over public sentiment, and which might have been perpetuated much longer by a discreet management, fell to the ground, or at least faded away into that degree of influence, which fairly attaches to a clever writer, according to the more or less skillful execution of his work.

What, on the whole, has been the tendency and influence of periodical writing in Great Britain, is a question too prolific of discussion for us to take up here. It may be generally affirmed of the two leading reviews, that they have shown the usual ductility which naturally belongs to such as depend on popular favor for their support, and that they have consequently more frequently followed than guided public opinion. It is also true, that the appetite for the short-lived notoriety, which is all that any article in a periodical work can promise itself, has stimulated the writer to aim too much at striking points, to say what is new, rather than what is true; and has more than once encouraged a flippant temerity of criticism, which proves its author to be utterly incapable of raising himself to the level of the work he depreciates.

With every defect, however, necessarily incident to so miscellaneous a concoction, both one and the other review may claim the credit of being the depositories of much valuable speculation on subjects of greatest interest and moment. The Edinburgh, notwithstanding the imputation, sometimes merited, of levity of manner, and indeed laxity of principle, has furnished many examples of a liberal philosophy in its disquisitions on government, and has discussed many questions of taste and general literature with singular ingenuity, eloquence, and richness of illustration. The Quarterly, with all its bigotry and dogmatism, has large claims on our consideration for the soundness of its erudition, and in particular the activity of its geographical researches, while the tone of literary criticism, although less dashing and presumptuous than its rival's, has been, on the whole, more conscientious and of a more uniformly healthful character.

It is singular that these two great journals, after having run along for so many years, the one as the supporter, the other as the constant impugner of administration, should have completely changed position. The position, not the principles, are changed, however, and the Quarterly still maintains the same resolute front as of yore, against revolutionary movement, reminding us of some gallant frigate, which, getting stranded in the action, still keeps her colors flying at mast-head, discharging her impotent guns at the enemy, one after another, with a spirit worthy of a better fate.

Review-writing, in the form we have been examining, has been pursued to a considerable extent in England, and to still greater in the modified form of magazines, whose existence indeed dates from a much earlier period. The most conspicuous of these, perhaps, is Blackwood's, a work whose bigoted tory-ism of principle presents a whimsical contrast with the dashing dandyism of its manner.

In our own country, we may be allowed to consider the introduction of reviews, on the whole, as salutary. As they have been hitherto conducted, they have served to invigorate the patriotic principle within our bosoms, and they have af-forded a shelter, long demanded, against the blasts of foreign criticism, which swept too rudely over our young nurseries of literature. They have done some service to the State, also, by affording a gymnasium, as it were, in which the literary tyro might try the strength of his arm, before venturing into more serious conflict. Periodical writing may be considered as better suited to the intellectual condition of this country than of any country in Europe, because, although up to a certain point there is a more diffused and equal civilization here, yet there does not exist, as there, the depth of scholarship which leads men to take an interest in more laborious and erudite researches. One thing may be observed in commendation of the course pursued by our periodicals, that it has generally, we may say indeed uniformly, been decorous and dignified, unstained by the vulgar party squabbles and brutal personalities, that dis-figure the best of those in the mother country.

[DEMOCRATIC CULTURE]

[A fourth passage from "English Literature of the Nine-teenth Century." Here is a characteristic mixture of patrician doubt and democratic faith, sympathy for English culture and loyal Americanism.]

The Newspaper opens another most prolific chapter in the literary history of our time. No machinery can be put in competition with this for importance, in the existing state of society. It may be said to have done for mind, what the invention of railroads has done for body, by opening a rapid communication between the most distant points, so that thought has been made to travel, or rather to flash like an electric spark, from one extremity of this vast community to the other. It is above all important in a Republic, and especially one of the immense territorial extent of ours, where the ready transmission of knowledge connected with public affairs, so essential to every individual, is greatly impeded by local distance. The free States of antiquity were so circumscribed in extent, that every citizen, that is, every one who took part in the conduct of affairs, could be brought at once within reach of the orator's voice; and something like a similar result may be said to have been effected in our extended community, by means of the gossamer machinery of the press.

At the present moment, there are probably three times as many newspapers published in this country as there are in Great Britain, and more than in all the States of Christendom united. Many, who have assumed the duties of editorship, are doubtless incompetent to it, and do a sensible mischief by inundating the public with crude and intemperate opinions. But these contradictory crudities serve in some degree to neutralize each other; and perhaps the advantage gained by the more active circulation of facts may be thought, in our practical common-sense community, to more than counterbalance any mischief resulting from opinions. It were much to be desired, however, that public patronage were sufficient to enable the editors of our newspapers to command the same extent of talent and accomplishment, with that which is put in requisition by the principal journalists of Europe.

The greatest evil resulting from the swarm of newspapers in this country, is the jeopardy to which, from the personal necessities of many of the editors, it exposes the independence of the press. The control of so potent an engine becomes a matter of such consequence in a government like ours, that a corrupt administration will hardly calculate the cost, by which to obtain possession of it. But the independence of the press is so vital a principle in a Republic, that when once it has been impaired to any considerable extent, the first blow to public liberty has been given. ***

History cannot fall within a survey of elegant literature, except so far as relates to its rhetorical execution. In this particular, some writers of the age, as Mitford and Turner, for example, have been so abominably perverse, that it would seem as if they were willing to try what degree of bad writing the public would tolerate, for the sake of the valuable matter it may contain. Others again, as Southey and Scott, blessed with a style at once perspicuous and picturesque, seem bent on counteracting these advantages, by a rapidity of composition, which sets at defiance everything like arrangement, conciseness, or proportion. But as if no speed of an individual, however great, could keep pace with the public appetite, associations have been formed for the purpose of expediting the movements of the press, through all its thousand channels. Everything now-a-days is done by association. The principle of concentrating a large mass on a given point, is found no less effective in civil than military matters, and an association is made the great lever by which most of the problems, whether in science or letters, are to be moved. Societies are organized for the diffusion of useful knowledge, of entertaining knowledge, and the like. The great object appears to be the civilization of the lower classes of society, up to the level, or near the level of the higher. It is found, that in proportion as government becomes more democratic in its form,—which is the regular progress of the age,—the necessity becomes stronger for rendering the people more intelligent. The failure of France, and the success of our own country, leave no room for skepticism on this head. Joint stock companies in literature are, therefore, instituted to enlighten the public by wholesale, as it were, and cyclopedias, libraries, magazines, and the like, pour forth in monthly, nay, weekly prodigality, from the indefatigable press, afforded at a price so low, as to secure them a place on every man's shelf. This, it must be admitted, as the worthy alderman said, is most excellent soup for the poor; quite good enough, indeed, much of it, for the most cultivated epicurean palate.

What the tendency of opening so many royal roads to knowledge may be, is a formidable question. It doubtless must contribute largely to the intellectual advancement of the middling orders in England. But it is highly probable that it involves, to a certain extent, the sacrifice of the highest order of talent and erudition; for the most highly gifted minds are largely enlisted in these enterprises; and if writers like Mackintosh or Sismondi can obtain a larger premium and a more ready popularity for these comparatively superficial productions, they will scarcely waste their hours in hiving curious learning, or embodying it in the results of patient meditation. But although the cause of literature loses something in this way, the cause of society may be thought to gain more. If fewer great works are produced, there are likely to be more good ones, good enough for ordinary practical uses. Works like these, shot up in a day, must expect indeed to die with the day. But the present age may be the gainer, although posterity should be the loser.

We can hardly close these remarks without adverting to the present literary prospects of our country, although we have too much consideration for the reader, to do more than glance at them. At first view, these prospects might appear unpromising, for nothing would seem more repugnant to success in the lighter and more elegant productions of literature, than the engrossing business habits of our community. The attention might be naturally turned from them by the brilliant career opened to talent in public and professional life, by the seductions of commercial adventure, by the large encouragement given to those sciences, which have the most obvious application to social life. Then, the constant subdivision of property allows little scope for that munificent individual patronage, which fosters the liberal arts in other countries; while this subdivision, moreover, reduces the number of such as can afford leisure for their cultivation. And, lastly, the ready importation of the most elegant articles of literary luxury, of every variety and of the highest finish, from England, leaves little encouragement for domestic industry; while our most enterprising publishers can hardly be expected to advance liberal prices on doubtful native productions, when they can import those, whose popularity has been already ascertained, free of cost, from abroad.

But with all these discouraging circumstances, a much more comfortable augury may be gathered, both from the internal consciousness of our own strength, and the results of past experience. Amidst every difficulty of situation, there is scarcely any path of active or contemplative life, in which we have not pushed our way, whether for purposes of profit or of pleasure, with more or less success. We are placed within the sphere of influences totally distinct from any in the old world, whether in relation to government, society, or the aspect of external nature. Some of these influences may be considered eminently favorable to intellectual action, and the bold and unchecked display of nature in all its eccentricity. Although a young people, moreover, we are furnished with an old and highly finished language, capable of conveying, in all its freshness, every variety of impression produced on us by the novelties of our situation.

With regard to the disastrous operation of foreign competition on our domestic industry, such are our natural buoyancy and enterprise, that it has hitherto been found to stimulate rather than depress it, in every department, whether physical or moral, to which it has been directed. Our popular patronage, too, though not on the same scale with that of the old world, has hitherto proved perfectly competent to the protection of works of real excellence. We may add, that our capacity for such productions in the highest kinds of ornamental literature, and in the collateral pursuit of the fine arts, opposed as they may seem to be to our habitual direction, is well illustrated by the fact, that we claim as our countrymen two of the most eminent writers of fiction of the present day, by the admission of the

English themselves, Irving and Cooper, and three of the most distinguished artists, Allston, Leslie, and Newton.

We will only remark in conclusion, what cannot be repeated too often, that the American writer, if he would aspire to the credit of originality, must devote his days and nights to the study of the models around him. Not that he should relinquish the rich inheritance which English genius has bequeathed to him, in common with his brethren across the water. But, however enriched the mould may be by foreign culture, the product of his fancy should be no exotic, but spring from native seed, if it would come to healthy maturity. The English writer may copy from books with less harm than the American, because he has the original models of these books around him, by which to correct his copies. But an American drawing from the same sources will, at best, produce but a second-hand imitation of nature. If he would be original, he must study the volume which nature herself has unrolled before him.

[SCOTT AND THE PROFESSION OF AUTHORSHIP]

From *Miscellanies*, pp. 234–243

[From "Sir Walter Scott," a review in the *North American Review*, XLVI, 431–474 (April, 1838). Reprinted in *Miscellanies*, 176–244. The student may well read into this selection Prescott's own feelings about the profession. The article as a whole is a good sample of his biographical method in criticism.]

Scott, with all his facility of execution, had none of that pitiable affectation sometimes found in men of genius, who think that the possession of this quality may dispense with regular, methodical habits of study. He was most economical of time. He did not, like Voltaire, speak of it as "a terrible thing that so much time should be wasted in talking." He was too little of a pedant, and far too benevolent, not to feel that there are other objects worth living for than mere literary fame; but he grudged the waste of time on merely frivolous and heartless objects. "As for dressing when we are quite alone," he remarked one day to Mr. Gillies, whom he had taken home with him to a family dinner, "it is out of the question. Life is not long enough for such fiddle-faddle." In the early part of his life he worked late at night, but, subsequently, from a conviction of the superior healthiness of early rising, as well as the desire to secure, at all hazards, a portion of the day for literary labor, he rose at five the year round; no small effort, as anyone will admit who has seen the pain and difficulty which a regular bird of night finds in reconciling his eyes to daylight. He was scrupulously exact, moreover, in the distribution of his hours. In one of his letters to his friend Terry, the player, replete, as usual, with advice that seems to flow equally from the head and the heart, he says, in reference to the practice of *dawdling* away one's time, "A habit of the mind it is which is very apt to beset men of intellect and talent, especially when their time is not regularly filled up, but left to their own arrangement. But it is like the ivy round the oak, and ends by limiting, if it does not destroy, the power of manly and necessary exertion. I must love a man so well, to whom I offer such a word of advice, that I will not apologize for it, but expect to hear you are become *as regular as a Dutch clock—hours, quarters, minutes, all marked and appropriated.*" With the same emphasis he inculcates the like habits on his son. If any man might dispense with them, it was surely Scott. But he knew that without them the greatest powers of mind will run to waste, and water but the desert.

Some of the literary opinions of Scott are singular, considering, too, the position he occupied in the world of letters. "I promise you," he says, in an epistle to an old friend, "my oaks will outlast my laurels; and I pique myself more on my compositions for manure than on any other compositions to which I was ever accessary." This may seem *badinage;* but he repeatedly, both in writing and conversation, places literature, as a profession, below other intellectual professions, and especially the military. The Duke of Wellington, the representative of the last, seems to have drawn from him a very extraordinary degree of deference, which we cannot but think smacks a little of that strong relish for gunpowder which he avows in himself.

It is not very easy to see on what this low estimate of literature rested. As a profession, it has too little in common with more active ones, to afford much ground for running a parallel. The soldier has to do with externals; and his contests and triumphs are over matter in its various forms, whether of man or material nature. The poet deals with the bodiless forms of air, of fancy lighter than air. His business is contemplative, the other's is active, and depends for its success on strong moral energy and presence of mind. He must, indeed, have genius of the highest order to effect his own combinations, anticipate the movements of his enemy, and dart with eagle eye on his vulnerable point. But who shall say that this practical genius, if we may so term it, is to rank higher in the scale than the creative power of the poet, the spark from the mind of divinity itself?

The orator might seem to afford better ground for comparison, since, though his theater of action is abroad, he may be said to work with much the same tools as the writer. Yet how much of his success depends on qualities other than intellectual! "Action," said the father of eloquence, "action, action are the three most essential things to an orator." How much depends on the look, the gesture, the magical tones of voice, modulated to the passions he has stirred; and how much on the contagious sympathies of the audience itself, which drown everything like criticism in the overwhelming tide of emotion! If any one would know how much, let him, after patiently standing

> "till his feet throb,
> And his head thumps, to feed upon the breath
> Of patriots bursting with heroic rage,"

read the same speech in the columns of a morning newspaper, or in the well-concocted report of the orator himself. The productions of the writer are subjected to a fiercer ordeal. He has no excited sympathies of numbers to hurry his readers along over his blunders. He is scanned in the calm silence of the closet. Every flower of fancy seems here to wither under the rude breath of criticism; every link in the chain of argument is subjected to the touch of prying scrutiny, and if there be the least flaw in it, it is sure to be detected. There is no tribunal so stern as the secret tribunal of a man's own closet, far removed from all the sympathetic impulses of humanity. Surely there is no form in which *intellect* can be exhibited to the world so completely stripped of all adventitious aids as the form of written composition. But, says the practical man, let us estimate things by their utility. "You talk of the poems of Homer," said a mathematician, "but, after all, what do they *prove?*" A question which involves an answer somewhat too voluminous for the tail of an article. But if the poems of Homer were, as Heeren asserts, the principal bond which held the Grecian states together, and gave them a national feeling, they "prove" more than all the arithmeticians of Greece—and there were many cunning ones in it—ever proved. The results of military skill are indeed obvious. The soldier, by a single victory, enlarges the limits of an empire; he may do more—he may achieve the liberties of a nation, or roll back the tide of barbarism ready to overwhelm them. Wellington was placed in such a position, and nobly did he do his work; or, rather, he was placed at the head of such a gigantic moral and physical apparatus as enabled him to do it. With his own unassisted strength, of course, he could have done nothing. But it is on his own solitary resources that the great writer is to rely. And yet, who shall say that the triumphs of Wellington have been greater than those of Scott, whose works are familiar as household words to every fireside in his own land, from the castle to the cottage; have crossed oceans and deserts, and, with healing on their wings, found their way to the remotest regions; have helped to form the character, until his own mind may be said to be incorporated into those of hundreds of thousands of his fellowmen? Who is there that has not, at some time or other, felt the heaviness of his heart lightened, his pains mitigated, and his bright moments of life made still brighter by the magical touches of his genius? And shall we speak of his victories as less real, less serviceable to humanity, less truly glorious than those of the greatest captain of his day? The triumphs of the warrior are bounded by the narrow theater of his own age; but those of a Scott or a Shakespeare will be renewed with greater and greater luster in ages yet unborn, when the victorious chieftain shall be forgotten, or shall live only in the song of the minstrel and the page of the chronicler.

But, after all, this sort of parallel is not very gracious nor very philosophical, and, to say truth, is somewhat foolish. We have been drawn into it by the not random, but very deliberate, and, in our poor judgment, very disparaging estimate by Scott of his own vocation; and, as we have taken the trouble to write it, our readers will excuse us from blotting it out. There is too little ground for the respective parties to stand on for a parallel. As to the pedantic *cui bono* standard, it is impossible to tell the final issues of a single act; how can we then hope to those of a course of action? As for the *honor* of different vocations, there never was a truer sentence than the stale one of Pope—stale now, because it is so true—

> "Act well your part—there all the honor lies."

And it is the just boast of our own country, that in no civilized nation is the force of this philanthropic maxim so nobly illustrated as in ours—thanks to our glorious institutions.

A great cause, probably, of Scott's low estimate of letters was the facility with which he wrote. What costs us little we are apt to prize little. If diamonds were as common as pebbles, and gold-dust as any other, who would stoop to gather them? It was the prostitution of his muse, by-the-by, for this same gold-dust, which brought a sharp rebuke on the poet from Lord Byron, in his "English Bards":

> "For this we spurn Apollo's venal son";

a coarse cut, and the imputation about as true as most satire, that is, not true at all. This was indited in his lordship's earlier days, when he most chivalrously disclaimed all purpose of bartering his rhymes for gold. He lived long enough, however, to weigh his literary wares in the same money-balance used by more vulgar manufacturers; and, in truth, it would be ridiculous if the produce of the brain should not bring its price in this form as well as any other. There is little danger, we imagine, of finding too much gold in the bowels of Parnassus.

Scott took a more sensible view of things. In a letter to Ellis, written soon after the publication of "The Minstrelsy," he observes, "People may say this and that of the pleasure of fame, or of profit, as a motive of writing, I think the only pleasure is in the actual exertion and research, and I would no more write upon any other terms than I would hunt merely to dine upon hare soup. At the same time, if credit and profit came unlooked for, I would no more quarrel with them than with the soup." Even this declaration was somewhat more magnanimous than was warranted by his subsequent conduct. The truth is, he soon found out, especially after the Waverley vein had opened, that he had hit on a gold-mine. The prodigious returns he got gave the whole thing the aspect of a speculation. Every new work was an adventure, and the proceeds naturally suggested the indulgence of the most extravagant schemes of expense, which, in their turn, stimulated him to fresh efforts. In this way the "profits" became, whatever they might have been once, a principal incentive to, as they were the recompense of, exertion. His productions were cash articles, and were estimated by him more on the Hudibrastic rule of "the real worth of a thing" than by any fanciful standard of fame. He bowed with deference to the judgment of the booksellers, and trimmed his sails dexterously as the "aura popularis" shifted. "If it is na weil bobbit," he writes to his printer, on turning out a less lucky novel, "we'll bobbit again." His muse was of that school who seek the greatest happiness of the greatest number. We can hardly imagine him invoking her like Milton:

> "Still govern thou my song,
> Urania, and fit audience find, though few."

Still less can we imagine him, like the blind old bard, feeding his soul with visions of posthumous glory, and spinning out epics for five pounds apiece.

It is singular that Scott, although he set as high a money

value on his productions as the most enthusiastic of the "trade" could have done, in a literary view should have held them so cheap. "Whatever others may be," he said, "I have never been a partisan of my own poetry; as John Wilkes declared, that, 'in the height of his success, he had himself never been a Wilkite.'" Considering the poet's popularity, this was but an indifferent compliment to the taste of his age. With all this disparagement of his own productions, however, Scott was not insensible to criticism. He says somewhere that, "if he had been conscious of a single vulnerable point in himself, he would not have taken up the business of writing"; but, on another occasion, he writes, "I make it a rule never to read the attacks made upon me"; and Captain Hall remarks, "He never reads the criticisms on his books; this I know, from the most unquestionable authority. Praise, he says, gives him no pleasure, and censure annoys him." Madame de Graffigny says, also, of Voltaire, "that he was altogether indifferent to praise, but the least word from his enemies drove him crazy." Yet both these authors banqueted on the sweets of panegyric as much as any who ever lived. They were in the condition of an epicure whose palate has lost its relish for the dainty fare in which it has been so long reveling, without becoming less sensible to the annoyances of sharper and coarser flavors. It may afford some consolation to humble mediocrity, to the less fortunate votaries of the muse, that those who have reached the summit of Parnassus are not much more contented with their condition than those who are scrambling among the bushes at the bottom of the mountain. The fact seems to be, as Scott himself intimates more than once, that the joy is in the chase, whether in the prose or the poetry of life.

[PROTESTANTISM AND THE ARTS]

From *Miscellanies*, pp. 265–272

[From "Chateaubriand's English Literature," a review in the *North American Review*, XLIX, 317–348 (October, 1839). Reprinted in *Miscellanies*, 245–293. François René, Viscount

de Chateaubriand (1768–1848), anti-revolutionist, sentimental
primitivist, expressed in his *Sketches* the passionate Catholicism
which he had more spectacularly exhibited in his *Genius of
Christianity* (1802). Prescott's review, as a whole, is a temperate but firm defense of British and Protestant æsthetic
psychology. The concluding remarks on English prose style
are particularly noteworthy.]

Our author pronounces the Reformation hostile to the arts,
poetry, eloquence, elegant literature, and even the spirit of
military heroism. But hear his own words:

"The Reformation, imbued with the spirit of its founder,
declared itself hostile to the arts. It sacked tombs, churches,
and monuments, and made in France and England heaps of
ruins." . . .

"The beautiful in literature will be found to exist in a greater
or less degree, in proportion as writers have approximated to
the genius of the Roman Church." . . .

"If the Reformation restricted genius in poetry, eloquence,
and the arts, it also checked heroism in war, for heroism is
imagination in the military order."—Vol. i., p. 194–207.

This is a sweeping denunciation; and, as far as the arts of
design are intended, may probably be defended. The Romish
worship, its stately ritual and gorgeous ceremonies, the throng
of numbers assisting, in one form or another, at the service, all
required spacious and magnificent edifices, with the rich ac-
cessories of sculpture and painting, and music also, to give full
effect to the spectacle. Never was there a religion which addressed itself more directly to the senses. And, fortunately for
it, the immense power and revenues of its ministers enabled
them to meet its exorbitant demands. On so splendid a theater,
and under such patronage, the arts were called into life in
modern Europe, and most of all in that spot which represented
the capital of Christendom. It was there, amid the pomp and
luxury of religion, that those beautiful structures rose, with
those exquisite creations of the chisel and the pencil, which
embodied in themselves all the elements of ideal beauty.

But, independently of these external circumstances, the spirit of Catholicism was eminently favorable to the artist. Shut out from free inquiry—from the Scriptures themselves—and compelled to receive the dogmas of his teachers upon trust, the road to conviction lay less through the understanding than the heart. The heart was to be moved, the affections and sympathies to be stirred, as well as the senses to be dazzled. This was the machinery by which alone could an effectual devotion to the faith be maintained in an ignorant people. It was not, therefore, Christ as a teacher delivering lessons of practical wisdom and morality that was brought before the eye, but Christ filling the offices of human sympathy, ministering to the poor and sorrowing, giving eyes to the blind, health to the sick, and life to the dead. It was Christ suffering under persecution, crowned with thorns, lacerated with stripes, dying on the cross. These sorrows and sufferings were understood by the dullest soul, and told more than a thousand homilies. So with the Virgin. It was not that sainted mother of the Saviour whom Protestants venerate, but do not worship; it was the Mother of God, and entitled, like him, to adoration. It was a woman, and, as such, the object of those romantic feelings which would profane the service of the Deity, but which are not the less touching as being in accordance with human sympathies. The respect for the Virgin, indeed, partook of that which a Catholic might feel for his tutelar saint and his mistress combined. Orders of chivalry were dedicated to her service; and her shrine was piled with more offerings and frequented by more pilgrimages than the altars of the Deity himself. Thus, feelings of love, adoration, and romantic honor, strangely blended, threw a halo of poetic glory around their object, making it the most exalted theme for the study of the artist. What wonder that this subject should have called forth the noblest inspirations of his genius? What wonder that an artist like Raphael should have found in the simple portraiture of a woman and a child the materials for immortality?

It was something like a kindred state of feeling which called into being the arts of ancient Greece, when her mythology was comparatively fresh, and faith was easy; when the legends of the past, familiar as Scripture story at a later day, gave a real existence to the beings of fancy, and the artist, imbodying these in forms of visible beauty, but finished the work which the poet had begun.

The Reformation brought other trains of ideas, and with them other influences on the arts, than those of Catholicism. Its first movements were decidedly hostile, since the works of art, with which the temples were adorned, being associated with the religion itself, became odious as the symbols of idolatry. But the spirit of the Reformation gave thought a new direction even in the cultivation of art. It was no longer sought to appeal to the senses by brilliant display, or to waken the sensibilities by those superficial emotions which find relief in tears. A sterner, deeper feeling was roused. The mind was turned within, as it were, to ponder on the import of existence and its future destinies; for the chains were withdrawn from the soul, and it was permitted to wander at large in the regions of speculation. Reason took the place of sentiment—the useful of the merely ornamental. Facts were substituted for forms, even the ideal forms of beauty. There were to be no more Michael Angelos and Raphaels; no glorious Gothic temples which consumed generations in their building. The sublime and the beautiful were not the first objects proposed by the artist. He sought truth—fidelity to nature. He studied the characters of his species as well as the forms of imaginary perfection. He portrayed life as developed in its thousand peculiarities before his own eyes, and the ideal gave way to the natural. In this way, new schools of painting, like that of Hogarth, for example, arose, which, however inferior in those great properties for which we must admire the masterpieces of Italian art, had a significance and philosophic depth which furnished quite as much matter for study and meditation.

A similar tendency was observable in poetry, eloquence, and works of elegant literature. The influence of the Reformation here was undoubtedly favorable, whatever it may have been on the arts. How could it be otherwise on literature, the written expression of thought, in which no grace of visible forms and proportions, no skill of mechanical execution, can cheat the eye with the vain semblance of genius? But it was not until the warm breath of the Reformation had dissolved the icy fetters which had so long held the spirit of man in bondage that the genial current of the soul was permitted to flow, that the gates of reason were unbarred, and the mind was permitted to taste of the tree of knowledge, forbidden tree no longer. Where was the scope for eloquence when thought was stifled in the very sanctuary of the heart? for out of the fullness of the heart the mouth speaketh.

There might, indeed, be an elaborate attention to the outward forms of expression, an exquisite finish of verbal arrangement, the dress and garniture of thought. And, in fact, the Catholic nations have surpassed the Protestant in attention to verbal elegance and the soft music of numbers, to nice rhetorical artifice and brilliancy of composition. The poetry of Italy and the prose of France bear ample evidence how much time and talent have been expended on this beauty of outward form, the rich vehicle of thought. But where shall we find the powerful reasoning, various knowledge, and fearless energy of diction which stamp the oratory of Protestant England and America? In France, indeed, where prose has received a higher polish and classic elegance than in any other country, pulpit eloquence has reached an uncommon degree of excellence; for though much was excluded, the avenues to the heart, as with the painter and the sculptor, were still left open to the orator. If there has been a deficiency in this respect in the English Church, which all will not admit, it arises probably from the fact that the mind, unrestricted, has been occupied with reasoning rather than rhetoric, and sought to clear away old prejudices and establish new truths, instead of wakening a transient sensibility, or dazzling the imagination with poetic flights of eloquence. That it is the fault of the preacher, at all events, and not of Protestantism, is shown by a striking example under our own eyes, that of our distinguished countryman, Dr. Channing, whose style is irradiated with all the splendors of a glowing imagination, showing, as powerfully as any other example, probably, in English prose, of what melody and compass the language is capable under the touch of genius instinct with genuine enthusiasm. Not that we would recommend this style, grand and beautiful as it is, for imitation. We think we have seen the ill effects of this already in more than one instance. In fact, no style should be held up as a model for imitation. Dr. Johnson tells us, in one of those oracular passages somewhat threadbare now, that "whoever wishes to attain an English style, familiar but not coarse, and elegant but not ostentatious, must give his days and nights to the volumes of Addison." With all deference to the great critic, who, by the formal cut of the sentence just quoted, shows that he did not care to follow his own prescription, we think otherwise. Whoever would write a good English style, we should say, should acquaint himself with the mysteries of the language as revealed in the writings of the best masters, but should form his own style on nobody but himself. Every man, at least every man with a spark of originality in his composition, has his own peculiar way of thinking, and, to give it effect, it must find its way out in its own peculiar language. Indeed, it is impossible to separate language from thought in that delicate blending of both which is called style; at least, it is impossible to produce the same effect with the original by any copy, however literal. We may imitate the structure of a sentence, but the ideas which gave it its peculiar propriety we cannot imitate. The forms of expression that suit one man's train of thinking no more suit another's than one man's clothes will suit another. They will be sure to be either too large or too small, or, at all events, not to make what gentlemen of the needle call a *good fit*. If the party chances, as is generally the case, to be rather under size, and the model is over size, this will only expose his own littleness the more. There is no case more in point than that afforded by Dr. Johnson himself. His brilliant style has been the ambition of every schoolboy, and of some children of larger growth since the days of the Rambler. But the nearer they come to it the worse. The beautiful is turned into the fantastic, and the sublime into the ridiculous. The most curious example of this within our recollection is the case of Dr. Symmons, the English editor of Milton's prose writings, and the biographer of the poet. The little doctor has maintained throughout his ponderous volume a most exact imitation of the great doctor, his sesquipedalian words, and florid rotundity of period. With all this cumbrous load of brave finery on his back, swelled to twice his original dimensions, he looks, for all the world, as he is, like a mere bag of wind—a scarecrow, to admonish others of the folly of similar depredations.

[HISTORICAL LITERARY CRITICISM IN EUROPE]

From *Miscellanies*, pp. 246–261

[A second passage from "Chateaubriand's English Literature." This passage represents Prescott's perennial interest in methods of historical literary criticism, and his recognition of German superiority in the field.]

But, notwithstanding the interest and importance of literary history, it has hitherto received but little attention from English writers. No complete survey of the treasures of our native tongue has been yet produced, or even attempted. The earlier periods of the poetical development of the nation have been well illustrated by various antiquaries. Warton has brought the history of poetry down to the season of its first vigorous expansion—the age of Elizabeth. But he did not penetrate beyond the magnificent vestibule of the temple. Dr. Johnson's "Lives of the Poets" have done much to supply the deficiency in this department. But much more remains to be done to afford the student anything like a complete view of the progress of poetry in England. Johnson's work, as everyone knows, is conducted on the most capricious and irregular plan. The biographies were dictated by the choice of the bookseller. Some of the most memorable names in British literature are omitted to make way for a host of minor luminaries, whose dim radiance, unassisted by the critic's magnifying lens, would never have penetrated to posterity. The same irregularity is visible in the proportion he has assigned to each of his subjects; the principal figures, or what should have been such, being often thrown into the background, to make room for some subordinate person whose story was thought to have more interest.

Besides these defects of plan, the critic was certainly deficient in sensibility to the more delicate, the minor beauties of poetic sentiment. He analyzes verse in the cold-blooded spirit of a chemist, until all the aroma, which constituted its principal charm, escapes in the decomposition. By this kind of process, some of the finest fancies of the Muse, the lofty dithyrambics of Gray, the ethereal effusions of Collins, and of Milton too, are rendered sufficiently vapid. In this sort of criticism, all the effect that relies on *impressions* goes for nothing. Ideas are alone taken into the account, and all is weighed in the same hard, matter-of-fact scales of common sense, like so much solid prose. What a sorry figure would Byron's Muse make subjected to such an ordeal! The doctor's taste in composition, to judge from his own style, was not of the highest order. It was a style, indeed, of extraordinary power, suited to the expression of his original thinking, bold, vigorous, and glowing with all the luster of pointed antithesis. But the brilliancy is cold, and the ornaments are much too florid and overcharged for a graceful effect. When to these minor blemishes we add the graver one of an obliquity of judgment, produced by inveterate political and religious prejudice, which has thrown a shadow over some of the brightest characters subjected to his pencil, we have summed up a fair amount of critical deficiencies. With all this, there is no one of the works of this great and good man in which he has displayed more of the strength of his mighty intellect, shown a more pure and masculine morality, more sound principles of criticism in the abstract, more acute delineation of character, and more gorgeous splendor of diction. His defects, however, such as they are, must prevent his maintaining with posterity that undisputed dictatorship in criticism which was conceded to him in his own day. We must do justice to his errors as well as to his excellences, in order that we may do justice to the characters which have come under his censure. And we must admit that his work, however admirable as a gallery of splendid portraits, is inadequate to convey anything like a complete or impartial view of English poetry.

The English have made but slender contributions to the history of foreign literatures. The most important, probably, are Roscoe's works, in which literary criticism, though but a subordinate feature, is the most valuable part of the composition. As to anything like a general survey of this department, they are wholly deficient. The deficiency, indeed, is likely to be supplied, to a certain extent, by the work of Mr. Hallam, now in progress of publication; the first volume of which—the only one which has yet issued from the press—gives evidence of the same curious erudition, acuteness, honest impartiality, and energy of diction which distinguish the other writings of this eminent scholar. But the extent of his work, limited to four volumes, precludes anything more than a survey of the most prominent features of the vast subject he has undertaken.

The Continental nations, under serious discouragements, too, have been much more active than the British in this field. The Spaniards can boast a general history of letters, extending to more than twenty volumes in length, and compiled with sufficient impartiality. The Italians have several such. Yet these are the lands of the Inquisition, where reason is hoodwinked, and the honest utterance of opinion has been recompensed by persecution, exile, and the stake. How can such a people estimate the character of compositions which, produced under happier institutions, are instinct with the spirit of freedom? How can they make allowance for the manifold eccentricities of a literature where thought is allowed to expatiate in all the independence of individual caprice? How can they possibly, trained to pay such nice deference to outward finish and mere verbal elegance, have any sympathy with the rough and homely beauties which emanate from the people and are addressed to the people?

The French, nurtured under freer forms of government, have contrived to come under a system of literary laws scarcely less severe. Their first great dramatic production gave rise to a scheme of critical legislation, which has continued ever since to press on the genius of the nation in all the higher walks of poetic art. Amid all the mutations of state, the tone of criticism has remained essentially the same to the present century, when, indeed, the boiling passions and higher excitements of a revolutionary age have made the classic models on which their literature was cast appear somewhat too frigid, and a warmer coloring has been sought by an infusion of English sentiment. But this mixture, or, rather, confusion of styles, neither French nor English, seems to rest on no settled principles, and is, probably, too alien to the genius of the people to continue permanent.

The French, forming themselves early on a foreign and antique model, were necessarily driven to rules, as a substitute for those natural promptings which have directed the course of other modern nations in the career of letters. Such rules, of course, while assimilating them to antiquity, drew them aside from sympathy with their own contemporaries. How can they, thus formed on an artificial system, enter into the spirit of other literatures so uncongenial with their own?

That the French continued subject to such a system, with little change to the present age, is evinced by the example of Voltaire, a writer whose lawless ridicule

"like the wind,
Blew where it listed, laying all things prone,"

but whose revolutionary spirit made no serious changes in the principles of the national criticism. ***

The Germans are just the antipodes of their French neighbors. Coming late on the arena of modern literature, they would seem to be particularly qualified for excelling in criticism by the variety of styles and models for their study supplied by other nations. They have, accordingly, done wonders in this department, and have extended their critical wand over the remotest regions, dispelling the mists of old prejudice, and throwing the light of learning on what before was dark and inexplicable. They certainly are entitled to the credit of a singularly cosmopolitan power of divesting themselves of local and national prejudice. No nation has done so much to lay the foundations of that reconciling spirit of criticism, which, instead of condemning a difference of taste in different nations as a departure from it, seeks to explain such discrepancies by the peculiar circumstances of the nation, and thus from the elements of discord, as it were, to build up a universal and harmonious system. The exclusive and unfavorable views entertained by some of their later critics respecting the French literature, indeed, into which they have been urged, no doubt, by a desire to counteract the servile deference shown to that literature by their countrymen of the preceding age, forms an important exception to their usual candor.

As general critics, however, the Germans are open to grave objections. The very circumstances of their situation, so favorable, as we have said, to the formation of a liberal criticism, have encouraged the taste for theories and for system-building, always unpropitious to truth. Whoever broaches a theory has a hard battle to fight with conscience. If the theory cannot conform to the facts, so much the worse for the facts, as some wag has said; they must, at all events, conform to the theory. The Germans have put together hypotheses with the facility with which children construct card-houses, and many of them bid fair to last as long. They show more industry in accumulating materials than taste or discretion in their arrangement. They carry their fantastic imagination beyond the legitimate province of the muse into the sober fields of criticism. Their philosophical systems, curiously and elaborately devised, with much ancient lore and solemn imaginings, may remind one of some of those venerable English Cathedrals where the magnificent and mysterious Gothic is blended with the clumsy Saxon. The effect, on the whole, is grand, but grotesque withal.

The Germans are too often sadly wanting in discretion, or,

in vulgar parlance, taste. They are perpetually overleaping the modesty of nature. They are possessed by a cold-blooded enthusiasm, if we may say so—since it seems to come rather from the head than the heart—which spurs them on over the plainest barriers of common sense, until even the right becomes the wrong. A striking example of these defects is furnished by the dramatic critic, Schlegel, whose "Lectures" are, or may be, familiar to every reader, since they have been reprinted in the English version in this country. No critic, not even a native, has thrown such a flood of light on the characteristics of the sweet bard of Avon. He has made himself so intimately acquainted with the peculiar circumstances of the poet's age and country, that he has been enabled to speculate on his productions as those of a contemporary. In this way he has furnished a key to the mysteries of his composition, has reduced what seemed anomalous to system, and has supplied Shakespeare's own countrymen with new arguments for vindicating the spontaneous suggestions of feeling on strictly philosophical principles. Not content with this important service, he, as usual, pushes his argument to extremes, vindicates obvious blemishes as necessary parts of a system, and calls on us to admire, in contradiction to the most ordinary principles of taste and common sense. Thus, for example, speaking of Shakespeare's notorious blunders in geography and chronology, he coolly tell us, "I undertake to prove that Shakespeare's anachronisms are, for the most part, committed purposely, and after great consideration." In the same vein, speaking of the poet's villainous puns and quibbles, which, to his shame, or, rather, that of his age, so often bespangle with tawdry brilliancy the majestic robe of the Muse, he assures us that "the poet here probably, as everywhere else, has followed principles which will bear a strict examination." But the intrepidity of criticism never went farther than in the conclusion of this same analysis, where he unhesitatingly assigns several apocryphal plays to Shakespeare, gravely informing us that the last three, "Sir John Oldcastle," "A Yorkshire Tragedy," and "Thomas Lord Cromwell," of which the English critics speak with unreserved contempt, "are not only unquestionably Shakespeare's, but, in his judgment, rank among the best and ripest of his works!" The old bard, could he raise his head from the tomb, where none might disturb his bones, would exclaim, we imagine, *"Non tali auxilio!"*

It shows a tolerable degree of assurance in a critic thus to dogmatize on nice questions of verbal resemblance which have so long baffled the natives of the country, who, on such questions, obviously can be the only competent judges. It furnishes a striking example of the want of discretion noticeable in so many of the German scholars. With all these defects, however, it cannot be denied that they have widely extended the limits of rational criticism, and, by their copious stores of erudition, furnished the student with facilities for attaining the best points of view for a comprehensive survey of both ancient and modern literature.

The English have had advantages, on the whole, greater than those of any other people, for perfecting the science of general criticism. They have had no academies to bind the wing of genius to the earth by their thousand wire-drawn subtleties. No Inquisition has placed its burning seal upon the lip, and thrown its dark shadow over the recesses of the soul. They have enjoyed the inestimable privilege of thinking what they pleased, and of uttering what they thought. Their minds, trained to independence, have had no occasion to shrink from encountering any topic, and have acquired a masculine confidence, indispensable to a calm appreciation of the mighty and widely-diversified productions of genius, as unfolded under the influences of as widely-diversified institutions and national character. Their own literature, with chameleon-like delicacy, has reflected all the various aspects of the nation in the successive stages of its history. The rough, romantic beauties and gorgeous pageantry of the Elizabethan age, the stern, sublime enthusiasm of the Commonwealth, the cold brilliancy of Queen Anne, and the tumultuous movements and ardent sensibilities of the present generation, all have been reflected as in a mirror, in the current of English literature, as it has flowed down through the lapse of ages. It is easy to understand what advantages this cultivation of all these different styles of composition at home must give the critic in divesting himself of narrow and local prejudice, and in appreciating the genius of foreign literatures, in each of which some one or other of these different styles has found favor. To this must be added the advantages derived from the structure of the English language itself, which, compounded of the Teutonic and the Latin, offers facilities for a comprehension of other literatures not afforded by those languages, as the German and the Italian, for instance, almost exclusively derived from but one of them.

With all this, the English, as we have remarked, have made fewer direct contributions to general literary criticism than the Continental nations, unless indeed, we take into the account the periodical criticism, which has covered the whole field with a light skirmishing, very unlike any systematic plan of operations. The good effect of this *guerilla* warfare may well be doubted. Most of these critics for the nonce (and we certainly are competent judges on this point) come to their work with little previous preparation. Their attention has been habitually called, for the most part, in other directions, and they throw off an accidental essay in the brief intervals of other occupation. Hence their views are necessarily often superficial, and sometimes contradictory, as may be seen from turning over the leaves of any journal where literary topics are widely discussed; for, whatever consistency may be demanded in politics or religion, very free scope is offered, even in the same journal, to literary speculation. Even when the article may have been the fruit of a mind ripened by study and meditation on congenial topics, it too often exhibits only the partial view suggested by the particular and limited direction of the author's thoughts in this instance. Truth is not much served by this irregular process; and the general illumination, indispensable to a full and fair survey of the whole ground, can never be supplied from such scattered and capricious gleams, thrown over it at random.

Another obstacle to a right result is founded in the very constitution of review-writing. Miscellaneous in its range of topics, and addressed to a miscellaneous class of readers, its chief reliance for success in competition with the thousand novelties of the day, is in the temporary interest it can excite. Instead of a conscientious discussion and cautious examination of the matter in hand, we too often find an attempt to stimulate the popular appetite by piquant sallies of wit, by caustic sarcasm, or by a pert, dashing confidence, that cuts the knot it cannot readily unloose. Then, again, the spirit of periodical criticism would seem to be little favorable to perfect impartiality. The critic, shrouded in his secret tribunal, too often demeans himself like a stern inquisitor, whose business is rather to convict than to examine. Criticism is directed to scent out blemishes instead of beauties. "*Judex damnatur cùm nocens absolvitur*" is the bloody motto of a well-known British periodical, which, under this piratical flag, has sent a broadside into many a gallant bark that deserved better at its hands.

When we combine with all this the spirit of patriotism, or, what passes for such with nine tenths of the world, the spirit of national vanity, we shall find abundant motives for a deviation from a just, impartial estimate of foreign literatures. And if we turn over the pages of the best-conducted English journals, we shall probably find ample evidence of the various causes we have enumerated. We shall find, amid abundance of shrewd and sarcastic observation, smart skirmish of wit, and clever antithesis, a very small infusion of sober, dispassionate criticism; the criticism founded on patient study and on strictly philosophical principles; the criticism on which one can safely rely as the criterion of good taste, and which, however tame it may appear to the jaded appetite of the literary lounger, is the only one that will attract the eye of posterity.

X. MISCELLANEOUS TOPICS

[ON BLINDNESS]

From *Miscellanies*, pp. 57–73

[From "Asylum for the Blind," a review in the *North American Review*, XXXI, 66–85 (July, 1830). Reprinted in *Miscellanies*, 57–87. The rest of the article is a historical discussion of philanthropy for the blind.]

There is nothing in which the moderns surpass the ancients more conspicuously than in their noble provisions for the relief of indigence and distress. The public policy of the ancients seems to have embraced only whatever might promote the aggrandizement or the direct prosperity of the state, and to have cared little for those unfortunate beings who, from disease or incapacity of any kind, were disqualified from contributing to this. But the beneficent influence of Christianity, combined with the general tendency of our social institutions, has led to the recognition of rights in the individual as sacred as those of the community, and has suggested manifold provisions for personal comfort and happiness.

The spirit of benevolence, thus widely, and oftentimes judiciously exerted, continued, until a very recent period, however, strangely insensible to the claims of a large class of objects, to whom nature, and no misconduct or imprudence of their own, as is too often the case with the subjects of public charity, had denied some of the most estimable faculties of man. No suitable institutions, until the close of the last century, have been provided for the nurture of the deaf and dumb, or the blind. Immured within hospitals and almshouses, like so many lunatics and incurables, they have been delivered over, if they escaped the physical, to all the moral contagion too frequently incident to such abodes, and have thus been involved in a mental darkness far more deplorable than their bodily one.

This injudicious treatment has resulted from the erroneous principle of viewing these unfortunate beings as an absolute burden on the public, utterly incapable of contributing to their own subsistence, or of ministering in any degree to their own intellectual wants. Instead, however, of being degraded by such unworthy views, they should have been regarded as, what in truth they are, possessed of corporeal and mental capacities perfectly competent, under proper management, to the production of the most useful results. If wisdom from one entrance was quite shut out, other avenues for its admission still remained to be opened.

In order to give effective aid to persons in this predicament, it is necessary to place ourselves as far as possible in their peculiar situation, to consider to what faculties this insulated condition is, on the whole, most favorable, and in what direction they can be exercised with the best chance of success. Without such foresight, all our endeavors to aid them will only put them upon efforts above their strength, and result in serious mortification.

The blind, from the cheerful ways of men cut off, are necessarily excluded from the busy theater of human action. Their infirmity, however, which consigns them to darkness, and often to solitude, would seem favorable to contemplative habits, and to the pursuits of abstract science and pure speculation. Undisturbed by external objects, the mind necessarily turns within, and concentrates its ideas on any point of investigation with greater intensity and perseverance. It is no uncommon thing, therefore, to find persons setting apart the silent hours of the evening for the purpose of composition or other purely intellectual exercise. Malebranche, when he wished to think intensely, used to close his shutters in the daytime, excluding every ray of light; and hence Democritus is said to have put out his eyes in order that he might philosophize the better—a story, the veracity of which Cicero, who relates it, is prudent enough not to vouch for.

Blindness must also be exceedingly favorable to the discipline of the memory. Whoever has had the misfortune, from any derangement of the organ, to be compelled to derive his knowledge of books less from the eye than the ear, will feel the truth of this. The difficulty of recalling what has once escaped, of reverting to, or dwelling on the passages read aloud by another, compels the hearer to give undivided attention to the subject, and to impress it more forcibly on his own mind by subsequent and methodical reflection. Instances of the cultivation of this faculty to an extraordinary extent have been witnessed among the blind, and it has been most advantageously applied to the pursuit of abstract science, especially mathematics.

One of the most eminent illustrations of these remarks is the well-known history of Saunderson, who, though deprived in his infancy not only of sight, but of the organ itself, contrived to become so well acquainted with the Greek tongue as to read the works of the ancient mathematicians in the original. He made such advances in the higher departments of the science, that he was appointed, "though not matriculated at the University," to fill the chair which a short time previous had been occupied by Sir Isaac Newton at Cambridge. The lectures of this blind professor on the most abstruse points of the Newtonian philosophy, and especially on optics, naturally filled his audience with admiration; and the perspicuity with which he communicated his ideas is said to have been unequalled. He was enabled, by the force of his memory, to perform many long operations in arithmetic, and to carry in his mind the most complex geometrical figures. As, however, it became necessary to supply the want of vision by some symbols which might be sensible to the touch, he contrived a table in which pins, whose value was determined principally by their relative position to each other, served him instead of figures, while for his diagrams he employed pegs, inserted at the requisite angles to each other, representing the lines by threads drawn around them. He was so expert in his use of these materials, that, when performing his calculations, he would change the position of the pins with nearly the same facility that another person would indite figures, and when disturbed in an operation would afterward resume it again, ascertaining the posture in which he had left it by passing his hand carefully over the table. To such shifts and inventions does human ingenuity resort when stimulated by the thirst of knowledge; as the plant, when thrown into shade on one side, sends forth its branches eagerly in that direction where the light is permitted to fall upon it. * * *

Blindness would seem to be propitious, also, to the exercise of the inventive powers. Hence poetry, from the time of Thamyris and the blind Mæonides down to the Welsh harper and the ballad-grinder of our day, has been assigned as the peculiar province of those bereft of vision,

> "As the wakeful bird
> Sings darkling, and, in shadiest covert hid,
> Tunes her nocturnal note."

The greatest epic poem of antiquity was probably, as that of the moderns was certainly, composed in darkness. It is easy to understand how the man who has once seen can recall and body forth in his conceptions new combinations of material beauty; but it would seem scarcely possible that one born blind, excluded from all acquaintance with "colored nature," as Condillac finely styles it, should excel in descriptive poetry. Yet there are eminent examples of this; among others, that of Blacklock, whose verses abound in the most agreeable and picturesque images. Yet he could have formed no other idea of colors than was conveyed by their moral associations, the source, indeed, of most of the pleasures we derive from descriptive poetry. It was thus that he studied the variegated aspect of nature, and read in it the successive revolutions of the seasons, their freshness, their prime, and decay.

Mons. Guillié, in an interesting essay on the instruction of the blind, to which we shall have occasion repeatedly to refer, quotes an example of the association of ideas in regard to colors, which occurred in one of his own pupils, who, in reciting the well-known passage in Horace, "*rubente dexterâ sacras jaculatus arces,*" translated the first two words by "fiery" or "burning right hand." On being requested to render it literally, he called it "red right hand," and gave as the reason for his former version, that he could form no positive conception of a red color; but that, as fire was said to be red, he connected the idea of heat with this color, and had therefore interpreted the wrath of Jupiter, demolishing town and tower, by the epithet "fiery or burning"; for "when people are angry," he added, "they are hot, and when they are hot, they must of course be red." He certainly seems to have formed a much more accurate notion of red than Locke's blind man.

But while a gift for poetry belongs only to the inspired few, and while many have neither taste nor talent for mathematical or speculative science, it is a consolation to reflect that the humblest individual who is destitute of sight may so far supply this deficiency by the perfection of the other senses as by their aid to attain a considerable degree of intellectual culture, as well as a familiarity with some of the most useful mechanic arts. It will be easier to conceive to what extent the preceptions of touch and hearing may be refined if we reflect how far that of sight is sharpened by exclusive reliance on it in certain situations. Thus the mariner descries objects at night, and at a distance upon the ocean, altogether imperceptible to the unpracticed eye of a landsman. And the North American Indian steers his course undeviatingly through the trackless wilderness, guided only by such signs as escape the eye of the most inquisitive white man.

In like manner, the senses of hearing and feeling are capable of attaining such a degree of perfection in a blind person, that by them alone he can distinguish his various acquaintances, and even the presence of persons whom he has but rarely met before, the size of the apartment, and the general locality of the spots in which he may happen to be, and guide himself safely across the most solitary districts and amid the throng of towns. Dr. Bew, in a paper in the Manchester Collection of Memoirs, gives an account of a blind man of his acquaintance in Derbyshire, who was much used as a guide for travelers in the night over certain intricate roads, and particularly when the tracks were covered with snow. This same man was afterward employed as a projector and surveyor of roads in that county. We well remember a blind man in the neighboring town of Salem, who officiated some twenty years since as the town crier, when that functionary performed many of the advertising duties now usurped by the newspaper, making his diurnal round, and stopping with great precision at every corner, trivium or quodrivium, to chime his "melodious twang." Yet this feat, the familiarity of which prevented it from occasioning any surprise, could have resulted only from the nicest observation of the undulations of the ground, or by an attention to the currents of air, or the different sound of the voice or other noises in these openings, signs altogether lost upon the man of eyes.

Mons. Guillié mentions several apparently well-attested anecdotes of blind persons who had the power of discriminating colors by the touch. One of the individuals noticed by him, a Dutchman, was so expert in this way that he was sure to come off conqueror at the card-table by the knowledge which he thus obtained of his adversary's hand, whenever it came to his turn to deal. This power of discrimination of colors, which seems to be a gift only of a very few of the finer-fingered gentry, must be founded on the different consistency or smoothness of the ingredients used in the various dyes. A more certain method of ascertaining these colors, that of tasting or touching them with the tongue, is frequently resorted to by the blind, who by this means often distinguish between those analogous colors, as black and dark blue, red and pink, which, having the greatest apparent affinity, not unfrequently deceive the eye. * * *

The faculty of hearing would seem susceptible of a similar refinement with that of seeing. To prove this without going into farther detail, it is only necessary to observe that much the larger proportion of blind persons are, more or less, proficients in music, and that in some of the institutions for their education, as that in Paris, for instance, *all* the pupils are instructed in this delightful art. The gift of a natural ear for melody, therefore, deemed comparatively rare with the *clairvoyans*, would seem to exist so far in every individual as to be capable, by a suitable cultivation, of affording a high degree of relish, at least to himself.

As, in order to a successful education of the blind, it becomes necessary to understand what are the faculties, intellectual and corporeal, to the development and exercise of which their peculiar condition is best adapted, so it is equally necessary to understand how far, and in what manner, their moral constitution is likely to be affected by the insulated position in which they are placed. The blind man, shut up within the precincts of his own microcosm, is subjected to influences of a very different complexion from the bulk of mankind, inasmuch as each of the senses is best fitted to the introduction of a certain class of ideas into the mind, and he is deprived of that one through which the rest of his species receive by far the greatest number of theirs. Thus it will be readily understood that his notions of modesty and delicacy may a good deal differ from those of the world at large. The blind man of Puisseaux confessed that he could not comprehend why it should be reckoned improper to expose one part of the person rather than another. Indeed, the conventional rules, so necessarily adopted in society in this relation, might seem, in a great degree, superfluous in a blind community.

The blind man would seem, also, to be less likely to be endowed with the degree of sensibility usual with those who enjoy the blessing of sight. It is difficult to say how much of our early education depends on the looks, the frowns, the smiles, the tears, the example, in fact, of those placed over and around us. From all this the blind child is necessarily excluded. These, however, are the great sources of sympathy. We feel little for the joys or the sorrows which we do not witness. "Out of sight, out of mind," says the old proberb. Hence people are so ready to turn away from distress which they cannot, or their avarice will not suffer them to relieve. Hence, too, persons whose compassionate hearts would bleed at the infliction of an act of cruelty on so large an animal as a horse or a dog, for example, will crush without concern a wilderness of insects, whose delicate organization, and whose bodily agonies are imperceptible to the naked eye. The slightest injury occurring in our own presence affects us infinitely more than the tidings of the most murderous battle, or the sack of the most populous and flourishing city at the extremity of the globe. Yet such, without much exaggeration, is the relative position of the blind, removed by their infirmity at a distance from the world, from the daily exhibition of those mingled scenes of grief and gladness, which have their most important uses, perhaps, in calling forth our sympathies for our fellow-creatures. * * *

Indeed, the cheerfulness almost universally incident to persons deprived of sight leads us to consider blindness as, on the whole, a less calamity than deafness. The deaf man is continually exposed to the sight of pleasures and to society in which he can take no part. He is the guest at a banquet of which he is not permitted to partake, the spectator at a theater where he cannot comprehend a syllable. If the blind man is excluded from sources of enjoyment equally important, he has, at least, the advantage of not perceiving, and not even comprehending what he has lost. It may be added, that perhaps the greatest privation consequent on blindness is the inability to read, as that on deafness is the loss of the pleasures of society. Now the eyes of another may be made, in a great degree, to supply this defect of the blind man, while no art can afford a corresponding substitute to the deaf for the privations to which he is doomed in social intercourse. He cannot hear with the ears of another. As, however, it is undeniable that blindness makes one more dependant than deafness, we may be content with the conclusion that the former would be the most eligible for the rich, and the latter for the poor. Our remarks will be understood as applying to those only who are wholly destitute of the faculties of sight and hearing. A person afflicted only with a partial derangement or infirmity of vision is placed in the same tantalizing predicament above described of the deaf, and is, consequently, found to be usually of a far more impatient and irritable temperament, and, consequently, less happy than the totally blind. With all this, we doubt whether there be one of our readers, even should he assent to the general truth of our remarks, who would not infinitely prefer to incur partial to total blindness, and deafness to either. Such is the prejudice in favor of eyes!

[THE MISSION OF DEMOCRACY]

From *Miscellanies*, pp. 294–305

[From "Bancroft's United States," a review of George Bancroft's *History of the United States*, Vol. III, in the *North American Review*, LII, 75–103 (January, 1841). Reprinted in *Miscellanies*, 294–349. Democracy is here discussed in historical perspective as a progressive force. The Federalist background of Prescott's thinking is obvious. The article should be compared with J. L. Motley's *Historic Progress and American Democracy* (1869), reprinted in the American Writers Series *Motley*. The concluding footnote of the selection was added in 1845.]

The celebrated line of Bishop Berkeley,

"Westward the *course* of empire takes its way,"

is too gratifying to national vanity not to be often quoted (though not always quoted right); and if we look on it in the nature of a prediction, the completion of it not being limited to any particular time, it will not be easy to disprove it. Had the bishop substituted "freedom" for "empire," it would be already fully justified by experience. It is curious to observe how steadily the progress of freedom, civil and religious—of the enjoyment of those rights, which may be called the natural rights of humanity—has gone on from east to west, and how precisely the more or less liberal character of the social institutions of a country may be determined by its geographical position, as falling within the limits of one of the three quarters of the globe occupied wholly or in part by members of the great Caucasian family.

Thus, in Asia we find only far-extended despotisms, in which but two relations are recognized, those of master and slave: a solitary master, and a nation of slaves. No Constitution exists there to limit his authority; no intermediate body to counterbalance, or, at least, shield the people from its exercise. The people have no political existence. The monarch is literally the state. The religion of such countries is of the same complexion with their government. The free spirit of Christianity, quickening and elevating the soul by the consciousness of its glorious destiny, made few proselytes there; but Mohammedanism, with its doctrines of blind fatality, found ready favor with those who had already surrendered their wills—their responsibility—to an earthly master. In such countries, of course, there has been little progress in science. Ornamental arts, and even the literature of imagination, have been cultivated with various success; but little has been done in those pursuits which depend on freedom of inquiry, and are connected with the best interests of humanity. The few monuments of an architectural kind that strike the traveler's eye are the cold memorials of pomp and selfish vanity, not those of public spirit, directed to enlarge the resources and civilization of an empire.

As we cross the boundaries into Europe, among the people of the same primitive stock and under the same parallels, we may imagine ourselves transplanted to another planet. Man no longer grovels in the dust beneath a master's frown. He walks erect, as lord of the creation, his eyes raised to that heaven to which his destinies call him. He is a free agent—thinks, speaks, acts for himself; enjoys the fruits of his own industry; follows the career suited to his own genius and taste; explores fearlessly the secrets of time and nature; lives under laws which he has assisted in framing; demands justice as his right when those laws are invaded. In his freedom of speculation and action he has devised various forms of government. In most of them the monarchical principle is recognized; but the power of the monarch is limited by written or customary rules. The people at large enter more or less into the exercise of government; and a numerous aristocracy, interposed between them and the crown, secures them from the oppression of Eastern tyranny, while this body itself is so far an improvement in the social organization, that the power, instead of being concentrated in a single person—plaintiff, judge, and executioner—is distributed among a large number of different individuals and interests. This is a great advance, in itself, towards popular freedom.

The tendency, almost universal, is to advance still farther.

It is this war of opinion—this contest between light and darkness, now going forward in most of the countries of Europe—which furnishes the point of view from which their history is to be studied in the present, and, it may be, the following centuries; for revolutions in society, when founded on opinion—the only stable foundation, the only foundation at which the friend of humanity does not shudder—must be the slow work of time; and who would wish the good cause to be so precipitated that, in eradicating the old abuses which have interwoven themselves with every stone and pillar of the building, the noble building itself, which has so long afforded security to its inmates, should be laid in ruins? What is the best, what the worst form of government, in the abstract, may be matter of debate; but there can be no doubt that the best will become the worst to a people who blindly rush into it without the preliminary training for comprehending and conducting it. Such transitions must, at least, cost the sacrifice of generations; and the patriotism must be singularly pure and abstract which, at such cost, would purchase the possible, or even probable, good of a remote posterity. Various have been the efforts in the Old World at popular forms of government, but, from some cause or other, they have failed; and however time, a wider intercourse, a greater familiarity with the practical duties of representation, and, not least of all, our own auspicious example, may prepare the European mind for the possession of Republican freedom, it is very certain that, at the present moment, Europe is not the place for Republics.

The true soil for these is our own continent, the New World, the last of the three great geographical divisions of which we have spoken. This is the spot on which the beautiful theories of the European philosopher—who had risen to the full freedom of speculation, while action was controlled—have been reduced to practice. The atmosphere here seems as fatal to the arbitrary institutions of the Old World as that has been to the Democratic forms of our own. It seems scarcely possible that any other organization than these latter should exist here. In three centuries from the discovery of the country, the various races by which it is tenanted, some of them from the least liberal of the European monarchies, have, with few exceptions, come into the adoption of institutions of a Republican character. Toleration, civil and religious, has been proclaimed, and enjoyed to an extent unknown since the world began, throughout the wide borders of this vast continent. Alas! for those portions which have assumed the exercise of these rights without fully comprehending their import; who have been intoxicated with the fumes of freedom instead of drawing nourishment from its living principle.

It was a fortunate, or, to speak more properly, a providential thing, that the discovery of the New World was postponed to the precise period when it occurred. Had it taken place at an earlier time—during the flourishing period of the feudal ages, for example—the old institutions of Europe, with their hallowed abuses, might have been ingrafted on this new stock, and, instead of the fruit of the tree of life, we should have furnished only varieties of a kind already far exhausted and hastening to decay. But, happily, some important discoveries in science, and, above all, the glorious Reformation, gave an electric shock to the intellect, long benumbed under the influence of a tyrannical priesthood. It taught men to distrust authority, to trace effects back to their causes, to search for themselves, and to take no guide but the reason which God had given them. It taught them to claim the right of free inquiry as their inalienable birthright, and, with free inquiry, freedom of action. The sixteenth and seventeenth centuries were the period of the mighty struggle between the conflicting elements of religion, as the eighteenth and nineteenth have been that of the great contest for civil liberty.

It was in the midst of this universal ferment, and in consequence of it, that these shores were first peopled by our Puritan ancestors. Here they found a world where they might verify the value of those theories which had been derided as visionary or denounced as dangerous in their own land. All around was free—free as nature herself: the mighty streams rolling on in their majesty, as they had continued to roll from the creation;

the forests, which no hand had violated, flourishing in primeval grandeur and beauty; their only tenants the wild animals, or the Indians nearly as wild, scarcely held together by any tie of social polity. Nowhere was the trace of civilized man or of his curious contrivances. Here was no Star Chamber nor Court of High Commission; no racks, nor jails, nor gibbets; no feudal tyrant to grind the poor man to the dust on which he toiled; no Inquisition, to pierce into the thought, and to make thought a crime. The only eye that was upon them was the eye of Heaven.

True, indeed, in the first heats of suffering enthusiasm they did not extend that charity to others which they claimed for themselves. It was a blot on their characters, but one which they share in common with most reformers. The zeal requisite for great revolutions, whether in church or state, is rarely attended by charity for difference of opinion. Those who are willing to do and to suffer bravely for their own doctrines, attach a value to them which makes them impatient of opposition from others. The martyr for conscience' sake cannot comprehend the necessity of leniency to those who denounce those truths for which he is prepared to lay down his own life. If he set so little value on his own life, is it natural he should set more on that of others? The Dominican, who dragged his victims to the fires of the Inquisition in Spain, freely gave up his ease and his life to the duties of a missionary among the heathen. The Jesuits, who suffered martyrdom among the American savages in the propagation of their faith, stimulated those very savages to their horrid massacres of the Protestant settlements of New England. God has not often combined charity with enthusiasm. When he has done so, he has produced his noblest work—a More, or a Fenelon.

But if the first settlers were intolerant in practice, they brought with them the living principle of freedom, which would survive when their generation had passed away. They could not avoid it; for their coming here was in itself an assertion of that principle. They came for conscience' sake—to worship God in their own way. Freedom of political institutions they at once avowed. Every citizen took his part in the political scheme, and enjoyed all the consideration of an equal participation in civil privileges: and liberty in political matters gradually brought with it a corresponding liberty in religious concerns. In their subsequent contest with the mother country they learned a reason for their faith, and the best manner of defending it. Their liberties struck a deep root in the soil amid storms which shook, but could not prostrate them. It is this struggle with the mother country, this constant assertion of the right of self-government, this tendency—feeble in its beginning, increasing with increasing age—towards Republican institutions, which connects the Colonial history with that of the Union, and forms the true point of view from which it is to be regarded.

The history of this country naturally divides itself into three great periods: the Colonial, when the idea of independence was slowly and gradually ripening in the American mind; the Revolutionary, when this idea was maintained by arms; and that of the Union, when it was reduced to practice. The first two heads are now ready for the historian; the last is not yet ripe for him. Important contributions may be made to it in the form of local narratives, personal biographies, political discussions, subsidiary documents, and *mémoires pour servir;* but we are too near the strife, too much in the dust and mist of the parties, to have reached a point sufficiently distant and elevated to embrace the whole field of operations in one view, and paint it in its true colors and proportions for the eye of posterity. We are, besides, too new as an independent nation, our existence has been too short, to satisfy the skepticism of those who distrust the perpetuity of our political institutions. They do not consider the problem, so important to humanity, as yet solved. Such skeptics are found, not only abroad, but at home. Not that the latter suppose the possibility of again returning to those forms of arbitrary government which belong to the Old World. It would not be more chimerical to suspect the Emperor Nicholas, or Prince Metternich, or the citizen-king Louis Philippe, of being Republicans at heart, and sighing for a democracy, than to suspect the people of this country (above all, of New England, the most thorough democracy in existence)—who have inherited Republican principles and feelings from their ancestors, drawn them in with their mothers' milk, breathed the atmosphere of them from their cradle, participated in their equal rights and glorious privileges—of foregoing their birthright and falsifying their nature so far as to acquiesce in any other than a popular form of government. But there are some skeptics who, when they reflect on the fate of similar institutions in other countries; when they see our sister states of South America, after nobly winning their independence, split into insignificant fractions; when they see the abuses which from time to time have crept into our own administration, and the violence offered, in manifold ways, to the Constitution; when they see ambitious and able statesmen in one section of the country proclaiming principles which must palsy the arm of the Federal Government, and urging the people of their own quarter to efforts for securing their independence of every other quarter— there are, we say, some wise and benevolent minds among us, who, seeing all this, feel a natural distrust as to the stability of the federal compact, and consider the experiment as still in progress.

We, indeed, are not of that number, while we respect and feel the weight of their scruples. We sympathize fully in those feelings, those hopes, it may be, which animate the great mass of our countrymen. Hope is the attribute of republics: it should be peculiarly so of ours. Our fortune is all in the advance. We have no past, as compared with the nations of the Old World. Our existence is but two centuries, dating from our embryo state; our real existence as an independent people little more than half a century. We are to look forward, then, and go forward, not with vainglorious boasting, but with resolution and honest confidence. Boasting, indecorous in all, is peculiarly so in those who take credit for the great things they are going to do, not those they have done. The glorification of an Englishman or a Frenchman, with a long line of annals in his rear, may be offensive; that of an American is ridiculous. But we may feel a just confidence from the past that we shall be true to ourselves for the future; that, to borrow a cant phrase of the day, we shall be true to our *mission*—the most momentous ever intrusted to a nation; that there is sufficient intelligence and moral principle in the people, if not always to choose the best rulers, at least to right themselves by the ejection of bad ones when they find they have been abused; that they have intelligence enough to understand that their only consideration, their security as a nation, is in union; that separation into smaller communities is the creation of so many hostile states; that a large extent of empire, instead of being an evil, from embracing regions of irreconcilable local interests, is a benefit, since it affords the means of that commercial reciprocity which makes the country, by its own resources, independent of every other; and that the representatives drawn from these "magnificent distances" will, on the whole, be apt to legislate more independently, and on broader principles, than if occupied with the concerns of a petty state, where each legislator is swayed by the paltry factions of his own village. In all this we may honestly confide; but our confidence will not pass for argument, will not be accepted as a solution of the problem. Time only can solve it; and until the period has elapsed which shall have fairly tried the strength of our institutions, through peace and through war, through adversity and more trying prosperity, the time will not have come to write the history of the Union.[1]

[1] The preceding cheering remarks on the auspicious destinies of our country were written more than four years ago; and it is not now as many days since we have received the melancholy tidings that the project for the *Annexation of Texas* has been sanctioned by Congress. The remarks in the text on "the extent of empire" had reference only to that legitimate extent which might grow out of the peaceful settlement and civilization of a territory, sufficiently ample certainly, that already belongs to us. The craving for foreign acquisitions has ever been a most fatal symptom in the history of republics; but when these acquisitions are made, as in the present instance, in contempt of constitutional law, and in disregard of the great principles of international justice, the evil assumes a tenfold magnitude; for it flows not so much from the single act as from the principle on which it rests, and which may open the way to the indefinite perpetration of such acts. In glancing my eye over the text at this gloomy moment, and considering its general import, I was unwilling to let it go into the

[ON BRITISH TRAVELERS IN AMERICA]
From *Miscellanies*, pp. 342–352

[From "Madame Calderón's Life in Mexico," a review in the *North American Review*, LVI, 137–170 (January, 1843). Reprinted in *Miscellanies*, 340–360. This selection is proof that Prescott's deep love of British civilization did not conflict with his patriotism. It deserves comparison with J. R. Lowell's similar "On a Certain Condescension in Foreigners" (1869). Madame Calderón, American wife of the Spanish Ambassador to the United States, was a good friend of Prescott, and supplied him with some of the local color which appears in his *Conquest of Mexico*. See the *Correspondence* for lively and interesting letters between the two.]

No nation, on the whole, has contributed so largely to these itinerant expeditions as the English. Uneasy, it would seem, at being cooped up in their little isle, they sally forth in all directions, swarming over the cultivated and luxurious countries of the neighboring continent, or sending out stragglers on other more distant and formidable missions. Whether it be that their soaring spirits are impatient of the narrow quarters which nature has assigned them, or that there exists a supernumerary class of idlers, who, wearied with the monotony of home, and the same dull round of dissipation, seek excitement in strange scenes and adventures; or whether they go abroad for the sunshine, of which they have heard so much but seen so little—whatever be the cause, they furnish a far greater number of tourists than all the world besides. We Americans, indeed, may compete with them in mere locomotion, for our familiarity with magnificent distances at home makes us still more indifferent to them abroad; but this locomotion is generally in the way of business, and the result is rarely shown in a book, unless, indeed, it be the ledger.

---

world with my name to it, without entering my protest, in common with so many better and wiser in our country, against a measure which every friend of freedom, both at home and abroad, may justly lament as the most serious shock yet given to the stability of our glorious institutions. [Prescott's note.]

Yet John Bull is, on many accounts, less fitted than most of his neighbors for the duties of a traveler. However warm and hospitable in his own home, he has a cold reserve in his exterior, a certain chilling atmosphere, which he carries along with him, that freezes up the sympathies of strangers, and which is only to be completely thawed by long and intimate acquaintance. But the traveler has no time for intimate acquaintances. He must go forward, and trust to his first impressions, for they will also be his last. Unluckily, it rarely falls out that the first impressions of honest John are very favorable. There is too much pride, not to say *hauteur*, in his composition, which, with the best intentions in the world, will show itself in a way not particularly flattering to those who come in contact with him. He goes through a strange nation, treading on all their little irritable prejudices, shocking their self-love and harmless vanities—in short, going against the grain, and roughing up everything by taking it the wrong way. Thus he draws out the bad humors of the people among whom he moves, sees them in their most unamiable and by no means natural aspect—in short, looks on the wrong side of the tapestry. What wonder if his notions are somewhat awry as to what he sees! There are, it is true, distinguished exceptions to all this: English travelers, who cover the warm heart—as warm as it is generally true and manly—under a kind and sometimes cordial manner; but they are the exceptions. The Englishman undoubtedly appears best on his own soil, where his national predilections and prejudices, or, at least, the intimation of them, are somewhat mitigated in deference to his guest.

Another source of the disqualification of John Bull as a calm and philosophic traveler is the manner in which he has been educated at home; the soft luxuries by which he has been surrounded from his cradle have made luxuries necessaries, and, accustomed to perceive all the machinery of life glide along as noiselessly and as swiftly as the foot of Time itself, he becomes morbidly sensitive to every temporary jar or derangement in the working of it. In no country, since the world was made, have all the appliances for mere physical, and, we may add, intellectual indulgence, been carried to such perfection as in this little island nucleus of civilization. Nowhere can a man get such returns for his outlay. The whole organization of society is arranged so as to minister to the comforts of the wealthy; and an Englishman, with the golden talisman in his pocket, can bring about him genii to do his bidding, and transport himself over distances with a thought, almost as easy as if he were the possessor of Aladdin's magic lamp, and the fairy carpet of the Arabian Tales.

When he journeys over his little island, his comforts and luxuries cling as close to him as round his own fireside. He rolls over roads as smooth and well-beaten as those in his own park; is swept onward by sleek and well-groomed horses, in a carriage as soft and elastic, and quite as showy as his own equipage; puts up at inns that may vie with his own castle in their comforts and accommodations, and is received by crowds of obsequious servants, more solicitous, probably, even than his own to win his golden smiles. In short, wherever he goes, he may be said to carry with him his castle, park, equipage, establishment. The whole are in movement together. He changes place, indeed, but changes nothing else. For traveling, as it occurs in other lands—hard roads, harder beds, and hardest fare—he knows no more of it than if he had been passing from one wing of his castle to the other.

All this, it must be admitted, is rather an indifferent preparation for a tour on the Continent. Of what avail is it that Paris is the most elegant capital, France the most enlightened country on the European *terra firma*, if one cannot walk in the streets without the risk of being run over for want of a *trottoir*, nor move on the roads without being half smothered in a lumbering vehicle, dragged by ropes, at the rate of five miles an hour? Of what account are the fine music and paintings, the architecture and art of Italy, when one must shiver by day for want of carpets and seacoal fires, and be thrown into a fever at night by the active vexations of a still more tormenting kind? The galled equestrian might as well be expected to feel nothing but raptures and ravishment at the fine scenery through which he is riding. It is probable he will think much more of his own petty hurts than of the beauties of nature. A traveling John Bull, if his skin is not off, is at least so thin-skinned that it is next door to being so.

If the European neighborhood affords so many means of annoyance to the British traveler, they are incalculably multiplied on this side of the water, and that, too, under circumstances which dispose him still less to charity in his criticisms and constructions. On the Continent he feels he is amongst strange races, born and bred under different religious and political institutions, and, above all, speaking different languages. He does not necessarily, therefore, measure them by his peculiar standard, but allows them one of their own. The dissimilarity is so great in all the main features of national polity and society, that it is hard to institute a comparison. Whatever be his contempt for the want of progress and perfection in the science of living, he comes to regard them as a distinct race, amenable to different laws, and therefore licensed to indulge in different usages, to a certain extent, from his own. If a man travels in China, he makes up his mind to chopsticks. If he should go to the moon, he would not be scandalized by seeing people walk with their heads under their arms. He has embarked on a different planet. It is only in things which run parallel to those in his own country that a comparison can be instituted, and charity too often fails where criticism begins.

Unhappily, in America, the Englishman finds these points of comparison forced on him at every step. He lands among a people speaking the same language, professing the same religion, drinking at the same fountains of literature, trained in the same occupations of active life. The towns are built on much the same model with those in his own land. The brick houses, the streets, the "sidewalks," the in-door arrangements, all, in short, are near enough on the same pattern to provoke a comparison. Alas! for the comparison. The cities sink at once into mere provincial towns, the language degenerates into a provincial *patois*, the manners, the fashions, down to the cut of the clothes, and the equipages, all are provincial. The people, the whole nation—as independent as any, certainly, if not, as our orators fondly descant, the best and most enlightened upon earth—dwindle into a mere British colony. The traveler does not seem to understand that he is treading the soil of the New World, where everything is new, where antiquity dates but from yesterday, where the present and the future are all, and the past nothing, where hope is the watchword, and "Go ahead!" the principle of action. He does not comprehend that when he sets foot on such a land, he is no longer to look for old hereditary landmarks, old time-honored monuments and institutions, old families that have vegetated on the same soil since the Conquest. He must be content to part with the order and something of the decorum incident to an old community, where the ranks are all precisely and punctiliously defined, where the power is deposited by prescriptive right in certain privileged hands, and where the great mass have the careful obsequiousness of dependants, looking for the crumbs that fall.

He is now among a new people, where everything is in movement, all struggling to get forward, and where, though many go adrift in their wild spirit of adventure, and a temporary check may be sometimes felt by all, the great mass still advances. He is landed on a hemisphere where fortunes are to be made, and men are employed in getting, not in spending—a difference which explains so many of the discrepancies between the structure of our own society and habits and those of the Old World. To know how to spend is itself a science; and the science of spending and that of getting are rarely held by the same hand.

In such a state of things, the whole arrangement of society, notwithstanding the apparent resemblance to that in his own country, and its real resemblance in minor points, is reversed. The rich proprietor, who does nothing but fatten on his rents, is no longer at the head of the scale, as in the Old World. The man of enterprise takes the lead in a bustling community, where action and progress, or at least change, are the very conditions of existence. The upper classes—if the term can be used in a complete democracy—have not the luxurious finish and accommodations to be found in the other hemisphere. The humbler classes have not the poverty-stricken, cringing spirit of hopeless inferiority. The pillar of society, if it want the Corinthian capital, wants also the heavy and superfluous base. Every man not only professes to be, but is practically, on a footing of equality with his neighbor. The traveler must not expect to meet here the deference, or even the courtesies which grow out of distinction of castes. This is an awkward dilemma for one whose nerves have never been jarred by contact with the *profane;* who has never been tossed about in the rough and tumble of humanity. It is little to him that the poorest child in the community learns how to read and write; that the poorest man can have—what Henry the Fourth so good-naturedly wished for the humblest of his subjects—a fowl in his pot every day for his dinner; that no one is so low but that he may aspire to all the rights of his fellow-men, and find an open theater on which to display his own peculiar talents.

As the tourist strikes into the interior, difficulties of all sorts multiply, incident to a raw and unformed country. The comparison with the high civilization at home becomes more and more unfavorable, as he is made to feel that in this land of promise it must be long before promise can become the performance of the Old World. And yet, if he would look beyond the surface, he would see that much here too has been performed, however much may be wanting. He would see lands over which the wild Indian roamed as a hungting-ground, teeming with harvests for the consumption of millions at home and abroad; forests, which have shot up, ripened, and decayed on the same spot ever since the creation, now swept away to make room for towns and villages, thronged with an industrious population; rivers, which rolled on in their solitudes, undisturbed except by the wandering bark of the savage, now broken and dimpled by hundreds of steamboats, freighted with the rich tribute of a country rescued from the wilderness. He would not expect to meet the careful courtesies of polished society in the pioneers of civilization, whose mission has been to recover the great continent from the bear and the buffalo. He would have some charity for their ignorance of the latest fashions of Bond Street, and their departure, sometimes, even from what, in the Old Country, is considered as the decorum, and, it may be, decencies of life. But not so; his heart turns back to his own land, and closes against the rude scenes around him; for he finds here none of the soft graces of cultivation, or the hallowed memorials of an early civilization; no gray, weather-beaten cathedrals, telling of the Normans; no Gothic churches in their groves of venerable oaks; no moss-covered cemeteries, in which the dust of his fathers has been gathered since the time of the Plantagenets; no rural cottages, half smothered with roses and honeysuckles, intimating that even in the most humble abodes the taste for the beautiful has found its way; no trim gardens, and fields blossoming with hawthorn hedges and miniature culture; no ring fences, enclosing well-shaven lawns, woods so disposed as to form a picture of themselves, bright threads of silvery water, and sparkling fountains. All these are wanting, and his eyes turn with disgust from the wild and rugged features of nature, and all her rough accompaniments—from man almost as wild; and his heart sickens as he thinks of his own land, and all its scenes of beauty. He thinks not of the poor, who leave that land for want of bread, and find in this a kindly welcome, and the means of independence and advancement which their own denies them.

He goes on, if he be a splenetic Sinbad, discharging his sour bile on everybody that he comes in contact with, thus producing an amiable ripple in the current as he proceeds, that adds marvelously, no doubt, to his own quiet and personal comfort. If he have a true merry vein and hearty good nature, he gets on, laughing sometimes in his sleeve at others, and cracking his jokes on the unlucky pate of Brother Jonathan, who, if he is not very silly—which he very often is—laughs too, and joins in the jest, though it may be somewhat at his own expense. It matters little whether the tourist be Whig or Tory in his own land; if the latter, he returns, probably, ten times the Conservative that he was when he left it. If Whig, or even

Radical, it matters not; his loyalty waxes warmer and warmer with every step of his progress among the Republicans; and he finds that practical democracy, shouldering and elbowing its neighbors as it "goes ahead," is no more like the democracy which he has been accustomed to admire in theory, than the real machinery, with its smell, smoke, and clatter, under full operation, is like the pretty toy which he sees as a model in the Patent Office at Washington.

CHRONOLOGICAL INDEX

The selections included in this volume are here arranged in the order of their appearance in Prescott's individual works, with an extra heading to take care of the passages from uncollected articles. The dates after the titles of books are those of original publication. The numbers in parentheses after the titles of selections indicate the pages of this volume on which the selections begin. In the case of Prescott's four histories, the references at the right indicate the location of individual passages. For the *Miscellanies* and "Uncollected Articles," the dates at the right are those of the original appearance of the material in the *North American Review*.